CHINA

A New Cultural History

D1738804

Masters of Chinese Studies

CHINA

A New Cultural History

CHO-YUN HSU

Translated by Timothy D. Baker, Jr.
and Michael S. Duke

COLUMBIA UNIVERSITY PRESS

NEW YORK

Columbia University Press wishes to express its appreciation for assistance given by the Chiang Ching-kuo Foundation for International Scholarly Exchange and Council for Cultural Affairs in the publication of this book.

Columbia University Press
Publishers Since 1893
New York   Chichester, West Sussex
cup.columbia.edu

Originally published as *Wangu jiangshan: Zhongguo lishi wenhua de zhuanzhe yu kaizhan*, Taipei: Yingwen Hansheng, 2006.
Written by Hsu Cho-yun © 2006
Illustrations by ECHO Publishing Co., Taipei © 2006
English-language edition published by arrangement with ECHO Publishing Co., Ltd., Taipei
Translation copyright © 2012 Columbia University Press

Library of Congress Cataloging-in-Publication Data
Xu, Zhuoyun, 1930–
[Wan gu jiang he. English.]
China : a new cultural history / Cho-yun Hsu ; translated by Timothy D. Baker, Jr. and Michael S. Duke.
p.   cm. — (Masters of Chinese Studies)
Includes bibliographical references and index.
ISBN 978-0-231-15920-3 (cloth : alk. paper) — ISBN 978-0-231-15921-0 (pbk.) — ISBN 978-0-231-52818-4 (electronic)
1. China—Civilization. 2. China—Relations. 3. China—Social life and customs. I. Title.
II. Title: Cultural history of China. III. Series.
DS721.X8813   2012
951—dc23
2011024504
♾

Contents

Chronology

10000–4000 B.C.E.

Neolithic cultures appear in various regions of Eastern Asia.
Agriculture develops in both the north and the south.

4000–2000 B.C.E.

Regional cultures interact with one another.
Cultures in the Yellow River and Yangzi River basins become dominant.
Urbanization and agriculture develop.

2000–1000 B.C.E.

The "Three Dynasties" begin with the legendary Xia dynasty.
The Shang kingdom (ca. seventeenth century–eleventh century B.C.E.)
    demonstrates state formation and hegemony.
The Kingdom of Western Zhou (ca. eleventh century–771 B.C.E.) expands
    its territory under decentralized control.
Bronze cultures flourish.

1000–300 B.C.E.

The collapse of the Zhou kingdom leads to multistate competition.
The Central Plain and Yangzi Valley cultures become clearly defined.
The Hua-Xia cultural identity emerges.
Confucius and Confucianism develop.
Daoism appears as a challenger and alternative to Confucianism.
States evolve toward independent monarchies and bureaucracy.
Urbanization and greatly increased social mobility occur.
Advancements occur in agriculture and technology.

300 B.C.E.–300 C.E.

Qin unification of China (221–206 B.C.E.).
Western Han (202 B.C.E.–8 C.E.) and Eastern Han (25–220 C.E.) dynasties.
The claim of a Tianxia universal empire supports imperial authority and bureaucracy.
The heritage of intensive farming and marketing networks provides an economic base.
Conflicts arise with a powerful and mobile Xiongnu empire on steppe land in the north.
China is connected with Eurasia by overland trade along the Silk Routes.
China expands its territory to the south and southwest.
Confucian scholars dominate the state bureaucracy.
The New Text movement is counterbalanced by the canonization of Confucian texts.
Buddhism enters China along the trade routes.
An indigenous Chinese response referred to as religious Daoism develops.
Massive peasant uprisings associated with Daoist sects take place.
The Han empire collapses.
The Three Kingdoms period (220–280 C.E.) is marked by continual interstate conflict.

300–600

Massive invasions of peoples from northern areas penetrate China.
The Western Jin dynasty (265–316).
Tribal states are established in the Central Plain and northern areas.

Northern States (420–581) include the Northern Wei, Northern Qi, and
Northern Zhou dynasties.

Courts are established for the Eastern Jin (317–420) and southern states
(420–589).

Xianbei (Särbi) and other northern peoples merge with the Chinese.

Chinese migrants settling in the south incorporate the indigenous cultures.

Buddhism is well accepted by all levels of society; Daoism develops further
in response.

Marine trade increases along with overland trade routes, supporting cultural
interactions beyond China.

600–1000

Political and cultural reunification of China under the Sui (581–618) and
Tang (618–907) dynasties.

China becomes a transregional power in the inner Asian and Asian-Pacific
regions.

Chinese cultural influences spread to Japan and Korea.

Buddhism flourishes in China.

Rivalry develops with newly expanded Islamic powers to the west.

The An Lushan Rebellion destabilizes imperial power.

China is torn by a long period of civil wars.

North China and South China become culturally differentiated.

Extended turmoil due to civil wars, referred to as the Five Dynasties
(907–960).

1000–1400

There is rapid rise and fall of dynasties: the Northern Song (960–1127),
Liao (Khitan; 916–1125), Jin (Jurchen; 1125–1234), Yuan (Mongol; 1271–
1368), West Xia (Tangut; 1038–1227), and Southern Song (1127–1276).

Song China is a member of an East Asian multistate community.

North China is ruled by conquest regimes from the north.

There is economic progress, technological advancement, and massive urbanization, along with refinement in the arts and literature.

The Cheng-Zhu School of Confucianism becomes the dominant Confucian orthodoxy.

Mongol expansion leads to conquest and the Yuan dynasty (1271–1368)

1400–1650

The Ming dynasty (1368–1644).

China proper regains independence from the Mongol conquest.

China withdraws from Inner Asia.

Asian-Pacific trade dominates foreign trade.

Cross-ocean trade routes are opened by European marine powers, to China's benefit.

China enters a new worldwide economic network with the influx of South American silver.

The urbanized South flourishes, and the North becomes impoverished.

Wang Yangming's school of liberal Confucianism arises.

Western culture enters China, including the use of firearms.

Liberalism in the late Ming surges before it is ended by massive peasant uprisings.

1650–1910

The Qing (Manchu) dynasty (1636–1911).

Mongolia, Tibet, and today's Xinjiang Province are incorporated into the Manchu empire.

Taiwan enters Chinese history as a Ming loyalist base and supports a community of Chinese migrants.

The Manchu empire is governed by a dual Manchu-Han administration.

Confucian scholarship becomes more conservative.

The population increases after the introduction of new crops from the Americas.

China continues to enjoy substantial economic benefit from foreign trade until imported opium creates a deficit.

China closes itself to Western culture in the eighteenth century.

The Opium War (1839–1842) leads to encroachment by Western powers.

The Taiping Rebellion (1850–1864) demonstrates the dangers of religious sects.

Taiwan conceded to Japan after China is defeated by Japan in 1895.

The Boxer Rebellion (1899–1901) further shows the weakness of the Qing government.

Attempts at reform within the Qing court are unsuccessful.

The 1911 Revolution ends dynastic China.

The Republic of China (1911–) and the People's Republic of China (1950–).

Initial goals of the Republican Revolution are unsuccessful.

Civil wars develop among regional warlords.

The Nanjing era (1926–1937) of Republican government is ended by the Japanese invasion.

Communist forces extend their control from the countryside to urban areas.

Civil War between the Nationalists and the Communists erupts after World War II (1945–1949).

China is divided along the Taiwan Strait.

Despotic government under Mao Zedong and the Maoist Communist Party.

The Nationalist Chinese government, after a bad start, is economically successful in Taiwan.

Economic reforms occur in the People's Republic of China from 1979 on, after the death of Mao Zedong in 1976.

Taiwan moves toward a liberal democracy in the late 1980s.

Political reforms in the People's Republic of China are aborted after June 1989.

Both the Republic of China (Taiwan) and the People's Republic of China flourish economically.

Communities of overseas Chinese people fully participate in an emerging global order.

Figures

Notes on the Translation

Timothy D. Baker, Jr. translated chapters 1, 2, 3, and 7; Michael S. Duke translated chapters 4, 5, 6, and 8 and the preface and afterword.

Official titles follow Charles O. Hucker, *A Dictionary of Official Titles in Imperial China* (Stanford, Calif.: Stanford University Press, 1985).

Pinyin romanization is employed, but we use dashes rather than apostrophes for words such as Xi-an (rather than Xi'an).

We indicate commonly known names in their pre-pinyin forms. For example, Chiang Kai-shek (rather than Jiang Jieshi) and Canton (rather than Guangzhou), etc.

CHINA

A New Cultural History

Author's Preface

What I have seen of the several-thousand-years-long river of Chinese cultural history is quite limited, as though I was standing on the bank and gazing at the river, sometimes seeing roiling rapids and sometimes calm stretches, but in the final analysis, catching a partial glimpse of only one time or place.

If we use rivers as a metaphor, the development of Chinese culture has been like the Yellow and Yangzi rivers. The headwaters of the Yellow and the Yangzi (*Changjiang*, "Long River") are not far apart in the Bayan Har Mountains of Qinghai Province, but one flows north and the other south. The drainage systems of these two mighty rivers traverse most of the territory of China before arriving at the same destination and pouring into the Yellow Sea and the East China Sea, eventually to join the Pacific Ocean. These two river basins, one in the north and one in the south, delimited two geographical environments and gave rise to two regions with distinctly characteristic cultures.

The dragonlike Yellow River follows a serpentine course—now gentle, now fierce—first raising its head and thrusting north, then lowering its mighty body and meandering east to pour into the great ocean. It carries with it tons of yellow loess sediment that it spreads out over the thousand-mile Central Plains, turning the sky black and the earth yellow, as the natural colors of the Chinese cosmos are often depicted. The Yellow River gave the Chinese rich, fertile soil—and a long series of devastating floods. In the Yellow River basin, the Chinese people sang happy songs, wept bitter tears, concentrated their great cultural creativity, and established their national race (*guozu*—a Chinese term that combines *guo*, "nation," with *zu*, "ethnic" or "racial" group). Thus, as a symbol of Chinese cultural history, the cover of this book is adorned with a picture of the Yellow River.

But perhaps the Yangzi River drainage system, with its many complicated, varied, and graceful tributaries, is an even more appropriate image for the long course of Chinese cultural change. The long Yangzi River originates as a tiny, thin stream flowing slowly down from Qinghai's Bayan Har Mountains. It first takes on the Jinsha (Golden Sands) River, then receives the flow of the Tuo, Min, and Jialing rivers of Sichuan before assimilating a number of waters pouring out from the high plateau on the Tibetan border with Gansu and Qinghai, where it becomes a mighty torrent. From there, the long river rushes east, and after it breaks through the 3,053-meter-high barrier of the Dabashan Mountains, it races and roars through the Three Gorges, with their steep cliff sides reaching to heaven, where the mysterious goddess mists of Shaman's Peak obscure the clouds and where tangled branches hang over the jade-green rocks above the rugged shoals and fleeting rapids. The river continues to flow east with tremendous power as it emerges from the gorges and pours straight on for hundreds of miles into the hills and lakes of Hubei and Hunan—by now, it has become a broad, powerful, bold, untrammeled, and truly great river. Flowing farther east, it takes in the southern rainfall of the Xiang, Zi, Yuan, Li, Gan, and Qing rivers of Jiangxi, Hubei, and Hunan, along with the yellow earth of the Central Plains carried by its greatest tributary, the Han. Across this graceful vista, the stars sinking into the plains, the moon rising over the eastern hills, the far-off trees and nearby hills, the islets in the stream and the sandbars are all beautiful beyond description. As the river flows south from this point, vast and boundless, the sun and moon shimmering on its surface, standing on the shoreline, one can see only the reflections of the mountains.

Beyond Nanjing, the river enters the sea, and the water rises and retreats with the high tides of Guangling and the ebb tides of Shicheng; sometimes, the river deposits silt to form sandbars that hinder its flow, and sometimes it flows so rapidly that it washes under its banks, splitting the rocks and causing landslides. Finally, the great river enters the East China

Sea at Shanghai, but at first the river and sea waters do not completely mix, and the river remains a long strip of green in the midst of the blue sea. The sea grows to its enormous size with the vast quantities of sand and water delivered by the river. The hundred waters have reached their destination, and all the rivers of the world are submerged in the seven seas.

From its origins as a thin stream, Chinese culture developed like the long Yangzi River, absorbing the resources of many tributaries along the way until it became a vast torrent racing toward the great ocean—and this great ocean is nothing less than humanity's collaborative creation: world culture.

The Chinese version of this book is a history compiled for this generation of Chinese readers; it is the story of the growth and development of Chinese culture and an interpretation of this long process. Over the course of this story, following the unfolding of Chinese history, the content of Chinese culture and the space occupied by that culture were continually changing as the "China" that was centered in the Yellow River basin moved step by step toward the "China" of world culture. On every stage of this journey, "China" faced other peoples and their cultures. After continuous contact and exchange, acceptance, or rejection, "China" transformed both itself and the cultures of its neighboring peoples. In the end, "Self" and "Others" blended together into a new "Self." This mutual interaction between "Self" and "Others" enabled Chinese culture continuously to grow over time and to occupy ever more geographical space. After several thousand years, from its beginnings in the Neolithic era, a complex pluralistic Chinese cultural system has finally taken shape.

Given this continual process of transformation, the story narrated here is a complex one, and the settings and main characters frequently change. It is just like the activities that take place on a public square: a few people discussing some issue may gradually attract a few others to join in, until, after several further turns of events, a very large crowd of people gather, but by then their discussion has left the original theme far behind. Of course, such a simile is too simple to describe adequately the complexity of cultural history.

This book's chapter titles benefit from the conceptualization given in Liang Qichao's (1873–1929) pioneering *Essays on Chinese History* (*Zhongguoshi xulun*, 1901). Like Liang, we consider the Chinese cultural sphere to have undergone a continual process of expansion, going from "Central Plains China" to "Chinese China," then to "China in East Asia" to

"China in Asia," and finally ending with our contemporary "China in the global context." Our age is different from Liang's day, however, and we can call on more materials on the history of Chinese culture, more knowledge of Chinese history, and the results of more research on the history of other cultures, all of which have expanded greatly in the past hundred years. Thus, for every phase of Chinese cultural history, this book not only offers its own periodization and its own understanding but also its own interpretations unconstrained by Liang's concept of that history.

Since this book concentrates on the development of the Chinese cultural sphere, it does not use the political system as its benchmark for periodizing Chinese culture, the way most general histories of China do. On this account, and for the convenience of the general reader, the dates of the various periods or eras in this book are given in the common-era system (that is, B.C.E., before the common era, and C.E., of the common era—formerly B.C. and A.D.) rather than using the traditional Chinese calendar or reign-period dating system. For further convenience, the beginnings and endings of the various periods are given in round numbers. Cultural changes take place gradually, and one cannot demarcate the elements making for such changes as neatly as one cuts bean curd. Thus, departing from the standard periodization, this book will discuss elements somewhat before and after changes in each major historical event.

For this reason, the year 1500 C.E. is employed as the limit of periodization for the first half of the book (chapters 1 through 5). That brings us exactly to the eve of the formation of a globalized economic system. The last three chapters tell the story of China's five-hundred-year struggle with repeated tidal waves of globalization. During these five centuries, Chinese culture nearly drowned, and the Chinese people had to learn how to ride the waves of great changes. This was a time when this great ethnic group—one quarter of the world's population—was compelled to invest its millennia of stored-up energy in the performance of a great tragicomedy of history!

Since the theme of this book is the development of culture, we have to discuss both the content and the extension of culture. In terms of the content of culture, special attention is paid to everyday culture, popular mentality, and social thought, particularly the patterns of daily life and the spiritual concerns of the common people. Orthodox Chinese history has always been a record of the activities of emperors, generals, ministers, sages, worthies, and famous individuals. Recently published general histories of China have not broken from this old practice of taking political history as a guiding principle and expending very little ink on everyday life. In shifting the focus of discussion, this book does not mean to devalue changes of dynasty, the rise and fall of national strength, or the institutional systems, wise words, and noble deeds of various ages. It is simply that all of these things have been well covered by earlier historians. The alternative focus of this book intends to fill the gaps left by most general histories of China.

Today's readers of history differ from those of the past. In this age, the common people, certainly most of those who have received a postsecondary education, may well be interested in history. By reading history, of course, they hope to gain an understanding of where they themselves and their contemporary style of life came from. This book discusses everyday life and the sequences of causes and effects of various cultural attitudes and ideas both to satisfy such readers' desires for knowledge and because the development of these elements of Chinese culture followed a long, slow process that is rich in meanings and implications worthy of the historian's investigation.

Chinese culture originally had a tradition of considering China (or Huaxia) to be on the inside and the various *Yi* barbarians (non-Chinese) to be on the outside. In modern times, from, say, the mid-nineteenth century on, nationalist historiography and nation building developed together as important phenomena of modern history, and modern Chinese historiography was not able to stand apart from this trend. The Chinese view of history inherited the above two elements and often embodied a Sinocentric view of Chinese culture—a belief that Chinese culture developed long ago in the remote past independently of the rest of the world. Chinese historiography paid little attention to events outside of China and even passed over without discussion the historical facts of exchanges between the Chinese and other cultures. The Chinese culture presented in this history, however, is a complex, multicultural system that accepted elements from many sources—an image quite different from the Sinocentric view. The chief characteristic of Chinese culture is not that it enlightened or assimilated its neighbors with its outstanding civilization. What is genuinely worthy of pride in Chinese culture is its capacity to tolerate, accommodate, and absorb elements from other cultures.

To make up for the misapprehensions stemming from the Sinocentric view, this book particularly focuses on the relationships between the "inside" and "outside" of the Chinese cultural sphere. Our theme will be not only to attend to the influences that Chinese culture had on other cultures but also to examine the many foreign influences on the process of Chinese cultural development. Aside from its scholarly interest, and at the risk of offending Chinese public opinion, one goal of this book is to argue, as much as possible, against some Chinese self-centered national biases and to persuade readers to alter these views. As stated above, today's world is gradually becoming one, and people living in every region of the globe must carry on some sort of communication with members of other societies and cultures. Excessive self-centeredness can easily lead to self-isolation, and that is not a normal or healthy attitude for oneself or for others. Thus, this book devotes a special section in each chapter to a discussion of the cultural exchanges taking place between China and the outside world at the time in question.

Besides discussing cultural exchanges, other sections compare some selected aspects in the development of Chinese culture with some other cultures. Such comparisons are helpful in explaining what aspects of cultural history are common to many cultures and what aspects are particular to China. The ancient philosopher Laozi said, "To understand others is to be clever, but to understand oneself is to be wise" (*Laozi* 33.1–2). This is in keeping with the Chinese proverb to "know oneself and others," but without some concrete comparison it is very difficult to achieve any genuine wisdom of self-understanding. In choosing various subjects for cultural comparison throughout the book, I do not mean to imply that they are the only contemporary phenomena worth examining; they are only chosen as representative examples.

The prehistory sections of this book do not privilege a "Central Plains" (the middle and lower regions of the Yellow River) concept of Chinese culture, and in the historical sections the so-called Central Plains concept of Chinese culture has several different definitions. In spatial terms, Chinese culture was highly portable. It expanded greatly from the middle reaches of the Yellow River and the Guanzhong Plain (the Wei River valley in modern Shaanxi Province) of the Qin and Han dynasties to include all of North China during China's middle antiquity, during the Sui and Tang dynasties. Then Chinese culture moved into the southeast during China's nearer ancient history of the Song, Yuan, and Ming dynasties, finally reaching its geographic limit in the southeastern coastal regions (including the island of Taiwan) of recent history. Furthermore, as a concept in the discussion of Chinese cultural history, the "Central Plains idea" has a connotation that differs from a discussion of political history.

In every age, Chinese culture as a cultural sphere transcends narrow political or regional definitions of "China." It is noteworthy that from middle antiquity on, Chinese culture comprised a cultural system that enjoyed the joint participation of many regions of East Asia. Discussions of the Chinese cultural system from chapter 4 on, then, are not limited to an understanding of only the region of "China proper." The many comparisons of China to other cultural areas serve to explain the special characteristics of Chinese history, while the presentation of various historical facts illuminate the contemporary historical background.

In sum, all of our contemporary cultural systems are merging and moving toward the formation of a world culture that has been created by and can be shared by all of humanity. Today, we are at the point where the great rivers all pour into the sea. When we look back at the thousand-years-long flow of Chinese history, that is our individual memory. When we look forward, we see an unlimited future, one that everyone should cooperate together to create.

The many rivers of the ancient past flow ceaselessly on, day and night, and I respectfully present this book as a salute to the countless generations of our ancestors!

Finally, many of the ideas I've employed in writing this book have benefited from the inspiration of a lifetime of teachers, friends, and students—I thank them all and ask their forgiveness for not being able to list all their names. During the process of writing, my friends at Hansheng Publishers have been enormously helpful, especially Wu Meiyun and Tang Shizhu, who worked extraordinarily hard on this project—I ask them to accept my heartfelt gratitude. My wife, Manli, offered constant encouragement, and she is responsible for the book's original Chinese title of *wangu jianghe*, "Rivers of the Ancient Past"! Finally, I want to thank professors Timothy D. Baker and Michael S. Duke for their very skillful and nuanced rendering of my Chinese into extremely readable English and for their expertise in compiling the "Suggestions for Further Reading" sections.

Prologue

In this book, three terms appear as key words throughout the whole text: "China," "Chinese," and "world." It is important to delimit their respective extents and contents, because all three terms change their constitutions from time to time.

"Chinese," in this book, refers to a nation that shares a common cultural heritage rather than to a racial entity or even a linguistic community. Such a cultural complex constantly absorbs influences from outside, blends various previously contending cultures, and revises as well as expands its own constituents into new patterns and emphases.

Likewise, "China"—the land wherein this multiethnic nation dwells—changes its boundaries from time to time, starting from the core area in the middle reaches of the Yellow River valley and finally taking in a vast stretch of land during the heyday of the Manchu dynasty in the eighteenth century C.E.

The "world" as perceived by the Chinese consists of China and the nearby vicinity as well as remote places far beyond. Thus, during the days of Confucius, the lakes and hills drained by the Yangtze River were in a foreign land, while in the sixteenth century C.E., Europe and America, from whence great amounts of silver were brought in, were regarded as the lands of "Others" far away, in contrast to the familiar neighboring

Japan, Korea, and Central Asia. In each period, the "world" made up of "We" and "Others" constituted a "world system" of interactions, both of peaceful interflows of materials, peoples, and ideas and of violent conflict and competition. A real "Global World System"—even though it first took shape when the enormous wealth flowed in and out of the New World of America after the new oceanic sea routes were opened—appears in human history only in our recent century.

If we put all three of these "floating" concepts together, it is the notion of "China" today, with a rather concrete geographic connotation, that may serve as an anchor to delineate "China" and the "world." Thus, the first chapter starts with a detailed narration of the geography of present-day China, setting the "stage" for the performances of various periods to take place.

Moreover, given the definition of "Chinese" as a cultural collectivity, much of the human activities taking place before the Neolithic cultures took shape are not regarded as relevant parts of the Chinese cultural heritage.

Such a delimitation also precludes those ancient humanoids in that part of our world, now being excavated as fossil records of human evolution, such as Peking Man, from being regarded as the genetic ancestors of the modern human population of the "Chinese." This realization has taken hold especially since the new theory of the African origin of a modern human race was proposed. Some archaeological data are included here simply because they deserve our attention as a particular period of human history on our "stage." Recent analyses of the Denisovan hominid remains found in Siberia, conducted by archaeologists and paleontologists from the Max Plank Institute, reveal that the Denisovans, who came to East Asia from Africa earlier than the Neanderthals, are genetically different from both the Neanderthals and "modern Man," while interbreeding between these three groups suggests that a hybrid between the Neanderthals or the Denisovans with the modern humans of African origin may have carried genes of the former in the latter. Solid evidence is still insufficient to verify fully these arguments.

The following chapters are a narrative of the long story of turns and changes in the flow of Chinese cultural history.

1

Prehistory

CHINA'S EARLIEST CULTURES ACCORDING TO
REGIONAL ARCHAEOLOGY

Long before the notion of what we now refer to as "China" took shape, mankind was already active in this region of the world. Under the primitive Paleolithic living conditions, the people here gradually developed an understanding of agriculture and of how to raise livestock and grow crops; they lived in groups and developed regional cultures. Through a lengthy process of division and recombination, their regional differences gradually coalesced into several broad streams of culture, providing a foundation for the subsequent development of Chinese civilization.

1. The Natural Geography of Chinese Culture

In discussing China's geography as part of its cultural history, we should note that in this sense geography is not like a map with clearly delineated political boundaries but is instead the spaces defined by the core characteristics of Chinese culture. This different sense of geography can be attributed to the differences between elements within cultural systems and elements defined by the outlines of political units. The latter have boundaries that can be clearly demarcated with landmarks, but the former are difficult to distinguish by clearly visible territorial limits.

The nucleus of Chinese culture was to develop within an area bordered on the north by vast stretches of desert and steppes, to the west by mountain ranges and high plateaus, and to the east and south by the open sea. China was separated from the rest of the world by these natural barriers. Particularly, the obstacles of the northern deserts and the high mountain ranges to the west have given Chinese culture an orientation toward the southeast. In Chinese mythology, this is indicated by the tale of the goddess of creation, Nüwa. After the earth was created, it is said that the heavens cracked, and although Nüwa patched them, the earth tilted toward the southeast. But in the geography of Chinese cultural history, matters are not so simple as having a predilection for a certain direction. Rather, the regions to all the points of the compass each have their individual structure, their own creative tendencies, and their communication with other regions. This situation gave rise to the complexity of Chinese culture, wherein the individual regional characteristics of each area are apparent, but at the same time, within these minor variations we can distinguish major underlying similarities.

From north to south, there are at least seven major cultural regions: the Mongolian region, of primarily deserts and steppes; the northeast, of mostly forests and mountains; the middle to lower reaches of the Yellow River, of primarily high plains formed by the yellow loess dust blown south from the Mongolian steppes; the middle and lower reaches of the Yangzi River, dominated by networks of rivers and lakes; the coastal regions stretching north to south along the seacoast together with the island territories; the southwest, primarily of high mountains, upland basins, and long valleys; and finally the northwest, composed entirely of tall mountain ranges and plateaus.

To begin with the two northern regions, in the Mongolian regions that spread across northern China, pastoralist herders move about in search of water and grass for their flocks; in the northeast, with its great rivers and dense forests, the people rely on fishing and hunting. The herders of the steppes and the peoples of the forested northeast began to come into contact and communicate with each other at a very early time, and their customs have both commonalities and differences. Their primary difference is that the northeastern peoples are not nomadic but tend to live in settlements, while their common aspects are that they are both dependent on herding and hunting, their men ready to gallop thousands of miles on horseback to make war on other regions. One of the most basic recurring

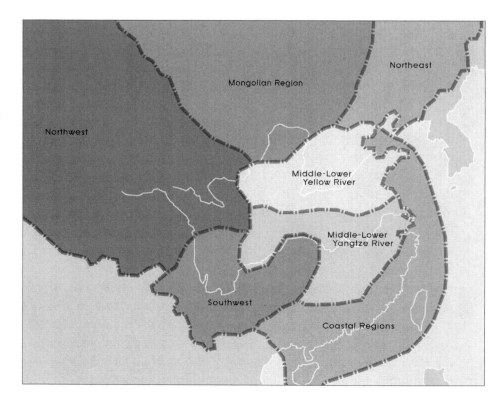

FIGURE 1.1 Major Divisions of Chinese Cultural Geography

trends of Chinese history is that these herders and hunters of the northeast have time after time raided the agricultural regions to the south in search of food and plunder. The borderline separating the farmers and the herders is the path along which the Great Wall stretches. Ever since antiquity, both war and commerce between the farmers to the south and the herder-hunters to the north have developed across this dividing line.

To the south, agricultural areas of China fall into two topographically distinct regions—the loess plateaus and plains along the course of the Yellow River and the middle and lower reaches of the Yangzi. These two great rivers both spring from the Bayan Har Mountains of Qinghai, their headwaters separated by less than a hundred miles. But they then flow apart, one northward and one southward, and thus their middle reaches are spread far apart, a separation that symbolizes the multifaceted cultural development of the Chinese heartland. Eventually, the Yellow River flows into the Bohai Sea, and the Yangzi into the East China Sea. These two mighty rivers, the water of one yellow and the other green, represent the two entirely different natural and cultural environments through which they flow.

The northern people of the Yellow River's loess plains, their faces bent toward the soil, the sun on their backs, eke out a harsh living, one where each measure of grain must be earned by the sweat of their brows. Since the soil must be thoroughly cultivated before it can be used for agriculture, the people of this region, with yellow soil filling the cracks in their callused hands, hold firmly to their native lands, unwilling to move from the fields they have so laboriously prepared. These hardworking and diligent people, so close to their land, have a relatively conservative nature.

But their neighbors to the south along the Yangzi are different. After leaving the high mountains of its origin, the Yangzi passes through hilly country, flows into the Four Gorges of Sichuan, and then bursts into the great southern plains, full of small lakes and rivers. The hills and forests here provide an ample supply of food and timber, and the banks of the lakes and rivers have an abundance of fertile land, so the people who live here have a less strenuous life and a more easygoing attitude. They are more willing to move about from one place to another and are less resistant to change. Their songs bring to mind light breezes wafting through forests or dancing brooks babbling through valleys.

The Yellow River culture of the north produced the highly regulated world of the Confucian scholar, who emphasized satisfaction with one's lot in life. In contrast, the southern regions brought forth a speculative intellectual culture, as exemplified by the dialectic arguments of Laozi and Zhuangzi, who questioned the nature of the universe we live in. This difference also appears in the visual arts. From as early as Neolithic times, the artistic forms of the Yellow River culture were staid, based on squares, triangles, and circles, whereas the most characteristic form in the art of southern China involved rounded, curvilinear designs.

These two large cultural areas were separated by but a few mountain ranges of not very great height, such as the Qingling and Funiu mountains, and there were many roads for communication between these areas. Thus, although the China of the Yellow River and the China of the Yangzi were distinct, there was a great deal of interchange, conflict, and mutual stimulation, through which the core of Chinese culture eventually developed. The combination of these two lines of development, one hard and one soft, one square and one round, one positivist and one relativist, enabled Chinese thought to develop according to different principles, helping it better adapt to changing times. Similarly, in artistic expression, the stone carvings of the north and the ink watercolors that were to develop later in the south present us with, on the one hand, a concrete portrayal of reality and, on the other, an abstract portrayal of feelings and ideas. Together, northern and southern directions combined to produce a rich and complex artistic tradition.

The eastern and southeastern boundaries of this core area of Chinese culture are formed by the Bohai Sea, the Yellow Sea, and the East China Sea. Beyond these seas lie the islands of Japan, the Korean peninsula, the Okinawan archipelago, and the Austronesian islands stretching south from Taiwan. This string of islands and the coast of the Chinese mainland combine to enclose an extended inner sea. The people along the shores of this sea, be they those of the Chinese mainland or those of the many islands, were constantly shifting from one area to another in patterns we have yet to fully understand. The coastal people moved to the islands in countless waves of migration, and the island people followed the ocean currents and seasonal winds to flow back and forth from north to south. The people living along the seacoasts relied on these ocean currents for their marine resources, while the low hills and riverbanks of the coastal region supported small areas of village agricultural life.

Given the division by the many low mountains and rivers, these agricultural villages along the coast relied on water—both the sea and rivers—for their communication, and this interchange led to the maritime culture of China's southeastern coast. As early as the Neolithic period, approximately 7500–1500 B.P. (Before the Present, a time scale used in archaeology that arbitrarily uses 1950 as the present), there was an ethnic differentiation between the people of the south, who are referred to as the Southern Mongoloid type, and those of the north, the Northern Mongoloid type. Moreover, the staple foods—taro and seafood for the maritime cultures and rice and millet for the mainland cultures—also clearly indicate a basic difference in lifestyles.

Here we should note that the maritime culture of China's southeastern coast was the origin of one of China's most fundamental traits, its reverence for jade. Traces of this culture of jade can be found all along the western shores of the Pacific, even as far north as the Bering Strait. Jade, along with gold from Central Asia, were to become the most treasured materials for artworks and prestige goods, this combination again expressing China's blend of maritime and mainland cultures.

Moreover, from the southeastern coastal regions, from the Yangzi's delta to the Pearl River delta, the inland waterways formed a network that was linked to the rock-lined harbors. Here, from the first millennium B.C.E., the cities and towns were closely located and densely populated, with relatively high standards of living. Thus this area has long been China's economic center, its main area for maritime imports and exports. The ancient cities of Yangzhou, Hangzhou, Mingzhou (modern Ningbo), Quanzhou, and Guangzhou (Canton), together with Macao after the sixteenth century, were the primary harbors for exports until the rise of the nineteenth-century treaty ports of Hong Kong and Macao in this same area. These harbors sent forth the finest products of China. Driven by trade winds across the ocean, silks and porcelains, teas and herbal medicines went out to many parts of the world. These ports also welcomed precious goods from Southeast Asia and, in modern times, a broad range of Western manufactured products. Through these imports and exports of the southeast, China long gathered the wealth of Pacific Asia. Then, for over a century, through these same ports it imported the manufactured goods of Europe and America, draining China's own economy dry. Under the influence of Westernization, these ports had an even greater influence, being largely responsible for bringing Chinese culture into the modern age and thereby fundamentally transforming it. As China now fully enters the modern world, this region fosters a two-way interchange in a manner not seen before in Chinese history. Much more so than the Silk Road, which was China's northwestern window for imports and exports, the southeastern coastal region has served as the vital link connecting China to the rest of the contemporary world.

We now move to consider the high mountain region of the southwest. Here, Yunnan Province is home to over fifty indigenous peoples, each with its own individual customs: one tribe for the upper mountain slopes, another tribe living on the shores of midlevel mountain lakes, while down in the valleys there is yet another tribe. These three different tribal cultures have distinct living patterns given their different environments. In the high altitudes, the people are forever climbing up and down the mountains, and they rely on the high notes of wooden flutes to call back and forth. They trade among one another, the tribes living on the upper slopes of the mountains exchanging their mutton and highland barley for the mushrooms and millet of the valley peoples. They also trade with the frequent horse caravans and salt merchants, who ply back and forth with products from the various regions and news of local events. Peoples from the lowland regions can enter the mountainous regions either along the narrow valley roads or the rivers to propagate the news and culture of the central regions while bringing the products of this region back to the central regions.

The northwest, stretching from Mount Tianshan to the snow-capped peaks of Tibet, is very high, dry, and cold, with the level areas covered by grasslands and the deserts punctuated by oases standing like lone islands. These oases each comprise a small city whose residents can support themselves through agriculture. It is also worth noting that there are two types of nomadism in this northwestern region: one the Tibetan transhumance pattern, where the herders take their flocks up to the mountains in the summer and then down to lower altitudes in the winter, and the other, prevalent in the high grasslands of Xinjiang and Qinghai, where the herders drive their cattle and sheep back and forth across the plains in search of water and fodder.

From ancient times, various peoples have come and gone from this northwestern region, moving for thousands of miles across its wastes, through its deserts, and over its mountain passes. We have records of travel through this region as early as the Han dynasty (206 B.C.E.–220 C.E.), along the routes that comprised the Silk Road, which served as a northwestern gate for imports and exports. Through this trading, China maintained contact with Central Asia, the Middle East, and Europe, enabling an intercourse that has continued over two thousand years. Along these pathways, Chinese silk fabrics were carried westward, and Western religions came eastward. Buddhism, Zoroastrianism, and others were all transmitted to China along this route. Thus China gained both the profits of trading and the intellectual stimulation of Western thought, which profoundly changed the modes of thought in Chinese culture.

Though it is true that the areas of China are geographically defined by natural barriers, there are always routes of communication across them. Within China, there are three or four east-west trade routes, while from north to south there are many mountain passes, and these are supplemented by north-to-south coastal navigation, following the seasonal winds and ocean currents. This situation can be compared with the great cultural difference that existed in the ancient Middle East. Although the two great civilizations of Mesopotamia and Egypt were fairly close to each other physically, being connected by the Levant, because of the different topographic characteristics of these two regions, the civilizations they produced were vastly different. China was similar to the Middle East in that its individual regions had many striking geographic restrictions. Here, the deserts, the steppes, the loess plateau, the hilly terrain, the lake regions, the rivers, and the high mountains each produced its own particular culture, attracting different groups of people to settle and put down roots in these areas. Considering China's history in detail, however, there is hardly a single local group of people that permanently settled in a region. Instead, these peoples moved in successive waves of migration, from east to west, from north to south, continually mixing with and influencing one another, leading to the development of a Chinese culture that displays fundamental similarities despite its minor local differences.

However, this in no way diminishes the importance of the minor differences across these local cultures, cultural differences that were produced by the necessities of local conditions. In the north, the people of the yurts gallop their sturdy horses across the plains and draw their longbows to shoot great eagles. The hunters of the forest regions live on their prey, raising peregrine falcons, shooting deer, and spearing fish. In the loess regions, the native people sing of the northwest winds and flowers in bold tenor notes, whereas the vibrato tunes of the southeastern operatic *kunqiu* have a soft indirectness—these two styles expressing the contrast between northern manly strength and the feminine softness of the south.

In sum, the world of China is both closed and open. Though each of its regions seems separate, they are all actually closely connected. It is as if on the great stage that is China, actors playing many roles join in with their own melodic themes. There are the nomad flutes of the herders on the steppes, the oxen horns of the hunters, and the bamboo mouth organs of the highlanders; the beating drums urging on the rowers along the rivers, the baritones of farmers in their fields, and the yodeling of the high mountain herders. Sometimes there are pounding rains and driving gales, sometimes the soft winds and light rains of the mild south, sometimes the whispering pines and rushing waterfalls of the mountains. All of these sounds mix together to produce a complex and rich polyphony. This music is the great "Human Comedy" of China, the drama of humanity that has been acted out on this stage for over ten millennia. And from this broad perspective, we can now consider some of the earliest actors to appear on this stage and their roles there.

2. The Extent of Paleolithic Man

The territory now occupied by China is vast, in effect a subcontinent with a very complex set of cultures that were internally differentiated yet interconnected over the great span of its history. Who were the first humans active in this vast area? Were they the same as the peoples who now inhabit these areas? Though these are questions that have yet to be completely resolved, in this section we will outline the prehistory of this region according to archaeological findings of the remnants of early man, showing how some of the broad outlines of Chinese history have their roots as early as the Paleolithic times (2.5 million to 12,000 B.P.).

Chinese archaeologists generally believe that, according to the physical characteristics of early human beings in East Asia, these early people must have had a highly consistent and progressive development within the regions of China. This conclusion is supported by the fact that the early techniques for making stone tools indicate very consistent traditions that clearly differ from those of Europe. The view is in accord with the theory of multiregional evolution, according to which human beings of each world region evolved independently from the early species of Homo sapiens existing in that area.

But more recent scholars have put forth the "Out of Africa" Theory to explain the evolution of contemporary humans. This is the view that all humankind had a common origin in the African continent, from which all later types evolved. Supported by investigations using molecular biology, this theory contends that the ancestors of all modern human beings emerged from Africa in a migration starting twenty thousand years ago, beginning the process that replaced the earlier Homo sapiens species that had lived in other areas, such as the Neanderthals of Europe. If this theory holds true, it would require major adjustments to the theories of Chinese archaeologists regarding human evolution and the development of Paleolithic techniques for stone tools in this area. Since the evidence to date is insufficient to prove or overturn either of these two theories, it remains a major issue of debate. However, there are considerable remains of Paleolithic man in Chinese regions, and a number of independently developed theories have been proposed in recent years. Perhaps with further discoveries in the field, the contradictions between these two theories may be clarified.

Currently, it is generally believed that in the hundred thousand years of the mid- and late Paleolithic period, the earliest hominids, who were present in East Asia before the arrival of more advanced peoples from Africa, had sufficient time to shift from one area to another, during which time later peoples could have moved in and out. So if this were the case, it is possible that the genes of these earlier peoples could have been transmitted to modern man. If the genes of the newly arrived early man mixed with those of the original local hominids and were then transmitted together, then these examples of early man would represent a common species with modern man, the same type of human. The newly arrived groups of humans from Africa would have mixed with the original inhabitants, creating a new hybrid species rather than being a new type of human that completely supplanted the original humans. This would be a position that combines the multiregional and single-origin views of evolution.

From Paleolithic traces found in various regions of China, it appears that over this long period of development, the Paleolithic period here did display a clear tradition of its own, distinct from areas to the west and south, beyond China's great northwestern plains and the Himalayas. During the 1940s, the American archaeologist Hallam Movius (1907–1987) proposed that the western cultural area of the Eurasian continent could be distinguished from that of East Asia, including China, by the fact that the former used stone axes that had been made by flaking from both sides, while the latter used scraping and chopping tools exclusively, without any tools similar to the bi-flaked stone axes of the West. Although Chinese archaeologists have recently claimed the discovery of some bi-flaked stone axes, calling into question the theory of a "Movius Line" between East and West, there is still considerable controversy over the various archaeological definitions of these stone axes, and a scholarly consensus has not yet been reached on this issue. But in general, because the western and eastern Paleolithic implements do have striking differences, it appears that the Paleolithic implements from Chinese regions clearly indicate the presence of individual traditions in areas of eastern Asia.

In fact, the term "Paleolithic" itself is subject to a broad range of definitions. But within the span of time from the appearance of the first hominids about a million years ago up to the emergence of modern man about

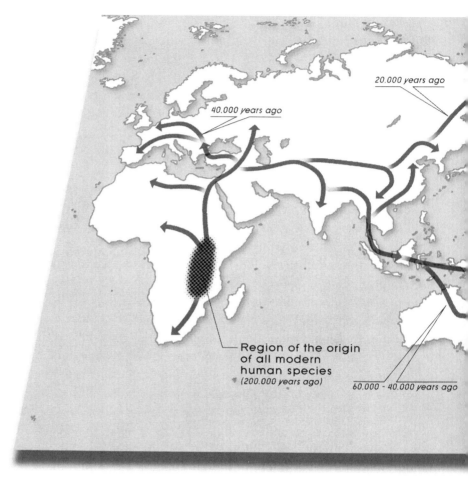

FIGURE 1.2 Map of Modern Human Species Distribution

a hundred thousand years ago, the Paleolithic is generally considered to be the period before humans had begun to grow their own food, though they had begun to make a variety of stone tools used for hunting and gathering.

The best-known remains of early Paleolithic man found in the regions of China are those of Peking Man, found at Zhoukoudian, a large natural limestone karst cave near Beijing. The traces of Peking Man that have been excavated include the fossilized bones of early hominids and indications of their way of life. In this site, the remains are stratified into numerous layers, the analysis of which indicates that five hundred thousand

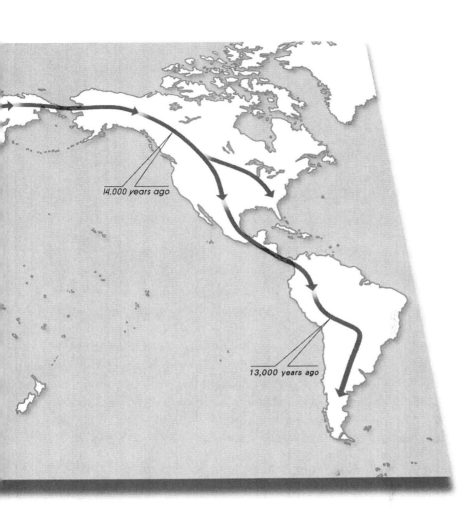

14.000 years ago

13,000 years ago

years ago Peking Man had begun to live there and continued to do so intermittently for more than three hundred thousand years.

The skulls of Peking Man had an average cranial capacity of 1,059 milliliters, somewhat smaller than the modern average of 1,400 milliliters. These hominids had the ability to use fire and may have known how to cook food with it. They employed direct chipping to produce stone tools, whose types include scrapers, pointed tools, choppers, carving tools, and hammers. Judging by information obtained from different cultural levels, the techniques for making these tools developed through a slow and gradual process of improvement. The remains found at Zhoukoudian indicate that the area went through several periods of hominid occupation. As demonstrated by the stone tools, together with stone implements for working bone and horn, it is clear that these early hominids already had a fairly high level of social life that relied on hunting and the gathering of local animals and plants.

But Peking Man was not the only type of early human in Chinese regions. Yuanmou Man from Yunnan, in the south of China, also lived five or six hundred thousand years ago. Their sites have burnt animal bones and fragments of charcoal, although according to the evidence we currently have, it is difficult to determine if these are the result of natural fires or indications of the deliberate human use of fire.

The Nihewan sites of central China near Yangyuan in Hebei, extending in time from the early into the late Pleistocene (roughly the same era as the Paleolithic but based on climate rather than on stone tools), have yielded stone tools and may have been campsites of early man near the higher elevations on lake shores. Lantian Man, who had physical characteristics similar to Peking Man, was found near the town of Lantian in Shaanxi and has been dated to between seven and five hundred thousand years B.P., though there are some who consider that it may be even earlier, between 1.1 and 1.15 million years B.P. Despite the geographical separation, the physical characteristics of Lantian Man and Peking Man are quite similar.

There are also numerous sites that have yielded remains of Paleolithic cultures akin to that of Peking Man, including Yuanxian and Shilongtou sites in Hubei, Guanyin Cave in Guangzhou's Qianxi County, as well as Jinniushan in Liaoning's Yingkou County. In each of these sites, we see a very strong consistency in the levels of workmanship on the tools, the physical characteristics of early man, and the time period of occupation. All the sites also indicate the frequent use of fire.

Closer to the present, the best-known discoveries of artifacts and physical remains of early man from the mid-Paleolithic are Dali Man from Shaanxi, Dingcun Man from Shanxi, Xujiayao Man from Shanxi, Maba Man from Guangdong, Tongzi Man from Guizhou, and Changyang Man from Hubei. Based on the fossilized remains of Xujia's Yao Man, these early humans would date from about one hundred thousand years B.P., since they were found in a stratigraphic level from the late Pleistocene. The New Cave at Zhoukoudian, where the remains of the much earlier Peking Man were found, is another location that contains remnants from

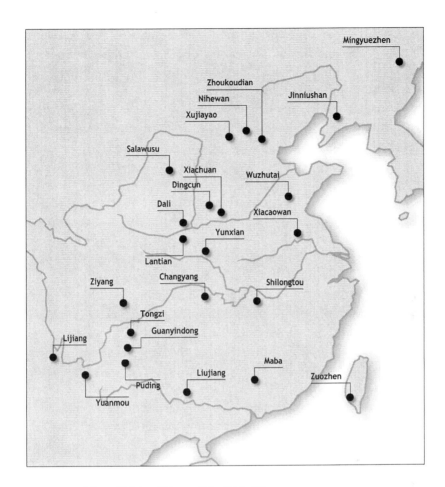

FIGURE 1.3 Map of Major Chinese Paleolithic Sites

the mid-Paleolithic, including human teeth within layers also containing stone tools, ash, and burnt animal bones. In each of these sites, the level of craftsmanship generally shows significant improvement over time, and the stone implements also demonstrate a gradually increasing degree of specialization.

The Paleolithic period, part of the late Pleistocene geological period, is approximately fifty to sixty thousand years B.P., and the physical characteristics of humans are already those of the late stage of *Homo sapiens*, very close to modern man. For example, the particular physical characteristics of Upper Cave Man from Zhoukoudian, much later than Peking Man, are especially close to Mongoloid racial characteristics. This indicates that these native Mongoloid humans may have been the common ancestors of the Chinese, the Inuit, and the American native peoples. By the late Pleistocene, these three races of modern man already show their distinguishing characteristics, though they had not yet divided into the branches that are today apparent. For example, the physical characteristics of Shangdingdong Man (Upper Cave Man) have certain aspects that are very close to some of the current branches of modern man and other aspects that are peculiar to them alone.

Liujiang Man from Guangxi already shares some of the physical characteristics of contemporary man, although the skeletons also show distinctly early traits. The physical characteristics of Liujiang Man seem to be similar to those of contemporary humans from southern China and Southeast Asia, including a relatively short stature, indicating that they may be an earlier form of the Mongoloid peoples. Similarly, the basic characteristics of Ziyang Man from Sichuan are very close to those of modern humans, though they also have a few characteristics of earlier humans, such as projecting brows and temporal skull plates. This indicates that Ziyang Man is probably a later period *Homo sapiens* of the Mongoloid type.

Skeletal and cultural remains of late Paleolithic man are found in almost all the northern and southern districts of China, for example, Hetao Man from Erdos in Inner Mongolia, Antu Man from Jilin, Xintai Man from Shandong, Lijiang Man from Yunnan, Xiacaowan Man from Jiangsu, Chuandong Man from Guizhou, Zouzhen Man from Taiwan, and others.

The chronology of China's late Paleolithic sites can be generally divided as follows:

1. The lower levels of the Salawusu riverbank sites in southern Hetao may date from as early as fifty thousand years B.P., while the upper levels are not earlier than thirty thousand years B.P., an approximate range of between fifty thousand to thirty-seven thousand years B.P.

2. Charcoal from the sixth level of the Dingshan Cave site of Anyang Xioananhai Beilou in Hebei has been carbon-14 dated to 24,100 B.P. ± 500 years (corrected), while charcoal and bone from the third and second layers have been dated to 11,000 B.P. ± 500 years (corrected). "Corrected" indicates that the dating according to the level of carbon-14 present in the

sample has been adjusted according to information on global carbon-14 levels obtained from tree rings and other sources.

3. In the three levels of the Qinshuixiachuan sites in Shanxi, the middle level has been carbon-14 dated to 36,200 B.P. + 3,500 years or − 2,500 years, while the upper level has material ranging from to 23,900 B.P. ± 1,000 years (corrected) to 16,400 B.P. ± 900 years (corrected).

4. Shangdingdong Man from Zhoukoudian has been dated by carbon-14 analysis on material from the same strata to 10,770 B.P. ± 360 years (corrected), indicating that this early man lived in this area until early Neolithic times.

In addition to the technique of direct chipping, during the late Paleolithic, humans in this area also began to use indirect chipping. This more advanced level of craftsmanship, whereby tools are chipped by an intermediate pointed object that is struck with a larger stone, enabled the creation of finer stone implements. By this time, humans could also create bone and horn tools that were ground and polished smooth, and they could drill holes. These fine stone implements include stone arrowheads, indicating that mankind also had developed the ability to hunt with a bow and arrow, which is perhaps the point at which humans first had the ability to extend their action beyond that provided by implements thrown directly by hand. Even more significant is the much wider range of shapes for the stone tools. These have been found in a number of different sizes and are made from stone, bone, and horn. The shapes include knives, shovels and digging tools, needles, and fish spears. The techniques for making them included sawing, cutting, shaving, grinding, and drilling. These techniques constituted the foundation necessary for the growth of Neolithic craftsmanship.

Another noteworthy aspect to Paleolithic culture is the development of mental or emotional life. A great many items for personal ornamentation from this period have been found, for example, drilled stone beads, the teeth of wild animals, and clam shells; even the flutes made out of fish and bird bones had carved designs and decorative colors. Most of these ornamental items were found placed beside human bones, indicating not only that mankind had developed an appreciation for beauty but also the possibility that they had developed the notion of a soul or afterlife. In line with this, the Shangdingdong Man of Zhoukoudian lived in the upper level of this cave and reserved the lower cave as a "burial ground," where skeletons were intentionally placed. Overall, Chinese late Paleolithic remains are quite numerous, widely distributed, and demonstrate many different types of artifacts. This clearly reflects an increased population, a broader territorial range, and lifestyles that were adapted to their environments, demonstrating that a number of different directions of cultural development had already emerged by this time.

3. The Emergence of Agriculture and Fixed Settlements

Given the lack of fixed sources of food during the primitive hunting-gathering period of the Paleolithic, it was difficult for early humans to maintain long-term abodes or establish communities, and so we do not use the word "culture" to describe life at that time. The first point at which we can properly refer to human life in terms of culture is after people had begun to produce their own food, either by tilling the soil or raising livestock. After the establishment of fixed sources of food, people tended to gather together more, gradually forming socially defined areas and groups. This increased level of cooperation fostered major advancements in the process of human development beyond the social life of nonhuman animals. Culture, as I use the term here, is based on human beings having a pattern of communal living and fixed sources of food and, furthermore, on their ability for abstract thought. The skills of this more advanced time period, however, predated the development of culture, being still within in the Neolithic period.

Archaeologists in the twentieth century originally distinguished major epochs according to the typical shapes of stone implements found in the respective periods. The Neolithic and the Paleolithic were distinguished in this way, and this pair of terms remains in use today. But since the English archaeologist Gordon Childe (1892–1957) proposed the change from gathering food to raising food as a revolutionary advancement in the process of mankind's development, this change has better served as a marker to distinguish these two periods. Despite the significance of this revolution, the process of development from gathering food to growing crops was a gradual one, and it would be difficult to determine a particular time when it had finally been completed. Although agriculture certainly has a vital role, the raising of animals is another important source of food, and so the use of food production as the criterion for the periodization of the Neolithic and the Paleolithic should include both agriculture and animal husbandry.

Once fixed sources of food had been established, the patterns of human living went through deep and far-ranging changes in response. The most notable of these was that humans began to establish fixed settlements. In the period of hunting and gathering, people needed to be constantly on the move in search of food; when the food supply in one area had been exhausted, they would move on to another area to find more sustenance. This constant movement to find food, without establishing a fixed abode, required a great deal of effort even for healthy adults, and life was even more difficult for the elderly and very young. This limited the populations of these groups of people living together. In contrast, after the development of agriculture people could establish communities, where they were born, lived, and died. In areas of pastoral herding, the major food source was livestock, which could move about, and so it would appear that the herders were not as limited as the farmers, who had to remain close to their fields. But the pastoralist pattern of following the supply of grasses and water had certain geographic limitations, since areas where fodder for livestock was available were restricted, and so unlimited movement would not be beneficial for the livestock. Therefore, although these peoples had no fixed abodes, there were certain defining patterns to their living space. Accordingly, the techniques discussed in this section concern the two main topics of agriculture and settled communities in prehistoric China.

The Emaokou site in Shanxi Province's Huairen is a workshop from the late Paleolithic where prehistoric man used chipping and flaking techniques to make tools from igneous rock. These stone implements include shovels, axes, and sickles, shapes that are already the same as those of early Neolithic tools. Shovels and scythes can be used for agriculture and thus might indicate that the people of the Emaokou site were agricultural. But in addition to cultivation for planting, shovels could have been used to dig for roots and other food gathered from the wild; in addition to harvesting grain, scythes could have been used to cut down wild fruit and branches. Thus these tools could well have been used by hunter-gatherers as well as by an agricultural community, and their presence at this site indicates the degree to which the transition from Paleolithic to Neolithic, though revolutionary in its degree of change, was still a gradual process.

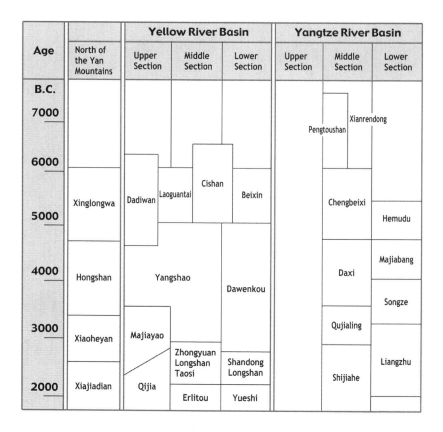

Age	North of the Yan Mountains	Yellow River Basin			Yangtze River Basin		
		Upper Section	Middle Section	Lower Section	Upper Section	Middle Section	Lower Section
B.C.							
7000					Pengtoushan	Xianrendong	
6000				Cishan			
	Xinglongwa	Dadiwan	Laoguantai	Beixin		Chengbeixi	
5000							Hemudu
							Majiabang
4000	Hongshan	Yangshao				Daxi	
				Dawenkou			Songze
3000	Xiaoheyan	Majiayao				Qujialing	
			Zhongyuan Longshan / Taosi	Shandong Longshan		Shijiahe	Liangzhu
2000	Xiajiadian	Qijia	Erlitou	Yueshi			

FIGURE 1.4 Major Neolithic Cultures in China

The appearance of agriculture in China depended on the discovery of foods that could be cultivated. In the northern areas, the earliest traces of agriculture found to date are from a period prior to the Yangshao culture (see figure 3) and are located along the middle and lower reaches of the Yellow River. Here, the Cishan and Peiligang sites from before 8000 B.P. have yielded implements that could be used for agriculture, such as flaked knives. The Cishan site, in Hebei Province's Wu-an, located where the flanks of Mount Taihang meet the North China Plain, occupies eighty thousand square meters and represents the site of an ancient town. The houses in this town are all round or oval in plan, with the floor level lower than the ground. Traces of post holes indicate their structure. The houses and storage pits are generally clustered in small groups, as if reflecting a secondary classification of living units, perhaps by clans. The houses generally contain stone mortars and pestles, axes, and diggers, all of which are for growing or preparing food. The site also has several hundred ash pits, many of which were used as storage pits for food supplies. These pits show considerable variation in depth. Some are as deep as five meters, and they contain decomposed food supplies of up to two meters deep, with a total storage capacity of over ten thousand kilograms, indicating a considerable scale of food production. Similarly, the two Henan sites of Peiligang in Xinzeng and Egou in Mixian, also on the alluvial plain of the Yellow River, have yielded stone mortars and pestles, axes, and diggers as well as the remains of food in storage pits. The time periods of these three sites are essentially very close to one another, around 8000 B.P. The Cishan and Peiligang sites are both about twenty-five meters higher than the river level, perhaps indicating that the alluvial plain of the Yellow River at that time was marshy and damp; the terraces not far from the river would have been more suitable for growing millet. The names of both these sites, as in many later sites, are also used to refer to a common culture, as expressed by similar artifacts, that can be seen in surrounding sites. At the Peiligang culture's site at Jiahu in Henan's Wuyang (from between 9000 and 7800 B.P.), agricultural production was significantly different from the Cishan culture as well as from other Peiligang sites. Although millet, which is grown in dry soil, was cultivated there also, the staple product was paddy rice, which is grown in wet fields.

Contemporary with these sites, the earliest site with evidence of agricultural production found along the Wei River in Shaanxi and Gansu is the Dadiwan site in Gansu's Qin-an, a site that is part of the Laoguantai culture (named after the Laoguantai site in Shaanxi's Hue County). The agricultural products found here are millet, from the family *Poaceae* (the family of grain-bearing grasses that includes barley and rice), and rapeseed, from the family *Brassicaceae* (the cabbage family). Although the Laoguantai site has not yielded grinding boards or grinding bowls, stone pestles were found, indicating that food production had developed to the point of grinding, probably with wooden mortars that did not survive. Stone sickles were not found, although stone knives were, indicating a cultural difference in the method of harvesting from the agricultural practices in Cishan and Peiligang.

All of these sites have yielded large quantities of pig bones and complete skeletons of dogs and suckling pigs, which shows that as early as 8000 or 9000 B.P. these animals had been domesticated. Furthermore, as shown

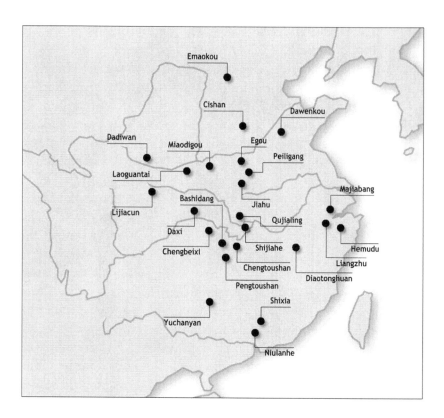

FIGURE 1.5 Geographic Distribution of Major Chinese Neolithic Sites

by the contemporaneous Cishan site, in addition to domesticated pigs and dogs, there were large quantities of bones from wild animals and aquatic animals that had been discarded after eating, showing that hunting and fishing remained important activities along with agriculture.

The areas south of the Qingling Mountains and the Huai River had a warmer climate with ample rainfall, and here early man developed rice cultivation. Recently, archaeologists have discovered that the earliest rice cultivation was along the middle reaches of the Yangtze, as indicated by the Yuchanyan site in Hunan's Dao County, where accelerated carbon-14 dating has indicated remains as early as 14,000 B.P.

Geologists working on the continental shelf of the East China Sea, which would have been dry land during periods when the sea level was lower, have found the silica remains of cultivated rice husks dating from 13,000 B.P. From the earlier levels at the Neolithic site of Diaotonghuan

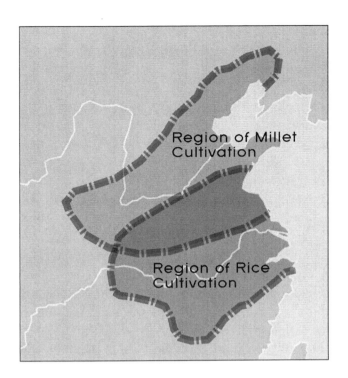

FIGURE 1.6. Distribution of Millet and Rice Cultivation

in Jiangxi's Wannian County, a joint Chinese-American team for agricultural archaeology has collected large quantities of silicized husks from both wild and cultivated rice, and these have been carbon-14 dated also to before 10,000 B.P. (corrected). Somewhat later are the Pengtoushan and Bashidang sites in Hunan's Feng County, of which the Pengtoushan site has been carbon-14 dated to 8000 or 9000 B.P. (corrected). The Neolithic site of Chengbeixi in Hubei's Yidu, which also has remains of cultivated food, is considered to date from 5700 to 5400 B.P. In the far south, at the Niulanhe site in Guangdong's Yingde City, archaeologists have collected the silicized husks from both short-grain *japonica* and long-grain *indica* strains of rice dating from between 11,000 and 7000 B.P. These traces come either from rice husks mixed into the mud plaster on walls or from grains embedded in the clay of pottery.

Within the area drained by the Han River in Shaanxi, the Lijiacun site in Xi County and the Laoguantai culture sites in Hejiawan, dated to between 6000 and 5000 B.P., also yield the remains of rice grains. In the

Chengtoushan group of sites in Hubei's Feng County are the remains of a very early settlement, within which there are indications of a rice paddy. This paddy may have originally been built slightly earlier than the Chengtoushan culture, and, since there was a ritual platform close to it, the paddy may have been for growing sacrificial rice.

From a somewhat later time period, the Hemudu culture's sites in Zhejiang on the southeastern seaboard, in addition to showing clear remains of rice grains, even have specialized tools for rice-growing agriculture, such as bone plows and water dippers. In the storage pits here, the rice grains and stems are piled to a depth of one meter, and these remains have been established as being from cultivated long-grain rice.

The traces of rice found at all these ancient rice-culture sites indicate not only that it is cultivated rice but also that the short-grain *japonica* rice commonly eaten in China was a hybrid of the long-grain *indica* rice. The wild rice growing in China is the ancestor of *indica* rice, and this wild rice is even more widely distributed in the warm and moist regions of Guangxi and Hainan Island. However, the earliest location for rice cultivation is not there but in the middle reaches of the Yangzi. This may be because in the tropical climate of southern China, like that of Hainan Island, food is more easily obtained year round, whereas the temperate climate of Hubei, Hunan, and Jiangxi has a winter season, when natural food sources are restricted. This seasonal variation would motivate the growth of higher-yield cultivated crops that could produce enough to be seasonally stored.

These sites with remains of rice cultivation also have yielded large numbers of bones from pigs, dogs, and water buffalo as well as pottery depicting shapes of pigs and chickens, indicating that domesticated animals and poultry had been developed by this time. Aquatic produce was also a food source, and there are clear signs of activities to gather it, contemporary with the agricultural practices. During the period of the Shijiahe and the Liangzhu cultures, the northern food staples of millet and corn were introduced to the south, clearly boosting the available food sources. Sheep, originally from the north, also appeared in the south as domestic livestock. In this same time period, the agricultural tools of the later Neolithic cultures in the middle reaches of the Yangzi River basin and along the southeastern seaboard all began to display particular characteristics according to their individual sites. For example, triangular stone plows are found in the Liangzhu culture's sites, whereas stone sickles and diggers are found in the sites of Guangdong's Shijia culture, probably because of different methods of cultivation in response to local conditions.

Indeed, both the climate and soil of the south differ markedly from the north, and these differences are reflected in their early buildings. In the Neolithic period, dwellings in the Yellow River basin are partly dug into the layer of loess soil, with an upper structure of wooden columns and beams covered by mud. In contrast, dwellings from the Yangzi basin Daxi culture are either recessed into the ground or have level foundations, are either round or square, and the wooden columns in the walls are connected by woven bamboo strips or poles, which are plastered inside and out with mud, forming a bamboo wattle-and-daub structure. Inside, the floor has a top layer of burned earth. This use of local materials to make bamboo, wood, and mud buildings can still be seen today in the rural areas of the Yangzi River basin. The buildings of Zhejiang's Hemudu culture show more basic differences in structure. Here, many wooden structural elements have been excavated, showing that in this region the early peoples already knew of techniques for wood mortise and tenon joinery, so that this region may have been the origin of China's traditional wooden post-and-beam architecture. At one of these Hemudu sites, the foundation of a long building—twenty-three meters long and seven meters wide, with a covered walkway 1.3 meters wide around it—was also excavated. A well made from wooden piles driven into the ground close together was also found at a Hemudu site. On the eastern shores of Dahai Lake in southern Inner Mongolia as well as on the high loess plateau of Shanxi, Gansu, Ningxia, and Shaanxi, cave dwellings in loess cliffs are found, indicating that these people were planning for a long-term, settled way of life.

From these observations, we can say in general that the peoples of China had developed both agriculture and settled communities by 6000 or 7000 B.C.E. The millet agriculture and loess dwellings of the north as well as the rice agriculture and wood-and-bamboo dwellings of the south were both responses to local conditions, and each area's artifacts had certain distinctive characteristics. In addition to the domestication of food grains, mankind had developed particular varieties of crops, livestock, and poultry. We can speculate that at this point, having established more stable means for acquiring food, people in China entered a new stage of cultural development, with more energy available to advance their social organization and mental life.

4. Relationships Between Regional and Local Neolithic Cultures

In the introduction, I used the Yellow and the Yangzi rivers as a broad and general metaphor for the different characteristics of Chinese cultures. These local differences arose as early as the Neolithic period, as each area of China developed its own early culture with its own local characteristics. These microcultures were like many small rivers that came together, each from its own area, combining to form a major cultural system. It was a process of evolution through constant interchange and melding together.

To discuss each of these Neolithic cultures and the ways they developed and related to one another, archaeologists analyze the material qualities, patterns, and shapes of the pottery produced by these cultures as well as the ways these early humans laid out their settlements. In this way, they define characteristics of these cultures and then further analyze the ways in which these cultures interacted, changed, and combined, thereby working toward a comprehensive theory of cultural systems. It is important to note that by the Bronze Age (variously reckoned in China as 3100 or 2000 to 771 B.C.E.), some of these separate Neolithic cultures were combining or mixing together, and thus the independent cultural systems in each of these areas were gradually melding to form the parts of what would become an overall Chinese cultural system.

Such interactions between local cultures and larger systems of regional cultures were described by the early archaeologist Su Bingqi (1909–1997) using the terms "region," "area," "locale," and "place." In his usage, "locale" and "place" refer to the smaller individual cultures; the term "area" refers to larger, unifying cultural systems; and the term "region" indicates even larger systems formed by the combination of area systems. Su Bingqi considered that China's Neolithic cultures were combined step by step from the local cultures of each area, finally forming more inclusive cultures that covered larger regions. He also considered that this was a very slow and complex process, one involving contacts, conflicts, intercommunication, integration, and division, as well as both rises and falls.

From the time humans developed agricultural techniques, which helped reduce the risk to their livelihood, mankind lived mostly in fixed settlements and thus also had more energy available for expressing emotional and intellectual capabilities. These two new aspects profoundly affected the ways of life of groups in all the regions, and these ways of life

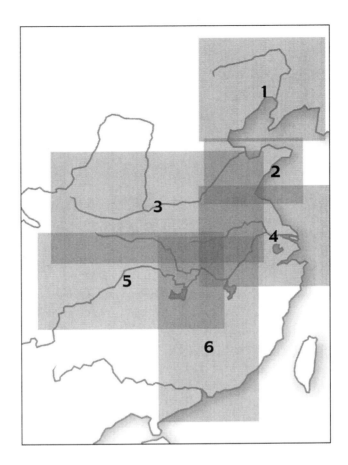

FIGURE 1.7 The Six Major Systems of Regional Cultures

gradually acquired the fixed characteristics that we refer to as "culture." As the food sources for human groups became better established, the population increased, and as the increased populations gradually outgrew their original settlements, they were forced to establish new ones. In this way, these people carried with them the culture of their original home places, so that the complexity of the culture could be progressively increased. However, the environment and the food sources of the new area would necessarily differ from their original home; so to accommodate themselves to the requirements of living in their new home, the original culture would need to undergo certain changes. When a local culture has expanded to a certain degree, the space that it occupies will come up against the space occupied by another culture, to the point where they mesh closely together. Thus between neighboring cultural groups there is bound to be competition and conflict, and this process takes place continually in each region. Between cultural groups there may also be intermingling that forms larger cultural groups covering broader areas, but these groups also retain differences along with their commonalities.

According to Sun Bingqi, Chinese archaeological cultures can be arranged into the following six large regional cultures: (1) a northern region with its center north of the Yan River and the Great Wall, (2) an eastern region with its center in Shandong, (3) a central plains region with its center where the Wei River joins the Yellow River and including southern Shanxi and western Henan, (4) a southeastern region with Lake Tai as its center, (5) a southwestern region with Lake Dongting and the Sichuan basin as its center, and (6) a southern region lying along the axis of a line from Lake Boyang down to the Pearl River delta. The borders of China as we know it today exceed the area covered by these six cultural groups in several locations, such as Inner Mongolia, Central Asia, the mountainous region of the southwest, and the offshore islands, with each of these outlying regions having its own group of cultures. The system proposed by Su Bingqi covers the main areas with the densest spacing of Neolithic sites, a region for which the most archaeological information is available and that has the clearest lines of cultural development. Accordingly, from the traces of these lines of development we can make out the process by which the early peoples of China coalesced into a larger, more complex constellation of cultures.

The local cultural groups of these major regions were formed by combinations and amalgamations of the different cultures within the individual areas. The formation of the large cultural groups led to conflict and competition between the different cultures within each group.

I begin with the northern region. Broadly speaking, this region could be composed of three general areas, the northwestern, northern, and northeastern. Strictly speaking, based on the evidence available from the northern region, this group of areas was centered on Liaoxi and the south-central part of Inner Mongolia. Considered in more detail, it could be divided into the four local areas of Zhaoyang in Liaoning, Zhaowudameng in Inner Mongolia, the local areas around Beijing and Tianjin, and Zhangjiakou. These local areas are spread along the line of the later Great Wall, the region where the agricultural and pastoral cultures over-

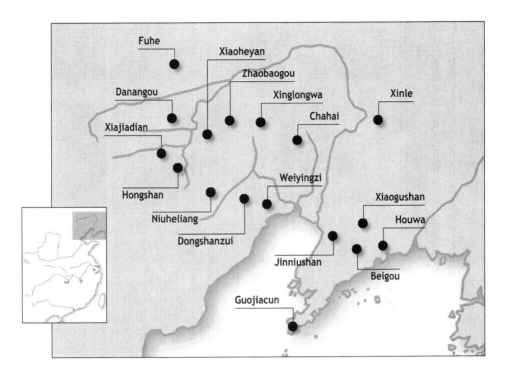

FIGURE 1.8 Major Archaeological Sites of the Northern Cultural Region

lapped and responded to each other. Here, the characteristic lifestyles define different local cultural aggregates, which coexisted and influenced one another. For example, though the Chahai site in Fuxin and the Xinlongwa site in Quhanqi, each from 6000 to 7000 B.P., are separated by only two hundred kilometers, each has its own distinguishing individual characteristics. Similarly, the subsequent Hongshan culture, which developed out of the Chahai culture and was centered on Chifeng, coexisted with the Fuhe culture, which was centered on Chaoyang. This line of development here continued even into the Bronze Age, where the earlier stratum of the Xiajiadian culture site and the later strata of that site partially intermix in the vicinity of Chifeng. In the earlier strata of the Xiajidian culture site, there are linked defense works in various locations, which may reflect conflict and competition with another culture. In some areas, two cultures are found, one earlier and one later, that show similarities; for example, the Later Hongshan culture site of Da-nanjiang shows traces of contact between the late-period Hongshan culture and the

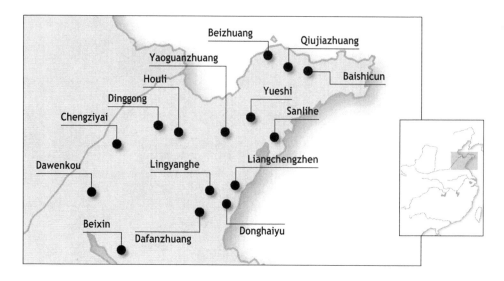

FIGURE 1.9 Major Archaeological Sites of the Eastern Cultural Region

earlier stratum of the Xiajiazhan culture. These two cultures have their own lines of development, but they also alternately had control of the core area, each advancing and retreating in turn, occasionally overlapping.

The second regional cultural system lies to the east, centered on the Shandong peninsula. Its Neolithic cultures have two main areas, the Luxinan and the Liaodong cultural sequences. Marking the beginning of the southwestern of these two cultural areas, a local agricultural culture dating from 7000 B.P. was found in Luxinan's Teng County. Also within this area, the subsequent Dawenkou culture left a number of sites spaced relatively closely together. These two cultures, together with the subsequent Shandong Longshan culture, formed an independent cultural sequence that had common aspects and extended over a four- to five-thousand-year period. The northeastern cultural area in the eastern region, located in the Liaodong area, had its own line of development, which also extended for five thousand years, from 7000 to 2000 B.P., and had certain particular local traits. Even though it is considered an independent cultural area, the Liaodong local cultures had aspects of both independent development and mutual influence with cultures of other areas, and they developed in tandem with each of the progressions of the southwestern Luxinan culture.

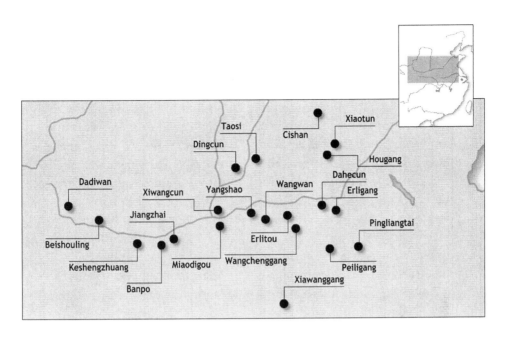

FIGURE 1.10 Major Archaeological Sites of the Central Cultural Region

The third cultural region is the North China Plain, centered on the areas of Guanzhong (the Guanzhong Plain, including central Shaanxi and western Henan), Jinnan, and Yuxi. Historically, the Chinese people have regarded this region as the heartland of Chinese culture, and archaeologically the Yangshao culture was long considered the fountainhead of Chinese culture. However, with increased archaeological finds, the concept of mutual influence and concurrent development of these six regional cultural groups has replaced the earlier concept of a single origin. Within this large region of local cultures on the North China Plain are several distinctive areas. For example, although the Western Longshan sequence is mainly a part of the North China Plain, this culture is also significantly related to the culture of the Xicui area, within the second of the six main cultural regions, the easternmost. Similarly, the local cultures to the east of Zengzhou had a very significant interchange with the Shandong cultures in the eastern region, and they too display signs of overlapping. Showing characteristics of independent internal development, the central area of this region saw a line of cultural development from the Baoji to the Zhengzhou cultures. In addition to the combined evolution of separate cultures, we can also see indications of internal division. For example, within the Yangshao culture of the central area are both eastern and western lines of development, with a western branch in Baoji and Sha-an counties and an eastern branch in Luoyang and Zhengzhou.

The development of the group of cultures in the central region, like the two regional groups of cultures mentioned above, covers a span of five thousand years, from 7000 to 2000 B.P. The early period of development around 6000 B.P. is referred to as the Yangshao period, while that around 5000 B.P. is the Late Yangshao period. In this extended development from the early to the Late Yangshao period, all local areas, large and small, were part of a clear line of development that led up to the Zhou culture. The western area of the central zone of the Yangshao culture had two local cultural sequences that developed concurrently within it after the culture of the earlier stratum of Beishouling in this area split into the Banpo culture and the Miaodigou culture. Both of these were located in the Guanzhong region, coexisted during the same time period, and influenced each other. Eventually, the Miaodigou culture developed more strongly, extending to the east as far as Zhengzhou, while the Banpo culture remained in the basin of the Wei River, allowing the Miaodigou to become the main stream of the regional Yangshao culture.

The ways of life of the Banpo and the Miaodigou were similar in that they both practiced a millet-based agriculture, although the Banpo had highly developed chopping tools and hunting implements. Artifacts of the Miaodigou type, in contrast, are primarily agricultural, with relatively few chopping tools or hunting implements. The garments of Banpo were all of animal skin; those of Miaodigou were made from woven vegetable fiber. Since the economy of Miaodigou was primarily agricultural, it may have been able to accumulate more resources, so that as these two cultures developed alongside each other, the Miaodigou type eventually became the stronger branch of the Yangshao culture. In the designs on Miaodigou painted pottery, the primary distinguishing characteristic is a rose design with a single stem with stylized leaves and petals. Su Bingqi believed that these stylized floral patterns of the Miaodigou might be closely related to the form of an ancient ideogram for flower, *hua*, which has also long been used by the Chinese people to refer to themselves, indicating that this culture began to be considered the origin of mainstream Chinese culture at a very early time.

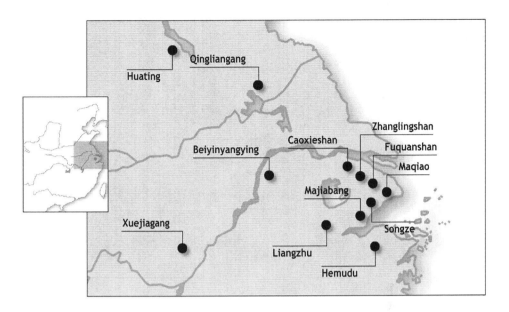

FIGURE 1.11 Major Archaeological Sites of the Southeastern Cultural Region

The fourth regional group of cultures is the southeastern group surrounding Lake Tai. This region is characterized by its many lakes and rivers, an environment entirely different from that of northern China. From Neolithic times, the people of this area relied on a rice-based agriculture supplemented by fishing and gathering other aquatic products. This region can be divided into several local areas, including the area of Lake Tai itself, the Ningzhen area, and the Wei River area, as well as their many local divisions. The cultural system of the Lake Tai area originated with the Majiabing culture of 7000 B.P. and the Liangzhu culture of 4000 to 5000 B.P. and extended down to the Wuyue culture of 3000 B.P., a period of four to five thousand years. An early high point of these cultures was in the ritual centers and ceremonial objects of the Liangzhu culture, which represent the most refined level of the Jianghan culture, as discussed further in section 6. Thus the Wuyue culture, which eventually became strong enough to compete with the cultures of the North China Plain during the Eastern Zhou period, had a long period of individual development. In the Ningzhen area, the Northern Yinyangying culture moved westward to the Xuejiagang culture in Da-an's Huiqianshan, where remains

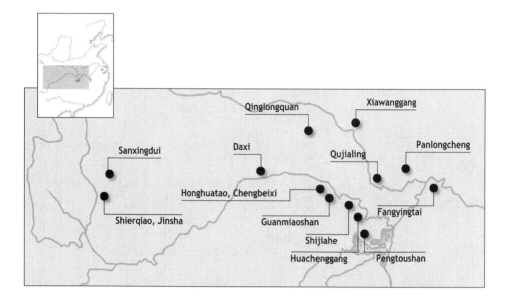

FIGURE 1.12 Major Archaeological Sites of the Southwestern Cultural Region

in the later stratum of the former already display characteristics in common with the later Erlitou culture of Hunan and the Erligang culture of Zengzhou in the North China Plain region. Thus, the Ningzhen area had established communications both to the east and west as well as to the north and south. Within the Wei River area to the north in this region, the Huating culture demonstrates the interchange between the Liangzhu and Dawenkou cultural sequences, since it formed its own local culture from influences of those outside cultures. Overall, the Liangzhu culture around Lake Tai was the leading cultural area of the southeastern cultural region, followed by the Ningzhen culture, which was based on the riverbanks, and the Huating culture of the seacoast.

The fifth regional culture region was centered around Lake Huting and the Sichuan basin in the southwest, and it can be divided in to two areas, the Jianghan Plain and the Sichuan basin. Agriculture in the Jianghan Plain began as early as 7000–8000 B.P., as found in the Chengbeixi and Pengtoushan sites of Hubin in Dongting, though even earlier indications may have been found at the Yuchanyan site in Hunan's Dao County. The culture of this area can be divided into three main local sequences: 1) the Daxi cultural sequence, as represented by the Daxi, Honghuatao, and Guanmiaoshan sites; 2) the cultural sequence to the north on the upper reaches of the Han River, represented by the Qinglongquan and Xiawangang sites; and 3) the Qujialing cultural sequence to the east, represented by the Fangyingtai and Qujialing sites. These three cultural sequences mutually influenced one another and were also influenced by the regional cultures to the north, on the North China Plain. For example, considering the Qinglongquan culture, the earlier strata indicate that it was influenced by the Yangshao culture from the north, and the middle stratum shows the influence of the Qujialing culture of the same northern system, whereas the later stratum shows influence from the Shijiahe culture of the southwestern Daxi cultural area. By the time of the Bronze Age, with the rise of the state of Chu, this Jianghan area became the main locus of what was later referred to as the Chu culture.

The cultures of the second area in this region, the Sichuan basin, can be divided into the Ba and the Shu cultures. Dating from between 6000–5000 B.P., the lowest stratum of the Sanxingdui site represents the origin of the ancient Ba-Shu culture. By 3000 B.C.E., entering the historical period (where we begin to use B.C.E. and C.E., as mentioned in the preface), this culture had divided into the dual systems of the Ba and Shu bronze cultures, which had independent communication with the Shang and Zhou bronze cultures of the North China Plain.

The sites of the sixth regional culture system are distributed generally along a line from Lake Boyang to the Pearl River delta in the south of China. The eastern subsystem lies along the seacoast and low hills from Zhejiang to Fujian and Taiwan. The central sequence is at the source of the Gan River, straddling Wuling and going into Beijiang, and the western sequence is centered where the Yanxiang River crosses Wuling and enters Xijiang. The pottery of all three of these sequences is characterized by stamped geometric designs, though each of these sequences has its own characteristics, and within each of these sequences there are even smaller cultural groups. The cultural interactions of the region were focused eastward, toward the coastal regions along the Pacific, where the island chains, combined with the north-flowing ocean currents and the seasonal winds, fostered communication between these mainland cultures and the oceanic cultures.

During the Neolithic, these six cultural regions, to greater or lesser extents, all had some degree of mutual influence. For example, the Later Yangshao culture of the North China Plain, the Qingliangang culture

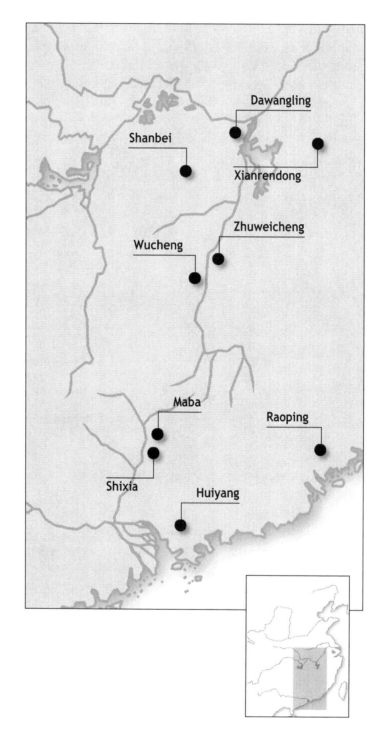

FIGURE 1.13 Major Archaeological Sites of the Southern Cultural Region

and various cultures of the Dawenkou in the eastern region, and the Qujialing culture of the southeastern region all lived almost as if they were close neighbors, with well-established lines of communication. By 4000 B.P., peoples of the Hongshan culture in the north moved along the Zhangjiakou route through the steppes and then shifted to the Fen River valley in Shanxi, there mixing with the Yangshao culture from the Guanzhong region, as seen in the Taosi site near the Fen River basin. This Taoshi culture combined influences from the northern Jianghan culture and cultures of the eastern seaboard. Through these processes of aggregation, the culture of the North China Plain developed more powerfully, so that it could take control as the leading force during the three dynasties of the Xia, Shang, and Zhou. Somewhat before 1000 B.C.E., the establishment of the Zhou dynasty (1045–256 B.C.E.) enabled the Hua-Xia culture of the North China Plain to blend with the eastern cultures and produce the mainstream culture of the Yellow River. Slightly later, the Chu culture pulled together the strengths of the Jianghan and the other southern cultures to form the mainstream culture of the Yangzi River. After another relatively brief period, the southeastern culture of Wuyue fought a long but ultimately unsuccessful military campaign against these two great cultures, furthering the process of cultural mixing. Finally, under the Qin dynasty (221–206 B.C.E.), the numerous cultural groups of China at last began to meld into a cohesive whole, but we should note that the numerous differences coloring the many peoples of China of today in fact have their roots long, long ago in these early Neolithic cultures.

5. Ancient Legends and Ethnic Divisions

Just as in other societies of the world, the traditions of Chinese cultures preserve a great body of myths and legends, which transmit stories of cultural heroes that have historical aspects to them. To the extent that we can sort out the different aspects of these legends, we can catch glimpses of historical developments that predate the historical record.

The main themes of the legends, familiar to almost all Chinese, include a great variety of these stories: Pangu establishing heaven and earth, Nüwa creating mankind from clay and repairing the split in the heavens,

Shen Nong bringing agriculture to the world, Youchaoshi showing mankind how to build, the Yellow Emperor establishing government, the transmission of rulership between the Five Emperors, and the actions of the rulers Yao, Shun, and Yu to cultivate able successors and then yield the throne to them. Although they may be commonly considered together, these legends in fact have distinctly different origins, and it was a long and gradual process that wove together the traditions of different ethnic groups into a body of myths. As such, they may embody the recollection of a time when Chinese society was first coming together, a recollection that can also be seen in the myths of many other societies.

For example, the story of the creation of the world by Nüwa is not recorded until the Han dynasty, and ethnologists have established that it originated with the peoples of southern China and has a very close relationship to creation myths found in the Indian subcontinent. Similarly, the earliest appearance of the story of Nüwa mending the heavens and forming mankind is found in the Chu culture of southern China. Moreover, the visual image of Nüwa joined with her elder brother, Fuxi, especially in the form so frequently seen in the Han, where their bodies are shown with the tails of snakes, may also come from the south and be related to legends of brother-sister coupling. But the variant of this story that connects Nüwa's repair of the heavens to the flood deity, Gonggong, striking the pillar supporting the heavens, Mount Buzhou, is related to the myths of cosmogenesis and the taming of floods. This group of stories is quite complex, and their central character, Buzhou, has a long and well-established tradition in northern China, one quite unrelated to the southern tradition of Nüwa.

The stories collected around the figure of the Yellow Emperor (Huang Di) are one of the most significant parts of the Chinese legendary tradition, and to this day he is revered by most Chinese as having established the identity of the Chinese people. But these Yellow Emperor legends include a great variety of different stories: the conflict of the Yellow Emperor with both the god of war, Chiyou, and the Emperor Yan; his systematic organization of the different images of cultural heroes; and his role as the forerunner of the Five Emperors and thus the common ancestor for all the later dynasties. Though the Yellow Emperor is an individual, he also represents a dynasty, and his opponents, the Emperor Yan and Shen Nong, stand for an earlier historical epoch. This multifaceted complexity shows that the body of legends surrounding the Yellow Emperor have diverse origins and methods of composition. Put as succinctly as possible, the Yellow Emperor is the ruler of mankind, and he bears the responsibility for overseeing the world and giving birth to culture. He is at the same time a deity and a controller of deities, able to dispatch gods and demons on his missions and with the superhuman powers of calling the winds and summoning the rain.

Since the legends surrounding the Yellow Emperor are so complex, organizing them and distinguishing the kernels of historical events within them is a demanding task. Furthermore, since the sites mentioned in these tales range across all of northern China, it is difficult to come to any conclusion as to the region from which these stories sprang. But despite these difficulties, there are some important clues. According to the section on the Five Emperors in the *Records of the Grand Historian (Shiji)*, the Yellow Emperor did not have a fixed abode, moving with a troop of armed followers from camp to camp. Furthermore, the original meanings of the two characters of the Yellow Emperor's alternate name, Xuanyuan, are both related to wheeled vehicles, whereas his enemy, the Emperor Yan, is also known as Shen Nong, or the god of agriculture. Thus these two opposing leaders may echo an early conflict between nomadic peoples and settled farmers. The sites of two important battles mentioned in these stories, Zhuolu and Banquan, are both located in the northern part of modern Hebei, the region where early agricultural and nomadic peoples would have come into contact. Indeed, in later times the advances and retreats of northern nomadic peoples also occurred along this belt. Thus the groups represented by the Yellow Emperor and the Emperor Yan may have originally been in northern Hebei.

Another enemy who fought against the Yellow Emperor, Chiyou, appears in these legends as a great villain. But up until the Han dynasty, among the deities of the Shandong region, one of the heroic leaders of the Eight Spirit Gods was this same Chiyou. These two strains of nomadic Yellow Emperor legends can be correlated with the locations of the Yangshao culture in the earliest agricultural sites of Cishan and Peiligang as well as with the lower stratum of Xia-period sites found across northern Hebei. Accordingly, most archaeologists view the legends as representing a prolonged conflict between these peoples, with the northern peoples represented by the Yellow Emperor emerging victorious in this struggle

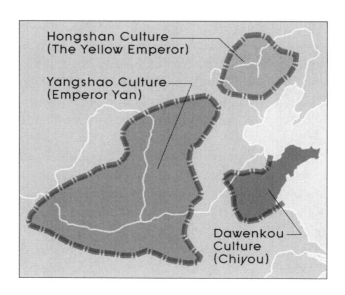

FIGURE 1.14 Early Neolithic Cultures of Northern China

and moving down into the agricultural areas to give up their warlike life for settled agricultural practices.

At the same time, if Chiyou originated in the Shandong peninsula, since he has long been identified with a martial deity there, he may represent the peoples of the early Dawenkou culture. In fact, although this group, known in historical times as the eastern Yi peoples, may have been defeated in their early attempts to move into Hebei, they remained a determined enemy of the Hua-Xia culture up until the historical period of the Zhou dynasty.

The body of legends surrounding the Five Emperors (Huang Di, Zhuanxu, Ku, Yao, and Shun) also mentions Taihao and Shaohao, and the state of Tan during the Spring and Autumn period (722–481 B.C.E.) was considered to be descended from Shaohao. In addition, the people of Tan considered themselves to be represented by the animal spirit, or totem, of a bird, and they used the names of birds to indicate government offices, as noted in the ancient *Zuo Commentary* (*Zuozhuan*, year 10 of Duke Zhao, 529 B.C.E.). Although it would be very difficult to assign to this ancient tradition a historical time period, it probably has its origins in a common folk memory. The Tan state that revered Taihao as their earliest ancestor was located in the Ji River basin. The original meaning of the characters in the names Taihao and Shaohao are related to the brightness of the sun. Moreover, inscriptions on pottery from Dawenkou culture sites are characterized by a figure representing the sun above the mountains, and this figure is similar to the character for *hao* in these two names. Based on these observations, it appears likely that there was a three-way competition between the cultures represented by Emperor Yan, the Yellow Emperor, and Chiyou—undoubtedly representing the Yangshao, Hongshan, and Dawenkou cultures. This conflict may have become associated with the body of legends surrounding the Five Emperors and then been transformed into the later concept of the reigns of three successive rulers (*sanhuang*, or Three Sovereigns: Heavenly, Earthly, and Human; or Fuxi, Nüwa, and Shen Nong) who preceded the Five Emperors.

Emperor Ku and his father, Zhuanxu, are generally considered to be less important members of the Five Emperors. But the *Book of Rites* (*Liji*), in its chapter on offerings (*jifa*), notes that the three early dynasties of Yu, Yin, and Zhou all revered Emperor Ku as their founder, and his cultural contributions are considered to include arranging the order of the constellations of stars. In ancient societies, astronomical knowledge was closely connected to both agriculture and religious beliefs, and so the Emperor Ku was a highly significant figure, and his prestige was based on religious powers. In the *Classic of Mountains and Seas* (*Shanhaijing*), the collection of early Chinese mythical materials, an Emperor Jun is said to have given birth to the sun and the moon, which may represent the same concept as Emperor Ku but assigning it a different name. This can also be understood as the establishment of a calendrical system, which in ancient times combined religion and astronomy. The *Classic of Mountains and Seas*, with its great combination of the strange and marvelous, appears not to be a product of the northern literary tradition and is more likely to have stemmed from the Jianghan culture of the Yangzi River.

China's earliest recorded poet, Qu Yuan (ca. 340–278 B.C.E.), was from the Chu region in the south during the Warring States period (476 B.C.E. to the unification of China by the Qin dynasty, in 221 B.C.E.). He referred to Zhuanxu as his ancestor, and Zhuanxu is also associated with the fire god Zhurong Baixing, an association supported by the original meaning of the characters in his other name, Gaoyang. The cult of Zhurong Baixing is popular in the Huai River area, between northern and southern China, and it may connect several ethnic groups. Following the Spring and Autumn period (after 481 B.C.E.), the Mie clan mixed with the Bai ethnic group of what is now Hubei, forming the state of Chu, which rose to such prominence that it could challenge the political and cultural domination of the northern Hua-Xia states.

Again, in the *Book of Rites*'s chapter on offerings, the contribution of Zhuanxu is said to be improving on the Yellow Emperor's task of "correcting the names of all things," thus demonstrating his connection with the Yellow Emperor tradition. Zhuanxu is also said to have commanded Chongli to divide the heavens and the earth into the realms of mankind and of the gods, a task that points to the diminishing power of the priestly class and the increasing strength of the secular world, though Zhuanxu overall maintains a great sense of sacredness.

In what is referred to as the Chu culture, the names and activities of deities in the writings of Qu Yuan are distinctly different from those of northern Chinese cultures. Although the Chu culture as such became distinct only as late as the Spring and Autumn period, it is not simply a product of the people who brought with them the cult of Zhurong Baixing. In fact, the culture of the Bai Man, the original inhabitants of the Jianghan area, also contributed greatly to the Chu culture. Determining the relationship between Zhuanxu and the southern shamanic religious tradition of Chu is extremely difficult. But it can be seen that the tradition of the Five Emperors developed only very gradually in the north, perhaps as a result of developments by the Chu peoples of the south, and the mixing of these two cultures was responsible for the admission of Zhuanxu as one of the Five Emperors.

The *Book of Rites* chapter on offerings lists many of the figures from ancient Chinese legends, indicating that by this time (extant texts date from the Han dynasty) they were considered worthy of inclusion in the formal record of religious observances. These figures include the deities who brought agriculture to the world—Shen Nong and Houji—as well as the water gods who controlled floods—Gun, his son Yu, and Ming, who was the legendary founder of the Shang dynasty (1600–1046 B.C.E.). So here, as in many other cultures, agriculture and water control (flood control) are represented by mythical heroes. In these early myths, Gonggong is the villain responsible for smashing Mount Zhou, which supported the heavens, causing heaven and earth to tilt, just as Chiyou did. Gonggong

is generally considered to be outside the mainstream of the northern legends, but this chapter of the *Book of Rites* mentions Gonggong as one
of the lords of early China and the father of Houtu, who was the god of
earth and is considered to be of very high rank. This series of reverential
references to Gonggong, a figure from outside the northern cultural tradition, is likely to be product of ancient cultural memories that were later
incorporated into a more organized set of legends.

The mass of ancient Chinese legends can be quite complex and con-
fusing, and they display many conflicting differences in the early textual
sources. But this is only natural, considering the diversity of these sources,
coming from both elite and commoner cultures, each with its own particular legends that were then edited through different processes and stages
into the various works. This section is much too brief to go into detail, and
we have presented only a small selection of figures from these legends to
illustrate how the heroic figures from disparate cultures were gradually
assimilated into a mythic system within which we can still distinguish the
traces of their origins. Given the lack of materials, it is also not possible
to develop a complete account of their relationship with cultural groups
from the archaeological record. But we can briefly sketch their connection, indicating how traces of these very early interactions can be found in
the legends still current in China today.

6. The Development of Early Complex Societies

The previous sections have discussed the formation and expansion of
village-based societies, the regionalization of Neolithic cultures, and the
formation of cultural groups. The subsequent societies, based on larger
settlements, were more complex, incorporating several village groups. In
addition to the increased size of settlements, the formation of cultural
groups led to the development of a greater sense of cultural identity in the
peoples of that time, so that they could coalesce into social groups bound
together by common beliefs. These two factors formed the basis for the
development of complex societies.

About five thousand years ago, according to the archaeological materials we currently possess, the complex societies emerging at that time
shared the following characteristics:

- Accumulation of greater wealth enabled more advanced training of craftsmen, who could create finer ritual implements.
- Ritual centers with dedicated ceremonial buildings could reflect different levels of importance in a social or religious hierarchy.
- As some individuals gained control over greater wealth or power, society was divided into more strata, and these hierarchies developed differently in the various regions of China.
- By the time societies had grown sufficiently complex, an upper social stratum with greater power had developed to handle the administration of these nascent states.
- The stratification of villages brought about more central villages with larger populations and concentrations of wealth, and these became both the official places of residence for more powerful individuals as well as regional trading and ritual centers. These larger settled areas were ancient cities, and many had provisions for defense, such as city walls or moats.
- To provide for this increased level of ritual and government, there were specialized individuals responsible for certain tasks, for which they required more developed knowledge of certain areas. In addition, writing or other symbolic systems may have developed, which is one of the main indicators of a culture having reached the level of civilization.

In the different regions of China, archaeologists frequently find Neolithic sites that stand out as distinctly different from the others, such as tomb 10 from the Dawenkou culture in Tai-an, Shandong, with its dazzling array of finely crafted funerary articles. The relics from this tomb include a jade axe head, an ivory comb, a drum covered with alligator skin, and numerous pieces of delicate white pottery—ritual articles and levels of craftsmanship that indicate both long-range trading and the power and wealth of the person buried in this tomb. That this was the location for a limited group of individuals controlling greater status and power in the Dawenkou culture indicates that this culture had developed centralized villages by that time, villages whose leaders had the discrimination and power to accumulate a great number of highly valuable possessions, many of which could be interred along with them after death.

This development of centralized villages can be seen even more clearly in the large settlement of Dadiwan Site A, located in Gansu's Qin-an Prefecture. This site contains the remains of numerous large buildings, in

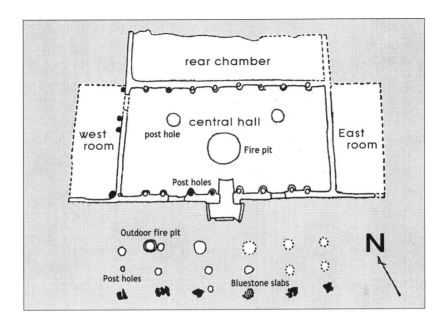

FIGURE 1.15 Plan of Dadiwan Building Site 901

particular building 901, at its center, on the northern slopes of a mountain. The urban area fans out downward to the south and is divided into a number of smaller districts, each indicated by the traces of a larger building surrounded by smaller ones. In particular, the foundations of building 901 show that a front hall faced south, with a chamber to the rear and flanking rooms to each side. The central hall is quite large, sixteen meters wide and eight meters deep, having an entranceway in the middle of the front wall, with steps down to ground level. The floor is a hard earthen material, compacted and polished smooth, and in the center there is a large round firepit two and a half meters across. In the southern and northern walls at the back and front of this hall there are post holes from eight columns that would have supported the roof, and behind the firepit, evenly placed to the right and left, are two even larger post holes. When complete, this would have been an awe-inspiring structure. Outside the front hall is a leveled area extending out about six meters, with a row of six pairs of columns in front, each pair of which has a bluestone slab to the outside. To the south of building 901, there are the indications of many large and small buildings in clusters, with smaller buildings around a larger one in the centers of these clusters. All of these dwellings face to the north, in the direction of building 901. The larger buildings in the centers of these clusters are typified by building 405, which is about fourteen meters wide and eleven meters deep, having a firepit in the middle and walls with large columns for the roof and smaller columns to stabilize the earthen walls. Just west of building 405 there is a much smaller building, about twenty-seven square meters in area, but with the same structural system of larger roof columns and smaller wall columns, essentially the same as building 405 but on a much smaller scale.

The larger residential areas of Dadiwan Site A show a hierarchy of three levels, and overall it appears to be a ritual or administrative center, what might be called a capital. Each of the smallest areas might have had a tertiary leader; building 405 might indicate a secondary level of leadership, and building 901 would be for the highest level, where the leaders of the lower levels might be called together, with the six pairs of columns and six bluestone slabs reflecting the social groupings. The firepits, both inside and outside building 901, would have been for sacrificial offerings. Outside the society of this capital city, there could also have been a corresponding hierarchy of organization down to the towns or smaller villages.

In northern China, along the southern regions of Inner Mongolia, western Liaoning, and northern Hebei, many sites of large-scale settlements have also been found, dating to more than five thousand years B.P. Collectively referred to as the Hongshan culture, in the Liaoning counties of Lingyuan and Jianping, as well as the neighboring Niuheliang site, covering an area of more than twenty square kilometers, are groups of stone burial cairns, stone altars, mountain altars, pyramids, and temples to female deities, comprising a great ritual center. The temples to female deities are identified as such by the presence of female figures of varying sizes shaped from clay. The larger figures remain only in fragments, such as arms, legs, or an ear, but these are sufficient to indicate that the figures originally would have been two to three times life size. There is also a largely intact head to one of these figures, approximately life size and quite realistic, with color applied to the face and round pieces of jade for the eyes. The smaller figures of female deities include many that are pregnant, displaying the power of fertility. Based on reconstructions from fragments, these temples to female deities contained figures of several different sizes—human size, twice human size, and three times human size.

They were arranged in an orderly fashion, with the largest of the figures in the center of the main shrine room, representing the main deity of this temple. To the extent that the world of gods represented here reflects the world of the people who created it, this human society would also have been organized in several strata.

Another site that shows very similar characteristics is the Kazuo Dongshanzui site from the Hongshan culture, also in Liaoning. Since the 1970s, groups of masonry structures have been excavated, including a fragmentary female figurine about one-third life size and two groups of smaller clay figurines of varying sizes representing pregnant women. The Dongshanzui site is also a ritual center for sacrifices and burials, though on a smaller scale than the Niuheliang site. These two sites, which date from similar periods and are separated by only tens of kilometers, indicate two different levels of ritual center. Overall, the Hongshan culture sites are distributed along the Daling River basin, extending north to the Xar Moron River of Inner Mongolia, south to the Bohai Sea, east to the Liao River, and west to the upper reaches of the Luan River. The large Niuheliang site is centrally located in this region, and its connection to the river valley means of communication make it an effective point of control.

The Hongshan culture burial cairns are located mainly along the Daling River and its tributaries, mostly on hilltop sites, and so some scholars refer to them as mountain tombs and to the collection of these cairns as burial communities. In these Hongshan sites, jade carvings are frequently found representing a great variety of mythical and real forms, including bear-dragons, pig-dragons, two-headed beasts, eagles, tortoises, hooked cloud shapes, and interlocking circles. The jade used in these carvings is excellent and the carving very fine, examples from the Niuheliang site being especially beautiful. Only with substantial wealth could so many pieces of such quality have been accumulated. The mausoleums and temples, together with the sacrificial altars, mountain altars, and pyramids, appear to be assemblies related to the stone tumuli, indicating a combination of burial and ceremonial rituals not simply limited to offerings to the individuals interred in the tumuli. These people of high status would have had positions of religious and ritual significance, and the opinion of the archaeologist Guo Daxun that this society had already progressed to the point of having a state government is not improbable. The foundation of this government would have been not just in administrative or military

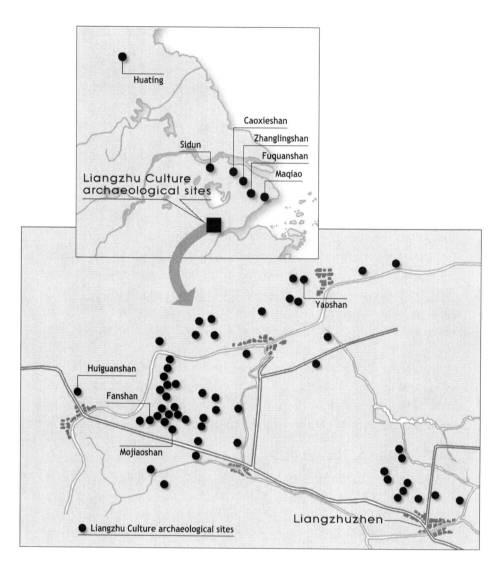

FIGURE 1.16 Major Sites in the Liangzhu Culture Cluster

power, but it must also have been based on religious ritual. The temples to female deities would have been at the center of this ritual system, as places for the worship of fertility or for shamanic rituals.

In southeastern China, the Liangzhu culture, which takes its name from the town of that name, in Yuhang County, near the modern city of Hangzhou in Zhejiang, has been dated to between 5300 to 4000 B.P. Sites of the Liangzhu culture are located mostly over a triangular area between the estuaries of the Yangzi and Qiantang rivers and Lake Taihu, although they also extend north of the Yangzi, into Jiangsu, with the Huating site in Xinyi County. But the greatest concentration of these sites is in Yuhang County, in the valleys between the towns of Liangzhu, Pingyao, and Anxi. Here, in just over thirty square kilometers, over a hundred large-scale sites have been found close together, leading it to be called the Liangzhu culture cluster of sites. Among these is one extremely large construction, the Mojiaoshan site, which has a large rammed-earth foundation that supported a great wooden structure, and in the southeastern area of the site is a fire altar that supported fires for long periods of time. The Mojiaoshan site lies at the center of the Liangzhu sites, surrounded by an especially high number of large tombs, indicating that this may have been the central area of that culture and the Mojiaoshan site the focus of that central area.

The large earthen burial tumuli of the Liangzhu culture rise up like small mountains heaped out of earth. One of these, the Fuquanshan site from Shanghai's Chingpu County, is a large pyramid ninety-four meters from east to west and eight-four meters north to south. Based on its original height, it would have used 25,920 cubic meters of earth, and a small lake nearby may have its origin in the excavation of this earth.

These grave sites have yielded a great number of jade ritual objects: *cong*, large jade tubes that combine a square exterior with a round inner shape; *bi*, flat discs with a hole in the center; *huang*, flat rainbow shapes; *guan*, round tubes of jade that can be small or long; and *yue*, ceremonial axes. There can be over a thousand of these in a single grave. Of all these ritual objects, the *cong* appears to have been the most significant. Fanshan's Tomb 12 contained a large jade *cong* weighing more than six kilograms, with human-animal faces carved on all four sides, together with small figures of deities riding on flying beasts. The same figures also appear on a jade *yue* from that tomb. One of the archaeologists specializing in Liangzu sites, Wang Mingda, believes that the animal faces frequently found on the Liangzhu jade *cong* are simplified representations of the deities riding flying beasts. Another archaeologist, Chang Kwang-chih (1931–2001), further contended that these designs indicate a shamanic communication with deities descending from the heavens, symbolizing the connection between heaven and earth. In the Liangzhu tombs, males were also frequently buried with a *yue* representing a weapon and perhaps symbolizing the military power of the deceased. This combination of symbolic items indicates how leaders in the Liangzhu culture could have wielded both religious and military power.

The Yaoshan site in Yuhang County is a small mountain topped with an altar. This altar is composed of several layers stepping up to the top, which is made of earth of the five symbolic colors, with a six-meter red square in the center and a three-meter-wide layer of gravel around it. South of the altar are arranged twelve tombs, half for men and half for women, with jade *yue* in the men's tombs. The nearby Huiguanshan site also has an altar very similar to the one at Yaoshan, surrounded by four large tombs. In both of these sites, the rear portions of the tombs were cut into the stratum of the altar, as if the tombs were built later in this manmade mountain with an altar on the top, so that climbing the tumulus was itself an offering to heaven.

The Mojiaoshan site is a large artificial earthen terrace, about 670 meters from east to west and 450 meters north to south; on top are blocks formed of earth from three mountains, Damojiaoshan, Xiaomojiaoshan, and Guishan. In the middle of these three blocks is a rammed-earth foundation of more than twenty thousand square meters, with two lines of post holes for giant columns. On the southern edge of this great terrace are large masses of fire-baked earth.

This site was clearly an architectural complex used for important ceremonies. Within a radius of about three kilometers, there are more than ten burial tumuli for high-status individuals from the Liangzhu culture, as denoted by the significant number of associated burials or the large number of ritual implements contained in the tumuli. Clearly, the Mojiaoshan site was of great ritual importance.

Far to the west, at Changzhou's Sidun site, there is an even larger manmade earthen terrace, of almost a square kilometer in area. In the very center is an altar raised about twenty meters and surrounded by a square internal watercourse. Outside of this is a less firmly compacted band of earth, used for the graves of high-status individuals. Outside of these graves is a level band of even less firmly compacted earth, upon which were built houses. Beyond this, centered on the altar, is a cross-shaped river bed connecting the inner moat with an outer one and dividing the graves and dwellings of the nobles into four quadrants. As the archaeological strata make clear, the watercourses had both defensive and communication functions, further adding to the complexity of this ritual center.

Many of these Liangzhu sites reflect a multilevel regional hierarchy. The area around Liangzhu in Yuhang was the center, the Sidun site was the next level outside of that, and the earthen mounds at Shanghai's Fuyuanshan sites were peripheral, lower-level centers. Large-scale sites such as Fanshan or Yaoshan, with large tombs or groups of tombs, were also parts of ritual centers, as indicated by the great number, variety, and quality of burial objects excavated. A number of the smaller earthen mounds at Fuyushan were also significant graves, although their scale was smaller and the grave articles of a lower grade, somewhat below that of the average small tombs from the more central Liangzhu culture, having only pottery and lacking jade. This difference in grave goods reflects the lower social or ritual rank of these peripheral centers.

Accordingly, the social structure of the Liangzhu culture was highly stratified and complex, with great wealth and significant organizational ability. The leaders of this society appear to have wielded both religious and military power. Furthermore, the area of the Liangzhu culture that extended north of the Yangtze and the Huating site of the Dawenkou culture in Jiangsu both reflect the interchange between these two cultures, with the Liangzhu culture being the main one and Dawenkou subordinate to it, perhaps indicating that the Liangzhu culture had conquered this northern area and subdued its people. If this inference is correct, it would indicate that the Liangzhu culture had already developed to the rank of a state based on the use of military force.

Based on the Yangshao culture of the Dadiwan site described above, together with the Hongshan culture along the Daling River and the Liangzhu culture of the Jiangnan region, we can see that five thousand years ago these societies had developed the ability to control large regions and command the energy of great numbers of people. These were societies of substantial wealth and multistrata complexity. Comparing these complex societies to the humans of ten thousand years ago, who were just mastering the ability to raise livestock or grow crops and had just started to live in settled communities, we can see that these five thousand years permitted great advancements, which led to the development of societies that had coalesced together and split into subordinate groups, developing highly complex governments and religions.

7. A Comparison with Cultural Developments in Ancient Mesopotamia

The culture of ancient Mesopotamia was perhaps the most advanced of the great ancient cultures. The beginning of this chapter discussed the origins of agriculture and settled communities in China, although archaeological evidence shows that the agricultural revolution and the rise of cities first appeared in Mesopotamia. But the cultures of China had some major differences from their slightly earlier Middle Eastern counterparts, and a brief review of the development of ancient Mesopotamia will help to give a perspective on the ancient cultures of China. In terms of agriculture, early cultures in northern China were based on the cultivation of millet, and the southern cultures grew rice; in contrast, grains such as barley, wheat, rye, and oats were the staple crops of Mesopotamia. Since these three types of agriculture had fundamentally different crops and methods of cultivation, it appears that they developed for the most part independently, without major influences from cultural dissemination. And this cultural separation is important to keep in mind when comparing cultures. Furthermore, the cultural contexts of these two major regions were of a significantly different scale. Although the ancient Chinese cultures spread over most of the area comprising the Chinese nation today, in contrast, ancient Mesopotamia was limited to a small area of modern Iraq, comparable in size to a single one of the several ancient Chinese cultures, such as the Dawenkou cultural group of Shandong. Accordingly, the cultural interactions that influenced ancient Chinese cultures were much more complex. Interactions that affected the rise and fall of the various areas of Mesopotamian culture were more limited—although relations with surrounding cultures, especially that of Egypt, do indicate a multivalent interaction with other major cultural regions.

According to the archaeological evidence we currently have for China, the development of agriculture in Mesopotamia occurred earlier than it did in China. In Mesopotamia, culture developed in the area between the Euphrates and Tigris rivers and in the downstream alluvial plain. Up to several decades ago, most theories on the development of civilizations considered that they all began in major river valleys—the Tigris and Euphrates, the Nile, the Indus, and the Yellow River. These were the "cradles of civilization," and the beginnings of agriculture in Mesopotamia lay in the river plains of the Fertile Crescent.

But more recent excavations at sites such as Hallan Cemi, in southeastern Turkey on the headwaters of one of the tributaries of the Tigris, have indicated that the development of agriculture may not have taken such a clear path. In this ancient townsite, though its inhabitants had yet to develop the cultivation of crops, bones from a great many yearling piglets were found, indicating that pork was a staple food. Carbon-14 dating from this site clearly indicates that it was occupied between 10,400 to 10,000 B.P., making it the earliest indication for the production of food by mankind. Similarly, from the Zawi Chemi Chandar site in the Zagros Mountains northwest of Mesopotamia, on the headwaters of the Euphrates, are indications that people had begun to domesticate bovine livestock by about 10,000 B.P. Somewhat later, about 9000 B.P., the growing of crops and raising of goats had become common, though hunting and gathering remained mainstays of the food supply. Moving up to 8000 or 7000 B.P., in the foothills of the Zagros Mountains many small agricultural settlements have been found, the most significant of which is the Jarmo site. Here, in addition to a grain-based agriculture, we also find evidence for the breeding of pigs. Other early sites from approximately this period revealing the beginnings of agriculture include Çatalhöyük, in the mountainous Anatolian region of Turkey to the northwest of Mesopotamia, and Jericho, of later Biblical fame, in the modern-day regions of Israel and Palestine. These sites are all very early cultures, some of which had yet to develop pottery and all of which retained the earlier practices of hunting and gathering.

In many areas over the foothills of the Zagros Mountains, the wild plants that were the origins of cultivated cereal grains can still be found, and it is from these families of wild grains that the people of ancient Mesopotamia selected strains that were better suited for cultivation. The earliest of these grains to be cultivated was rye, followed by similar grains such as einkorn, emmer, two-rowed and six-rowed barley, and the grain commonly known today as bread wheat, as well as species of beans. In these regions, goats, sheep, dogs, and pigs were also raised. Thus, by 8000 B.P. highland Anatolian regions had a well-formed system of agriculture that could provide the basis of later developments in agricultural and settlement patterns in the cultures of Europe, North Africa, and the West Asian regions around the Persian Gulf.

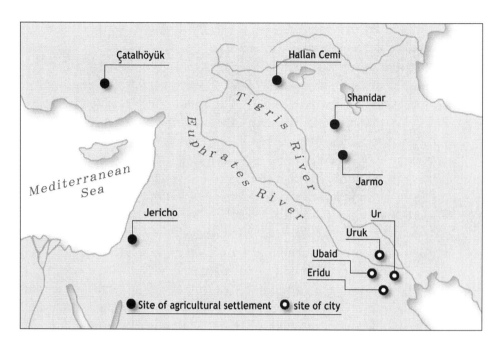

FIGURE 1.17 Major Cultural Sites in Mesopotamia

The history of cultivated crops and domesticated animals in Mesopotamia begins one to two thousand years earlier than similar levels of agriculture in China currently known to archaeologists. But because the early crops cultivated in East Asia are entirely different, China must have had a separate agricultural revolution. The main sites for millet-growing regions of North China, the Cishan and Peiligang cultures, are found in the foothills of the western Taihang Mountains, running through Hebei, Shanxi, and Henan, not in the eastern coastal or alluvial areas that were home to later, more developed cultures. In the mountainous regions of northern China, wild strains of millet that could have provided the basis for the later cultivated crops are still common. This upland origin of agriculture shows a trend very similar to the development of cultivated grains in Mesopotamia. Many varieties of millet successively became important cultivars, and they remain in cultivation up to the present time. The early varieties of wheat grown here, with the exception of a few minor strains, have also remained in cultivation. Of the rice-growing sites in the south, the earliest may be Yuchanyan, which lies to the west, in a basin surrounded by mountains in Hunan's Dao County. The current type of paddy rice commonly grown in China has its origins in wild varieties of the moist and swampy regions from Yunnan to Guangdong. Both the round-grain and the long-grain types of paddy rice grown in China today are derived from these early wild varieties. Thus agricultural developments in both northern and southern China, though independent, follow a pattern similar to that found in the Middle East.

Although agriculture developed in upland regions, not in great river valleys, it was in the lowland regions that civilization was to develop. Five thousand years before the present, the lower alluvial plains of Mesopotamia had developed many agricultural settlements. An ample supply of water is necessary to obtain good yields from wheat, and since the foothills of the Zagros Mountains are not steep and receive sufficient rainfall, wheat can be grown there. But the more level areas of the alluvial plain, with their better soil and greater supply of river water, are even more productive. To develop higher yields from crops such as bread wheat, early peoples began to rely on river water. Thus the agricultural practices that had originated in highland areas of the Zagros Mountains in the eastern Mediterranean regions flourished in the many agricultural settlements that grew up along the banks of the Euphrates and the Tigris.

These more developed early settlements appeared in many areas, but they were most closely spaced in the southern alluvial plains of Mesopotamia. About five thousand years before the present, the beginnings of an urban economy can be seen in the Ubaid culture, which arose on the lower reaches of the Euphrates, some distance upstream from the marshlands at the river's estuary. This process of urbanization was very gradual, progressing from collections of neighboring small settlements, from which emerged a more centrally located settlement that gradually became a central town within a constellation of smaller towns. This central town could effectively collect resources and manpower and thereby improve living conditions. The alluvial plains of Mesopotamia are very low and level, with good soil, but there was little stone for building, and it had to be acquired from other areas. In addition, since the vegetation on these plains was mostly low, with few large trees, most timber also had to be brought in from elsewhere. Because of the low and level topography, flooding occurred frequently, and the water table tended to be slightly saline, making it unsuitable for agriculture. Thus these early cultures needed to establish irrigation systems that could cleanse the alkaline soil. Long-range trading and techniques of water control were within the abilities of the towns that emerged in this region, and they also enabled cultures to grow beyond the scale of these early collections of towns, leading to the development of transportation and networks of communication. Based on the Ubaid culture, a number of cities developed in this southern region, the most important of which were Ur, Eridu, and Uruk.

At this point in time, defensive city walls were built, along with the development of urban markets and greater wealth. But even more significant were the specialized branches of knowledge that people of these cities developed, such as the ability to calculate astronomical calendars to support agriculture and the tools for the measurements and calculations necessary for trade. Religious beliefs also grew more complex, including the worship of the sun, moon, and stars, and these religious beliefs not only provided explanations for natural phenomena but also formed the foundation of the new fields of knowledge. Altogether, this brief sketch indicates how the Mesopotamian cultures had formed a highly developed, large-scale civilization by 5000 to 4000 B.P., a civilization that was multifaceted, with a complex social hierarchy and division of labor.

This pattern of development in Mesopotamia was similar to that of Neolithic cultures in China such as those of Hongshan, Liangzhu, or Yangshao. Though agriculture in these two regions of the world evolved independently, both areas had similar agricultural revolutions and saw the resulting evolution of complex societies. But as we have noted, archaeological discoveries in China show there were two main parallel directions of cultural development, one in the north and one in the south. At the same time, we should also note two aspects of the Chinese situation: first, in the north, agriculture began in the Taihang Mountains, whereas the complex society of the Hongshan culture arose around the Liao River in Manchuria; second, in the south agriculture began in an upland basin of Hunan, whereas the complex society of the Liangzhu culture arose in the lower Jiangnan regions. Agricultural development and complex societies thus appear at this point to be two separate stages of the early cultural evolution in both the Near East and in China, though a clearer understanding of their relationship must await further archaeological discoveries.

This chapter discusses four areas: geography, legends, archaeology, and a comparison between the developments in Mesopotamia and China. These seemingly independent topics are grouped in one chapter because they reveal certain patterns of convergence toward larger homogenized cultural entities.

The section on the geography of this part of East Asia demonstrates how such a vast stretch of land is subdivided into several areas and regions having a different types of terrain.

Local environments demanded that the peoples who lived there make certain adaptations, and thus local "cultures," including livelihoods, social organization, and views on nature and man, gradually took shape.

The legends, some remnants of which survive in later literary sources, are envisioned as relics of collective memories that reveal how the ancient peoples recorded their experiences in the names of heroes and their memorable deeds. These legends are rather simplified and distorted versions of their history before they had the skill to write self-conscious history. For instance, the relationship between Huangdi and Yandi was sometimes that of siblings and sometimes that of contenders. Such stories may reveal the struggles and then the unions between two groups of peoples who lived near each other and experienced a long process of contention and merging. Likewise, the story that the Zhurong league of eight groups with different surnames were descendents of children born to the same mother is likely a justification of the alliance of eight otherwise unrelated peoples. These stories may reflect the fact that the ancient peoples might have constantly regrouped themselves into larger groups, given their lengthy associations.

The discussions on archaeological information generally benefit by adopting the profound analysis conducted by Su Bingqi, who recognized a process whereby local cultures merged into more inclusive and more complex ones occupying larger areas and then later grouped into identifiable regional cultural complexes. No fewer than a half dozen of these major archaeological cultural regions have been identified in the late phase of the Chinese Neolithic.

The patterns of change apparent in both legends and the analysis of archaeological materials in the case of ancient China appear consistent. A comparison of the Chinese case with that of ancient Mesopotamia seems to support the idea that such a pattern may represent a rather common confluence and convergence of local into regional cultures that is shared by peoples who expanded and enriched the cultures of smaller areas through a process of contact-conflict and interactive reshaping of their otherwise individual local heritages.

In conclusion, it seems that the scenario of constant merging of smaller cultural entities to form larger and more inclusive ones may be a rehearsal for the process of the long-range development of Chinese cultural history, with the many turns and changes throughout several thousands of years that entails. This process will be explored in detail in the following chapters of this book.

Suggestions for Further Reading

GENERAL REFERENCES

Blunden, Caroline, and Mark Elvin. *The Cultural Atlas of China*. New York: Facts on File, 1983.

Chan, Wing-tsit. *A Source Book in Chinese Philosophy*. Princeton, N.J.: Princeton University Press, 1963.

De Bary, Wm. Theodore, and Irene Bloom, eds. *Sources of Chinese Tradition*. Vol. 1: *From Earliest Times to 1600*. 2nd edition. New York: Columbia University Press, 1999.

Ebrey, Patricia Buckley, ed. *The Cambridge Illustrated History of China*. 2nd ed. Cambridge: Cambridge University Press, 2010.

Elvin, Mark. *The Retreat of the Elephants: An Environmental History of China*. New Haven, Conn.: Yale University Press, 2006.

Mair, Victor H., ed. *The Columbia Anthology of Traditional Chinese Literature*. New York: Columbia University Press, 1994.

Mair, Victor H., Nancy S. Steinhardt, and Paul R. Goldin, eds. *Hawai'i Reader in Traditional Chinese Culture*. Honolulu: University of Hawai'i Press, 2005.

Needham, Joseph, et al. *Science and Civilization in China*. Cambridge: Cambridge University Press, 1954–.

Owen, Stephen, ed. and trans. *An Anthology of Chinese Literature, Beginnings to 1911*. New York: Norton, 1996.

Owen, Stephen, and Kang-I Sun Chang. *The Cambridge History of Chinese Literature*. 2 Vols. Cambridge: Cambridge University Press, 2010.

Rawson, Jessica, ed. *The British Museum Book of Chinese Art*. London: Thames and Hudson, 1992.

Ropp, Paul S., ed. *Heritage of China*. Berkeley: University of California Press, 1990.

Sivin, Nathan, ed. *The Contemporary Atlas of China*. New York: Houghton Mifflin, 1988.

Sullivan, Michael. *The Arts of China*. 4th ed. Berkeley: University of California Press, 1999.

Tuan, Yi-Fu. *A Historical Geography of China*. Piscataway, N.J., Aldine Transaction, 2008.

Watson, William. *The Arts of China, 900–1620*. New Haven, Conn.: Yale University Press, 2000.

Wills, John E. Jr. *Mountain of Fame: Portraits in Chinese History*. Princeton, N.J.: Princeton University Press, 1994.

1. PREHISTORY: CHINA'S EARLIEST CULTURES ACCORDING TO REGIONAL ARCHAEOLOGY

Allan, Sarah. *The Shape of the Turtle: Myth, Art and Cosmos in Early China*. Albany: State University of New York Press, 1991.

Bagley, Robert. *Ancient Sichuan: Treasures from a Lost Civilization*. Princeton, N.J.: Princeton University Press, 2001.

Barker, Graeme. *Agricultural Revolution in Prehistory: Why Did Foragers Become Farmers?* Oxford: Oxford University Press, 2006.

Bellwood, Peter. *First Farmers: The Origins of Agricultural Societies*. Malden, Mass.: Blackwell, 2005.

Birrell, Anne. *Chinese Mythology: An Introduction*. Baltimore, Md.: Johns Hopkins University Press, 1993.

Chang, Kuang-Chih. *The Archaeology of Ancient China*. New Haven, Conn.: Yale University Press, 1986.

——. *Art, Myth, and Ritual: The Path to Political Authority in Ancient China*. Cambridge, Mass.: Harvard University Press, 1983.

Chang, Kuang-Chih, and Pingfang Xu. *The Formation of Chinese Civilization: An Archaeological Perspective of Ancient China*. New Haven, Conn.: Yale University Press, 2006.

Liu, Li. *The Chinese Neolithic: Trajectories to Early States*. Cambridge: Cambridge University Press, 2005.

Loewe, Michael, and Edward Shaughnessy, eds. *The Cambridge History of Ancient China: From the Origins of Civilization to 221 B.C.* Cambridge: Cambridge University Press, 1999.

2

The Emergence of Chinese Civilization

THE SIXTEENTH THROUGH THIRD CENTURIES B.C.E.

Though Chinese civilization had begun to take form even earlier, from the Shang to the Zhou dynasties, the Hua-Xia culture of early China more fully coalesced. Even more significantly, the Confucian system of thought in the north and Daoism in the Yangzi River basin had begun to develop and influence each other, forming the core of a Chinese way of thought. Thus many of the ways of understanding the questions of human life and what lies beyond emerged at this time.

1. Beginnings in the Bronze Age

The use of bronze and the war chariot brought deep and far reaching changes to the early Chinese cultures. Of these two advances, bronze left signs of its development, which we are better able to trace, whereas archaeologists have found few clues to indicate the early development of chariots. Nevertheless, these two major advances are likely to have appeared in China within the same time period, and they may both have been transmitted in stages through Central and Inner Asia.

Bronze is an alloy of copper and smaller amounts of tin. Pure copper itself is relatively soft, tin and lead are even softer, and all three have relatively low melting points. But after they have been melted together, the mixture acquires a very rigid structure and can be cast into a great variety of shapes. The earliest traces of copper implements have been found at the Cayonu Tepesi site, dated to around 7000 B.C.E., in southeastern modern Turkey, on one of the small tributaries of the Euphrates flowing from the southern edge of the Anatolian Mountains. The copper implements found there were made by hammering pure, naturally occurring copper to make both utilitarian and decorative items, including needles, awls, brooches, and beads. Since this site is not far from areas still rich in copper, the items found there are most likely to have been produced locally rather than obtained through trade. The subsequent Halaf culture, also in Anatolia, used free copper until the middle of the sixth millennium B.C.E., when the center of civilization shifted down into the plains of the Tigris and Euphrates rivers. The Halaf culture was a well-developed, irrigation-based agricultural system that supported a string of settlements with a complex society and temple buildings. This civilization, which began in the late seventh millennium B.C.E., made finely crafted pottery vessels that were decorated using color and fired in kilns at high temperatures. Following the decline of the Halaf culture, the main centers of development were the Ubaid culture (4300–3500 B.C.E.) and the Uruk culture (3500–3100 B.C.E.) along the Tigris and Euphrates rivers, where copper items are frequently found. By this point, the Middle Eastern Bronze Age had developed. All of the cultures in this region were characterized by complex societies centered on cities, and they had specialized craftsmen, ritual leaders, and highly trained warriors. Thus in this region of Eastern Asia, the development from primitive items of native copper to articles of bronze took place over at least two thousand years, culminating in a Bronze Age culture in the fourth millennium B.C.E.

Considering early metallurgy in the Chinese region, a small bronze knife cast from a pottery mould has been excavated from the Majiayao-period strata of the Linjia site in Dong County, Gansu. The Majiayao period runs from 3100 to 2700 B.C.E., making this knife the earliest bronze object found in China. But more commonly occurring artifacts made of bronze are not seen until the Qijia sites of Huangiangniangtai in Wuwei County, Yongjing Dahe, and Taiweijia in western Gansu, where knives, chisels, awls, axes, and augers made of copper have been found. The earliest bronze mirror found in China was recently unearthed at a site of the Qijia culture, which carbon-14 dating estimates to have lasted from 2050 to 1915 B.C.E. Most of these objects were made by cold hammering red copper, but this mirror was of cast bronze, indicating that the development of bronze in China followed a less direct course than in the Middle East. Moreover, the appearance of an early bronze culture in China occurs at least a thousand years later than it does in western Asia, and the Qijia culture, where these earliest objects are found, lies at the eastern terminus of the trade route to China from western Asia.

In the northern regions of China, knives and decorative items made of copper have been excavated at a string of Beijiang sites, including the Siba culture, Zhukaigou culture, and the lower strata of the Xiajiadian. These items display a high degree of uniformity and have been dated from the early to the middle of the second millennium B.C.E. Given their location and sequence of dates, it appears that these sites mark the path by which the use of bronze entered China. In the interior of China, the Longshan sites in Henan and Shandong have also produced a number of very early copper items. Another Longshan site, at Dengfeng Wangfenggang in Henan, has produced the fragment of an object cast from a bronze alloy that included both tin and lead, dating from the first half of the third millennium B.C.E.

So how did ancient China develop the use of bronze? Was knowledge of these techniques an indigenous development, or was it transmitted from western Asia? The dates and areas above tend to indicate that technical knowledge transmitted from outside China must have been a very important part of the process. Copper implements from Neolithic China, both primitive items hammered from free copper and those cast of bronze, are found in many areas, and their pattern of distribution indicates that articles found in western China tend to be earlier than those from the east. Thus we can speculate that bronze technology was introduced from the west, but in the process of transmission the craftsmen in China did not receive a complete knowledge of the alloys or casting techniques used. Thus the production of bronze implements may have been independently developed in various areas, beginning with the primitive hammering processes, before achieving the full techniques of casting bronze. The existing pottery techniques of Neolithic China were quite highly developed by that point, and the techniques necessary for high-temperature kilns to fire pottery had been mastered at an early date. The skills needed to cast bronze could have been rapidly developed based on this pottery technology, since it would have enabled both smelting metals to make alloys and firing pottery molds at high temperatures. As a result, by the time of the Shang dynasty (1600–1046 B.C.E.) bronze castings were available for a great many different types of objects, which were made in large quantities and to very high standards. From the end of the Longshan culture to the beginning of the Shang was but several centuries, an astonishingly brief period for the development of this complex technology.

Although cutting tools made from bronze castings are much sharper than those made from stone or bone, because bronze is more easily fractured it is less effective for agricultural implements to till the soil or fell timber. Accordingly, the use of bronze tools did not necessarily lead to an increased standard of living. But bronze weapons are much more lethal than those made from more primitive materials. This can explain several phenomena of Bronze Age cultures, such as the emergence of a specialized military and more complex social groups, together with a greater concentration of resources and their unequal distribution. Since copper and the other metals were very difficult to obtain, and since the various skills needed for casting required extensive training and organization, the production of these more effective weapons could be manipulated and controlled by a small group of people who could then bring the larger social group under their control. This led to the concentration of valuable materials and to cultural segmentation. In China, the era traditionally known as the Three Dynasties (discussed below, in section 3) was the period when states emerged and took form, and this development had a clear relationship with the time when bronze technology evolved.

Exactly when wheeled vehicles appeared in China is still difficult to determine. Based on the archaeological evidence uncovered to date, the war chariots of the Shang dynasty were similar in form to those of western Asia, Egypt, and the Indian subcontinent. But in China no evidence has been discovered of more primitive wheeled vehicles, and signs of the chariot's developmental process have not been found. This would indicate that wheeled vehicles were introduced from outside China, and it is a reasonable assumption that knowledge of both wheeled vehicles and the use of bronze entered China at the same time. Chariots and bronze weapons are both used in warfare, and they were both important to the mobile and warlike tribes of the northern steppes. War, in addition to its destructive power, can also serve as a means of exchanging knowledge and resources between cultures. In the middle of the third millennium B.C.E., there were great movements of peoples in western Asia, South Asia,

Eastern Europe, and northern Africa. The Hyksos people invaded Egypt, the Medes established their kingdom in western Asia, there was an ethnic change in the Greek peninsula, and waves of Aryans entered the Indian subcontinent. Most of these movements were marked by signs of the war chariot.

Though China was somewhat removed from these great changes, given its remote location in eastern Asia, the Central Asian steppes permitted free movement, and so China, too, could be influenced by these movements of peoples to its west, influences that most likely included the use of chariots. At the same time, these new technologies underwent independent local development that brought them to a high standard, leading to the rapid development of a Chinese bronze culture clearly distinct from its counterparts to the west. This phenomenon of an interchange with external cultures stimulating native technologies to bring about creative changes is not infrequent in human history; the many changes in China that arose during the third millennium B.C.E. are prime examples of it.

2. The Shang Dynasty as the Core of Ancient Chinese Culture

According to traditional Chinese historiography, the three dynasties of the Xia, Shang, and Zhou represent the fountainhead of Chinese culture. The consciousness of a Chinese culture based on the Central Plains is also derived from this notion of a central cultural core. But the Xia history is essentially legendary, since it has yet to be supported by clear archaeological evidence. Though the Erlitou site in western Henan's Yanshi City, near Luoyang, is sometimes taken to be a confirmation of the existence of the Xia dynasty, it is only the legendary association of this location with the Xia that would identify the traces of buildings for large-scale public ceremonies found here as part of a Xia-dynasty royal capital. The archaeological evidence itself has no direct indication to show that this early Bronze Age city is a Xia capital.

In contrast, since the discovery of the Yinxu remains at Anyang in 1928, the Shang sites have included a large number of both buildings and graves, together with a treasure trove of oracle-bone inscriptions that record events from that period, confirming the traditional historical accounts of the Shang. Accordingly, this section takes the rise of the Shang kingdom as the period in which the core of Chinese culture took form and developed.

According to calculations based on traditional historical sources, the Shang kingdom held sway for over six centuries, from the eighteenth to the twelfth centuries B.C.E. According to current archaeological materials, this period is divided into the three periods: Proto-Shang, Early Shang, and Late Shang. The region over which the early forms of the Proto-Shang culture are found includes the eastern foothills of the Taihang Mountains in Hebei and the vicinity of Weihu City, north of the Yellow River in Henan. These sites are adjacent to locations that have been traditionally considered to be sites of the Xia dynasty, such as the area of the Erlitou culture, although these two cultures have marked differences. On the other hand, sites from the Early Shang in the vicinity of Zhengzhou in Henan are quite similar to remains from the Erlitou culture. This could indicate that influences of the more advanced Erlitou culture enabled the Proto-Shang culture, which was quite similar to late Neolithic cultures, to begin developing into the great power that was characteristic of the Early Shang.

The main body of the Early Shang culture, whose largest center appears to have been the Erligang site, had territories branching over a very wide area. It extended over the whole of Henan, together with parts of Shandong, southern Shanxi, central Shaanxi, and northwestern Anhui. This comprises the area traditionally regarded as North China's Central Plain, though the Early Shang's extent is even greater than the plain per se, extending far to the north, as represented by the western Gaocheng Taixi site in Hebei; to the south, down to the Yangzi region, taking in central and eastern Hubei; and to the west, stretching to Fufeng and Qishan counties in Shaanxi. Its furthest reach is indicated by the Shang culture of the Dayangzhou site in Jiangxi's Xin-gan County, a site whose local characteristics are so distinct that it serves mainly to indicate the outermost fringe of the Shang cultural sphere. The great extent of these regional territories demonstrates the power of the Early Shang culture; it had at this early point developed governmental and military strength no less significant than the later Shang kingdom.

The Late Shang period covers the two hundred years from the fourteenth to the twelfth centuries B.C.E., and its most significant archaeological material comes from the sites around its capital near Anyang, which,

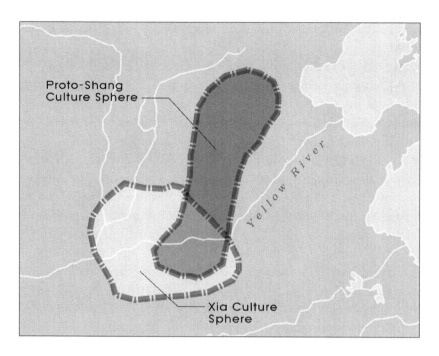

Proto-Shang
Culture Sphere

Yellow River

Xia Culture
Sphere

FIGURE 2.1 Regions Covered by Xia and Proto-Shang Cultures

according to later histories of this era, was established by the Shang king
Pan Geng. Apart from this site, archaeological work on the Late Shang
has been concentrated on the area of Hunan, and thus its full geographical extent is not clear. But the oracle-bone inscriptions from Anyang, as
discussed below, indicate that the Late Shang kings dominated essentially
the same area as did the Early Shang.

Two of the defining characteristics of the Late Shang are, first, the extensive written records in the form of oracle inscriptions and, second, the
development of Shang royal power, as shown by these inscriptions. The
emergence at this time of writing and highly defined kinship relations are
milestones in the development of Chinese civilization and represent the
demarcation between prehistory and history.

The beginnings of writing in China had already appeared before the
Shang. At Neolithic sites such as Jiahu in Henan's Wuyang County, Jiangzhuo in Shaanxi's Lintong County, and in particular the Dawenkou culture in Shandong, symbols carved on bone and pottery have been discovered. Although there is no consensus on the uses of these symbols, it is

clear that they were intended to convey information and were not simply for decoration. Among the pottery markings from Dawenkou, there are many that bear a striking resemblance to later Chinese characters. In particular, the repeated combination of an abstract indication of a sun above a mountain had a clearly established design. This symbol, moreover, has been found written in a consistent fashion on pottery shards at sites separated by several hundreds of kilometers, indicating that these symbols already may have served the rudimentary function of written language.

The oracle inscriptions found at the Anyang Yinxu site have already developed well beyond direct pictorial representations. The pictographic characters for animals, for example, are simplified to indicate some representative characteristic of the animal being designated, and the drawings are consistently based on a full-length profile view. In fact, we can also see most of the six basic ways of forming characters: *xiangxing*, a pictographic representation of an object; *zhishi*, an ideographic representation of a concept; *huiyi*, a combination of two pictograms to represent a third meaning; *xingsheng*, a combined form in which one part indicates the basic category of meaning and the other part indicates the sound; *jiajie*, in which an originally pictographic or ideographic character is used in place of a conceptual word with the same sound; and *zhuanzhu*, in which characters with different meanings have derived similar forms from an original phonetic character. The sentence forms of these inscriptions, moreover, indicate that there is already a clear grammatical structure to the written language; it is not just a free representation of speech. The writing on these oracle-bone inscriptions has already reached a high level of maturity. The characters found on bronze vessels from the Shang have ritual functions, and they tend to be more complex and closer to realistic representations of objects, although they display a level of abstraction beyond simple drawings of the objects. Thus, we can deduce from the maturity of the Shang writing system that it must have had its predecessors in an extended period of development, and similarities with later written Chinese indicate that the later writing system evolved from it. But recent archaeological discoveries have shown that, beyond the simple writing variants seen in the southern Chu culture of the Warring States period, there might have been other systems of writing different from the one seen today. Just as the Shang writing system developed to become the only surviving mature writing system, so did the Shang culture also form the main stream of ancient Chinese culture.

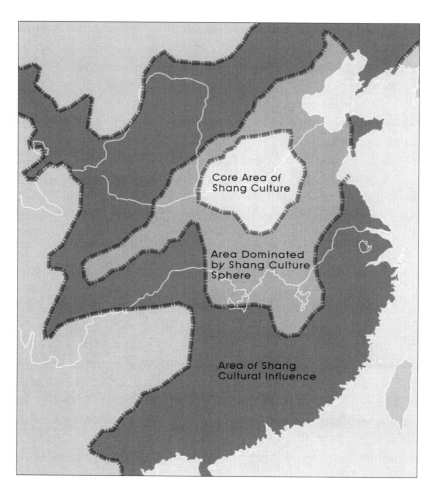

FIGURE 2.2 Regional Influence of Shang Culture

The oracle-bone inscriptions record a great variety of activities involved with Shang government administration, reflecting the direction in which this state evolved over its last two centuries. Though the governmental power of the Shang king was originally of a rank similar to the religious power of the masters responsible for the oracular divinations, during this late period the king brought religion under the control of government. He referred to himself as "the lower god *xiadi*," in the same frame of reference as the main Shang deity, the "High God *Shangdi*." The Shang kingdom was hierarchically organized, with the Great City Shang at its center, surrounded by territories within the capital district given to relatives and descendents of the king, outlying territories under royal control, territories of nobles who paid allegiance to the king, and then allied regional kingdoms in the four directions.

As seen by the "eastern tours" of the Shang king recorded in these inscriptions, during the Late Shang, the eastern territories controlled by the feudal nobility were part of the main body of the Shang state; the outlying kingdoms, which had originally been enemies of the Shang, had fallen under the influence of Shang military superiority. The government of the Shang kingdom was composed of a hereditary class of lower officials, which gradually developed into an administrative system with five departments. The emissaries of the Shang king had considerable powers, being able to lead armies and set up the administration of the outlying districts. The numerous sacrificial victims found in great numbers in tombs of Late Shang kings indicate the great power of these rulers, while the rich troves of architectural elements and ritual vessels that were also buried with the kings manifest the great wealth and artistic refinement of the Shang court. A government of such strength and organization naturally took the lead in the cultural development of China at the time and formed the core of its culture.

Bronze Age Shang society had a complex structure based on ethnic connections; thus restricted by regional and family lineage limitations, it could not expand its territory. The religious system of the Shang was based on offerings to ancestors and also to local guardian spirits of mountains and rivers. This combination of deities was a result of the Shang expansion to outlying areas, absorbing the gods of different ethnic groups and incorporating their cultures. The overall structure of royal offerings that can be seen in the record of divinations contained both a new ritual system and an older one, both of which were maintained together. The older system was composed of offerings strictly limited to the lineage of the Shang kings. The later system included a complex group of deities, including the spirits of natural forces, great individuals (such as great shamans), and ancestors. But this newer system also had a reduced schedule for ritual offerings, and in it offerings were made only to the earliest ancestor and the five generations previous to the present time. When the newer religious system appeared, the Late Shang was already in its final stages, and the characteristics of this religion are closely related to the kingdom's expansion. It appears that by then the Shang kingdom had developed beyond its original regional and ethnic basis to move toward a more general and unifying national culture.

The two centuries of Late Shang rule constitute the last segment in the history of the Shang people. But from the archaeological remains at Anyang and the oracle-bone record, it is clear that the Shang kingdom had developed beyond being just one of the many ancient regional states, and, likewise, Shang culture had become the center of the Chinese regional cultures. This formation of a core culture helped progressively to absorb regional cultures and move toward the multifaceted Chinese culture of later times.

3. The Chinese Cultural System, Western Zhou Political Structure, and the Concept of the Three Dynasties

In the twelfth century B.C.E., according to traditional accounts, the small Zhou kingdom located in the Guanzhong region of central Shaanxi defeated the mighty Shang kingdom in a single battle and then replaced it as the ruler of China. But the establishment of the Zhou dynasty was not, as traditional history portrays it, simply a change of dynastic house; it constituted a complete renewal of the cultural system and structure of government. This was a shift that established some of the basic characteristics of the Chinese cultural system that developed later.

From their vantage point, the Western Zhou (1045–771 B.C.E.) victory over the Shang would have been completely unforeseen. The origin of the Zhou people has been explained in a number of ways, and there is as yet no definitive version. It is clear, though, that in the process of their development into a powerful ethnic group they absorbed a great many elements from other cultures that had deep and multifaceted influences on them. Based on the archaeological evidence to date, what is referred to as the Proto-Zhou period is narrowly defined as the time when the Zhou people lived in the Qishan Mountains of western Shaanxi, here beginning to coalesce but without arriving at a stage that could be referred to as a kingdom. But before they settled there, traditionally under a leader called Gong Liu, the Zhou people went through a period of nomadic existence. During this period, they moved southward from northern Shaanxi, coexisting with the landowners of the Guanlong region while also absorbing influences from their neighbors to the west and cultures to the east.

Traditional accounts transmitted by the Zhou themselves state that their ancestor Houji was responsible for introducing agriculture to humankind, although agriculture was abandoned by later generations of the Zhou, who lived a nomadic life in the north for several centuries, returning to a settled life under Gong Liu. The twists and turns of Zhou development through this period include stays in various locations and movements along different routes that are now almost impossible to reconstruct. In my opinion, the Zhou were originally an agricultural people in southwestern Shanxi who moved along the edge of the Yellow River and, at one stage, resided in the region around the bend of the Yellow River, where they took up a pastoralist way of life. Later on, during the Gong Liu period, they moved south into the river basin and readopted agriculture in the more fertile and well-watered region of the Qishan Mountains. Thus the Zhou ethnic and cultural origins were much more diverse than those of peoples in the Qishan region, and they had acquired ethnic components and cultural elements from the different areas and stages of development they had passed through.

Although the development of a Zhou state in the Qishan region gradually led to a Zhou kingdom that was one of the regional powers to the west of the Shang, this new culture was subservient to the Shang. There was also technological influence—archaeological evidence indicates that the Zhou techniques of bronze casting were heavily influenced by those of the Shang. The Zhou religious rituals used the written forms of Shang divination, and the Zhou also worshipped some of the Shang deities. In the records of Shang divinations, the Zhou appear to be one of the western regional states, and there were extensive marriage ties between nobles in the two governments. The relationship was essentially one between a small tributary state and a more large, powerful state. But this smaller state, after developing increasing strength during the reigns of Gu Gong, King Wen, and King Wu, was able to defeat the Shang state in battle. The Zhou people must have been astounded at their own victory, and the *Book of Documents* (*Shangshu*) records a number of texts from the early Zhou that discuss the reasons behind this remarkable turn of events. In sum, they put forth the theory that "the will of Heaven is not constant, and virtue alone is as close as your kin," concluding that the Shang lost power because their morals had been corrupted. The purported evils of the Shang included drinking to excess, debauchery, having no sympathy for their common subjects, and running away in the face of defeat. But the question of how much these alleged failings actually influenced the ability of a small state to conquer a much larger one is by no means easily answered.

The concept of the Mandate of Heaven (*Tian ming*) proposed by the Zhou can be understood in two senses: the first is that a ruling state must adhere to a definite set of moral principles, and the second is that there is a force higher than that of mankind that watches over and judges the affairs of mankind. These viewpoints, concepts that were to be fundamental in the political theory of Chinese government after this, had not appeared before the Zhou. The notion that the legitimacy of a particular regime depended on moral values and that a heavenly force passed judgment on its actions was a radical departure from the previous strictures of ancestral or clan-based deities. It was a movement toward a more universal understanding of government, one based on the idea of a transcendent power. To receive the Mandate of Heaven, a ruler had to accept the obligation of conforming to and promulgating the moral responsibility handed down by heaven (*tian*), and it is only by conformance to this moral good that heaven determines if the ruler is fit to retain the mandate. This is a lofty ideal, one that is indeed difficult to realize in the world, but it could be conducive to social order, and the promotion of this ideal by the Zhou was an epochal event in the development of Chinese culture. It was a far cry from the notion of worldly affairs being arbitrarily determined by the random caprice of deities, and this concept must have passed through an extended period of evolution before reaching this stage of maturity.

When the smaller population of the Zhou state, which tended to lie mostly in its western regions, was confronted by the problem of governing the much larger masses of people in the vast regions to its east, it was necessary to devise a structure for government administration. The solution was to use a system of territories ruled by members of the royal house as a means of protecting the Zhou center. This political system, termed *fengjian zhidu* in Chinese and usually referred to as "feudalism" in earlier Western scholarship, was based on two main points: first, that crucial areas would be protected by being held by members of the royal family, who would be loyal and assist one another in forming a large network of control; and second, that cooperation would be fostered by accommodation to the differences between different cultural groups. It was, in effect, a military colonization by the Zhou people, who sent garrisons to the newly conquered areas, where the commanding Zhou kinsmen and rela-

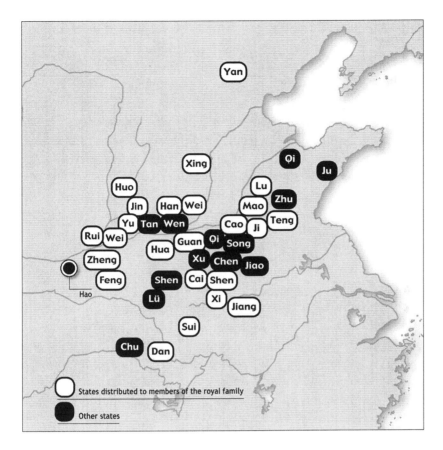

FIGURE 2.3 The Geographic Position of Major Western Zhou States

tives were bestowed with the hereditary power to govern these subordinate states.

The first few generations of Zhou rulers—including the kings Wen and Wu, the Duke of Zhou, and the kings Cheng and Kang—continuously distributed territories under this *fengjian* system to members of the royal house with the surname Ji and to an allied clan with the surname Jiang. At the same time, they set up subject kingdoms under rulers from the east who had marriage alliances with them. In addition to military displays and the distribution of economic benefits, the relationship between subject lords and the Zhou kings in the *fengjian* system relied on the ties of clan lineages that were manifested in ritual offerings to the royal ancestors, including the payment of tribute, royal audiences, the presentation of gifts, intermarriage, and the bestowal of rights to govern territories. These means continued to strengthen the web of family relationships that bound together the early Zhou kingdom.

This political system of the Western Zhou unified many levels of control in the new and old states through a network of family alliances. Thus the relationships between states were not simply those of greater and lesser but were more like the relationships between uncles and nephews or aunts and nieces. The moral weight and ethical requirements of these relationships did much to promote filial behavior between the states.

The sons and younger brothers who were granted territories by the Zhou kings would move to these territories, taking with them troops from the royal Ji clan, together with some of the conquered Shang people and specialized artisans such as ceramic workers or musicians. These people would settle in the capitals of these territories and were referred to as "people of the state" (guoren). The native inhabitants of these areas would be moved outside the city walls or to cities of their own. The leaders or upper social levels of these native peoples often intermarried with the new leading group that had been granted control of the area. Apart from this mixture of native peoples and new rulers, there were other native peoples with other cultures who lived in more remote areas and had originally inhabited the eastern regions from the earliest times, and they were referred to as "savages" (yeren).

There were at least two or three types of states created by the Zhou in the fengjian system, and there were even more ethnic groups that combined to make up a complex multicultural social structure. Through this distribution of subject states, China went through a process of cultural amalgamation during this early period of the Western Zhou. The upper strata of society in eastern China generally acquired a high degree of cultural uniformity as a result of this structure, whereas distinctions between the original cultures of the earlier states were preserved among the lower strata of society, giving them much more individuality.

With the new understanding of the Mandate of Heaven, it was not sufficient for the Zhou to simply criticize the Shang for their moral failings and upbraid their own younger generation. They needed to create a theory of history that would explain the events of the past and give direction for actions in the present. There are many passages in both the Book of Songs (Shijing) and the Book of Documents (Shangshu) that refer to the Shang's loss of the Mandate of Heaven as an indication of the operation of this principle. In the "Greater Odes" division of the *Book of Songs*, for example, there is a section of verses referred to as *"Dang,"* in which King Wen, who ruled the Zhou before they conquered the Shang, criticizes the last Shang king for his immorality. The well-known last line from this section states, "You need not look far to find a lesson from history for the Shang; it lies in the last generations of the Xia." Here the Zhou are finding a precedent for the fall of the Shang in the actions of the preceding dynasty, the Xia, and this section describes the evil behavior of both dynasties and their rulers in accordance with a stereotyped pattern. But there are also passages in the *Book of Documents* indicating that the Zhou considered the Xia to have been their forerunners.

An early theory by Fu Sinian (1896–1950), based on archaeological data from excavations in the 1930s, proposes an east-west dichotomy between the Shang and the Xia. According to this theory of cultural opposition, the Zhou people had a common western identity with the Xia and considered the Shang people to be "eastern barbarians." This would provide an explanation for why the Zhou people claimed the much earlier Xia dynasty in the West as their original ancestors, as that would provide legitimacy for the ruling Ji clan of the Zhou and indicate that the previous Shang dynasty had been of questionable legitimacy.

Seen in this light, the traditional account of the dynastic sequence of the Xia, Shang, and Zhou would be essentially a version of history fabricated by the Zhou. Moreover, archaeological excavations have yielded no conclusive evidence of either the geographical area or the time period of the Xia, much less any sense of what its political or social system might have been. Thus the Xia culture, if it actually existed, may have had few characteristics to distinguish it from other cultures of the time, and its identification may have been a political move on the part of the Zhou to set apart the Xia as the first stage of what they referred to as the Three Dynasties. By the time of the Eastern Zhou (771–256 B.C.E.), the Three Dynasties era was already considered a golden age of civilization, and the term itself appears to have originated in the Eastern Zhou, since it first appears in several sections of the *Book of Documents*, all of which date from the Spring and Autumn period, at the beginning of the Eastern Zhou. There are several possible explanations for the origin of this historical construction. It may have been a political move on the part of the Zhou to establish a legitimate lineage for their dynasty, positioning themselves as the third in a sequence of linked dynasties. Or it may have been an attempt to embody a moral vision, projecting an idealized view of a succession of dynasties onto the distant past, one that could be bathed in the golden light of nostalgia. For example, the "Duke Ling of Wei" passage from the *Analects* of Confucius (*Lunyu*) extols the concept of the Three Dynasties and the part that the three founders of the Zhou—King Wen, King Wu, and the Duke of Zhou—had in this process. By doing so, the concept of the Three Dynasties is reinforced as both a historical truth and a moral example for later governments.

4. The Role of Regional Cultures in Forming a Chinese Cultural Order

In 771 B.C.E., King Ping and the Zhou court moved the royal capital eastward to a location less vulnerable to attack by western peoples, marking the change from the Western to the Eastern Zhou. From this point until the unification of China under the first Qin emperor, China went through five centuries of political and cultural change. Although the Eastern Zhou timeline is traditionally broken into two parts, the Spring and Autumn (722–481 B.C.E.) and the Warring States (476–221 B.C.E.) periods, these two are in fact part of a continuous line of development, and there is little to indicate a significant break between them. The political history of this time, sometimes referred to as the Five Hegemons and Seven Martial States (*wuba qixiong*), was a turbulent time when the balance of power shifted constantly between states that nominally owed allegiance to the Zhou king but in fact were striving either to attain dominance and replace the Zhou ruler or simply to maintain their own identity in the face of aggression by their neighbors. The focus of this book is not the complex military and political strategies played out during this period, which can be found in other histories of early China, but rather the underlying decline of the *fengjian* system and the cultural changes that derived from it.

The fall of the Western Zhou was not as simple as moving a royal capital; it marked the demise of an entire social order. This is traditionally described by the phrase "the rites were ruined and the music shattered" (*li huai, yue beng*), and its effects on the development of Chinese culture were profound. To better understand these changes, we should recall the *fengjian* system at the height of the Western Zhou, as described in the previous section. In this period, the system of granting territories to feudal nobles served both to help protect the Zhou capital and to extend its administration over a large area. To consolidate this feudal network, the Western Zhou developed a system of rituals to display the combination of its royal power and ethnic system, which were in fact two sides of one coin. This ritual system included a great range of ceremonies for granting feudal territories, official visits of homage to the Zhou king, ancestral offerings, and marriages, among others. It was a common culture shared by the upper stratum of this feudal society. When the Western Zhou nobles took charge of a feudal territory, their courts included people from both the Zhou and the Shang, members of the main Ji and Jiang clans, and people from other clans, and they would most likely have also included peoples from the original upper classes of the region in question. The upper strata of society in these feudal territories were extremely complex ethnic mixtures. For example, the state of Lu was composed of Zhou, Shang, and Yan peoples; the Qin state had Zhou, Xia, and Shang peoples.

Despite this original ethnic mixture, after several centuries of accommodation, the upper stratum of Zhou nobles had fused into a common culture. As archaeological findings show, there was a shared standard for the ritual objects to be placed in the tombs of each rank of feudal nobility. These sets of bronze offering vessels included nine, seven, or five large cauldrons (*ding*) that were matched with eight, six, five, or four smaller containers (*gui*). Together with the size of the tomb and the richness of other funerary objects, the burial practices accurately indicate the feudal standing of the individual. Moreover, ritual inscriptions that were typically placed on shallow ewers (*min*), found throughout most of the feudal states, follow highly formulaic patterns of wording and content, indicating the degree to which ways of thought among the upper stratum of society had also become unified across the various feudal states.

The literature surviving from this time also demonstrates this shared culture of the elite. For example, the *Zuo Commentary*, a historical narrative commenting on events of the later Eastern Zhou, quotes extensively from the *Book of Songs*, a collection of various types of poetry that had taken shape in the earlier Eastern Zhou. Based on this and on the frequency with which quotations from the *Book of Songs* appear in other texts, it is clear that these quotations were an important component in a common medium of communication among the educated elite. Furthermore, an analysis of the types of poems that are quoted in the *Zuo*

Commentary shows that the great majority were from sections that celebrate ceremonies of the feudal courts, not sections that describe common life. These poems were thus part of a limited and defined body of literature that was the basis of upper-class education.

Combining what we know from bronze inscriptions and funerary objects with what can be seen in the early works of literature and history, it is clear that during the Eastern Zhou the feudal nobility and the religious rites were part of a single system: the principles of government were the same as the principles that bound together family clans. The basic forms of social relationships—ruler and minister, father and son, husband and wife—were combined with a system of moral principles—loyalty, filial piety, benevolence, honesty—to define norms of proper behavior. Overall, the materials surviving from this period give a clear picture of the richness and structure of a complex culture that by this time was shared by the upper stratum of feudal society across China.

Although the Zhou kings continued to rule after the Western Zhou, it was sovereignty in name only; by the time of the Eastern Zhou, their power was no longer sufficient to rein in the feudal network of great eastern states. The phrase "the rites were ruined and the music shattered" describes not merely a loss of standards of behavior or a decline in the authority of government; it was rather that the very fabric of society was becoming unraveled. Already by the Spring and Autumn period, the nobles had assumed an increasing degree of independence, and the royal court had little meaningful control over their actions. The power within each of the states had, moreover, been delegated to lower levels of the feudal nobility by the first half of the Spring and Autumn period, following the Western Zhou model of granting territories to members of the royal family. By the middle of this period, each of the states had a hierarchy descending from the ruler down to government officials, and although there were some titles in common, each state tended to develop its own hierarchical positions for the feudal nobility and administration. As the Spring and Autumn period shifted into the Warring States period, the functions of government were delegated to a new class of hereditary officials.

The power struggles between the states affected not simply the nobility but also this new class of officials, since defeat of their state could mean the loss of their positions and their means of livelihood. Two hundred years of social change had brought about a fundamental reorientation of

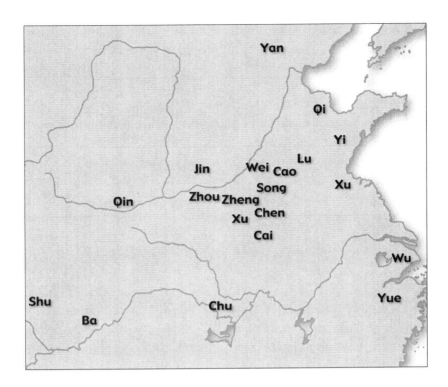

FIGURE 2.4 The Various States of the Spring and Autumn Period

the feudal order, and the rising and falling of feudal nobles helped the culture that had originally been limited to the highest levels of society to penetrate and mix with the middle and lower social strata.

It was from this class of nobles who had lost most of their actual power that Confucius (traditionally dated 551–479 B.C.E.) came. Seven generations earlier, one of his ancestors had been prime minister for the state of Song (in present-day Shandong). The Kong family fell from power in the next generation, following power struggles within Song. His father moved to the state of Lu, where he was essentially a person trained in the military arts but cut off from his connection to a particular state. One of many children, Confucius became a member of the *shi* class of scholar-officials in the middle ranks of the Lu state administration. Like Confucius, members of this class were not simply low-level members of the ruling class but were trained to maintain actively the culture of the nobility, and, moreover, they worked to disseminate this culture to lower strata of society. The best known of these fallen members of the feudal aristocracy, Confucius worked to reinterpret this culture to give a new, more universal meaning to the ideals and moral values of the upper crust of feudal society.

But the effects of this breakup of the Zhou feudal system were not limited to ideals and moral values; the gradual decline of the aristocratic noble class was accompanied by changes in the economic structure of society. In opposition to the earlier system of large agricultural estates, the Spring and Autumn period saw significant expansion in the use of different natural resources, thus reinforcing independent entrepreneurship. The resulting urbanization and commercialization led to the development of a new social stratum of merchants whose wealth enabled them to acquire high social status. This social change was accompanied by the development of a new culture that rose on the foundations of the earlier, fading aristocratic culture.

We can see traces of this cultural evolution in bronze vessels from Qi, a large state at the base of the Shandong peninsula, whose capital, Linzi, was the wealthiest and most populous city of the Warring States period. Though it had been originally granted to members of the Jiang clan, the Tian clan replaced them as rulers of Qi and used their economic resources to solidify their hold on that position. Enough bronze vessels with accurate dates have been found in many areas of Qi for a significant trend to be seen. It is clear that the numbers of ritual vessels gradually decreased, while the vessels for other uses increased, and these nonritual vessels appeared in new shapes and with new styles of decoration, styles that became increasingly ornate and inventive later in the period. This trend is indicative of a more secular society replacing the earlier one based on ritual, a shift toward the popular and away from the sacred. This trend of the Qi bronze vessels is also apparent in other areas, and it clearly reflects the dissolution of the earlier feudal structure. This change also may have led to the increasing number of human sacrifices found in Qi tombs after the Spring and Autumn period. Human sacrifices in burials had been one of the distinguishing elements of Shang culture, and its absence during the Zhou was one aspect that set this culture apart from its predecessor. The reappearance of this custom at this time in Shandong may indicate that the indigenous traditions of the eastern Yi peoples were beginning to resurface as the cultural control exercised by the Zhou feudal system disintegrated.

Considering this situation from a multistate viewpoint, the upper strata of the Zhou feudal culture were initially quite consistent. There was originally a high degree of standardization to the bronze ritual vessels of the nobility in northern areas, although this gradually became less apparent in the Spring and Autumn and Warring States periods. In the far northern state of Yan, which had been cut off from the central Zhou court for an extended period of time, the bronze vessels showed characteristics of the northern indigenous cultures. The feudal state of Jin, originally limited to the lower reaches of the Fen River, expanded gradually until, under Duke Wen, it established hegemony over the other states, a position it maintained for a hundred years. Even before the point during the Warring States period when Jin was divided into three linked states, its territory already included many of the indigenous cultures of Shanxi, and there was extensive intermarriage with these peoples. Then, when it had expanded and split into three separate states, it included even more of the northern Yi cultures, which mixed with the Han culture. Finally, when King Wuling of Zhao adopted the military uniforms of the indigenous peoples and increased the use of cavalry, this was a clear cultural change and was noted in the historical records.

But there were also examples running contrary to this trend of increased localization, such as the smaller state of Zhongshan, which was established in the Hebei region by the Xianrong people during the Warring States period. Although excavations have shown that this state preserved many of its earlier cultural attributes, such as the use of tents and camp stoves, the tomb of its ruler and his wife conforms completely to the ritual system of the Zhou nobility. This example, since it was preserved so completely, clearly shows the dual nature of this cultural blending, whereby instead of overriding the local or indigenous culture, the mainstream Chinese culture existed alongside of and mixed with it.

During the Spring and Autumn and the Warring States periods, the Zhou culture became the primary component of the mainstream Chinese culture, as the aristocracy fell and its traditions permeated the lower and middle levels of society. But at the same time, the cultures of local areas began to crop up within this greater cultural matrix, as the rise of urbanization and commercialization affected popular culture. This occurred in the north, in the south, and eventually in the representative Hua-Xia culture of the Central Plain, as we will discuss in the following section.

This was a period of time between when the Shang dynasty held nominal sway over many areas and when China was finally unified under the Qin and Han dynasties. The unified mainstream culture and the diverse local cultures existed side by side for long periods of time, as did the sacred aspects of the ideal culture and common aspects of the popular cultures. These two divergent trends meshed together and stimulated each other, making Chinese culture richer and more multifaceted.

5. The Formation of the Core of Chinese Thought: Confucian Teachings and the Debates of the Hundred Schools

Most civilizations tend to have one particular strand that forms the core of their system of thought, and with Chinese civilization it is the teachings of Confucius and their subsequent developments. If a relatively advanced culture such as that of the Shang falls to a less advanced one, such as the Zhou, this transition can lead to deep introspection by contemporary intellectuals. When the educated elite of the Shang made their transition to the Zhou, they probably continued work very similar to what they had done in the previous dynasty: predicting the future by cracking tortoise shells, maintaining state archives, examining the heavens—and thereby establishing the foundations of religion, history, and astronomy. As they handled these affairs, they could not help but reflect upon the causes that led to the small state of Zhou suddenly overcoming the great northern Shang dynasty. The answer of the time was that the Zhou had received the Mandate of Heaven, that receiving it depended on moral virtue alone, and that "the Mandate of Heaven is beyond all common considerations, and it is only virtue that that is essential." This is the first time we see the idea that moral virtue is greater than individual fate.

This concept of the Mandate of Heaven helped the Zhou to confirm their reign, to convince the descendents of the Shang to support fully the new dynasty, and thereby to expand the Shang-Zhou cultural system across northern China. But later, with the dissolution of the Western Zhou and the crumbling of its feudal system, this sense of self-confidence also evaporated, along with the sense of mastery it was founded on. Thus a new way was needed to explain the concept of the Mandate of Heaven, and Confucius appears to have been the person to supply this new understanding.

The *Book of Changes* (*Yijing*), a text that originated in this period, was originally a book of divination. Its core of pithy statements used to predict the future, together with the beginnings of commentaries on them, appears to have first been assembled around the time of the Shang-Zhou transition. As the *Yijing* presents it, fate is not blind, there is a great degree of choice open to mankind, and an individual can alter his fate by these choices. The attitude underlying this idea of the individual's ability to change his fate is closely related to the way that the concept of the Mandate of Heaven developed in the political context of the Zhou expansion. We do not know if the traditional attribution of portions of the *Yijing* to the hand of Confucius is correct, but in his words as recorded in the *Analects*, the Mandate of Heaven is the fate of an individual, not of a dynasty. Confucius himself had been oppressed, yet he could say, "Heaven has given me this Mandate. Heaven has given life to me, has given me a responsibility. Now that I have this responsibility, how can my persecutors control me?" From this standpoint, the Mandate of Heaven is no longer the affair of a government; it is each individual's mission, a responsibility that must rise above the restrictions of particular circumstances or the natural world.

Later, after Confucian teachings had become the officially sanctioned school of thought, the "Doctrine of the Mean" (*Zhongyong*) section in the *Book of Rites*, which was compiled during the Han dynasty, could enlarge upon this view, stating, "the Mandate of Heaven is called human nature; to follow human nature is called the Way (*Dao*), refining the Way is called education." (*Zhongyong*, 1; Wingtsit Chan translates the first line as "What Heaven [*T'ien*, Nature] imparts to man is called human nature." *A Source Book in Chinese Philosophy*, 98.) It was previously difficult to grasp clearly the meaning of this passage or its intellectual background, but in 1993 a large number of texts written on bamboo strips were discovered in the Guodian tombs near Jingmen City in Hubei. One of these texts in particular, the "Human Nature Originates from the Mandate" (*Xing zi ming chu*), helps us to understand the development of the concept of the Mandate of Heaven—although from this point on, it is more appropriate to translate "Mandate" as "Fate." The first sentence states, "Human nature originates from its mandate, and this mandate descends from Heaven." In this context, heaven is not an omnipotent deity with a consciousness or will but rather a gathering together of universal powers, and from this source of power each individual has an innate endowment. The concepts of mandate and heaven thus mutually accommodate each other. The Guodian texts were written down around 300 B.C.E., much earlier than the *Book of Rites*, so this passage may provide a missing link to fill in our understanding of the development of the concepts of fate and human nature.

If Confucius's understanding of fate and human nature was similar to that in the Guodian text, then his view would be that mankind has essentially only a single type of collective endowment, although each person has a particular nature, an individual endowment. It is from this perspective that we may better understand why Confucius used the idea of "humanity" (*ren*) as the core concept of his teachings. This term appeared before it was used by Confucius, but with different meanings. For one, it indicated a sense of mental consciousness, a sense of being awake instead of benumbed, and for another, a sense of being fine or wonderful. For example, a line from the *Book of Songs* describes a handsome man who arrives driving a chariot as being "truly beautiful and *ren*," praising his appearance and bearing. In this early example, the term *ren* does not denote a person's inner character, and it is not an essential part of the basis of individual human nature; it is instead an adjective describing a feeling and a characteristic of a person's physical form. Confucius, however, gives this term a radically different meaning, one that relates to the totality of an individual's personality. This becomes one of the basic propositions of human thought, the notion that each individual has a natural endowment and that this endowment naturally expresses itself in this person's character. This is the fate that each individual has received from heaven. These three linked concepts—fate, human nature, and humanity—together form the foundation of all of Confucian teaching.

In the sense given to this term by Confucius, *ren*, or humanity, is the natural endowment of an individual, and its expression is an indication of their character. So how does one become a "noble and humane person"? This quality of humanity is seen as something that everyone possesses, like a seed that can sprout and grow into a healthy plant if given the right circumstances. But even though the teachings of Confucius in the *Analects* are based on the concept of humanity, he rarely speaks of it to define it in an overall sense. Rather, his hope is that each person can develop an individual sense of humanity and give it the chance to develop to its fullest potential, so that one can become a "noble and humane person." Ideally, if there are many of these "noble and humane persons," society will become purified, and it will be based on the highest level of personal character.

But in the *Analects* there are few places where Confucius speaks directly about his ideals for society.

The Warring States period produced many thinkers of many different schools, most of whom put forth ideals for individual and social life influenced by the teachings of Confucius. One of the earliest of these thinkers was Mozi (ca. 470 B.C.E.–ca. 391 B.C.E.), who is sometimes said to have been a student of Confucius before he left to establish his own school of teachings. Whether or not he actually met with Confucius, his teachings are influenced by those of the earlier master, some developing Confucian ideas further and some diametrically opposed to them. The core of the Mohist school of thought is the concept of "rightness" (*yi*) and that, in the context of a social group, common justice should be based on a spirit of "universal love" (*jian-ai*). When people thus care for one another, there would be no partiality, and a commonly held belief in justice would be the basis of society. In this focus on the social aspect of individual life, Mohist teachings are clearly supplementing an area that is less developed in Confucianism.

The second great teacher in the Confucian lineage was Mencius (Mengzi, 372–289 or 385–303/302 B.C.E.), who was faced with the challenge of countering the popularity of the school of Mozi. This competition was one motivation for his further development of the unified concepts of humanity and rightness (*renyi*) as the common principles of selfhood and society. An additional line of development that is essential to Mencian thought is his view that people are basically good (*shan*); that their innate, natural state is one of goodness; and that it is this goodness that enables them to express their humanity and rightness (*ren* and *yi*).

Another very significant figure in the development of early Confucianism was Xunzi (ca. 312–230 B.C.E.), whose focus was the importance of education and self-cultivation. In contrast to Mencius, he considered that human nature was originally blank or neutral and that it was necessary for individuals to go through a process of training and education until they had been nurtured into cultivated people truly capable of humanity. In his school of thought, humanity is not a natural ability that can be taken as a matter of course; it is an accomplishment that can be attained only through a process of thorough training. Education is not simply the acquisition of knowledge, but the individual personality must also be developed by conforming to the ways of behavior in Confucian ritual before he can truly express his humanity.

These early Confucian scholars were not only debating to counter the communal doctrines of the Mohist school. They also needed to rebut the individualistic doctrines of the earlier thinker Yang Zhu (370–319), a line of thought that formed a part of the later Daoist school of thought. Although Yang Zhu's concern with the individual and human nature may share a common origin with the teachings of Confucius, in the Daoist teachings, this individualism was carried to a much greater extent, wherein concerns for society were almost nonexistent, the focus being entirely on individual experience. From this perspective, the innate human capabilities are much vaster, and one can not only work toward a sense of goodness but also seek a sense of integration with the natural world that is completely independent of human standards or regulations.

This particular direction in understanding the individual was developed even further in the teachings of Zhuangzi (fl. fourth century B.C.E.), which focus on each individual's own nature. It is from this individual nature that cognition and moral values emanate. In this sense, the Confucian concept of benevolence was extended toward communalism with the teachings of Mozi and toward individualism in the schools of Yang Zhu and Daoism. By the Warring States period, Xunzi had assimilated communalism into the Confucian teachings, with rites (ritual, *li*) as the norm for bringing people together in society and humanity (*ren*) as a confirmation of the value of human nature. During this same general period, Zhuangzi and the other celebrated Daoist philosopher Laozi (fl. fourth century B.C.E.) were further affirming the primacy of individual experience and values, with little concern for the interaction of individuals in society.

During the late Warring States period, these competing directions of thought about the individual and society went through a period of intensive debate, cross-fertilization, and change. If we are to find a common direction in these developments, it would be the movement away from a mystical view of human nature and fate toward more deeply considered and rationalistic views of human existence and its meaning.

During the time when Confucius was teaching, he seems to have felt a kind of transcendental power, and this was precisely the so-called mandate (*ming*). Confucius was unwilling, however, to discuss this much further. Thus, aside from the events of the human world, in the realm of mystery, Confucius "never discussed prodigies, feats of physical strength, unnatural disorders, or spirits" (*guai, li, luan, shen*; *Lunyu* 7.22). It is this gap in Confucian teachings that was partially filled by the doctrines of the Five Agents (or agencies, elements, or phases) (*wuxing*) and of yin and yang. Chinese cultures had been concerned with the relationship between the individual and the cosmos as early as the Neolithic period. These ancient Chinese beliefs can generally be divided into two aspects, the worship of deities and the respect for ancestral spirits. Since the feudal structure of the Zhou dynasty was based on a network of family lineages, respect and worship of the ancestors became an important part of the Zhou system of government. Belief in spirits was partly fused with nature worship, although it also was a component of official state ritual. The worship of ancestors and of nature were both concerned with basic relationships between mankind and nature as well as between individuals and their transcendental abilities. These schools of the Five Agents and of Yin-Yang that developed during the Warring States period were cosmological systems based on these two levels of human existence.

The Yin-Yang school of thought must have been the earlier of the two, since archaeological findings indicate that from a very early period Chinese people had developed the idea of a polarity between two opposite and complementary characteristics. This doctrine of a mutually supportive dualism seems to be one of the basic characteristics underlying all of Chinese culture. In contrast, the origin of the Five Agents theories, though it is still a topic of contentious debate, appears not to be earlier than the Bronze Age. The experience of casting metal and firing glazes for pottery may have introduced the Chinese to the concept of transmutation in the natural world—and to people's ability to manipulate these changes. At the same time, developing astronomical knowledge of the five planets related to the concept of a cyclical movement within the five elements.

These two schools of thought both seek to explain phenomena of the natural world, and the two are closely related. In addition, they both see human affairs as one facet of the cosmological system, a viewpoint that has a close affinity with the Daoist affirmation of nature. It may be these similarities that inspired the later development of more religiously oriented schools of Daoism to incorporate Five Agents and Yin-Yang concepts into their teachings.

In general, two directions appear in Chinese thought following the Spring and Autumn and the Warring States periods. First was the Confucian order, centered on a humanistic view of the world, and this was followed by a naturalistic view centered on the Five Agents and Yin-Yang theories. But these two directions of thought continued to influence each other, and they shared several common concerns, such as fate, human nature, and *qi* (material force), that continued to receive attention throughout later periods of Chinese history. These two basic considerations, human affairs and the natural cosmos, interacted with each other to form a complex system, extending through higher and lower levels of society as well as expanding or contracting within themselves. Later, the development of the fundamental doctrine "Heaven and Mankind are one" sprang from this historical origin. Moreover, the concern with understanding processes of change, visible in the influence of the *Yijing* or in the debates of Warring States thinkers, later appears in the concerns with situational and organic development that are characteristic of Chinese ways of thought. With their concern for overall or holistic organization and analysis, it is best not to consider the so-called Hundred Schools of Thought during the Warring States as separate schools with their own independent lines of development. Rather, it is important to see that the extended debates during this period combined to form the foundation for the Chinese thought of the following two millennia.

6. Rise of the South: Development of the Yangzi River Basin and Its Merging with the Central Plains

The division between North China, of the Yellow River basin, and South China, of the Yangzi River basin, is marked by the Qinling Mountain range and the Huai River, which flows from them eastward to the Pacific. The natural environments to the north and south of this division differ clearly, and from ancient times the cultures in these two macroregions differed in their traditions and their lifestyles. Beginning in the Neolithic period, northern agriculture was based on millet, while the south relied on rice as its staple. The buildings in the north were generally built of rammed earth, while those in the south used timber frames with walls of wattle and daub. In all the basic aspects of material culture, fundamental regional differences are apparent.

Naturally, there was interchange between these two areas. For example, southern rice has been found in northern regions of millet agriculture, traces of rice husk likewise have been found at the Jiahu site of the Peiligang culture near Wuyang in Hunan, and the cultivation of millet had similarly spread deep into the south. To compare the levels of cultural development in these two areas, in the south there were vast ceremonial centers, demonstrating the highly sophisticated organizational ability of southern societies, which enabled them to develop such indications of movement toward a national government. But the large-scale governmental organization that is evident in the northern Shang and Zhou cultures did not develop in the south. It was in the north that the Zhou feudal system, built on the foundations of Shang culture, could organize human and economic resources and develop one of the major civilizations of the ancient world.

The assimilation of the southern regional cultures into a central cultural body was a slow and gradual process, and it was not until the political unification of China under the Qin and Han empires that a Chinese culture, unified but including regional characteristics, began to emerge. Following this unification, Chinese cultures display a high degree of homogeneity, and this section describes the step-by-step process of cultural development during the Warring States period.

The interest in southern culture on the part of the Zhou began in the early part of the dynasty, as indicated by sections in the *Book of Songs* titled "South of Zhou" and "South of Shao." As the Zhou distributed their feudal kingdoms, they moved down the Huai and Han rivers, creating a zone of kingdoms stretching from north to south through the areas of southern Henan, northern Hubei, Anhui, and Jiangsu—a zone that remains connected by common customs and ecology even today. But despite its southern expansion, the Zhou feudal system was never able to penetrate deeply into the Yangzi River regions and much less into regions such as Jiangnan or Lingnan farther south.

As early as the Neolithic, independent cultural systems had developed in the Yangzi basin. During the Western Zhou, areas lying to the north of the Yangzi were controlled by the powerful Yunmeng and Pengli royal houses, which ruled over a region full of lakes and crisscrossed by rivers; the area covered by water was much greater than it is today. Records from the Spring and Autumn period refer to these peoples generally as the Bai Man (numerous indigenous peoples) or, further south, the Bai Yue (the numerous peoples of Yue). This collective name does not really designate one genuine ethnic group, but the Bai Man were the main ethnic collective in the kingdom of Chu, which rose to prominence during the Spring and Autumn period. The Bai Yue, then, refers to several southern ethnic groups of the late Spring and Autumn through the Qin and Han. They include the Minyue, the Dong'ou, the Luoyue, the Xi'ou, and others. These groups, however, have yet to be defined in terms of their physical or linguistic anthropology.

As the southern cultures gained power, this influence was centered on the kingdom of Chu, which enters the written historical record in the very early years of the Spring and Autumn period. The oracle-bone record from the Shang does include the character for Chu, and according to tradition, the Chu people assisted the Zhou in their conquest of the Shang. But the exact connection between these peoples and the kingdom of the same name that appears suddenly in the historical records is not clear. The clan name of the Chu royal clan was Mie, which was one of the eight traditional surnames of Zhurong, the god of fire. The concept of surnames was clearly different from that in later times, at that time indicating a tribal allegiance, and the eight surnames of Zhurong were clans that had traditionally sworn an oath of allegiance to one another. According to tradition, these eight clans originated from six sons of the same mother, three of whom were born from her right side and three from her left side; the other two clans were added later. Originally active in the area between Henan and Shandong, these eight clans would be considered northern peoples, and during the Spring and Autumn period the Eight Clans of Zhurong had established small kingdoms in this northern area. The Mie clan, however, migrated south into northern Hubei, to an area along the upper reaches of the Han River, and established the kingdom of Chu.

Though we do not understand the process of this migration, two of the other clans of Zhurong from the Shandong region, the Xu and the Shu, also moved south and eventually settled in the area around Anhui and Jiangxi. We can conjecture that before forming a large-scale nation, these groups had been driven south by the superior military forces of the Shang and the Zhou. Some of these smaller groups submitted to become feudal territories of the larger northern powers; others moved south to develop in their own directions. The Mie clan moved into the region of the Bai tribes, mixing with the original inhabitants and forming what was perhaps the first kingdom of this southern region, a kingdom that gradually grew in power to dominate the area. As this kingdom of Chu grew, it not only took in the area between the Yangzi and Han rivers but even swallowed up the Zhou feudal kingdoms along the Han and Huai rivers, to the point where it could compete for power with the northern states.

The growing strength of Chu incited determined resistance from the northern kingdoms. By this point, the northern kingdoms had fallen under the control of first the kingdom of Qi and then the kingdom of Jin, which replaced the Zhou kings in terms of actual power. This competition between north and south drew both of them to muster all of their resources in an extended back-and-forth conflict. To the east of Chu, the kingdoms of Wu and Yue also rose up to contend in the struggle between north and south. This long-term competition between regions eventually led to the amalgamation of a Chinese cultural system, drawing in the influences of the southeastern regions. The southern development was thus part of a process of broad cultural expansion whereby the central culture grew in both size and complexity as it drew in peripheral territories.

The details in this saga of opposition and resistance by the south over periods of war and peace are included in most histories of ancient China, and so we will not go into them here. Significant for the narrative at hand are the various contributions of the southern regions to the process of forming a Chinese cultural system.

First of all, we must consider the question of why it was that the northern regions first moved in the direction of forming large-scale governmental systems and then imposed these systems on the southern regions. With its warm climate, fertile land, and abundant water, South China is naturally very productive. But even though its natural resources should have enabled the kingdom of Chu to resist the north, it eventually lost its independence and fell under the control of a northern government. From a cultural standpoint, the main reason for this was probably the north's more developed literary system, which was supported by a more powerful military force that forced the south to adopt the northern system of writing after a unified government was formed. Archaeological work in recent decades has yielded numerous texts from the Chu culture, written on bamboo strips, in which the character forms and grammatical structure are essentially the same as texts from the north. Where there are differences in the script, they are mostly in cases where the characters are used to represent the sounds of words in the spoken language, which varied greatly between regions. One reason contributing to the Chinese development of a single writing system is the fact that Chinese characters are graphic representations and thus are more adaptable and less restricted by linguistic changes than exclusively phonetic writing systems.

Thus, through the vehicle of this written language, Chu culture absorbed the northern administrative system and traditions of scholarship. But despite this cultural merging, the Chu culture retained its identity and did not necessarily conform to northern notions of orthodoxy. In cases where it did accept northern traditions, it developed viewpoints independent of the mainstream.

The political institutions of the Chu people arose when the Zhou feudal system was falling apart, its official cultural traditions were collapsing, and the feudal domains were developing their own governments. Although the northern states were moving in the direction of self-government, however, they were not able to break away from their original forms of government. For example, within the Zhou dynasty's family-based feudal structure, the government and the clan system had a reciprocal relationship, and as the individual states grew apart from the Zhou court, they each developed their own system of officials and noble families that was, in effect, a secondary feudal structure. In contrast, the Chu government, apart from the Zhou royal house itself, had far fewer families of hereditary nobility. Moreover, as Chu annexed the Zhou feudal territories, instead of maintaining the family-based feudal structure already in place there, the Chu court dispatched officials to act as county administrators of the newly acquired domains, similar to the system of provincial officials with temporary postings, a system that was to become customary for later dynasties. In this sense, the Chu governmental structure was a forerunner of the system of prefectures and counties of later imperial China.

In terms of systems of thought, the Confucian tradition generally formed the mainstream in northern areas, with the Mohist school acting as a corrective opponent. Then from the late Spring and Autumn into the Warring States period, the Chu kingdom fostered the development of most of the schools that contended with the Confucians, such as the Daoists and the Agriculturalists, as well as the Confucian reformers such as Xunzi and the Mencian school recently discovered from newly excavated bamboo texts. This situation is an example of how, with their growing independence and activity, peripheral subcultures could in turn affect the mainstream culture of the core from which they originated.

In their ritual systems, the Chu kingdom adapted some aspects from the northern states and rejected others. Both the festival rituals and the literary tradition were generally taken from the northern culture, but the ritual objects used in the south indicate a clearly separate tradition.

The ritual bronzes excavated from southern regions—referred to as Chu vessels, Qi vessels, or the Huai style—clearly represent a southern genre, while the lively decorations on recently excavated lacquerware have no precedent in northern areas. The artistic tradition of soft and sinuous lines that developed in the south was a polar opposite to the northern decorative tradition, which appears hard and somewhat awkward in contrast. The artworks from the eastern kingdoms of Wu and Yue also have their own style, distinct from both the north and from Chu, as seen in the linear decoration and stylized script found on its bronze swords.

As the southern languages took literary form, though rational prose works were less suited to express their differences from northern standards, poetry that was rhymed and could be chanted to express personal emotions became an excellent vehicle to display the special characteristics of the south. A genre of prose poetry known as *cifu* developed in the south, in distinct contrast to the northern form of poetry, as exemplified by the *Book of Songs*. These *cifu* are full of long, drawn-out sounds and means of expression more characteristic of the south, such as comparisons to flowers and beautiful women. In the most famous of these collections of poetry, the *Songs of Chu* (*Chuci*), characters such as rejected councilors, mountain spirits, and beautiful goddesses float through the clouds. Deities in the later religious schools of Daoism retain much of the vitality of the southern tradition, whereas northern deities tended to be more abstract and conceptual, with fewer distinct personal characteristics.

As these different aspects of southern culture show, Chinese culture was enriched by the ways in which the south first developed on its own and was then absorbed into the mainstream culture. The origins of the southern cultural tradition were just as early as those of the north, its vitality was just as great, and it can hardly be considered inferior to that of the north. When these two cultural systems met and fused, they produced a richer and more complex whole.

7. Ordering the Populace: The Organization of Government and Daily Life

While the Zhou feudal structure gradually disintegrated during the Spring and Autumn and Warring States periods, a new concept of the state and society emerged step by step. One of the aspects of this new type of government was the system of recording the population according to where their family lived, referred to as the household registration system, which has continued through more than two millennia of Chinese history up to the present.

The most pressing need that brought about this household registration was warfare. With the dissolution of the feudal system that followed the eastward relocation of the Zhou capital under King Ping, the rulers of individual states increasingly began to assert their autonomy and to expand their domains by annexing territory from neighboring states. The amount of warfare that took place during this period was staggering. One of the main historical resources for this period is the *Spring and Autumn Annals*, a text attributed to Confucius's editing of the historical annals for the state of Lu, which recorded events in most of the Zhou feudal states. During the two centuries of time it records, more than fifty states were conquered and absorbed by their more powerful neighbors. The Seven Martial States of the Warring States period, together with four or five weaker states such as Lu, Wei, and Zhongshan, were all that remained after the others had been conquered. The seven main states then contended between themselves until the kingdom of Qin conquered "all under heaven," in 221 B.C.E., and finally the area covered by Chinese culture was under a single government. In the five hundred years between the beginning of the Eastern Zhou in 771 B.C.E. and the founding of the Qin empire in 221 B.C.E., there was no respite from the warfare of strong states conquering the weak and large states conquering the small. In this process, the diffused control of Zhou feudalism changed step by step into the centralized kingdoms of the Warring States. The states developed the means to control effectively their natural resources and mobilize their manpower, turning them into tightly organized militaristic entities.

The first step in changing the political structure of these states was that governments with a more comprehensive regional scope gradually replaced the earlier leadership by feudal cities, and the early division of China into prefectures and counties (*junxian*) appeared in several of these states. The first divisions into counties may have occurred at the beginning of the Spring and Autumn period, when the kingdom of Chu reorganized the Zhou feudal territories it had already assimilated into what were referred to as counties (*xian*) and appointed a county lord (*xian gong*) to rule over them. Although the term for duke (*gong*) used here is the same as that used to denote one of the highest levels in the feudal structure,

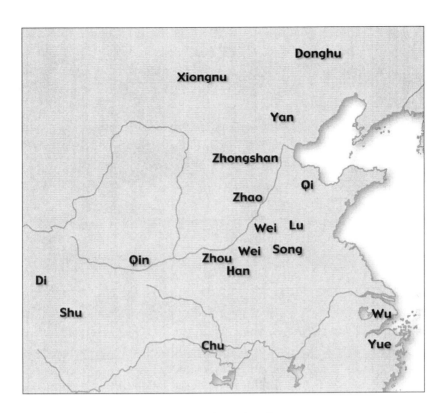

FIGURE 2.5 The States of the Warring States Period

when used by the kingdom of Chu, it had a very different meaning. The dukes in this case, like their feudal counterparts, were persons of great importance appointed by the king to rule over an area, but the main difference was that these were not hereditary positions. Chu was not one of the Zhou feudal states, its domain was not within the region covered by the central Chinese culture, and it was thereby less limited by the conventions of feudal organization that affected the northern states. Its rapid rise to being one of the dominant powers may have been related to its ability to organize more effectively the territory it controlled. Other states, too, began to adopt this form of organization. In the middle of the Spring and Autumn period, the state of Jin reorganized its territory along similar lines. There, the clans of six powerful and wealthy ministers (*qing*) each controlled a large territory and therein established a number of counties to administer.

Some of these counties were smaller feudal dukedoms that had been absorbed by Jin as it expanded, and some were areas that had formerly been under the control of the military. By the time of the Warring States, another state, Wei, had established military districts called commandaries (*jun*) at strategic locations on the frontier. These commandaries, such as that of Xihe, could be subdivided into a number of counties (*xian*), and they were of critical importance in protecting the state. Toward the end of the Warring States period, the state of Qin was systematically reorganized into a structure of commandaries and counties (*junxian*) under the plan of its prime minister, Shang Yang (d. 338 B.C.E.). Then, when Qin had conquered and unified all of the Chinese states, the entire nation was reorganized into this same system. Subsequently, for more than two thousand years a two-tiered system of large commandaries, or areas very similar to them, subdivided into counties became the standard organization for local administration.

This new organization of commandaries and counties had essential differences from the earlier feudal system. First, governmental decrees were issued from a central source; second, officials on temporary postings replaced the hereditary nobility. Under the Zhou feudal system, control by the rulers over their territory filtered down indirectly through a series of levels, and none of these levels—whether of kings, dukes, or high officials—held complete authority over an area. In addition, under the Zhou, there was a social class of nobility that included everyone from the king down to the high officials, and so the people were essentially divided into two distinct classes. In contrast, under the new system of commandaries and counties, apart from a few ruling and noble families, the people were all essentially commoners. These common people were all organized under the system of household registry, and the population of China was recorded in this way. The upper strata of society did not rise to the level of nobility, the lower strata did not sink below the level of commoners, and no one was completely free from the responsibility to provide annual labor and pay grain taxes to the state.

Under the Zhou feudal system, the nobles and high officials all had territory under their hereditary control, and this territory included the people who worked the land. The agricultural workers were distributed by their lord to work the plots of land, and the harvests were considered public property, with a small remainder left to the workers. Similarly, the nobles retained a certain amount as they passed the harvest upward in tribute to the king. This pyramid of economic distribution allocated resources to all of the levels of society in a system of ownership that was, at least nominally, permanent and unchanging. When the feudal system collapsed, the ruling authority declined level by level. The feudal princes (*zhuhou*) no longer paid tribute to the king, and the high officials no longer paid tribute to the public treasury. This dissolution of authority progressed to the point where powerful officials in the states of Jin and Lu even appropriated the royal lands to divide up among themselves.

These changes in the actual ownership of property in turn changed the ways in which ownership was understood, and with the expansion of commerce, people who were not nobles could become wealthy and own large tracts of land. As the population swelled, upland areas were opened for agriculture in order to support the additional people, and these new agricultural areas were obtained through labor, not feudal grants. In addition to the population attached to a state through feudal grants, there were also the native inhabitants of these newly opened areas, and these people were called "people of the wilds" (*yeren*, but not with the usual connotation of being uncivilized), since the areas prior to feudal grants were called wilderness (*yedi*). Because the taxes collected by the state were based on the household registry, these indigenous peoples also had the right to work agricultural land. As a state increased its power through the collection of taxes, the common people were obliged to pay tribute in grain and to provide an annual period of corvée labor, in return receiving the right to own land, a right that had originally belonged to the state. Thus, by being enrolled in the household registry, the common people were no longer bound to the large feudal tracts of land under the feudal manors, and the possibility of owning their means of livelihood was opened to them.

With the incessant conflict of the Warring States period and resulting loss of life and property for the various states, it was necessary for the states to do all they could to bolster their resources. Increasing their manpower was especially important. In *Mencius*, the king of Wei expresses his great concern about maintaining the population of his state, saying that he would spare no pains to attract immigrants from other states. This is an indication of the mobility of common people during the Warring States period and their ability to move to places where living conditions were better. The desire to restrict this mobility as the feudal strictures binding commoners to the land broke down was another major reason behind the system of household registration.

Especially in ancient times, a state's effectiveness at waging war was directly related to the sheer size of its armies as well as its military skills. During the Zhou feudal period, the military leaders in the field drove chariots, with foot soldiers acting as their assistants, but chariots were limited by the terrain they could pass over. With the greater geographic scope of conflict during the Warring States period, the importance of foot soldiers also increased, with the field of battle expanding beyond the loess plains of northern China to include more hilly and swampy terrain. In the level northern areas, the use of cavalry was also developed to supplement the leaders' chariots. A large state would often claim to have a million foot soldiers led by a thousand chariots and supplemented by ten thousand cavalry, while weaker states would purport to have at least one tenth that number. The need to field forces of this size, even though they were not permanently maintained as are modern standing armies, consumed a great part of a state's resources. There were also expenses beyond the direct maintenance of the armed forces. The state of Qi, for example, attached great importance to military skills and richly rewarded soldiers who had made significant contributions. The state of Wei used a highly effective, well-trained, and well-equipped professional army, but its soldiers were exempt from taxation and corvée labor for life, creating a great burden for the state. The state of Qin combined its military and agricultural systems. Since every male of draft age was required to serve in the army, Qin recruited commoners to immigrate from the neighboring state of Jin to handle the agricultural work, so its own men could form a large standing army. Thus Qin could more easily support its large and well-trained army than could Qi or Wei. In addition to bolstering its food supply, Qin also developed a system of nobility based on military achievement, whereby soldiers who distinguished themselves would receive not merely honors but also enemy captives as slaves for their use. Military conscription was by no means limited to Qin; in this period, all of the states were well aware of the other's tactics and quickly imitated successful strategies. These large armies of several hundred thousand or a million soldiers could not have been assembled without an organized means of conscription—and again the household registry was an essential part of this.

Under the Zhou feudal system, there was a sharp division between the level of society that held power and the level of society under the ruling class's control. The system of punishments did not reach as high as the aristocracy, and the system of ritual did not include the commoners. The legal system was quite clear on this issue, and since the social system of ritual and punishment was not universal, a universal legal code was not appropriate. It was not until the system of statewide household registration had come into effect that complete legal codes began to be implemented consistently. The Warring States school of philosophy referred to as Legalism (*Fajia*) was concerned primarily with the means by which a government could be most effectively implemented. It focused on both how a civil service could be established and how a legal code could be accepted by the people. Legalist thinkers such as Shang Yang and Wu Qi (d. 381 B.C.E.) realized that for a legal code to be effectively promulgated, it must be both impartial and strict, effective across all strata of society.

Since the common people were freed from the feudal system and could leave the control of feudal towns or manor farms, they needed a new means to establish their individual identity. During the Zhou, the distinction of family names, originally separated into two parts, the family name or surname (*xing*) and the clan name (*shi*), was reserved for the nobility alone. As the feudal system began to disintegrate, some of the noble families who had fallen out of that class still retained their family name as the sole marker of their former status. As social mobility increased and established communities dispersed, individuals without a permanent residence increased, and they required a marker to distinguish them from others in that situation. In addition, within the system of household registry, family names were needed to distinguish the family units that were registered. Thus for several reasons, this former privilege of the feudal nobility became accessible and used by commoners. By the Warring States period, the distinction between *xing* and *shi* was no longer observed, and they both came to be equivalent to what we now know as a family name or surname. The older *xing* and *shi* could also indicate a person's place of origin, profession, special characteristics, or nickname. In the historical records of the Warring States, however, there are individuals without a family name and who use only a given name, and this can be seen even into Han times. Changing one's family name was also quite common. The general use of a family name as an essential part of an individual's personal identification, however, was not commonplace until the Qin and Han dynasties.

Under the feudal system, commoners were tied to the soil, and individuals were essentially members of a local social group. Under the system of household registration, the nobility lost their function as local leaders, but as communities did not necessarily have a social structure, the local elders tended to assume a leadership role. The increased role of local elders, as seen from references in Warring States records, was closely related to the increased importance of social cohesion.

To sum up, following the disintegration of feudal society, as the common people began to shed their feudal domination, opening the possibility for greater personal identification, the role of the former feudal structure was transferred to the state. The individual within the early Chinese system of household registry was substantially different from the individual in ancient Greek city-states and even further from our current idea of citizens in a nation-state. Though the people of this time had greater possibilities for status and were members of large social bodies, they could not necessarily share in the rights of these social bodies. Through two thousand years of Chinese history, from the Warring States period up to the present time, there was essentially little change in the system of household registry.

8. Conditions of Daily Life and Seasonal Festivals

Although the many finely crafted and beautiful archaeological materials from this period indicate the high material standards of the life of the nobility and display the finest of Chinese culture, they tell us little about how most common people lived. This section focuses on the daily life of the common people, not on praising the high level of Chinese artistic achievement.

The characteristics of daily life over the great time span covered in this chapter—more than a thousand years from the early Shang dynasty to the end of the Warring States period—of course show great differences according to time and place. To give a clear picture of one particular moment in this epoch, we focus on the Eastern Zhou during the Spring and Autumn and the Warring States periods, particularly the latter, since we have more historical materials from this period. Although there were changes in daily life over time, in early periods these changes were generally very slow and gradual, and the differences over several centuries were not great.

We begin our discussion with food, one of the most basic requirements of human life. As noted previously, the northern staple was millet and the southern was rice, a distinction that remained clear through this period. Wheat, which originated in the Mesopotamian region, had already entered China by the Neolithic Age and was common by this time. Large-scale irrigation projects had been constructed in northern China by the Warring States period, and since millet is very drought resistant, it is likely that the irrigation was needed to support wheat. In the south, irrigation was used to cultivate paddy rice, which germinates in flooded fields.

All of these grains can be easily boiled after their hulls are removed, though steaming also seems to have been a common method of preparation—numerous earthenware steaming pots (*zeng*) have been discovered. These would have had a bamboo basket in the middle so that the grain above would have been steamed and the food below boiled. Grains cooked in a steamer cauldron (*li*) would have had the consistency of very thick porridge. Other archaeological findings indicate that the grinding of grains into flour began during the Warring States period and gradually became common during the Han dynasty. In addition to being a staple at meals, the other main use for grains at this time was to brew alcoholic beverages. The use of yeast in alcoholic fermentation had begun much earlier in China, and the preparations could be filtered after fermentation. Filtering out the dregs was clearly a well-developed practice by the Spring and Autumn period, since there is a record of Duke Huan of Qi (r. 685–643 B.C.E.) requesting the state of Chu to pay tribute in the form of a special herb that could be used for filtering and perhaps flavoring liquor.

Beans were another important food staple. They may have originated in Shanxi and then been adopted in other areas, spreading rapidly and becoming popular as farmers discovered that growing beans could make the soil more fertile. In addition, since the area under cultivation during the Warring States period increased at the expense of area for grazing livestock, there was less protein available from meat. Beans offered an alternate source of protein.

The cultivation of fruits and vegetables was also significant in Confucius's day, and there are special agricultural terms found in the *Analects* that indicate that by the Spring and Autumn period cultivation had reached a level of sophistication that included advanced skills requiring a great many years to master. Archaeological findings of seeds and references in the *Book of Songs* indicate that many varieties of vegetables had become important crops by the Warring States period. The cultivated varieties of vegetables that had been bred by this time included, among many others, gourds, squash, leeks, green onions, garlic, celery, turnips, ginger, water chestnuts, lotus seeds, and sunflowers. The products from trees included peaches, plums, apricots, pears, various citrus fruits, persimmons, Chinese dates (jujubes), chestnuts, and hazelnuts. In addition, there were many varieties of ferns and other plants that were gathered from the wild. Although these probably were not gathered in sufficient volume to be normally a staple part of the diet, when crops failed wild plants, fruits, and nuts became very significant food sources.

Meat, on the other hand, was enjoyed primarily by the upper classes. The oracle-bone records from the Shang dynasty mention frequent sacrifices, including up to hundreds of cows or sheep, as well as hunting expeditions that could bring in large animals such as tigers and rhinoceros in addition to the more common prey of deer. Hunting was mostly under the control of the nobility, and the *Book of Songs* mentions that when the lord of a manor went hunting, he would take the larger wild boars for his share, leaving the smaller ones for the farmers who had assisted in the hunt. In addition, the common people might occasionally take a few smaller animals to supplement their diet, and the *Book of Songs* also notes that when friends met it was customary to cook a rabbit. Excavations at the Shang capital Anyang yielded two large bronze cauldrons, one inscribed as being for beef and the other for venison, indicating that cattle and deer may have been the most representative types of domestic and wild sources of meat at that time. Other animals kept for their meat included sheep, pigs, and poultry, and the means of cooking included boiling, roasting, and baking. Horses and dogs may have originally been kept for their meat, though by this time they were probably used mostly for transportation and as guard animals, respectively.

The bronze vessels of the nobility were primarily used for ritual offerings, and so even for the upper classes the daily preparation of cooked food would have been in earthenware utensils. Finer pottery was made with white clay and, beginning in the Shang dynasty, there was glazed ware of protoporcelain. The common people's pots were far from this standard, and there were only a few types. The materials varied with what was locally available, and the making of pottery was a specialized profession. In the Warring States book of *Mencius*, it says that potters and metal casters were craftsmen who could exchange their wares with one another. By this point, it appears that the common people had access to professionally produced wares whose quality did not vary too greatly. The pottery workshops and bronze foundries that produced these goods expanded greatly from the Spring and Autumn through the Warring States eras, as indicated by the frequency with which their remains are found in archaeological excavations.

The types of clothing depended on the wearer's social status as well as on the season and region. Silk, although it originated in China, was expensive and generally worn only by the upper classes and the wealthy. Fabrics woven from vegetable fibers, such as hemp or the kudzu vine, less expensive and coarser, were commonly used by ordinary people, most of whom wore clothing made from these poorer materials in both winter and summer, though in areas of pastureland, sheepskins were available. The wealthier, by contrast, could wear light furs to keep warm in winter and scarlet slippers with tinkling rings of jade. The *Book of Songs* records how women were responsible for producing silk, from raising the silkworms to weaving and dying, to make splendid garments that the ordinary people could wear only in their dreams.

In terms of domicile, elegant family housing compounds were formally laid out around several courtyards, with a central hall approached by a low flight of steps and chambers with corner rooms to the side. In the north, beginning in the Neolithic period, buildings were constructed mainly of rammed earth compacted between board formworks, whereas buildings in the south had timber frames filled in with wattle and daub. By the Zhou dynasty, these two construction types had been combined, so that the main framework was timber and the walls were rammed earth. In better buildings, the roofs were of clay tiles, while those of average construction used mud plaster. By Zhou times, house floors were raised slightly above ground level and made of rammed earth, and even the common people no longer lived in the pit houses that had been common up to the Shang. But the poor still lived in hovels with dirt walls and chinks of windows made from broken tiles, in stark contrast to the great halls under roofs decorated with elegant tiles that housed the wealthy. Large structures, though they used columns for internal support and might appear from the outside to have several stories, were actually raised up on internal earthen platforms; actual multistory construction did not appear until the end of the Warring States period.

To understand seasonal changes, fragmentary descriptions for the life of the ordinary people through the seasons of the year can be found here and there in historical materials. Up to the Spring and Autumn period, calendrical systems tended to vary by region. Although the Zhou calendar was used for official rituals during that dynasty, the earlier Xia calendar, Shang calendar, and the calendar of Xuanxu all continued to be used in various areas. Material from the *Book of Songs* shows that when different calendars coexisted, the monthly sequence could differ by as much as two months. Moreover, descendents of many of the earlier tribes that lived apart from the Chinese cultural system may have used very different systems to mark the passage of days and years. To take the festival marking the advent of spring as an example, regions would use different dates, just as they would use different ceremonies to celebrate it. In the state of Lu, people would rid themselves of bad spirits from the old year by bathing in the Yi River. The state of Song would enact the religious ritual of *gaomei* on the first day of spring to ensure the fertility of its people. And in a more direct celebration of fertility, people in the states of Zheng and Wei would celebrate the arrival of a new year by free coupling between men and women in forests along the riverbanks.

The festivals of each area had their own particular aspects. In celebrating the god of the earth, the whole state of Lu would indulge in mad revelry that even the ruler could not resist going out to observe. This celebration of the earth god was certainly not an official government ritual for the state of Lu and was more likely to have been one remaining from the earlier indigenous inhabitants of this area. In addition to seasonal rites, there was also worship of particular areas. The mulberry groves in the state of Song were considered sacred places, a point agreed upon by both the ancient traditions and ceremonies of the time. Other states also had sacred places, especially mountains, such as Mount Tai in Lu or Mount Huotai in Jin. Thus we can get a general idea of the religious beliefs of that time, though few of the details have been preserved in the historical materials.

Overall, the customs and living conditions in the various regions of ancient China continually mixed with one another. At the same time, even though the upper classes were moving toward cultural unification, the regional characteristics of individual areas tended to be preserved by the lower strata of society. Up through the Warring States period, Chinese culture tended to preserve its diversity, and there was little visible consistency across the regions. The government might ordain a single standard, but the common people retained their diverse customs both in their quotidian activities and in their celebrations of special events over the course of a year.

9. Ancient Civilizations in China and the Middle East

Within the period of time covered in this chapter, there was a general tendency for the regional cultures of China to blend together. In the north, the far-reaching kingdoms of the Shang and Zhou dynasties had each forged different groups of people into a state under a unified governmental system. As a result, the aspects of civilization supported by these kingdoms absorbed and transformed the cultures of the local ruling classes to forge a single cultural order. The military forces unleashed during the Spring and Autumn and Warring States periods spread these cultural and political orders over a greater field, in the north extending to the frontier grasslands and in the south beyond the Yangzi. In doing so, the central culture was enriched by absorbing many influences, through interaction with groups of people who originally had very different cultural practices. Most importantly, in this period Chinese culture assumed the essential characteristics that it would retain through all its developments and changes over the next two millennia.

While China was undergoing this process of amalgamation, civilizations in the Middle East were taking a different course of development. The ancient civilizations of the Tigris-Euphrates and Nile rivers had displayed brilliant accomplishments in many fields and then declined, whereas Greece and Persia, which had previously been insignificant and peripheral, rose to become the major cultural actors in the West. Originally the nuclei of very vigorous cultures, the civilizations of the Tigris-Euphrates and Nile did not expand significantly beyond their original geographic areas. Within those limits, they formed great and lasting cultural constellations until they began to disintegrate, eventually disappearing to await the archaeological excavations and deciphering of lost languages, which revealed an almost vanished chapter in ancient history.

To compare the trajectories of development in China and the Middle East, it is helpful to first consider the effects of geography. The main feature of northern China is the Yellow River, which links three distinct regions: the high loess plateau of Shanxi, Shaanxi, and Gansu provinces; the loess plain along the middle and lower reaches of the Yellow River; and the alluvial plain where it flows into the Bohai Sea. Although there are mountainous areas within these three regions, there is little to form either a serious barrier to communication or a formidable natural defense.

The south, centered on the Yangzi, Han, and Huai rivers, presents an entirely different landscape, one dotted with numerous lakes and marked by the slow meandering of many rivers. To the north of this region, there are river systems passing through the Wuling Mountains, facilitating communication between the north and the south. The Sichuan Basin, on the other hand, is cut off by steep mountain ranges that separate it from both the north and the south, and the southwestern and northwestern regions are also outside of the northern and southern macroregions. The middle and lower reaches of the two great river systems are the representative areas for both north and south, and with their environmental differences, both developed characteristic variations in the ways of life of their peoples. Despite the differences in these two cultural systems, there has always been a great deal of communication between them, leading to continual competition and cross-fertilization, stimulating the development of each. Their combination formed a dynamic cultural system that continually drew in and absorbed influences from all directions, maturing and deepening its identity.

The terrain of the Tigris-Euphrates region differed markedly from that of China. It was protected by high mountain ranges to the north and sweltering deserts to the southwest, which formed effective barriers to invasion, while to the east was the Persian Gulf, bordered by only a narrow strip of level land in what became Persia and is now Iran. To the northwest, the land steps gradually upward to what is now the Anatolian uplands of Turkey. To the southwest, on the other side of what was to be called Palestine, was the Mediterranean, and between this region and the deserts of the Arabian peninsula was a narrow corridor of communication that led to the Egyptian civilization along the Nile.

Egypt's territory stretched out along the banks of the Nile, and where it was not surrounded by desert wastes, it was hemmed in by cliffs of bare rock. On the southern edge of Egypt, the upper reaches of the Nile are impassable cataracts that tumble through steep gorges. In terms of land area, these two Middle Eastern civilizations were not large; taken together, the extent of the Nile *and* the Tigris-Euphrates civilizations was comparable to that of the southern region of ancient China along the Yangzi, Han, and Huai rivers. The two civilizations were separated by a great desert, and marine communication was also limited, because, although there is clear sailing inside the Red Sea, when ships exit it to the southeast, the passage is broken by rocks, with only a few safe shipping lanes. So although contact between these two great early civilizations of the West was not inconsiderable, they did not interact as closely nor with the same frequency of communication as did the northern and southern cultures of China. During this historical epoch, the Assyrian empire invaded Egypt, and during the New Kingdom period of Egyptian history, Assyrian control reached to the east of the Red Sea. Following the decline of these two early civilizations, this area saw the rise of the Persian empire and the Hellenistic empire of Alexander, each of which in its time succeeded in uniting the Middle East. But these conquests were able to pull together these lands under a single government for only a limited time, achieving little in the way of cultural synthesis. Thus an overreaching and lasting cultural nucleus was never formed in the Middle East during ancient times.

Accordingly, the individual regional cultures of the Middle East developed independent systems of writing. The cuneiform writing system that developed in the Tigris-Euphrates region evolved from a pictographic system to an alphabetic system, one that could be used by other peoples to write their own languages. The hieroglyphic system of writing that developed in Egypt somewhat later than cuneiform used entirely different principles to construct its written words.

These two systems of writing followed completely independent courses of development with essentially no possibility of mutual influence. In contrast, the two macroregions of China produced a single writing system that developed continuously. The origins of the Chinese characters date back to as early as the Neolithic, and by the Shang and Zhou dynasties, the system of characters was fully mature.

By the time the cultures of northern and southern China were crossing paths, the south could not develop its own writing system and instead accepted the one used by the north, even though the Chu culture of the south had its own identity. Although the Warring States period saw great political fragmentation, the system of written language was highly consistent, despite some relatively minor differences in the forms of some characters, and so the documents produced by these local cultures could be easily read by others. The importance of this single writing system in the unification of the Chinese regional cultures can hardly be overemphasized.

Turning now to the ways of thought in these two ancient Middle Eastern civilizations, texts of the Tigris-Euphrates cultures show a constant underlying concern with dualism: fresh water and brackish water, mountain

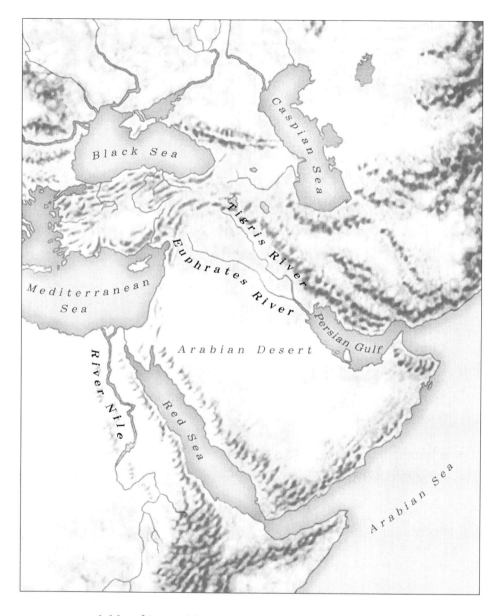

FIGURE 2.6 Map of Ancient Mesopotamia and Egypt

rains and dry winds, agriculture and herding, down to the basics of light and dark or life and death. Motifs of irreconcilable oppositions constantly recur. This stream of thought developed into the dualism of Zoroastrian beliefs that contributed to the foundation of later Middle Eastern religious concepts. Even in the Christian beliefs that were to emerge much later, ideas of death and rebirth and of the goodness of God and the evil of Satan are not far removed from these origins.

Ancient Egypt's worldview probably evolved prior to the Mesopotamian concept of dualism. Its regions, irrigated by the Nile, formed a self-contained environment wherein all phenomena were seen as parts of a harmonious system, so that the pharaoh and the sun god were two stations for a single entity, the ultimate arbiter of all affairs. Deities may have differed according to local customs, but they formed parts of a consistent theological system, and each had his or her own roles and responsibilities. Aspects of the world such as day and night or life and death were seen as part of continuous cycles, not as oppositions or conflicts. The worldview based on Egypt's self-sufficient vision of itself, nourished in the self-contained world of the Nile, may have made its people complacent. And this complacency was challenged during the New Kingdom, as Egyptian civilization came in greater contact with the cultures of other regions, making it increasingly difficult for Egyptian culture to maintain its former self-assurance.

Considered in relation to these two cultures of the Middle East, we can see that the culture of ancient China also gradually developed a fundamental viewpoint based on a resolution of dualities. Concepts such as yin and yang, male and female, superior and inferior, active and still—all of these were oppositions, yet they were also seen as reciprocal and balanced. It is perhaps the *Yijng*, a text that began to take form in the early Zhou, that best expresses the kinetic interplay of phenomena and the accommodation between opposites that mutually grow and decline in harmony with each other. This is a viewpoint radically different from those of the two great ancient civilizations of the Middle East. It is also a viewpoint that would better enable the Zhou to build a political system, as they did when they replaced the Shang as rulers of China. They were thus better able to accommodate the remnants of the Shang administration within the new feudal system, divide the kingdom among feudal princes who ruled over states that covered the territory of China, and coexist with the indigenous inhabitants of these areas. In this way, the political order of the Zhou closely reflected its culture. There are similarities between the Chinese worldview and the understanding of continuity and cyclical change in the Egyptian worldview, though the Chinese is more tolerant and accepting of external viewpoints. Such similarities also exist with the understanding of the Tigris-Euphrates civilization, although the Chinese view of change or growth and decay resolves the conflicts inherent in a strictly dualistic viewpoint.

During the Warring States period, Confucius promoted the idea of humanity (*ren*) in order to situate the understanding of human nature within a cosmological framework, using humanity as the primary means to unify the human order with his system of thought. This enabled understandings of the cosmos, human society, and human thoughts and emotions to be connected within Confucian philosophy. Throughout human history, the ultimate questions on issues such as the boundary between heaven and man, the space of life and death, or the distinction between good and evil have been matters of concern. As the German philosopher Karl Jaspers (1883–1969) pointed out, history is marked by occasional breakthroughs by various civilizations in understanding these transcendental issues. It was his contention that there was an "axial age," a time period within the one discussed in this section, and it was during this axial age that the major religions and philosophies of the world established their foundations. The individuals who put forth these ideas included the Buddha (ca. 563–483 B.C.E.), Confucius, the Greek philosophers, and the Hebrew prophets. We should also note that the two ancient Middle Eastern civilizations of Egypt and Assyria are not represented in these breakthroughs. Instead, what were at that time very insignificant and peripheral cultures, those of Greece and Israel, set the initial course of the two streams of thought that would later combine to form the Christian tradition that continues to underlie most of Western civilization.

China also witnessed breakthroughs in the realm of thought. After the transition from the Shang to the Zhou, which occurred somewhat earlier than Jaspers's axial age, the ideas of the Mandate of Heaven and moral standards and of the productive dualities expressed in the *Yijing* were fundamental for Confucius and the later Warring States thinkers. Using a common written language, Chinese thinkers of this period engaged in an extended debate on a series of interconnected ideas that had developed in the context of these fundamental notions.

In the civilizations of the Middle East, there was a similar foundation of basic notions that supported the later breakthroughs. For example, the monotheistic religion that the pharaoh Akhenaton (1380–1362 B.C.E.) attempted to institute, the Zoroastrian notions of conflict between good and evil, the notions of death and the afterlife seen in popular religions—all these foreshadowed the later Judeo-Christian tradition. When the breakthroughs to new cultural developments in the Middle East did occur, however, it was after a long and winding transition from the earlier ways of understanding, and the new ways of thought emerged in what were essentially different cultural contexts.

Speaking generally of the situation in China, the process whereby the peoples of the major regions interacted with one another fostered an extended and continuous development through a common written language. With the major advances of this period in establishing the key concepts of Chinese systems of thought, concern for human life and human society were structured by an understanding of complementary duality, leading to the major modes of thought that developed within the Chinese cultural system.

Suggestions for Further Reading

Chan, Wing-tsit. *A Source Book in Chinese Philosophy*. Princeton, N.J.: Princeton University Press, 1963.

Cook, Constance, and John Major. *Defining Chu: Image and Reality in Ancient China*. Honolulu: University of Hawai'i Press, 1999.

Ehrenberg, Margaret. *Women in Prehistory*. London: British Museum Press, 1989.

Falkenhausen, Lothar von. *Chinese Society in the Age of Confucius* (1000–250 B.C.): *The Archaeological Evidence*. Berkeley: University of California Press, 2006.

Graham, A. C. *Disputers of the Tao*. New York: Open Court Press, 1989.

Hsu, Cho-yun. *Ancient China in Transition*. Stanford, Calif.: Stanford University Press, 1965.

——. *Western Zhou Civilization*. New Haven, Conn.: Yale University Press, 1988.

Keightly, David. *The Ancestral Landscape: Time, Space, and Community in Late Shang China, ca.* 1200–1045 B.C. Berkeley: University of California Press, 1999.

Lewis, Mark Edward. *Writing and Authority in Early China*. Albany: State University of New York, 1999.

Li Feng. "'Feudalism' and Western Zhou China: A Criticism." *Harvard Journal of Asiatic Studies* 63, no. 1 (June 2003): 115–144.

———. *Bureaucracy and the State in Early China: Governing the Western Zhou.* Cambridge: Cambridge University Press, 2009.

———. *Landscape and Power in Early China: The Crisis and Fall of the Western Zhou, 1045–771 B.C.* Cambridge: Cambridge University Press, 2009.

Loewe, Michael, and Edward Shaughnessy, eds. *The Cambridge History of Ancient China: From the Origins of Civilization to 221 B.C.* Cambridge: Cambridge University Press, 1999.

Nylan, Michael, and Michael Loewe. *China's Early Empires: A Reappraisal.* Cambridge: Cambridge University Press, 2010.

Rawson, Jessica, ed. *Mysteries of Ancient China: New Discoveries from the Early Dynasties.* London: British Museum Press, 1996.

Schwartz, Benjamin. *The World of Thought in Ancient China.* Cambridge, Mass.: Belknap Press, 1985.

Shaughnessy, Edward. *Before Confucius: Studies in the Creation of the Chinese Classics.* Albany: State University of New York Press, 1999.

Thorp, Robert. *China in the Early Bronze Age: Shang Civilization.* Philadelphia: University of Pennsylvania Press, 2006.

3

China Comes Into Its Own

THE THIRD CENTURY B.C.E. TO THE
SECOND CENTURY C.E.

The third century B.C.E. to the second century C.E. was a critical period of
metamorphosis for China. It expanded from the central area of the North
China Plain in all four directions, setting out its basic territorial extent.
The Qin-Han imperial government established a nation that covered "all
under heaven," one that was supported by intensive agriculture, a commercial network, and a bureaucratic civil service. From this setting, the
characteristics of Chinese culture emerged. Based on the stability of an
all-encompassing government, China was able to maintain an extended
conflict with the nomadic peoples to its north. During this same period,
the established Confucian doctrines were challenged by Buddhism as it
entered and melded with Chinese civilization.

1. A Universal State System

In little more than a decade, from 230 to 221 B.C.E., the state of Qin conquered the six other states remaining at the end of the Warring States
period, absorbing them to unify finally all of the regions that were parts of
the Chinese cultural system. Under Qin rule (221–207 B.C.E.), the system
of commandaries and counties (*junxian zhidu*) was applied consistently to

all areas, and standardization was imposed on many aspects of daily life, including weights and measures, written characters, and the axle span for wheeled vehicles. Qin Shihuangdi, the First Emperor of Qin (r. 221–210 B.C.E.), was, in aspects from the mundane to the profound, one of the most influential individuals in all of Chinese history.

Seen from the perspective of the Warring States period, China's unification was all but inevitable. Mencius had already said that "all under heaven" was destined to be one, and the seven states remaining at that time were bent on conquering one another to fulfill their ambition of controlling their entire world. Political unification and cultural unification are difficult to separate, and Chinese culture had been gradually taking form through the close interactions between the various states over the Spring and Autumn and Warring States periods. The debates of the Hundred Schools of thought revealed the extent to which China was becoming a single intellectual community. Archaeological remains show that it is not easy to isolate regional characteristics in material culture, since differences in the arts and crafts were not great. The forms of the written language in various regions also showed a basic consistency, with relatively minor differences, and so when the First Emperor unified the writing system, it was more a matter of simply taking care of the externals.

The Seven Martial States at the end of the Warring States period insisted on their sovereign rights within clearly demarcated boundaries, and the people living there had clear national identities. These territorial states were already essentially similar to the nation-states that were to develop later in Europe. By applying the system of commandaries and counties over the entire kingdom, the First Emperor was simply extending the scale of the previously disparate application of governmental revolutions that had been taking place during the Warring States period. The Qin empire was doing little more than consolidating the basic structure common to the seven great states and applying it at a greater scale.

In its basic character, the Qin empire was an extension of the former Qin state, and the changes it adopted were primarily superficial. The title of emperor, or *huangdi*, was chosen by the First Emperor himself simply to place himself at a higher level than that of the feudal Zhou kings. The administrative structure was altered to incorporate subdivisions of six, and the color black was given precedence because of its place in the cycle of the Five Agents as they were applied to the Qin and its preceding dynasties. This concern with numbers and colors indicates how the theory of a cyclical change of the dominant agency, one replacing another in sequence, could be applied to the earlier concept of the Mandate of Heaven, which had relied on the notion of morality alone.

Local government officials under the Qin were generally military officers, which indicates the contrast between the Qin policy of domination and the earlier Zhou policy of accommodation. During his lifetime, the First Emperor began the construction of his mausoleum, whose funerary temple faces east, as do the soldiers of his terracotta army. These phenomena show how Qin, despite its strength, remained in many aspects a frontier state and not a truly all-encompassing empire. Nations of the ancient world that could be considered world empires, such as Rome, Persia, or China, tended to share a view that humanity all over the world was one and that sovereign commands from the center of the empire would emanate to various regions, which were never subdivisions of that sovereignty. From this viewpoint, a world empire would stretch from one side of "all under heaven" to the other, and within it there could be delegations but not subdivisions of imperial authority. In line with this, the rock inscription of Langya indicates that the Qin emperor considered himself lord of all within the four directions. It says: "To the west are the shifting desert sands; to the south the far kingdom of Beihu; to the east the Eastern Sea; to the north the distant land of Daxia. Of all the places marked by the footprints of mankind, there is none that is not subject to my rule." This idea that "all under heaven" was subject to a single monarch was subsequently expressed even more concretely during the Han dynasty (206 B.C.E.–220 C.E.).

The systems of government adopted by the early Han were not essentially different from those of the Qin. It was not until after a period of quiet during the reigns of the first four emperors, a period when China recuperated from the turmoil of the previous centuries and restored calm and prosperity, that Han imperial power was universally put in place under Han Wudi (the Martial Emperor, r. 141–87 B.C.E.).

As Han imperial power was becoming more pervasive, it was also gradually becoming more open and public. The founder of the Han, Liu Bang (Gaodi, Emperor Gao, r. 202–195 B.C.E.) was originally a commoner; without even a large family estate, he did not have a good understanding of what was necessary to rule all of China. In the early Han, important government officials and the royal family together formed a ruling class. Most of the high officials came from this group, and the prime ministers

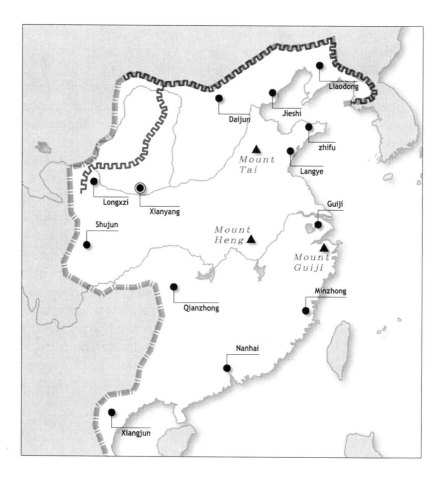

FIGURE 3.1 Map of Qin Dynasty China

were generally nobility. Under the Han government, there were no feudal grants of land except to reward exceptional military achievement, making the governing class a relatively limited body. Empress Dowager Lü (Lü Taihou, r. 195–180 B.C.E.), who ruled after Liu Bang, reduced the status of feudal kings who were not part of the Liu clan, so that apart from the royal family in the state of Changsha, the regions of China were all governed by descendents of the Liu clan. Then, following the Rebellion of the Seven States in 154 B.C.E., which had been supported by members of the royal family, the royal clan gradually lost power in the court. As a result, the central and regional officials came into office because of their qualifications rather than because a family member had previously held office, opening up the ruling class.

But during the reign of Emperor Wu, although the process of selecting officials according to their qualifications had not yet been systematized, the court included people from very diverse backgrounds. The local administrators were generally "able and virtuous" individuals from that region, and some of these local administrators, even a poor woodcutter such as Zhu Maichen (d. 115 B.C.E.), could rise to high government positions. To administer their newly opened frontier territories, the Han continued the Qin system of government, dividing its peripheral territories into different levels, including the *dao* (circuit, the official designation of a district or *xian* in a frontier area) and the dependant states (*shubang*). Similar to the interior districts, their leaders would often be former chiefs of the local people. The leaders of these semiautonomous areas had various titles. In the western regions, they were under the supervision of a proctor-general (*duhu*); the Xiongnu to the northwest and other tribes in the southwestern regions who had "returned to rightness" (*guiyi*) all had their own chieftain leaders. This system later extended to become the Tang dynasty's system of "loose reign" (literally, "haltered and bridled") prefectures (*jimizhoufu*, loosely controlled areas ruled by tribal chieftains) for border areas and then the Ming-Qing system of aboriginal officers (native chieftains, *tusi*) to govern areas of ethnic minorities. Thus there were areas of Chinese political power that lay between that of the all-encompassing empire and the autonomous state, and this structure could be clearly seen as early as the Han.

Thus, in relations with its neighbors the Han dynasty did not draw sharp borders to set itself off from others. The Great Wall was a line of defense, not the limit of a nation that covered "all under heaven." The diplomatic policy of confirming relations by marrying daughters of the imperial family to rulers of neighboring nations conformed to the general intent of cultural expansionism, and the purpose of military expeditions was that nations should willingly submit and receive the benefits of relations with China. The blurry borders were constantly shifting as the vassal states were gradually Sinicized, and areas of indigenous peoples within China blended with the rest of the nation as Chinese culture entered along with government control and the influx of Han Chinese settlers. From the Han dynasty onward, the population of China generally followed a course of continual expansion.

Over four centuries of relative peace, a common body of Chinese culture took form as ideas, skilled people, products, and natural resources continually spread throughout the nation. Thus it is that one of the Chinese terms for their culture is the "culture of the Han people" (*Han wenhua*). The great majority of the Chinese people, regardless of their origin, continue to call themselves *Han ren*, that is, "people of Han" or "Han Chinese" (the term used in this book), long after the political power of the Han dynasty passed away.

As this dynasty developed, two major differences emerged between its imperial system and that of the Qin. One was the government bureaucracy and the examinations to select its officials, which formed the beginning of a bureaucratic stratum of society that remained strong throughout later Chinese history. This social stratum differed from the aristocracy in that it was much more accepting of talented individuals, so that persons in power generally had a higher level of ability. The examinations also helped increase the representation of different regions among government officials. Accordingly, the officials were sometimes closely allied with the emperor and sometimes strongly opposed to him, and many of the government policies and events were shaped by this tension and conflict between these two loci of power.

The second distinguishing characteristic of Han imperial government was that the imperial power had to face the inevitability of dynastic change. The First Emperor of the Qin had expected that his descendents would reign after him for countless generations over thousands of years. In contrast, the early Han emperors were constantly concerned with the possibility of change in the Mandate of Heaven. The cycles of destruction and production in the Five Agents theory, together with the constant alternation of yin and yang, were used to rationalize the previous sequence of dynasties. The Confucian scholars who made up the main body of government officials used this idea of cosmic laws governing the change of dynasties as a means to restrict the emperors' power. As a result, these scholars had difficulty avoiding close involvement with government policy and did not develop a tradition of pure scholarship. This tendency to challenge imperial power, however, declined after the Han. Even by the Eastern Han (25–220 C.E.), imperial power was much less restricted by ethical ideals, since it had forbidden the study of omens, which had formerly been used to support scholars' claims of imperial shortcomings.

The national system that developed during the Qin and Han dynasties was extremely large and complex. Like any such system it had its center and its periphery and its upper and lower levels, although there was continual adjustment and intermixing between different actors in the system. With its great strength, the Qin dynasty had completely controlled the distribution of natural resources, although a great deal of these resources had been expended in the construction of monuments, palaces, and the emperor's great mausoleum. The fortunes of this dynasty had risen and fallen with incredible speed, and this example stood as a constant warning to the Han.

In the early Han, scholar-officials such as Jia Yi (201–169 B.C.E.) and Lu Jia (240–170 B.C.E.) persistently used the fall of the Qin in their essays to admonish the emperor. The proper balance of power between the core of government and its periphery was also an important issue in Han times. The metaphor of a strong trunk and weak branches underlay many policies of the central government, but whenever the central government encountered difficulties, the local powers were quick to challenge its authority. Outside the realm of government administration, there were also struggles with the private sector. Commercial interests that exploited natural resources were at odds with the central government, and there was a tension between rural agricultural interests and those of urban commerce and manufacturing. More broadly, there was a relationship of both opposition and support between the society and the government. The organized great family clans were especially contentious vis-à-vis the state.

Generally speaking, after the divisiveness of the Spring and Autumn and Warring States periods, the Qin and Han dynasties finally succeeded in shaping China into a large and unified structure. Moreover, because this system under the Han could be adjusted and changed, it became more complex and nuanced. Along with this increasing openness and complexity, the imperial system displayed great resilience in the face of its own instability.

2. Advanced Agriculture and Its Market Network

Agriculture was the most important aspect of production in China. Neolithic agriculture primarily used slash-and-burn or swidden cultivation, in which the cultivated fields were shifted to new locations as the soil lost fertility after a few growing seasons. Subsequent advances in agricultural techniques during the Shang dynasty varied greatly according to region. The large feudal estates of the Spring and Autumn period were farmed mostly by serfs, which tended to limit individual initiative. With the collapse of the Zhou feudal system, smaller individual farms began to appear, and these independent farmers, both tenants on the former feudal estates and pioneers who had opened up highland areas, were able to retain what remained of their crops after paying taxes. This made individual farmers more willing to put effort into their farming and try new methods and tools that could boost efficiency and obtain higher yields from their land.

This move toward agricultural development can already be seen in texts from the Warring States period; for example, there are discussions of aspects such as soil fertility and the closeness of planting in many chapters of *The Spring and Autumn Annals of Lü Buwei* (*Lüshi chunqiu*, ca. 239 B.C.E.). These various advances combined to produce a labor-intensive and highly developed form of agriculture, one of the earliest in history and one that evolved through a very extended period of development.

In this period of advanced agriculture, there was considerable regional variation in the techniques of production according to the local climate and soil as well as the level of cultural advancement. During the Han dynasty, the population increased dramatically as the nation recovered from the turmoil of the Warring States, and there were some areas, such as Guanzhong, the "Land Between the Passes," the middle and lower reaches of the Yellow River, and the Shandong peninsula, where the population density made for a very small amount of arable land per capita. This large supply of labor but limited amount of agricultural land stimulated the development of a more carefully considered and labor-intensive agriculture.

Intensive agriculture required more water and better soil, which were supplied by irrigation, fertilization, and soil improvement. Advanced tools were also developed, such as improved plowshares, wheeled seeders, and different shapes of hoes and sickles. The new methods to better utilize the growing period included the interplanting of different crops, crop rotation, deep plowing, and constant, intensive weeding as the crops grew. Farmers also developed higher-yield strains of plants through techniques such as seed selection and selective breeding. The combination of these advances led to the development of a highly systematic and productive agriculture during the Han dynasty.

FIGURE 3.2 An Illustration of the Ridge and Furrow Rotation in the Daitian System

The *daitian*, or "alternating fields," system of the Western Han was a method of managing long strips of cultivated land by regulating the distances between ridges and furrows and using the dirt from the furrows to build up ridges for planting. This made cultivation more efficient and also improved ventilation and irrigation of the crops. The next stage of advancement, which gave this system its name, was to switch the locations of furrows and ridges when the crop type being planted was changed. This combination of crop rotation and close planting maintained the soil's fertility. The combination of more fertile soil and intensive labor on small plots of land, referred to as *quzhong* (area planting), made it possible to obtain relatively high yields from smaller areas of fields. The *quzhong* techniques were a very particular agricultural practice, and although this term was not used in later periods, much the same principles were followed, and the *daitian* system became the standard agricultural practice.

These advanced agricultural techniques required large amounts of manpower, a need that increased greatly during the seasons of intensive cultivation. The great discrepancy between the labor needed at peak seasons and that needed at slack times meant that nonagricultural activities were required to keep the people productive throughout the year. One aspect of Han society that helped mobilize manpower was the clan system, which organized individual family lines into large groups. There were different tasks for men and for women; it was traditionally said that "men plow and women weave." In practice, women and men both handled a broad range of work. In addition to a great miscellany of household tasks for women, they also provided supplemental labor during busy seasons of farming, and the thread they spun and cloth they wove were important products of the agricultural sector. In slack times, the men worked at the many handcrafts needed to support life on the farm, making items such as tools needed for making cloth, agricultural implements, pottery, processed food, and local specialty products.

Raising poultry and livestock was another important aspect of agriculture, and pigpens and fishponds were basic elements of Han farm compounds; the other main types of livestock were cows, sheep, dogs, and chickens. Outside of the compounds were allotments of land for cultivation, though there was much less land allocated to grazing or woodlots than in European agriculture. Thus the Chinese diet depended much more heavily on beans and grains to provide protein and other nourishment. These factors gave China's agriculture, foods, and rural landscape characteristics quite different from those of Europe, and as they were gradually transmitted to other East Asian areas, they formed a broad genre of East Asian agriculture.

Intensive agriculture and the handcrafts practiced in the farm compounds were mutually complementary, with the former providing food and the latter providing the other necessities of life. Furthermore, the products of handcrafts could be sold or bartered to supplement the farmers' income. In line with this economic development of agriculture, the urban economy expanded greatly from the Warring States period to the early Han, and the wealthy individuals portrayed by Sima Qian (ca. 145 or 135–86 B.C.E.) in the *Records of the Grand Historian* were able to amass considerable fortunes through various combinations of industry and commerce. During the reign of Emperor Wu of the Western Han, as part of a government policy to suppress the growing influence of business people, especially heavy taxes were levied on the urban workshops, which bankrupted most of the larger enterprises. The resulting gap in the production of articles of daily life was taken up by handcrafts of the agricultural sector.

These products of farmsteads acquired a fairly widespread distribution, for which a system of collection and distribution was necessary, allowing the circulation of specialized, local products. Accordingly, as they were traded at local marketplaces the shipment and sales of these items followed the routes of highways, creating an economic distribution system, as I discussed in my earlier book, *Han Agriculture*. This economic system, which was incrementally established within this network of local marketplaces, reflected and was supported by a road network that connected the small rural fairs with the larger towns and cities. This concept is central to the geographical "central-place theory" that is discussed below and more specifically in the work of C. K. Yang (Yang Ch'ing-kun, 1911–1999) and G. William Skinner (1925–2008) on the local market economy of North China.

Since the Warring States period, there had been a network of main trunk roads covering most of China, as described in the section of the *Records of the Grand Historian* that contains the biographies of wealthy entrepreneurs. This network of trunk roads had two main centers. One was Chang-an, the imperial capital in the west, and the other was to the east, in Luoyang and Xingyang in Henan, which were strategically located on river routes. These two centers formed the major east-west axis of trade during the Han. In the west, the highway built by the First Emperor, the Straight Road, led north to the lands enclosed by the great bend of the Yellow River, while to the south the Baoye Road led toward Sichuan. In the center was the main north-south road, linking the Yellow River to the Han River and the Yangzi; in the east, another road led to the southern reaches of the Yangzi, today's Jiangxi and Fujian.

The major Han cities were all located on this network of main roads. Branching off from the main roads were smaller roads that served local areas, such as the plain around the city of Chengdu, where the western road network branched off. These points of connection or termination along the roadways were generally the capitals or principal cities of the prefectures and counties. In rural areas, smaller roads branched off, leading to towns and villages, and the spacing of roadways reflected the density of population. Though these smaller roadways changed through time, the routes of the main trunk roads remain major communication lines by roadway, railway, and canal even up to the present.

All areas of China at the time were connected by this commercial network of collection and distribution. Tied together by these roadways supporting various levels of exchange, China's economic system became stable and highly integrated, acting even more strongly than the government to support the connections between regions. Government orders moved along these roadways as well, linking all of the areas of higher and lower levels of administration, and the educated individuals who were to become officials traveled along them from the provinces to the capital. These roadways permitted control over the economic factors of natural resources, manpower, and communications. Areas along them were the

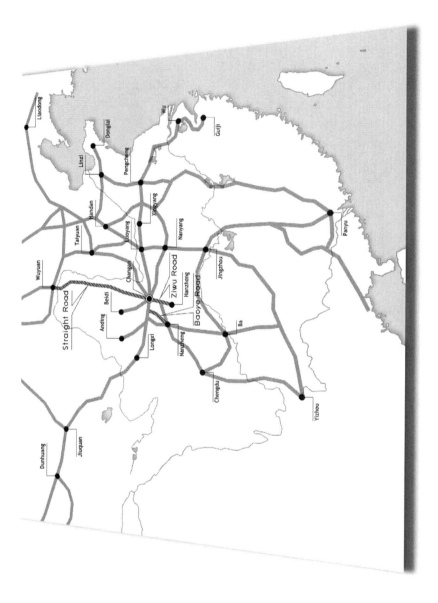

FIGURE 3.3   Major Cities and Roadways of the Han Dynasty

most prosperous, and areas further from them were served more poorly, so the hinterlands at the extreme ends of the roadways were left in poverty, because of the limited flow of resources. Areas beyond the reach of the road network were blank spaces on the map of China of that time.

We should note that though these blank areas were not necessarily far from the urban centers, they remained poorly connected to the government decrees, and cultural advancements were much slower to affect them. Compared to the cultural level of the central area, they could have been frontier outposts. In the complex, large-scale system of a nation that included "all under heaven," they were the most unstable elements. During Qin and Han times, these areas first raised the banners of popular revolt that could lead to the fall of an empire. These agrarian disruptions, such as those led by Chen Sheng (or Chen She, d. 209 or 208 B.C.E.) and Wu Guang (d. 209 or 208 B.C.E.) beginning in Yunmeng County of Hubei, or the Xinshi bandits, who rose up from a village in Nanyang, also in Hubei, all began far from the network of roadways. The rebellion of the Way of the Celestial Masters (or the Way of the Five Pecks of Rice), a Daoist sectarian movement beginning around 142 C.E., and the peasant revolt of the Yellow Turbans in 184 C.E. both started in remote rural areas far from the main roadways, and the central government remained unaware of them until all the military resources of the empire were required to stamp them out. Another indication of the importance of the road network is that the battles that determined the fate of these popular uprisings often took place at critical points along the main trunk roads.

Looking at this period in overview, the intensive agricultural practices developed during the Qin-Han period and the local handcraft industry that developed in tandem with this form of agriculture were important parts of the foundation of a national economic system. This large-scale economic network relied on a network of roadways that stretched throughout the nation, and the areas with poor connections to this network were the cultural borderlands of the empire.

3. Completion of the Chinese Cultural System

Chinese philosophical schools, beginning with the humanism of Confucius in the Spring and Autumn and Warring States periods, saw both continuous development and bitter conflicts in the contention of the so-called

Hundred Schools, each of which claimed its own victory in the debates. After the Qin unification, the Legalist school was the only one to receive official approval, and the others were all oppressed to varying degrees. With the recuperation following the establishment of the Han dynasty, Daoism became the mainstream line of thought, and the other Hundred Schools became merely the domain of specialized scholars. Then, following the reign of Emperor Wu of the Han, Confucianism rose to ascendancy, overshadowing the other schools and becoming the officially sanctioned way of thought. This, it seems, is the commonly accepted view of this history. Yet from a broader viewpoint, it could be said that rather than simply struggling for supremacy, all the pre-Qin schools of thought were converging like rivers flowing into a sea to form a multifaceted Chinese way of thought.

This process of intellectual integration proceeded in tandem with the development of stable government and the economic network described in the previous sections. Warring States philosophers such as Zhuangzi, Xunzi, and Han Feizi (ca. 280–233 B.C.E.) each criticized various aspects of the other schools of thought during that period, and although this criticism was based on significant differences between the schools, it also to some degree initiated the process of integration. King Hui (d. 319 B.C.E.) of the Warring States kingdom of Liang asked Mencius, "how can this world be stabilized?" Mencius replied, "it must be stabilized into a single entity" (*Mengzi*, book 1A.6). This viewpoint may be taken to refer more broadly than to just the political situation, indicating his view of the need for integration in the schools of thought as well. Two subsequent texts from this period of the Qin and early Han, *The Spring and Autumn Annals of Lü Buwei* and the *Huainanzi* (second century B.C.E.) are examples of this drive to pull together the various schools of thought. These encyclopedic compilations knead together schools of thought such as the Confucian, Daoist, Yin-Yang, and Five Agents, blending them with more practical aspects of knowledge, such as astronomy, geography, government, and ritual.

The organization of the earlier of these two books, *The Spring and Autumn Annals of Lü Buwei*, expresses the desire for unification. The whole work is divided into twelve records (*ji*), eight views (*lan*), and six discourses (*lun*). The twelve records are based on the traditional division of a year into four seasons and each season into three periods, with philosophical aspects grouped according to this division of the natural cycle. The three periods of spring are concerned with life, those of summer with ritual and music, those of autumn with war and punishment, and those of winter with death. Each one of these sections contains discourses on related aspects of human affairs and philosophy. This arrangement expresses a view of the completeness of the universe and of the unity of heaven and man. The second part of its structure, the eight views, discusses phenomena organized according to a logic different from that of the natural calendar. The third part of its structure, the six discourses, is concerned with human behavior ranging from ethics to agricultural production, explaining the principles of harmony that underlie them. This work was compiled from the work of scholars of all the Hundred Schools under the direction of the First Emperor's prime minister, Lü Buwei. Although this text incorporates a vast range of materials, the various views are smoothly brought together, and the material is quite consistent, demonstrating the work of synthesis it must have entailed.

The later of these two works, the *Huainanzi*, is also a work that combines the views of many schools, although Daoism is the primary influence running through the text. The material here is not organized with the regularity of the *Spring and Autumn Annals of Master Lü*, but there are twelve chapters denoted as "teachings" (*xun*), covering fields such as "The Primal Way," "Astronomy," "Topography," "Mountains," "Forests," and the "World of Mankind." The book thus ties together various aspects of the natural world and the human world with a view of how human affairs form a part of universal processes.

The ways in which sections of these two books are structured also express the political direction of the time in which they were produced, a period that saw the Qin unification and the establishment of the Han empire. Moreover, the emphasis of the contents on notions such as a Great Unity (*Da yitong*) and the interconnectedness of universal processes together with the conduct of human affairs provides an ontological foundation for the emerging view of a nation that would govern all the known world.

A third text, the *Luxuriant Dew of the Spring and Autumn Annals* (*Chunqiu fanlu*), attributed to the noted scholar Dong Zhongshu (179–104 B.C.E.) in the middle of the Western Han, should be discussed separately from the *Spring and Autumn Annals of Master Lü* or the *Huainanzi*. This slightly later book is structured around the concept of a mutual resonance between heaven and man, and, similar to the other two texts, it brings together Confucian, Daoist, Legalist, Yin-Yang, and Five Agents thought from the pre-Qin thinkers into a grand and complex structure, generating complete individual systems for the movement of heavenly bodies, the cycle of four seasons, human ethical principles, forms of government, and even human physiology and psychology. These systems are assembled in a highly ordered way and closely coordinated with one another, balanced through a sense of normative standards together with the principles of yin and yang and the Five Agents. The abstract principles of yin and yang are expressed in concrete terms such as higher and lower, respected and humble, male and female, ruler and minister; where there is an excess or insufficiency in any of these, it is considered abnormal and in need of rectification. The Five Agents are expressed in the various natural processes of creation and destruction and the movement of one process replacing another, and deviations from these processes are likewise considered aberrations. In this view, just as society and the individual have the ability to influence each other, so do nature and mankind.

This systematic body of theory fuses a great range of different disciplines of the time, from cosmology, numerology, and primitive shamanism to Confucian ethics, Legalist government, Daoist ontology, and the Yin-Yang and Five Agents theories. In this intellectual universe, one founded on both permanence and change, the smallest local changes can reflect a loss of balance in the overall system, similar to the way in which, according to magical beliefs, humans can bring about changes in their universe through very small and seemingly inconsequential actions. In such a well-regulated system, it is conceivable that future events can all be foreseen and that departures from normalcy can be returned to their proper states by the appropriate arrangements. Thus, the universe as seen by Dong Zhongshu is similar to Newton's physical universe: both have an order that can be followed, both can be understood by human beings, and both can be influenced by human action.

The cosmology of Dong Zhongshu had a profound effect on both the academic and government practices of the Western Han, and those who followed it had a deep belief in the idea that dynastic changes were determined by the Mandate of Heaven. There were certain things that were appropriate for a particular time and certain things that were not; the virtue of the Han dynasty would eventually decline, and it would be replaced by another that received the Mandate of Heaven. Though the emperor's position might be supreme in the human order, in the order of the cosmos it was following a cycle like that of the seasons, which held it to a law of inevitable change. Accordingly, disasters or unusual events both natural and manmade were all seen as solemn portents of an impending change in the mandate. After the Han, there were some scholars who held firmly to this doctrine, and in response to the theory about renewal of the Mandate of Heaven, even emperors took measures to conform with cosmological changes. In the latter part of his reign, Emperor Wu of the Western Han would change the title of his reign period every four to six years, to signify a new and more appropriate beginning. Emperor Ai (r. 7–1 B.C.E.), toward the end of the Western Han, even changed his name to Emperor Liu of the Great Peace Displaying Holiness (*chensheng Liu taiping huangdi*), so that the house of Liu could retain the mandate. Wang Mang (45 B.C.E.–23 C.E.), who established his own brief Xin, or New, dynasty (9–23 C.E.) during the interregnum between the Western and Eastern Han, interpreted or even fabricated many auspicious omens intending to prove he had already received the mandate as the new emperor. Then Liu Xuan (Gengshidi, d. 25 C.E.), the member of the house of Liu who led the rebellion overthrowing Wang Mang, titled his first reign period *Gengshi*, "a change to a new beginning," to indicate his hope for receiving the mandate.

This concept of a cycle in which things return to their beginnings is clearly expressed in the Han calendrical system. There were by Qin times many different systems in current use for beginning the year and calculating its end. Most were named for previous dynasties, including the Xia calendar, the Shang calendar, and the Zhou calendar, as well as the Zhuanxu calendar, which became the standard used during the Qin dynasty. Within a single feudal kingdom there could even be different calendars used by the lords, the ministers, and the ordinary people, but there were efforts to have all the subjects of the empire use a single system, the royal calendar, to indicate the legitimacy of imperial rule. In the early years of the Han dynasty, during the reign of Emperor Wu, Luoxia Hong (156–87 B.C.E.) and others established a new standard calendar, called the Great Beginning Calendar (*taichu li*). This was based on complex mathematical calculations that pulled together the solar year and the lunar year of twelve lunar cycles, compensating for the difference by inserting an extra month during certain years. Toward the end of the Western Han, the scholar Liu Xin (ca. 46 B.C.E.–23 C.E.) introduced an even more complex calendar, called the Three Unities Calendar (*santong li*), which extended the Great Beginning Calendar to include not only the solar and lunar years but also the movements of the sun, the moon, and the five known planets, seeking to find a common beginning for all of these cycles. During the Han, this idea was applied as a means to establish a theoretical basis for a more elaborate understanding of the relationship between astronomical events and human affairs, which related to the thought of Dong Zhongshu and others who had faith in the relationship between heaven and man. Sima Qian, in the *Records of the Grand Historian*, described this view as "examining the border between heaven and man, and understanding the changes of ancient and modern times." The greater system of the cosmos and the lesser system of human affairs in both ancient and modern times were linked together into a unified whole.

As the Confucian scholars of the time absorbed these theories, they broadened their base of knowledge to include ancient and contemporary studies of the heavens and the earth, and they used this knowledge in their exposition of sagely ideals in the rules and responsibility of human conduct. Along with this view of a mission of individual responsibility, the New Text School (*jinwen xuepai*) of interpreting the Confucian classics sought to change the government through their interpretation of these texts. Their ideal sage was, of course, Confucius, and there was no place in their views for an imperial ruler such as the First Emperor. The sources they viewed as classics were not only the canonical Confucian classics but also the large body of cryptic and prophetic works referred to as *chenwei*, which were believed to support the standard classics. These Confucian scholars saw their role not simply as the interpreters and spokesmen for universal laws but as more active critics of the government and the ruler, explaining the future results of current policies based on cosmological theories. For this reason, many of Dong Zhongshu's close students were executed because of imperial displeasure with their criticisms. Despite this, the classical scholars of the New Text School persisted in passing down their views from teacher to student and developed a special branch of scholarship that continued to produce apocryphal *chenwei* texts throughout the Western Han.

In the latter part of the Western Han, this type of scholarship and its political applications were exceptionally contentious, to the point that after Wang Mang had usurped the throne to establish his own new dynasty, the armed forces that arose to overthrow him used *chenwei* texts to establish their own legitimacy. This direction of Western Han Confucianism came close to establishing a religious sect: it had its founders and clerics, its classical scriptures, and its apocalyptic warnings. The significance of Western Han Confucianism is, however, broader than just the formation of new religious beliefs. Over a period of more than a century, these Han scholars labored on many fronts but maintained a consistent direction of seeking basic universal principles that would demonstrate a cosmological unity and could be extrapolated to form rules for the world they lived in.

With the establishment of the Eastern Han, a new direction in scholarship rejected this earlier work as being lax and mystical, and the work of interpreting the classics shifted to extended discussions of minute details or the production of elegant essays, suppressing the earlier search for worldly justice and the rules of the universe. During the Eastern Han, there were still individual social critics, such as Wang Chong (27–ca. 100 C.E.), and groups that banded together in protest, as seen in the Disasters of Partisan Prohibition (*danggu zhi huo*), which repressed, imprisoned, and executed students and scholars in 166 and 169 C.E. But the continuity and strength of the heroic Western Han vision of the authority of Confucian scholarship had passed away.

4. Popular Beliefs

Previous sections in this chapter discussed the cultural systems established by scholars of the time, systems that had profound influences on the later developments of Chinese culture. Apart from that intellectual world, many ancient beliefs were preserved by the common people in different areas. These beliefs or views tended to be highly localized, much simpler, and orally transmitted. The centralized imperial government had tried many times, with little success, to unify these local beliefs, and there is scant notice of them in the historical records.

According to the "Record of the Feng-Shan Sacrifices" in the *Records of the Grand Historian*, following the Qin unification, the government established a Bureau of Temples (*ci guan*) that was responsible for recording and organizing the places of worship over the entire nation. These sacred sites, famous mountains, great rivers, and supernatural beings represented earlier beliefs of long standing. Yongzhou, for example, had over a hundred places of worship dedicated to heavenly bodies such as the sun, moon, Orion's belt, the Big and Little Dippers, Venus, Mars, Jupiter, Saturn, and the twenty-eight lunar "mansions" in the sky through which the moon passes each month as well as to natural forces such as the wind and the rain. By the Western Han, the imperial capital Chang-an had dozens of these places of worship; the rest of the nation had thousands in total. In the *Book of Rites* (*Liji*), the chapters "Meaning of Sacrifices" (*Jiyi*) and "Methods of Sacrifices" (*Jifa*) have extensive lists of the different sacrificial rituals to mountains and rivers, along with a description of their general characteristics as the objects of worship by the common people. Famous mountains and great rivers were found in all areas, and each locale naturally had its own particular ceremonies. At the same time, there were some observances common to most of China. For instance, the ritual referred to as *di* (using the same character as in *Shangdi*, "supreme ancestor") and the offerings to heaven and earth, which went by different names in different areas, had been held since ancient times throughout China. With the political unification of the Qin-Han empires, there was an attempt to unify the diversity of these rituals and draw them into the greater cultural sphere described in the previous sections of this chapter. For example, the numerous locations in Guanzhong where the *di* ritual was performed were organized in conformance with the five directions and five colors, which were an extension of the Five Agents theory.

After the founding of the Western Han, the imperial government again attempted to standardize the local religions. In addition to bringing the ritual procedures and texts under the control of government officials, it also sought to put all the local shamans, both male and female, under palace control. Although the great variety of shamans, who were identified with particular lakes, rivers, mountains, trees, and other locations, could still maintain the distinctive characteristics of their individual rituals, the central government sought to exercise control over their activities.

Moreover, there were offerings made throughout all areas of China to a great variety of figures who had distinguished themselves through their intelligence, moral uprightness, or contributions to the public good. The "Methods of Sacrifices" chapter of the *Book of Rites* lists figures such as the leaders of ancient tribes, astronomers who had named the stars in the sky or organized the calendar, farmers who had made important advancements in agriculture, warriors who had killed great numbers of the enemy, engineers who had tamed the floodwaters, and mythical founders of the earliest dynasties. It is a list of offerings that must have been compiled from diverse sources. During the Han, offerings were also occasionally made to more recent historical individuals. For example, Liu Zhang (d. 177 B.C.E.), who reigned as Prince Jing of the Western Han feudal state of Chengyang (r. 178–176 B.C.E.), had a folk religious rite with its own shaman established to him two centuries later in the interregnum between the Western and Eastern Han. There likely were many other minor local religious traditions like this one honoring Liu Zhang that appear nowhere in the historical record.

Offerings to mountains and rivers can be considered a type of nature worship, one whose deities often took human form and who could transform into individual heroes who were also protector spirits. The mountain god for the city of Jianye (modern Nanjing) at the end of the Eastern Han was Jiang Ziwen (fl. Eastern Han), who had actually been a "District Defender" (*xianwei*) in the region. The sacred places that formed a part of this nature worship were known for their mystical emanations. One of the more commonly seen emanations was cloudlike wisps of *qi* energy (*yunqi*), and divination through its observation was a specialty of geomancers in the Qin-Han period, as is evident from a number of archaeologically excavated texts. One of the fragmentary manuscripts found at Dunhuang described divination by *yunqi* for military use, arranged as a reference for a commander in the field. Similarly, a manuscript from the Mawangdui tombs, excavated in the 1970s, was titled "Miscellaneous Divinations by Astronomy and the Weather" (*Tianwen qihou za zhan*).

Qi was understood as having two aspects. The first type is lighter and referred to as cloud *qi* (*yunqi*). It was considered a transcendental, universal power. The second *qi* is denser, referred to by Mencius as "floodlike *qi*" (*haoran zhi qi*), and is present in the human body. In Qin-Han thought, these two types interact with each other in a variety of transformations and were generally combined to form the concept of a fluid power or vital force referred to simply as *qi*. There were significant differences in the way this energy is understood. For example, in the cosmology of Dong Zhongshu, human abilities, including *qi*, can affect universal processes, whereas in the intellectual system of the *Huainanzi*, these human abilities can only adapt themselves to the universal cycles. The concept of *qi* has been a key component in Chinese traditional medicine from the Han down to the present, particularly in practices such as acupuncture (*zhenjiu*) and breathing exercises (*tuna*). Medical treatment was inseparable from the broader cultivation of health and longevity, as seen in the early exercises combining movement and breathing called "guiding the breath" (*daoyin*), which was a forerunner of modern martial arts such as Tai ji quan.

In addition to having this natural power, the mountains and rivers were also considered the haunts of strange creatures. An encyclopedia of these fantastic beasts, the *Classic of Mountains and Seas* (*Shanhai jing*), was edited in the Western Han from pre-Qin materials and describes eerie beings inhabiting remote mountains, forests, rivers, and lakes. These creatures have strange forms, such as human bodies with animal heads, animal bodies with human heads, or many heads on a single body, and each beast has its characteristic activities. Illustrations of similar hybrids together with explanations also appear on a Chu silk manuscript from the Warring States period that was excavated from a tomb in Zidanku near Changsha in Hunan. In Warring States texts, there is no shortage of these part-animal, part-spirit creatures, and the *Classic of Mountains and Seas* appears to be essentially a compilation of these legends, organizing them into an imaginary and highly detailed geographical space. The local religious cults of the Han, described above, also incorporate some of these creatures, such as the Chen Bao, worshipped in the state of Qin and variously described as a pair of children, hedgehogs, or roosters. From time to time over seven centuries this spirit was described as being about four or five *zhang* (about ten meters) in length, emitting a red and yellow light, and making a sound that was echoed by wild chickens.

These legends are reflections of Qin-Han occult beliefs that supernatural and natural phenomena can foretell either good fortune or disaster. The emperors worshipped these beings to prevent calamities in the land, and the common people were always hoping to attract good luck and avert the bad. This world of the supernatural generally was integrated with the human world to the point where the two were indistinguishable. It is an attitude that differs widely from the ideal order that underlies the integration of these two worlds seen in the cosmology of Dong Zhongshu, which is neatly organized by the balance of yin and yang and the cycles of the Five Agents. These types of folk beliefs pay little attention to cultivating moral virtue but instead use ceremony to fend off ominous influences and maintain peace and prosperity.

There was also a belief that if an individual could accumulate enough refined *qi*, he could extend his life and become immortal. Both the Qin First Emperor and Emperor Wu of the Han did their utmost to find methods and drugs to attain immortality. The imperial household was continually adopting rituals from local beliefs and inviting to court spiritual masters who promised the ability to extend life. Magic islands in the far seas and sacred mountains throughout China were likely places to search for mystical sages or herbs that could promise immortality.

Emperor Wu associated his own search for longevity with another matter, the *feng shan* ceremony performed on Mount Tai, which he considered essential for maintaining the Han's Mandate of Heaven. With so public a purpose, this might have been a widely attended ceremony that could inspire reverence in his subjects, but instead it was a closely guarded secret, and essentially nothing is known of its contents to this day. For the most important part of the *feng shan* ceremony, Emperor Wu set off to ascend the mountain alone, accompanied only by his chariot driver, and not long after coming back down the mountain, his driver died from unknown causes— apparently a victim of the emperor's compulsion to achieve longevity.

Likewise, the common people were not necessarily uninterested in obtaining immortality. Wang Ziqiao, from the Eastern Zhou dynasty, and An Qisheng, from the time of the Qin-Han transition, are but two of the individuals who were claimed to have become immortal. On the many bronze mirrors found from the Han, the most frequent inscription is a supplication for longevity. The individual regarding himself in the mirror would see below his image the words, "Above is an immortal who will never know old age."

No one can live forever, but the interest in cultivating long life during the Qin-Han period led to ideas of improving the bodily *qi* as well as advances in medicine and breathing exercises. And since death inevitably brings an end to the hopes of life in this world, people of that time strove to develop a human world beyond this life, one that would be truly imperishable. The First Emperor's mausoleum contained an imperishable world that his spirit could inhabit: it took the form of a map of the empire that he ruled, and he was guarded in the hereafter by troops of terracotta soldiers. In the rock-cut Mancheng tombs of the Western Han feudal kingdom of Zhongshan, King Jing and his wife were encased in suits made of jade plaques sewn with gold thread, intended to prevent decay, and all the necessities of daily life were set out neatly within their chambers. Everything was included, from containers of fine wine to a latrine. Even the tombs of well-to-do commoners during the Han were decorated with fine ceramics, carved stone sarcophagi, and wall frescoes, all preserving the joys of life in the present, frozen in eternity for the tomb's occupant. There were even documents that simulated deeds for these tombs, which would extend the occupants' ownership rights into the next world. Naturally, an afterworld such as this had its own government bureaucracy, one mirroring that of the human world and controlled by its own official guardians.

Rather than there being a simple division between the worlds of life and death, there was a continuous interplay between them. This is vividly portrayed on the painted silk funeral banner from the Mawangdui tomb of Lady Dai, which depicts the afterlife in three parts. The upper part has the sun and moon, together with a three-footed raven, as described in the *Classic of the Mountains and Seas*; in the middle, which is the realm of mankind, Lady Dai moves upward toward eternity accompanied by her lady-in-waiting; and the lowest part of the banner is an underworld controlled by a monster in human form. From top to bottom, these three levels are fluidly connected by a tree of life and by the intertwined forms of serpentine dragons: although there are divisions, the banner graphically expresses that the three realms are continuous and not distinct.

In the upper strata of Chinese culture, rational intellectual debates established a structure for concepts of the cosmos, human knowledge, and moral values. Though there were differences between the various schools of thought, they were all concerned with essential issues of the human world. At the same time, concerns of the human order were intertwined with the order of the cosmos to produce a complex, multilayered system. In this system, all of the myriad affairs of heaven and earth are essentially gradations of the human world; it is complete and unified, just like the ideal government of the empire itself.

On the other hand, the cosmological understandings of the common people described in this section were transmitted from much more ancient periods, and they embodied a reverence for human life and its preservation as well as dread and respect for supernatural powers. The concepts of vital force (*qi*) and vital essence (*jing*) in living beings may not be immediately apparent, yet they symbolize and embody the core of human life. In all the places on earth, none lacked many kinds of strange beings, each of which manifested the *qi* and the essence of its life. Just as there may be many forms of being in the life and death of the human world, the afterlife is simply an extension of the present world, in which movement returns to stillness and change returns to permanence.

5. Northern Nomad Cultural Interaction with Chinese Culture

The northern regions referred to in this chapter include the steppes to the north and south of the Mongolian desert, the northern and southern mountains of Xinjiang, and the vast expanse of Central Asia. Although the environments, inhabitants, and ways of life in these regions differ from one another, in comparison with the cultures of China to their south, they have certain common characteristics of a steppe culture.

Contrary to the general impression of life in this region as one of simply moving the herds to follow available grass and water, the nomadic life developed a complex economy with particular characteristics. Growing crops and pasturage are two of the basic ways people produce food, and they were the means by which peoples developed beyond the hunting and gathering stage and began to have more settled means of production. There are six types of livestock in traditional Chinese agriculture that supplement crops: horses, cattle, sheep, dogs, chickens, and pigs, the last two being the most important. In traditional European agriculture, in addition to raising crops and livestock, forests are also maintained, so that planting, pasturage, and hunting and gathering from the wild together form the basis of an agricultural economy. In Inner Mongolia and Xinjiang, there was also small-scale farming of drought-resistant plants such as hulless oats to supplement the livestock.

The nomads lived on food provided by their livestock, such as cattle, sheep, camels, and horses, with the last two serving both as transportation and food. The migrations of these nomadic peoples in Mongolia and Xinjiang are of varying lengths, given the cold, dry climate of these regions, which makes the grasses recover very slowly from grazing. Their nomadic way of life is thus based on the need to accommodate a very short growing season.

The Mongolian region has evidence of an early microlithic culture, one that used very small stone points, generally only about a centimeter long, in their hunting and fishing. Neolithic sites in Mongolia indicate that agriculture developed relatively late and that it remained at a relatively undeveloped stage. Expansion of the agricultural societies to the south could have forced some peoples into the more unreceptive environment that lay on the border between the agricultural and nomadic peoples. In this environment, they would have had no choice but to abandon their sedentary life for one based on moving with their livestock in search of water and forage. In the area along the Yingjin River, which flows through the Aohanqi region of Inner Mongolia near Chifeng, archaeologists have discovered Lower Xiajiadian sites from approximately 2000 B.C.E., including a string of rock fortresses. The archaeologist Su

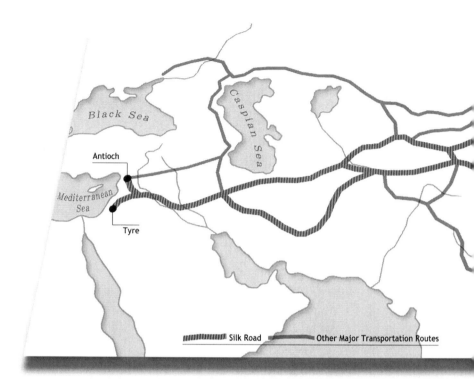

FIGURE 3.4 Routes of Han Overland Communications with the West

Bingqi believed that these structures were intended to separate peoples of differing ways of life, and this area lies close to the later border between nomadic and agricultural peoples where the Great Wall was to be built. Thus, the nomadic cultures of these northern regions could date back as far as four thousand years ago.

Since these nomadic peoples moved over great distances, the tribes would continually come into contact with one another, and this interaction would lead to a sustained interchange of products, tools, language, and ways of thought. Thus, in the broad spaces of the Eurasian grasslands, the ways of life, languages, and religions of tribes living in different areas acquired many fundamental common features underlying the superficial differences. Accordingly, the inhabitants of the grasslands could coalesce into larger tribes, occasionally forming large military bodies. The peoples referred to as Xiongnu or Huns in the historical records of the Qin-Han period were representative of these nomadic empires. The later Mongol

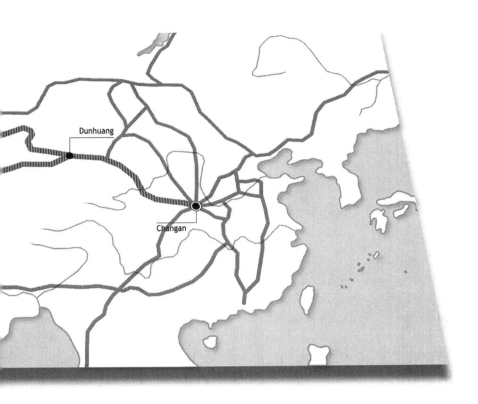

empire of Chinggis Qaghan was another great gathering of these grassland tribes. In addition to these two prominent and better-organized examples, the tribes of northern and central Asia often formed and disbanded swift troops of cavalry to harass the agricultural states to the south.

The inhabitants of Xinjiang today are primarily the Uyghur, who live in towns, and the nomadic Kazakhs of the grasslands, a division similar to the ancient one between urban settlers and nomads. Early official contact between these western regions of Serindia and the Chinese court was led by Zhang Qian (195–114 B.C.E.), who was sent as an emissary by the Han Emperor Wu, and by the general Ban Chao (32–102 C.E.), who led a number of military campaigns in this region during the early Eastern Han. Their records indicate that by this time the area contained both settled and nomadic kingdoms. The settled kingdoms were generally city-states located around oases and were primarily agricultural; the nomadic kingdoms were tribes that raised livestock on the grasslands. Since the climate of Serindia is better than that of the Mongol areas, the nomadic tribes did not need to move such great distances to maintain the supply of water and grass for their livestock. In these regions, the social structure was a complex interaction between the many nomadic pastoralist tribes and the settled agricultural communities around the oases, and so it was more difficult to form large nomadic empires like the Xiongnu (Huns). When this area was being opened to China during the Han, the Chinese relied on the city-states for vital aid in their campaigns against the Xiongnu. These oasis city-states were also vital nodes of communication, since they provided stable resting points along the routes of the Silk Road, which was one of the main trading and cultural links between China and the West.

Considering the larger regional scale, the overland line of communications between China and the West now referred to as the Silk Road was actually a complex network of roadways. To the north was another main route that ran along the edge of the Mongol grasslands to arrive at the Tianshan mountain range and Mount Wulaling. Its eastern terminus was far east in what is now northeastern China and Siberia; to the west one branch ran to what is now Russia, and a more southerly branch ran through the Central Asian kingdoms. This route was in fact older and more direct than the better-known Silk Road to the south, and it served as a means of communication in stages between East Asia, Central Asia, and Europe before the Silk Road developed. The earliest use of transportation by horse or mule cart probably spread along this road, moving east from the Mesopotamian region to East and South Asia and west to North Africa and Europe. Although the earliest use of wheeled vehicles in China has not yet been established, it was probably about 2000 B.C.E., and their use, along with the knowledge of bronze and iron metallurgy, was likely to have been introduced along this northern grasslands route.

There was also a southeastern route following the gorges from Sichuan to Yunnan and connecting what is now the grasslands of Qinghai (Kokonor, Blue Lake) to the Silk Road, then running south to what is now Myanmar and India. This road was more difficult, since it had to cross mountains and rivers, but it was still used, since it was the only overland link to these southern regions. The Sanxingdui culture, located near the modern city of Guanghan in Sichuan, in the vicinity of this route, was closely contemporary with the Shang dynasty. A culture with broad trade linkages, its bronze masks have Central Asian characteristics, and shells excavated from its sites originated in the southern seas. Even further south, artifacts from the Shizhaishan site of Jinning County in Yunnan have distinct similarities with the northern grassland cultures. It was along this route that Zhang Qian probably passed during his journey to India during the Han.

Through these routes, China had extensive dealings with Central Asia and South Asia as well as indirect contact with western Asia. From earlier times, the various peoples who advanced and retreated throughout areas to the north and the west of China influenced one another greatly, and the influence of the central culture of China entered these areas through the Gansu Corridor (the border between present-day Gansu and Xinjiang) beginning as early as the Neolithic period. North of the line of the later Great Wall, Chinese peoples steadily moved into the grassland areas. The early twentieth-century scholar Wang Guowei (1877–1927) established that various early northern peoples, such as the Xianyun or Hunyu, were the ancestors of the Xiongnu, although the regions inhabited by these early peoples were the northern areas of the modern provinces of Shanxi and Shaanxi—to the south of the line of the Great Wall. During the Warring States period, there was further pressure on this area because of competition between the three great states of Qin, Zhao, and Yen, which all expanded their territories northward, pushing the boundary of Chinese peoples further into this region. Faced by this incursion, various northern tribes, such as the Xiongnu, the Donghu, and the Dingling, gradually coalesced to form a powerful empire that stretched across the Mongolian regions. On the western frontier of China, the Yuezhi peoples, who originally lived in the Gansu region, left this area because of pressure from both the Chinese peoples and the Xiongnu, moving westward into Central Asia and later founding the Kushan Empire (ca. first to third centuries C.E.). All of these movements worked in a chain reaction, with one group moving into an area as another moved out. By the Eastern Han, the Xiongnu's military power had been crushed by the Chinese armies, and the remnants moved westward, gradually absorbing indigenous tribes of the areas they moved through. Gathering strength in this process, they eventually threatened Europe, and by the time Attila the Hun (ca. 406–453 C.E.) was moving toward Rome in the mid-fifth century, his peoples had been away from their homeland for four centuries. The shock waves of this broad movement caused most of the tribes on the European mainland to move as a result, and what was referred to as the "Barbarian

Invasion" was in fact a complex concatenation of movements by tribes each pressed by others.

Apart from warfare, these tribes also had frequent contacts that carried trade and cultural influences. The Silk Road was a result of China's opening up of these western regions, and beginning in the Han dynasty, China exported great quantities of silk fabric and imported Western items in return. Foods now common in China, such as grapes, onions, or watermelon, together with aspects of daily life such as the common two-stringed fiddle-like instrument (*huqin*) or magic shows of the common people, were introduced to China as part of this trade.

A fundamental change in the Chinese diet that came about as a result of this East-West communication was the increased use of wheat products in addition to the traditional staples of millet and rice. Wheat had been introduced to China from the Middle East as early as the late Neolithic. Before the Eastern Han, wheat in China was prepared similarly to the other grains, by boiling or steaming the whole kernels. Then in the Eastern Han, techniques of grinding wheat into flour, introduced from the West, became more commonly available, and there are many contemporary references to water-powered mills used for grinding wheat. By the end of the Eastern Han, the influence of this new technique on the diet of the common people is indicated by the many references to "soup pastries" (*tangbing*), which refer to noodles, not what we now consider pastries, although baked cakes also appeared at this time. This dietary revolution gradually made wheat and barley, along with millet, the staple foods of North China.

Another far more unfortunate result of this cultural interchange was the introduction of Western diseases into China. During the Eastern Han, large-scale epidemics swept over North China. The terrible epidemic of the late first century C.E., which killed great numbers of people, was probably brought back by troops returning from duty at outposts along the Silk Road. About the same time an epidemic referred to as the Antonine Plague swept the Mediterranean world from 165–180 C.E., likely brought back by Roman legions returning from campaigns in Parthia. Whether these two plagues were attributable to the same disease cannot be established, but they are indeed indications of the common results in both the East and the West of expanding communications. Plagues in China recurred throughout the Eastern Han, and it was at this time that major advances in Chinese medicine were made, as seen in *On Cold Patho-*

genic Damage (*Shanghan lun*) of Zhang Zhongjing (ca. 150–ca. 219 C.E.), which focuses on infectious diseases. Overall, the population of North China was reduced substantially by these plagues, and this may have been a factor in the contemporary shift in the balance of power between north and south.

6. Chinese Culture Moves South

China's move to the south was completely different from its move to the north or to the west, which were areas where the dominance of pastoralism restricted China's traditional agricultural economy. To the south, as in the other areas, were many non-Han inhabitants of numerous ethnic backgrounds. Although the level of agricultural development varied substantially, generally speaking, rice cultivation in areas to the south of the Yangzi was not as intensively developed as in areas to the north, and many areas retained more primitive traditions of farming. As Han people entered the south, a process of assimilation occurred, leading to developments at many levels. Compared to the conflicts and antagonism that occurred in northern regions, the south was drawn progressively into the Han cultural sphere.

During the Warring States period, even though territory south of Lake Dongting was nominally under the state of Chu, there was little actual administrative control over this area. With the Qin-Han unification, government control spread southward, with the system of commandaries and counties extending as far as Lingnan ("south of the mountains," a region that includes modern Guangdong, Guangxi, Hunan, and Jiangxi provinces). The actual administration was limited to points along the lines of communication, and areas to either side of the main trunk roads were largely controlled by the indigenous peoples. The most significant of these indigenous peoples was the Baiyue (the "hundred Yue"), who lived along the southeastern coast and may have been related to the Yue people, who are recorded as having lived there. They may also have a close relationship to the people of Vietnam, since their languages are both part of the Austronesian linguistic system. During the Qin, military campaigns to the south conquered the southern Yue area around Guangdong and established the administration of prefectures and counties. But with the fall of the Qin, this area rose up and established itself as an independent state administered by Han officials who ruled over the local Yue people. Han records indicate that these peoples, who lived also in Fujian and Zhejiang, had established kingdoms, although they may not actually have been at the scale of true kingdoms.

During the reign of Emperor Wu in the Western Han, military expeditions that were part of his southern expansion brought these areas more completely into the Han dynasty's empire. It is also significant that large numbers of Yue peoples migrated to the area between the Yangzi and the Huai rivers. Although it is difficult to estimate the population that moved, it appears the first migration may have included forty thousand people, and the second involved as many as two or three hundred thousand, an extremely large number of people for that time. Despite the large number of Yue peoples who moved to the Yangzi region, many continued to live in the more remote regions of their original homeland, coexisting with the Han people who had moved in to colonize the regions close to the main roads.

From the late Western Han up to the middle of the Eastern Han, expansion into the south was a major aspect of government policy. At this time, there were two groups of indigenous peoples, the Man and the Shanyue ("mountain Yue"), both of whom lived in areas away from the main roads. Despite their cultural differences—the Shanyue most likely were descendents of the original inhabitants, and the Man were people who had moved in from southwestern areas to fill areas vacated by the earlier Yue migrations—the two groups were united in their long-term opposition to settlement by Han immigrants.

The main wave of Han settlers to the south probably took place from the first to second centuries C.E., attributable at least in part to the plagues that were sweeping the north at that time. An even more significant cause may have been the increasingly strict government controls in the north, which made it more difficult for the common people to avoid military conscription and taxes there than in the south, which was distant and thus less supervised by the central administration. Though it is impossible to estimate the numbers of these immigrants, the scale of this migration is indicated by the substantial increase in the number of commandaries and counties that are recorded for the south from the beginning to the end of the Eastern Han, indicating the significant increase of households under government administration. As this administration became stronger and penetrated deeper into the mountainous hinterland, the road system increased from a few main trunk roads to a web that spread over the region. This development progressed in a steady and orderly way, and the Han immigrants were not able to rely continually on superior military force. For example, as the southern expansion began in the early Eastern Han, the troops sent to suppress resistance by the Wuxi "barbarians" (*man*) were decimated by disease, probably either malaria or the waterborne parasite schistosomiasis.

The Han settlers who slipped by in small groups into the south to open up new land in the hilly terrain must have suffered from the same diseases as the soldiers, although it is also possible that, in the process of gradually moving southward, the Han settlers intermarried with the local Man and Yue peoples and thus developed better immunity to these diseases than the troops, who simply marched in. This cultural assimilation also would have produced a population that, though not yet incorporated into the regional administration of the imperial government, did comprise a group more amenable to the ensuing immigration and government control.

The final large-scale effort to organize the area to the south of the Dongting and Poyang lakes and the mountainous territory of Wannan and the southeastern seacoast came under the Eastern Wu kingdom (222–280 C.E.) during the Three Kingdoms period. At this point, the incursions were not, as before, by northerners moving into southern territory but rather by the southern kingdom of Wu opening this territory to take large numbers of men and whatever wealth that could be converted to movable assets. At this time, Wu was in a desperate struggle with the northern kingdom of Wei (220–265 C.E.), and the people and resources from this newly opened territory were vital to their resistance.

Opening up the southwestern regions occupied by the Yi people was a particular concern of Emperor Wu of the Western Han, as part of his strategy to enter Serindia through the southwest. Given the limitations of geographical knowledge at the time, Emperor Wu was unaware that the high Tibetan plateau and the Himalayan Mountains formed an almost impassible barrier. This mistake was attributable in part to the fact that there was a route connecting China to South Asia, as discussed in the previous section, traversing the mountain ranges to link the northern grasslands and southwestern China. Even though Emperor Wu was unsuccessful in crossing the southwest to penetrate the western regions, his actions to open this territory resulted in China's acquisition of a large area of forest land and its indigenous population.

Part of this region, referred to as Ba-Shu during the early Han, was composed of two relatively small areas of the Sichuan basin, one the Chengdu plain and the other a strip of land that ran along the Yangzi River valley without penetrating deeply into the southwest. A route through this territory was part of the program of expansion into the southwest, and this went not only south but also westward to the Tibetan Plateau; thus this development was supported by the two main regional trunk roads.

The chapter "Southwestern Barbarians" (*Xinan yi*) of the *History of the Former Han* (*Han shu*), in recording this process, also describes aspects of many of these southwestern cultures, including their clothing, customs, and tribal names. But since this information is very sketchy, it is difficult to make associations with peoples in this area today, and we should also realize that since that time the peoples in this area have gone through almost two thousand years of movement and assimilation, which have greatly changed their cultures. The mountain forests of southwestern China are dense, its mountains high and valleys deep, and the cultures of the peoples in the different areas have always been clearly separated. Ethnological studies have found that in areas such as Yunnan, the high mountains may have one ethnic group, the valleys another, and the region around the high lakes in between yet a third.

The three routes into the southwest radiated from Chengdu to form a network. The first went to the Mekong River, which leads south to Vietnam; the second to the Yangzi and the Xi rivers, which lead west through Guangxi; and the third went directly west, toward the Tibetan plateau. During the Han, side roads expanded off these main routes to form a network that supported the many new prefectures and counties that were being established, though this network was much less dense than what developed in the areas of Hunan, Jiangxi, Guangdong, and Fuzhou. In contrast to those denser roadways, the people who used this network serving the hinterlands were not primarily Han immigrants but rather the indigenous peoples, together with the Han government officials and troops who governed them and oversaw the process of cultural assimilation to the Han majority.

We should also note that in the Han province of Jiaozhou, now a part of northern Vietnam, the prefectures and counties had much closer connections with the Guangdong region and to a much lesser extent with the newly opened areas in the southwest. This situation, in which the far south had a much better developed administrative network than areas closer to the central government, contrary to the general trend throughout China, was a result of the difficult terrain in the southwest.

This particular pattern of development in the southwest is indicated by the fact that its administrative units are referred to as *dao* (circuits), which originally meant road. In the southwest, development proceeded from isolated points, extending along lines and then expanding into areas that became administrative units. The process is like that of settlement, where traders gradually expanded into this area, followed closely by immigrants, who were followed by military force and government administration. This Han movement of linear expansion followed by control over an area was similar to that of later areas of expansion, as in the northeast or northwest, although the process was much clearer here because of the difficult topography in the southwest.

The first wave of immigrants played an especially important role in settling the southwest, one similar to that of earlier immigrants into Sichuan. As part of that earlier process, the family of Sima Xiangru (179–117 B.C.E.), a famous poet of the Western Han, had been sent to the Sichuan area during the reign of the First Emperor as part of his program to open up this area. In addition to collecting salt, smelting iron, and doing business deep in indigenous territory, the activities of immigrants included abducting native peoples, who were then sold as servants to Han settlers in the region. Similarly, as southeastern areas such as Kuaiji (Shaoxing in modern Zhejiang) were opened up during the Han dynasty, Han people were the first to enter, with a variety of commercial motives. The well-known official Zhu Maichen (?–115 B.C.E.), the prefect of Kuaiji, was a Han Chinese who had moved into the Yue area and helped the Han open it up.

In current terms, this was colonization by the imperialist Han state, and countless groups of indigenous peoples were affected in this way by the Han empire. Restricted by their limited economic resources, most of these people were subsistence farmers in forested mountain areas and unable to compete with the stronger economic backing of the Han immigrants. The ability of the Han people to open up these areas was based first on their commercial activities, second on their clearing marginal land for agriculture, and third on their military and administrative strength.

Of course, many of these indigenous peoples continued to live in this region. For example, during the late Tang dynasty, an extremely short people with very dark skin, clearly different from the Han peoples, lived in Hunan's Dao County. The oral traditions of the Saisiyat indigenous

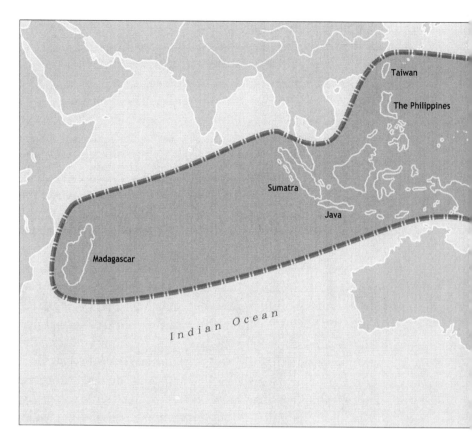

FIGURE 3.5 Extent of the Austronesian Languages Group

people in Taiwan retain legends of short pygmylike people, and, personally, I suspect that some of the very short Pacific islanders may have some ethnic connection with them. These scattered clues indicate that, even though the cultural traditions of these indigenous groups in the southwest were erased by assimilation with the Han, their traces remained for quite a long time.

Another piece in this puzzle lies in our understanding of the Austronesian language group, whose speakers extend all the way from Taiwan to Easter Island in the east, Madagascar in the west, and New Zealand in the south. The divisions within Austronesian languages are closely related to the movements of peoples in this area over the past two thousand years, and the origins of these peoples, whose movements across the chains of

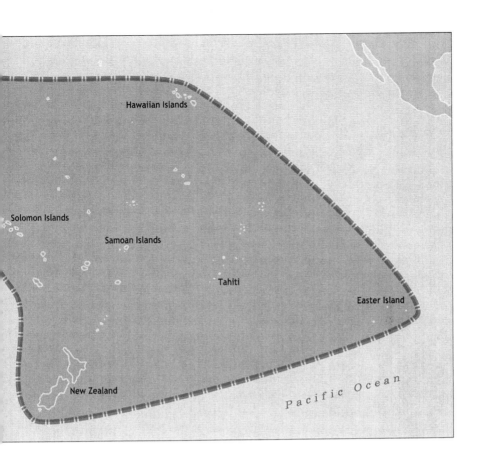

Pacific islands followed the ocean currents, can now almost certainly be traced to Taiwan. But even before that, their earlier origin may have been mainland China. Although we cannot yet prove that peoples from southern and southwestern China migrated first to Taiwan and then to the Pacific islands, there are many similar cultural features that can be observed, though further confirmation must await DNA testing.

To make a best guess about this process, it appears that although a great many of the native peoples were assimilated as the Han peoples moved into the south, some of the ethnic groups were pushed steadily southward, and, for those who were pressed to the seacoast, the nearest places of refuge were the islands of Taiwan and Hainan. Since the Philippine islands are not far from Taiwan, and since the Southeast Asian islands of Malaysia are also not distant from Hainan, this hypothesis is not impossible. Should it be confirmed, it would indicate that the slow and inexorable movement southward that began during the Qin-Han period had effects that extended far into the South Pacific. It is a significant research topic in world history but one that has yet to receive the attention it deserves.

As this section has discussed, the westward expansion of China and the Xiongnu created shocks that touched off great waves of migration that swept through Central Asia and Eastern Europe. These movements eventually resulted in what in European history has referred to as the barbarian invasions, and it had long-lasting effects on the ancient Mediterranean and European world. Just as ethnic groups flowed southwest into the Eurasian continent, other groups may have flowed to the southeast into the Pacific islands, creating the cultures now found there. The movement southward into the Indian subcontinent by South Asian peoples is similar, although these South Asian migrations did not extend as far and thus had little influence on South Pacific islands at this point. The earliest origin of the great Austronesian language group may have been on the Chinese mainland, and even today the language groups of southern China are extremely complex and change dramatically from one mountain valley to another. It is clear that these dialects preserve many ancient traits, and if sufficient linguistic studies could be made, I am confident that the dialects of Zhejiang and Guangdong could be shown to have close relationships with the ancient language of Yue and that this ancient language would also be related to that of the peoples who set off from Taiwan to the Pacific islands. The previous view of the opening of southwestern China was one that almost exclusively considered it from the viewpoint of the Han settlers. But considered from a broader viewpoint, it had global effects.

7. Buddhism Enters China, and Religious Daoism Comes Into Being

The introduction of Buddhism was one of the greatest influences on Chinese culture throughout its history. This was the first time that China was significantly influenced by an outside civilization, and it led to profound changes in the characteristics of Chinese civilization. Before the entrance of Buddhism, religious beliefs in China were primarily concerned with offerings to deities, who were primarily nature gods, and veneration to the ancestors, which was related to the development of strong family ties. These beliefs in deities and ancestral spirits were not founded in clear religious doctrines, concerns about the ultimate purpose of life, or explanations about the afterlife. The arrival of Buddhism from India not only supplied these aspects to its believers but also stimulated the development of a native religious creed, religious Daoism.

The question of exactly when Buddhism entered China has not yet been definitively answered. According to traditional historical sources, Buddhism first appears in the historical records during the reign of Emperor Ming of the Eastern Han (r. 57–75 C.E.), when the emperor had a dream of a golden deity and one of his ministers presented to him a Buddhist icon as explanation. This story indicates that there must have already been some knowledge of Buddhism at that time, and there are archaeological indications that Buddhism had entered China as early as the Western Han. The carvings of the Leshan cliff tombs in Sichuan and the rock carvings of tombs at Mount Kongwang near Xuzhou in Jiangsu have both been dated to this early period. More controversially, the recently excavated Tianxingggguan Tomb 2, which has been dated to the Warring States period, yielded artifacts which are said to resemble the Buddhist mythical bird called the Kalaviuka (*miaoyin niao*) and artistic forms of the lotus throne, which is frequently found in Buddhist iconography. Although there remains room for debate, it points to the possibility that Buddhism may have entered China at a very early date. Moreover, the development of a religion as it enters a new cultural environment can be very slow and gradual before it emerges as an influential force. Thus the definitive points noted by historians may have been preceded by a lengthy period of gestation in the new environment.

When the Silk Road opened to increased trade with western areas, Buddhism was already flourishing there. But despite official communications such as Zhang Qian's diplomatic missions to the West for Emperor Wu of the Western Han, it seemed this new religion had not yet attracted Chinese notice, since there is no mention of Buddhism in historical records such as Sima Qian's chapter in the *Records of the Grand Historian* on the Central Asian kingdom of Ferghana (*Dayuan zhuan*) or the chapter in the *History of the Former Han* on Serindia (*Xiyu zhuan*). Much less is there any sign of its spread within China. However, at some point Buddhism was brought into China by merchants who traveled along the Silk Road, planting seeds that would germinate and grow in Chinese soil.

Since this was a process that probably took place largely among the common people, the educated elite took little notice of it. Thus even as late as the Eastern Han, there is no mention of Buddhism in the writings of important scholars such as Wang Chong, Wang Fu (ca. 78–163 C.E.), and Zhong Changtong (180–220 C.E.). Nevertheless, by this time there were already individuals such as Yan Fotiao (fl. 181 C.E.), who is traditionally said to have been the first Chinese ordained as a monk. The Eastern Han Prince Ying of Chu and General Ze Rong (d. 195 C.E.) sponsored mass ceremonies whose participants numbered in the tens of thousands, thus demonstrating that Buddhism had firmly taken root in some areas of China by that time.

But if religious developments were of little interest to the intelligentsia, they certainly did not escape notice by the central government. In the late Western Han, the supernatural *chenwei* writings that had been used for political purposes such as protest against government policies or to propagate ideas about a change in the Mandate of Heaven were a reminder of the potential threat of mysticism. Given the concern about potential threats to imperial power from religious movements, the Eastern Han court gave its official approval only to Confucian studies.

At this time, there remained a few groups of Confucian scholars who continued the apocryphal tradition of the *chenwei* and considered the classics in terms of their truth or falsity. The mainstream Confucian study of the classics during this period focused on detailed study of phrases and words in these texts, producing studies that could easily run to many tens of thousands of words. But this consideration of minutiae was not ultimately satisfactory to the scholars' intellectual desires, and from the late Eastern Han through the Wei-Jin period, a school of metaphysical thought referred to as the Dark Learning or Neo-Daoism (*xuanxue*), that is, metaphysics, developed. Investigating areas of study little considered by Confucian studies, this Neo-Daoism considered questions such as epistemology and ontology, the relationship between ability and original nature, and the distinction between being and nothingness.

With the rise of Neo-Daoism, Buddhism in China absorbed some of its teachings. On the one hand, Buddhism was originally concerned with similar issues such as the reality or illusoriness of phenomena, the being or emptiness of basic substance, and fundamental questions about the ultimate concerns of human life. On the other hand, the technical vocabulary developed by Neo-Daoism also proved to be effective for translating Indian Buddhist concepts into equivalent Chinese ones by matching concepts between the two doctrines, referred to as "matching the meaning" (*geyi*). Thus compatible notions are used to render certain Buddhist concepts that are particularly difficult to translate. The earliest known Buddhist text in Chinese, the *Sutra of Forty-Two Chapters* (*Sishier zhang jing*), dating from the early Eastern Han, is far from a cogent explanation of the direction of Buddhism and appears to be the simple notes used by missionaries. With the development of more translations of Buddhist scriptures, it became apparent that the terminology borrowed from Neo-Daoism would be necessary to help the Chinese grasp the deep meanings of this new religion. With the extensive use of the *geyi* translation technique, what had been a foreign religion began to take on a native appearance.

Although there had been religious movements in China before the entry of Buddhism, they had not included a defined set of religious doctrines, nor had they established a clearly organized body of believers. In addition to the earlier offerings to deities and ancestors, there had been the ceremonies of the state religion. In these beliefs, the idea of the Mandate of Heaven and personal morality were closely integrated, and they had developed to the verge of being a transcendental religious faith. The concept of the Mandate of Heaven, however, remained attached to the world of government in the debate over the legitimacy of government authority or policies. The myriad offerings to heaven and earth, to the mountains, rivers, and other deities, had been largely appropriated into a system of official ceremonies. The original transcendental quality of the nature worship had, to various extents, become ancillary to the national government and its bureaucratic administration. The belief in ancestral spirits, which also had very ancient roots, was concerned with issues of life and the afterlife, and the Chinese reverence for ancestors had a distinctly religious feeling. The view that the ancestral spirits would not accept offerings from those outside the family greatly limited the ability of this belief system to expand into a more public and universal religious creed.

Chinese culture did have some traditions that came very close to developing into what might be considered religions. One of the earliest was that of the Warring States thinker Mozi (ca. 470–ca. 391 B.C.E.). The Mohist doctrines have a strong religious sentiment, with ideas of respect for the deities and the High God (Shangdi) and a clear organization of believers under leaders called "strong men" (literally, "sons of steel," *juzi*). As another example, the Western Han doctrines of the reciprocal relation between heaven and man, together with the related *chenwei* movement, elevated Confucius to the level of an "uncrowned king" whose status approached that of the founder of a religion and prophet. This movement was not without a group organization, and the Confucians of that time could also form a semireligious body, one that would have placed itself higher than the power of government. Despite these two opportunities, the early schools of thought in China did not develop into religions, and with the entry of Buddhism from India during the Han dynasty, China developed two organized religions: the foreign belief Buddhism and the native belief Daoism.

The emergence of religious Daoism (*daojiao*) is intimately connected to two popular communal cults of the late Eastern Han, the Way of Great Peace (*Taiping dao*, or Yellow Turbans) and the Way of the Celestial Masters (*Tianshi dao*). At the end of the Eastern Han, the nation was wracked by uprisings of armed groups of peasants, similar to the rebellion led by Chen Sheng and Wu Guang at the end of the Qin or the Red Eyebrows uprising at the end of Wang Mang's Xin dynasty. In these latter two examples, there were no religious beliefs associated with the massive armed uprisings apart from some superstitions used to mislead the people, and their organization was unrelated to any particular creed. In contrast, both the Way of Great Peace and the Way of the Celestial Masters were large-scale communal movements inspired by religious beliefs and headed by masters of those religions. Before these two movements, there had been Daoist religious proselytizing and organized groups, but when these two groups arose, one after the other, their influence shook the entire empire. Although the Way of the Celestial Masters was not as large, it was much better organized as a social body, and, as a result, it was much more able to sustain itself over a long period of time. These massive peasant uprisings at the end of the Eastern Han were stimulated by religious movements, and these movements evolved into China's native religion of Daoism.

When the Way of Great Peace and the Way of the Celestial Masters emerged, the earlier pre-Qin Daoist philosophical thought (*daoxue*) of Laozi and Zhuangzi was not an integral part of their religious doctrines. When the early Daoist religions began, they were instead based on the Chinese traditions of spirit worship, organized into a structure similar to a government bureaucracy and integrated with the tradition of shamanistic mediums to communicate with the deities. In this heavenly bureaucracy there was an Official of Heaven, an Official of Earth, an Official of the Law, a God of Thunder, and a God of Mount Tai; there were gods to represent all the powers of nature, each with his organizational responsibilities carefully established. With this strong organization, religious Daoism was able to draw in other medical or supernatural techniques of the Han. The techniques described in the previous section of searching for earthly *qi* or breathing exercises to support bodily *qi* could be incorporated. In addition, the shamanistic practices of summoning spirits evolved into Daoist incantations, and the practices aimed at longevity or immortality were the foundation for the development of Daoist alchemy.

In the realm of rituals and ceremonies, the early Daoist practice of burning incense gradually extended to the later regulations for Daoist monks, which also borrowed greatly from Buddhism. Other practices of self-cultivation, such as sitting in meditation to reflect on one's errors, as well as a ritual of self-confession with frequent prostrations to indicate complete submission, owe a great deal to practices within both the Buddhist and Confucian traditions. The subsequent development of Daoism is largely based on the foundation laid during its seminal development during the North-South dynasties, since the doctrines and canons had not been codified in the Eastern Han.

As seen in the *Classic of Great Peace* (*Taiping jing*), Daoism at the end of the Han was both a call for great peace and a form of gnosticism with a millennial belief in the coming apocalypse, a concept that had also appeared in the Qin-Han political theory of the cycle of Five Virtues (*wude*), the political expression of the Five Agents. The ideas of cosmic cycles and of predestined fate can be said to have points in common, although the inevitability of an apocalypse is different from the mechanism of cyclic movements. Under the leadership of Zhang Jue (d. 184 C.E.), the Way of the Heavenly Peace considered itself as a harbinger of the apocalypse, with the slogan "The Yellow Heaven is imminent" referring to both their rebellion and the apocalypse—and alluding to the yellow turbans they wore. At the same time, they cast themselves in the role of saviors, and this connection between the concepts of an apocalypse and a world savior is a characteristic of Central Asian apocalyptic religions. In early Indian Buddhism, the Mahayana belief in rebirths through various bodies and various worlds was a transformative process that originally took form in Central Asia. The Way of Heavenly Peace was different from these in that it also planned for the operation of a new order in the human world,

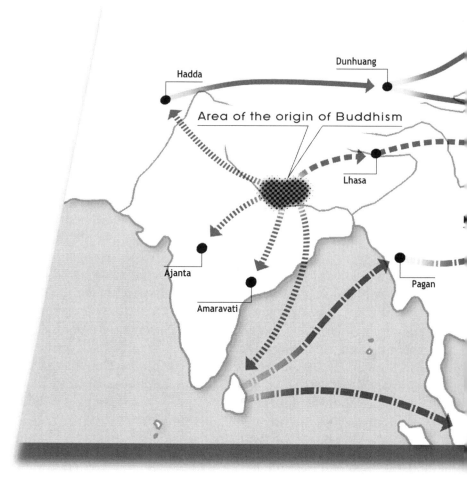

FIGURE 3.6 The Spread of Buddhism Into China

and this new theocracy was intended not to satisfy the social order but ultimately to save its believers from the coming calamity.

The origins and development of Daoism, as described in this section, can be seen as a reflection of the entrance of Buddhism to China. In this sense, as people accepted this foreign religion, some were stimulated by these new religious views to combine and restructure various views that had previously existed in China. The first wave of development for this new religion had been in the traditions of mystic adepts (*fangshi*) and sha-

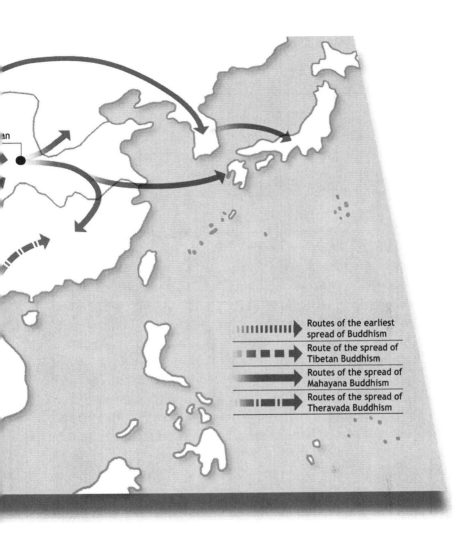

‖‖‖‖‖‖‖▶	**Routes of the earliest spread of Buddhism**
▪ ▪ ▪ ▪ ▶	**Route of the spread of Tibetan Buddhism**
▬▬▬▶	**Routes of the spread of Mahayana Buddhism**
▪▬▪▬▶	**Routes of the spread of Theravada Buddhism**

manistic arts (*wushu*), to which various foreign millennial and redemptive beliefs had been grafted. This belief was set into motion by the strength of mass movements that were searching for a new society and a new world order.

Thus, the importance of the entrance of Buddhism into the Chinese world is hardly less than that of the teachings of Christ in the Mediterranean world. Since not all of China was converted to Buddhism, a religion that combined beliefs native to China could also emerge. From this point onward, Chinese spiritual life was formed by the mutual interaction of the three great traditions of Confucianism, Daoism, and Buddhism.

8. Daily Life During the Qin-Han Period

Although a picture of daily life during the Qin and Han dynasties can be assembled from textual sources, it does not measure up to the details we can find from archaeological materials. These include the carved wall panels from tombs and representative objects that were placed in these tombs as offerings. They are especially valuable, since they show the living conditions of various levels of society. Unlike the predisposition of literary sources to focus more narrowly on the educated elite, archaeological materials cover a much broader spectrum of society, and thus they form the basis of much of this section's discussion on the basic necessities of food, clothing, shelter, and transportation.

Clothing at the beginning of the Qin-Han unification was especially marked by regional differences. The hats worn in Chu were entirely different from those worn in the north. Liu Bang, the founder of the Han, was a native of Chu and preferred the short caps worn there; after the Han was established, this Chu style became common. The male figurines buried in Qin tombs are often consistently dressed in military uniforms, though there is a great deal of differentiation in their hairstyles, reflecting the possibility of individual choice. Although in the Warring States period men generally wore a short skirt similar to a kilt, with the cloth folded over in layers, King Wuling of Zhao (340–295 B.C.E.) was known for wearing the long pants and shirts with narrow sleeves associated with foreigners, since they were more convenient when shooting arrows from horseback. Unfortunately, the lower garments of Qin tomb figurines are not clearly visible, since they were generally draped over, but it is known that as short clothing became more common, trousers were generally worn.

The literature of that time indicates that men during the Han tended to wear broad and ample clothing, and stone engravings on tomb walls show clearly that men wore wide robes with large sleeves, the left lapel folded over the right (as in men's jackets today). Servants wore clothing with narrower sleeves, as it was more convenient for working. To give them more flexibility in their tasks, manual laborers wore even shorter upper and lower garments, as seen on the stone figure of an agricultural worker holding a winnowing fork found at Dujiangyan, near Chengdu. In the stone carvings of northern and southwestern areas, the physical features of ethnic minorities are often seen, together with many varieties of clothing different from that worn by Han people. The scholar Xing Yitian has shown that when the Han artists depicted ethnic minorities, they worked with a preconceived set of images for the way that ethnic minorities should dress, and as a result they sometimes made errors and showed an ethnic minority wearing the wrong costume.

Women's clothing was more varied than men's, with special attention paid to the many styles and ornaments for their hair, a characteristic true across many cultures and times. Generally, women wore their hair high on their head and dressed in long skirts, with slanting lapels folded left over right, as with the men. The sleeves hung down loosely from a high tunic that showed off their figure, unlike the more ample coverings seen in later periods.

Though the stone engravings do little to indicate the types of fabrics from which Han clothing was made, literary materials indicate that the most common were silk, kudzu cloth (something like hemp), and linen. Furthermore, the clothing recovered from Mawangdui Tomb 1 of Lady Dai from the Western Han indicates an extremely high level of skill in weaving patterned fabrics. Furs could be worn in cold weather, though only by the wealthy. There is little information on the types of footwear used, although they would probably have been removed when entering a room, with socks worn indoors.

The diet of Han times is well indicated by both archaeological and textual information. The food offerings from the Mawangdui tomb of Lady Dai show that at least some wealthy people ate a fairly large proportion of wild foods. In contrast, the Eastern Han text *Monthly Instructions for the Four Classes of People (Simin yueling)* indicates that people of the middle classes consumed very little wild food, instead eating a diet composed almost entirely of cultivated plants and livestock. Whether this difference in food is attributable to differences in social class, time period, or region is difficult to distinguish.

The engraved stone tomb panels from the Han frequently show scenes of banqueting as well as food preparation in kitchens, clearly indicating the methods of cooking and serving. In the dining halls, in front of the seating mats are utensils for eating, such as cups, plates, ladles, and spoons, but the large tripod cauldrons used in pre-Qin times are not seen. The stone engravings also show offerings of household goods arranged before the deceased, not the formal and systematic arrangements of ritual vessels seen in pre-Qin tombs. Thus it is clear that by Han times a basic change in the manner of dining had taken place from the earlier use of large common vessels to a style of presenting food in smaller dishes arranged before the seating mats. Of the miniature objects of daily life used as offerings in Han tombs, among the most common are stoves, which are shown in detail, with fire doors and holes on the top for pots, looking as if they were ready to start cooking. Compared to later stoves, there tend to be more holes for pots, and the stovetop is quite large, sometimes with all the necessary cooking utensils, such as knives, forks, spatulas, and ladles carved into the pottery. The most frequent terms for cooking used in the Han are steaming, boiling, roasting, and broiling (*zheng, zhu, kao,* and *zhi*), all long since very common. There is, however, one new character, *chao,* which is similar to the modern character of the same sound that indicates stir frying, and if this connection is correct, it would indicate that as early as the Han all of the most typical means of preparing Chinese food were already in use. The cooking pots of this time were still thick and heavy, although later on they tended to become thinner, perhaps to accommodate the stir-frying method of cooking, which required more rapid heating. This means of preparation, in which the food was cut into small pieces and cooked rapidly, may also have had the advantage of requiring less fuel.

The main staples of the Han diet were still millet, rice, barley, wheat, and beans. Wheat was initially eaten as kernels, although by the Eastern Han milling into flour had become common, which was, as explained above, a development introduced from Serindia. Beans were already a staple in the pre-Qin period; in the Han they were initially eaten boiled in place of rice, and they were later treated as a side dish to accompany other foods. Prepared *doufu* (tofu, or bean curd) was eaten in the Han. Its invention is traditionally ascribed to Liu An (179–122 B.C.E.), a king of Chu and author of the *Huainanzi.* Although there is no proof for this, the legend may indicate a southern origin for this food, which is supported by a rock carving found at Dahuting in Mi County of Henan that is considered to represent the preparation of tofu. The origin of tofu requires further clarification, but the use of beans or wheat prepared with bacteria to make a cultured drink is frequently mentioned in literature.

In terms of drink, alcoholic beverages were a significant part of the diet. As discussed by the Eastern Han annotations by Zheng Xuan (127–

200 C.E.) to the classic text *Rites of Zhou* (*Zhouli*), alcoholic beverages were graded into five levels, not, it seems, by alcohol content but in terms of how thick or watery they were. Alcoholic distillation was not known by the Eastern Han, and the sediment was simply strained out. This type of beverage would not have had a high alcohol content, perhaps in the range between wine and beer. People of Serindia made wine from grapes, but this practice was not adopted in China, even though grapes were cultivated as fruit.

The tea plant itself is native to the southwestern regions of China, and the use of tea as a beverage had become popular by the North-South dynasties. A book on the popular culture of this period, *The Slave's Contract* (*Tongyue*) by Wang Bao (fl. 85 B.C.E.), mentions that tea leaves from Wuyang in Sichuan were a commercial item, and it is likely that tea drinking had become common by the Han.

To understand Han living quarters, there is a vast amount of information provided by the offering models found in Han tombs. The literary sources describe dwellings of the wealthy, with high halls and broad rooms, pavilions and towers. Representations in material objects show some platforms with two stories, which have rooms on both floors and which may be connected by internal stairs. The farm compounds frequently depicted in the offering models show watchtowers that clearly are multistory structures. For timber joinery, the traditional *dougong* system of brackets to join columns and beams had become generally used for both multistory dwellings and platforms.

According to the imperial memorial submitted by Zhao Cuo (ca. 200–154 B.C.E.) during the Western Han, the typical arrangement of houses in areas for immigrants in rural prefectures is one central room flanked by two smaller ones, one on each side. This is confirmed by the offering models of houses, which indicate a size that would include one central room and two flanking rooms, and so it appears that this arrangement was standard during the Han. The models of farmhouse compounds generally have a latrine and a pigsty, sometimes with a sow and her piglets, indicating that human waste was probably used as feed for the pigs. There are also some models of tilled fields and ponds with water chestnuts, fish, and turtles. These arrangements reflect the multiple use of natural resources to increase agricultural output.

The scenes of eating and drinking at banquets in the large halls within homes of wealthy people always show guests seated on floor mats. Cups and bowls are arranged before the guest of honor, who is seated in the center, with singing and dancing girls to one side. Some of the depictions of these halls show them surrounded by balustrades and with short flights of stairs down to the ground, but the relationship between the large halls and smaller private rooms is not clear. The stone panels also sometimes show a courtyard with a hall inside it, clearly composed of a central room and two flanking rooms. The watchtowers mentioned above were used as defensive fortifications, and the figure of a soldier is sometimes included in the depictions. But the relationship between the watchtowers and the main halls is difficult to reconstruct from the depictions.

Beyond the standard arrangement of dwelling, a great variety of other building types are shown in Han tomb art. Some panels depict city streets, probably showing an intersection with market shop fronts on the four corners, indicating that the arrangement of marketplaces was quite different from that of dwellings. Some tombs of prefecture heads in distant areas have panels showing domed structures like yurts. Bronze artifacts from the ancient Dian kingdom in modern Yunnan include models of oval houses, which probably indicate the type of buildings used by non-Han peoples.

In terms of conveyances, the stone panels also show a great variety of horse-drawn vehicles, and the tombs also contain models of them. The carriages of important officials, either two- or four-wheeled, would have a single shaft connected to the carriage and would be drawn by horses. Carts for carrying heavy loads would be drawn by oxen, harnessed between two shafts. The various means of drawing vehicles by horses or oxen is discussed in detail by texts of the Qin-Han period. After the North-South dynasties, the single-shaft type of vehicle was no longer used for either horse-drawn or ox-drawn carts, and wheeled vehicles all have two shafts.

There are a few models and depictions of boats from the Han, for example in depictions of land and water battles, and most of the boats are relatively small. The ponds included in tomb offerings will sometimes model a small boat on the water, perhaps used for gathering fish or plants from the pond. Literary descriptions of boats in the south tell of banks of rowers and, like a racing boat, flags and a coxswain to direct the rowers. This type of boat could also be used for naval battles, and the Han military expedition to the south included what were referred to as "spear boats" (*gechuan*). These were probably small craft, but the Han military also had large warships, as indicated by the term "admiral of storied ship" (*louchuanjiangjun*), which appears in historical sources, although no models or representations have been found. The meaning of this term is not clear, and it could mean a large ship with several decks, or it could simply be the ship used by a commander, not one that was especially large or fast for use in battle.

These engraved stone slabs show a great variety of scenes from daily life, such as the tilling of fields, hunting, and salt collection, providing a vivid portrait of the life of the common people. There are also descriptions of everyday life in literary sources, such as the *Monthly Instructions for the Four Classes of People*, mentioned above, which describes life throughout one year on the large estate of an official during the Eastern Han. This book gives detailed information on the daily work and leisure of masters, the young and the old, servants and other workers. These activities include tilling the fields, seeding, weeding, irrigation, harvesting, growing fruit, the offering rituals of the master, large family gatherings, the purchase and sale of goods, education, and the children's leisure time. It is a complete picture of life in the family and of the four traditional classes of people: scholars, farmers, workers, and merchants (*shi, nong, gong, shang*). Similarly, Wang Bao's *The Slave's Contract*, although it is an entertainment piece, describes agricultural and market businesses, providing a lively account of the adult male work force. It tells of the childbearing and year-long work without respite of agricultural laborers, raising animals, carrying water, gathering firewood, and going to market to buy and sell. When the literary sources are considered in the light of objects from material culture, many misinterpretations of the texts can be avoided and correct interpretations confirmed, since the way tools are used can be seen clearly from the illustrations. For example, the distinction between the animal-drawn seeder and the traditional plow can only be clarified by reference to the images.

The life of the Han people was better and their standard of living in daily activities much higher than that of people in other parts of the world at that time. Moreover, the diverse activities of daily life in Han China formed the basic model that was to be developed over the next two thousand years.

9. The Han Empire and Imperial Rome

Over the two centuries before and two centuries after the beginning of the Common Era, the Han and Roman empires stood like great peaks at the eastern and western ends of the known world. They were both more

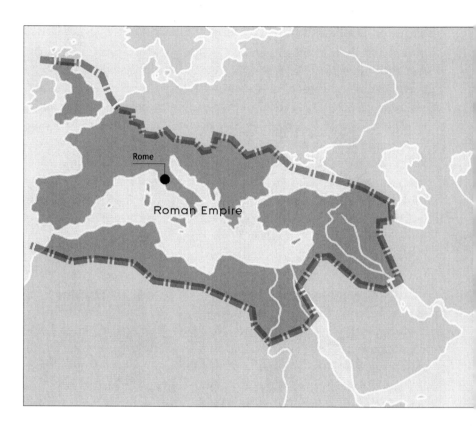

FIGURE 3.7 Map of the Extent of the Western Han and the Roman Empire

extensive than any empire the world had known before, and although there was little direct communication between them, they each were aware that over extreme distances lay another mighty nation with a thriving population and vibrant culture. The respect in which the Chinese held Rome can be seen in their term for that land, *Da Qin*, or Great Qin, indicating that it was of the same rank as the Qin empire itself. The ultimate end of the Silk Road was Rome in the West and Chang-an in the East, and thus these two empires were linked through innumerable points of stopping and transfer along the way. To the south, the other great civilization of India was developing on the subcontinent, although it cannot be compared with those to the west and east in terms of global influence. The historical processes of the rise and fall of these two great empires have some important differences that can help to develop a deeper understanding of China itself.

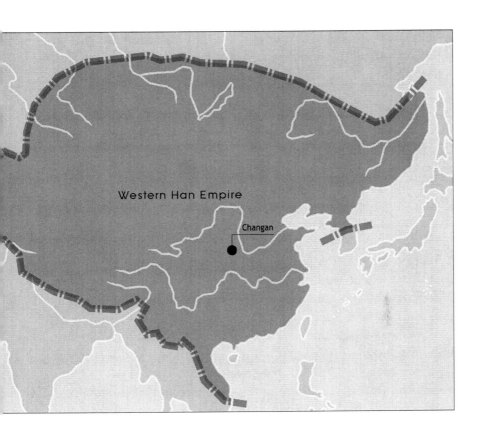

Western Han Empire

Changan

During the Warring States period prior to the Qin-Han unification, China had already been moving toward unification for several centuries. As noted in section 3, in reply to King Hui of Liang, who had asked, "how can this world be stabilized?" Mencius's answer was that "it must be stabilized into a single entity." The Qin conquest of the other six major states was little more than a marker in a historical process, and the rise of the Han dynasty was likewise another point in that process, not simply a separate entity. The Roman unification of the Mediterranean world was similarly an extension of the unification of Hellenistic culture that had begun to tie together this region, and Rome was doing little more than taking up the reins of a historical process already in motion. Cultural unification in both cases preceded political unification as the basis for the rise of a great empire. The mighty undertakings of assembling both the eastern and western empire involved powers at both center and periphery, relying on superior arms and military strategy for the success of the conquests. These were aspects in common between the two empires.

However, the processes of conquest differed in each case. When the Qin conquered each of the six states, there was a great slaughter of that state's soldiers, making it unnecessary to leave divisions of troops there to guard the conquered territories. Qin administrators were used to govern, of course. For example, the well-known Shuihudi Tomb 11 in Yunmeng County of Hubei belonged to a man who had been an official for the Qin, sent to Chu as an official and not as a member of a military guard force. As Qin fell, the various military uprisings that put an end to this empire then moved south, without placing guards on the original Qin territory. With Liu Bang's victory in the ensuing struggle for supremacy with Xiang Yu (232–202 B.C.E.) and the rise of the Han empire, most of the early prefecture governors were appointed based on their former military service. By the time of Emperor Wu, a hundred years later, this system was much less significant, and favoritism and nepotism often gave members of the social elite more convenient entry to government positions or faster advancement in that system. Sometimes, even important local administrators were no longer selected from a group of meritorious officials. Yet there is no record of guard troops being needed to maintain control over internal territories. In later history, it is only in campaigns against outside ethnic groups that military force was needed to control territory within China, though there were mobilizations of troops to put down peasant uprisings in the provinces.

In contrast to the situation in China, the Roman legions were formed mainly of men from farming families in the Roman homeland on the Italian peninsula. The Roman military expeditions were led by important generals, and the legionnaires generally followed their officer's orders to remain in the conquered areas to guard them. As a result, group after group of young Roman men left the Italian peninsula only to settle in the new territories as the governing elite. The population of able-bodied men on the Italian peninsula thus dropped, which required that large numbers of slaves be imported to perform the agricultural work. Accordingly, there were significant changes in the population of the original Roman territory, accompanied by occasional increases in the status of slaves and their being granted Roman citizenship. This problematic situation is largely attributable to the continued insistence of the Roman Empire on maintaining its military strength and control of conquered territories.

Another main difference between the situations of Rome and China was that even before political unification, China had developed a consistent system of territorial government composed of prefectures and counties. As early as the Spring and Autumn period, when the great states of Qin, Chu, and Jin expanded and absorbed new territory, they dispatched officials to govern it rather than using a system of hereditary feudal grants. Before unification under the Qing, all seven of the states had individually adopted a two-level system of prefectures and counties to administer their territories. The commanders of these territories were generally not native to the regions they were governing, although their staffs were generally composed of the more talented local individuals. The central government also dispatched prefectural governors to oversee the administration. This system had its origins much earlier and had developed over an extended period of time, so communications worked quite effectively. Once this mechanism for control was in place, the states of China relied much less on long-term deployment of military troops and so were able to administer larger areas and greater populations.

The Roman situation was quite different. The Mediterranean coastal regions were generally dominated by the Hellenistic cultural world, which included the original territory of Rome. The peripheral regions, including what is now the Middle East and northern Europe, were inhabited by peoples of entirely different backgrounds, and so the local governments tended to be based on much different structural models. The empire of Alexander the Great (356–323 B.C.E., r. 336–323) had risen and then fallen to pieces immediately upon his death before any substantial cultural unification. Because of this, the territories seized by Roman legions, including the fragments of Alexander's empire, each had distinct and different characteristics. It was impossible for Rome to unify its territory as China had done, through a consistent structure of prefectures and counties, and it had to employ different means of governance in different areas, using the preexisting local administrations as best it could to maintain cooperation. Rome ruled over a patched-together system of subject states, relying on its military force to control its colonies. It had conquered the world on horseback, and it proceeded to rule it in the same way. This method was naturally highly unstable, and with time the Roman forces stationed to guard the territories used their responsibility as a means toward their own profit, as their loyalty to their mother country was no longer undivided. Strong colonies would have the troops return to Rome, or the guard troops closer to Rome would turn to control the government; the problem of military forces vying for control of the government became a chronic problem in the late Roman Empire.

Looking at the Chinese situation according to the development of schools of thought, we can see that Confucianism was undoubtedly the mainstream of the Hundred Schools during the Warring States period. Then during the Qin empire, Legalism formed the intellectual foundation for governing the empire, though Legalism also contained strong Confucian influences. After the rise of the Han dynasty, Daoism became dominant for a time, although in the end a combination of a strong Confucian exterior with Legalist concepts at the core was adopted. Confucian scholars continued to rely on their superior position in government and society to propagate Confucian teachings, so that eventually these Confucian views displaced Legalism as the core school of thought, and the culture of the common people also became suffused with Confucian values. In the outlying areas, through the dedicated influence of local officials, Confucianism eventually gained a great ability to assimilate native cultures. In addition to this, the graphic as opposed to phonetic nature of the Chinese writing system helped to overcome the separation caused by differences between local dialects and the national language. Hence, although it had a teeming population spread over a large area with many local differences, China could preserve a fairly high degree of consistency in its shared culture. Dynasties would rise and fall, but the common cultural identity would have the strength to hold together this body of peoples.

Roman culture was largely a further development of Hellenistic culture, and the mainstream thought of upper-class Roman citizens before the arrival of Christianity was Stoicism, which is in many ways similar to Confucianism. Today, when we read the discourses on virtue of Cicero (106–43 B.C.E.), one of the great thinkers of early Rome, we still have a sense of their validity. Rome chose to maintain its vast empire through armed force, not to cherish its earlier intentions and establish a strong intellectual tradition. As a result, the native cultures of the conquered regions and the native intellectuals continued to go their own ways. For example, in Judea the rabbis maintained the strength of Judaic religion and culture by depending on the power of their Roman rulers, and thus, for example, the rabbis were able to order the death of Jesus with the complicity of the Roman prefect. The Latin language and its phonetic script was, along with Greek, the language of the upper classes throughout the Roman Empire. Because the semiliterate masses of common people held on to their native tongues, however, Latin did little as a tool for cultural unification.

After the reign of Constantine the Great (306–337 C.E.), Christianity gradually gained strength throughout the Roman Empire, and based on its persuasiveness as a universal religion, it infused the late Roman Empire with its great cultural conviction. This was sufficient to pull together the formerly disparate parts of the Roman world so they could finally coalesce into a consistent cultural body. But that lasted only a brief time, and the eastern empire soon diverged under the Eastern Orthodox church, and the Middle Eastern and North African territories were conquered by Islam, creating new cultural entities. When the so-called barbarians invaded from the northeast, these foreign ethnic groups were converted to the Christian culture, and thus after a period of several centuries a complex cultural revival sprang up. This broke apart the cultural body that remained from imperial Rome and altered the common culture of Christianity, so that Europe could become a multicultural region with numerous ethnic groups in their own nation-states. Seen from the perspective of China, the problem of Rome lay not with the fall of a dynasty but with its fundamental cultural transformations.

By the time all Europe had become Christianized, despite the more structured aspect of the Catholic Church and the universal direction of its doctrines, there were still strong movements either to retain native beliefs or to reject certain Church dogmas. The Church was ruthless in its opposition to these divergent beliefs and entrenched itself firmly throughout Europe. Although there were deep divisions and struggles for power between the secular government and the Church, the alliance of feudal lords, knights, and clergy formed a tripartite bloc that controlled all levels of society. The Christian saints had displaced or absorbed the earlier deities, and the rites and holy days of the Church replaced those native to various areas. For many centuries, the intellectual and spiritual life of Europe could accept few ideas that differed from its own. As the power of the Vatican and the bishops increased, the clerics and monastic orders became like a giant bureaucratic civil service, though with a less professional and more multicentric structure.

In comparison, China had existed as a Confucian world since the Han, and because Confucianism was a philosophy of the human world, the metaphysical and religious dimensions in which it was weaker were supplied by Daoist philosophy and religion, together with the imported religion of Buddhism. Confucianism is a much less exclusivist way of thought, and it coexisted and complemented these two religions, making a space in Chinese culture for different centers of gravity or vertices of activity. The Confucian scholar-officials had a relationship with the court that was both cooperative and in opposition: on the one hand, there was a strong strain of professionalism that inspired those working in the official bureaucracy, but Confucianism also discussed the proper limits of the monarch. The ideal Confucian world was to be found not in heaven but in the human world. After Confucian scholar-officials had served in the court, they could retire to the provinces to continue their studies as gentleman scholars. By maintaining this order, they exerted at least as much influence as the clergy in Europe. As a result, over the course of the past two thousand years, the common people of China may have enjoyed a greater degree of material and spiritual ease than those of Rome or Europe.

In its economic activities, the Roman Empire, like Qin-Han China, combined a vast network of local economies into an enormous economic system. Under the Pax Romana, vessels plied from the Danube to the Straits of Gibraltar, while overland transport reached westward throughout Europe and eastward to Asia. There was no place so remote that it did not share, at least to some extent, in this great network of exchange. The Mediterranean was the high road of the Roman Empire, and the lands surrounding it were its core territory. Despite the existence of this long-range commerce, the trading of almost all goods, whether in large quantities, such as olive oil, wine, hides, or salt, or in small quantities, such as household articles, tended to be handled within the local regional markets.

The economic network of Han China has been described in a previous section. In contrast to the Roman Empire's maritime traffic, its goods moved along a network of main roads and branches and rivers and canals that handled the collection and distribution of agricultural and other products between the countryside and urban centers. These well-established lines of communication formed a network that led the regions of central China to become highly interdependent and develop into a collective body. In contrast, the old saying that "All roads lead to Rome" applied only to the main east-west roads in the northern half of the Italian peninsula. Although the Mediterranean shipping routes led smoothly from port to port, they were by nature much less effective in establishing a fixed network of land transportation than a permanent cross-country highway system maintained and controlled for ready communication. By comparison, at a very early period China had woven together the form of a communications network that could expand gradually and organically—and that was not easy to disrupt. If, as happened from time to time, it split into regionally focused networks, they could be reunited easily. Thus, at the points in its history when China was divided, economic reunification was accomplished through political unification.

Viewed from the standpoints of government, culture, and economy, although the empires of ancient Rome and Qin-Han China have their points in common, when considered more closely, the differences are even more fundamental. As discussed in this chapter, the political empire, cultural sphere, and economic network of China were closely intertwined and worked mutually to support one another, leading to a more stable and coherent whole. The order of the Roman Empire was less stable and its cohesion not as long lasting, so that when its political order disintegrated, the regions it had governed—Europe, the Middle East, North Africa— each developed in very different cultural directions, fostering a system of ethnically distinct nation-states.

Suggestions for Further Reading

Bielenstein, Hans. *The Bureaucracy of Han Times*. Cambridge: Cambridge University Press, 1980.

Ching, Julia. *Chinese Religions*. New York: Orbis, 1993.

Csikszentmihalyi, Mark. *Readings in Han Chinese Thought*. Indianapolis, Ind.: Hackett, 2006.

Di Cosmo, Nicola. *Ancient China and Its Enemies: The Rise of Nomadic Power in East Asian History*. Cambridge: Cambridge University Press, 2004.

Hardy, Grant. *The Establishment of the Han Empire and Imperial China*. Westport, Conn.: Greenwood Press, 2005.

Hinsch, Bret. *Women in Early Imperial China*. Totowa, N.J.: Rowan and Littlefield, 2002.

Hsu, Cho-yun. *Han Agriculture*. Seattle: University of Washington Press, 1980.

Kieshnick, John. *The Impact of Buddhism on Chinese Culture*. Princeton, N.J.: Princeton University Press, 2003.

Kim, Hyn Jin. *Ethnicity and Foreigners in Ancient Greece and China*. London: Duckworth, 2010.

Lewis, Mark Edward. *The Early Chinese Empires: Qin and Han*. Cambridge, Mass.: Belknap Press, 2007.

Lloyd, G. E. R., and Nathan Sivin. *The Way and the Word: Science and Medicine in Early China and Greece*. New Haven, Conn.: Yale University Press, 2002.

Loewe, Michael. *Chinese Ideas of Life and Death: Faith, Myth, and Reason in the Han Period*. London: George Allen and Unwin, 1982.

———. *Divination, Mythology, and Monarchy in Han China*. Cambridge: Cambridge University Press, 1994.

Owen, Stephen. *The Making of Early Chinese Classical Poetry*. Cambridge, Mass.: Harvard University Asia Center, 2006.

Queen, Sarah. *From Chronicle to Canon: The Hermeneutics of the Spring and Autumn, According to Tung Chung-shu*. Cambridge: Cambridge University Press, 1996.

Raphals, Lisa Ann. *Sharing the Light: Representations of Women and Virtue in Early China*. Albany: State University of New York Press, 1998.

Wang, Aihe. *Cosmology and the Transformation of Political Culture in Early China*. Cambridge: Cambridge University Press, 2006.

Yu, Ying-shih. *Trade and Expansion in Han China: A Study in the Structure of Sinitic-Barbarian Economic Relations*. Berkeley: University of California Press, 1967.

[4]

China in East Asia

THE SECOND TO TENTH CENTURIES C.E.

The rivers roll on without cease as the China of the North China Plain strides forward to become East Asian China. During the period covered in this chapter, the immigration and internal migration of neighboring peoples transformed the face of ancient China while greatly enriching its ancient culture. At the same time, this long series of changes brought about a renewal in Chinese styles of eating, dressing, dwelling, and traveling, laying a firm foundation for the Chinese style of living of later generations.

1. The Collapse of the Qin-Han Empire

The destruction of the Qin-Han imperial system, which had lasted from 221 B.C.E. to 220 C.E., was not merely the breaking apart of a great political system; it was also the end of the ancient Chinese social order. During the Qin-Han era, the Chinese cultural sphere expanded into the most important areas of what would later be known as China proper; its boundaries were basically set, and the principal elements of the Chinese people were established. For a time, they were known as "the people of Qin" (*Qinren*) and, afterward, as "the people of Han" (*Hanren*).

After half a century of turmoil, the Eastern Han (25–220 C.E.) split into the three kingdoms of Wei, Shu, and Wu. During this period, also given the intrusion of non-Chinese peoples from the north, the north and south were ruled separately for over two centuries, during the era of the North-South dynasties (317–589). It was only at the end of this long period that the Sui (581–618) and Tang (618–907) dynasties established a new social order. During this era of division, Chinese culture was torn apart, and then its political, cultural, economic, and other aspects of life were re-organized—all of which led to an expansion of its area of inclusion and the creation of a Chinese cultural sphere within which nearly all of the various ethnic groups of East Asia participated.

In terms of world history, this process of development is similar in many ways to the great transformation attendant on the fall of the ancient Roman Empire. As that empire's social and political order came to an end, the cultural sphere of Christianity took its place, and its area of inclusion extended beyond the Mediterranean. The renowned historian Edward Gibbon (1737–1794) studied the collapse of the Roman Empire and detailed its causes in his celebrated *Decline and Fall of the Roman Empire* (1776–1778). In this section, I want to adapt Gibbon's method of analysis to discuss the general similarities between the decline of the Roman Empire and that of the Qin-Han imperial system.

I'll begin with a consideration of Qin-Han localism. Ever since the Qin dynasty thoroughly implemented the system of administrative commanderies and counties, the various administrative districts of China had very little political independence as compared to the same sorts of districts under Roman rule. The Qin dynasty perished, and the remaining six states were unable to create a united empire. When the Han dynasty was established, the ruling house of Liu eliminated all the kings or marquises (*wang* or *hou*) with surnames different from theirs. After the rebellion of the seven *fengjian* lords (called the seven feudatories in earlier scholarship) was put down in 154 B.C.E., the various Liu kings (sometimes called princes) never again had any substantial power. During the Wang Mang era of the Xin, or New, dynasty (9–23 C.E.), the central power lost control of the provinces, but the entire country did not come apart, and, later on, when many local strongmen took up arms to contend for power, they had no intention of partitioning the country. In all this, the Chinese situation was quite different from the Roman case, in which the "barbarians" brought great disorder to the ancient empire and divided it up into separate political entities.

In the Qin and Han commandery and county system, each commandery had a small population and limited territory, and none of them was able to become a great power in its own right. The provincial regions (*zhou*) of the Later or Eastern Han (25–220 C.E.) evolved from their early watchdog role into geopolitical units with substantial and relatively great administrative power. The chief magistrates of these provincial regions were, nevertheless, still members of the regular bureaucracy and appointed by the central government; furthermore, the Eastern Han practiced a rather strict system of avoidance, whereby local men were not permitted to occupy the position of chief magistrate in their home area. For these reasons, although each provincial region had sufficient resources to be independent, their chief officials could not arbitrarily appropriate the territory under their control.

Local power increased greatly during the Han, primarily because the strength of the local great families steadily increased. In pre-Han Confucian thought, the virtues of humanity and rightness (or justice, *ren* and *yi*) were uppermost, but during the Han the value of filial piety (*xiao*) was rapidly elevated to the supreme position. This change was intimately connected with the development of patriarchal clan organizations. Han clan organization was quite different from the clan groupings that existed under the Qin *fengjian* system (*fengjian* is sometimes referred to as "feudal," but most recent scholarship simply uses *fengjian*); it was mutually reinforced by geographical affinities with village or neighborhood units. Powerful clans in the same district also used the concept of filial piety to maintain their internal cohesion while at the same time contracting marriages and friendships that created social power alliances. These local great families became the only social powers that could restrain the power of the imperial rulers.

In the Han dynasty's system of political power, the civil bureaucracy and the imperial power were originally two complementary forces. The civil officials of the Han were, however, also members of various Confucian groupings, and their Confucian beliefs contained some idealistic principles that did not predispose them to unconditionally serve the interests of the emperor. Thus, the civil bureaucracy with its Confucian concepts was sometimes able to serve as a balance to the power of the emperor.

In the Han local government, the chief magistrates came from outside the areas they oversaw, but their subordinate officials and clerks came from "worthy and able" (*xianliang*) local people. They had to have the support of the powerful great families for their appointment and to execute their administrative duties, and this made for a balance at the local level between governmental political power and the forces of society. Eastern Han provincial regions and commanderies were the administrative units that had actual control over resources, and thus the alliances of great families made it possible for them to gain real power over large areas of regions and commanderies through their patronage appointments of local officials.

At the beginning of the Han, groups of meritorious officials (*gongchen*) monopolized both the central government chancellorships and the highest local government positions (magistrates receiving two thousand or more measures of grain), but their power gradually declined from the time of Han Wudi (the Martial Emperor, r. 141–87 B.C.E.). Wudi's economic policy was to curtail the development of the rich and powerful merchants, and thus, early in the Han, the policy of varied levels of appointment and frequent forced transfers almost completely eliminated the local rich families and others who had the power to influence society. With these changes, the great families of ranking scholar-officials (the *shidafu*, also known as the gentry or literati) constituted the only force that could contend with imperial power. After Wudi, the selection of able and worthy men for office was gradually institutionalized, and the emerging recruitment system provided the bureaucracy with a mechanism for self-selection and proliferation through patronage. The relationship between officials and their dependents was very close, creating a mutually supportive patronage network. Although one's selection and rise to office was in the hands of the higher central government officials, it was not uncommon for one to gradually rise by means of a minor provincial appointment.

Thus, the great scholar-official families of the Eastern Han had rather strong local characteristics. Local consciousness gradually arose in the second half of the Eastern Han as many areas developed their own local "public opinion" (*yulun*)—the convention of the "village criticism and hamlet election" (*xiangping lixuan*). Local consciousness was also seen in these provincial districts' self-praise and their satirical comments on other districts. Most of this type of writing has been lost, with only titles or short excerpts being preserved—for example, *The Records of Jizhou* (*Jizhou ji*) and *The Elders of Xiangyang* (*Xiangyang qijiu zhuan*).

The emergence of administrative power and local consciousness in all of these provincial areas was a gradually unfolding process; no particular historical event marked a definite turning point. Nevertheless, this tendency was quite obvious—so much so that, in the last stage of the Eastern Han, the central government tried to prevent local powers from evolving into legally legitimate administrative units. Thus, the central government rigorously enforced the avoidance policy, whereby neither a local person nor even a relative was allowed to hold the position of district chief magistrate. The general trend was, however, already established that local great families were closely combined to control local resources.

The Yellow Turban (Way of Great Peace) uprising of 184–185 gave these great families a further excuse to organize their own military forces. Dong Zhuo entered Luoyang in 189 with the emperor in tow, the central government collapsed, local great families hurriedly roused their troops, and thus began a civil war for possession of former Han lands. The empire was divided into the three kingdoms of Wei, Shu, and Wu, with their foundations being precisely the strength of powerful local strongmen such as Yuan Shao, Cao Cao, Sun Ce, and Liu Biao.

This situation was unique to the end of the Han. When the Roman Empire collapsed, there were no powerful clans with local consciousness who were also embedded in the civil bureaucracy and its recommendation system. There, autocratic military rulers appeared, but China did not have such a problem. Eunuch control of the imperial guards and thus of the government was actually a product of a malformation of imperial rule, and it paralyzed the central government, but it was not necessarily enough to destroy the entire Qin-Han imperial order. Dong Zhuo leading the Jingzhou army into the capital, dominating the court for several years, and sacking Luoyang in 190 was certainly a case of military interference in government, but there is no record of late Han generals acting this way before Dong Zhuo and Cao Cao. The Eastern Han never experienced the Roman situation, where military dictators gave rise to a new emperor every three days. In Chinese history, it was rather the regional military governors (*jiedushi*) of the late Tang and Five Dynasties who proclaimed themselves emperor and usurped the throne of the Son of Heaven in a manner similar to generals usurping the throne at the fall of the Roman Empire.

Gibbon particularly emphasized the rise of Christianity during the decline of the Roman Empire. Buddhism entered China during the Eastern Han, and after several hundred years of development became one of China's most important belief systems; it also stimulated China's native religious Daoism (*daojiao*, as opposed to *daoxue* or philosophic Daoism) and challenged Confucianism's (*rujia*) primacy as the cultural mainstream. In terms of a particular religion carrying a great deal of weight and having a great influence on the culture of a society, the rise of Buddhism in China and of Christianity in Rome can certainly be considered together, but in China, Confucianism did not in any sense come to an end because of the rise of Buddhism. Meanwhile, China also saw the rise of the autochthonous religion of Daoism, and the pluralist nature of this religion is strikingly different from the Roman world's movement toward the monotheism of Christianity.

As Rome declined, many border peoples invaded in a manner similar to the invasion and occupation of North China by five northern steppe peoples (the five Hu or non-Chinese northern "barbarians") during the fourth to sixth centuries. The Eastern Han had expended a great deal of energy controlling the Xiongnu peoples to their north and the Qiang (proto-Tibetan) peoples in the west. In the earlier Western Han, under Emperor Wudi, China mobilized vast resources and crushed the Xiongnu's great nomadic steppe empire (in 127 and 119 B.C.E.). Thus, by the end of the Eastern Han the Xiongnu no longer posed a serious threat. The Qiang population was small, and their strength was not very great. They did cause considerable trouble for the Eastern Han, going into rebellion several times, but the resources needed for China to deal with them was nowhere near what the two Han dynasties had to expend to repel the Xiongnu. The Qiang settled in several areas of China proper, for the most part in present-day Sichuan and Gansu in the west as well as parts of Shaanxi and Shanxi provinces. The incursions of other northern peoples into China, the "five Hu ravage China" (*wuhu luanhua*), took place after the collapse of the Qin-Han imperial order and as a result rather than as a cause of it.

From the pre-Qin era to the beginning of the Han, China had a relatively well-developed urban economy. Beginning in the reign of Han Wudi, however, the structure of China's economic system gradually began to rely on small peasant production, handicraft industry, and market forces. With the further integration of a nationwide network of roads, all the areas of the country became mutually dependent to a high degree, and this economic pattern continued to exist throughout China. Integration of the economic system further stimulated the unification of China's cultural order.

In marked contrast to China, the economic hubs of Rome's Mediterranean world were its great cities situated along a vast system of roads that provided for the urban circulation of large amounts of goods arriving from the far-flung empire. The economy of the Roman Empire was certainly not founded on peasant villages. The economies of the Near East could also be divided into those of Central Asia, South Asia, and North Africa. They were not necessarily integrated with the Mediterranean area into a single economic bloc. Thus there were both economic and cultural reasons why the Eastern Roman Empire broke away from Rome. If we compare the two imperial orders of China and Rome, China's was the more stable, because of its internal economic integration.

The Chinese cultural order that took shape in the Qin-Han era did not really undergo any fundamental changes because of the collapse of the Eastern Han empire. In striking contrast, the changes in Europe after the fall of the Roman Empire were extremely violent and far reaching. China experienced three hundred years of gradual change after the fall of the Han and was then reintegrated into the Sui-Tang cultural order. In this regard, the historian Arnold J. Toynbee (1889–1975) called the Sui-Tang era "China's Second Kingdom." This new order, just like that of the Qin and Han, was a universal order of a universal empire. In contrast, the universal order of the Roman Mediterranean was transformed into the Christian world order and a multistate system. Christendom retained its universal or at least ecumenical character, but under a system of multiple states; the contemporary national state gradually emerged but forever lost the characteristics of a universal empire.

The cultural order of China established during the Qin and Han did not disappear with the fall of the Eastern Han. The three-hundred-year era of the Three Kingdoms, the Wei, Jin, and North-South dynasties, witnessed the reconfiguration of this universal order. The order established in the Sui and Tang was a continuation and a broadening of that of the Qin and Han, during which many elements of the Qin-Han synthesis were transformed and readjusted but not eliminated.

2. China's Relations with Surrounding Peoples

The collapse of the Qin-Han imperial order initiated great changes in the distribution of the various East Asian ethnic groups. Our discussion of these momentous events will focus separately on the north and the south, beginning with the north.

Clashes of arms took place between the Qin and Han empires and the nomadic steppe empire of the Xiongnu for over a century. During the Eastern Han, the Xiongnu separated into northern and southern factions. The Northern Xiongnu soon dispersed, a part of them drifting far away, to emerge in the history of Europe a few centuries later when Attila the Hun's (406–453) armies brought terror to the hearts of the people of Rome. This long journey across Central Asia and the disturbances it caused initiated a reorganization of many Central Asian ethnic groups. In the process of separation and regrouping, the Xiongnu continuously incorporated elements of the local peoples they passed through, so much so that by the time they reached southcentral Europe their ethnic composition was no longer the same as it was when they had left the North China steppes.

The Southern Xiongnu gradually moved into China's border regions and became Sinicized (*Hanhua*; the neologism "Hanicized" is sometimes used now). During this period of incursion by non-Chinese ethnic groups, the Jie people were also subordinate to the Xiongnu; they established the Later Zhao, the earliest of the five non-Chinese conquest regimes to occupy part of North China, which lasted from 319 to 351.

As the power of the Xiongnu diminished, other non-Chinese ethnic groups began moving eastward into North China. Among them were the Qiang and the Di. These two peoples, situated beside the Silk Road, took advantage of the decline in the Han Chinese population to enter gradually the Eastern Han border commanderies. At first, they served as tenant farmers for the Han Chinese, but, as their numbers increased, they developed into self-sufficient tribes. The route of Qiang immigration followed the Wei River valley out of Shaanxi into the high plateau of Shanxi and all the way to present-day Hebei. The Di and the Qiang also established powerful conquest regimes, among which the Early Qin kingdom (351–394) of the Di peoples nearly united all of North China.

In China's northeast, the Xianbei (Särbi) took advantage of a power vacuum in the southern Gobi Desert and moved in several waves through the Liao River basin and the Greater Khingan Mountains into the areas formerly occupied by the Xiongnu as well as China's You, Ji, and other commanderies in the Hebei region. One Särbi group cut across the southern Gobi, turned south, and reached the Ordos area (the southern bend of the Yellow River)—an astonishing distance. The Särbi people, including the Tuoba (Tabgatch), eventually became the most powerful of the five non-Chinese ethnic groups, founding the Northern Wei dynasty (386–534). Then the dynasties of the Northern Zhou (556–581) and the Northern Qi (550–557) split off from the Northern Wei, the three collectively termed the Northern dynasties. Together these three dynasties transformed the divisive situation of the Sixteen Kingdoms of the North into three unified conquest dynasties. The Sui and Tang empires were the continuation of these three states.

During this period, North China absorbed many non-Chinese ethnic groups, or Hu peoples. In the last stages of the Eastern Han, because of many natural and manmade disasters as well as frequent epidemics, the Han Chinese people of the north either moved away or died, and the population decreased greatly. It is impossible to give definite figures on this decline given a paucity of historical records, but estimating from those records that we do have, the Han Chinese populations of the regions of You, Ji, Qing, Bing, and Si may have declined by a third to even a half! Even greater numbers of Hu people moved in to populate the areas where the Han Chinese population was decreasing, and, for that reason, ever more Han Chinese people fled into exile in the south. The vast migration and resettlement of people that occurred during these two centuries represents the greatest population movement in Chinese history.

The northern Hu and Han Chinese ethnic groups gradually intermingled in a process of hybridization that differed according to time and place. At first, during the era of the Sixteen Kingdoms, the conquest regimes were not very stable. The Han Chinese who remained in the north at that time concentrated in their villages, where, under the direction of several great families, they built fortification for self-protection. Behind these deep moats and high ramparts they created a series of autonomous areas where they continued to maintain their Han Chinese culture and resist the incursions of the Hu peoples. After a while, however, the Hu

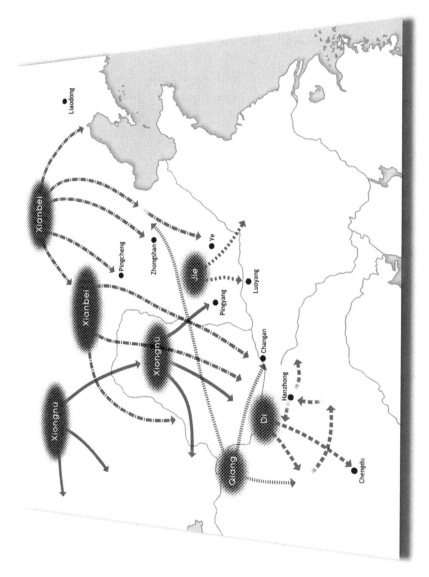

FIGURE 4.1 Geographical Spread of the Five Hu Groups

people settled in and gradually became Sinicized, and, at the same time, the great Han Chinese families increasingly began to participate in the Hu regimes. The blending of Hu and Han cultures was a back-and-forth process that eventually resulted in the creation of a new hybrid culture in medieval North China.

The direction of acculturation was in general toward the Sinicization of the Hu peoples, the deliberate policy of Sinicization of the Northern Wei regime being an obvious example. The Tuoba (Tabgatch) nobility almost universally intermarried with great Han Chinese families, spoke Chinese, read the Chinese classics, and ruled their country by means of a Chinese-style bureaucratic system. On the other hand, however, the Särbi-speaking Tabgatch who remained behind in the Six Garrisons of Dai in the north held on to their own customs; the Han Chinese who settled in these border regions acquired Hu ways of life. When the Rebellion of the Six Garrisons erupted in 524 and the northern Tabgatch attacked Luoyang, strictly speaking it amounted to a culturally conservative northern bloc attacking a Sinicized central plains bloc in the Yellow River valley. What had come to distinguish these two groups was not race but way of life! Neither the conservative nobility of the Northern Zhou nor the Northern Qi could avoid Sinicization once they settled in the central plains. This tendency continued into later times. After the An Lushan–Shi Siming Rebellion of 755–763 (hereafter referred to as the An Lushan Rebellion) was put down, the regional military governors (*fanzhen* or *jiedushi*) in the Hebei region were actually Han Chinese who had been acculturated into Hu ways.

As wave after wave of Hu peoples entered North China, new steppe peoples repeatedly vied for leadership behind them on China's wide northern and western borders. The names given here are what the Chinese called them. The Gaoche (a branch of Xiongnu), Maoran (a Tatar people), Tujue (or Türks, a spelling used to distinguish them from the modern Turks of Turkey), and Huihe (Huihu) alternated as masters of the steppes. The Dangxiang (Dangxiang Qiang, Minyak, later called Tanguts), Tubu (Tibetans, from Bod), and Tuyuhun (Mongolian-speakers related to the Uyghurs) also arose in the west. At the beginning of the Tang, the Tujue empire was the most powerful in North China, no less so than the former Xiongnu empire; by the era of the late Tang and Five Dynasties (907–960), the Qidan (Khitan), a Turko-Mongol people with a Proto-Mongolic language, had replaced them. The Tubu occupied the high plateau of western Tibet and conquered Qinghai (Kokonor), Hehuan, and parts of modern Sichuan and Yunnan; for a time, they were equal to the Tang dynasty. The Baizu state of Nanzhao (738–937) in Yunnan was originally a Tubu dependency and later became a veritable power in the south. The Huihe arose in the western steppes and were able to situate themselves between China and the Tubu, where they developed into a powerful people who could not be ignored. During the Sui and Tang, the Tujue Türks interfered in Chinese affairs, and the Tang court had to rely upon Huihu and Tubu support to suppress the An Lushan Rebellion.

Superficially, the great power of the Tang gave it the appearance of a genuine Heavenly Qaghan (*Tiankehan*) ruling over Hu dependents, and the Tang government did establish loose-reign prefectures (*jimizhoufu*, loosely controlled areas ruled by tribal chieftains) all along their northern and western borders in order to bolster this impression. Most non-Chinese tribal chieftains accepted the ranks and titles conferred on them by the Tang state, and China often called upon one group to fight against another similar group. Nevertheless, in a deeper sense, during this period of medieval Chinese history, China had already become part of a multistate system in East and northeastern Asia and could not stand apart from the many powerful nations involved in it, among which China was only one. On the international gameboard, where many-sided competition flourished, some rising while others fell, China was not the only driving force.

The development of the south followed a different pattern than that of the north. During the Eastern Han, the population of the northern regions continually diminished. At the same time, new commanderies and counties were constantly being established in the Yangzi River valley as Han Chinese continued to migrate into the south and as the control of the central government over more southern areas increased. The original inhabitants of the south were subjected to the pressure of this Han Chinese immigration, and sometimes they resisted with force—the revolt of the Wuxi *man* "barbarians" in present-day Hunan being a prime example. The Eastern Han government mobilized a large military force, fought a lengthy battle, and incurred very heavy losses before finally putting down this uprising. Similar large and small military confrontations frequently occurred, and many small-scale battles between the southern aboriginal peoples and the Han Chinese immigrants may not have been entered in the historical records.

This Eastern Han tide of migration may have been the result of overpopulation and land scarcity in the central plains of the Yellow River valley and the "Land Between the Passes" (Guanzhong) in Shaanxi. It more likely occurred, however, because the natural environment of the south was much better than that of the north. Given the length of the agricultural growing season, the number of days of sunshine, and the amount of rainfall, the crop yield per unit of land in the Yangzi's drainage area was much higher than that in the Yellow River valley. The only impediment was that the many forests and wetlands in the Yangzi River valley required a greater expenditure of labor to clear for farming. The development of the south generally followed the river valley, and newly established commanderies and counties stretched southward in a line on both sides of the main roads. A map of the Eastern Han would show these administrative areas everywhere throughout its territory, but in fact the remote regions were still mainly populated by indigenous peoples, with the Han Chinese inhabitants rather few in number.

These indigenous peoples of the Yangzi River basin in the south were called Yue, Xi, Dong, Man, Liao, and so on, appellations that varied according to place but do not explain their origins. We can only conjecture that from the pre-Qin to the Qin and Han eras they were dispersed over a wide area; perhaps they had a certain relationship to the ancient Warring States kingdom of Yue, or perhaps they were related to the various Miao (Hmong or Mong) and Li (Hlai or Sai) peoples of later times. The ethnographic and archaeological materials we can rely on today are insufficient, and no hypothesis can stand as definitive. All we can say for certain is that when these aboriginal peoples were subjected to the pressure of Han Chinese immigration, some of them were wiped out and some of them were driven further south, but most of them were so acculturated and assimilated into the Han Chinese way of life that it later became very difficult to separate the two groups. This process went on generation after generation during China's long southward migration. The acculturation of Taiwan's so-called plains or lowland tribes (*Pingpuzu*) into Han Chinese culture is a similar recent event that happened almost before our eyes.

There were many separate instances of Han Chinese people migrating to the south. The Eastern Han experienced several epidemics that led people to flee their homes. During the Yellow Turban uprising, the situation was quite chaotic; warfare in the north was endemic during the Three Kingdoms era (220–265); a similar situation prevailed during the two Jin dynasties (Western, 265–317; and Eastern, 317–420); and the central plains were in great disorder after the sack of Luoyang by northern invaders in 311. The Huai River valley was also a battleground during the North-South dynasties (420–589). The Sui and Tang finally established relative peace for over a century, but with the An Lushan Rebellion, war raged on for years in the central plains and the north. All of this warfare impelled the Han Chinese in the north to flee to the south in great numbers.

Northern Chinese great families were the chief nuclei of this flood of refugees. They gathered up their dependents and fled south in large numbers. Many great families that had supported the regime of the Three Kingdoms state of Wu rose to power in just this manner. The great families of Wang and Xie formed the nucleus of those groups moving south after the disastrous 311 sack of Luoyang. The Three Kingdoms' great houses of Zhu, Zhang, Gu, and Lu already occupied the best lands in Wujun (modern Suzhou), so these immigrants could only settle farther south, in the Kuaiji area. When no great families were available to lead those refugees who fled into present-day Hunan and Jiangxi, some formidable leaders, known as "refugee commanders," would emerge from their ranks. In southern regions, where many refugees from the same local northern district gathered, they followed the Eastern Jin system and established immigrant (*qiao*) commanderies and counties within the preexisting southern administrative territories. The creation of these separate districts probably slowed the process of assimilation of the northerners and the local people. During the Eastern Jin and the various southern dynasties of Song, Qi, Liang, and Chen, their territories finally began to be consolidated under a single administrative system.

As mentioned above, the course of the southward migration followed the main transportation routes. In general, the people of Qingzhou and Xuzhou in the Eastern Jin entered Wujun and Kuaiji from the upper Huai River (in modern Anhui)—they included many members of the southern dynasties' social elite. It was from the population that remained north of the Yangzi that the northern governments recruited their armies. During the Three Kingdoms era, part of the population of the central plains and Jingzhou (modern Hubei) went into Shu (modern Sichuan), and some crossed the Yangzi and went south. After 311, the refugees following this route skirted the Xiang and Gan rivers (in modern Hunan and Jiangxi, respectively) and gradually began to develop those areas—the early arrivals usually took the easily accessible land, and the latecomers had to move on to more remote areas. In the process of this long and gradual southern migration, the Han Chinese eventually populated the southeast and China's southern coastal regions.

The last great wave of southward migration took place from the Sui to the Five Dynasties, when Han Chinese fleeing various disturbances in the central plains populated the Yue and Min regions—modern Guangdong and Fujian provinces. The contemporary Hakka ("guest households") people are the descendents of one or another of these unspecified waves of migration. No doubt they would settle in a place for some time, multiply in number, and then be forced once more to send their young off in an unending stream of southward migration. The immigrants and the native peoples sometimes fought and sometimes intermingled, but most of the non-Chinese peoples of the south were eventually assimilated into Han Chinese culture. There were, however, many ethnic minorities living in remote mountain areas who preserved their own cultural identities. These peoples, such as the Miao (Hmong), Yao, Zhuang, and Yi, still exist today. Furthermore, when the Three Kingdoms state of Shu-Han opened up the area of Nanzhong in modern Yunnan, Guizhou, and southern Sichuan, they employed the resident ethnic minorities as army recruits to fight and protect the Hanzhong basin (modern Shanxi) and Ba-Shu (modern Sichuan). This is another example of a group of non-Chinese people being moved to the north.

Whether in the north or the south, the migrations of different ethnic groups continued without cease, as did their intermingling and hybridization. The entire process did not progress in only one direction, however. The general direction was that of northern Hu peoples moving into North China and northern Han Chinese moving toward the south. The general trend of acculturation was Sinicization or hybridization in both the north and the south. There were also frequent repetitions, with populations moving in and out of various regions. During the process of Sinicization or hybridization of non-Chinese peoples, there were also similar instances of Han Chinese becoming hybridized through the adoption of aspects of non-Chinese cultures. The Chinese way of life during the Sui and Tang dynasties was very different from the Chinese culture of the Qin and Han, because it embodied a great many elements of the cultures of non-Chinese peoples from both the north and the south.

In the Chinese social-class structure from the Eastern Han to the North-South dynasties, the hereditary noble clans and the great families were very powerful. There were contemporary reasons why this power of the great families formed during the Eastern Han. First, after the founding of the Eastern Jin in 317, the Han Chinese great families in the north protected themselves behind their fortifications, while in the south, they led the immigrants. In both cases, they had much popular support, and the government could not interfere with them. Second, when the northern Hu peoples entered China, they were generally organized into tribes. When the tribal chiefs adopted a sedentary lifestyle, they controlled most of the population, and their descendents also became known as "great families." The refugee commanders of the southern immigrants were also transformed into local strongmen, just as the chiefs of the indigenous people remained local leaders. All of these centers of power weakened the ruling power of the central government and created a situation in which society was more powerful than the state. Thus the southern dynasties had to rely upon the support of the great families and the local powers. The Northern Zhou (557–581) reorganized its government in order to accommodate this preexisting power structure. It was not until the Tang dynasty that the power of these great hereditary families gradually declined. Thus, the social structure of medieval China was intimately related to the great migration of peoples discussed in this section.

3. The Further Influence of Buddhism

Medieval China witnessed the gradual development and indigenization of Buddhism and its successful adaptation to Chinese culture. The first stage of this process was a dialogue between the two cultures, in which the incompatible elements were adjusted and harmonized. The second stage involved the creation and flourishing of a Sinified Buddhism on Chinese soil.

During the North-South dynasties, the non-Chinese Hu people entered North China and established political regimes at the same time as the arrival of Buddhism. The educated classes of northern Han Chinese developed into local great families protecting themselves behind their fortifications, and Confucianism lost its political support as an official ideology. Thus the Buddhist monks had ample room to operate freely and without hesitation. In the south, the governing regimes were influenced by local powers and were unable to protect the former state ideology. All these factors created space for this foreign religion to develop.

The Buddhist scriptures, or sutras, were written in ancient Sanskrit and Pali, and their translation into Chinese created many grammatical and semantic misunderstandings. At first, both the translation and preaching of these texts was the responsibility of foreign monks. Among them, Kumarajiva (344–413) and his followers were without peer, and their contributions to the translation of Buddhist scriptures was immense. The brilliant Chinese monks who later participated in this translation effort understood even more the difficulties involved. The Eastern Jin monk Dao-an (312–385) promulgated his theory of "five ways of losing and three difficulties of transmitting the original meaning" to explain why great care had to be taken with the situational and linguistic differences in translating these texts. Although the translation work during the North-South dynasties made important contributions, the great Tang monk Xuanzang (602–664) nevertheless carried out another large-scale translation project. Relying on much better editions of the Buddhist scriptures, he corrected many mistakes in earlier translations. Nevertheless, because of the Chinese terms that resulted from the translation method called "matching the meaning" (geyi—taking terms from Daoism to explain Buddhist ideas), one could still not escape the problems created by such nonliteral translations. Given the early difficulty of finding suitable Chinese equivalents, the translated Buddhist sutras also contained many transliterations of Sanskrit words that made it extremely difficult for the reader to understand the original meaning. Since nonliteral translations could be inaccurate, and because transliterations were easily misunderstood, it was difficult to avoid many far-fetched interpretations of Buddhist ideas.

As a foreign religion, it was natural that Buddhism would encounter some resistance over the course of its development in China. Many non-Chinese rulers of the North-South dynasties greatly respected non-Chinese Buddhist monks. This practice easily offended the Chinese literati's sense of cultural nationalism. At the same time, when Buddhism first entered China, the so-called Pure Land of the West (Paradise) was easily confused with India. The uninformed then wondered whether when the Chinese were reborn they first had to spend time in India and endure one more difficulty on the way to paradise. With greater understanding, such uninformed questions eventually disappeared.

In terms of social etiquette, whether or not Buddhist monks had to salute the temporal rulers also gave rise to much discussion. In India, the social status of the Brahmin caste of teachers, scholars, and priests, which included Buddhist monks, was higher than that of the Kshatriya caste of kings and warriors. Thus monks were not required to salute their temporal masters. The ruler of China was, however, the Son of Heaven, and the land and all its inhabitants belonged to him. Everyone was a subject of the Son of Heaven, so how could Buddhist monks not pay homage to him? A similar problem was the violation of Confucian principles of filial piety involved in one's leaving home to become a monk or a nun. In these ways, the behavior of Buddhist monks gradually came into direct conflict with China's Confucian teachings.

The celebrated Eastern Jin monk Huiyuan (334–416) tactfully explained away these two problems with his theory of mediation. He advocated a separation of monks and nuns—people who had left home forever—and lay believers, who remained within their families. Since monks and nuns had already abandoned this secular world, they should not be restrained by its worldly customs. Taking China's traditional culture into consideration, Huiyuan also pointed out that the "the principles of loyalty and filial piety are manifest in the sutras." As time went by, Chinese rulers came to tolerate a certain relative autonomy for the Buddhist clergy, exempting them from taxes and military service. After the Tang dynasty, though, the Buddhist clergy was regulated and administered by the government.

Huiyuan reconciled the conflict between filial piety and leaving home to become a Buddhist monk by asserting that when an individual finds the way, his meritorious works will "benefit all under heaven." Thus, even though one may abandon the parent-child relationship, that "will not violate the rules of filial piety." The Buddhist concept of retribution (*bao*, reward and punishment), whether in this life or a later one, is always an individual matter. In the Chinese cultural context, with its emphasis on family ethics, retribution (good or bad) was not just personal but could be passed on from father to son for generations within a family group. Nevertheless, by the Tang dynasty, the change in Buddhism from complete violation of Chinese culture to full accommodation was obvious. For example, in both story and ceremony, *Mulian Rescues His Mother* (from Hell) subsumed the Chinese concept of filial piety within the Buddhist concept of reward and punishment.

During the North-South dynasties, the Buddhist theory of the indestructibility of the soul (*shen bumie lun*) became a contentious issue. Reincarnation is an important Buddhist doctrine: when one dies in this life, the soul still has to go through a series of six levels of reincarnation from Hell at the bottom to Heaven at the top. One can only escape misery and pain by achieving Nirvana. Traditional Chinese culture also had a concept of the soul, but Wang Chong (27–97) and others questioned whether the soul could exist outside the body. Fan Zhen's (450–510) treatise *The Destruction of the Soul* (*Shen mie lun*) represents the most extreme position in this debate. He compared the soul to the sharpness of a knife, the knife representing the body: when there is no knife, where can the sharpness reside? Emperor Liang Wudi (r. 502–549) summoned a group of scholars to refute Fan Zhen's arguments. The Buddhist interpretations continued to rely on Huiyuan's formulation that when a torch (the body) is reduced to ashes, the flame (the soul) can be passed on and continue to burn. This analogy does not really agree with the Buddhist philosophy of the twelve links in the chain of existence, nor can the torch-fire analogy necessarily refute the knife-sharpness analogy. Both arguments rely on metaphors for body and soul; they do not employ epistemology to solve directly the problem of the body-soul relationship. Of course, even today we are unable to fathom the meaning of life from contemporary biological science.

By the fourth century C.E., Buddhism was firmly established in China. Chinese monks had replaced foreign monks as the main force in translating and teaching the scriptures and organizing the Buddhist community. Among them, Dao-an, Huiyuan, Faxian (337–422), and Daosheng (?–434) made the greatest contributions. The previous practice of non-Chinese monks using the name of their country of origin as a Chinese surname, such as Zhu (India) or Kang (Samarkand), was now replaced by Chinese monks taking Shi (for Buddhist) as their surnames.

We have reliable records of no fewer than ten Chinese monks who set off for India to learn more about Buddhism. Faxian, who traveled from 399 to 414, is the most celebrated, because he actually made it all the way to India, where he studied for several years. He was the first Chinese monk to return to China with a collection of sutras. By that time, there was in China a fairly complete collection of scriptures from both the Mahayana and Hinayana (Greater Vehicle and Lesser Vehicle) traditions of Buddhism; there were many Chinese translations, and the faithful no longer had to worry about their sources being too fragmentary. Temple organizations and monastic regulations were also quite well developed. There were already quite a few Chinese Buddhist schools by the fourth century, and those that were to become most prominent—Pure Land, Chan (Zen), and the Disciplinary School—had already started to develop.

To cite one example of the development of Chinese Buddhism, Zhu Daosheng's opinion that "everyone has the Buddha nature within" gave rise to the theory that every sentient being can become a Buddha. His startling assertion may have been influenced at the time by suggestions contained in the six-chapter *Nirvana Sutra* (*Nihuan*) that Faxian brought from India and translated in 418, and it may have also coincided naturally with the Mencian idea that everyone can become a sage. When various Chinese versions of the *Nirvana Sutra* (*Daban niepan jing*) were transmitted to the south, the idea that all sentient beings had the Buddha nature within became widespread. Zhu Dao-an's theory of sudden enlightenment, the starting point for the later school of Chan (Zen) Buddhism, may also have been influenced by Mencius.

Buddhism flourished greatly at that time. According to Yang Xuanzhi's *Records of the Monasteries in Luoyang* (*Luoyang jialan ji*), completed in 547, Buddhist temples were everywhere in the city. As evidence of Buddhism's prosperity south of the Yangzi, we have the Tang poet Du Mu's (803–852) line, "in the South are a hundred and eight temples." Whether it is Liang Wudi "flattering the Buddha"—being a devout believer—or Northern Zhou Wudi (r. 560–578) "killing the Buddha"—suppressing Buddhism—both actions attest to the overwhelmingly dominant position of the faith.

After Xuanzang returned from his pilgrimage to India with a trove of sutras, China's collection of Buddhist classics was quite comprehensive. Xuanzang's translation of these Buddhist texts was a great achievement not only for the propagation of Buddhism but also for his introduction into China of Indian thought and scholarship, such as logic (*yinmingxue*). Many Buddhist schools proliferated from the North-South dynasties to the Tang. They were distinguished either by their dominant scriptures or by their particular doctrines. The result of the competition between these various schools was that those with very difficult theoretical doctrines, such as the Consciousness Only School (*weishi zong*), did not survive, while those that did last were characterized by relatively simple and easy-to-practice beliefs. The Tang development of Chan (Zen, meaning meditation) Buddhism was extremely rapid, beginning with the rise of the Northern School, with Shenxiu (600–706) as its great patriarch. The Southern School arose shortly after, and its sixth patriarch, Huineng (638–713), brought Chan Buddhism to the height of popularity. From then on, Chan, Pure Land, and the Disciplinary School became confirmed as Sinified forms of Buddhism. These three schools of Chinese Buddhism were also transmitted to Korea and Japan, after which Buddhism became one of the common characteristics of East Asian culture. From its entry into China in the first century B.C.E. up to the Tang dynasty, about one thousand years, Buddhism had become completely integrated into Chinese culture.

As Buddhism entered China, the organization of religious Daoism took shape, and the two proceeded along similar paths. Religious Daoism was a Chinese cultural reaction to a foreign religion. At the same time, it also appropriated the organizational system and ceremonies of Buddhism to transcend the limitations of popular beliefs. The Daoist religion was (and still is) extremely complex. Under an overall umbrella of pre-Qin Daoist quietism, nonaction (*wuwei*), and respect for nature (*ziran*), it encompasses many elements of Chinese culture stemming from different historical backgrounds. These include shamanism and nature gods, magic and divination, fortune telling, Yin-Yang and Five Agents (*wuxing*) theory, breathing exercises, alchemy, and the quest for immortality.

The development of religious Daoism gradually unfolded during the North-South dynasties. In the Eastern Jin, Way of the Celestial Masters (*tianshi dao*) Daoism flourished in the coastal regions. For generations, prominent families, such as that of the celebrated calligrapher Wang Xizhi (303–361), worshipped the Celestial Master. The rebels Sun En (?–402), Lu Xun (?–411) and Xu Daofu (?–411) organized the lower classes and revolted under the banner of the Five Bushels of Rice sect; their rebellion lasted from 398 to 410. These two examples demonstrate how the Daoist religion could transcend class barriers and appeal to different elements of society precisely because its complexity made it able to satisfy their differing spiritual needs. During the Jin and North-South dynasties, the theoreticians of religious Daoism—Ge Hong (283–363), Tao Hongjing (456–536), Kou Qianzhi (365–448), and Lu Xiujing (406–477)—established theological systems, practiced alchemical methods of refining cinnabar (mercuric sulfide) as an elixir of immortality, and set out rules and regulations for Daoist organizations, thus bringing theoretical order to religious Daoism.

In general, the Talisman (*fulu*) School inherited some of the practices of exorcism, sorcery, and witchcraft from traditional Chinese beliefs. Developing late Han popular religious beliefs, during the North-South dynasties it became one of the most important centers of Daoist religious activity. The Alchemical (*danding*) School carried on the traditional search for the elixir of immortality that had begun during the Warring States period (475–221 B.C.E.). Both the First Emperor of Qin and Han Wudi had been obsessed with obtaining immortality this way. The quest for outer alchemy (exterior cinnabar, *waidan*) was related to medical practices and involved ingesting cinnabar as an elixir. The quest for inner alchemy (interior cinnabar, *neidan*) involved training one's physical constitution through breathing techniques in order to prolong life. A large body of chemical knowledge was amassed as a result of these alchemical practices, about which we have a great deal of archaeological material going all the way back to the pre-Qin era. Ge Hong and Tao Hongjing were *waidan* practitioners of the Alchemical School; Kou Qianzhi was a *neidan* practitioner.

Late Han religious Daoism was still in its popular stage and lacked any developed theology. The integration of Daoist theology and the pre-Qin Daoist philosophy of Laozi and Zhuangzi was gradually completed during the North-South dynasties. From then on, the concepts of emphasizing the natural (or self-so, *ziran*) and reverence for Nature (also *ziran*) became fundamental tenets of religious Daoism. In its principles of conduct, religious Daoism followed Confucian ethics and morality, thus exhibiting the characteristics of an indigenous Chinese religion.

Ever since the Yellow Turban uprising, religious Daoism continued to embrace a religious sense of apocalypse and redemption. From the North-South dynasties on, a millenarian desire for a final apocalypse and salvation, such as that of Li Hong (fl. 290) and others, was often the impulse behind large-scale popular revolts. Although the Celestial Master Daoism led by Sun En and Xu Daofu did not particularly highlight the idea of a savior, nevertheless it expressed the faithful's hope for apocalyptic redemption and release from this world through its concepts of the "Water Power" and rebirth, which brought together Chinese traditional beliefs in the forces of nature—Heaven, Earth, and Water—as Three Powers that govern human life with the Buddhist idea of rebirth in the Pure Land of Amitabha Buddha.

The surname of the Tang royal house was Li, supposedly the same as the Daoist founder Laozi, and thus the Tang rulers spared no effort to venerate Laozi and promote Daoism. Ironically, it was precisely because the Tang Daoist masters were in such a superior and comfortable position that, except for adding some minor embellishments to the lore of religious Daoism, they made no genuine contributions to Daoist doctrines. The next major breakthroughs for religious Daoism came during the Song, Jin, Yuan, and Ming dynasties.

Since medieval times, the Alchemical School of religious Daoism served as a vehicle for the rich and well-born to search for immortality, and its primary byproducts included many achievements in chemistry and medicine, especially pharmacology. The Talisman School served the popular masses as a vehicle to ward off evil, and for this reason it was often a key element in many armed peasant uprisings. Pre-Qin Daoist philosophy provided the theological foundations of religious Daoism, while its ideas of physical and spiritual cultivation were adopted by the literati class to compensate for their absence in contemporary Confucianism.

The development of Daoist religion during the North-South dynasties can even be said to constitute an overall reorganization of traditional Chinese culture. With the melding of Confucian morality, Daoist philosophy, and popular beliefs and the addition of Buddhism's ceremonies and clerical and monastic organization, a syncretic religious system comprising many disparate elements came into being. The Daoist pantheon was in principle based upon the apotheosis of the forces of nature and of people who had benefited humankind, but the names of the gods were different from those of ancient China. From medieval times on, this great panoply of gods and goddesses continually grew and overlapped with the various incarnations of the Buddha to create a vast and popular Buddho-Daoist hierarchy of deities.

From medieval times on, Confucianism, Buddhism, and Daoism were all integral elements of Chinese culture. Among the three, Buddhism and Daoism sometimes competed and sometimes merged. Confucianism believed in serving the secular world; Buddhism and Daoism wanted to escape from mundane human existence. These two trends were mutually opposed yet also mutually complementary. Their legacy remains with us to this day.

4. Literature and the Arts

By the Eastern Han, the political order of the Qin-Han empire was aging, and Confucian scholarship was no longer vibrant. Excessively concerned with trivialities, Confucianism gradually lost its leading role in Chinese culture. As these two sources of authority declined, individual consciousness gradually came to the fore. Devotees of Eastern Han Neo-Daoism discussed man's individual character and ability (*caixing*) and debated whether ability (*cai*) and nature (*xing*) were identical or different. They also searched for the particular characteristics of one's individual authentic self, while society affirmed the autonomy of individual personality by valorizing men of singular or extraordinary conduct and independent character. This atmosphere had a great influence on cultural creativity.

From the Eastern Han to the Tang, China experienced extreme political turmoil, and the ordinary people suffered from the ravages of war. This was, as seen above, also an age of intense encounters between Chinese and foreign cultures. The shock of these culture clashes also provided considerable opportunity for the expression of individual ability. As a result, there were outstanding achievements in literature, art, music, and so on.

In literature, from the Eastern Han through the Tang, regulated verse (*lüshi*) and quatrains (*jueju*) of five or seven characters per line matured and became the mainstream of traditional Chinese poetry. Even though the Song poets wrote some extremely fine verse, they never surpassed the Tang in lyric poetry.

Before the Eastern Han, Chinese poetry consisted of the *Book of Songs* (*Shijing*, twelfth to seventh centuries B.C.E.) in the north and the *Songs of Chu* (*Chuci*, third to second centuries B.C.E.) in the south. The *Shijing* poems are mostly written with four characters per line and range in theme from court ceremonial odes to regional folk songs. The "three hundred poems" (actually 305) of the *Shijing* took shape during Confucius's time (551–479 B.C.E.) and, as a literary and moral textbook, became required reading for the literati. Poetic compositions that expressed the poet's individual thoughts and feelings were almost never again seen in the ancient classics. The *Chuci* contained both songs chanted at shamanistic religious ceremonies, like the "Nine Songs" (*Jiuge*), and politico-erotic lyrical outpourings, like Qu Yuan's (340?–278 B.C.E.) "Encountering Sorrow" (*Lisao*). The other works in the *Chuci*, by writers like Song Yu (ca. 290–ca. 223 B.C.E.), were few and mostly imitative.

The *Chuci* was written in long and short lines that often had an exclamatory particle—*xi*, *xie*, and so on—inserted between two lines. Neither of these ancient poetic traditions employed five- or seven-character lines. The Han Music Bureau poems (*yuefu*), by contrast, contained many penta- and heptasyllabic poems, and we sometimes encounter quotations from similar songs in the historical records. For example, both the "Song of the Great Wind" attributed to Han Gaozu (Liu Bang, 247–195 B.C.E.)

and Li Yannian's (?–87 B.C.E.) "Song of Beautiful Women" are in penta-syllabic verse.

Since the Chinese language is monosyllabic, lines of verse were at first made up of two beats plus three beats forming a segment, with two or three segments ending in a pause, or caesura. Odd and even beats would alternate to avoid monotony. Perhaps these long lines evolved into the shortest combinations as poems based on couplets of five or seven char-acters per line. These penta- or heptasyllabic folk songs were sung in a completely natural, unselfconscious fashion, with no need to follow pre-scribed rules of prosody.

In the Eastern Han, this form was gradually taken up by literary men for the creation of individualistic lyric verse expressing their own feelings (*qing*). The poets of the Jian-an era (196–220 C.E.) produced many fine poems that still move us because of their honest expressions of sadness or regret for the brevity of human life. From that point on, the poetic style of the two Jin and the North-South dynasties gradually broadened in scope to include lyrical expressions of individual ambitions and even discussions of Neo-Daoist metaphysics. The poets whose works continue to be read and anthologized today include Xie Lingyun (385–433), Tao Qian (Tao Yuanming, ca. 365–427), Yu Xin (513–581), and Bao Zhao (414–466).

As Buddhism entered China at this time, Indian languages came to in-fluence Chinese poetry and linguistics. Sanskrit and Pali texts were highly inflected and polysyllabic, and Indian literature also had a long oral tradi-tion of chanting its epics and sutras. As these texts were translated into Chinese, it was necessary to employ monosyllabic Chinese characters one by one in place of phonetic letters in an attempt to transmit the ineffable meanings contained in the long, polysyllabic Indian technical terms. This led to a Chinese interest in their own language and gave rise to the sys-tem of "spelling out" the pronunciation of Chinese characters, known as *fanqie*, in which a character is represented by two others: one character represents the initial sound and one character the final sound and the tone. The sound of every Chinese character could be analyzed into an ini-tial consonant plus a medial and final containing the tone (and thus, the rhyme). A phonetic "spelling" or *fanqie* of the character *tian* (field, rising tone) would work as follows: it would be represented by the character *tu* (disciple) plus the character *nian* (year, rising tone); thus, *t-* + *-ian* (rising tone) = *tian* (rising tone and rhyme). Once the Chinese had the concept of *shengmu*, the rhyming part of a Chinese syllable (literally, "mother of sound"), they were able to produce much more appropriate and accurate rhymes—the fundamental element of Chinese verse.

Chinese is also a tonal language. Monosyllabic Chinese characters have to rely on their phonetic tonal inflection in order to distinguish their semantic meaning. Around 483–493, Shen Yue (441–513) of the Southern Qi dynasty established that northern Chinese had four tones, which he called level, rising, departing, and entering (*ping, shang, qu, ru*; the *ping* later changing to *yinping* and *yangping*). Southern Chinese dialects were found to have more than four tones. Following this understanding of tonal qualities, Chinese poetic lines came to be written with a symmetry between level (*ping*) and deflected (non*ping*, or *ze*) tones and alternations of the first and second lines, thus increasing the musicality of the verse. The use of antithetical or parallel constructions (*duizhang*) was characteristic of lines of Chinese verse. In the fourth century C.E., with the exhaustion of the Jian-an style and the shallowness of Jin thought, feelings were unequal to poetic diction, and poets sought to refine the formal qualities of verse. Antithesis and parallelism were clever techniques of prosody, and from then on, the fully developed and elaborate form of regulated verse emphasized antithesis and parallelism between level and deflected tones.

The Tang dynasty represents the height of *shi* lyric poetry. Using regulated verse as a foundation, Tang poets, with Du Fu (712–770) as the greatest master, could arrange many rhymes into very long poems. They could also cut eight-line regulated verse into quatrains having one or two sets of antithetical couplets. Tang quatrains are short but powerful and express profound meanings with great brevity, thus mastering the formal restraints of the genre. Regulated verse (also known as new-style verse, *jintishi*) has very strict rules of prosody, and it was a great challenge to the poets to achieve artistic variation within the rules. That is why many regulated poems, and especially *pailü* (long poems repeating the quatrain many times in multiples of twenty lines), even by celebrated masters, could sometimes not escape piling up repetitive phrases. Li Bo (701–762) and Du Fu also wrote many old-style poems (*gutishi*) to free themselves from the restrictions of regulated verse.

After the High Tang, Yuan Zhen (779–831) and Bo Juyi (772–846) advocated the freedom of writing new *yuefu* emphasizing content (often social criticism) over formal properties. *Yuefu* (from "Music Bureau") were originally popular folk songs that were written down as poems. Tang *yuefu* aimed at escape from poetic regulations and were the creations of individual poets. The Late Tang saw the appearance of the long-short verse style (*changduan ju*) that departed even further from the limitations of five- and seven-character verse and paved the way for the later lyric verse (*ci*) and aria (*qu*) forms.

This transformation of regulated verse illustrates the dialectical relationship between freedom and the rules of prosody. Literature should have the expression of content as its principal aim, but it also entails a search for beautiful forms to communicate that content. Thus, the expression of rich content within the limits of formal regulations is one of the greatest tests of any poet's skill. Formal rules grow old with much use, and then the poets have to break through the limits of the extant form, return to content as the principal element, and try to establish the new rules of a new form. This is the artistic cycle of breakthrough to promotion to further breakthroughs. In the history of Chinese culture, the age under discussion in this chapter exhibited tremendous cultural energy, which is attested to by eight centuries of transformation in poetic styles and prosodic regulations.

Parallel prose (*piantiwen*) was a companion genre to regulated verse. Its precursor was the Han rhyme-prose (or prose poem, *fu*), whose precursor was the "Encountering Sorrow" (*Lisao*) or *sao*-style in the *Chuci*. Han *fu* were full of elaborate descriptive narration in very florid rhetoric and involved exhibitions of great erudition, but they were not suitable for theoretical discussions. In general, Han *fu* was still a form of free prose or *sanwen*. After the Wei-Jin era, writing that was belletristic and used for the expression of feelings was called *wen*, while utilitarian prose came to be known as *bi* (literally, "writing brush"). These styles were distinguished by both content and form. Following the trend toward increasing formalism, *sanwen* essay-style prose evolved into parallel prose—not only did it employ more flowery diction, but it gradually came to be characterized by parallel and antithetical sentence constructions and melodies suitable for chanting like poetry. In addition to these formal properties, parallel prose relied on the use of copious allusions and metaphors for the figurative expression of its themes. Thus the readers of parallel prose had to posses great interpretative ability in order to unravel and explain the similarities hidden in many layers of metaphor and allusion.

This literary genre could neither directly express the author's meaning nor accurately narrate events and ideas. It was instead a literary game played by the literati of the great families to exhibit their mastery of profound erudition and graceful expression. This genre, in which the expression of emotion and the narration of events was quite incompatible, lasted for eight generations. It was not superseded until Han Yu (768–824) advocated a return to the straightforward ancient-style (*guwen*) prose essay of the Qin and Han and initiated the Ancient Rose Movement. From then on, parallel prose was confined to ceremonial use. Han Yu's literary revolution may actually be compared to the May Fourth Movement of the early twentieth century in its influence on Chinese cultural history.

The development of parallel prose and regulated verse was attributable to the literati's excessive search for formal rules until form overshadowed content or content was altogether ignored. Both of these trends were a result of the literati's desire to express their individual self-consciousness by concentrating their energies primarily on literary techniques. The literati had become a privileged class that dominated both higher education and the literary stage. In a narrow competitive arena, they strove to produce works of flowery, decorative, elegant, and dainty beauty and paid scant attention to literature's original communicative purpose. This kind of competition finally came to an end when the High and Mid-Tang witnessed a literary reform. The Mid-Tang was a period of transformation, during which men of letters broke through the great clans' monopoly of literature and knowledge. The social-class base of literati and scholars was broadened, and literature, no longer a word game played by a minority nobility, again became a tool for the expression of philosophical and moral ideas.

Cultural factors external to literature also had some influence on literature at this time. After Buddhist sutras written in Indo-European phonetic alphabets entered China, the Chinese first came to understand the particular tonal character of their language. Phonology developed out of that knowledge and laid the foundation for the *ping-ze* system and the distinctive rhyme schemes of the new-style poetry. The designation *yuefu* is only a general term, and many popular songs from different times and places continually offered Chinese poets new resources of creative vitality.

A similar creative situation could be seen in other literary genres. Fiction (the usual English translation of *xiaoshuo*, "petty talk") was at first held in contempt in ancient times as unworthy of a gentleman's consideration. Nevertheless, oral stories were avidly listened to and transmitted among the popular masses, and some of them were eventually written down by the literate minority. Tales of the supernatural (*zhiguai xiaoshuo*) were especially widespread during the Jin and North-South dynasties, and the reason for this is not hard to imagine. The Buddhist classics contained many stories known as *jataka* tales, which were employed for preaching and explaining the meaning of the work in question. Although Confucians, following Confucius, did not normally speak of "prodigies, force, disorder, and gods" (*guai, li, luan, shen*) (*Analects* 7.21), at a time when Buddhism permeated Chinese life, Chinese literati also took great pains to describe strange and unusual supernatural happenings. When teaching the Buddhist sutras, each session began with a story as an introduction to the main text. Since the populace wanted these stories, the literati had an incentive to write them. Besides supernatural tales, anecdotes and other gossipy works also provided rich materials for popular enjoyment. The Tang dynasty had a large and prosperous urban population, and the streets and market areas were a hotbed for the growth of popular stories. Thus, in the High and Mid-Tang a new genre of stories called *chuanqi*— "transmitting the strange"—arose in such great numbers and such high quality that they far surpassed the earlier *zhiguai xiaoshuo*. Familiar titles such as "The Curly-Bearded Stranger," "The Story of Cui Yingying," and "The Kunlun Slave" paved the way for the Song tradition of oral storytelling and the great Yuan and Ming novels.

The period from the Wei and Jin to the Sui and Tang was one in which writers actively responded to both internal and external conditions to extend continually the scope of literature and transform the nature of many literary genres. Similar changes also took place in other nonliterary arts, such as painting.

Most of the Han painting that survives today consists of silk paintings from the ancient state of Chu and human figures painted on stone tomb walls and tiles. The earliest famous painting preserved today is a Tang and a Song copy of an illustration of Zhang Hua's (232–300) *Rules of Conduct for Palace Women*. The painting is attributed to Gu Kaizhi (ca. 344–405), and, although it is impressive, when we compare the depiction of women's clothing to the flowing apparel painted by the great masters Wu Daozi (ca. 685–758) and Cao Zhongda, we find Gu's work to be less elegant and vivid. The folds in the robes of the Northern Wei Buddhist statues from Dunhuang and those from the northern dynasties discovered in 1996 in the Longxing Temple in Qingzhou, in Shandong Province, are extremely delicate and lifelike. Such Buddhist art lent great impetus to the remarkable changes in Chinese art and painting that took place from the Jin dynasties to the Sui and Tang. There was landscape painting in the Jin, but it was still in the early stages of development and cannot compare with the fine lines and blue-green landscape colors of the Tang masters Li Sishun (651–716) and his son Li Zhaodao.

Examining the Buddhist paintings from Dunhuang, we see that landscape painting gradually developed out of the painting of people and stories into an independent genre, a process closely tied to Buddhist art. Buddhist art came from outside China and was part of a popular tradition, and thus it influenced the upper-class Chinese literati artists through both the stimulation of foreign art and the expansion of the social base for artistic creativity and appreciation.

External influences were even more apparent in the performing arts. As non-Chinese peoples continually entered China from the end of the Eastern Han, the numbers of Buddhist believers rapidly increased, and the popular songs and dances of non-Chinese people from Central Asia and the eastern end of the Silk Road streamed into China. The Chinese accepted not only new musical instruments but also fresh new melodies and dances. The music of the northern dynasties was mainly from India, Kucha (Khocho), and the Western Liang (with Dunhuang as its capital), while of the court music (*yayue*, "elegant music") of the Tang, nine parts out of ten came from abroad—from India, the western regions (mostly modern Xinjiang), Central Asia, Yu (ancient Burma), Nanzhao, and Korea. This new music and instrumentation basically replaced the traditions of China's ancient music of bronze bells, stone chimes, pan pipes, drums, zithers, and so on. Foreign music and dance was performed both at court and among the people and also effectively broke down the previous elite-popular distinction.

In sum, in the five centuries from the Jin through the Sui and Tang, the cultural life of China in both literature and the arts underwent a profound transformation. The influence of non-Chinese artistic elements and the changes in social structure greatly broadened the social base of participation in cultural activities. The cultural ethos of this period was very different from that of the classical era of the Qin and Han, and it opened the way for many cultural developments of the Song, Ming, and even recent times.

5. Astronomy, Mathematics, and Medicine

Traditional Chinese culture made many significant contributions to the fields of mathematics, astronomy, and biology that are important to contemporary science, but of course ancient Chinese scholars did not employ modern scientific methodologies or concepts in their investigations of nature. Chinese culture had its own complex, multilayered theories of the universe. Ever since Dong Zhongshu (179–104 B.C.E.) synthesized the ancient knowledge up to his day and organized a vast cosmological system of mutual correspondences, the Chinese mode of thinking was influenced for centuries by this theory of interactive correspondence between nature and human beings. In this section, I will discuss the impressive scientific achievements made in medieval China under the influence of this concept of the cosmos. We must acknowledge at the outset, though, that none of these accomplishments laid the foundation for the appearance of modern science in Chinese culture. Medieval China's scientific achievements were in the final analysis limited by Chinese culture and history.

Ancient Chinese astronomy was inseparable from calendar making. Because the movement of heavenly bodies was used to record time, Chinese calendar making involved blending together records of heavenly phenomena and the establishment of an official calendar of the seasons. China's traditional calendar was a mixed solar and lunar system. From the inception of the *huntian* theory that the sky (or heaven) was like an eggshell and the earth a yolk, to the invention of the armillary sphere in the Eastern Han, to Li Chunfeng's (602–670) "Linde Calendar" of 665 in the early Tang, calendar makers of every age had done their best to combine the common multiple of measurements of the true length of a solar year, the exact length of a lunar month, the orbital periods of the five largest planets, and the year-month-day cycle of Heavenly Stems and Earthly Branches (*ganzhi*) in order to trace back the origin of time. This sort of calendar making represented a metaphysical system of the cosmos. To calculate these various periodic cycles, calendar makers developed astronomical observations and built the armillary sphere as a model to demonstrate the orbits of the heavenly bodies. Everyone from Zhang Heng (78–139) in the Han to Zeng Yixing (683–727) in the Tang relied on this important instrument.

Many mathematical problems grew out of Chinese astronomy. Beginning with the *Measurements of Zhou* (*Zhoubi suanjing*), China also had a long tradition of mathematics books dealing with practical calculations such as land area, volume of food crops and field work, distance, and time as well as calculations of averages for various sets of data. From these various practical calculations involving simple addition, subtraction, multiplication, and division, Chinese mathematicians developed plane and solid geometry, trigonometry, and algebra. Books called "classics of mathematics" (*suanjing*) were collected from Han times on. During the Tang dynasty, the government established a Mathematics School to train experts in mathematics, and these so-called Erudites (*boshi*) edited and annotated ten famous "classics of mathematics"—*Measurements of Zhou, Nine Chapters on the Mathematical Art* (*Jiuzhang suanshu*), *The Sea Island Mathematical Manual* (*Haidao suanjing*), Sunzi's *Mathematics* (*Suanjing*), *Five Divisions of Calculation* (*Wucao suanjing*), Xia Houyang's *Mathematics* (*Suanjing*), Zhang Qiujian's *Mathematics* (*Suanjing*), *Arts of Combination* (*Zhuishu*), and the *Continuation of Ancient Mathematics* (*Jigu suanshu*). China's ancient tradition of mathematics having been thus reorganized, a firm foundation was laid for the theoretical mathematics of the Song, Yuan, and later times.

In the fifth century, Zu Chongzhi (429–500) calculated the value of *pi* as somewhere between 3.1415926 and 3.1415927—at the time the most accurate calculation in the world. It would not be until the fifteenth and sixteenth centuries that Islamic and French mathematicians would produce a more accurate value. Based on the *Nine Chapters on the Mathematical Art*, Zu Chongzhi also calculated the volume of spherical objects. He not only produced a method of calculation but also a theorem very similar to that of the sixteenth-century Italian mathematician Bonaventura Cavalieri's (1598–1647), an important foundation of infinitesimal calculus. The *Sui History* (*Suishu*) mentions that Zu Chongzhi could also calculate linear and cubic equations, but his methods have been lost. The work of Zu and his son Zu Geng was contained in the book *Arts of Combination*, which the Tang Mathematics School used as a textbook; it was also transmitted to Japan and Korea but has not survived.

Wang Xiaotong (fl. 623) was an early Tang mathematician who compiled the *Continuation of Ancient Mathematics* included in the ten classics of mathematics. This work contains twenty sections that, except for one on calculating the position of the moon, primarily concern problems of practical measurements for building dikes and dams, erecting granaries, and digging ditches. Wang Xiaotong's geometry developed solutions for cubic equations and quadratic equations with two variables. In the West, a similar use of numerical values to solve cubic equations had to wait until the thirteenth century.

From the examples of Zu and Wang, we can see that medieval Chinese mathematics was oriented toward practical problem solving. It did not rely on deductive logic to open up mathematical theory. Thus, Chinese mathematics had its own internal limitations, and even though it produced some brilliant achievements long before the rest of the world, these remained isolated breakthroughs that were not built upon to develop modern and systematic theoretical mathematics.

Medicine and pharmacology were also important elements of traditional Chinese scholarship. As with astronomy, Chinese medical theory was also based upon the metaphysical cosmological theory that regarded the blood vessels of the human body as a miniature universe within the great universe and posited a correlative relationship between the greater system of nature and the lesser system of the body. During the Eastern Han, Zhang Zhongjing (ca. 150–219) compiled *On Diseases of Heat and Cold* (*Shanghan zabing lun*), an empirical study of disease symptoms, but Chinese medical theory never freed itself from the Yin-Yang and Five Agents theories. Thus, it could only bring together symptoms and medical prescriptions to seek the best cures from empirical data. From the Jin through the Tang, many celebrated works, such as Ge Hong's *Collected Prescriptions* (*Zhouhou fang*), Tao Hongjing's *One Hundred Prescriptions* (*Zhouhou yibai fang*), and Sun Simiao's (541/581–682) *Ten Thousand Golden Remedies* (*Qian jin fang*), all collected and classified disease symptoms and recorded the best curative prescriptions. Sun's work listed several thousand efficacious prescriptions classified according to various types of illness. *Ten Thousand Golden Remedies* and a later supplement contained thirty chapters concerning various departments of medicine such as internal medicine; gynecology; pediatrics; eye, ear, nose, and throat; diseases of heat and cold; trauma; setting fractured bones; and emergency medicine. Sun also discussed nutrition and nurturing life as well as diagnosis by taking the patient's pulse, medical prescriptions (similar to modern pharmacology), and acupuncture. From the Tang on, Sun was known as the Sage of Medicine.

Chinese medical theory was metaphysical and mysterious, and, if it had not been for these collections of clinical diagnoses and medical applications, Chinese medicine might not have been so successfully practiced for a thousand years. Chinese medicine developed out of clinical practice, and thus the tradition established from the *Collected Prescriptions* to the *Ten Thousand Golden Remedies* constitutes a vast record of effective clinical practices. Leaving aside its metaphysical theories, this is still an outstanding curative system with an extremely long pedigree.

Chinese medicine and mathematics both followed the line of practical problem solving and, although producing exceptional achievements, they could not transcend clinical practice and practical calculation to rise to the level of the science of pathology and scholarship based on the application of deductive logic.

Chinese intellectuals' search for the subjective authenticity of the self during this long medieval period was not limited to literature. Scholars who applied themselves to scientific investigation were also dissatisfied with merely solving practical problems. They strove to develop abstract concepts through the application of logical thinking. The significance of Zu Chongzhi's search for *pi*, the ratio of the circle's circumference to its diameter; for mathematical formulas for the area of objects; and for a theorem for the volume of spherical objects all transcended practical utility. Based on the concept of limits or boundaries, Liu Hui (fl. 263) measured the area of polygons in an attempt to approach an accurate measure of the volume of cylindrical objects. His logic was that of the fundamental concepts of contemporary analytical geometry and calculus. In his *An tian lun*, Yu Xi (281–356) put forth the idea that the sky (heaven) is empty and the earth is solid and that the heavenly bodies all move in their own regular orbits, thus overcoming the limitations of the *huntian* eggshell sky and egg-yolk earth theory. In his "Linde Calendar," Li Chunfeng swept away the confusion caused by the long seventy-six-year cycle of *zhang* (nine years) and *bu* (four *zhang*) in Chinese calendar making. He directly relied on the true length of the solar year (from winter solstice to winter solstice) and the first day of the moon of the first of the twenty-four periods (*jieqi*) of the lunar year to accurately calculate the calendar year. In the eighth century, Zeng Yixing, Nangong Shuo (fl. 707), and others measured the differences in the sun's shadow in different places north and south and used these concrete figures to correct the mistakes in written records. According to their data, they also estimated the radius (*huchangdu*) of the Earth's meridian. Had they gone just a little further, they could easily have demonstrated that the Earth is round.

Medieval Chinese medical practitioners also sought to discover the etiology of diseases. Early in the Sui dynasty, Chao Yuanfang (fl. 609) and others compiled *The Origins and Symptoms of Diseases* (*Zhubing yuanhoulun*), containing 1,739 entries cataloging the origin, pathology, symptoms, and changes in various illnesses. Aside from about three hundred entries on various forms of treatment, the rest of the entries hardly touch upon curative methods—they are rather deductive pathology and symptomatology of various illnesses.

The study of medicinal plants resulted in the compilation of many important classics of pharmacology, or *bencao*. The Han *Shen Nong's Materia Medica* (*Shen Nong bencaojing*) was probably a pharmacological work compiled by Zhang Zhongjing and others. Zhang Hongjing found it an overly large and confused work, and so he reorganized it into 365 items and added his own further collection of 365 items on the medical practice of famous physicians to produce his *Collected Commentaries on the Materia Medica* (*Bencaojing jizhu*). Although still a pharmacopoeia, it was also a taxonomy of medicinal materials of animal, mineral, and vegetable origins.

In the early Tang, Su Gong (Su Jing, fl. seventh century) collected the work of twenty-two experts in his *Revised Materia Medica* (*Xinxiu bencao*). He divided most of the known pharmaceuticals into nine major categories—minerals, grasses, woods, birds and beasts, insects and fish, fruits, vegetables, grains, and "well-known but not yet used" medical materials—describing their appearance, special characteristics, and uses, complete with illustrations. This vast seventh-century pharmacopoeia specializing in botanical materials was effectively an encyclopedia of medical botany. The taxonomy used paved the way for that of Li Shizhen (ca. 1518–1593) in the Ming dynasty. Thus, Tang materia medica (*bencauxue*) represented a great advance over simple descriptive lists of herbs.

All of these achievements in mathematics, astronomy, and medicine demonstrate that the contemporary search for knowledge was not completely restrained by practical concerns. As scholars strove to solve practical problems, they continually raised standards and broke new ground. As knowledge became more specialized and communities of experts developed, some scholars engaged in intensive study of individual fields. During the Jin and North-South dynasties, scholarship was monopolized by the upper classes, but even then there was a community of scholars who were able to benefit from mutual interaction. During the Sui-Tang era, the government established specialized schools and regularly organized scholars into teams to edit books such as *Revised Materia Medica*. Reaching this critical level of scholarly concentration gave great impetus to the development of higher knowledge.

The Tang dynasty had many contacts with the outside world, especially with Indian culture and its astronomy, mathematics, and medicine, which had entered China along with Buddhism. In general, Indian scholarship had a great influence on these same fields in China, but Chinese advances also relied on China's own native traditions. In short, the Indian influence on Chinese science never matched the influence it had on religion, philosophy, and literature.

6. Medieval Food, Clothing, Dwelling, and Transport

Different ethnic groups continually entered medieval China, bringing with them new customs and new ways of life. Chinese ways were greatly influenced by this contact, and everyday Chinese lifestyles underwent great changes during this period.

In dietary practices, the gradual introduction of wheat products was an important change. Ever since the invention of agriculture in the Neolithic age, northern China's main staples were various varieties of millet. From the pre-Qin era, wheat, barley, and oats were also among the main food grains, but they were not as common as millet, which still remained the most commonly eaten grain during the Han dynasty. The whole grains of wheat were at first steamed or boiled and eaten like rice and millet. Perhaps it was primarily because the outer shell of wheat (the chaff) was too rough and hard to digest that it did not become widely popular at the time. As mentioned in the previous chapter, in the Eastern Han the milling of wheat flour gradually became a common practice.

The word *bing* (flat cake) is a general term for a large number of food items made with wheat flour—including today's thin round cakes (*bao-bing*, eaten with Peking duck), steamed buns (*mantou*), noodles (*mian-tiao*), and so on. The Song *Imperial Digest of the Taiping Reign Period* (*Taiping yulan*, 976–983) quotes the "Rhyme-prose on Bing" (*Bingfu*) of the Western Jin writer Shu Zhe (?–300), in which the character *bing* is written with *mai* (wheat, for the meaning) and *bing* (together, for the sound), thus demonstrating that *bing* were made from wheat. Shu Zhe lists many types of food, the preparation of which would be hard to guess, but he particularly states that these names came either from local neigh-borhoods or from faraway places. He also points out that in ancient times people ate wheat before they started to make *bing*. Some names he lists, like *an-gan* (or *an-gan-te*) and *junü* (a pastry made of fried flour and honey) are surely transliterations from non-Chinese languages.

The *Important Arts of the People* (*Qimin yaoshu*), compiled during the Northern Wei (around 533–544), has a chapter entitled "Preparation of *Bing*" that cites various recipes from the *Classic of Food* (*Shijing*). From them we can see that baking yeast was already known; many of these *bing* were made with yeast, but others were not. The methods of cooking *bing* of various shapes included baking, frying, boiling, and steaming. Some-times leavened dough in ten-inch strips was rolled thin, boiled, and dried; other times two-inch gobs of dough were boiled at a high flame and eaten or rolled into dumplings, boiled, dried, and eaten later in soup. What Shu Zhe calls *mantou* (today's solid steamed rolls) were probably stuffed *baozi* (steamed buns), *laowan* (wrapped rolls) may refer to *tangbao* (juicy steamed buns) filled with spicy minced meat, and *tangbing* (soup *bing*) were probably noodles in soup. Noodles were made either like today's knife-cut noodles, by rolling the dough flat and cutting it in strips, or perhaps by first baking it and then cutting it into strips like today's braised flat cakes; it is hard to say for certain. During the Three Kingdoms and Jin times, rich families often used water power to turn millstones, keeping part of the flour for their own use and possibly selling the rest. At that time, most water-powered mills were used to grind wheat into flour. Since rice and barley can be eaten without milling, the frequent appearance of these mills amply demonstrates the ubiquity of wheat consumption.

During the Three Kingdoms, the Qiang (proto-Tibetans) and Di planted a great deal of wheat, and the great Shu-Han army of General Jiang Wei (202–264) may even have eaten Tibetan wheat. Tang census records of Kucha and Hexi (west of the Yellow River, modern Shaanxi and Gansu) show wheat to be the main crop, thus demonstrating how highly devel-oped wheat agriculture was in western China at the time.

Wheat was first domesticated in the Fertile Crescent and spread east-ward, crossing Central Asia into China. On this account, the migration of Qiang and Di peoples into China from the Eastern Han onward probably helped to establish wheat products as the main staple of North China. Thus, from the Han through the Tang, many *bing* were already for sale in the public markets. One, called *hubing* (barbarian cakes), probably a kind of baked sesame cake, was very popular, and its name is proof of its foreign origin.

Many varieties of vegetables that were eaten with the wheat staples also entered China from the West. The most commonly seen today include spinach, rape greens, lettuce, celery, and carrots (called "barbarian turnips")—they came to China from the North-South dynasties through the Tang. Even more food plants came into China proper from the south. The *Record of Southern Flora* (*Nanfang caomu zhuang*) of Ji Han (263–306) lists the fruits and vegetables of southern China and Southeast Asia. Among the better known items are lychee fruit, betel nuts, and plantains. It goes without saying that Tang materia medica also contain many such lists of foreign plants.

We have already mentioned China's tradition of stir frying or sautéing in chapter 3. This cooking technique was even more widespread in medieval times. But the non-Chinese ethnic groups that immigrated from the north during the North-South dynasties and the south during the Tang dynasty continued to prefer their own methods of barbequing and roasting; this way of cooking also had considerable influence on Chinese cuisine.

During the North-South dynasties, northerners drank yogurt and ate beef and lamb, southerners drank tea and ate fish, and both ridiculed the other's customs. By the Tang dynasty, though regional differences remained, culinary customs had blended together and old divisions disappeared. Take tea for example: it was originally produced in southwestern China. Wang Bao's (fl. 73–49 B.C.E.) Han poem *The Slave's Contract* (*Tongyue*) already lists tea as a commercial market product of Sichuan. Drinking tea was extremely widespread in the south during the North-South dynasties and then gradually spread north. Lu Yu's (733–804) *Classic of Tea* (*Chajing*, 760), a major work on Tang tea culture, records the varieties of tea leaves and how to make tea. The most famous tea service set is that uncovered by archaeologists from the Gate of the Law Monastery's Underground Temple in Shaanxi Province near the Tang capital of Xi'an. It contains many utensils for grinding, filtering, and boiling tea. In general, Tang people drank tea after grinding the leaves into powder, sprinkling some into boiling water and boiling it for a while, sometimes adding other flavoring ingredients. The "ground tea" (*leicha*) that Hakka people drink today may be a remnant of this Tang method. At the end of the Eastern Han, there were many large epidemics, because diseases easily spread from the uncultivated, dank, humid jungles of the south. The practice of boiling water for tea serendipitously provided protection from disease germs; after tea drinking became common, China did not experience epidemics on such a large scale.

Wine was also a very important drink. Tao Yuanming loved to drink, and the wine he drank was probably brewed from millet. The Tang poet Li Bo was a celebrated drinker said to have an enormous capacity, perhaps because, not being brewed by distillation, the alcohol content of his grain-based wine was not very high. So-called thick wine (*choujiu*) drunk in Shaanxi today may be brewed by this old process; it is only slightly more alcoholic than sweet fermented rice (*jiuniang*).

Grapes entered China via the Silk Road as early as the Han. Census records from Tang Xizhou (modern Xinjiang) demonstrate that grapes were frequently cultivated there. Wang Han's (fl. 713) famous line—"Grape wine, sweet wine, in a moonlight cup"—is still read today and reminds us that the arts of brewing grape wine arrived from Central Asia. Female entertainers of non-Han origin were as numerous as flowers in the markets of Chang-an, and the young men who came to see them and order silver bottles of good wine were quite likely drinking grape wine. We do not know for certain what a "moonlight cup" refers to, but it might mean a cup made of glass. Glass was a Eurasian product, and the art of glassmaking was brought by He Chou to China during the Sui dynasty; from then on, Chinese glassblowing factories made household utensils.

To sum up, the dietary practices of the Tang were very different from those of the Han. All of the most important elements that entered China at this time completely blended into Chinese culinary culture and formed a single tradition of Chinese cuisine that everyone took for granted, no longer asking about the provenance of its individual elements.

As for clothing, the Han Chinese generally wore long robes with loose sleeves, did their hair up in various styles, and wore a variety of hats or caps. Although clothing of non-Han people (*hufu*) had already entered China by the time of King Wuling of Zhao (340–295 B.C.E.) during the Warring States period, and coarse hemp jackets and knee-length pants were worn by workers and servants, the Chinese mainly wore loose-fitting gowns. From the North-South dynasties through the Tang, the clothing of northern non-Chinese peoples arrived, and Chinese dress for both sexes gradually changed in the direction of narrow sleeves and close fitting open cross-collar upper garments and pants or skirts for men and women, respectively.

Of course, each age had its own popular fashions, and women's fashions changed frequently, just as they do today. The general direction of change in women's clothing was toward long skirts with flowing sleeves that fit the body better than Han dress. From the North-South dynasties to the Tang, when women went out horseback riding, they wore veils (*mili*) that covered their entire body. The veils gradually developed into long trailing skirts called *weimao*; by the Mid-Tang, they began to wear "barbarian hats" (*humao*) that revealed their faces and their hairdos. Women's loose sleeves and long skirts grew gradually less restrained, and by the Mid-Tang women's upper garments were characterized by décolletage in a most liberated fashion, bearing witness to the rather free and open lifestyle of Tang women. Men's headgear gradually changed from caps called *guan* to cloth, turbanlike head wraps called *putou* and then to hats with regular shapes and styles (modern *maozi*).

Han Chinese generally wore shoes called *lü*; those with thick soles were known as *xi*. When reinforced with a shoemaker's last (a device shaped like a foot for holding shoes), they were called *fuxi* (double xi). When they went outside, they wore wooden clogs (*ji*) with two spikes for walking on muddy roads. Leather military boots were worn by Western Zhou times, and the Han Chinese also made women's boots. During the North-South dynasties, southerners wore clogs; northerners wore leather boots with high tops for horseback riding. After the Mid-Tang, the boot tops became shorter and developed into our common low-top shoes. The clogs worn in the south gradually developed into a bootlike clog called *xueji*. The Japanese custom of wearing clogs today is one carried on from the Tang dynasty.

Most Han Chinese clothing was made from silk or hemp, but the well-to-do wore woolen coats in the winter. Leather was used only for armor and helmets and not for ordinary clothing. Wool and felt were used for tents but not for clothing. The Tang Chinese, however, wove wool clothing. An even more important change was the increasingly common use of cotton cloth in the south. Archaeology demonstrates that raw cotton could already be woven into fine cotton cloth and even velvet. The wool of the north and the cotton of the south gradually became the main materials used to make clothes for the general population; silk remained the chief material for more expensive clothing. With intricate methods of weaving and embroidery, Chinese silk products—including light silk, satin, damask, and gauze—developed into an elegant and refined art form.

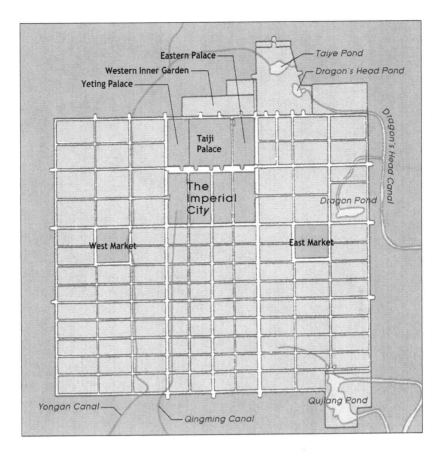

FIGURE 4.2 The Quarters of Tang Dynasty Chang-an

The North-South dynasties and the Tang already had multistory build-ings, built using wood-frame architecture. Buddhist pagodas appeared from outside to have eight or nine levels, and, inside, they actually did rise to at least three or four stories. Multistory houses were also not uncom-mon. Not only did the imperial family's palaces have spacious landscape gardens, but even rich commoners had large private gardens. Buddhist and Daoist temples also had such gardens, which ordinary people could walk in and enjoy: forerunners of today's public parks. Medieval cities, such as Luoyang in the Northern Wei and Chang-an in the Tang, were divided into square-shaped urban wards (*fang*). The Japanese city of Nara, modern Kyōto, was modeled on Tang Chang-an, and the urban unit *ma-chi* in modern Japanese cities is a remnant of Tang customs.

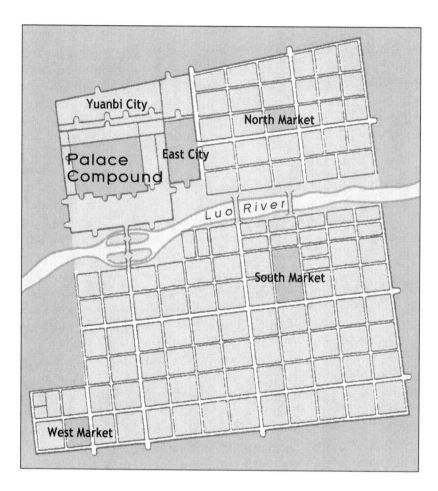

FIGURE 4.3 The Quarters of Tang Dynasty Luoyang

Styles of indoor living also underwent great changes during this time. The ancient Chinese sat on woven mats and had to take off their shoes when entering the house. Indoor furniture was primarily limited to low tables. During the Three Kingdoms, as northern customs entered China, beds (first called barbarian beds) and folding stools, both elevated above the floor, came into general use. In keeping with these innovations, traditional low tables were replaced by high tables similar to those in use today. The non-Chinese northern people wore boots and did not remove them upon entering a room; this practice soon spread over the entire country. Only Tang beds still had mats for sitting on and small low tables to lean upon. It was generally the custom to have a complete furniture set of tables, chairs, benches, beds with curtains, and pillows. In the early Tang, musicians still played sitting on mats on the floor, but the celebrated painted scroll "Night Revels of Han Xizai" by the Southern Tang (937–975) master Gu Hongzhong depicts the host, guests, and musicians sitting on chairs, clearly demonstrating the change that had taken place.

There were great changes in vehicle construction over this period. All ancient vehicles—whether war chariots manned by standing soldiers or comfortable carriages for riding while seated—had a single axle on a single shaft and were drawn by horses. Carts for carrying heavy loads were pulled by oxen or horses harnessed to both sides of the shaft. Beginning in the North-South dynasties, single-axle vehicles gradually disappeared, and all carts began to be pulled by animals hitched to multiple shafts. War chariots went out of use, but in the Tang, Fang Guan (fl. eighth century) did once employ the "Spring and Autumn war chariot strategy," using two thousand oxcarts to attack an enemy. The result was a great defeat that made Fang a laughingstock. During the North-South dynasties, northerners rode horses all the time; southerners feared horses as greatly as tigers. Tang elite men and women were both skilled equestrians, and polo (*po-luoqiu*, obviously a Central Asian word) was a common exercise for both sexes. The masses rode donkeys and mules, and in the Tang one could also rent a donkey for long trips, just as we rent cars today.

Chinese medieval ships and boats—junks—included everything from small sailing boats to multistoried ships, and their sails and masts could be seen everywhere on inland rivers and the open seas. Tang communication with foreign lands was highly developed, and foreign ships arriving from Persia, Arabia, India, and Southeast Asia docked at the great international port cities of Guangzhou (Canton), Yangzhou, and Mingzhou (modern Ningpo). Large-scale Chinese oceangoing ships already employed stern-mounted rudders. Indian ships seem to have imitated this directional rudder invented by the Chinese, but the Chinese never seem to have learned to use the Arab's three-cornered sail. During the North-South dynasties, there was even a "thousand-mile boat" powered by peddling like a bicycle, but it was never widely used and is only mentioned sporadically in Tang and Song records.

To sum up, everyday life in medieval China—dress, cuisine, dwelling, and transportation—was extremely different from that of ancient times. The key to the difference was primarily the influence of non-Chinese peoples from the north who continually entered China, for several hundred years bringing elements of Central Asian culture along the Silk Road. The scope of these changes over a period of seven to eight hundred years was both deep and broad, as all the changes beginning in the north eventually made their effects felt in the south. Perhaps only the changes taking place in China since 1840 can compare to these changes in the everyday lifestyle of medieval Chinese people.

7. Economic Transformation

Trade arises in human history whenever production develops for consumption and exchange with a market mechanism as its center of activity. The amount of consumption depends, of course, on the size of the population, and the market depends on the available transportation system. If there is a high volume of consumption, it will naturally stimulate both the volume and diversity of commodity production. The economic patterns of the first half of China's medieval period (the Southern Jin and North-South dynasties) and that of the second half (the Sui and Tang dynasties) were quite different. Both the conditions of population and transportation underwent great changes between the first and the second half of China's medieval period.

China was divided during the Jin and North-South dynasties: the "five Hu ravaged China," the north was pitted against the south, warfare was endemic, and the population perforce decreased. Furthermore powerful great families, whether Chinese or non-Chinese, took over land and populations and created self-enclosed communities. The result of such a population structure was a return to a natural economy (one in which money is not used in the exchange of resources). The Han dynasty had a relatively developed market economy, one based on money as the medium of exchange, especially in the cities. In the first half of the medieval period, however, silk and grain became mediums of exchange as well commodities of consumption. The economic functions of the cities declined, while production and the limited amount of exchange that remained was centered in the farm villages. Although there were still some handicraft products like porcelain and silk items, both the quality and the volume of commodities at this time did not compare with those of the second half of the medieval period.

The economy of the Sui and Tang was able to develop very rapidly given two factors: population growth and ease of transportation. The former provided a market for consumptions; the latter strengthened the mechanism of exchange.

To consider population growth first, the census systems of the North-South dynasties were defective. The number of people was out of sync with the number of registered households; naturally this was because of deliberate concealment to avoid of taxation, corvée labor, or military service. Furthermore, since there were several different political regimes operating at any given time, there was really no such thing as an overall population figure. Once the Sui dynasty was established, they conducted a new census in order to include more people. In 606, there were approximately nine million households and forty-six million people in the entire country. These figures should represent the population when the North-South dynasties were united as one polity. The census figures of several periods after that had their ups and downs, with the peak population occurring during the *kaiyuan* and *tianbao* reign periods (713–756) of Tang Xuanzong. The "Food and Traded Goods" chapter of the *Encyclopedic History of Institutions* (Tongdian, 801) states, however, that the real number of households should have been thirteen to fourteen million. Using this figure to calculate the population at the same ratio as the 606 figures would produce an overall population of almost eighty million people during the High Tang! During this period, before the breakdown of the equal-field system (*juntian zhidu*) of government land tenure and allocation, most people had ample means of support, and their consumption capacity was naturally much greater than during the chaotic age of division. There were several wars early in the Tang, but from the reign of Empress Wu (r. 683–705) to the *kaiyuan* era (713–741), the nation was at peace, government income was high, and the state was quite prosperous. This large population base and high volume of consumption stimulated productive capacity and led to both a higher quality and a greater volume of commodities.

The second condition favorable to market growth was the transportation network. We can observe the contemporary network of roads by noting the Sui and Tang establishment of administrative subdivisions. The Qin and Han took commanderies as the largest unit, with several counties per commandery. They also sent central government officers—censors (*yushi*) in the Qin and inciting officers (*cishi*) in the Han—out to inspect the work of the local chief magistrates. The Eastern Han *cishi* developed into the chief magistrates of provincial regions (*zhou*) who lived out their terms in the place they governed; their title was later changed to *zhoumu* (district pastor). The Jin and North-South dynasties followed without change the Han system of districts, commanderies, and counties, a system that divided the country into large and small administrative units.

In the Sui and Tang, the circuit (*dao*) appeared as another such unit. At various times for various administrative reasons, the Sui rulers established several temporary circuits, such as Hebei *dao*, Henan *dao*, and Huainan *dao*. As the name implied, these circuits were temporary extensions of the central government that extended forward along transportation routes. From the examples just mentioned, we can see that they moved forward along roads to the north or south of the Yellow and Huai rivers. Before the founding of the Eastern Han, Emperor Guangwu (6 B.C.E.–57 C.E.) regarded the entire north as one northern *dao* and the entire south as one southern *dao*. Among the Tang dynasty's local administrative subdivisions, the circuits were regarded as geographical units. Tang Taizong (r. 626–649) established ten circuits. After that, the number of circuits increased or decreased; sometimes there were as many as fifteen or seventeen, more or less planned out following mountain valleys or river channels.

The fifteen circuits during Tang Xuanzong's reign (712–756) included the Chang-an capital territory, the Luoyang capital territory, Henan, Hebei, Hedong, Longyou, Shannan Dong, Shannan Xi, Jiannan, Guannei, Huainan, Jiangnan Dong, Jiangnan Xi, Qianzhong, and Lingnan. Chang-an and Luoyang formed the center of two overlapping transportation networks. Yizhou (modern Chengdu) and Yangzhou made up another fan-shaped radiation from the southwest to the southeast.

The Tang dynasty once had five capitals (*jing*) and five cities (*du*), and they established and abandoned them at different times. In addition to Chang-an and Luoyang, there were five large metropolitan areas: Fengxiang, Jiangling, Taiyuan, Hezhong (Suzhou), and Yizhou. These large cities were each the center of a secondary transportation network. On another level, Hongzhou, Tanzhou, Daming, Suzhou, and Guangzhou made up a further set of local centers. Other cities with large populations that occupied various strategic points grew into prosperous busy urban areas that made up another level of transportation centers. In short, during the period of its greatest flourishing in the *kaiyuan* and *tianbao* eras, the

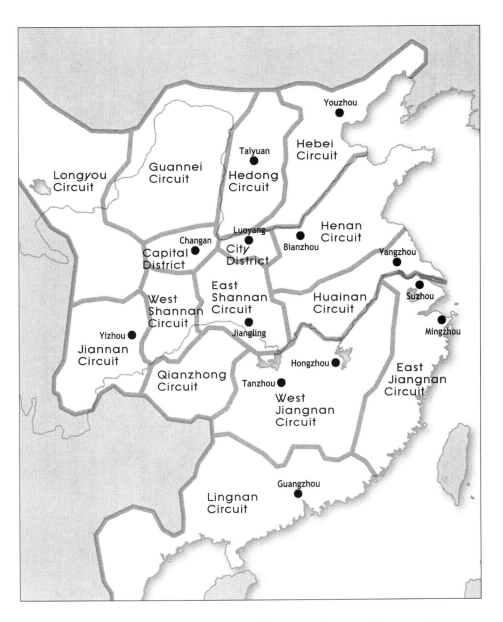

FIGURE 4.4 The Fifteen Circuits (Dao) and Important Commercial Regions of the Tang Dynasty

Tang dynasty had four transportation centers linking the entire country into one vast network of roads.

Besides the overland road system, there were also many navigable rivers and manmade shipping canals. For example, the Tongjiqu Canal, from Luoyang to the Huai River, completed in 605, and the Yongjiqu Canal, from south of the Qin River to the Yellow River and north to Zhuojun (modern Beijing), completed in 608, brought together different water systems. People moved and goods were transported over this vast transportation network, which provided extremely beneficial conditions for market exchange. Government post stations and rest houses serving civilian travelers were fully provided for in conjunction with this transport network, and there were mules for hire for long journeys. During such prosperous and peaceful times, travelers did not need to carry provisions or weapons for self-defense. Long-distance travel was extremely convenient, and goods flowed freely around the country.

Silk remained the most commonly traded commodity in the Sui and Tang. Under the equal-field system, the peasants received private fields (*yongyetian*) that they could retain and residential garden fields (*yuan-zhaitian*), which were primarily mulberry fields, with some left over for household use. Peasants paid their taxes according to the *zu-yong-diao* system of taxes: in grain (*zu*), in kind (*yong*), and for corvée exemption (*diao*). *Diao* taxes were paid in silks, cotton, and hemp. Thus silk was produced all over the country. During the North-South dynasties, silk functioned as both commodity and currency. The Sui and Tang monetary system was based on fairly reliable copper cash, but silk could still circulate as a compensatory payment for goods or as salary for work performed. Silk was a very important item of foreign trade and for the bestowal of gifts. Chinese silk was transported by camel caravan over the Silk Road to far-off Central Asia, where it was processed and sold all over Europe. The Chinese also traded silk for horses on their western and northern frontiers. In general, all these exchanges were of bolts of raw or coarsely woven silk; when the peasants paid their taxes in silk, they may have worked it a bit, but it should probably not be considered a genuine manufactured commodity.

Naturally, when silks became trade goods, they were more carefully manufactured. The central government's production of silk products was primarily assigned to the Directorate for Imperial Manufactures, while small-scale private production was carried out as a cottage industry and generally performed by peasant women. Large-scale silk workshops carried on more professional production, and some of them had up to five or six hundred looms on which highly skilled workers wove silk damask.

The Tang dynasty's textile industry had a well-defined division of labor. The manufacturing process of the Weaving and Dyeing Office under the Directorate for Imperial Manufactures was divided into four departments—weaving, cording, spinning, and dyeing. Products were also ranked according to quality: there were eight kinds of thick, loosely woven silk called *juan* and nine varieties of cotton cloth. Many varieties of cloth were produced, including at least cotton; *juan*; coarse silk (*shi*); fine gauze (*sha*); damask (*ling*); coarse gauze (*luo*); satin (*jin*); fine, thin silk (*qi*); and coarse hemp cloth (*he*). All of these were further divided according to manufacturing techniques and workmanship. To give one example, in Ye County, Henan, they had the "three twists and five knots" weaving process, employing eight looms to produce "eight-shuttle-damask." Contemporary weaving techniques could easily handle simple to complex weaves from flats, to twills, to satin quality; using the weft (horizontal) threads to create flower patterns was also common. Archaeology has unearthed many examples of Tang textiles whose delicate weaving and superb embroidery testify to the maturity of their textile arts. The gauzes discovered in the Gate of the Law Monastery in Shaanxi, for example, are so light and thin that you can make a fist around several yards of fabric!

Tang textiles were not limited to silks. Archaeology has uncovered many examples demonstrating that the products of cotton-, hemp-, and wool-weaving techniques were of very high quality. Tang cotton cloth was called "white layered cloth." Cotton weaving began in the western regions and gradually diffused to southwestern and central China. In Emperor Xuanzong's time, "white layered cloth" was already on sale in the markets of Chang-an, but it was thought to be from Guangdong and Guangxi and was called "Guiguan cloth," from Guiguan in Lingnan. Woolen cloth was used for floor rugs; softer wools were also made into clothes. All these textiles could be dyed by various techniques, such as pressing between two boards, wax dyeing, and tie dyeing. The finished products, like the Buddhist banners found at Dunhuang, were quite striking and beautiful products of handicraft art.

Tea, wine, and sugar were three more important agricultural products. As mentioned above, Wang Bao's Han poem *The Slave's Contract* mentions tea being sold at markets in Wuyang in Sichuan (modern Pengshan County) during the Western Han, and drinking tea was widespread in the south during the Jin dynasties. Growing and processing tea became professionalized during the Tang just as tea workshops separated off from cottage industries—there were famous locally produced teas throughout the Jiannan and Jiangnan regions. There were very many varieties of tea, which were sold in special tea markets. Bo Juyi's celebrated poem "Lute Song" (*pipa xing*) mentions a tea merchant from Xunyang who traveled to Fuliang (both in modern Jiangxi) to buy tea and did not return home for months. The lute player tells him: "From morning to dusk, my colors faded. . . . Grown old, I married a merchant. / Merchants value profit, are indifferent to separation. / Last month he went off to buy tea in Fuliang, / And left me to wait in an empty boat at the mouth of the river."

As a valuable commodity, the volume of tea sold was also quite large. The Tang government levied a 10 percent tea tax wherever tea was produced or transported. According to the "Food and Traded Goods" chapter of the Tang histories, Emperor Dezong began taxing tea in 793, and four hundred thousand strings of cash could be collected in just one year. Thus, the value of tea sold must have amounted to at least four million strings of cash.

Wine brewing was also a long-standing Chinese technology, grains having been made into wine (or liquor) since ancient times. Tang viticulture and perhaps enology derived from Kucha in Central Asia. Wines and liquors were also such valuable commodities that early on the Tang government levied taxes on them as well.

Ancient Chinese sweeteners included honey, maltose, and sugarcane juice. The technique of refining sugar from sugarcane was introduced from India at the beginning of the Tang. Sugar could not be produced as a peasant cottage industry but required rather large-scale factories, and thus the process was a completely professional operation, from refining to marketing.

Ceramic ware or porcelain, known to the world as china, is a Chinese specialty. As early as the Neolithic era, the technique of pottery making developed in different places around the world. But China particularly developed the industrial art of firing fine white kaolin clay at very high temperatures and painting on glazes to produce semitransparent, true porcelain ware. In the medieval era, Chinese porcelains were sold everywhere from South Asia in the west to Korea and Japan in the east, and the artisans of these various locals tried unsuccessfully to copy Chinese methods of ceramic production. The Yue kiln (in Yuezhou, Zhejiang) already made true porcelain during the Han; in the early medieval period, southern celadon (grayish jade green) porcelain was brought to a very fine quality, but not much was produced, and it did not become widespread. Ceramic production was very highly developed during the Sui and Tang, when techniques for controlling kiln temperatures and glazing reached an extremely high proficiency. There were famous kilns in both in the north and south, the most celebrated being the white porcelain of Xing kiln in the north (modern Hebei) and the celadon of the Yue kiln in the south.

Many other areas—Yaozhou, Dingzhou, and Ruzhou in the north and Dingzhou, Wuzhou, Yuezhou, Shouzhou, and Hongzhou in the south— all had famous kilns. During the medieval period, there were very many northern kilns, but in general northern ceramics gradually declined, and the south eventually became the chief ceramic manufacturing area. This shift was aided by the greater availability of high-quality kaolin clays in the south. That there were still some famous kilns in the north in Tang times was probably because the people were well off and market demand encouraged the manufacture of ceramic goods. After the An Lushan Rebellion, the center of Tang economic activity shifted south. The harbors for sea transport of ceramics were all in the south, and there were ceramic industries in Zhejiang, Jiangxi, Fujian, Guangdong, and Funan. This overseas trade supported the best southern kilns; the northern kilns fell behind.

Porcelain production is a very specialized technology that requires good-sized factory operations. Being further limited by the availability of suitable clays and abundant fuel for stoking the fires, ceramic kilns were naturally concentrated in certain locations that possessed all the necessary conditions, and thus these regions became porcelain-producing areas. Each of these regional kilns also had its own very characteristic product. Because porcelain was both heavy and easily broken, overland transport of ceramics was too costly. It was necessary to ship this precious cargo on inland rivers to ports, where they could be transferred to oceangoing vessels. Inland southern areas of porcelain manufacture were generally located near river-transport facilities, as Hongzhou and Yuezhou goods were shipped along the Gan and Xiang rivers respectively to Quanzhou and Guangzhou, where they were put out to sea.

Paper is a well-known Chinese invention. History records that Cai Lun (ca. 63–121) invented paper during the Eastern Han, but archaeological finds indicate that paper already existed during the Western Han, and there are ancient characters that may mean "paper" going back as far as the Warring States period. Bamboo writing slips were still in use during the Jin dynasties, in the third to fifth centuries C.E., and thus paper was not yet widely employed. Paper was, however, in universal use during the Sui and Tang, with government and private paper factories throughout the country, most of them in the south. The Tang government ordered that paper be presented to the throne from many areas, including Julu (modern Hebei), Puzhou (Shandong), as well as modern Jiangsu, Zhejiang, Anhui, Hunan, Sichuan, and Guangdong. Chinese papermaking materials included rattan, bamboo, moss, hemp, kudzu cloth, paper mulberry bark, and winter daphne bark; used cotton and old netting could also be employed in manufacturing paper pulp. Papers from different locals had their own special characteristics and usages.

Papermaking techniques were divided into the production of raw paper (*shengzhi*) and finished paper (*shouzhi*). Raw paper consisted of pulp that was merely spread out and baked to dry. Finished paper was produced by rolling, pounding, sizing (adding powdered starch), and applying glue. Papers for special uses could be made by adding colors or sprinkling on gold dust. Strong hemp-based paper was long lasting and was used for official documents and imperial orders. Bamboo-based paper was light and smooth and was used for writing letters. Waxed and died yellow, paper could resist spoilage by insects; it could even be made into clothing and armor to be used in funeral rituals.

Chinese methods for making paper very quickly spread to Korea and Japan, where many traditional papermaking techniques are still used today. During the reign of Tang Xuanzong, General Gao Xianzhi (d. 755) was defeated by an Arab army at the Battle of Talas in 751. Tang artisans skilled in papermaking were taken captive, and their art was transmitted to the Arab world. Soon after, paper made in Samarkand (in modern Uzbekistan) became famous throughout Eurasia, replacing deer skin and Egyptian papyrus. From that point on, the techniques of making paper gradually spread throughout Europe.

In this section, we have basically traced China's medieval economic situation from the stagnation of the first half to the last half's lively economic activity. The motive force behind these changes was a combination of the reunification of China accompanied by stable internal conditions, an increase in population and concomitant consumer demand, and sufficient natural resources, labor power, and a large and convenient transportation network. The consumer demand of China's internal market was enough to stimulate production and lead to a prosperous economy.

After Han Wudi, the productive forces of the Han dynasty were in part contained in peasant cottage industries, but government factories occupied a dominant position. By contrast, Tang consumer products such as silks, ceramics, paper, tea, wine, and sugar were primarily produced in private factories, and the government collected taxes and tributes from these enterprises. These private, nongovernmental enterprises concentrated both labor power and capital and carried on a tradition of cumulative technological improvement. Given market conditions and the availability of raw materials, particular industries were usually concentrated in particular geographical locations, and this distribution adumbrated the future development of commercial cities after the Song dynasty. Possessing a sufficiently large internal market, silks, ceramics, and paper gradually became available for export overland and on the high seas, and thus the Chinese economy gradually joined other Asian economies to form a pan-Asian economic sphere.

Within this sphere, something similar to modern technology transfers took place. For example, Chinese learned the art of glassmaking, sugar production, and grape wine enology from Central Asia, while Central and Western Asians learned paper-, ceramic-, and silk-making techniques from China. Korea and Japan adopted Chinese industrial arts on an even greater scale and fully integrated them into their own cultural traditions. During the Tang dynasty—the second half of China's medieval period—trade and technology transfers outpaced China's internal economy, and the overall Chinese economy blended into a larger Asian economy.

8. Ethnic Relations in Medieval China

During the second half of the Eastern Han, non-Chinese ethnic groups, collectively labeled *Hu*, gradually entered China from the west and the north as a prelude to the "five Hu ravage China" (*wuhu luanhua*) era. At the same time, the Han Chinese population of the Yellow River basin began migrating southward toward the Yangzi and Huai river valleys and Lingnan, initiating a huge population shift from which South China emerged as China's main population center. (I use "Han" throughout this section to indicate ethnic Chinese. Some contemporary scholars prefer the earlier "Hua." Either term refers to an ethnic group that, like "white" or "Caucasian Europeans" and "Americans," is made up of many diverse strains absorbed over a long period of time.)

The Xiongnu Qaghan Kuansai, who came to China in 33 B.C.E., during the Eastern Han, to take Wang Zhaojun as his bride, led the first migration of pastoral people into China. The movement of Qiang (proto-Tibetan) and Di peoples into China was a more salient phenomenon. The Qiang, who lived west of China, originally did not have a complex leadership structure, just local strongmen who acted as tribal chieftains. Such scattered groups of non-Chinese people often did corvée labor for the Han. There were many large-scale epidemics during the second half of the Han, during which the Han Chinese population decreased, and these Qiang people stepped in to provide labor to clear border lands for great Han families in Xizhou (modern Gansu). Later on, according to the biographical sections of the *History of the Later Han (Hou Hanshu)*, the Qiang moved eastward from the western provinces into the "Land Between the Passes" (Guanzhong), following the river valleys of modern Shanxi all the way to the foothills of the Taihang Mountains running down the eastern edge of the loess plateau in Henan, Shanxi, and Hebei provinces. In this area of great Han Chinese population decline, the Qiang provided much needed labor power. Several other non-Chinese peoples besides the Qiang and Di entered the Chinese labor market at this time; these included the Xiongnu and the Jie people, who also migrated into China proper looking for work in order to survive after the breakup of their tribal groupings. A considerable degree of cultural conflict and intermingling was of course implicit in this ethnic dispersal and gradual movement into China. The non-Chinese peoples who entered China undoubtedly accepted Han Chinese culture, but not completely, and thus China's northern frontier provinces were home to considerable cultural diversity (today we would say they became multicultural).

Liu Yuan (?–310 C.E.), the founder of the Former Zhao (one of the Sixteen Kingdoms), has always been the model for non-Chinese state building. After immigrating to China, he reunited his tribal group, and, although he became a Xiongnu leader, his authority was based on support from the Han regime. Liu Yuan was well versed in the Chinese classics, put himself forward as a descendent of the Han practice of "peace and kinship" (*heqin*) marriage alliances with non-Chinese groups, and even usurped the dynastic surname Liu. His actions bear witness to both the acculturation and the cultural conflicts of that time.

The life experience of Shi Le (274–333), the founder of the Later Zhao, is another fascinating example. This youth of the Jie people once served as a tenant farmer for a Han great family in Bingzhou (modern Hebei and Shanxi). At that time, there were as many as a thousand such Xiongnu and other non-Chinese tenants working in some provinces in the Taiyuan (Shanxi) area. During the chaos before the establishment of the Later Zhao, Shi Le tried to lure some other non-Chinese to follow him into Jizhou (modern Hebei), ostensibly to look for work but with the real intention of selling them into slavery. His plan backfired when he himself was taken prisoner, slapped in irons, and sold as a slave! These stories of Liu Yuan and Shi Le clearly demonstrate the confused process of change in North China (Shanxi and Hebei) at a time when various ethnic groups were falling apart or trying to reconstitute themselves and establish Chinese-style states.

When the northern Hu peoples dispersed and made their way into China, they set up kingdoms with names like Han, Zhao, and Qin and usurped the Chinese title of emperor—while at the same time calling themselves Great Qaghan. The composition of these "state" regimes were not purely Xiongnu, Jie, or Di, because the populations they ruled over were of mixed ethnic origin.

The situation of the Xianbei (Särbi) people was different from that of the others. They were originally an ethnic group living in the northeast that had already moved into Youzhou and Jizhou (modern Liaoxi and eastern Hebei) during Wei-Jin times. When the Sima notables disputed the throne in a civil war known as the Revolt of the Eight Princes (291–306), several groups of Särbi joined the fighting, and the Murong group established a state in North China. The Xianbei scope of operations was quite extensive—their descendents now live all over Inner Mongolia. In yet another example of ethnic blending, after 311, a portion of the Murongs moved west into the area of present-day Gansu and Ningxia, joined with the Dangxiang Qiang, and formed a new mixed-ethnic Mongolian-speaking group known as the Tuyuhun.

Another group related to the Särbi (Xianbei) was the Tuoba (Tabgatch), who gradually migrated from their ancestral home in the Greater Khingan Mountains into today's Inner Mongolia. The various non-Chinese groups having entered the central plains, no powerful pastoral peoples were left south of the Gobi. The Tuoba (Tabgatch) took advantage of this opportunity to create a large tribal federation, move into China, establish the Northern Wei state, effectively controlling North China. The Tuoba represented an amalgamation of different ethnic groups both before and after establishing the Northern Wei. It was the general rule on the steppes that whenever a powerful group appeared, other smaller ethnic groups would coalescence around it to establish a collective ethnic identity. The Xiongnu, the Tujue (Türks), and the Mongols all followed this pattern.

Northern Han Chinese assisted in the establishment of the Northern Wei dynasty, and Chinese great families worked with the Tuoba (Tabgatch) rulers on the basis of their shared interests in maintaining a stable dynasty. At the same time, there was a high degree of mutual assimilation between Chinese and Tabgatch cultures. It reached its apogee when Emperor Xiaowen moved the Northern Wei capital to Luoyang and became almost completely Sinified. By the same token, the steppe culture also exerted a considerable influence on Han Chinese culture—sitting on chairs at tables being only one striking example from everyday life. This process of assimilation was aided by the frequency of Chinese and non-Chinese intermarriages, leading to mixed ethnicity; the blood lines of both the Sui and Tang ruling houses soon consisted of Han and non-Han elements.

The Han Chinese living in the north were considerably acculturated to non-Han cultures. By the end of the Northern Wei, the Tabgatch soldiers who had remained behind in the Six Garrisons of their northern area called Dai, holding on to their old ethnic customs, were quite alienated from the Tabgatch who had entered China and greatly assimilated to Han Chinese culture. When the dynasties of the Northern Zhou and the Northern Qi split off from the Northern Wei, the Yuwen family of the former tried hard to combine the Tabgatch and Han Chinese cultures, while the Gao family of the latter, said to be Han Chinese from Bohai, paradoxically promoted non-Han over Han culture so much that the Sinicization of Hebei was not as great as that in the Guanlong area of modern Shanxi, Shaanxi, and Gansu. During the Sui and Tang, Hebei was often considered non-Chinese territory, and it was not surprising that the An Lushan Rebellion started in Yuyang, Hebei, in 755. The 524 Rebellion of the Six Garrisons was also an attack on a Chinese-style state by a people from the steppe. Significantly, among the Six Garrisons troops there were not only

Tabgatch but also other non-Chinese peoples and even "barbarized" Han Chinese. The Six Garrisons' invasion of Luoyang can thus be interpreted as a conflict between peoples developing in opposite directions, bringing about another rift between Chinese and non-Chinese.

Following the time-honored pattern of pastoral steppe peoples—confederation, breakup, separation, and reconfederation—different regimes of non-Chinese peoples, such as the Rouran (related to the Särbi/Xianbei) and Tujue (Türks), repeatedly rose and fell suddenly on the steppes north and northwest of China. These steppe peoples continued to have both peaceful and warlike relations with the Chinese regimes. Some of the recently defeated peoples would even submit to Chinese governance, settle in China, and become Sinified. The Tang government frequently established loose-reign prefectures (*jimizhoufu*) to accommodate such non-Chinese peoples.

There were quite a few such immigrant prefectures at that time, the greatest number of them in places including Lingzhou, Xiazhou, Shuozho, Daizhou, Youzhou, and Jizho in present-day Shaanxi, Gansu, north Hebei, and southern Inner Mongolia. There were as many as a hundred such immigrant settlements in some of these areas, accommodating peoples such as the Tujue, Tiele, Dangxiang Qiang, Tuyuhun, Sogdians, Mohe, Xi, Shiwei (proto-Mongolian), Khitan (Chinese Qidan), and Koreans from the kingdom of Silla.

During the early Tang, when the dynasty was very strong, many non-Chinese peoples paid allegiance to it and also settled inside the boundaries of China even without being given a loose-reign prefecture. For example, in 636, during Tang Taizong's reign, the Eastern Tujue (Türk) leader Ashina She-er led some ten thousand troops to surrender to the Tang and became a Tang general in Lingzhou; Li Simo, another Ashina Türk, was granted the surname Li and settled with many people in the border prefectures of Shengzhou and Xiazhuo. When the Tuyuhun were defeated by the Tubu, the Chinese settled them in Shuofang and several areas east of the Yellow River. During the *kaiyuan* era (713–741), many other peoples, such as the Huihe, Pugu, Tonglo, and Bayegu, also settled in Shuofang and several areas south of the Yellow River. In sum, there were non-Chinese peoples living throughout an area from Shaanxi and Gansu in the west to modern eastern Mongolia, northeastern Hebei, and western Liaoning in the east. Some of them settled as a coherent group and some as independent families. In the end, most of these non-Chinese peoples learned settled agriculture, became Sinified, and melded into the Chinese nation.

Before the process of assimilation was complete, however, many of these non-Chinese peoples provided soldiers for the Chinese empire. Generals on the Tang borders were almost all descendents of non-Chinese people, as were the generals on both sides of the An Lushan Rebellion. An Lushan was himself a mixed-blood non-Chinese of Sogdian- or Iranian-Turkish origin from Yingzhou (modern Liaoning). Even before the rebellion, the military regions of Lulong and Fanyang, near modern Beijing, were all governed by non-Chinese generals. At the same time, the generals who fought for the government, such as Li Guangbi, Pugu Huai-en, and Geshu Han were all non-Chinese. General Guo Ziyi's Shuofang army had to have military assistance from the Huihe people in order to put down the rebellion.

After the death of An Lushan and Shi Siming, military leaders in Hebei continued to venerate them and to occupy many garrison towns. Although they ostensibly acknowledged the Tang state, the Hebei area was so "barbarized" that it was like a foreign country—the common people had never even heard of Confucius. The Turko-Mongol Khitan (Qidan) arose at the end of the Tang, and in 938, during the Five Dynasties, Emperor Shi Jingtang of the Later Jin ceded sixteen northern prefects to them.

From that point on, throughout several hundred years of the Khitan Liao, Ruzhen Jin, and Mongol Yuan conquest dynasties Hebei was ruled by non-Chinese peoples. The essential nature of the An Lushan Rebellion, then, was similar to that of the 524 Rebellion of the Six Garrisons—it was another example of a "barbarized" (huhua) area attacking the Han Chinese central government. The rebellion being put down with the aid of non-Chinese troops meant that this war was actually one fought on Chinese soil between different non-Chinese armies.

Ethnic relations were extremely complicated in the northwest. The Tang loose-reign prefectures were all under the nominal command of the Protectorates General of Anxi ("pacify the West," western Gansu), but this did not reflect reality, because the Tang central government's commands could hardly reach so far. The fortunes of the local Tujue, Huihe, Sogdians, and so on rose and fell all along the great Silk Road, which ran some six hundred miles along the Gansu Corridor (also called the Hexi, or West of the Yellow River, Corridor) west from Lanzhou to the Jade Gate (the border between Gansu and Xinjiang). This area, anciently known

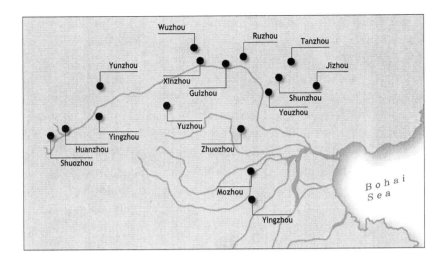

FIGURE 4.5 The Sixteen Northern Prefects of Yanyun

as Liangzhou (modern Gansu), was of tremendous strategic importance to China and was always guarded by Chinese garrison armies so that, no matter what changes occurred in the western regions west of Gansu, the Chinese could always maintain the upper hand along the Gansu Corridor. Even after the 311 chaos in the north, Lü Guang (338–399), an ethnic Di from Liangzhou, was able to found the Later Liang dynasty on China's western frontier and preserve Chinese culture and institutions—a feat that matches that of the Nanzhao in Yunnan.

Throughout the Tubu expansion in this area, Shazhou and Guazhou (modern Dunhuang and Xinjiang) were able to protect themselves, given the penetration of Han Chinese culture along the Hexi Corridor.

Another similar example was Qarahoja (Chinese Gaochang, modern Xinjiang). Living in an environment shared by a multitude of non-Chinese peoples, the Qu family regime of Qarahoja managed to preserve Tang customs for a long time. Archaeological evidence indicates that they even practiced the equal-field system of land tenure. Since it was an extremely important place on the Silk Road where many Han Chinese continuously resided, it is not surprising that Qarahoja was able to preserve so many Chinese ways.

Many non-Chinese peoples also immigrated into the Sichuan basin. During the Three Kingdoms' Shu-Han dynasty, when Zhu Geliang opened up the area of Nanzhong and made soldiers out of the "fierce" Man "barbarians," many of the Man had immigrated into Hanzhong (modern Shaanxi) from the north. When the Shu-Han collapsed, many Shu people moved southward. The Xue clan, for example, moved into Shanxi and became a powerful family during the three Jin dynasties. On the eve of the destruction of the Western Jin, many Di and Qiang people moved into Sichuan and settled throughout the areas recently depopulated by the exodus of Shu people. During the Tang, Jiannan in Sichuan was known as a rich and fertile area; its importance as a defensive backup evidenced by the emperors Xuanzong and Xizong (r. 873–888), who both fled into Sichuan to avoid danger. When the rising Tubu established the kingdom of Nanzhao in 738, Sichuan was again on the front line of the Tang empire. When the Tubu raided Jiannan, they captured Han Chinese and took them back with them. Even in the absence of a strong enemy, the non-Chinese tribal peoples living throughout Sichuan often captured one another's people and sold them into slavery. After being sold on several times, a person could never return to his native place. The Yi people of the southwest, for example, were once divided into the Black Yi and the White Yi, the Blacks being the masters and the Whites the servants, a situation that certainly resulted from the buying and selling of neighboring peoples into slavery during this medieval era.

South of the Yangzi, the ethnic situation was quite different from it was in the north. From the Eastern Han on, northerners continually migrated southward, and the southern aboriginals the Han Chinese encountered at the time were mostly called Yue—a generic term for non-Han peoples of South China. During the Eastern Jin and Nanzhao, finer distinctions were made—southern peoples were then divided into Xi, Dong, Man, and Liao. Neither the physical nor linguistic characteristics of these peoples can be readily ascertained today. Generally speaking, these southern aborigines were agriculturalists, and they were rapidly acculturated under the relentless pressure of the more powerful Han Chinese culture and economic forces; they soon became part of the registered, taxable population. There were always some groups, however, who lived deep in the mountain valleys or who deliberately moved on to escape the regions settled by the Han Chinese—these groups made up the post-Tang Miao (Hmong), Man, Yao, Dong, Li (Hlai, Sai), and Yu people, who lived on small marginal plots of land. Under these conditions, ethnic relations in the south were much less confrontational than they were in the north;

some clashes were inevitable as the Han Chinese moved south, but they were not nearly as violent.

As the Han Chinese moved south, they divided into early settlers and latecomers, and conflict often broke out between the two. The Jiangnan (south of the Yangzi) area was already well populated during the Three Kingdoms; after the catastrophe of 311, the new southern immigrants established the Eastern Jin regime. At first, the original inhabitants of this Wu area (modern Jiangsu) were quite unhappy about northern immigrants taking over. It was only the conciliatory policies of the statesman Wang Dao (276–339)—especially his employment of local notables—that made the Wu people acquiesce to Eastern Jin rule. The great families moving south with the Jin were not allowed to buy up land in Wujun (modern Suzhou); they could only move further south to develop Kuaiji—another example of conflict between earlier and later immigrants.

If not traveling as an intact clan or lineage, these northern immigrants would form ad hoc groups. Refugee or migrant commanders would emerge at the head of these new collectives; when the group settled somewhere, these men would take on the role of powerful local leaders. Orders from the central governments of the southern dynasty of Song, Qi, Liang, and Chen usually could not reach present-day Jiangxi and Hunan, not to mention Guangdong and Fujian. The northern migrants generally moved south along the Xiang and Gan river valleys or split off on various tributaries, forming a treelike pattern as they opened up the fertile agricultural areas to cultivation. Towns and cities grew up one after another at the most important intersections along the route. The aboriginal peoples generally lived in the countryside and the mountainous regions that made up the gaps in this network of roads. The same language was spoken along the main roads, but dialects of Chinese that were highly influenced by aboriginal languages proliferated in the countryside. The route followed by today's Kejia (guest households) people followed the main road, and their tense relations with the indigenes along the way from 311 on remains an element of their collective memory.

There were many different ethnic groups living throughout Guangzhou and Jiaozhou (an area including northern and central Vietnam and parts of Guangxi); in medieval times, the Han Chinese could not penetrate very deeply into their lands. Each village settlement had its own powerful leader, many of whom accepted Chinese government titles, in effect creating another kind of loose-reign prefecture—the Xians of

Gaoliangzhou being a prime example. In Yunnan, Zhuge Liang could only cooperate with the aboriginal leaders; the best that could be done was to give Meng Hu (of Nanzhong) an official position in Chengdu. Local powers were deeply entrenched and not easily shaken. I'll discuss the kingdom of Nanzhao later, as part of the international situation during China's medieval era.

To sum up this section, in the medieval period, China experienced seven to eight hundred years of ethnic realignment. During this time, the Han (*Hanren*) population of China absorbed many cultural elements from numerous non-Han peoples from both north and south and emerged as a new and very large, pluralistic nation (or people, *minzu*). This people or nation was not so much a race defined by blood relationships (a term that is much less in use in today's scientific community) but a people both identified by a unified cultural tradition and exhibiting great cultural diversity.

9. China's Medieval Foreign Relations

At the beginning of its medieval period, China was subject to non-Chinese (*Hu*) incursions from the north, east, and west, and the northern frontier was a frequent battleground. At first, these non-Chinese peoples invaded China just after the breakup of their own organized political power (the Xiongnu) or before they had actually established any large-scale political organization (the Qiang). Peoples such as the Xianbei (Särbi) and Tuoba (Tabgatch) that entered China later did so while in the process of forming large political entities. Some of them, adapting to the Chinese imperial model, went through a long process of reorganization: they either left the tribal society behind and organized themselves on the Chinese model or continued their own cultural traditions (the northern Särbi Six Garrisons), attacked the Sinicized central government, and underwent a second Sinicization.

For all these reasons, in the early medieval period, China's foreign relations on its northern borders was subject to alternating pressures. Every time the current major steppe power entered China, a new ruling power would appear behind it to reorganize the remaining steppe people. As an obvious example, after the Tuoba entered China, the Rouran and the Tujue (Türks) rose up in the southern Gobi, and the Sogdians became active in Central Asia. Not yet having grown into powerful steppe empires, these newly risen powers constituted a border threat to contemporary China but had not yet formed a multistate system. The Northern Wei and the Northern Zhou and Northern Qi that followed it continued to practice the traditional Chinese tactic of making alliances with distant peoples to attack those who are near—using the Tujue to control the Rouran, for example. By the Sui-Tang unification, however, a powerful and widespread Tujue (Türks) empire had come into existence.

Commercial traffic on the Silk Road remained heavy in spite of the rise and fall of the many political entities along the way. Merchants continued to transship their goods to all the cities on this long commercial highway. At the time, there was really no powerful empire in Central Asia, even though the power of the Rouran and the Tujue loomed large. On China's western frontier, the Tuyuhun, however, had cut off the Silk Road. The Persian empire and the Northern Wei and Northern Zhou had no direct contact, there being several different peoples living between them in Central Asia. The Tubu were not yet powerful, and the Shu-Han governing mechanisms gradually ceased to function in the southwest under the southern dynasties; Nanzhong in modern Yunnan, Guizhou, and southern Sichuan were not strong enough to become a major regional powers. Beyond the East China Sea, although the Japanese reception of Chinese culture had made no great leaps, the Korean peninsula was divided into three kingdoms that had already made sea voyages to conduct relations with the Eastern Wu (222–280) and the southern dynasties. This is why the names of many Japanese objects still begin with Go (Chinese Wu). In short, during the Wei-Jin and North-South dynasties, China looked inward, and many peoples gathered within China, but it had not yet developed a very great outward momentum.

In the second half of the medieval period, the Sui and Tang dynasties unified China, and many important changes occurred on China's borders; these two historical trends combined to gradually create a pan-Asian order with China as its central element.

The first important change was in the power relations between China and the steppe peoples. The Tujue (Türks) formed a large and very powerful steppe empire; near the end of the northern dynasties, it was the most powerful state in Asia. On the eve of unification, both the Sui and Tang fought with the Tujue, being sometimes victorious and sometimes defeated. In the chaos at the end of the Sui, when many people contended for the throne, local powers in the north, including Tang Gaozu (r. 618–626), all called themselves vassals of the Tujue and hoped to employ the Tujue as their rear guard. But shortly after that, the Tujue fought each other and split into eastern and western factions; the Western Tujue further divided into ten tribes. The Eastern Tujue were defeated by Tang Taizong; their leader, Xieli (Illig) Qaghan (r. 620–630) was taken prisoner; and the Eastern Tujue devolved into a number of subject peoples under Tang suzerainty. In 630, several leaders of these northwestern peoples came to Chang-an, urging Taizong to accept the illustrious title of Heavenly Qaghan (*tian kehan*) and have a road built—a royal road for ease in visiting the Heavenly Qaghan—which was actually the northern route of the Silk Road from today's Inner Mongolia to northern Central Asia. This honorific title of Heavenly Qaghan was unprecedented and symbolized the great power of the Tang over the steppes at that time. This power could not be preserved for long, however; after the An Lushan Rebellion, China was no longer able to control its northern border. The Tiele and Huihe gradually developed into powerful Central Asian nations, and near the end of the Tang, the Khitan (Qidan) people arose to establish a great northern nation that embraced both Chinese and non-Chinese cultures—the Liao empire (907–1125).

When Tang Taizong defeated the Eastern Tujue (Türks), he established the two area commands (*dudufu*) of Dingxiang and Yunzhong in their Shanxi homelands (near modern Datong). The Tang rulers generally established loose-reign prefectures (*jimizhoufu*) and protectorates general in the areas of non-Chinese peoples who surrendered to them; their top official posts continued to be filled hereditarily by local ethnic leaders. These administrative units were actually self-governing entities in which the Tang state simply granted meritorious appointments and official titles; they were quite different from genuine Tang local governments. Nominally, these *jimizhoufu*, *duhufu*, and *dudufu* at various levels were attached to the various prefectures of China proper, such as Hebei, Longyou, Jiannan, Jiangnan, and Lingnan. The Tang empire could not hold on to its far eastern and western border regions for long; after Gaozong's reign, the areas under Tang control shrank in size. Tang power was at its height during the *kaiyuan* and *tianbao* reign periods (713–756) of Tang Xuanzong. The four Anxi garrisons established in 658—Kucha, Kashgar, Khotan, and Karashar—were still in Chinese hands and well guarded. The Andong ("pacify the East") protectorate general in the east, from the Korean peninsula west to the banks of the Liao River, would never again return to Pyongyang's control. This system of loose-reign prefectures, constituting the periphery of China proper, may be considered an assertion of Chinese sovereignty over non-Chinese peoples on China's borders.

If the non-Chinese peoples living in the loose-reign prefectures fought one another, the Chinese would often resettle the losers in immigrant prefectures (*qiaozhoufu*) in China proper, allowing them to retain their original leaders. Most of these immigrant prefectures were in present-day Gansu, Shaanxi, and Shanxi. These areas maintained their self-governing nature for longer or shorter periods—some very quickly disbanded or were Sinified; others remained self-governing for several generations. The Huihe, for example, fought a civil war in the ninth century, after which one group of them settled in Taiyuan, in Shanxi, where they maintained their independent status for some time before being absorbed by the Shatuo (Western Tujue) Türks leader Li Keyong (856–908).

The system of loose-reign prefectures did not exist during the Han dynasty. The Han protectorates in the western regions (modern Xinjiang) were staffed by officers from the central government, whose job was to control the various nations on China's western border. The agricultural colonies with garrison soldiers, like the commandants of various areas in Hexi, Dunhuang, and Juyan, were all part of this border-defense system. Non-Chinese minority people's commanderies and counties existed in the Han, and district (*dao*)-level officials took charge of newly submissive non-Chinese peoples. The Shu commandery (modern Sichuan) had several such districts for the accommodation of "southwestern barbarians." Eventually, these districts were given county (*xian*) status. The leaders of these non-Chinese peoples were often given honorific titles such as "Righteous Commander of Yue" and so on. The Tang system was not completely original: there had been a few loose-reign prefectures during the Sui. The Ming aboriginal-office system, with tribal chieftains, *tusi*, as leaders, was quite similar to the Tang setup, but the minority peoples were distributed throughout the provinces of China proper. In the northeast, in Jianzhou and elsewhere, the Ming established guard offices (*yasuo*) staffed by local leaders and nominally under the command of similar offices in China proper—this was most similar to the Tang system of *jimizhoufu*.

The Tang empire also extended its power to another outer ring of foreign countries that it invested (*cefeng*) with titles of rank. Relations

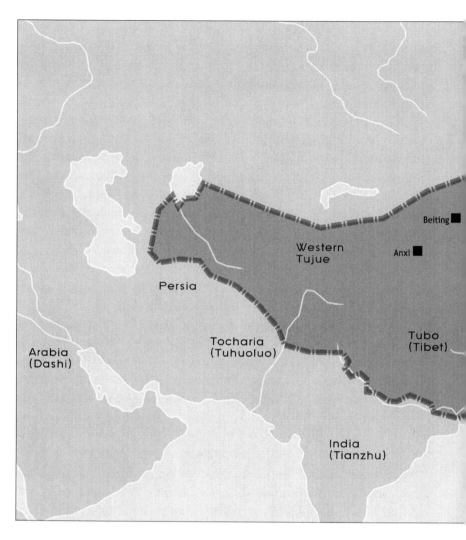

FIGURE 4.6 Map of the Extent of High Tang Cultural Influence in Asia

between China and the three kingdoms on the Korean peninsula had been close since ancient times, and China had often intervened in the affairs of the region. The Sui and Tang made two unsuccessful military attempts to conquer the Korean peninsula, but from the time of Tang Taizong, there was a great deal of contact between China and the Korean states, and the Koreans adopted Chinese culture to a high degree. From then on, Korea or the Korean states were often the most friendly nations

within China's supposed power-investiture system (*cefeng zhidu*). In later times, when Japan invaded Korea, China came to its defense.

Japan was an independent country, but it was regarded as belonging within Tang China's investiture system. There was much contact between the Liu Song dynasty (420–479) and Japan. During the Sui dynasty, Japan began to send emissaries to China. After the promulgation of the Taika Reform Edict in 645, Japan established the Ritsuryō criminal and administrative code system, based on the Tang model, employing Chinese Confucianism and Legalism as understood in Japan. The government administration was reorganized in a Chinese style, and scholars, learned monks, artisans, and so on were dispatched to study in China. At this time, the Japanese also developed their alphabetic *kana* script, which was based on Chinese-character script. Japan was indeed another country greatly influenced by Chinese culture. The Mohe people also established the kingdom of Balhae (Bohai, 698–926) on China's northeastern border.

All of these nations to the east of China—Goguryeo (Gaogouli, 37 B.C.E.–668 C.E.), Baekje or Paekche (Baiji, 18 B.C.E.–660 C.E.), Silla (Xinluo, 57 B.C.E.–935 C.E.), Japan, and Balhae—at some point accepted many Chinese immigrants. Leaving aside the legend of Jizi fleeing the ancient Shang dynasty to rule Korea for the Zhou dynasty, from the Eastern Han through the North-South dynasties, because of the unstable situation in China, many Chinese from the Liaodong peninsula escaped to Korea. The Han even established several commanderies, such as Lelang, Daifang, and Xuantu, on the Korean peninsula, where these people could live. When the Sui emperor Yangdi's (r. 569–618) attack on Goguryeo was defeated, he lost a large Sui army; they remained behind to live on the Korean peninsula. During Japan's Yayoi period (ca. 500 B.C.E.–300 C.E.), many Chinese immigrated to Japan, primarily settling in the Kyushu area. According to a Japanese legend, a descendant of Qin Shihuangdi, Gong Yuejun, led a group of Chinese across Korea to settle in Japan. They were known as "people of Qin." (*Qinren*). Another son of the Han emperor Lingdi, Azhi Shizhu, is also said to have led some Han Chinese to settle in Japan. They were known as the "new Han people" (*xin Hanren*). To this day, some Japanese still have the surnames Qin and Wu and call themselves *Qinren* and *Wuren*. Significantly, Kyushu was the starting point for many Japanese missions to China, and the emissaries were for the most part from Kyushu. Thus, it is likely that Chinese immigration to Kyushu was a spur to Japanese visits to China.

Politically, China's relations with all of these East Asian nations came under the investiture system, while culturally, it was a case of them imitating Chinese ways. The same was true of the industrial arts, though each country developed its own special characteristics. For example, the Koreans excelled in weaving cotton and the Japanese in metallurgy, and both produced products of a higher quality than the Chinese versions. Korean and Japanese Confucianism and Buddhism developed very rapidly, both inheriting the Chinese traditions and establishing their own new ones. In their trade relations, however, the East Asian nations could not match the scale or influence of China's trade with the west across the Silk Road. This was to a large extent because Chinese, Korean, and Japanese products were too similar and thus unable to fill any mutual needs or create any mutual economic dependence.

From the Han dynasty on, Japan and the states of the Korean peninsula often accepted titles from the Chinese. Take Goguryeo as an example. The Han granted the title King of Goguryeo, while the Eastern Jin granted many military titles similar to Chinese titles, such as Commissioner with Extraordinary Powers, Commander-in-Chief, General Who Pacifies the East, King of Goguryeo, and Duke of Lelang—the Koreans had both Chinese official titles and the five noble ranks. In 57 C.E., the Japanese were granted a golden seal with the inscription "Han King of the Wonu" (Han Wonu guowang). During the Liu Song dynasty, Japanese tribute envoys began to carry diplomatic credentials and called themselves Military Commissioner with Extraordinary Powers and Commander-in-Chief, and added many military titles relating to the states of the Korean peninsula: Great General Who Pacifies the East and King of the Japanese. The Liu Song rulers refused to accept most of these titles, allowing only Great General Who Pacifies the East and King of the Japanese. Actually, the king of Paekche already had the titles of Military Commissioner with Extraordinary Powers, Commander-in-Chief, and King of Paekche. From all this, it would seem that the Japanese already had expansionist ambitions; they hoped to use these nominal Chinese titles to legitimize their control of the Korean peninsula, on the one hand acknowledging Chinese sovereignty while secretly planning to establish their own hegemony in the region. At that time, the investiture system was not an empty ceremony but rather a genuine allocation of hierarchical power. The Tang dynasty was much more powerful than the Liu Song, but they did not make Japan into a loose-reign prefecture. Thus, Japan was not brought into the second circle of the Chinese imperial structure but relegated to the third circle of tributary states.

China's relations with the Tubu kingdom of Tibet and the kingdom of Nanzhao were of a different sort. Tubu was large nation established by the Qiang people on the Tibetan plateau; it rose to power at about the same time that the Sui and Tang reunified the Chinese empire. At the beginning of the Tang, Tubu was already very strong, and so in 641

Tang Taizong sent Princess Wencheng (ca. 623–680) to be married to the Tibetan king Songtsän Gampo (605?–650). The Tibetan king also took a Nepalese princess as his bride, the two marriage alliances symbolizing Tibet's cultural and political position between China and India. At this same time, Chinese armies defeated the Eastern and Western Tujue Türks, making the might of the Heavenly Qaghan felt all the way to Central Asia; the four Anxi garrisons marked the western extremity of Chinese power. After unification of the Tubu kingdom, the Tibetans conquered Nepal and then tried to extend their power into China's western regions. They were repulsed by the Chinese defenses along the Gansu Corridor and went southwest through the Karakorum Range, where they encountered a matriarchal kingdom (Dongnüguo), took over the salt trade, and spread into the southern part of China's western regions. Under Tang Gaozong and Empress Wu, China several times lost and regained its four western garrisons. China's strategy was to isolate the Tibetans and the Tujue Türks outside of this long defensive line and thus keep the Silk Road open.

At this time, the Sassanid empire (226–651) of Persia was already threatened by the rise of Arab states such as the Umayyad caliphate (661–750); Chinese historical records call them *Dashi* (a term more appropriate to the Tajik people). Thus, Central Asia became the site of multistate conflicts. The concern of the combatants was not exclusively the profits from the Silk Road trade; even more important was territorial expansion and control of this area of frequent warfare. The chief economic beneficiaries of the Silk Road were the small oasis states and the steppe nomadic pastoralists. The Tibetans, Arabs, Tuqishi (Western Turks), and Huihe all set their sights on the collection of taxes along the Silk Road. As a large East Asian empire, China always tried to maintain its hegemony in the western regions. China succeeded in weakening the Tujue Türks and the power of other steppe peoples, but its armies were too far from home, supply lines were too long, and although generals such as Guo Yuanzhen (656–713) scored some victories, Gao Xianzhi suffered a decisive defeat at the Talas River in 751. Chinese power was at its height from 713 to 756, but after the An Lushan Rebellion, the western regions and Longyou joined in the civil strife. With the Chinese armies and the Huihe cavalry fighting in the east, the Tibetans gained an opportunity to expand into the western regions. After the rebellion, Tubu became a great Tibetan empire and occupied the formerly Chinese-controlled territory west of Fengxiang in Shaanxi. The Tibetans then attacked Chang-an, and the Tang signed a treaty in

783 marking Jinglong in the north and the Dadu River (which flows from Kokonor to Sichuan) in the south as the borders between Tubu Tibet and Tang China.

China was used to exercising suzerainty over its neighboring countries, and subordination like this to the Tibetans was seldom seen. In Central Asia, China's strategy had been to unite the Arabs (*Dashi*) and the Huihe to control the Tibetans. Dezong's (779–805) celebrated Chief Minister Li Bi (722–789) originally had planned to do this but was never able to carry it out. The Helong and Hexi areas of modern Shaanxi and Gansu remained under Tibetan control, even though Zhang Yichao of the Dunhuang area betrayed the Tibetans and submitted to China in the late ninth century. The western borders of the Song dynasty could not extend beyond Weizhou in northwestern Sichuan. Tibetan culture transmitted Buddhism and united the local and the Indian cultural traditions, but Chinese culture had little opportunity for development in the Tibetan areas.

Nanzhao was a newly risen state on China's southwestern border. It is believed to have been founded by the Baizu people (in Chinese, *Baipu*), descendents of the Ailao of the Han era. They are said to have been a tribe settled in Yunnan, Guizhou, and southern Sichuan, with six leaders or subgroups, the *liu zhao*. They were once thought to be ethnically related to the Thais, and they were influenced by both Chinese and Tibetan culture. The Mengshi *zhao*, also known as the southern *zhao* (*nanzhao*), united the six *zhao* in the early eighth century to form the kingdom of Nanzhao. Emperor Xuanzong granted their leader the title King of Yunnan, and Emperor Dezong made its leader king of Nanzhao. They were quite independent of China; situated in China's southwestern border area as well as in modern Thailand, Myanmar (Burma), Vietnam, and Laos, they unified the various non-Chinese peoples of the area into a large state. During its ascendancy, the Tang government established many loose-reign prefectures in this region and put them under the Jiannan circuit. When the Nanzhao rose, they sided with the Tibetans against the Chinese given their cultural affinities and helped them in the encirclement of Jiannan. Situated in the mountainous regions of the southwest, the Nanzhao had a long trade route that is now known as the "Third Silk Road," which brought together northwestern and southwestern China and extended to the southcentral peninsula and Mandalay Bay in the northern part of the Indian Ocean. They were not direct traders but mainly transshipers of salt and copper from the south in exchange for northern and Chinese products.

Tibetan Tubu and Nanzhao were within the greater realm of the Tang empire, but they were very independent and not within the Tang investiture system. These two states arose during the Tang era and lasted for quite a long time. It was not until the Qing dynasty that the central government of China had truly close relations with the Tibetan kingdom. The successor state of Nanzhao was Dali, which also remained quite independent during the Song and Yuan dynasties. The Mongol Yuan established Prince Liang's fief there, but the area was first made a province during the Ming dynasty, and many of the Ming aboriginal offices (*tusi*) originated in the Yuan era.

To sum up this section, Sui-Tang China was the hub of a vast international network. Relying on its superior cultural and economic strength, it carried out many military campaigns that for a time vanquished the northern steppe peoples and created an impregnable empire. It employed non-Chinese peoples in a system of loose-reign prefectures to create a buffer zone around the empire while relying on an investiture system to absorb neighboring peoples into its imperial structure. Farther away, however, were the independent Tibetans, Huihe, and other groups with whom China was unpredictably sometimes at peace and sometimes at war. The world of East Asia, with China as its leader, came into frequent contact with Central Asia and South Asia, led by first the Persians and later the Arabs. Following the international policy of attacking nearby neighbors and maintaining friendly relations with more distant nations, this area became a place of multinational relations. The world of South Asia, with India as its leader, had cultural and economic contact with Central Asia, but its contact with East Asia was primarily cultural. Most important was the transmission of Buddhism across Central Asia into China, after which China directly imported the religion and other aspects of Indian culture by means of land and sea journeys to India, passing it on in turn to Korea and Japan. East Asian commercial products were traded by land and sea to the Middle East, from where they were shipped to Europe, and the profits of the Silk Road were shared by the nations of Central Asia and the Middle East. The seagoing merchants of Persia, the Arab states, the Jews, and India all profited from a similar sea trade. The harbors of the small Southeast Asian states along the sea routes also profited from this trade, but they had to wait until the Tang-Song transition to become truly wealthy.

During the first half of its medieval period, China had looked inward, but after amassing sufficient cultural and economic capital, it opened out in the second half to become the cultural, economic, and political center of East Asia.

10. A Comparison of the Tang and Islamic Empires

The Tang empire and the Islamic caliphates belong to the same era, except that the Abbasid caliphate lasted from 750 to 1258, much longer than the Tang dynasty. Both empires represented a political order and a cultural sphere. Their borders came together in Central Asia, and their combined territories included the three continents of Asia, Europe, and Africa—that is, most of the civilized world as it then existed. Only Europe north of the Mediterranean and the Indian subcontinent were not within the area of control of these two great powers. The Tang dynasty came into conflict with the fledgling Abbasid caliphate when its armies defeated a Tang expeditionary force in Central Asia. Much later, the lands controlled by the Abbasid caliphate were taken over by the Mongols when Hulagu Qaghan's troops sacked Baghdad in 1258.

As is well known, under the leadership of the Prophet Muhammad (ca. 570–632), the world of Islam grew very rapidly from a new religious sect on the Arabian peninsula to a great empire spanning three continents, a feat rarely seen in human history. When Muhammad died in 632, Islam had already conquered part of the Arabian peninsula. His first four successors were known as *caliph* (successor or representative, in Arabic). They were primarily religious leaders, and their political power was secondary and much less important than their military prowess. All four were Muhammad's relatives and had been with him from the beginning; they received their power through election. At first, only Muslims (followers of Islam) from the holy cities of Mecca and Medina had the right to vote in these elections, but this power was later extended to all Arab converts.

The second or Umayyad caliphate (660–750) had its capital at Damascus and was founded by members of the same family as Muhammad;

their caliphs passed on the throne to their sons. The Umayyad was a caliphate of Arabs within which Arab Muslims held the highest rank; Muslims of other ethnic groups were next in status, with non-Muslim peoples (infidels) next and slaves (mostly prisoners of war) on the bottom of the hierarchy.

The Abbasid caliphate passed from father to son. Arab culture was its common culture. Other ethnic groups, however, whether of Persian, European, or African origin, were still allowed to participate in this great cultural system, but the distinction between Muslim and non-Muslim was maintained.

The social structure of the Tang empire was quite different. Before the Tang, the various ethnic groups fought one another, there were ethnic inequalities during the North-South dynasties, and there were even inequalities within the Han Chinese themselves, between the great noble families and the common people. After a couple hundred years of turmoil and intermixing, Tang society basically returned to the Han practice of regarding all registered households as members of the polity. By the beginning of the Tang, the distinction between Chinese and non-Chinese was virtually gone (though recent scholarship has shown the Tang Chinese to have been aware of ethnic differences), and after the middle of the Tang, the superior status of the great families gradually disappeared. Tang scholars who entered the imperial bureaucracy through the examination system gradually made up a new literati class. Though it was still difficult for poor scholars to compete with the scions of wealthy families, entrance into this new literati class was in theory open to all men of talent. Thus, the class divisions of the Tang empire were much less rigid than in the Islamic world.

At first, the governmental structure of the Islamic world was rather loose. Under the first four caliphs, every newly conquered area was only required to pay its taxes; local rule could be carried on in the local fashion, with the previous ruling stratum taking its orders from the central Islamic power. The Umayyad caliphate used a "divide-and-rule" system. They followed Persian and Byzantine precedents and divided the empire into a number of provinces that they allowed to be ruled very much in terms of their own traditional methods.

The Abbasid caliphate, however, developed into a centralized power. Its power base was in the east, in Khorasan, an area of central and western

Afghanistan to the west of the upper and middle reaches of the Amur River; southwestern Türkmenistan (Turkmenia); and northeastern Iran. Its capital was Baghdad.

The entire Islamic world was rapidly Arabized, and Arabic became its common language, but everyone throughout the caliphate's empire was regarded as one of the caliph's people. As Allah's (God) spokesman on earth, the caliph monopolized all power—religious, legislative, military, and administrative—in his single person. The center established four departments to administer these four forms of power, and every province also had the same four departments, and they took their orders from the corresponding central department. The central government had a police intelligence system for ferreting out information and an attached postal system that could reach anywhere in the far-flung empire to deliver orders to subordinates and bring information back to the center. The central government's control was quite secure.

The Tang empire followed the political system it had inherited from previous dynasties; the emperor ruled on the basis of the Mandate of Heaven and with the assistance of a large civil bureaucracy. The organization of the civil bureaucracy at the center involved three institutions: a policy-making Secretariat, a policy administration Department of State Affairs, and an evaluation Chancellery. Later on, the top officials in the Secretariat and the evaluation Chancellery merged into a pool of chief ministers that met to discuss policy. Policies were carried out by six ministries—Personnel, Revenue, Rites, War, Justice, and Works—and judicial power was directly responsible to the emperor. The religions of Buddhism and Daoism coexisted; the ideas of Confucianism made up the cultural mainstream. China had nothing comparable to the Islamic theocratic power. Even when Daoism was designated the national religion, Daoist priests and Buddhist monks were regulated by a special bureau of the Ministry of Rites.

As for the social status of the military, from the beginning of Islam, every member of the religion was considered a soldier, and all Islam was a military organization. The armed forces grew under the Umayyad caliphate, but not every Muslim was necessarily a soldier. All military forces, including those non-Arab contingents, were under the control of Muslim officers. The regular standing army was professionalized and received a fixed stipend, but in times of military emergency, all Muslims could be

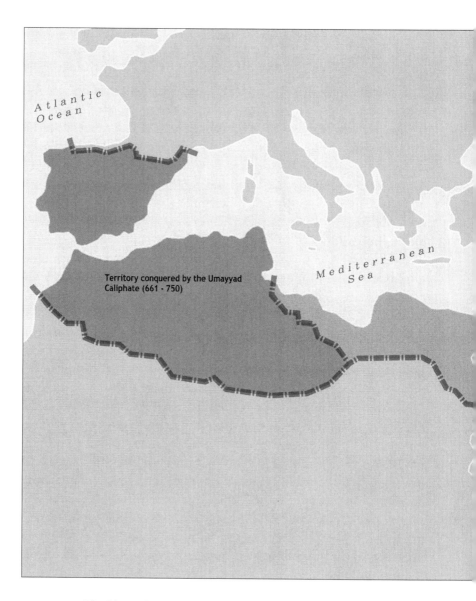

FIGURE 4.7 The Islamic Empire, 632–945

subject to military conscription. The Abbasid caliphate had a powerful imperial palace guard under the direct control of the caliph. They were drawn first from Berbers and Bedouins and, later, from all the various eastern peoples. In the end, the most powerful troops were made up of professional Turkish military men; eventually, the officer corps was mainly

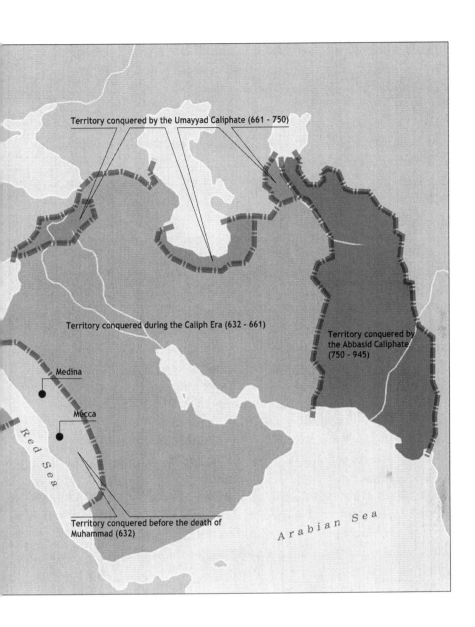

Territory conquered by the Umayyad Caliphate (661 - 750)

Territory conquered during the Caliph Era (632 - 661)

Territory conquered by the Abbasid Caliphate (750 - 945)

Medina

Mecca

Red Sea

Territory conquered before the death of Muhammad (632)

Arabian Sea

staffed by these Turks. Some palace guards were commanded by palace eunuchs. In the late years of the Abbasid caliphate, overbearing Turkish generals made and deposed the rulers and reduced the young caliphs to their political puppets. Many provincial governors also annexed the territory under their command. The title of sultan, originally meaning "commanding officer," came to equal that of caliph, and eventually the title sultan replaced caliph as leader of the Islamic world.

The status of the military under the Tang dynasty went through a similar process of change. At first, they carried on the Northern Zhou conscription system, in which the hereditary soldiery derived from the ranks of the powerful families whose wealth came from landed property. They practiced agriculture in normal times and were called up for military service when needed. The recruitment of a highly skilled cavalry of mounted archers began in Xuanzong's time, when the professional standing army came under the emperor's direct command. The troops under the command of regional military governors on the borders mostly derived from non-Chinese peoples. Thus, the An Lushan Rebellion was a case of non-Chinese border troops attacking the central government. After the rebellion, not only did these regional military governors commanding troops in outlying provinces in Hebei annex their territories, but similar defense commands (*jiezhen*) were established in the interior and set the stage for dynastic collapse and the rise of the Five Dynasties. There were also large Armies of Inspired Strategy established in the capital in 753 under the command of the palace eunuchs. The eunuchs of this palace guard repeatedly deposed the emperors, took unauthorized control of the government, and led the Tang dynasty toward destruction. Thus, these two great empires both conducted large-scale border wars that led to such great enhancement of military power that it could no longer be controlled by the central government.

These two great empires also gave birth to brilliant and flourishing cultures. Islam was originally an Arab religion of the desert, but it was able to absorb doctrines from Persian Zoroastrianism, Eastern Orthodox Christianity, and Judaism and combine them into one simple religious system of submission (Islam literally means "submission") to one true god (Allah). Over the course of its expansion, the Islamic governments ordered the translation into Arabic of large amounts of Greek, Persian, and Indian literature, philosophy, and scholarship, thus greatly enriching the content of their increasingly significant language. Through the careful selection of materials, Arab scholars both inherited past knowledge and produced original results, leading to important and greatly admired accomplishments in astronomy, mathematics, historiography, and literature.

During this time, Indian Buddhism, Central Asian Zoroastrianism, Manichaeism, and Christianity all entered China by way of foreign merchants. After the Tang replaced the North-South dynasties, it naturally maintained Chinese culture as the mainstream, but it also enriched that culture by absorbing many elements of non-Chinese people's cultures. The cultural accomplishments of the Tang era were also remarkably brilliant. Tang society was quite open, and non-Chinese were given much room to display their talents—a Korean could become a general (Gao Xianzhi), a Vietnamese could become a chief minister (Jiang Gongfu, fl. 760s), and a Japanese could serve the court (Chao Heng, Abe no Nakamaru, 698–770). This employment of non-Chinese is quite similar to the Abbasid caliphate's use of non-Arabs in important offices.

These two empires had great vitality and originality. They were both able to absorb the best of many cultural traditions, extend their sway over an extremely large area, weave together many disparate strands, acculturate many different peoples, and create a universal medieval world order. These universal world orders were both able to bind together and maintain a multicultural empire for over a thousand years.

In terms of their central guiding ideas, however, the two empires differed greatly. The central idea of Islamic culture was (and still is) unconditional submission to and worship of one true god. Because Allah was the only true god, the Islamic religion was essentially exclusionary. Absolute submission also meant that the status of the human person was also very low. With Confucianism, Daoism, and Buddhism combined comprising the central ideas of the Chinese universal world order, the human person (*ren*) was respected, and the human heart/mind (*renxin*) was regarded as the seat of observation and understanding of the universe. The Buddhist precept that "the external world is created by the mind" (*jing you xin zao*) and the Confucian idea that "affairs depend upon human action" (*shi zai ren wei*) were combined in Chinese thought. If we compare Islamic and Chinese culture on these points, the former emphasizes the transcendent power of God while the latter emphasizes the human being's inner perfection or perfectibility. This point is enough to demonstrate that these two cultural traditions are very different and thus quite difficult to compare. If they exhibit certain points of similarity, such as late-stage domination by the military, this is probably related more to the division of labor and balance or imbalance in their political systems than to their cultural system per se.

Suggestions for Further Reading

Barfield, Thomas J. *The Perilous Frontier: Nomadic Empires and China, 221 B.C. to A.D. 1757.* Oxford: Blackwell, 1989.

Benn, Charles D. *Daily Life in Traditional China: The Tang Dynasty.* Westport, Conn.: Greenwood Press, 2001.

Bol, Peter. *This Culture of Ours: Intellectual Transitions in T'ang and Song China.* Stanford, Calif.: Stanford University Press, 1992.

Chen, Jo-shui. *Liu Tsung-yüan and Intellectual Change in T'ang China, 773–819.* Cambridge: Cambridge University Press, 2006.

Chiu-Duke, Josephine. *To Rebuild the Empire: Lu Chih's Confucian Pragmatist Approach to the Mid-Tang Predicament.* Albany: State University of New York Press, 2000.

De Blasi, Anthony. *Reform in the Balance: The Defense of Literary Culture in Mid-Tang China.* Albany: State University of New York Press, 2002.

Di Cosmo, Nicola. "Ancient Inner Asian Nomads: Their Economic Basis and Its Significance in Chinese History." *Journal of Asian Studies* 53, no. 4 (November 1994): 1092–1126.

Hartman, Charles. *Han Yü and the T'ang Search for Unity.* Princeton, N.J.: Princeton University Press, 1986.

Hymes, Robert. *Way and Byway: Taoism, Local Religion and Models of Divinity in Sung and Modern China.* Berkeley: University of California Press, 2002.

Lewis, Mark Edward. *China's Cosmopolitan Empire: The Tang Dynasty.* Cambridge, Mass.: Belknap, 2009.

Liu, Xinru, and Lynda Norene Shaffer. *Connections Across Eurasia: Transportation, Communication, and Cultural Exchanges on the Silk Roads.* Boston: McGraw-Hill, 2007.

Loewe, Michael. "China's Sense of Unity as Seen in the Early Empires." *T'oung Pao* 80 (1994): 6–26.

——. "Imperial Sovereignty: Dong Zhongshu's Contribution and His Predecessors." In *Foundations and Limits of State Power in China*, ed. S. R. Schram, 33–57. London: University of London, 1987.

Owen, Stephen. *The Great Age of Chinese Poetry: The High T'ang.* New Haven, Conn.: Yale University Press, 1981.

Pearce, Scott, Audrey Spiro, and Patricia Ebrey, eds. *Culture and Power in the Reconstitution of the Chinese Realm, 200–600.* Cambridge, Mass.: Harvard University Asia Center, 2001.

Rothschild, Harry N. *Wu Zhao: China's Only Woman Emperor.* New York: Pearson Longman, 2008.

Sivin, Nathan. *Medicine, Philosophy, and Religion in Ancient China: Researches and Reflections*. Aldershot: Variorium, 1995.

———. *Science in Ancient China: Researches and Reflections*. Aldershot: Variorium, 1995.

Twitchett, Denis C., ed. *The Cambridge History of China*, vol. 3: *Sui and T'ang China, 589–906 A.D.*, part 1. Cambridge: Cambridge University Press, 1979.

Zürcher, E. *The Buddhist Conquest of China: The Spread and Adaptation of Buddhism in Early Medieval China*. 3rd ed. Leiden: E. J. Brill, 1972 [1959].

China in an Asian Multistate System

THE TENTH TO FIFTEENTH CENTURIES C.E.

From the tenth to the fifteenth centuries, Chinese civilization expanded beyond East Asia and encountered many challenges, conflicts, and amalgamations with other civilizations. The expansion of several non-Chinese peoples, especially the western march of the Mongols, brought China and the West closer together, into one Eurasian field of interaction. China's economic network expanded, and Chinese thinking grew into a substantially complete system of thought. After this transformation, China and East Asia were virtually indivisible.

1. Late Medieval China and the Multistate System

In the usual alignment of Chinese history, the Tang and Song are grouped together as unified dynasties. In reality, though, the Song dynasty was only one member of contemporary international society and did not compare to the early years of the Tang. We have already discussed in the previous chapter the situation of the Tang from the reign of Emperor Taizong to Xuanzong—how China was the most powerful empire in East Asia at the time and how, relying on the title of Heavenly Qaghan, China set up loose-reign prefectures, bringing many diverse ethnic groups under the hegemony of the Tang empire. Precisely because the Tang empire was so all-embracing, many non-Chinese peoples were able to move freely into China proper. When some of these peoples lost a war on the steppes and saw their ancestral lands conquered, they would then move into China and settle in the various loose-reign prefectures, mostly in modern Shaanxi, Gansu, Shanxi, and Hebei. Many such peoples on the northern borders lived close to the mountain passes; whether as traders or as soldiers, they lived among the Chinese. China's northern provinces of modern Inner Mongolia, Liaoning, and Hebei were heavily influenced by non-Chinese culture, a situation that led to the An Lushan Rebellion and the establishment of independent prefectures (*fanzhen*) after the rebellion, when non-Chinese culture continued to dominate the area. It was on this basis that the confrontation between China and the peoples of the north, despite the Great Wall's separation of steppe and arable land, moved south with the removal from Chinese control of a large area of north-central China.

Although the period following the Tang is known as the Five Dynasties (907–960), the Later Tang and Later Jin were founded by Shatuo Türk military factions, while the Later Han and Later Zhou (from which the founder of the Song came) represented the power of such combined Chinese and non-Chinese military leaders as mentioned above. During the Five Dynasties, the central plain was the site of chaos and war and under constant pressure from the Khitan people. After the establishment of the Song dynasty (Northern, 960–1127; and Southern, 1127–1279), they could never escape this Khitan (Later Liao dynasty, 947–1126) pressure. After the Later Jin ceded the Sixteen Prefectures of North China, from Datong to Youzhou, China's northern line of defense was pushed back to the northern and central areas of modern Hebei and northeastern modern Shanxi. The Liao dynasty was replaced by the Jurchen Jin (Gold, 1115–1234) dynasty, they in turn were replaced by the Mongol Yuan (1271–1367) dynasty, and China's northern defense lines steadily retreated south, first to the Yellow River and then to the Jianghuai region of the Yangzi and Huai river basins. After the rise of the Mongols but before the defeat of the Jurchens, the Song and these two peoples struggled for control of former Chinese territory from north to south.

The Southern Song was able to maintain its position in the Jiangnan (south of the Yangzi) region given the prosperous economic situation that had developed in the south after the end of the An Lushan Rebellion. Nine of the ten southern states of the Five Dynasties and Ten States

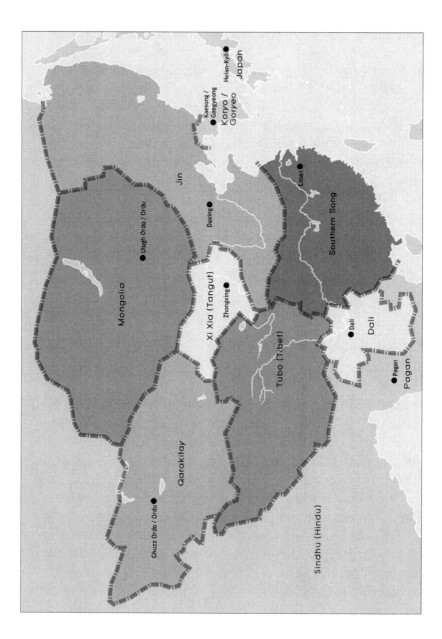

FIGURE 5.1 Map of Asia During the Southern Song

period (the Wu, Min, Southern Tang, Wuyue, Southern Han, Jingnan, Chu, Former Shu, and Later Shu) were established by the Han Chinese. The Song versus the Jin and Yuan represented a long-term confrontation between Chinese and non-Chinese peoples. During all this time, the Song was in the weakest position. After several military defeats at the hands of the Khitan Liao, the Song-Liao Treaty of Shanyuan was concluded in January 1005, which brought about a hundred years of peace, paid for by the Song's large annual payments of silk and silver to the Liao. Although not as bad as the Later Jin situation, the Song emperor still had to suffer the humiliation of calling himself the "younger brother" of the Liao leader. Of course, the Song fared even worse with the Jin and the Yuan, the Northern Song brought to an end by the former and the Southern Song by the latter—without even being given the chance to be called "younger brother"!

To the west of the Song was the Tangut people's state of Xi Xia in the original Tang home of the Turkic Tuyuhun people, a Xianbei (Särbi) noble group that for some time ruled over the Qiang. The area occupied by the Xi Xia, where Mongolia and the Tibetan plateau come together, was home to many diverse groups, and the Tanguts of the Xi Xia were themselves a hybrid people. The small state of Xi Xia survived for over two hundred years in the Western Regions; they defeated the Song, and after 1042, the Song also agreed to pay tribute to them in exchange for peace.

The Tubu (Tibetans) gradually rose to power on the Tibetan plateau during the Tang dynasty, absorbing elements of Indian and Chinese civilization and developing into a large state to the west of the Tang. During the An Lushan Rebellion, the Tubu invaded Hexi, Longyou, and northwestern modern Sichuan. The Tang made eight treaties with them, and the two sides assumed positions of equality, but Tubu armies made repeated raids into Guanzhong and Jiannan, and the Tang could do little to stop them. During the Song, given the constant encroachments by the Huihe, the Tubu Tibetans were not as strong as before; they eventually sent tribute and declared themselves servants of the Liao. Song-Tubu conflict did not last long, and at least the Song did not have to suffer the humiliation of defeat by them.

In the southwest, the state of Nanzhao also arose in Tang times, unifying the six *zhao* (tribes) in modern Yunnan, absorbing Chinese, Tibetan, and Buddhist cultural influences and creating a unique cultural mix. At the beginning of the Song, the Duan family carved out a large section of the southwest (modern Yunnan, Guizhou, Sichuan, and parts of Myanmar), replaced the Nanzhao, and established the successor state of Dali. It remained independent from 937 to 1253, when it was conquered by the Mongols as part of their conquest of the Song.

To the east, the Korean peninsula had long received Chinese cultural influences and was deeply Sinified. After many unsuccessful campaigns by the Sui and Tang, the various Korean states—Silla, Paekche, and Goguryeo—all accepted Chinese titles and presented tribute to China. The Korean peninsula was united in 936 by the Goryeo dynasty (918–1392), during the Song. Goryeo continually presented tribute to the Song, Liao, Jin, and Yuan; while the Southern Song maintained itself in southern China, Goryeo also kept the sea lanes open between the two states. Although Goryeo was thoroughly Sinicized, it was not under Song suzerainty, and its so-called presentation of tribute was mainly for the sake of trade.

Japan readily accepted Chinese cultural influences, and, after the 645 Taika Reform, the Japanese writing script, bureaucratic system, laws, and religion all imitated Chinese forms. During the Sui-Tang era, Japanese leaders actually asked the Chinese to confer titles on them in order to have their political power legitimized by the largest empire in East Asia. During the Song, Liao, Jin, and Yuan eras, Japan no longer received such titles from mainland political powers.

The nearest area on China's southeastern border was the Annam peninsula (*Jiaozhi*; *Giaochâu* in Vietnamese), modern Indochina. The Han dynasty established the prefecture of Jiaozhou in the northern part of this region. During the time of the Southern Dynasties, Jiaozhou was considered outside China's borders, but it was again governed by China during the Sui and Tang. During the chaos at the end of the Tang, the central government's writ no longer extended to Jiaozhou, and the region became independent. Early on, Champa and Khmer presented tribute to China for many years, and then in 1119 and 1120 the Song bestowed the title of king on the region's leader, acknowledging its independence. Soon after the establishment of the Southern Song, the emperor granted the title of king of to the local ruler. Again in 1162, the Song granted the Vietnamese leader Li Tianzuo the title of King of the Southern Pacified Region (*Nanping wang*) and Protectorate of Annam (*Annam duhu*), titles functionally the same as those of the ruler of a loose-reign prefecture. In 1174, the Song granted Li the title of King of Annam, and from then on the Annam peninsula ceased to be a Chinese prefecture.

Thus, if we survey the internal and external realities facing the Song, we see that it occupied a weaker position in its relations with the Liao, Jin, Yuan, and Xi Xia and did not have real suzerainty over Goryeo, Japan, or Dali. And although the states of Annam frequently presented tribute to the Song and accepted Chinese titles, this was only done to maintain trade relations; Song suzerainty over these states was an empty formality, and the Song lacked the power to make it real.

Song China was no longer the center of the East Asian world, a world where many nations now competed on the international stage and in which China was in an inferior position vis-à-vis its powerful northern neighbors. In that international arena, alliances and betrayals or war and peace were intimately connected to a nation's economic interests and military strength. The Song paid annual tributes to stronger neighbors, purchasing peace with its wealth. The arrangement of relative status though tribute and the granting of titles could also maintain trade stability by relying on international relations to obtain economic advantages.

Han and Tang China employed a network of concentric circles, with China in the middle, to arrange international relations with its neighbors. It was a rational pattern made from following its ancient cultural and political order of five or nine relationships, in which China always occupied the center and established a hierarchy of political entities and relative international relations. The investment and tribute systems served to arrange other nations in relation to the superior Celestial Court of China. The Han allied marquisates (*guiyi houwang*) that were bestowed upon non-Chinese chieftains and the Tang loose-reign prefectures, in addition to frontier garrison troops, were all methods of maintaining the efficacy of China's universal imperial order. This ideal order had already collapsed after the Mid-Tang, and China proper during the Song dynasty no longer represented a universal imperial order. The Liao, Jin, and Yuan dynasties (some scholars call them "conquest dynasties") all represented the incursion of non-Chinese nations into lands formerly controlled by China. They had to maintain their own political traditions but could not avoid adopting an imperial structure; with this combination, they were unable to develop into universal empires. Although the Mongols swept across Eurasia and established a vast military empire, they were unable to organize it into a universal order, and it broke up into a number of local khanates.

The Song occupied China proper and maintained China's political traditions, but the universal imperial dynasty was for them only a historical memory. The Tang sense of difference between ethnic groups was not too strong, but the ethnic divide in the Song was very sharp. The sense of individual ethnic consciousness and the idea of universal empire were fundamentally incompatible.

In the late medieval period, Central Asia included more than just the countries on China's immediate border, and the relations between the Central Asian states were closely related to developments inside China. When the Tang dynasty was strong, the loose-reign prefectures under the command of the protectorates of Anxi and Beiting extended far into Central Asia, and Tang power reached all the way to Afghanistan. After the mid-Tang decline, China could no longer attend to Central Asia, and it reverted back to an area of multistate conflict.

In general, two important events occurred in the struggle for Central Asia at this time. The first was the rise of an Islamic Arab empire and the way its expansion into Central Asia changed the developmental pattern of the tribal groupings there. The second was that many pastoral empires or tribal confederacies rose and fell on the steppes north of China, and the defeated tribes all migrated toward Central Asia to join in the region's multistate conflicts.

Were it not for the rise of the Arab Islamic empire, these northern tribes moving into Central Asia might well have gradually blended in with the local inhabitants, as the Xiongnu did in earlier times, or simply moved farther west. But because the Arabs had established a major empire in Central Asia, the tribal peoples migrating west from North China into this area were forced to organize themselves into large empires and settle there. Thus, after the collapse of the pastoral empire of the Huihe Qaghan (related to the Uyghurs) north of the Gobi Desert, its remnant people moved into the area of the Ili and Syr Darya rivers and established the Khwarezmian empire (840–1211), which, in spite of some vicissitudes, managed to last nearly four centuries. The Khwarezmians constantly fought with the Sāmānī dynasty (819–999), a Persian-speaking Islamic polity. Many of the Tujue Türks who originally resided in North China became Islamic soldiers. One of their leaders was the governor of Khorasan, an eastern part of the Islamic empire. In 962, he claimed the area for himself and established the Ghaznavid Turkic empire (962–1041). The progeny of the Tujue (Türks) and the Huihe fought each other for a long time in Central Asia. The Khwarezmian leader styled himself the Chinese Qaghan. Literally, the title in Chinese was Peach Blossom Stone (*taohuashi*) Qaghan, because in the Tujue lexicon *taohuashi* (probably a transliteration of a Turkic word) referred to Song China. From this, we can see that even though the Huihe had been independent for several hundred years, they still admitted that they came from China.

When the Liao dynasty collapsed, a member of the royal house, Yelü Dashi (1087–1143), led a remnant force westward and established the Kara Khitai (Black Khitans), or Western Liao, dynasty (1132–1218, in modern Kazakhstan), whose chief opponents were the Seljuk Turks. The name Khitan or Khitai carried west by the Kara Khitai developed into the term Cathay, which stood for China in European languages.

The last great assault on China, Central Asia, and farther west was the Mongol invasions. Wave after wave of Mongol cavalry arose from China's northern steppes to attack and conquer all of the Central Asian states, setting their aim on the very heart of the Islamic empire.

Using the broadest definition of "China," we can say that the peoples of the Khwarezmian and the Kara Khitai states entered Central Asian history as a result of the migration of peoples out of China and their embroilment in the multistate conflicts of that area. This area was ultimately Islamicized, but the various larger or smaller regional states did not on this account organize themselves into a world power. Different ethnic identities ensured that multistate conflict would remain the dominant element in the region.

During the Five Dynasties and the Song, China proper took on the structure of a late medieval, pluralistic, multistate society made up of powerful pastoral empires and newly risen states in both the north and the south. Although these various states were not part of a universal imperial order, nevertheless they also did not follow the developmental trajectory of premodern European nation-states. Thus, the states of eastern Central Asia and East Asia did not create a genuine international society of sovereign national states.

2. Conquest Dynasties and the Chinese World

The Khitans, Jurchens, and Mongols established three dynasties on the territory previously ruled by China: the Khitan Liao dynasty (947–1125), including the Western Liao (Kara Khitai, 1132–1218); the Jurchen Jin (Gold) dynasty (1115–1224); and the Mongol Yuan dynasty (1271–1368). If we count only the time from the beginning of the Liao to the end of the Yuan, it comes to over four hundred years. After the Yuan emperor Shundi (r. 1333–1368/70) returned to Mongolia, the offspring of Chinggis Qaghan still maintained the Yuan dynasty there. Chinggis Qaghan's fifteenth-generation descendent, Dayan Qaghan ("the Great Yuan Emperor," Batu Mönke, ca. 1464–ca. 1532), unified Mongolia for a time, and the title of qaghan persisted into the seventeenth century, but there were too many tribal groupings, and power was too dispersed for the Mongols to become ever again a unified political power.

The Mongols and the Ming dynasty continued to struggle against each other for some time. Notably, in 1449, the Western Mongols (Oyirats) under Esen (d. 1455) massacred a Chinese army at the Tumu garrison (modern Hebei) and took the young Ming emperor Yingzong prisoner (1449). From that time until Altan Qaghan (Chinese Anda, ca. 1507–ca. 1582) accepted the Ming title of Prince Who Follows Righteousness (*Shunyi wang*) in 1571, the Ming and the Mongols carried on a north-south confrontation. In light of all this, one might even be justified in calling the tenth to the sixteenth centuries the era of China's *second* North-South dynasties!

Chinese historical records are written from the Han Chinese point of view, and these three conquest dynasties founded by non-Chinese peoples are generally considered to be foreign invaders rather than orthodox dynasties. Nevertheless, after four to five hundred years of north-south conflict, during which a large portion of former Chinese territory was controlled by northern peoples, and given that the composition of the Chinese people and elements of their culture experienced a good deal of change, Chinese history cannot avoid paying attention to these dynasties.

The attractions of Chinese culture were very great, and after these non-Chinese peoples moved into Chinese territory and settled there for some time they generally became Sinified. In their non-Chinese lands, however, these conquest dynasties had a very large amount of territory and peoples whose Sinification was not very genuine. This was especially true of the empire founded by Chinggis Qaghan. These peoples, having been rapidly brought into the vast Mongol empire as a result of whirlwind military campaigns, had very complicated cultural backgrounds. The Mongol-ruled Chinese territory was only the easternmost of several Mongol khanates. The Liao and the Jin were not as powerful as the Mongols, but their methods of unification provided an example for the Mongol system and may be discussed together.

The steppe lifestyle was completely different from that of settled agriculture. Thus, when the northern nations took over land and people south of the Great Wall, they had to have a method for differentially governing them. After the Liao received the Sixteen Prefectures of North China from the Later Jin, they set up a system of dual administration. They governed the northern steppe peoples through a Northern Chancellery and the southern sedentary people (mostly Chinese) through a Southern Chancellery. The people living in the Sixteen Prefectures continued to carry on their Chinese cultural life. The Jin and the Yuan copied this dual administration system of the Liao with very few changes. The Jurchens left few people in their original home in the northeast, and the rest were rather quickly Sinified, but the Mongol situation was very different. After Chinggis Qaghan destroyed the Jin, he gave the task of conquering China to General Prince Mukhali (1170–1223); he followed Jin precedents and retained the original Chinese administrative structure of prefectures and counties.

The Jin had stationed military units (normal Jurchen institutions) called *meng-an* and *mouke* to protect the administration of these Chinese prefectures and counties. The Mongols also stationed similar allied army units to protect important locations—transliterated as *tanmachi jun*, these were Khitan, Jurchen, and Chinese soldiers who had joined the Mongol armies. Although the Yuan dynasty had Chinese armies numbering in the thousands in the Hebei and Shaanxi regions, nevertheless they assigned overseers called *darughachi* (in Chinese, *daluhuachi*) to watch over these local military units and almost all administrative units. The Qing dynasty also employed banner troops as territorial garrisons in strategic locations under the command of Manchu generals.

The Mongols conquered the Southern Song after their armies were already very advanced on their western conquests and were thus scattered throughout Central Asia, the Middle East, and the northwest. At first, the Mongol troops that entered Chinese territory under General Prince Mukhali represented only a small portion of Chinggis Qaghan's vast armies. After campaigning for years in the west and dividing their armies, it remained for the great khans Möngke, Güyüg, and Khubilai to lead the Mongol armies in China. Many of the troops were allied army units (*qian jun*, another name for *tanmachi jun* mentioned above) recruited in northwestern and Central Asia, thus making them armies with diverse and mixed ethnic compositions. With the rise of the Ming dynasty, the Mongol regime was reduced to the population north and south of the Gobi Desert, and they retained only six of this type of military unit called *tümen* (Chinese *wanhu*, "ten thousand families," alluding to their putative size). The descendents of those allied armies all remained in China, and, for this reason, the composition of the Chinese population absorbed many foreign elements.

Not only was there this change in the composition of the population in the Mongol-ruled Chinese territories, but as the Mongols continued their western conquests, they pressed the men of many lands into their allied armies to continue their western march. They did this in Chinggis Qaghan's time, and the western khanates continued this method of constant conquest and expansion. The population of this entire Eurasian land mass, now known as Inner Asia, was greatly transformed by these rapid Mongol conquests, and it lost its medieval makeup.

Not only the Mongol conquests had this effect of ethnic transformation. When the Jurchens destroyed the Khitan Liao, Yelü Dashi led a remnant group west to establish the Kara Khitai (Western Liao) near the Chui (Chuy) River (in modern Kyrgyzstan and Kazakhstan). The Kara Khitai was for a time the most powerful nation in Central Asia. When the Mongol (or Turkic) Naiman people were defeated by Chinggis Qaghan in 1204, their Prince Kuchlug (?–1218) took refuge in the Western Liao. In 1211, he usurped the Western Liao leadership in a coup d'état, and the dynasty was destroyed when the Mongols killed him in 1218. All of these events brought about a transformation and realignment of the power of the peoples of the northwest. In sum, the entrance of the Liao, Jin, and Yuan into China and their rise and fall had a deep and lasting influence on the peoples of East and North Asia.

The peoples of the steppes were usually divided into tribes, with an area of pasturage separating them, and with no confederated affiliation. Generally, when a powerful leader emerged, he would unite the many steppe tribes by means of his sweeping power and then establish a commonly shared ethnic consciousness. The Xiongnu during the Qin and Han, the Xianbei during the Northern Dynasties, and the Tujue during the Sui and Tang all united the steppe pastoralists into great empires (or confederacies). These great empires went through a cycle of increasing power and then dispersal, with a loss of ethnic allegiance, until they were reunited by yet another powerful emerging force. The three great empires of Abaoji (Khitan Liao), Aguda (Jurchen Jin), and Chinggis Qaghan (Mongol Yuan) emerged one after another on the steppes. The Liao, Jin, and Yuan dynasties all assimilated Chinese practices, with the Mongols also absorbing cultural elements from the Huihe (Uyghurs) and the Tibetans, elements even more suitable to their pastoral nomadism. Although the Mongols returned to their homeland after the rise of the Ming dynasty, the several centuries of their acculturation did not come to an end. Even while fighting with the Ming, the later Mongol Yuan dynasty was influenced by the transmission of Tibetan Buddhism. Although their political system broke down into several dispersed tribal groupings, they still remained connected through the medium of Lamaist Buddhism and both their classical and later Mongolian writing systems. From this time on for several hundred years, the Mongols were the only nation (ethnic group) occupying the northern steppes of China.

At the same time, although the Jurchen Jin's hegemony did not last long before they were replaced by the Mongols, nevertheless a struggle for control of Chinese territory still continued in the Jurchen's homeland in northeastern China. In the end, Nurhaci (1559–1626), the leader of a Jurchen group later to become the Manchus, won out, and Manchuria became the seat of great power in the northeast. The Manchus and the Mongols had sometimes fought each other, but in the long run their relations were more friendly than confrontational. Tibetan Lamaist Buddhism was the main cultural element bringing these two steppe peoples closer together. The second important element that encouraged a common consciousness for these two peoples was the Manchu adoption of the Mongolian script for writing their language. When the Manchu Qing dynasty entered China, it repeated the experience of the Liao and Jin, but the Manchu's close relations with the Mongols was something never seen before in a conquest dynasty. This was an extremely important change in North Asia—from then on, the steppe region no longer witnessed the cyclic rise and fall of nomadic confederacies.

In contrast to this Manchu-Mongol relationship, the three khanates created by the sons and heirs of Chinggis Qaghan were not only at odds with the Mongol Yuan but also fought more than cooperated among themselves. The khanates possessed great military might, but they were never able to unite. They were even culturally assimilated, especially

Islamicized, by the peoples they conquered. Although when he rose to power in Central Asia, Timür (Tamerlane, Timür the Lame, 1336–1405) kept the descendants of the Chagatai line as Timurid khans, he took the Islamic title of sultan for himself. In the same manner, the Mughal empire in India (founded in 1526 by Babur, a descendent of Timür on his father's side) was also an Islamic state. The Tatars (in Chinese, Dada) in central Europe and Russia also lost their Mongol ethnic consciousness.

Ruled by three successive conquest dynasties, China was profoundly influenced by their cultures. Before the medieval era, the northwest was a Chinese cultural hinterland. From the Song through the Ming (later medieval to early modern times), Chinese culture, with Confucianism as the mainstream, moved continually south. After the post–An Lushan governor generals usurped their northern prefectures and the Liao took over the Sixteen Prefectures in the north, the north was ruled by non-Chinese for a long time. The Khitan Liao employed Han Chinese officials—men like Liu Shouguang (872–959, the founder of the short-lived state of Yan, near modern Beijing) and Han Yanhui (a governor general who served under Liu)—to rule Chinese territory. Thus the Han, Liu, Ma, and Zhao families, all descendents of meritorious officials, grew into powerful families under the Liao. Having led military campaigns for some time, they were quite different from the hereditary great families of the Sui and Tang eras. As the Liao, Jin, and Yuan succeeded each other, the prominent families of Shandong and Hebei were caught in the middle of the north-south conflict and subsequently developed into regional warlords in North China. Among them, the Yan, Shi, Wu, Zhang, Li, Wang, and Dong families changed leaders and allegiances often and fought one another for generations. These regional generals were later called "hereditary lords" after they surrendered to General Prince Mukhali, from 1217 to 1223, in exchange for a grant of hereditary control of their forces; they finally became a regular part of Khubilai Qaghan's military system.

This pattern was seen not only in Hebei. Such regional power centers also existed in Shandong and Guanlong. Near the end of the Yuan, Chaghan Timür (?–1362) and his adopted son Kökö Timür (?–1375), *semu* (see below) men from the Western Regions, united the power of people in their region to contend with powerful Mongol officials. They defeated them, but later on ironically fought for the Mongol Yuan cause all the way to the end of the dynasty in China. These regional warlords, like Zhu Yuanzhang (1328–1398), Chen Youliang (1320–1363), and Zhang Shicheng

(1321–1367), who later fought under the banner of the Red Turban Rebellion, were all born commoners without any high-ranking support. Zhu Yuanzhang was the first commoner since Liu Bang to take the imperial throne, but he did it in a manner quite different from the Sui-Tang dynastic transition. One reason for this was that the collective power of the hereditary great families no longer existed. The three conquest dynasties had wiped out the traditional power of the northern Chinese great families. From the Six Dynasties on, there were no great hereditary families within the borders of Song China. With their demise, national power based on a powerful social elite was fatally weakened. Community or regional forces relying on popular religion as their organizing principle began to arise everywhere to challenge the imperial power.

In sum, the effects of rule by three conquest dynasties on the societies of both the northern steppe peoples and the Han Chinese had very important long-term significance. On the one hand, the steppe peoples' ethnic consciousness was strengthened. On the other hand, great changes occurred in Han Chinese society. The new relationship between Han Chinese and the northern steppe peoples and the clear demarcation between north and south in China proper are a direct result of developments during this four-hundred-year late medieval period leading into the early modern era.

3. Formation of an East Asian Economic Sphere

After the political order established by the Heavenly Qaghan was replaced by a pluralistic multistate system, the economic relationships between various parts of East Asia did not actually become estranged. On the contrary, during the Song and Yuan dynasties, the various states of East Asia developed very closely knit economic networks.

After the An Lushan Rebellion, North China was a battleground, but the east-west trade routes continued to prosper. Many large nomadic groups were in constant contact on the steppes; they fought one another but also exchanged goods and people. Sogdian merchants traveled throughout Central Asia and beyond. Archaeology has unearthed copious records of business accounts and contracts that give us a glimpse of a thriving commercialism. Communication hubs, like Qara-hoja (modern Xinjiang) and Guazhou and Shazhou on the Hexi (Gansu) Corridor (the

Northern Silk Road)—all very small states—were quite able to maintain their independence. Their ability to do so in the middle of an area of violent ethnic strife was certainly attributable to the economic power they obtained from their strategic locations on that main east-west commercial thoroughfare.

China's north and northwest was the locale for an early struggle for hegemony between China and the Tujue. Then, later on, China and the Huihe (Uyghurs), Tubu (Tibetans), and Dashi (Arabs) maneuvered for power in this area. Though the trade routes were not as open and unobstructed as they would have been under the unified rule of a single regime, a considerable movement of people, goods, and information followed the fortunes of these various wars. During the late medieval period, North China gradually came to be dominated by a few very large political entities: the Khitan Liao, Jurchen Jin, Tangut Xi Xia, and Mongol Yuan, while the Mongol khanates stretched westward and the vast and rapidly developing Arab empire Islamicized Central Asia. These great political powers maintained order in their own territories and used their considerable economic clout to carry out large-scale official trade relations. A most striking example was China's exchange of silk for horses. This Tang exchange with the Huihe (Uyghurs) was extremely large. The Song dynasty's treaties with the Liao and Xi Xia included large annual payments of silk, with which the Chinese bought peace; at the same time, a brisk border trade of tea for horses also thrived. China's annual payments of silk reached the costly amount of some one hundred thousand bolts. The Liao and Xi Xia sold this silk along to the Western world and made a very tidy profit in the bargain. Indeed, these international treaties effectively amounted to a process of coercive long-range exchange.

The Mongol armies raced west and south, extending their great power from the east to Central Asia and on across Eurasia. Their wars of conquest were extremely brutal, but, on the other hand, the Mongols were very supportive of the commercial activities and handicraft industries of the people they conquered. The courier routes of the Mongol khanates were efficient and unobstructed. Even in times of mutual struggle, the khanates rarely blocked the trade routes, and thus vigorous long-distance commercial activity continued. During the Mongol Yuan dynasty, Central Asian merchants served the Mongols and even held offices in the Mongol regime. They were collectively labeled *semu*, Chinese for "colored eyes" (that is, not brown); the term is usually translated as "people of varied categories" and was applied to western and Central Asians given special privileges under their administrative system. These merchants were employed primarily for their ability to write and keep accounts, things that the Mongol cavalrymen were not very good at. *Semu* could be applied to almost anyone from the West; it included Sogdians, Arabs, Jews, and other Europeans—if there really was a Marco Polo in Yuan China, he, too, would have been a *semu*! The vigorous commercial activities of these merchants trading between East and West, whether by land or by sea, are evidence that a large economic sphere was in the process of formation.

The main commodities of medieval China's international trade were silk, porcelain, tea, and iron wares. Silk was the most important export commodity during the Tang, but in Song times Central Asia, Japan, and Korea had all become good at silk weaving, and China no longer monopolized the market. Song porcelain production, however, made great progress. The famous Tang kilns were in the north, but after the Five Dynasties, porcelain production in the south became both more abundant and sported a greater variety. The Chinese iron-smelting industry also made great strides in the Song. According to the *Song Collection of Essential Documents* (*Song huiyao*), iron smelting reached the impressive figure of one hundred and fifty thousand tons, fully two times the amount of iron produced in Europe at that time! Song tea production also increased greatly as tea became a drink enjoyed by the general population. This tea was also transported from North China to become an internationally traded commodity. Some local specialty products, like salt from the southwest, were also important commodities to be sold to the north. Nine of the ten states in the Five Dynasties and Ten States period were in the south. Since the south was not the locale of violent struggles for the imperial throne, the southern economy was very prosperous. The above-mentioned porcelain, iron, and tea were all primarily southern products.

It was much easier and safer to ship commodities for trade abroad by sea than by the arduous overland route. Chinese porcelain, for example, was transported by sea and sold in Southeast Asia and India, while its ultimate destination was via the Persian Gulf or the Red Sea for sale in the Middle East and transshipment and sale in Europe. The mountains of porcelain shards found at Al Fustat in Egypt (near modern Cairo), the first Red Sea transfer port, bear witness to the large scale of the east-west porcelain trade. Owing to the large foreign market, many areas in the south produced porcelain. There are no kilns in today's Hunan, but during the

Five Dynasties and the Song, porcelain produced in Hunan was shipped to Guangzhou and almost exclusively intended for the foreign market. At Wazhaping ("the Plain of Shards") near modern Changsha, archaeologists have located the ruins of many kilns surrounded by piles of shards. Many of these shards have painted on them patterns obviously intended for the Middle Eastern market; they may be regarded as early trade porcelain. The Five Dynasties state of Chu in modern Hunan was small and weak, but it could maintain itself as one of the ten southern states because of its thriving foreign trade. The four big townships (*zhen*) of Song times grew large and important because of their economic strength. Both Jingdezhen as a center of porcelain production and Foshanzhen's iron smelting prospered thanks to their important local product. These two commercial products had large internal and foreign markets, and consequently these areas prospered for hundreds of years.

Many harbors on China's southern coast were involved in international trade. From the Han dynasty on, large numbers of foreign ships docked at Guangzhou and Jiaozhou (north and central Vietnam and parts of Guangxi). Song-dynasty Annam was an independent country, but Guangzhou remained as prosperous as ever. Even though Guangzhou's Middle Eastern merchants had been massacred during the Huang Chao Rebellion (874–884), they still regarded the city as a most important trade center. The insignificant state of the Southern Han relied on the accumulated wealth of Guangzhou to sustain itself.

Quanzhou was an important international trade port throughout the Tang, Song, and Yuan dynasties, and many Middle Eastern merchants took up residence there. People with the surnames Guo and Ding in modern Quanzhou can still trace their Islamic origins. The Zaytun (the Moslem name for Quanzhou) of Marco Polo was one of the greatest ports of that era. Fujian no longer produces porcelain, but at the time it also had many kilns producing for the foreign market; their remains still bespeak their flourishing in the past. The Five Dynasties state of Min, with its small size and meager population, was another place that prospered at the time from overseas trade. Wuyue was also a small state, but their famous kilns were the most prosperous at the time; most of them, like the Longquan kiln and the Ge kiln, were located in Zhejiang. Mingzhou (modern Ningpo) was also a famous international port. Thus, the small state of Wuyue was able to construct a seawall and irrigation works and become a peaceful and prosperous realm that enjoyed the longest reign of the ten southern states. The extent of foreign influence in Wuyue can be seen from the fact that contemporary Zhejiang even had a Manichean Theological Academy. For similar reasons, the states of Wu and Southern Tang on the lower reaches of the Yangzi were not only centers of wealth in the southwest, but ships could come straight up the river and thus make Yangzhou another important international port. Hongzhou (modern Nanchang) was also a place of northward transshipment from Fujian, serving as an international trade entrepôt. The Southern Tang was the richest of the ten southern states, and the foundation of its wealth rested on its internal and external commodities markets. The states of Former Shu and Later Shu in Sichuan were not only rich in resources, but their exchange of tea and salt for horses with Hexi and Tibet was also extremely profitable. When the Song armies were short on horses, their needs were supplied from the southwest.

We can see from all of the above that late medieval China carried on international trade in natural resources and commercial products in both the north and south. Who were the winners in this international trade? In the north, China traded silk and tea for horses, furs, and leather products. After the An Lushan Rebellion, the Tang government bought Huihe (Uyghur) horses with silk, but the Song rulers made annual payments of silk to the Liao and Xi Xia—a trade at great expense with no financial profits at all! China's northern neighbors did not take all of this silk for their own use. Great amounts of it passed through the various Central Asian countries on its way to the Middle East and Europe, where it was sold at great profit. Ever since the Islamic empires established their hegemony in the Middle East and Central Asia, they had served as middlemen, making hefty profits on eastern commodities including Chinese silk, porcelain, paper, and South Sea spices. Middle Eastern Arabs also tried to imitate Chinese porcelain production, but to no avail; they did, however, process the silk and sell it on to many places at a very good profit. Jewelry was the main item the foreign traders brought to China. These precious gems, pearls, and jades were produced in Africa and Southeast Asia, the pearls coming mainly from the warm waters of the Indian and Pacific oceans. The Middle East did not really have any commodities that could be sold, but the Arab and other traders served as middlemen who sold others' products in China at very high prices. Chinese history and literature are full of stories about the jewels and great wealth of these Middle Eastern merchants. Thus, the Islamic world of the Middle East took advantage of its favorable geographic position to monopolize the profits of the east-west trade and maintain their cultural efflorescence and economic prosperity. The Middle East lost its geographic advantage after the opening up of maritime trade on the Pacific Ocean, and the gradual decline of the Islamic world after the fifteenth century was directly related to this change in patterns of world trade.

There were important differences between the maritime trade from the southeast and that from the south. Chinese foreign trade goods, silk, porcelain, paper, metals, and so on were not only shipped to the Middle East; they were also traded at many points along the way. Departing from southeastern ports, medieval ships navigated northward, hugging the coastline on their way to Japan and the Korean peninsula. Most of the products of these two areas were quite similar to Chinese products and did not fill any basic mutual needs. Japan and Korea exchanged luxury goods like Korean satins and Japanese swords for Chinese luxury goods like porcelain, paper, and even materials for the construction of Buddhist temples. The chief import from Japan during the Song dynasty and the most worthy of our later attention consisted of copper bars for minting coins!

The South Sea trade was on a much greater scale than the trade to Japan and Korea. The long sea route started from the South China Sea and followed the Indochina and Malay peninsulas to modern Indonesia. From there it went north along the Malay peninsula and crossed the Bay of Bengal to Ceylon where it turned south for a while and then north along the Indian subcontinent, crossing the Indian Ocean to enter finally the Persian Gulf or the Red Sea. There the goods were loaded ashore and transferred to the Mediterranean port of Alexandria. Thus, the ocean trade route reached all the way to the Middle East and indirectly linked up with the Mediterranean and Europe; nearer at hand were Annam, Champa, Khmer, and all of modern Southeast and South Asia. Not only Chinese but also Indian and Arab ships plied this sea route, carrying as much as several hundred tons of cargo. Although they hugged the coastlines, they also navigated by compass. Many-masted sailboats could even sail against the wind. Chinese merchant ships already had watertight cabins and stern-mounted rudders and were able to navigate relatively certain courses with considerable safety. Besides the ship captain's own goods, Chinese merchants could also reserve a place for their goods and ride along with them to the port where they were to be sold. Then they would load up on other commodities and return to their starting port, where they would sell them.

This sort of trade involved sailors, merchants, brokers, and government customs offices. Many foreign merchants who traveled the trade routes took up long-term residence in Chinese ports. There were foreign merchants living in "foreign quarters" (fanfang) in Guangzhou, Quanzhou, Mingzhou (Ningpo), and even inland transfer ports like Yangzhou and Hongzhou (Nanchang).

For the same reasons, Chinese merchants also had to take up residence in various places in Southeast Asia. It is said that the overseas Chinese born in today's Malacca can trace some eight hundred years of oral history, thus demonstrating that they have been there since Song and Yuan times. At the beginning of the Ming dynasty, when Zheng He (1371–1433) made his seven long sea voyages, his sailors, his knowledge of navigation, and even his shipbuilding techniques were all based on the long-distance shipping experience of the Song and Yuan dynasties. After Zheng He, the Ming government closed the country off from international intercourse, but the Chinese merchants and common people continued to associate with their counterparts in Southeast Asia. Thus, many Chinese settlements in Southeast Asia continued to exist and established an unbroken tradition of trade with that area. According to the Song huiyao, the most important areas visited on these southern trade routes included the Arab states of Java, Champa, Borneo, Mindoro, Samboja (Sri Vijaya), and Kalimantan. China exported gold, silver, strings of coins, lead, tin, various kinds of silk, and various grades of porcelain; it imported spices, rhinoceros horn, ivory, coral, amber, pearls, high-quality iron, tortoiseshell, tortoise skin, giant clams, agate, crystal, foreign fabrics, elm gum, and medicinal plants.

The most noteworthy items in this list of Chinese imported goods are the spices; gold, silver, and strings of coins are the most notable exports. The Song dynasty imported great quantities of spices. In Taizong's (r. 976–997) time, the government collected spices to make up its financial shortfall—the maritime trade supervisor of Guangzhou, Mingzhou, and Hangzhou collected over 354,449 pounds of frankincense (high-quality incense) alone! Marco Polo described the flourishing nature of trade in Zaytun (Quanzhou) in the following manner: "If one ship laden with spices entered the port of Alexandria, there would be a hundred such ships entering Zaytun harbor." Although the amounts cited may well be

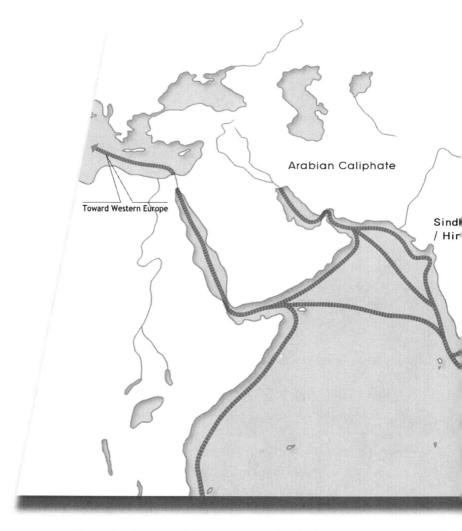

Arabian Caliphate

Toward Western Europe

Sind
/ Hir

FIGURE 5.2 Map of the Oceanic Silk Road in Late Medieval China

exaggerated, they are sufficient to represent the immense prosperity of this spice trade. Spices can be divided into those used for fumigation and those used for flavoring food. In medieval times, Buddhism and other religions from the east all ceremonially burned incense, and the practice of burning incense at home was also widespread. The recipes in the early medieval book *Important Arts of the People* (*Qimin yaoshu*, 533–544) use only onions, ginger, celery, and orange peel as flavorings, but Song cuisine already made use of pepper ("barbarian pepper" in Chinese), fennel,

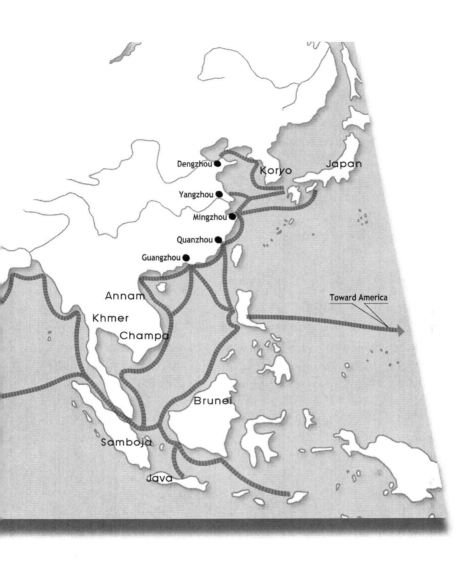

and other spices. By that time, it would seem that the Chinese used spices in about the same abundance as contemporary Europeans.

China's three most significant exports were gold, silver, and strings of cash, all of which can be regarded as payment for imported commodities. The Song dynasty already had a highly developed monetary economy and no longer used silk as a currency for commodity purchases, as in the Tang. Gold and silver, being expensive metals, already served as both commodities and currency; copper strings of cash were strictly common currency. The Song government calculated its taxes in copper cash, and a tremendous amount of it was in circulation. As Lien-sheng Yang (1914–1990) pointed out, more copper was cast during the Song than any previous dynasty. Indeed, the Song government restricted the use of copper for everyday utensils to ensure a sufficient supply for minting coins. China had to import copper from Japan and Korea to make up for its own lack of that metal. There were most probably two reasons for the Song dynasty's currency shortage. The first is the great development and huge size of the Chinese economy itself, requiring that a considerable amount of currency be in circulation, and second is the fact that Chinese copper cash had become the chief currency in circulation throughout Southeast Asia. The commercial economy of the Song was certainly highly developed. That commercial taxes were the government's most important tax demonstrates that purchasing power was very great and supply and demand very lively. At the same time, while the countries of Southeast Asia were growing ever more prosperous from their long-distance trade, most of them were newly emerged states that lacked or had insufficient amounts of their own currency. The Liao and the Xi Xia both imported Song currency and forbade the export of copper, and even the Jin and the Yuan relied on Song currency. A great deal of Song currency has also been unearthed in Japan; thus archaeological evidence shows that Chinese copper cash had become an international medium of exchange.

From the discussion in this section, we can see that medieval China had not only entered the overall Asian economic network but had become a major commodity provider in the long-distance overland trade between East and Central Asia. Chinese currency had also become an international medium of exchange in contemporary maritime trade. With China at its center, the economies of East and West were in the process of coming together in an integrated network.

4. A Pluralistic Economic Network

The political and economic centers of China both shifted during the medieval period, gradually developing into a pluralistic and multicentered arrangement. During the first half of the Tang, the political center was along an axis from Chang-an to Luoyang, but this area did not produce enough foodstuffs to satisfy the consumption needs of the large population. Food grains had to be shipped in from the southeast by inland waterways and canals. After the An Lushan Rebellion, the two capitals were severely damaged, and, with the governor generals occupying Hebei and the Tibetans and Uyghurs encroaching in the west, the capital areas had to rely even more on the support of the southeast.

Following the precedent set during the Five Dynasties, the Song dynasty established its capital at Bianliang (Kaifeng in eastern Henan) primarily for ease of canal transport from the south. During the Northern Song, Hebei and Guanzhong were on the front lines. With the Khitan Liao occupying the Sixteen Prefectures of North China (from Datong to Youzhou), Beijing ("the northern capital," Damingfu) became the most important northern defense garrison. With the rise of the Xi Xia, Guanzhong, Huanqing, and Yansui all became frontier garrisons; Xijing ("western capital," the former Chang-an) was also a western defense garrison.

Ten thousand imperial guards were stationed in Bianliang, but they could not really defend the city and lacked the economic resources to maintain themselves, so the political center had to depend on the wealth of the southeast. During the Northern Song, the southeast was not only rich in agricultural products—many important manufactured products, such as silk, porcelain, iron smelting, and bronze casting, were all located south of the Yangzi—but the most important foreign trade ports were also in the south.

Thus, after 1127, the Southern Song was not only protected by mountains and rivers, but it was also more prosperous than the Northern Song. The economic and political centers of China proper were divided, and the economic center had shifted to the southeast.

The Sui dynasty built the north-south Grand Canal in response to the difficulty of supplying food grains to the capital, but the canal also provided a means of transportation for southeastern agricultural and industrial products. This helped turn China's northern population into an internal market for the southeast. At the same time, the Khitan Liao and the Xi Xia established themselves on China's northern borders, where their abundant populations also had strong purchasing power. Thus, not only was the Song dynasty an internal market, but the Liao and Xi Xia, taking advantage of China's north-south transport, also grew into a market supplied by the southeast. All of this naturally provided a powerful stimulus to southeastern economic development.

In Han and Tang terms, two big changes had occurred. On the one hand, given the rise of the Liao dynasty and the Xi Xia state (and the

Jin and Yuan to follow the Liao), the political center of greater China had split into a multicentered arrangement. On the other hand, China's southeastern region as a whole had leapt forward to become the extremely influential foundation of economic production for all of greater China.

At the time, the south could be divided into several distinct economic regions, each with their own special characteristics and regional centers. The southeast included the lower reaches of the Yangzi and was the largest and probably the most prosperous region. Its chief products were silk, cotton, and rice. The Five Dynasties states of Wu and Southern Tang became rich and independent on the basis of this wealth. The population of this region was quite large; they transported goods both by sea and via the north-south canal, and the lakes and rivers of the interior formed a major network of water transportation. The major cities were Yangzhou and Jiankang (modern Nanjing).

The Zhejiang region borders on the southeast. The Five Dynasties state of Wuyue established itself there and profited from silk, fishing, salt production, and porcelain manufacturing carried out in the celebrated Ge and Longquan kilns. The chief port in this area was Mingzhou (Ningpo), and its major city, Hangzhou, was the true capital of the Southern Song despite its hopeful designation as Xingzai (the European's Quinsai), meaning "temporary residence of the emperor."

The modern Fujian region was the Five Dynasties state of Min. Though small and weak, it achieved independence based on its lucrative foreign trade. Quanzhou was an international trading port; Marco Polo (calling it Zaytun) described it as the largest port in the contemporary world. Merchant ships embarking from Quanzhou went as far as the Persian Gulf and the Red Sea, trading at all of the ports of Southeast Asia and India they visited along the way. Fujian no longer produces porcelain, but at the time it produced large amounts of fine china for foreign trade.

Jingdezhen in Jiangxi was already a major center of porcelain productions and sent its wares along the Gan River to Quanzhou for transshipment to foreign markets. At the same time, foreign merchants came to Quanzhou and then traveled overland to Jiangxi and further north, making Jiangxi vitally important to the Fujian region. Hongzhou (Nanchang) was also a major southeastern city. When the Jurchen Jin pursued the Song armies at the fall of the Southern Song, they invaded the south along a route that followed the Gan River.

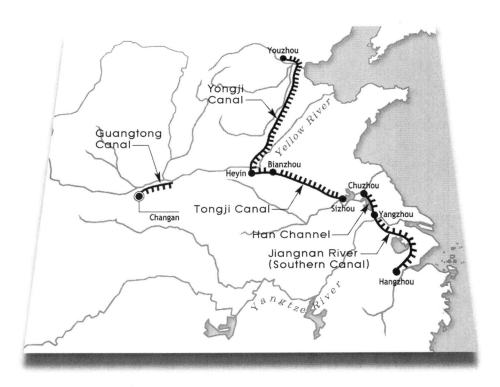

FIGURE 5.3 The Grand Canal in Sui and Tang Times

Fujian and Zhejiang share a common border area that is easily reached from the sea or over the Xianxia Mountains. Relations between the two areas were so close that many members of the Southern Song royal family took up temporary residence in Quanzhou. Farther south from Fujian is Lingnan, the seat of the Five Dynasties state of Southern Han.

Guangzhou was an international port that had been full of foreign ships since Qin and Han times. The center of the Guangdong area was Guiguan (Guangxi) on the West River; it was also connected to the Xiang River via the Ling Canal, which carried Hunan porcelain to Guangzhou for shipment abroad. Yue or Guangdong (Canton) was also prosperous and world famous early on. The economic strength of this area was just as great as that of the lower Yangzi region.

The prefecture of Jiaozhou in modern Vietnam was already independent in Song times; the Song government invested their leader with the title of King of Annam, however, and the area still remained within the greater Chinese economic sphere.

Dali in Yunnan, the successor state to Nanzhao, was independent throughout the Song. The area relied on its profits from tea and salt to buy horses from the steppe peoples. Copper bars and jade were the chief commodities traded between Dali and the Song, and they also sold horses to the Song.

The interior of Yunnan could also be divided into several distinctive areas, such as the Lake Dian (or Kunming Lake) and Lake Erhai regions. When the Mongols invaded China, they circled around, following the southwestern trade route, and attacked the Song from the rear at this point.

The Sichuan basin was known as the "heaven-blessed province" because its salt and agricultural products were abundant enough to supply itself and many other surrounding regions. It was an economic region in itself, given its major cities of Chengdu and Bazhou (modern Chongqing). During the Northern Song, Sichuan was Guanzhong's rearguard defense against the Xi Xia; during the Southern Song, Sichuan commanded the upper reaches of the Yangzi and provided defense support to the Hubei area.

Most of these areas had rich economic resources. By contrast, during the Northern Song, the Shaanxi and Gansu area made up an outer ring surrounding and protecting Guanzhong and the capital area. With its dense population and government expenses, the capital area was forced to rely on the rich resources of the above-mentioned economic regions. During the Southern Song, the Jiangsu and Anhui areas were on the front line of defense; they were even less able to provision themselves and had to rely on economic support from the central government.

Most noteworthy about the Song economy was the extremely large commodity flows between different economic regions. Song commercial taxes were remarkable—vast amounts of goods passed through the major land and water transportation hubs, and a prodigious amount of tax was collected. There were more than a dozen major cities throughout the country where the government's commercial tax revenues amounted to more than thirty thousand strings of cash per year. According to the *Song huiyao*, in the 1060s and 1070s (during the Northern Song), ten northern prefectures, including Damingfu (Beijing) and Luoyang, provided thirty to forty thousand strings of cash per year in commercial taxes, and thirteen southern prefectures, including Yangzhou, Hangzhou, and Suzhou, each provided approximately fifty thousand strings in commercial taxes. The commercial taxes of these twenty-some cities accounted for over one-fourth of the revenue from that source. Adding in the various cities of Sichuan and the particularly large capital city of Bianliang (Kaifeng), there were over thirty urban areas in which commercial tax collection was concentrated. Thus, we can see that the cities were the engine of the Song dynasty's economic vitality.

There seem to be two reasons for this urban economic vitality. First, the various areas all had specialty products that were mutually supportive, and second, the urban areas all maintained fairly large-scale government and private handicraft workshops. This reflects the fact that industry was no longer scattered throughout the rural areas and that the urban population had greatly increased.

Also noteworthy was the great change in the structure of Song cities. Tang cities inherited the earlier practice of division into square-shaped walled and gated districts. Song cities, however, followed an open street pattern. From the twelfth-century scroll painting *Spring Festival Along the River (Qingming shanghe tu)* and the 1147 book *Dream of Splendors Past in the Eastern Capital (Dongjing Meng Hua lu)*, both recalling the Northern Song capital, we can see long rows of shops and crowds of people bustling up and down the streets.

Besides industrial and commercial activities, Song cities also offered many entertainments and leisure activities, from jugglers and other street performers to professional theaters. Marco Polo's account of the flourishing, lively, and exciting nature of the cities of Yuan China is in complete accord with Chinese records. Not only was this the usual situation in Song cities, but the cities of the Liao, Jin, Xi Xia, and Dali all followed similar patterns.

Many contemporary Chinese cities are in the same place as their Song and Yuan predecessors, but they are not necessarily the same medieval cities. Some cities—including Beijing (Damingfu), Nanchang, Changsha, Wuchang, Shaoxing, and Ningpo—that developed in the tenth to thirteenth centuries were rebuilt during the Ming dynasty, but their street patterns are quite similar to their Song models. Even Nanjing, Guangzhou, and Quanzhou were built on the foundations of their Song and Yuan city models. Thus, the urbanization of the Song and Yuan dynasties represents a major milestone in Chinese history.

Although the southern regions of the Song dynasty were very strong economically, thanks to the excellent Song administrative system, they did not separate into independent powers. The Song administrative units, in order of size, were circuit (*dao*), prefecture (*zhou*), military prefecture (*jun*), and finally county (*xian*). None of the local administrators at each level were given complete or overall power. Officials at the same level had more than one superior; they might have a transport intendent, judicial commissioner, governor commanding troops, associate executive official, or deputy working with or above them. The power of the Song central government over the provinces rested on its control of finances. The central government established supervisors (*jianguan*) to oversee the collection of taxes on various industrial products in the provinces. At the same time, there was a very lively trade in many areas, and on that account the economies of many administrative cities developed greatly. Many places that were originally not cities but were strategically located near mountain passes, ferry crossings, bridges, and harbors, or in periodic market areas just outside the walls of administrative cities, also developed into prosperous new commercial markets.

In the Northern Song, Zhuxian (in Henan), Hankou, Hukou (in Jiangxi), Qingjiang (in Hubei), and Wuwei (in Anhui) were all great cities teeming with merchants and far outshining their nearby administrative cities. As mentioned above, the *Spring Festival Along the River* scroll wonderfully depicts the lively commercial and entertainment activities of these Song cities. All of this demonstrates that the economic strength and the flow of goods in the Song was a powerful force that integrated the entire nation in a vast network of markets. During the Wang Anshi (1021–1086) reforms of the 1070s, the most powerful administrative unit was the Finance Planning Commission (*zhizhi sansi tiaolisi*), which, from 1069 to Wang's death in 1076, granted financial powers to the chief minister. The commission was much more powerful than the personnel or military organs of the government. Thus, the Song government relied on its economic development as an integrative force to overcome any centrifugal local economic powers and maintain national unity and a commonly shared market network.

Throughout Chinese history, military men have seized territory to aggrandize themselves and divide the nation; the Tang regional military governors' seizures of northern areas was a prime example. Taking the Tang example as a warning, the Song government did everything possible to emphasize the civil bureaucracy and downgrade the military. Gener-

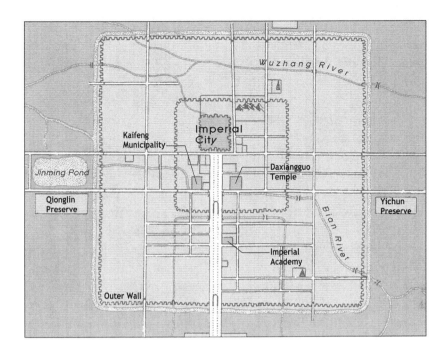

FIGURE 5.4 Map of Kaifeng in the Northern Song

als were not allowed to occupy territory with their troops. The Southern Song generals who commanded troops—including Yue Fei (1103–1142) and Han Shizhong (1089–1151)—suffered persecution no matter how loyal they were.

The Song had a palace army of one hundred thousand troops, but they had very little fighting strength, and the central government was thus forced to rely on other military units with genuine fighting ability. For this reason, local armed military units facing the Liao, Xi Xia, and Jin remained under the command of hereditary warlord leaders.

After the fall of Bianliang to the Jurchen Jin in 1126, loyalist irregulars in the Taihang Mountains, Anhui, and Shanxi and the Fujian militia of the Southern Song developed into the quite numerous Huyi (Tiger troops) regional army. These armed units operated outside of the official Song armed forces and might even be considered a sign of Song pluralism. Such armed groups could only capture a limited amount of local economic resources, however, and thus the possibilities for Tang-style regional takeovers was proportionally restrained.

When the Jurchen Jin and the Mongol Yuan occupied China, their ethnic military organizations—*meng-an*, *mouke*, and *darughachi*—were stationed all around the country. Nevertheless, they still lacked a Song-style mechanism for controlling all of the nation's resources. For this reason, a number of Han Chinese warlords, like the commanders of the Han army in Hebei, were able to control all of the resources of some provincial areas.

To sum up this section, in the larger international sense, late medieval China was no longer leading a "heavenly qaghan" system; it was instead part of a system of mutually independent states that squared off and fought one another. In terms of China proper, the Song dynasty's government, economic, and military affairs constituted three disparate power sources that mutually controlled the others in a complex pluralistic arrangement. Furthermore, there were also several regions within China's collective system that set themselves up as individual units. It was neither the governing nor the military power but rather the economic market network that served to bring this collective enterprise together as an integrated whole. Contemporary China was a vast and complex collective organism, and its great economic power supplied the force that integrated this pluralistic enterprise.

5. The Chinese Intellectual Class During and After the Song Dynasty

After the rule of military men in the late Tang and Five Dynasties, Song Taizu (Zhao Kuangyin, 927–976, r. 960–976) did not want ever again to have to face the threat of generals usurping imperial power. After he dismissed all of his most trusted generals in the spring of 963 "with one cup of wine," Song political power relied on the huge civil bureaucracy, which was supported by the Confucian gentry literati class (*shidafu*). From then on, a tradition of emphasizing the civil over the military became the norm in China and was suspended only during the Mongol Yuan dynasty. During the Song, Confucian scholars (*rusheng*) entered the civil bureaucracy through the highly competitive examination (*keju*) system that tested their knowledge of the ancient classics and their ability to express themselves in writing.

Although from Empress Wu (r. 683–705) on, the Tang dynasty already employed the "presented scholar" (*jinshi*) examination as an opening to the civil service, the powerful hereditary families were still strong in Tang times, and the scions of great families had an advantage over scholars with less exalted pedigrees. During the chaotic warfare of the late Tang and Five Dynasties, when powerful generals usurped government power, the great hereditary families declined, never to rise again.

In the Song administrative system, members of the imperial house and sons of high-ranking officials often entered the bureaucracy through the *yin* privilege (*biyin*, without going through the examination system), but their official careers were not necessarily smooth after that. Members of the Song royal family had to rely on their own competitive abilities once in office, and by rule they could not hold the office of chief minister. Throughout the Song dynasty, only two men of the royal family—the future emperor Zhao Kuangyin, while governor of Kaifeng, and Zhao Ruyu (1140–1196) of the Southern Song—occupied the position of chief minister. All of the most famous officials of the Song—including Su Xun (1009–1066), Su Shi (1037–1101), Su Che (1039–1112), Song Jiao (Song Xiang, 996–1066), Song Qi (998–1061), Fan Zhongyan (989–1052), Wang Anshi, and Wen Tianxiang (1236–1283)—relied on their outstanding literary talent and knowledge to rise above the rank-and-file literati without the benefit of powerful family backgrounds. One of the main practices that made this possible and assured that the Song examination system was able to identify real talent was that the examination papers were sealed to hide the examinees' names from the examiners; this prevented favoritism and guaranteed that the examinees had to rely on their genuine knowledge and ability to pass.

The Song official class received better treatment from the emperor than it had in previous dynasties. It is said that Song Taizu left instructions to his heirs not to put *shidafu* to death. Although factional struggles were fierce in the Song, officials on the losing sides were generally only demoted and/or banished; they were rarely in danger of execution. High officials who were pushed out of office were frequently given sinecures as supervisor of a temple. Song generals did not, however, receive such decent treatment, as the case of Yue Fei amply demonstrates.

Once a Song scholar became a scholar-official, however, he was a member of the bureaucracy for life and could never change that status. Su

Dongpo is a good example of this. He was famous all his life, and everyone thought his talent deserved his elevation to the rank of chief minister, but his official career was not a smooth one. Aside from a stint as Hanlin drafting officer (secretary to the emperor), he spent his whole life in exile, having been banished all the way to the island of Hainan. In earlier dynasties, he could have resigned to live in retirement like Tao Yuanming, without being mired down in the bureaucracy. Song scholar-officials did not have such freedom. Thus, although the Song literati were treated extremely well, they were dependent on the government all their lives.

Song factional struggles occurred repeatedly, and scholar-officials came and went. Thus dedicated reformers such as Fan Zhongyan and Wang Anshi were merely able to improve a few of the faults in the system they inherited.

The status of the Song intellectual class did not rise simply because the imperial government respected scholars; it also rose because this great number of educated men constituted a large social base. Here are two examples: When the celebrated historian Sima Guang (1019–1086) resigned his post as chief minister, the populace sighed in admiration, and when he returned to office, they greeted him with public congratulations. Again, when the Jurchen Jin invaded China and Li Gang (1083–1140) was removed from office by the appeasement faction, students of the Imperial University rallied in protest, and many common people joined in with them. That the common people would participate this way demonstrates that the Song scholar-official literati were no longer an aristocratic class divorced from the lives of ordinary people. The intellectual class was more numerous and their social base broader, because education and knowledge were more widespread.

The greater dissemination of education was related to the school system. Ever since the Han dynasty established the Imperial University, every dynasty has had such an institution of higher education, but not all of them lived up to their name. Local schools are frequently mentioned in the *History of the Former Han* "Biographies of Upright Officials" (*Shunli zhuan*), the best known being the commandery school established by Wen Zhongweng in Sichuan. During the chaos of the Wei-Jin and North-South dynasties, officially established schools remained in name only. Higher education was revived in the Tang, when schools were established in the capital and the provinces. The curriculum was not limited to the Confucian classics but also included mathematics, medicine, and calligraphy. During the high point of the *kaiyuan* era, there were more than sixty thousand students in the whole country; although a large number, this represents only 0.1 percent of the population. After the An Lushan Rebellion, most of the schools were destroyed, with only the Confucian temple still left standing.

The Song dynasty revived education, and both central government and provincial schools were reestablished. Two things are notable about Song official education: first, the schools set up a lecturer system so the students had regular teachers, and second, the government allotted land to provide for the schools' expenses. With steady instructors and landed property, government education under the Song had a much firmer foundation than in the Han to Tang period.

A central idea behind Fan Zhongyan's so-called Minor Reforms of the *qingli* (1043–1045) reign period was to train a professional bureaucracy and thereby improve the quality of local government. The establishment of schools was a focal point of these reforms. Wang Anshi's New Policies (or Major Reforms) of the 1070s had little to say about schools, but Cai Jing's (1047–1126) *chongjing* reign period (1102–1106) reforms under Emperor Huizong (r. 1100–1125) brought education to the fore again by having students trained by local officials and then sent on to the Imperial University. The university itself was also divided into the Three Colleges (Outer, Inner, and Superior), in order of excellence, with scholarships provided for the best students. The student population expanded to more than two hundred thousand. After the fall of the Northern Song in 1126, all of these plans were abandoned, but school education was still carried on to some extent, as the schools had the lecturer system and their own landed property to sustain them.

The foundation of Song school education rested on academies (*shuyuan*), private family schools (*jiashu* or *sishu*), and local community schools (*shexue*). Scholars lectured to students in academies that could be managed by either the government or private individuals. The number of Buddhist monasteries expanded rapidly during the Tang dynasty. They were often located in the most beautiful mountain areas, and famous monks frequently expounded the scriptures and taught religion in them. Tang scholars took up the practice of studying in these monasteries, given the low cost of lodgings and peaceful surroundings for study. Song Confucian scholars followed the tradition of these monasteries when they set up their academies. The chief lecturers were even called "mountain masters" to reflect the mountain monastery origins of the academies, and their chief officers were termed abbot, even more obviously displaying their origins in Buddhist monasteries.

The academies usually had their own landed property, which was supplied either by the government or by private individuals. The students in the academies came and went quite freely, and there were no fixed degrees, as in today's universities. The academies were havens of independent instruction, but several of them were the center of instruction in one of the many schools of Song Neo-Confucian doctrine. The most famous Song academies, like Zhu Xi's (1130–1200) White Deer Hollow Academy and Lu Jiuyuan's (1139–1191) Elephant Mountain Academy, were academic centers for their particular school of thought. The famous rules of the White Deer Hollow Academy—on learning and human behavior—established the pattern for future academies. Confucianism emphasizes both speech and action, and the academies practiced both teaching by lectures and dialectic question-and-answer discussions and teaching by personal moral example. Scholars from different schools of Neo-Confucian thought would travel around to meet and discuss their similarities and differences with members of other academies. The Jiangxi Goose Lake Conference of 1175 between Zhu Xi and Lu Jiuyuan was the most celebrated of these meetings, but it was also said that there were so many participants in a similar meeting between Zhu Xi and Zhang Shi (1133–1180) at Zhang's Yuelu Academy near modern Changsha that their horses drank all the water in the academy's large pond.

At their height, there were more than two hundred Song academies, and many of them still exist to this day. If one really wants to compare the university education systems of Europe, the Middle East, and China, it would be more reasonable to use these Chinese academies instead of the Imperial University as the unit of comparison. As academic organizations and seats of learning, these academies were at the "research academy" level and should certainly have an important place in any universal history of academic thought.

In family education, a single clan would invite a teacher to teach their young men. The smaller establishments were nothing more than household schools (*sishu*), but there were also large schools supported by grants of clan land. Education was one of the projects supported by Fan Zhongyan's celebrated charitable estates. During the Southern Tang, the

Chen family of Jiangzhou (in Jiangxi) and the Hu family of Hongzhou (Nanchang) had extensive libraries that were open to both clan members and outsiders and constituted another organization for family education. Some of the above-mentioned academies were supported by government grants of land; others were supported by private grants of landed property, housing, and libraries. Fan Zhongyan, for example, donated land to the Yingtianfu Academy (near the city of Shangqiu, in modern Henan).

From the Song on, the *sishu* family school was the model for popular education; it was the clan school and the community school, and both clan members and local men studied there. Family and community schools provided the basic foundations for education; students there learned how to read and write, so that they could go on to study other important subjects in the government schools.

The academies were institutions of higher education where students and scholars discussed profound intellectual questions and urged one another on to polish their characters and maintain firm moral principles and aspirations. The curriculum of these educational units emphasized the Confucian classics as well as poetry, prose, and some elementary mathematics. There were specialized official schools for studies other than the classics, such as mathematics, calendrical studies, drawing and painting, medicine, and so on—the Song and Qing both established an official painting academy (*huayuan*). If a private school taught specialized subjects, this was generally carried out in a master-disciple context.

Besides the Confucianists, Buddhists and Daoists also had monasteries and temples, where they transmitted knowledge of the classics and ceremonies of their thought and religion. All of these traditional practices continued until the twentieth century, when Chinese education underwent reforms in light of the new knowledge of Western educational systems.

There were many diverse schools of Neo-Confucian thought during the Song. There were regional schools in the Northern Song, and in the Southern Song there was the celebrated division between Zhu Xi's School of Principle (*lixue*) and Lu Jiuyuan's School of Mind (*xinxue*), the two sometimes characterized as the idealists and the rationalists, respectively. During the Yuan dynasty, Zhu Xi's interpretative commentaries on the Four Books, *Great Learning* (*Daxue*), *Doctrine of the Mean* (*Zhongyong*), *Analects of Confucius* (*Lunyu*), and *Mencius* (*Mengzi*), which he established as the core of Confucian teaching, became the official Confucian state orthodoxy. It was not until the rise of the Wang Yangming (Wang Shouren, 1472–1528) School of Mind that there was any major theoretical rival to the Zhu Xi orthodoxy.

There is no way to ascertain the exact numbers or the literacy rate of the educated stratum in the Song. From the number of books published and handed down, it would seem that the circulation of literary collections and the numbers of men involved in the Song academies must have been closely related. The techniques of Chinese woodblock printing originated with the making of rubbings from characters or pictures engraved on metal, stone, or brick. Even the stamping of engraved seals can be considered a form of early printing, but printing done with whole blocks of wood completely filled with carved characters constituted true printing. The earliest works printed in large numbers were probably Buddhist or Daoist religious books. The earliest printed book known to archaeologists today is still a Buddhist sutra from the seventh century.

Besides Buddhist sutras, almanacs, and lexicons, poetry and prose works also began to be printed around that time. During the Five Dynasties, Feng Dao (882–954) supervised the woodblock printing of the *Nine Confucian Classics* (*Rujia jiujing*) in 932, the earliest systematic arrangement and printing of these canonical works. The Wu family of the Later Shu printed the Confucian classics as well as specialized works such as *Selections of Refined Literature* (*Wenxuan*, 520s, English title as translated by David R. Knechtges), *Record for Early Learning* (*Chuxue ji*, ca. 700), and *Master Bo's (Bo Juyi) Six Collections* (*Boshi liutie*) for the benefit of scholars. The last two are encyclopedic references that were used to prepare for the civil-service examinations.

There were more printed books from Sichuan and south of the Yangzi (Jiangnan) during the Five Dynasties, probably because of the advanced economies of these regions. During the Northern Song (around 1040), Bi Sheng (ca. 970–1051) invented the earliest movable-type printing, using ceramic characters in an iron frame on iron plates. From then on, movable-type printing methods were transmitted to Korea, Japan, Annam, Xi Xia, Liao, Jin, and Mongolia.

Movable-type printing was much faster and convenient than woodblock printing, because each character was separate and could be rearranged and used repeatedly. After its invention in 1140 and further improvements in the thirteenth century, printed materials were produced in much greater numbers. Song books were no longer limited to Confucian,

Buddhist, and Daoist classics; they included many genres, including histories and geographies, alchemy and occult arts, poetry and prose, drama, and medical and pharmaceutical treatises. All of these works proliferated given the inexpensiveness of movable-type printing.

Beside the Sichuan of the Five Dynasties era, there were centers of Northern Song printing in Bianliang (Kaifeng), Linnan (Hangzhou), and Fujian, and Huzhou (in Zhejiang), Jizhou (in Jiangxi), and Suzhou were added during the Southern Song.

The most famous private library at the time was the Yu family's establishment in Jianning in Fujian; it was said to have been operating for five hundred years. There was a Yu family library in Fujian's Jian-an in the eighteenth century. In the twentieth century, the Yu family's collection was said to contain ten thousand volumes (*juan*), and the library was known as the House of Ten Thousand Volumes (*wanjuanlou*). There were many other book printers and sellers, such as the Chens and Yins of Linnan, the Huangs of Jian-an, the Lius of Mosha, the Ruans of Fujian (Minhou), and others in Sichuan, Shanxi, Jianghuai, and Huguang (covering parts of modern Hubei, Hunan, Guangxi, and Guizhou) that specialized in books on particular subjects, such as medicine; others printed a wider range of books. During the Yuan dynasty, aside from religious books, very many works for popular reading—plays and novels, including illustrated editions—were printed. With the perfection of movable copper type and color printing, the Ming printing industry flourished even more.

The large number of readers was closely related to the easy availability of reading matter, and this large number of literate people laid the foundation for the expansion of the learned stratum of society. Exactly how many people were there in the Song intellectual, literate classes? We have no way to obtain a reliable figure. Nevertheless, given the three factors of the Song patronage of literature and art, the widespread availability of education, and a thriving printing industry, and assuming that there were thousands of men per generation at the top level of advanced scholars and officials, we can make an educated guess. There should have been at least ten times as many educated people in the middle range, including Confucian students, monks, and Daoists, and another ten times as many on the lowest level of the literate population, including students and merchants. Thus, the literate population during the Song dynasty must have surpassed that of any previous age.

The social status of the Song literate, educated stratum was also higher than in past ages. The Tang literate population was not as great a percentage of the total as in the Song, and the status of local great families was also subject to powerful political influences. Tang literati held positions of leadership in local areas due to the great size of their clans, but Song scholars generally relied on their own personal abilities to obtain the right to speak and the respect of the local people. Song villages often had village compacts (*xiangyue, sheyue*), in which membership was established on the basis of the Confucian tradition of respect for family and neighbors. Confucian ethical concepts were deeply embedded in popular society, and this made scholars important members of these village-compact organizations. The people of the Song had a neoclassical turn of mind; they made copies of ancient ritual vessels (*liqi*), and their officials advocated ancient rites (*li*). One of these ancient rites was a village drinking ceremony in which common people offered their respect to the educated stratum. The high respect in which the Chinese educated stratum was held in late imperial times began in the Song dynasty and returned in the Ming and Qing after a temporary decline during the Mongol Yuan dynasty.

6. Pluralism and Integration in Late Medieval Thought

Confucianism (*Rujia*) and Daoism (*Daojia*) were the mainstream of Chinese thought, but over the several hundred years since the introduction of Indian Buddhism during the Han dynasty, the medieval era witnessed a great deal of accommodation and blending of these three currents of thought. Buddhism and religious Daoism often experienced persecution, however, especially under Emperor Wudi of the Northern Zhou (r. 560–578) and the Tang emperor Wuzong (r. 840–846), when Buddhist monks and monasteries suffered very greatly. Some organizations inspired by religious Daoism were militarily suppressed because of their violent antigovernment activities. The early Daoist religious sects of the Way of Heavenly Peace (*taipingdao*) and Celestial Master Daoism (*tianshidao*) and the many religious secret societies (like those of Li Shun and Hundred Year Li) frequently arose to resist the government. As for Confucianism, Confucian scholars were always a reserve army for the civil bureaucracy, and Confucian theory was always part of the orthodox government education. Shackled to the yoke of government orthodoxy, however, for a long time Confucian scholars lacked the opportunity to produce outstanding talents.

Things changed after the Tang dynasty, when Buddhism flourished. After Xuanzang's large-scale translation of Buddhist sutras, Buddhist doctrines proliferated—from the Ideation Only (*weishi*) School to Chan (Zen, or Meditation School) and Pure Land (*jingtu*) Buddhism. In the long run, as Chen Yinke (1890–1969) has pointed out, although the extremely Indian types of Buddhism, such as the Ideation Only School (also known as the *Faxiang*, or Dharmalakshana, School) continued to proliferate after taking root in Chinese cultural soil, nevertheless, those schools like Chan and Pure Land that were more heavily influenced by Chinese culture eventually developed into the most important schools of Chinese Buddhism.

Religious Daoism, on the other hand, was an autochthonous Chinese religion that developed out of a belief in shamanism. In its early stages, it was challenged by the foreign religion of Buddhism and spurred on to develop into a religion with an organized church structure. Thus, the ceremonies and structure of the Daoist church reflect a Buddhist influence. From medieval times on, the content of Daoism was all inclusive, reaching into medicine, alchemy, and so on and far more rich and complex than Confucian thought, which was primarily concerned with the social and political order of *this* world. At the same time, foreign religious ideas, such as Manichaeism's concepts of apocalypse, redemption, and the end of the world, also influenced religious Daoism, and it grew into an amalgam of native and foreign thought.

Buddhism, a religion that came to China from abroad and absorbed Chinese elements, and Daoism, a native religion that absorbed external influences, were both able to blend together all of these disparate elements to form major religious doctrines.

As Tang cultural development continued surging forward, Confucian thought could and did not remain unchanged. Han Yu (768–824) and Li Ao (774–836) began to pioneer changes in Confucian thought. Facing the challenge of Buddhist metaphysical thought, they attempted to devise a theory to rival it from within the practical and pragmatic Confucian tradition. The *Great Learning* and the *Doctrine of the Mean* were originally only two chapters in the *Book of Rites* (*Liji*), but Han Yu and Li Ao extracted their discussions concerning human nature and passions (*xingqing*) and moral behavior (*dexing*) and raised them to the level of transcendent metaphysical doctrines. They particularly cited the *Mencius* in support of their ideas. Its discussions of the human heart-mind (*xin*) and human nature (*xing*) as well as sudden enlightenment (*dunwu*) gave it a sense of mystery that could be developed in tandem with Buddhist ontology and epistemology.

The Song Neo-Confucian thinkers went far beyond Han Yu and Li Ao. Zhou Dunyi (Lianxi, 1017–1073) and Shao Yong (Kangjie, 1011–1077) appropriated the Diagram of the Great Ultimate (*Taijitu*) and various other ideas from the *Book of Changes* to construct a Confucian ontology. With his assertions that "the Dao is the Great Ultimate" and "the heart-mind is the Great Ultimate," Shao Yong paved the way for later Neo-Confucianists to connect the human heart-mind (*xin*) to the Dao (the Way). Such a unity of phenomena and perception (or knowledge) was also a major concern for Buddhist thought. Just this set of ideas is presented through the metaphors of the Storehouse of the Thus-come (*Rulaizang*) in Tiantai Buddhism and Celestial Lord Indra's net (*Yintuolo wang*) in the Huayan School.

Zhang Zai's (1020–1077) unity of heaven and man (*tian ren he yi*)—"Enlarging his heart-mind, one can embody (comprehend) everything under heaven" (*da qi xin ze neng ti tianxia zhi wu*)—unified the ontology of the cosmos and human ethics. Heaven's nature (*tianxing*) and human nature (*renxing*) can both be identical to the Way of Heaven—"heaven's innate goodness was originally my innate goodness" (*tian liangneng jishi wu liangneng*)—as both are interconnected by means of the Dao. Passages in his "Western Inscription" (*Ximing*)—"All people are my brothers and sisters" (*min bao wu yu*) and serving heaven and earth in his life, then "in death I will be at peace" (*sheng shun si ning*; Wing-tsit Chan's translation, in *Sources of Chinese Tradition*, 524–525)—brought the progressive changes in human life and death, the nation, society, the cosmos, and time all together under one system.

Although the "Western Inscription" is a short prose essay, the scope and profundity of its content is sufficient to represent the main elements of post-Song Neo-Confucian ontology and ethics. Its importance is no less than that of the "Lord's Prayer" (Matt. 6:9–13) of Christianity or the *Heart Sutra* (*Prajñāpāramitā Hrdaya Sūtra*) of Buddhism. These three simple yet profound essays represent the essence of their respective modes of thought.

Zhu Xi (1130–1200) was the great synthesizer of Confucian thought, his main thesis being that principle (*li*) is the foundation (*benti*) of all things (all phenomena). Principle resides in concrete material things. First there is principle; then it can be actualized into material force (*qi*) and bring about the "ten thousand things" (*wanwu*, or everything). The nature (*xing*) of each phenomenon is different, but its natural endowment of principle is always comprehended within the great Dao. Principle in Zhu Xi's philosophy follows the positive or activist strand of the Confucian tradition; it is practical and related to this world. Zhu's so-called Reason (*daoli*) is completely different from the Buddhist idea that the nature (*xing*) of things and events is empty (*kong*)—this is the fundamental difference between Confucianism and Buddhism.

Zhu Xi's contemporary Lu Jiuyuan (Xiangshan, 1139–1193) regarded the heart-mind (*xin*) as principle. Lu's School of Mind went back to Mencius's statement that "he who exerts his mind to the utmost knows his nature; he who knows his nature knows heaven (nature)" in believing that if I can exhaustively exert my mind, I can penetrate the Mind of Heaven (Wing-tsit Chan's translation of *Mencius* 7A.1, from *A Source Book in Chinese Philosophy*, 585). This school paved the way for the vast system of Wang Yangming's (Wang Shouren, 1472–1528) School of Mind.

A debate continued within Confucianism on the similarities and differences between Zhu Xi and Lu Xiangshan, and their opposition was very similar to the debate in Buddhism between the Consciousness Only and Chan schools. First, this was because of the inner logic of their beliefs. Second, ever since Han Yu and Li Ao began this discussion in the Tang, Confucianism was greatly influenced by Buddhism and Daoism and could not but follow the same path in their mutual dialogue and disputation. This demonstrated the unavoidable mutual influences and divergences in the development of the overall pluralistic system of Chinese thought at that time.

The development of Buddhist thought after the Song went from the realm of the elite toward the level of the common people. The celebrated Tang monk Zong-mi (780–841) saw five stages in the development of Buddhism from the profound to the shallow, and it was the popular post-Song Pure Land School that he regarded as most shallow. In recent times, the Chan (Meditation) School is the only form of Buddhism pursued by scholarly people; the mass of the faithful simply think of good and evil karma and believe that "the body is originally empty, and emptiness is the root of everything."

That Buddhism developed in this way is probably related to the wider dissemination of knowledge from the Song on. As discussed above, the common use of printing together with the accelerated urban development of the Song period made it possible for many urbanites to learn from written materials. As the base of its believers widened, it would have been extremely difficult for Buddhist doctrine not to become relatively simplified to accommodate the demand of the masses for a "wisdom" they could understand. Buddhist sutra teaching activities and the publication of illustrated editions were actually on the increase from Tang times on. The popularization of Buddhism had long since begun, and the social and economic developments of the Song only accelerated the process. Along with this tendency, the Confucian emphasis on the practical affairs of this world naturally reduced Chinese Buddhism's mystical and otherworldly aspects.

From the Song on, the Daoist religion also developed in the direction of increasing popularization. Because the surname of the Tang ruling house was Li, supposed to be that of Laozi, they patronized religious Daoism. Reign periods such as Taizong's "great peace flourishing nation" (*taiping xingguo*) and Zhenzong's "great middle auspicious omens" (*dazhong xiangfu*) were replete with the aura of Daoism. Tang and Song emperors believed in and favored Daoist masters who employed their mystical arts to seek long life for them. Lin Lingsu (1075–1119) and others like him who were favored with appointments by Song Huizong (r. 1100–1126) sought riches and honors in more or less the same manner. Most post-Song Daoist religious activities, however, such as ceremonial sacrifices, involved prayers for good fortune. Regardless of whether they sought to protect the nation or pacify the people, they were all directed toward the well-being of the nation, the local district, or the general masses. This tendency was quite different from simply pleasing the emperor or seeking individual blessings, and the shift in this direction was probably attributable to the rise in social status of the mass of commoners from the Song on.

With the disaster of 1126, the Song ruling house moved south, and the north fell under Jurchen Jin and Mongol Yuan rule. In the north, newly formed sects of religious Daoism inaugurated a new direction for the religion. The Quanzhen (Complete Truth), Taiyi (Great Unity), and Zhenda

(Truly Great) sects in the north were all primarily centered on popular activities and no longer carried on the palace's mystical-arts tradition.

The most remarkable of these northern sects was the Quanzhen sect, founded by Wang Chongyang (1112–1170) in the area under Jurchen Jin rule. Quanzhen masters, including Qiu Chuji (Changchun, 1148–1227), organized and educated the northern people under anarchic conditions. They opened agricultural fields, made Daoist temples (Daoguan) centers of activity and gathered people there, maintained social order, and preserved Chinese cultural traditions in their regions. According to a record carved on a contemporary stele, the Quanzhen doctrines and the actions of their priests were as "deferential as Confucianism, as diligent as Moism, and as compassionate as Buddhism"—that is, they combined the best of the Three Teachings. While the north was ruled by militaristic non-Chinese peoples and hereditary warlords like the Zhang, Yan, Shi, and Wu families, these Quanzhen priests worked among them to admonish, educate, and generally alleviate their depredations against the suffering people. Qiu Chuji's advice to Chinggis Qaghan, resulting in a lessening of Mongol severity in China, is the most famous example of such activities.

The Taiyi and Zhenda sects also worked hard to protect the Chinese masses and preserve the roots of Chinese culture. After entering the sect, Taiyi priests all adopted the surname Xiao to commemorate the founder, a practice influenced by the Confucian idea of filial piety. This practice is actually an expression of Confucian family ethics far removed from the individualism of Daoist philosophy. Rather, it combines Confucianism and Daoism by maintaining a Daoist otherworldly stance while attempting the Confucian salvation of this world—thus going far beyond the inner logic of the religion.

Besides the major traditions of Confucianism, Daoism, and Buddhism, popular religious sects of various kinds were very active from the Song on. Ever since the Yellow Turbans gave rise to religious Daoism during the Han, popular religious beliefs always existed in China, sometimes underground, other times out in the open. With the Silk Road well traveled, non-Chinese peoples immigrating to China, and the Tang dynasty's extensive commercial activity in Central Asia, many Central Asian religions had an opportunity to enter China. Nestorian Christianity and Islam were the main religions that arrived during the Tang. Terms such as *yelikewen* (Christian) and *huihui* (Moslem) are regularly seen in Yuan writings.

Other religions that are often overlooked are Zoroastrianism (*Xian jiao*) and Manichaeism (*Moni jiao*); they were all popular in Central and Inner Asia at the time. These apocalyptic religious sects had many characteristics in common with Christianity and Islam: they all believed in a dualistic cosmos, a struggle between good and evil, a millenarian end of days or millennium, the coming of a savior (messiah), and salvation through faith. Some of these beliefs also entered the major religions, as in the case of the Buddhist belief in the coming of the Buddha Maitreya, a cheerful Buddhist Messiah.

The hope of salvation offered by these revealed religions was the most important demand of popular belief. Fang La (Fang Xi, ?–1121) of the Song was a "vegetarian-serving-devils" Manichaean, as were the Red Turbans of the Yuan and the Ming-Qing White Lotus Society, and they all held similar beliefs. Small popular religious groups that were usually inconspicuous could suddenly rise up and develop into very large movements of peasants and lower-class urbanites. Such religious movements were perhaps not unrelated to various Daoist and Buddhist sects. For example, could the Quanzhen sect's frequently convened Lotus assemblies and Golden Flower assemblies be perhaps related to the later White Lotus sect (*Bailian jiao*)? And was the White Lotus sect related to the Lotus Society (*Lian hui*) of medieval Buddhism? Were Han Shantong (?–1351) and other members of the late Yuan White Lotus sect known as "Bright King" (*mingwang*) given their connection with Manichaeism (the "bright sect," or *Ming jiao*)?

These apocalyptic or millenarian religious sects combined all the beliefs mentioned above with the mysticism of Chinese culture, such as material force (*qi*), fate or predestination (*yun*), and the unity of heaven and man (*tian ren he yi*), to form some very important characteristics of the Chinese people's style of thinking. It is worth observing here the interesting phenomenon that, although in Confucian thought women's status is below that of their fathers and husbands, in these popular religions the Unborn Mother (*Wusheng laomu*), Guanyin, Mazu, and the leaders of many religious activities often bore the title of "Holy Mother" (*Shengmu*).

From the above, we can see that by this time Confucianism, Daoism, and Buddhism were intimately connected by syncretism and mutual borrowings that resulted in one vast system of Chinese thought. At the same time, from the end of the Tang on, the hereditary great families and their upper social class that had developed in the Eastern Han were in decline. By the Song era, such powerful families as had existed in the early Tang were no more. Replacing them were the urban residents (not the same as contemporary European city people) and the local gentry (*xiangshen*), who dominated cultural activities.

Under the rule of conquest dynasties, China's traditional great families of ranking scholar-officials could not maintain their power, and it fell to powerful leading clans to preserve order in the local areas. The supporters of Confucian, Daoist, and Buddhist thought primarily consisted of these local gentry. The overall trend in Song, Yuan, Ming, and Qing times was for a greater number of people to participate in Chinese cultural activities than was the case in medieval times, and the social status of these people was also lower. Popular beliefs were even more rooted in the lower strata of the villages and urban areas.

All of this pluralistic interaction can be regarded as a homogenization of the Chinese style of thinking during the Song to Qing eras of near ancient and early modern history. The modern thought of the Western world that came to China from the sixteenth century on came into contact with this type of syncretic Chinese thinking.

7. Late Medieval Science and Technology

During the Song and Yuan dynasties, Chinese science developed to levels so high that it occupied the premier position among the nations of the contemporary world. The historian of science Joseph Needham regarded the year 1500 C.E. as the great divide. Before 1500, European science and technology could not compare with China's, but after that date, Europe developed modern science and technology and transformed the nature of human culture.

This section discusses the development of several aspects of science and technology and examines the rise and decline in this realm of China as compared to Europe. The background causes of this problem are extremely complex, including not only looking at what elements China lacked but also discussing what conditions arose in Europe in modern times. Scientific changes involve both the inner logic of scientific thinking and the available social conditions. In like fashion, the development of any new technology also requires a certain chain of technical clues, together with the social and economic conditions favorable for its emergence.

Traditionally, Chinese mathematics was closely related to practical astronomical and calendrical calculations such as land measurement, estimations of crop storage, and civil engineering. Chinese mathematics developed greatly from the Qin-Han to the Sui-Tang periods and achieved many outstanding accomplishments, discussed elsewhere in this book. During the Tang dynasty, Chinese mathematics was greatly influenced by Indian sources such as the *Brāhman Mathematics Sutra (Poluomen suanjing)* and the *Brāhman Calculation Methods (Poluomen suanfa)*, which came into China at that time. Gautama Siddha (Qutan Xida, fl. eighth century) introduced the *Navagraha (Nine Planets) Calendar*, Greek projective geometry, the tables of sine functions from Indian trigonometry, and the Indian concept of zero. Indian terms for extremely large numbers (immeasurable numbers, numerous as the sands of the Ganges) and extremely short durations (a snap of the fingers, a twinkling of the eye) as well as the concept of infinity all had an influence on Chinese mathematics.

To sum up, in the Sui-Tang era, the government established special schools for the training of mathematical talents and had all the mathematical treatises collected together as the *Ten Classics of Mathematics (Shibu suanjing)*. The hard work and the explications of mathematicians were sometimes lasting and sometimes lost. In spite of the emergence of scientific geniuses such as Shen Kuo (1031–1095), whose work inspired scientists and mathematicians of later dynasties, the Northern Song court was not interested, and it was not an era of mathematical development.

During the Southern Song and Yuan dynasties, a burst of talent appeared in late medieval Chinese mathematics. The "Four Geniuses" of the Song and Yuan all made important contributions. The *Mathematical Treatise in Nine Sections (Shushu Jiuzhang)* (1247) of Qin Jiushao (1202–1261) records numerical solutions to higher-order equations (for powers higher than cubes) and contains remainder theorems for congruent equations. The works of Li Ye (1192–1279) and Zhu Shijie (1249–1314), appearing in the middle and late thirteenth century, also discuss systems of single equations and of multivariable equations as well as methods of successive substitution for multivariable higher-order equations, known in Chinese as the *Tianyuanshu* (heavenly-origin method) and the *Siyuanshu* (four-origins method). Zhu Shijie also went a step further by developing the solution to higher-order arithmetic series into a new method of interpolation. His discovery predated Newton's formula for the interpretation of polynomials (expressions of more than two algebraic terms, such as the sum of several terms of different powers of the same variable) by more than three hundred years. Yang Hui (ca. 1238–1298) of the Southern Song further developed Shen Kuo's work into a method for harmonizing higher-order arithmetic series.

Yang Hui also took the unprecedented step of publishing some texts for commercial use to teach merchants how to properly employ arithmetic! Li Ye moved into the hills of Hebei to avoid the chaos of his time, but students came from all over to study with him. Zhu Shijie lived somewhat later than Li Ye and may also have come from Hebei. He styled himself Yanshan (meaning Mount Yan, in Hebei) and is said to have traveled widely before settling down in Yanzhou and spending the rest of his life teaching mathematics. They both wrote mathematics textbooks that taught the subject from elementary to advanced levels.

Computations in ancient China were generally made using counting rods arranged in three rows. The operations of addition, subtraction, multiplication and division were performed by moving the rods around to different positions. Chanted mnemonic formulas (or incantations, *gejue*) gradually developed in the Tang and Song as aids to calculation. During the Song, the three rows of rods were more simply arranged horizontally into one row. Many simple mnemonic formulas for arithmetic calculation appeared for use with different units (such as catties and taels); Zhu and Yang themselves produced many of these easy-to-use formulas.

The abacus, using beads instead of rods, appeared during the Yuan dynasty and is still in use today. Tao Zongyi's (1316–1403) *Records Compiled After Retiring from the Farm* (*Zhuogenglu*) contains some popular sayings involving the abacus, and thus it must have been in common use by the 1366 date of compilation of this book. There is still no definitive answer, however, as to exactly when computation using the abacus was invented. Since the Four Geniuses of the Song and Yuan never mention it, but as it was already commonly used at the end of the Yuan, therefore it must have been invented sometime near the middle of the fourteenth century. With the appearance of the abacus, the flourishing of Chinese mathematics came to an end. Were these two phenomena related? Did the use of a simple tool for calculation that required little thought eliminate most people's incentives for mathematical speculation? This is a question worth considering.

That the Four Geniuses of the Song and Yuan all lived in chaotic times and had to scramble to save their lives makes their extraordinary accomplishments all the more remarkable. Especially noteworthy is that Li, Zhu, and Yang all gathered disciples and students to whom they taught mathematics, and they all came from one area in the southwestern corner of modern Hebei. This part of Hebei seems to have been a center of mathematical teaching and research. Both Zhu Shijie and Yang Hui wrote mnemonic formulas to aid in mathematical study and works especially intended for commercial use. Furthermore, the famous mathematicians Guo Shoujing (1231–1316), Liu Bingzhong (1216–1274), and Liu's disciples such as Wang Xun (thirteenth century) and Zhang Wenqian (1216–1283) were all from Hebei. This, too, is worth pondering. If many talents live in the same area, did they produce a critical mass such that by intellectual interaction they set off a chain reaction of development? Did the practical needs of society also help to maintain a group of talented teachers and researchers who were not dependent on the government schools?

During the same period, the Yuan dynasty brought in many Moslem intellectuals from Central Asia to work in China. Perhaps the famous Persian scholar Jamal al-Din ibn Muhammad al-Najjari (thirteenth century) introduced Moslem astronomy at that time. Seeing that the library of the Yuan Directorate of Moslem Astronomy contained many books of Moslem mathematics, it is safe to say that Islamic mathematics—including geometry and algebra—came into China at that time. Another thing to note here is that from oldest times Chinese mathematics did not have a number for zero but simply left an empty space. The Indian numeral zero was transmitted to China during the Song, but Chinese mathematics still did not employ it. The numeric zero began to be used for calculation during the Song and Yuan dynasties. All the numbers recorded in the Yuan-era magic number (magic square, *huanshu*) chart discovered at Xi-an are written in Arabic numerals, including zero. In light of this, we may wonder if the stimulation of foreign culture had not finally overpowered the tradition of China's ten mathematical classics.

Astronomy and mathematics are sister subjects, and in the Chinese cultural tradition astronomy, calendrical studies, and mathematics are even more closely related. During the Song, Chinese astronomy relied on new scientific instruments to obtain reliable numerical data. Shen Kuo's 1088 *Dream Pool Essays* (*Mengxi bitan*) discusses his use of an inflow clepsydra (water clock, greatly improved by his design) to make more accurate measurements of astronomical phenomena.

Guo Shoujing of the Yuan dynasty was both a mathematician and astronomer and made important scholarly contributions in both fields. He was particularly concerned with instrumental observations, and he manufactured many astronomical instruments, including a simplified armillary sphere, an improved gnomon (the part of a sundial that casts the shadow), sighting tubes, and measuring instruments aimed at obtaining accurate data on the position and movement of heavenly bodies. Before the invention of the telescope, Guo Shoujing's astronomical instruments were the most accurate observational tools in the world.

Chinese astronomy was originally concerned with practical measurements, but to reach such a high level of accuracy, besides building on its past traditions it also received great stimulation from the Islamic techniques of astronomical measurement. The Persian Jamal al-Din ibn Muhammad al-Najjari, active in the Yuan and of a slightly older generation than Guo Shoujing, was brought to court by Kublai Qaghan to work in the Moslem Directory of Astronomy and edit the *Gazetteer of the Unified Great Yuan* (*Da Yuan yitongzhi*). He also manufactured seven types of astronomical instruments and replicated Greek and Persian tools for astronomical observation. The astronomical system introduced by Jamal was very different from the Chinese system, and the Yuan court obviously employed both the Moslem and Chinese systems of observation and of calendar making—as well as two independent groups of astronomical officials. Guo Shoujing's Chinese system was greatly influenced by the availability of these new instruments. Thus the design of many of Guo's instruments, especially his simplified armillary sphere, surpassed the traditional Chinese styles in a manner that took advantage of both Chinese and Moslem characteristics—for example, removing many unnecessary spheres and changing from a hundred-degree to a 360-degree graduated scale. While manufacturing so many astronomical instruments, Guo still maintained the same practical concerns as the mathematicians mentioned above. Above all, he carried on the Chinese calendrical tradition of assuring that the movement of the heavenly bodies was in accord with all of the other elements of time that went into making the Chinese calendar (see chapter 4).

These northern scholars lived in an area conquered by non-Chinese peoples, and perhaps they had given up on the Chinese scholar's habit of trying to achieve merit and fame through Confucian practices. Thus less restrained by orthodox thinking, they had a relatively more liberal attitude toward the pursuit of learning. At the same time, their learning focused on the practical. In a chaotic age, practical knowledge could be relied on to earn one a living, just as the northern mathematicians mentioned above taught in local schools and wrote mnemonic formulas for popular use. Guo Shoujing's learning was not limited to astronomy and mathematics. He also used his surveying and computation skills to search for the origins of rivers and to construct canals. All of this demonstrates that at the time there were a number of practical-minded Chinese scholars whose style of living was quite different from the traditional literati who recited poetry and read the classics.

We have already discussed the great expansion of the economy during the Song dynasty. Vigorous market demand brought about a considerable advance in the techniques of production. Contemporary multicultural contacts were also an element in this technical development. The Mongol Yuan fought campaigns everywhere with a great deal of slaughter, but they very much valued technical talent. From the age of Chinggis Qaghan on, every time they conquered new territory they took away the most skillful artisans, and any technically proficient prisoner usually escaped death. Thousands of artisans followed the Mongol armies and interacted with other skilled artisans and craftsmen wherever they went. The Yuan central and local governments set up many government offices to watch over and administer these registered artisan families, and they produced many kinds of tools, clothing, and other material articles on an unprecedented scale.

Since these artisans had many opportunities to learn from one another, and also given their specialized division of labor, many of them were very highly skilled. The common defects of these government offices, such as fraud and extortion, were difficult to prevent, and thus the workers lacked a positive motivation for production. Many of the various financial officials of the Yuan, such as the Tibetan Sangha (?–1291) and others, were extremely adept at becoming wealthy through taxation and extortion. They often employed West Asian and Central Asian (*semu*) merchants to supervise production, and under this system the artisans employed various methods, such as buying low and selling high, to create some space for their own economic activity. The nature of these government-established production units changed over time, and some artisan families were even able to escape registration and regain their freedom.

With these changes, Yuan industrial production evolved from a centralized to a decentralized form. In the centralized stage, production techniques made some noticeable progress, while in the decentralized stage, the workers returned to private production and developed an extremely positive work ethic. This was not planned change but rather an unanticipated transformation that greatly increased the technological efficiency of production.

The Song weaving industry, for example, was already quite well developed. As the Mongols moved toward the west, they brought with them textiles of gold thread and fur from Central Asia, and Chinese brocade appeared even more resplendent by contrast. Weaving families not only belonged to government offices but were also attached to noble houses. The quantity of textiles produced by Yuan governmental and private workshops was very great, efficiency was very high, and the quality of this great variety of goods was extremely fine. Another noteworthy event that occurred at this time was the introduction of the technique of cotton weaving by the commoner woman Huang Daopo from Songjiang, who traveled to the island of Hainan in the second half of the thirteenth century and learned it from the Hlai (Li) people. She disseminated her knowledge throughout Jiangnan, and thus the cotton weaving of southern China provided another useful fabric for making Chinese clothing.

Song iron smelting was also highly developed, and the quantity of iron smelted in the Song was the highest in the contemporary world. Yuan smelting and casting increased even more. In Khubilai Qaghan's time, twice as much iron was smelted as in the Northern Song—up to ten million tons per year. Yuan smelting technology also improved. First, they used porcelain and clay to construct furnaces that could withstand much higher temperatures. Second, they were able to produce fine steel, known as *bintie*, having a high carbon content. They may have been influenced by Arab smelting methods, but this idea remains to be studied.

The Chinese porcelain industry was always nonpareil. Neither the Persians nor the Arabs were able to produce Chinese-style pure porcelain, which was fired at very high temperatures. Song porcelain wares of the Jun and Ru (Henan) and Longquan (Zhejiang) kilns were highly prized and expensive Chinese exports for many years. New and improved techniques appearing in the Yuan and Ming, such as the "color under the glaze" (*youxiacai*) technique, produced prized porcelains like the famous "blue and whites" and "red under the glaze." The Middle East and Europe were unable to copy these Chinese techniques. The blue pigment for Ming blue-and-white porcelains was, for a long time, however, obtained in Central Asia; it was not until the mid-Ming that the Chinese began to purchase this material from Southeast Asia. Judged by the origin of materials, Moslem blue-and-white porcelain was greatly inferior to that made in China. Porcelain produced in China did, however, use many Islamic decorative motifs, such as pearl or rosary patterns, that bear witness that they were still intended for sale in the Islamic world. Thus Chinese "color under the glaze" porcelain was intimately related to the Islamic world both in the origin of its materials and its commercial market.

China was the first in the world to produce gunpowder and gunpowder weapons. Firearms had already been used in battle during the Song. The Mongol Yuan carried Chinese firearms on their westward conquests; using firearms combined with cavalry tactics, their armies established the largest empire in history. In the siege of Baghdad, Mongols used explosive shells of steel corresponding perhaps to modern-day bombs. At the decisive six-year siege of Xiangyang (Hubei, 1267–1273), the Mongols employed Moslems to operate powerful new counterweight trebuchets, designed in Iraq, that could fire three-hundred-kilogram projectiles into the city. This was another turning point in world military history, and it brought together both Chinese and Islamic weapons of war. Song artillery originally fired projectiles out of a tube using ballistic principles similar to today's rockets and missiles. The Song invented gunpowder cannons known as "fire tubes" (*huotong*). The renowned Southern Song prime minister and general Yu Yunwen (1110–1174) used them in the 1161 defeat of the Jurchen Jin armies at Caishiji in Anhui. The Mongols later followed Song models to manufacture similar cannons known as *huochong*. The oldest cannon in the world today is one of these bronze *huochong*, from 1332, from the Yuan dynasty. By Ming times, firearms and cannon were commonly used weapons of war. The Europeans, however, had superior weapons, and during the Ming, the Portuguese "great red cannon" (*hongyi dapao*, originally meaning "red barbarian cannon") was much more powerful and efficient than the Chinese *huochong*. This weapon proved decisive in the Manchu victory over the Ming.

We can sum up the above discussion of the development of science and technology during the Song and the Yuan under three headings: multi-cultural stimulus, expert specialization, and market demand. All three elements enabled the Mongol Yuan to make great progress on the basis of the foundation laid by the Song.

8. Daily Life in Late Medieval China

Many works of Song and Yuan art and literature have survived to this day and provide rather direct historical materials concerning daily life in those dynasties. For example, the *Night Revels of Han Xizai* by the Southern Tang (937–975) master Gu Hongzhong reflects a gathering of literati from the Five Dynasties to the early Song. The scroll painting depicts their dress, furniture, and articles of daily use, as well as the gestures of female entertainers singing and dancing for them. Even though we have only later copies of Zhang Zeduan's (1085–1145) scroll painting *Spring Festival Along the River*, mentioned above, it still provides a clear and very detailed panorama, almost like a motion picture, of twelfth-century life in the Song capital of Kaifeng (Bianliang). Although literary works lack illustrations, they can reflect the human psyche and emotions even better than paintings. We have many Song anecdotes or jottings in note form (*biji xiaoshuo*); their rich contents include not only classical allusions but also many details of daily life. The dialogues of Yuan drama are also full of the colloquial speech of ordinary people, which is especially moving and realistic. Ming fiction greatly elaborated on Song and Yuan stories; both their short stories and long novels all serve as material for the description of everyday life. Thus, both art and literature can provide abundant material for writing history.

In general, Song men wore loose-fitting and comfortable sleeveless jackets and long gowns. Their work clothing was usually a short shirt with a cloth belt and half-length trousers for easy movement. Song men also wore tight-fitting cloth wraps on their head. At home, they usually wore headpieces something like hair nets. Women's lives underwent the greatest changes, as the practice of foot binding gradually became common from the Five Dynasties on. Song elite women were quite different from Tang women in physical appearance. The full-bodied and healthy look of Tang women became slender and elegant in the Song. However, the women of the northern ethnic groups, whether Khitan, Jurchen, or Mongol, did not adopt the Han ideal of soft and tender feminine beauty. In like manner, the men of these northern peoples retained for the most part their own ethnic traditions in clothing and appearance. For example, Liao tomb murals show the men using various hairstyles that all differ from those of contemporary Han Chinese.

For transportation in the north, both men and women rode on horseback. Southerners also rode horses but used sedan chairs too. Carriages or carts were mostly used for heavy loads and were pulled either by oxen or men. There were many oxcarts in the Chinese regions; they were slow but could carry very heavy cargo. There were not very many horse-drawn carriages; they were generally reserved for ceremonial use and rarely for daily transportation of people.

Song ships and boats, especially in the south, were highly developed. From small fishing boats to large oceangoing ships, they can all be clearly seen in contemporary paintings. In general, small junks with sails and oars were used on inland waterways; oceangoing vessels were multisailed ships of enormous size. The structure of these large Song ships can be clearly seen from the originals that are on display in the Quanzhou Museum of Maritime Transportation, opened in 1959. Song maritime excursions on the Indian Ocean and around Southeast Asia were part of a triangular relationship with Indian and Arab voyagers. Chinese ships, with their central rudders, firm stabilization, and watertight compartments, as well as their use of the compass and advanced techniques of navigation by means of the stars, were the most able seafarers in the contemporary world. Chinese flat sails, no matter how many were used, could not, however, match the Arab three-cornered sails in their ability to navigate into the wind.

In the area of food and drink, the Song introduced early-ripening rice from Champa and thus gained nearly an entire additional season's harvest. This new rice also had thin hulls with less chaff, greatly increasing the edible portion. In northern and central China, wheat replaced millet as the staple grain. Millet and the newly developed sorghum both became secondary food grains and were often relegated to fodder for livestock. Beans that had served as a grain food in ancient times now became a side dish. An especially important change was that bean curd (*doufu*) became a common staple from the Five Dynasties on. Thus foods made from wheat and beans, such as vegetarian muscle (*mianjin*) and soybean skin (*doupi*), also became common daily foods. The introduction of these vegetarian proteins was, of course, closely related to the Buddhist vegetarianism and proscription on killing living animals.

As early as ancient times, Chinese ate many fermented foods, such as salted bean paste. In the Song Chinese and the northern people's diets, there were other chemically processed foods, and they both pickled fish, meats, seafood, fruits, and vegetables. Virtually all the things used to conserve foods today—sauces or pastes, vinegar, wine, oil, and honey—could be found during the Song and Yuan eras. From the Song on, the Chinese imported distilling techniques from Central Asia and were then able to distill white liquors (whiskeylike brews) with very high alcohol content. The northern peoples loved to drink; there was even an official in charge of liquor in attendance at the banquets of the Mongol Qaghans. According to Persian and European travelers' diaries, the Mongol court served a variety of drinks, including strong liquor fermented from grain, grape wine, and koumiss, made from fermented mare's milk. Some Song Chinese also acquired a taste for this Mongol beverage.

Ancient Chinese sweeteners were limited to honey and sugar made from grains. Although they may have used sugarcane juice quite early on, they did not know how to make sugar. The technique for refining sugar was an Indian invention. Imported to China in the late Tang, sugar became very common during the Song.

Ancient Chinese cooking did not employ very many spices, but the Song imported great quantities of spices from Southeast Asia. The value of these spices was the highest among Song commercial imports, and they were used in medicine, religious ceremonies, and cooking. Acting as a middleman, China also exported spices to the Liao and the Xi Xia, but the Chinese themselves also used these spices to flavor and preserve food. Most of the spices used in Chinese cuisine today could be found during the Song and Yuan eras. Using spices to flavor and preserve meat products was the most common practice. There was continual interaction between the north and the south at this time, and the northern people's meat-eating customs also influenced the food tastes of the southerners. Although the northern ethnic groups ate some fish—the Khitans and Jurchen were adept at both hunting and fishing—the Chinese in the south consumed much more seafood. It may actually be that these northern people yearned for southern seafood, because when the Song entertained their diplomatic envoys, they invariably served them delicacies from the sea.

From the information on Song eating and drinking customs found in books such as the *Dream of Splendors Past in the Eastern Capital (Dongjing menghua lu*, 1147), *The Record of a Millet Dream (Mengliang lu*, ca. 1300), *A Record of the Splendors of the Capital City (Ducheng jisheng*, ca. 1300), and *Past Events in Hangzhou (Wulin jiushi*, ca. 1280), cities in the Song not only had restaurants and wine shops, but there were also many peddlers who carried their wares around on their shoulders and set up food stands, selling cakes and pastries on the streets. The scroll painting *Spring Festival Along the River* also depicts these urban activities. From their presentation in contemporary stories and novels, we can see that the delicacies and the cooking methods of the Song and Yuan and of the present day are quite similar: pan frying, sautéing, deep-fat frying, quick stir frying, boiling, broiling, baking, and steaming were all common methods of cooking. As for meat, in general the northerners ate primarily beef and lamb; the southerners ate more pork and chicken. Fruits and vegetable consumption depended on the local conditions—tangerines, oranges, pears, and peaches were the most common. Song cultivators were most particular about their oranges: some even wrote guide books on the subject in order to demonstrate the high quality of their horticultural techniques.

Many works on food therapy, nourishing life, and curing illness appeared during the Song and Yuan eras. Chen Zhi's (Song) *Book on Serving and Providing for Our Elders (Yanglao fengqin shu)* and Zou Xuan's (Yuan) continuation entitled *New Book on Nourishing Our Elders (Shouqin yangsheng xinshu)* both contain detailed discussions of dietary information aimed at older people; they also discuss foods and beverages with high nutritional value. As a Yuan-dynasty imperial dietitian, the eunuch Hu Sihui (fl. 1314–1330) wrote the world's first book on the science of nutrition—*The Principles of Correct Diet (Yinshan zhengyao*, 1330). Hu collected many materia medica, valuable and tested medical prescriptions, and materials on the properties of various foods. He also introduced Indian, Tibetan, and other people's foods and compiled lists of staples like thin and thick soups, flat cakes, gruel, and congee and other comestibles such as grains, land animals, fish, fruits, and spices. Altogether, he classified and discussed the use or avoidance of over three hundred items, in terms of their main characteristics, effectiveness as medicine, and good and bad properties. In all of this, Hu brought food therapy and medical therapy together into one vast nutritional compilation.

Traditional Chinese medicine can be divided into two systems: theoretical ideas and practical prescriptions. The prescriptions (*fangji*) found in the works of men such as the Sui court physician Chao Yuanfang (fl. 610) and Sun Simiao (541/581–682), the author of the *Ten Thousand Golden Remedies*, follow the "inner canon" (*neijing*) or corporeal medicine tradition and were carefully prepared after collecting records of practical experiences both with medicines and in clinical observations.

Song medicine had a more theoretical bent, but the northern areas of Yan and Zhao (Hebei and Shanxi) blazed a new trail. Then the "Four Geniuses" of the Jin and Yuan established a new milestone in the history of Chinese medicine. Liu Wansu (1120–1200) studied contagious diseases and their relation to environment and local climate. Zhang Zihe (1156–1228) pointed out that many traditional ancient prescriptions were ineffectual in curing contemporary diseases. Li Dongyuan (1180–1251) paid special attention to the digestive problems of the sick. And Zhu Danxi (1281–1358) also remarked that ancient prescriptions were not suitable for contemporary diseases; he also stressed the importance of good nutrition in the treatment of illness. All four of these physicians emphasized understanding their patients' physical condition and then prescribing medical treatment accordingly. Their basic concept was very close to the ideas of food therapy and using dietary supplements to restore health. The Four Geniuses of the Jin and Yuan all came from northern China, in an area near to that of the northern school of mathematicians. This was a Han Chinese area, but it had been under non-Chinese control for many years, and the power of the Southern Song government could not reach it. In such a border entrenchment, cultural traditions may have been weakened so that scholars could break through received ideas and strike out in new directions to come up with original scientific concepts.

To sum up, we can say that thanks to the cultural flourishing of the Tang dynasty, daily life in the Song was also thriving and diverse. Two reasons for this were the many multicultural contacts and the vast size of China's border areas. From the end of the Tang to the Southern Song, the Han Chinese continued their southern migration. Nine of the Sixteen States and the Five Dynasties were in the south. The Southern Song culture was concentrated in the south, and thus the resources of various southern localities developed greatly and the resources of Southeast Asia were also brought through trade into China. Three northern conquest dynasties succeeded each other in controlling North China and extending their boundaries as far as today's northeast, Mongolia, northwest, and Central Asia. The Mongols set up a vast empire that stretched across Eurasia, and the natural and cultural resources of this empire were available to supplement China's own resources; from them, the Chinese chose the best and the brightest and greatly enriched the culture of their daily life. Thus, in times of peace, the living standards of most Song and Yuan people was quite abundant. From the Ming on, the way of life of the Chinese people was basically fixed, and it was not until the intrusion of modern Western industrialism and urban culture that China would once again experience a great tidal wave of change.

9. The Transformation of Late Medieval China and East Asia

In the traditional view, this period of late medieval Chinese history belongs to the Song, Liao, and Jin dynasties, but of course history is a continuation. Many of the changes that took place during this period originated during the Five Dynasties or can even be traced back to the middle of the Tang. And this period of history did not come to an end with the Mongol Yuan. In the traditional China-centered periodization, the Song dynasty is considered orthodox, and the regimes established by northern peoples are considered foreign conquest dynasties. We will, however, consider this situation, in which several nations fought against one another, as a sort of close mutual interaction in East Asia. Although one might also consider this another era of North-South dynasties, it seems more fitting to understand the changes taking place at this time as a process of gradual integration in the Asia Pacific region. The elements of this integration did not only include the Han Chinese agriculturalists and the nomadic northern nations struggling with one another on the East Asian land mass. They also included the nations on the shores of the Pacific Ocean, from Japan to Southeast Asia, that established relations of acceptance and rejection with the continental nations (or ethnic groups, *zuqun*). This process of regional integration lasted some five or six hundred years. In the later stages of change, the modern European, the Middle Eastern, and the Asia Pacific regions all experienced mutual interactions on an even greater scale and with even more wide-ranging consequences. Finally, today, in the world that we experience, nations have gradually moved in the direction of global integration.

The Song Chinese living in Chinese-controlled areas also went through some complex and profound changes during this period. The structure of cities changed, and with that, the relationship between the cities and the countryside. The great clan (*zongzu*) organizations that had held sway since the end of the Han gradually devolved into smaller clans (*jiazu*) with much closer blood ties. The social status of these new clans was no longer as high as that of the former clan organizations. Concomitantly, although the individual members of society enjoyed more freedom, they no longer had the same sort of collective "family" organization to rely on.

This phenomenon was reflected in the symbiotic relationship between the Song literati and the imperial bureaucracy. From the Han to the Tang, the literati class had great clan backgrounds and the support of local power holders. Thus, they could be relatively independent in the face of imperial power. The Song literati, however, felt it their mission to participate actively in public affairs to improve the people's livelihood, and they had to serve in the imperial bureaucracy to have any hope of accomplishing this mission. Song Neo-Confucianism was really not a purely academic matter; its intrinsic motivation was to try to achieve the Way of a "sage on the inside and a king on the outside" (*neisheng waiwang*). Since the literati no longer had the support of powerful great clans, they had to travel around teaching, making like-minded contacts and putting together large networks of social relationships. Every time there was a factional struggle during the two Song dynasties, the scholarly world was deeply involved on both sides of every issue.

With their almost complete control of the civil bureaucracy, the Song Confucians had an unprecedented opportunity to put their ideals into practice. Unfortunately, the fierce struggles between many "party" factions (*dangpai*) in and out of power at court rendered the realization of Confucian ideals ultimately impossible.

During this period, the mutual interactions between Confucianism, Buddhism, and Daoism were greater than in the past. As a result of this closer interaction, the "Three Teachings" underwent much syncretic harmonization. Buddhist schools of foreign origin were replaced by native Chinese schools; the Daoists eclectically chose elements from both Confucianism and Buddhism to produce a new Daoist religion. Song

Neo-Confucianism represented a turning point in the history of Chinese thought, and it developed to the level it did in part from the stimulus it received from Buddhism and Daoism. Simply put, Song intellectuals, whether Confucian, Daoist, or Buddhist, were all primarily concerned with the affairs of this human world. We could say that they had changed their focus from the mystical ideas of Wei and Jin to this-worldly pragmatism, or from the sacred to profane, everyday existence.

The rulers of the northern ethnic groups (Khitans, Jurchen, Mongols) were mainly tribal military leaders, and intellectual activity was not their forte. After they came in close contact with Chinese culture, however, the Liao, Jin, and Yuan dynasties all produced men who were profoundly influenced by it. In general, the Liao Khitans were in contact with Chinese culture for the longest time, and this contact gradually produced many Khitan scholars who possessed considerable literary talent. Yelü Chucai (1189–1243), who lived under all three dynasties (Liao, Jin, and Yuan), first earned Chinggis Qaghan's trust through his shamanistic activities. His greatest contribution, however, was in advocating that the Mongol Yuan adopt the Chinese style of government structure. From Khubilai Qaghan on, because he took China as his main area of rule, the Yuan government structure underwent a thorough Sinicization. The Yuan dynasty adopted the Chinese examination system and civil bureaucratic organization, and Han Chinese scholars were able to take advantage of them and rise into the Yuan elite. At the same time, greatly Sinicized intellectuals also appeared among the Mongols and the *semu* (Western and Central Asian) ethnic groups. While all of this took place, however, the Mongols continually maintained a dual administration, in which the Mongols and other northern people always occupied a higher status in their branches of the civil service than the Han Chinese in similar offices.

In areas outside of China on the northern steppes and Central Asia were many khanates (Mongol-ruled kingdoms) that had been established by Chinggis Qaghan. These khanates were also deeply influenced by the local cultures of the conquered peoples. In both intellectual activities and government mechanisms, they underwent Persianization, Islamicization, and even Indianization. Thus, the great Mongol empire was diverse and multicultural, and we should not think that the way the Mongols ruled China was representative of the common situation throughout their empire.

When Chinese scholars study the Mongol Yuan culture, they use Chinese-language records as their main sources, but these documents were usually written by Han Chinese, and thus we need to consult other sources to compensate for the possible biases in the Chinese-language records. Yuan cultural activities were characterized by interactions between Chinese and non-Chinese culture, and there were also areas where these separate cultures coexisted in the same realm of activity. For example, in the Yuan capital Dadu (modern Beijing) was a Moslem astronomical observatory, and traditional Chinese astronomical observations were going on there at the same time. These two distinct systems were never united to form a single new astronomical system.

Because of urbanization, changes in the relations between cities and the countryside, and other complex factors, the common people's lives underwent a great transformation during this period. One of the most notable changes was that clan organizations were no longer the main elements in the social community; they were replaced by regional village associations (*xiangshe*). In earliest Chinese history, the word *she* (modern society, association) was probably an organization for belief in the god of the soil. In the Qin to Han period, a *she* became the smallest unit in village administration. From the end of the Han, as the great clans and powerful men took control of the villages, local power was organized in a fashion recalling the *fengjian* system of the past, and the common people became the slaves or indentured servants of great families. From the middle of the Tang dynasty, these semi-*fengjian*-style local social structures were gradually transformed into collective community bodies.

During this process of transformation, perhaps stemming from the community activities of Buddhist temples and monasteries, the center of community cohesion also changed. In response to different conditions and demands, these collective communal bodies took on different social functions. Then still other social functions would come into existence in some of them and become a part of their organizational structure. Take the worship of the "Holy Mother" (*Shengmu*) on Mount Rao between Shanxi and Shaanxi, for example. This was a very large network that straddled the borders of several counties in Shanxi and Shaanxi and contained eleven associations (*she*), each of which was composed of at least ten villages. Reliable inscriptions on stone tablets concerning this religious practice can be traced back to Tang times, and their historically traceable collective activities go back to 1069, during the Song dynasty. The primary activity of this network was ceremonial praying for rain, but it also functioned in the collective areas of local markets, defense, and irrigation works. Similar organizations, all called *she*, included the Bow and Arrows in the northwest border area; the Loyal and Righteous in the Taihang Mountains, who resisted the Jin; and several Southern Song Benevolent Associations (*yishe*). The Daoist temples of the new Daoist sects in Hebei and Shandong (like the Complete Truth sect) became the center of their communities. Chan Buddhist temples and monasteries (like the Nongchansi, or Agricultural Chan Monastery) also functioned as community centers. All of the village compacts (*xiangyue* and *sheyue*) as well as clan property and benevolent lands (*yitian*) sponsored by Song Confucians were also intended to supplement the power of the state and lend more solidarity to local communities. From the Song dynasty to this day, whether in the north or the south, collective community organizations have generally combined religious belief, irrigation work, and market exchange into one vast social network. The Society for the Worship of Mazu in southern China (including Taiwan) is a contemporary example.

The conquest regimes of the northern peoples always began with tribal structures, but as soon as they grew into empires, they had to reorganize their people and their government. For example, the *tümen* (Chinese *wanhu*, ten thousand families) system of the Jin and the Yuan was a military organization created out of the breakup of tribal groupings; later on, the *tümen* came to guard particular territory and developed into a sort of *fengjian* system. The tribal people who belonged to these organizations were transformed into the ruling strata of these areas and dominated the conquered population. This was a three-step process of coming together, reorganizing, and dispersing again, during which the enfeoffed or occupying ruling elements were gradually indigenized and mixed with the local people to form a new ethnic identity that later became alienated from their original ethnic structure.

Conquest brought about this ethnic mixing and a great deal of population migration. As the Mongols rapidly expanded, the original groupings from their steppe homelands dispersed into the vast conquered territories. The Mongol's allied armies (*tanmachi jun*) of Khitans, Jurchen, and Chinese soldiers in the Western Regions followed the Mongol military movements and were stationed on Chinese territory. There they intermarried with the Han Chinese, took Chinese surnames, and in the end became a new element of the general Chinese population. Similar migrations taking place at this time were the oriental peoples (*dongfangren*) moving into Central Asia and the northern Han Chinese moving into southern and southeastern China. During this process of melding together divergent ethnic groups, the ancient Chinese practice of using blood ties to define ethnicity was gradually transformed into one relying on geographic concentration. Even though individual members of society might still be attached to their native land and reluctant to leave it, their prescriptive status as a member of a particular blood-related group had already been replaced by individual ascriptions of identity. As this period of time experienced a rather high degree of urbanization and a considerable development of industry and commerce, peasants who left their villages and migrated into the cities would take up industrial and commercial occupations and lose their indigenous identity. Individual migration thus brought about both autonomy and a sense of loss or alienation at the same time.

Within the Mongol empire, the princes of the various khanates spread out over the vast Eurasian continent. Conflicts between these Mongol princes (descendents of Chinggis Qaghan) eventually brought to an end the largest empire in history. After several generations of reorganization, the Mongol khanates no longer considered "Mongol" to be their common ethnic identity. During this same period, Tibetan Lamaism combined many elements of Tibetan Buddhism, gradually expanded its scope of influence, and finally became the new ethnic identity of the peoples of the East Asian steppe regions. From the point of view of the spread of religious power, the rapid expansion of Islam and Lamaism are most worthy of historical investigation.

To sum up, the changes that took place internally and on China's borders during the four to five hundred years since the tenth century were of vast scope and profound influence. To say that they brought about a comprehensive transformation of the character of Chinese society would not be an exaggeration. The Japanese historian Naitō Konan (1866–1934) argued that Song China was a "modern" society. The validity of this attribution depends, of course, on one's definition of "modernization." If one defines "modernization" simply as the appearance of urbanization and individual autonomy such as occurred in Western Europe, then we can see the outlines of "modernization" in the period from the Song to the Ming. Chinese historians of the 1950s tried very hard to locate the "sprouts of capitalism" in China. If we define capitalism simply as the corporatization (*qiyehua*) of commerce and industry, this change was also incipient from the Song to the Ming. Chinese cities at that time, however, were quite different from the free cities of Europe. A Chinese person's "individual autonomy" was still tied to strong collective community organizations and was of a sort very different from European "individual freedom." China's remarkable industrial and commercial development was large in scale and complex in practice, but the operational procedures of European capitalist corporations were not really carried on in China. Both the Naitō hypothesis and the "sprouts of capitalism" theory are based on events in the history of Europe (especially Western Europe); they cannot be used to explain the trajectory of Chinese history, nor can they establish a universal history of human society.

Every geographical area has its own characteristic model of historical development, depending on local conditions. Although there are some common elements in the development of human societies, the unique elements are greater. Historical research is quite engrossing, however, as one finds differences amid the similarities and goes on to attempt to explain the origin of these special characteristics. In the Song, Liao, Jin, and Yuan periods, each dynasty developed its own distinctive characteristics, because they were involved in mutual interactions between different state systems and two quite distinct northern and southern cultures.

Song China could no longer consider itself the universal Celestial Court, and for that reason it exhibited a new inwardness. The men of Song emphasized the distinctions between Chinese (*Hua*) and barbarians (*Yi*), and Song history writing is replete with discussions of them. Song literati admired the past and often exhibited neoclassical tendencies. Song Neo-Confucianism traced its doctrines back to Confucius and Mencius, and the Song style of learning from the ancient classics initiated the tradition of Chinese archaeology. All of these phenomena can be understood as the Song elite's search for the proper position of Han Chinese culture within a multistate system.

By contrast, the culture of the northern non-Chinese peoples looked outward. The conquest dynasties completely annihilated other peoples or were forced to absorb the "other" into their ethnic group. Thus, the boundary of their self-created identity was repeatedly ruptured and new boundaries established. This can be seen in all aspects the northern ethnic regimes, including land area, ethnic identification, as well as trade and economic and cultural exchange.

Between the north and the south, these inward-looking and outward-looking tendencies mutually clashed and stimulated each other, not only influencing their political domains but also contributing to the establishment of East Asian cultural and economic spheres. As the modern world system took shape, similar processes of development could be seen, but the processes are only similar, and each area continued to maintain its own unique characteristics.

Suggestions for Further Reading

Allsen, Thomas. *Culture and Conquest in Mongol Eurasia*. Cambridge: Cambridge University Press, 2004.

Brook, Timothy. *The Troubled Empire: China in the Yuan and Ming*. Cambridge, Mass.: Belknap Press, 2010.

Chaffee, John W. *The Thorny Gates of Learning in Sung China: A Social History of Examinations*. Cambridge: Cambridge University Press, 1985.

Chan, Hok-lam, and Wm. Theodore de Bary, eds. *Yuan Thought: Chinese Thought and Religion Under the Mongols*. New York: Columbia University Press, 1982.

Chan, Wing-tsit. *A Source Book in Chinese Philosophy*. Princeton, N.J.: Princeton University Press, 1963.

de Bary, William Theodore, et al., eds. *Sources of Chinese Tradition*. New York: Columbia University Press, 1960.

Ebrey, Patricia Buckley. *The Inner Quarters: Marriage and the Lives of Chinese Women in the Sung Period*. Berkeley: University of California Press, 1993.

Gernet, Jacques. *Daily Life in China, on the Eve of the Mongol Invasion, 1250–1276*. Stanford, Calif.: Stanford University Press, 1962.

Holcombe, Charles. "Re-Imagining China: The Chinese Identity Crisis at the Start of the Southern Dynasties Period." *Journal of the American Oriental Society* 115, no. 1 (January–March, 1995): 1–14.

Hymes, Robert P., and Conrad Schirokauer. *Ordering the World: Approaches to State and Society in Sung Dynasty China*. Berkeley: University of California Press, 1993.

Kuhn, Dieter. *The Age of Confucian Rule: The Song Transformation of China*. Cambridge, Mass.: Belknap Press, 2009.

Langlois, John D. Jr., ed. *China Under Mongol Rule*. Princeton, N.J.: Princeton University Press, 1981.

Levine, Ari Daniel. *Divided by a Common Language: Factional Conflict in Late Northern Song China*. Honolulu: University of Hawai'i Press, 2008.

Lewis, Mark Edward. *China Between Empires: The Northern and Southern Dynasties*. Cambridge, Mass.: Belknap Press, 2009.

Liu, James T. C. *China Turning Inward: Intellectual-Political Changes in the Early Twelfth Century*. Cambridge, Mass.: Council on East Asian Studies, Harvard University, 1988.

——. *Reform in Sung China: Wang An-shih (1021–1086) and His New Policies*. Cambridge, Mass.: Harvard University Press, 1957.

Mote, F. W. *Imperial China 900–1800*. Cambridge, Mass.: Harvard University Press, 1999.

Smith, Paul Jakov, and Richard von Glahn, eds. *The Song-Yuan-Ming Transition in Chinese History*. Cambridge, Mass.: Harvard University Asia Center, 2003.

Standen, Naomi. *Unbounded Loyalty: Frontier Crossings in Liao China*. Honolulu: University of Hawai'i Press, 2007.

Twitchett, Denis C., and Herbert Franke, eds. *The Cambridge History of China*, vol. 6, *Alien Regimes and Border States*, 907–1368. Cambridge: Cambridge University Press, 1994.

Twitchett, Denis C., and Paul Jakov Smith, eds. *The Cambridge History of China*, vol. 5, *The Sung Dynasty and Its Precursors*, 907–1279, part 1. Cambridge: Cambridge University Press, 2009.

[6]

China Enters the World System, Part 1

THE FIFTEENTH TO SEVENTEENTH CENTURIES

During this period, China enters completely into the world order. The opening of oceanic transport and the increasing frequency of Eurasian overland contact bring China into the world economy. A favorable balance of trade keeps its economy growing rapidly for three hundred years, and China leaps ahead to become the most prosperous region in the world! Stimulation from abroad also prompts China's intellectual world to reevaluate traditional Chinese culture. This is a great effort somewhat analogous to the European Enlightenment, but, unfortunately, it does not last long.

1. Rigidity of the Chinese Cultural System During the Ming Dynasty

The periodization of this chapter goes back to 1500 C.E., or, specifically, the momentous year of 1492, when Christopher Columbus (1451–1506) landed on the an island off of the North American continent somewhere in the present-day Bahamas. From that point on, no people anywhere could remain isolated from the rest of the world. Of course, we choose the year 1500 not as a fixed date but as a round number to symbolize a momentous historical change.

This designated point in time represents the first period of modern world history. Contemporary China, then midway through the Ming dynasty (1368–1644), did not realize that the rivers of human history were now about to flow together. China still thought of itself as the so-called Middle Kingdom, and the Chinese people were still completely engrossed in Chinese culture. The most momentous historical event of this period was the final collapse of the Mongol Yuan dynasty (in 1368) and the reestablishment of a dynasty ruled by ethnic Han Chinese. Thus, our narrative of historical changes taking place during this period must of necessity begin with the founding of the Ming. The objects of our investigation are the various internal and external changes during the nearly three hundred years of the Ming.

When the founding emperor of the Ming, Zhu Yuanzhang (Ming Taizu, the Hongwu emperor, r. 1368–1398), drove them north of the Great Wall, the Mongols lost only their control over Chinese territory. The great Mongol empire had long since collapsed into a number of indigenized qaghanates. The Mongol remnants who ruled the Northern Yuan in Mongolia after 1370 remained a strong enemy of the Ming, and the Ming could never relax their northern border defenses. Today's world-renowned Great Wall of China was not built by the Han dynasty; it is rather a border defense against the Mongols and was constructed during the Ming period.

This long border wall passes through the Nine Garrisons of the northern Ming border—from the Shanhai (Mountain and Sea) Pass in Liaodong Province, it meanders westward all the way to the Jiayu Pass in modern Gansu Province. Extending far into the distance, there are even places that have both inner and outer walls. Such walls have existed in China ever since the Warring States of Yan, Zhao, and Qin set up frontier fortresses. The first Qin emperor connected the disparate elements of this defensive construction project to produce the magnificent and celebrated "Great Wall of China." From an examination of the ruins of the oldest Great Wall, we can see that the Qin-Han wall was not a single continuous edifice. It was most likely an array of mutually supporting fortresses. In mountainous areas, signal fires were maintained on the spine of the high mountains, while on the level ground fortresses took advantage of the terrain, such as trenches or thick brambles, to create defensive

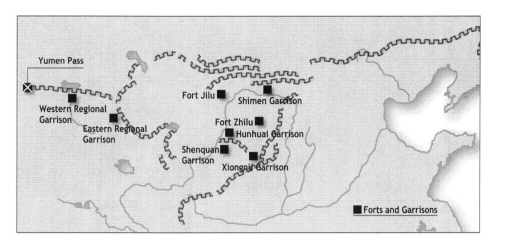

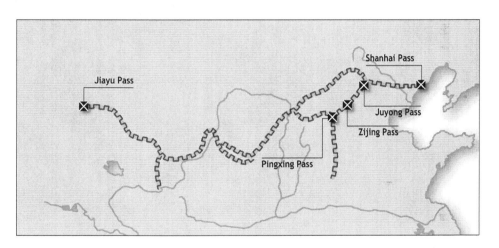

FIGURE 6.1 The Qin and Han Dynasty Great Wall (top); The Ming Dynasty Great Wall (bottom)

structures. Whenever they saw the northern enemy advancing, they could very quickly pass the information along using this long distance, in-depth, early-warning system. This allowed the crack Chinese garrison troops (such as those stationed at Youbeiping Prefecture in modern Liaoning Province) to quickly mobilize for defense against any attacking enemy.

This defense line did not completely seal off the border. The Chinese regularly traded with the northern Hu people, and the prefectural governors routinely conducted cavalry maneuvers on the border. In battle, the

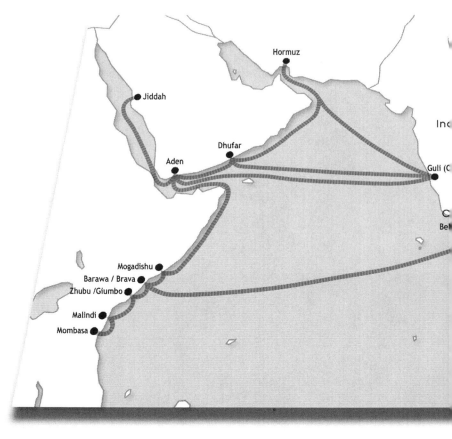

FIGURE 6.2 The Voyages of Zheng He

Chinese armies would attack (or counterattack) from different directions, considering going on the offensive to be the most effective defense. The northern people's pastoral lands and the Chinese agricultural areas were not walled off psychologically; the border was an open area across which each side moved.

In any case, Ming Taizu (Hongwu) and Taizong (the Yongle emperor, r. 1403–1425) led large northern military expeditions, after which there were no more. When the Mongols attacked, the Ming armies simply relied on the wall and guarded the passes. After the mid-Ming, the Manchus began to rise in the northeast outside the wall, where the Ming had established three garrisons in Jurchen territory (the Jianzhou Garrisons). The Ming army's defense line was originally north of the wall, but after

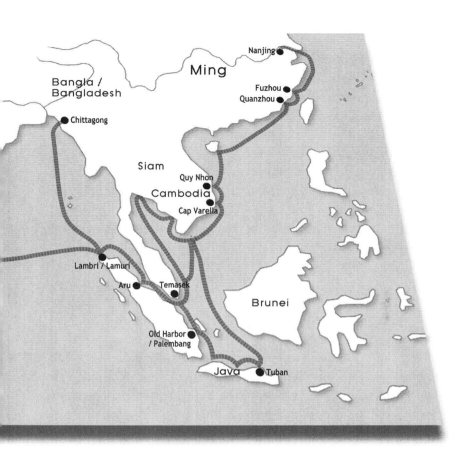

suffering several defeats, they retreated south, behind the wall; still they could not prevent the Manchus from breaking through the passes and entering Chinese territory. In the end, the Great Wall was unable to hold back the Manchu invaders.

In Chinese history, the Tang dynasty extended north of the Great Wall, and the northern peoples of the Liao, Jin, Yuan, and Xi Xia spilled over south of the wall. The Qin, Han, and Ming all employed the Great Wall as their northern line of defense, but the Qin and Han garrisons were more open; the Ming wall was more sealed up. The Great Wall was like a levee, however, and in times of great pressure it could collapse. Psychologically, this border wall separated the Han Chinese from the Hu barbarians, and the Chinese world behind it was closed in protectively upon itself.

Facing the ocean in the south, Ming China vacillated between attitudes of openness and isolation; in the end, they chose the latter. At the beginning of the Hongwu reign, the Yuan style of openness to the outside still remained, and ocean communication flourished. In Hongwu's fourth year (1371), when Japanese adventurers harassed the coastal border regions, China issued the first prohibition on entering or leaving by sea. Only the three Maritime Trade Commissions of Guangzhou (Canton), Quanzhou, and Ningpo remained open to receive oceanic trade. During the Yongle emperor's reign, Zheng He (1371–1433) led great armadas on seven expeditions to the South Seas, from 1405 to 1433. Although Yongle's motivation for sponsoring these expeditions is a subject of historical dispute, at least he had an attitude of openness to the outside. After the Xuande emperor (Zhu Zhanji, r. 1426–1436), the Ming government never again supported such external activities. After the middle of the dynasty, the incursions of Japanese pirates grew increasingly rampant, and in 1523 the Ming court closed the last three remaining trading ports and completely forbade foreign trade goods to enter China.

The policy of closing the country off to foreigners was impractical. Not only was it impossible to stop the oceanic trade, which had gone on for so long, but it also forced Chinese merchants to connive with the Japanese to set up coastal bases for carrying on illicit trade without government permission. These international adventurist groups represented something between merchant organizations and pirate bands. What the Chinese official records called "Japanese pirates" were not made up solely of Japanese; many Chinese also joined them and shared the risks in order to make a profit.

By this time, the world had already experienced great changes. The first Europeans to cross the seas to the east were the Portuguese and the Spanish, but soon the Dutch crisscrossed the oceans to join in the competition. The Arabs were no longer the main players in the game of international trade and communication.

An international trade network was coming into being. It brought the great continents of Europe, Asia, Africa, and the Americas, along with several Pacific island nations, including Indonesia and the Philippines, together into one huge economic system. The Ming government did not take cognizance of these momentous changes and thus continued to guard their coastal borders and maintain an official prohibition on ocean trade. Even though many Chinese merchants directly and indirectly entered into trade throughout Fujian, Zhejiang, and Guangdong, and although Chinese emigrants had already set up overseas Chinese settlements in Southeast Asia, the Ming government never acknowledged this reality. They simply denounced these activities as illegal. In sum, the Ming government's attitude to the sea remained one of defense and isolation.

Ming China's great land mass, numerous population, rich resources, and ample monetary surplus made it one of the richest countries in the contemporary world. But even with such great national strength, there is nothing to say about Ming China on the international stage. The Mongols in the north remained a dangerous threat to the dynasty. The Ming even suffered the capture of the Zhengtong emperor (Yingzong, r. 1436–1450) by the Oyirat or Western Mongols at Tumubao in September 1449. The Altan Qaghan (Anda in Chinese, ca. 1507–ca. 1582) attacked the Ming borders at will, and the Ming could do little to prevent it. Had it not been for the moderating influences of Lamaist Buddhism on the Mongols, China's northern borders would have had no peace at all. In the east, Japan continuously imported Chinese culture, but ever since General Fan Wenhu's (fl. thirteenth century) invading ships were wrecked by a hurricane, Chinese arms never reached Japanese territory. When Hideyoshi Toyotomi (1536–1598) invaded Korea in 1592 and 1595, the Chinese came to its defense, and their combined forces saved Korea. When Zheng He's armadas sailed to Southeast Asia, they only put in at small countries that could not resist them. The major military success of the Ming armies was, ironically, the destruction of South Sea colonies set up by overseas Chinese. They rounded up the Chinese leaders of places such as Palembang (in modern Sumatra, then known as Old or Great Harbor) and forcibly repatriated them. Before the Tang, Annam (Jiaozhi, later Vietnam) had been a Chinese province for a long time, but at the beginning of the Song it was a large border nation ranked as a tributary state and acknowledging China as its legitimate suzerain. There was civil war in Annam during the Ming, and the Lê family came to power. Ming forces intervened twice between 1406 and 1418, setting up provincial administration commissioners, but in 1418, Lê Loi led a successful revolt against them. After ten years of warfare with very heavy losses, the Ming was forced to accept the Lê regime.

All of this reflects the defensive and inner-directed attitude of the Ming dynasty, a dynasty that lasted over two hundred and seventy years yet cannot at all compare to the great national grandeur of the Han and Tang dynasties. One of the reasons for this can be found at the very beginning of the dynasty, when Zhu Yuanzhang (Taizu) issued his Ming "house law," entitled "Ancestral Injunctions" (*Huangming zuxun*), in which he ordered his descendants not to change lightly his institutional system. Succeeding emperors actually violated these "injunctions" in many ways, but nevertheless this key document still set the tone for a Ming government system that was very difficult to reform.

The Yongle emperor Chengzu was a very competent man, but except for seizing the imperial throne and moving the capital to Beijing, he did not bring about any meaningful improvements in government. The Hongxi emperor Renzong and the Xuande emperor Xuanzong, who followed Yongle, lived lives of self-cultivation with no great accomplishment; the style of their "Ren-Xuan rule" was representative of Ming conservatism. The high administrative officials of those days—men such as the "Three Yangs" (Yang Pu, 1372–1446; Yang Shiqi, 1365–1444; and Yang Rong, 1371–1440)—were all experienced and knowledgeable statesmen, but after the Zhengtong emperor Yingzong (r. 1436–1450), the Ming house never produced another capable emperor. Consequently, all their talented ministers exhausted themselves trying to make up for the faults of the emperors and were too worn out to accomplish any important reforms. Among the high officials, only a small number of individuals, such as Grand Secretary Zhang Juzheng (1525–1582) and Liu Daxia (1436–1516), were gifted administrators who genuinely wanted to improve the government. In the end, they accomplished very little. Zhang Juzheng's reforms, however admirable in such a dynasty, brought about a short-lived amelioration of the chronic ills in the civil bureaucracy but did not achieve any real governing breakthroughs.

After the Song's emphasis on the civil over the military came the militaristic Mongol Yuan regime. The Ming dynasty followed the Song and established a civil bureaucracy staffed by Confucian literati. The Ming examination system employed the so-called eight-legged essay (*bagu wen*) to examine the literati on their understanding of the Confucian classics. At the same time, Zhu Xi's Neo-Confucian interpretations of the classics were adopted as orthodox, and the anticheating apparatus was also greatly refined, with the intention of producing orthodox and standardized interpretations of the classics. As a result, the examination system became a test in formalism and dogma; it was not intended to develop the meaning and implications of the classics and even less to arrive at any new interpretations of these texts. This style of testing and selection was much execrated—although that system was also adopted by the Qing dynasty.

The Ming examination system produced the civil government bureaucracy and also nurtured an elite stratum in society that monopolized most resources, and both of these phenomena led to cultural conservatism. In the over two hundred and seventy years of the Ming, it was not until the latter half of the dynasty that there was any strong reaction to the above-mentioned orthodoxy. Before Wang Yangming (1472–1529), Confucian thought was limited to Zhu Xi's school, and before the literary style of the Wanli era (from 1573 to 1620) changed, Ming literature, art, and calligraphy were all characterized by a stultifying conservative stability in keeping with the so-called Cabinet Style (*taige ti*) of Ming officialdom, which in China has been synonymous with literary dullness ever since.

Zhu Yuanzhang abolished the office of chief minister and concentrated all power in his (the emperor's) hands. After that, the relationship between the civil bureaucracy and the emperor no longer maintained any semblance of the balance present during the Han and the Song dynasties. Absolute imperial power protected imperial conservatism to the point that any ideas that questioned the validity of the system would be suppressed. When an emperor was weak, incompetent, or uninterested in government, his absolute power would fall into the hands of his close attendants, the palace eunuchs. Thus after the "Ren-Xuan era," instances of eunuch persecution of civil officials and Confucian scholars are repeatedly recorded in the histories. The greatest harm brought about by the Ming eunuchs' usurpation of authority was not their terrible corruption but that they destroyed the vitality of Chinese culture and thought.

After the middle of the Ming, the intellectuals and the general public began to engage in various forms of resistance to this stifling milieu. Some of the individual events are discussed below, but here I note that there were many areas of conflict between the forces of resistance and the powers of absolute suppression. During a century of struggle between them, the talent and cultural vitality of China was totally exhausted. As a result, the late Ming had no reserves with which to face the newly developing world order. There were too few people who were even aware of these momentous changes and none who had any inkling of how Ming China should deal with the new world knocking at its gates.

To summarize, after liberation from the Mongol Yuan dynasty, no new vitality emerged from Ming China. The regime hid behind its image as a great "Celestial Kingdom," turned away from the Mongol-style importation of foreign cultural elements, and practiced a single-minded cultural protectionism based on the concentration of power in the person of the emperor. Political power was the absolute power of the emperors, the system of thought was Zhu Xi–style Neo-Confucian orthodoxy, and social control and influence was totally monopolized by the gentry elite in their red silk sashes. Ming China was one vast and monolithic cultural system that repressed any opportunity for the rise of internal forces of revision. For some time, foreign influences could not shake this moribund system. During this period, Chinese culture retained some exquisitely refined elements, but this stultifying system lacked the ability to adjust to emerging changes and in the end was destined to collapse in the face of them.

If we trace the origin of Ming China's rigid cultural order, we can say that it began over a century earlier, when Southern Song culture began to turn inward and ceased to unfold. The Song era created elegant and exquisite cultural works in both art and literature that are still greatly admired today, but these cultural accomplishments were primarily a manifestation of a process of continual breakthroughs and reorganizations of preexisting models. The Southern Song mode of thinking that gave Confucianism a theoretical system is a great accomplishment in human intellectual history. This form of Neo-Confucianism, with Zhu Xi's thought as its core, was, however, primarily aimed at making oneself a "sage on the inside" (*neisheng*) so that one could become a "king on the outside" (*waiwang*). In other words, the goal was to make a positive difference in the governance of society. Since the scholars had insufficient power, however, becoming a "king (on the outside)" was impossible, and they were left only as "sages (on the inside)." This Song situation was inherited by Ming scholars. The orthodox Wang Yangming School of Neo-Confucianism placed its hopes even more profoundly on one's inner nature (*xinxing*, heart or mind and nature).

Another cause of the Ming situation was the Mongol Yuan conquest dynasty's complete reliance on military force as the source of their power — absolute political power — and their suppression of the most important aspects of Chinese culture. Zhu Yuanzhang drove the Mongols out of China, but he took over their dictatorial and authoritarian system of political control. The Ming civil bureaucracy was enslaved by imperial power and could not act as a balance to a completely unrestrained emperor. They could not even successfully resist the rapacious abuses of power on the part of the palace eunuchs. The scholars protested ardently and were even willing to die to uphold their ideals, but usually their remonstrance ended in bloody sacrifice. Time after time they explained the spirit of their ideals, but they were unable to withstand the power of absolute monarchy. The price of their feeling of helplessness was a loss of dignity. The repressive imperial power smothered any possibility of flexibility, and Chinese culture and society moved step by step toward rigidity. After the Wanli emperor died in 1620, resistance to and self-reflection on this rigid system arose in the areas of scholarship, culture, and society. Those brave souls who struggled for freedom at that time were like moths throwing themselves into a lamp's flame. They left behind both a record for which we can still admire them and some profound food for our present-day thought.

2. Population and Life Resources

China's population today is over 1.3 billion and accounts for one-fourth of humanity. Rapid population growth began to be apparent during the Ming dynasty, and it was also during the Ming that China's material resources greatly increased.

According to official statistics, the population of the Han dynasty reached fifty to sixty million at its height, and from then on the population of the various dynasties fluctuated. The official figures from the various dynasties are not, however, very accurate. The figures for the Three Kingdoms era are surprisingly low, probably because the great clans controlled the population. The estimated Song figure of seventy to eighty million is also unreliable. The estimated population at the beginning of the Ming is one hundred million.

Thus, in the fifteen hundred years or so from the Western Han to the early Ming, the population had only doubled in size. By the mid-Ming, the population is estimated to have been one hundred and fifty million, and by the end of the dynasty it is said to have grown to around two hundred million. That means the population doubled again in just over two hundred years! More conservative estimates for these same times are sixty to seventy million, then eighty to ninety million, and finally over one hundred million—the rate of population increase was even faster in the eighteenth century. In the most recent fifty years, China's population growth rate has been more than double. This tendency for China's population to grow so rapidly began during the Ming dynasty.

China's territory during the Ming was larger than that of the Song, having added the southwestern region, the northeastern region, and much of Hebei. The food production of these areas alone was still not enough to support the population growth that occurred after the mid-Ming. From the Han and Tang on, Chinese food grains mainly consisted of the glutinous millet, wet rice, and sorghum, which had been cultivated for centuries, as well as several new varieties of rice and millet; added to these were some increasingly common products made from wheat flour. Early ripening and high-yield Champa rice was imported during the Song dynasty and was of great assistance in supplying the needs of the south. As the Ming dynasty began, many new food grain crops were brought into China and provided good sources of nourishment for much of the population. At the same time, given their different suitable environments for cultivation, many areas that hitherto were not suitable for growing food grains became able to produce an abundance of them. Thus, the improved agricultural prospects of the Ming cannot simply be explained by the extension of its territory.

The most important food crops imported at this time were sweet potatoes (or yams) and corn (zea maize). Sweet potatoes were introduced to Southeast Asia from America in the sixteenth century, and a few decades later they entered China, where they soon became widespread in both the north and the south—their diffusion was quite rapid. Sweet potatoes have a variety of local names, such as "foreign potatoes" (*fanshu*), "earth melons" (*digua*), "red potatoes" (*hongshu*), "white potatoes" (*baishu*), and so on. They were brought into various areas in Fujian Province from Southeast Asia during the Wanli era. According to Chen Shiyuan's (Qing, Qianlong era, 1736–1795) *Cultivation of Golden Yams (Jinshu chuanxilu)*, the vines were first imported from the Philippines and then planted widely in Fujian. At the same time, sweet potatoes were brought into Guangdong from Vietnam and cultivated widely in areas such as Dongwan and Dianbai counties. Shortly after that, the Ming scientist Xu Guangqi (1562–1633) transported the crop from the south up the Yangzi River to various places around the country; many local varieties soon began to appear. Officials in Fujian originally regarded the sweet potato as a stopgap during times of poor harvest or famine, but it gradually became a staple crop. Sweet potatoes grow in almost any soil, and thus the vines could be planted in hilly, sandy, and isolated areas. Sweet potatoes have a high nutritional value, and the leaves can serve as fodder for livestock; they soon became an almost universal crop.

Corn, or maize, was another food crop that rapidly became widespread throughout China. Corn is called "jade rice" (*yumi*) in Chinese, along with many other names, such as "jade millet" (*yushushu*), "precious pearl rice" (*zhenzhumi*), "wrapped grain" (*baogu*), and so on. It was first cultivated as zea maize by South American aboriginal peoples. The *Daily Jottings* (*Liuqing rizha*) of Tian Yiheng (fl. 1570), from the mid-sixteenth century, contains a detailed record of the form and appearance of corn and tells us it was originally known as "foreign wheat" (*fanmai*)—we can thus see that corn had been in China for some time. Tian's *Daily Jottings* also discusses the cultivation of this "foreign grain" in his native Hangzhou. It was probably first grown and transmitted north from Fujian and Guangdong to become common in areas such as Hangzhou. Corn can be grown in rather hilly areas, does not require too much care, and is easy to harvest and store; it too soon became a widely cultivated crop, especially in the many hilly areas of southern and southwestern China.

Peanuts (*huasheng*, born from flowers), also called "dropped peanuts" (*luo huasheng*) and "long-life fruits" (*changshengguo*), originated in South America. One of their characteristics is that when simply dropped on the ground they will begin to grow (hence the name *luo huasheng*); they can be cultivated in sandy and both saline and alkaline soils, making them an ideal crop to grow on newly reclaimed coastal land. Peanuts are mentioned in local gazetteers from Jiangnan (South of the Yangzi) during the Jiaqing reign period (1522–1566); from this, we can see that the crop entered China no later than the importation of sweet potatoes. Peanuts are very rich in fatty substances and thus an excellent source of edible oil, making them a widely cultivated crop.

Potatoes, called "horse bell yams" (*malingshu*), "foreign taro" (*yangyu*), "earth beans" (*tudou*), and other names, were introduced into Fujian and Taiwan during the Ming. They were soon after transported to the various provinces of the southwest and, during the Qing dynasty, to the north. They are cultivated extremely widely today, but during the Ming they were not as widespread as sweet potatoes.

Another well-known tuberous or root (rhizome) plant is taro (*yutou, yunai, maoyu*); the *dunchi* of Bashu (Sichuan) during the Han dynasty was probably taro. It too was considered at the time as a food to be eaten during times of famine. Taro is, of course, the principal food crop of many Austronesian aborigines (from Taiwan, Philippines, Hawaii, and so on). Although taro was present in China quite early on, it never became a very important crop. Being high in carbohydrates but low in protein, its nutritional value could not match that of sweet potatoes or yams.

Of the abovementioned crops that entered China during the Ming, corn, sweet potatoes, and peanuts were the most important. Corn and sweet potatoes are rich in carbohydrates and can be used as staples during deficiencies of rice and wheat. Peanuts provide vegetable oil, providing the Chinese diet with another source of edible oil besides the traditional soybean and rapeseed oils. These three crops can all be cultivated in sandy soils, thus transforming many areas hitherto regarded as useless into agricultural land. Southern and southwestern China has many mountainous areas and seaside or riverside areas with newly reclaimed soil—with these crops, all of them could become very fertile, and the Ming cultivated many sandy and dike-protected fields.

Besides these staples, other vegetables newly arrived in Ming China— pumpkins, tomatoes, carrots, kidney beans, and chili peppers—all greatly enriched Chinese cuisine. The Ming had many crops—sesame seeds, soybeans, peanuts, rapeseed, and tea seeds—that could be pressed to produce edible cooking oils. Animal fats were only used to prepare very special dishes. Fibers for textiles that had long since been used in China included silk and kudzu, and cotton and ramie became widespread during the Ming. Cotton and Java cotton, or ceiba—the kapok tree—was long known in South China. After the techniques for separating cotton from its seeds was introduced by Huang Daopo of Songjiang, who learned it from the Hlai of Hainan Island during the Yuan, cotton cultivation spread very rapidly from southern to northern China. Thus the very tall ceiba or kapok cotton tree was gradually bred into the widely cultivated cotton plant.

Chinese cultivation techniques, including grafting branches to rootstocks, were already well known by the publication of the early medieval book *Important Arts of the People* (*Qimin yaoshu*, 533–544). That the Ming knew various techniques of asexual reproduction was probably related to their widespread cultivation of sweet potatoes. Ming cultivation of ramie, mulberry, and sugarcane all employed these techniques.

As mentioned previously, so many species of crops were cultivated and the methods of cultivation became so diversified that Ming China was able to open up for cultivation many hitherto marginal areas as cotton fields and so on. On the one hand, this greatly increased the Ming dynasty's total area of cultivation. On the other hand, because of such changes in land usage, especially changes to the use of marginal lands, the overall ecology of the land was seriously affected.

Ming population statistics are not really accurate. Ming estimates of the number of *mu* under cultivation (one *mu* equals one-sixth of an acre) relied on the "fish-scale" land-registry system (*yulince*), so called because the fields resembled fish scales. The exact boundaries of a square of cultivated land were easy to see and thus its production easy to audit. According to an official Ming survey, it is estimated that during the thirty-year reign of the Hongwu emperor, from 1368 to 1398, the land under cultivation in the whole nation expanded rapidly from three million to more than eight million *qing*. At 16.7 acres per *qing*, that would be from 50.1 million to 133.6 million acres. From then on, although the cultivated acreage fluctuated, it generally remained around five to six million *qing* (83.5 million to 100.2 million acres); the late Ming figure of somewhat more than seven million *qing* (116.9 million acres) is, on the whole, a reliable number.

The amount of tax grain collected from the whole nation gradually increased from twenty million *shi* (bushels) in the early Ming to over thirty million *shi*; then, between the Hongzhi and Wanli emperor's reigns, from 1488 to 1620, it declined to around twenty-six or so million *shi*. Given that under the Ming system the gentry and the imperial family were exempt from grain taxes, the national grain tax figures cannot reflect either the population growth or the increase in cultivated acreage. Because the gentry was exempt from taxes and corvée labor, and because many poor peasants became tenant farmers for the gentry, according to Gu Yanwu's (1613–1682) *Records of Daily Learning* (*Rizhilu*) in the Jiangnan area of China south of the Yangzi, nine out of ten fields were cultivated by tenants, and only one out of ten peasants was an independent cultivator. Although landlords controlled most of the land, they did not organize it into large landed estates or latifundia but allowed their tenants to continue to cultivate small plots of land—the landlords just sat back and collected the rents.

A peasant family of the Ming dynasty generally cultivated around ten *mu* (or 1.7 acres), but some families had only around half that much land. Based on the production capacity per officially recorded *mu* at that time, although the overall production of grain staples was greater than that of the Song and Yuan dynasties, it would still be insufficient to support the entire population of the nation. The solution to this discrepancy is most likely that many terraced fields, sandy fields, fields protected by dikes, underwater turnip fields, and fenced-off fields were not included in the fish-scale (or flat-farm) land-registry system of total national acreage.

The small-scale farmers worked every nook and cranny of their land. In general, they used the mountains for wood fuel, had gardens for vegetables, dug fish ponds in low-lying areas, and piled up mud to create bases to plant fruit trees—all this work created a circulating small-scale ecological system. Bananas, lychees, and pineapples in the south and jujubes (Chinese red dates) in the north were all brought into the agricultural production network in this manner. Government regulations at that time encouraged peasant families to plant fruit trees.

In the early Ming, the government repeatedly urged on agricultural production, mandating that peasant farmers with five to ten *mu* of land must plant at least half a *mu* of mulberry bushes and/or cotton; those with more than ten *mu* (1.7 acres) had to plant double that amount. They also ordered the garrison troops each to plant one hundred mulberry bushes and, according to the local conditions, to plant persimmon, chestnut, and walnut trees. Farmers who grew mulberry, jujubes, and fruit trees were all exempt from various taxes. The ostensible rationale for planting these fruit trees was "to prepare for harvest shortfalls" and for planting mulberry and hemp was "to clothe the world," but the real reason was to encourage the common people to work hard to increase their life resources.

The Ming population distribution may also be related to the distribution of food resources. Ever since the Southern Song, the population south of the Yangzi and Huai rivers had been very high. Warfare and famines were frequent in the north during the Yuan dynasty, and the population declined precipitously. At the beginning of the Ming, the government moved many people from south of the Yangzi north to the middle and lower reaches of the Yellow and Huai rivers to make up for the population scarcity there. When the Yongle emperor moved the capital to Beijing in 1403 (changing Zhu Yuanzhang's Beiping, "pacifying the north" or "defeating the Mongols" to "northern capital"), the population directly administered by Beijing increased. Both troops from military garrisons and civilians from coastal settlements were moved north in accordance with this policy of "opening up the middle." This was quite a large population migration.

Despite this, after the mid-Ming, in general more than half of the total population lived in the south; the various provinces in the north had only one-third as many people as the south. The southwestern provinces actually had from one-fourth to one-third of the total population. The new food grains, fruits, and vegetables brought into the Ming first developed in the south and then gradually diffused to the rest of the nation. Jiangnan and the southwest received the benefits of these new crops before the north, so much so that the greater south (including Jiangnan, Huanan, and the southwest) were able to support an extremely large population despite having extensive areas of mountainous land.

In sum, the Ming population growth and increase in acreage under cultivation went hand in hand. The early Ming was a period of recuperation during which government policy actively encouraged increases in life-sustaining resources. During the mid-Ming, new plants imported from outside increased the number and varieties of food crops, and the area of cultivation was also expanded. Small peasant cultivators worked very hard and efficiently from a base of intensive farming to develop one vast and integrated production system of domestic animals, aquatic produce, distribution of fertilizer, and land management.

3. Great Waves from the Ocean

The Ming attitude to its coastal regions has already been described in section 1. Here we will go into greater detail, focusing on the Chinese people's own activities on the high seas. Part of this exposition will include the entrance of the island of Taiwan into both Chinese and world history.

Near the end of the fifteenth century, Europeans began to explore the sea routes east toward Asia. They were so motivated because the Ottoman Empire had captured Constantinople (the capital of the Byzantine Empire, now Istanbul) in 1433, cutting off the overland Eurasian trade routes. The Europeans had no choice but to seek out ocean routes to the East. In 1488, the Portuguese explorer Bartolomeu Dias circumnavigated Africa via the Cape of Good Hope, and in 1498 his compatriot Vasco da Gama entered the Indian Ocean. By crossing the Indian Ocean, they could reach India, Southeast Asia, China, and Japan. The Spanish mon-

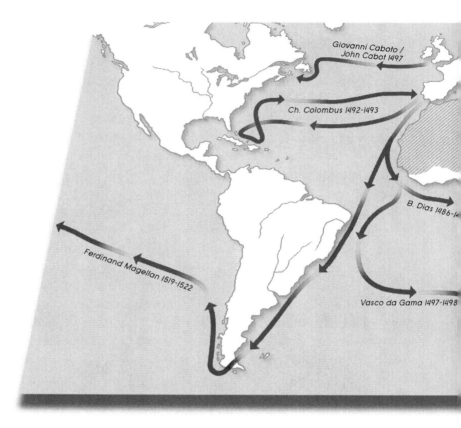

FIGURE 6.3 Ocean Shipping Lanes from the Fifteenth to Sixteenth Centuries

archs Isabella and Ferdinand sent Christopher Columbus west across the Atlantic Ocean in search of a direct route to Asia, but he inadvertently encountered (not "discovered") the American continent (first landing somewhere in the Bahamas) in 1492. The history of these momentous events is, of course, well known to everyone today.

The opening of the sea routes brought all of humanity together into one economic network. China borders the Pacific Ocean in the east and was the principal destination for the Europeans. Facing this new, global situation, China underwent many great changes. The most profound and immediate effect was that the Chinese themselves took to the seas. They entered the competition for power in the Asia Pacific region and opened up many overseas Chinese settlements.

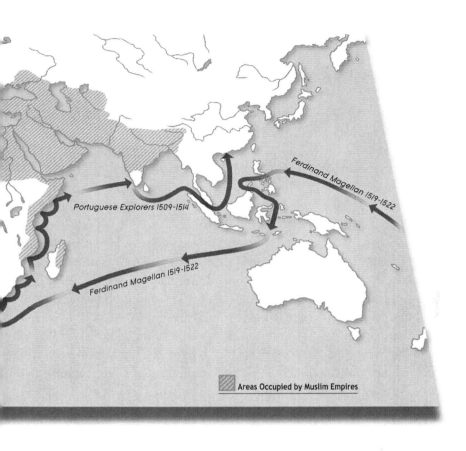

Portuguese Explorers 1509-1514

Ferdinand Magellan 1519-1522

Ferdinand Magellan 1519-1522

Areas Occupied by Muslim Empires

Earlier on, during the Song and Yuan dynasties, the "oceanic silk road" was well traveled by merchant ships from Persia, India, and Arabia passing back and forth between China and the Middle East. At the same time, Chinese merchants sailed to the Red Sea and the Persian Gulf plying their wares. In 1340, during the reign of the Yuan emperor Shun, the Moroccan Muslim scholar Ibn Battuta (1304–1368/69) boarded a large Chinese oceangoing vessel in Calcutta and traveled to Quanzhou (in Fujian, Marco Polo's Zayton). Ibn Battuta would have seen thirteen such large Chinese ships moored in Quanzhou at that time, each one having five stories and able to accommodate a thousand people. Song writings record the constant travels of these ships laden with goods, and we can see how enormous they were from the one complete ship that was dug up at Quanzhou. Ming Chengzu (Yongle) dispatched the eunuch Zheng He on seven expeditions to the South Seas from 1405 to 1433, and the grand scale of his armadas has been remarked upon ever since. Actually, the size of these ships in Zheng He's time was not unprecedented, because earlier in the Song and Yuan such large oceangoing vessels had also been built to sail the busy trade routes.

Since the Song and Yuan, the sea route between China and the Middle East had been well traveled by ships from many nations. In general, this sea route went from the various harbors of Quanzhou and Guangzhou, hugging the shore past the south end of the Malay peninsula, past Malacca and into the Indian Ocean, where it went by Ceylon (now Sri Lanka) toward Calcutta. Sometimes the route would divide, with some ships sailing for the Persian Gulf or the Red Sea and some toward Africa, landing in Mombasa (in modern Kenya). In several important entrepôts along this international sea lane, Chinese, Indian, and Arab merchants and sailors could transfer goods and passengers.

The various ports of call along this East-West trade route made a great deal of profit from the Song and Yuan on. From this lucrative trade, several small new nations came into being in Southeast Asia and along the coast of the Indian Ocean. When the Chinese sailed toward the South Seas (Nanyang; also Xiyang, Western Ocean, in the Ming), they did not stop at the large offshore islands of Taiwan or Hainan. Thus, the development of Taiwan did not take place during the Song and Yuan nor even the early Ming dynasties but had to wait until after the opening of the great sea routes. Hainan was never actually on this great sea route and remained merely a Chinese island in the Southern Sea.

Following the sea routes established during the Song and Yuan, some Chinese began to settle in areas overseas. In 1369, the second year of Zhu Yuanzhang's reign, the Ming court summoned various nations (states) to pay tribute and designated some fifteen states—including Japan, Korea, the Ryukyu Islands, Annam, Kampuchea (Cambodia), Siam (modern Thailand), Champa, Sumatra, Java, Samboja, and Borneo—as states not subject to attack. In 1371, Zhu forbade Chinese living on the coasts to go to sea. At the time, the Xinghua garrison commander, who had been personally dispatching people to sea for trading purposes, was reprimanded by imperial decree. In 1374, Zhu abolished the Maritime Trade Commissions in Quanzhou, Guangzhou, and Mingzhou. All of these actions reflect Zhu's attitude of isolation, and although these policies were sometimes carried out laxly, this basic attitude did not change until 1567, when the Longqing emperor Muzong officially rescinded the interdiction on Ming people going to sea.

During the first half of the Ming, then, the Chinese people were forbidden to emigrate, though it was practically impossible to prevent them from leaving. Besides, during the Song and Yuan, many Chinese had already gone abroad and set up communities; the government just did not acknowledge their existence. We can still observe their behavior on the basis of scattered information. For example, in 1402, when the Yongle emperor ascended the throne, he sent emissaries to various states with an official edict informing them that he was now emperor. When these emissaries returned, they reported that several non-Han peoples (*yi*) lived on the coastal islands and that "unscrupulous Chinese soldiers and civilians have secretly joined with them as bandits." At that, the emperor sent further emissaries with another official edict ordering the various states to send these miscreants back to China.

In 1404, Yongle issued an edict forbidding the people to go to sea. Those civilian vessels that had already gone to sea were all rerigged into single-deck flat boats. The following year, he sent emissaries to Palembang (in modern Sumatra) to extradite Liang Daomin, the so-called king of Samboja (also in Sumatra), and his followers who had absconded from Guangdong—this was just before Zheng He put to sea (in June of that year). When the emissaries returned to court with "king" Liang Daomin and his followers, they also offered some local products as tribute. The court then rewarded Yang and his people with some expensive silk cloth. This official ceremonial recognition was equivalent to the gifts given to small states that offered tribute, and so we can see that the overseas Chinese of Sumatra (Palembang, Samboja, and Srivijaya) had already set up a good-sized colony, one equal to a small state. For several years after that, the "pirate leaders" Liang Daomin and Chen Zuyi regularly sent their sons to the Ming court. In 1406, however, Zhen He captured the "pirates of Palembang" Chen Zuyi and two others and took them back to court, where Yongle ordered them beheaded.

In the same year, the Ming court established a Pacification Office (*xuanweisi*) in Palembang and appointed the Moslem Shi Jinqing as pacification commissioner (*xuanweishi*) of the Palembang region. The Ming court's policies toward Palembang were changeable, but the fact that it eventually awarded its overseas Chinese leaders status similar to an

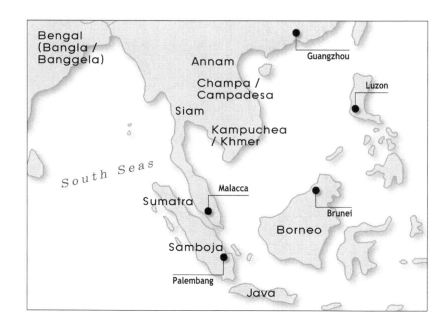

FIGURE 6.4 The Ming Dynasty South Seas

internal Ming rank demonstrates the sizable scale of the Chinese colony there; the Ming court could no longer ignore its existence.

There were overseas Chinese settlements like Palembang in more than one area of Southeast Asia. Malacca (Melaka in Malay) is on the Malay peninsula, which divides the Pacific and the Indian oceans. After the opening of the great sea routes, it was used as a transshipping center for, chronologically, the Portuguese, the Dutch, and the British. Overseas Chinese had lived and established trade centers there as early as before the Ming; they survived three successive European rulers and still remain to this day.

There are many historical examples of Chinese living abroad serving as tribute bearers for the states they lived in. For one, in 1436 and 1438, during the reign of the Zhengtong emperor Yingzong, Java sent several tribute missions to the Ming court, and all of the emissaries were Chinese from Longxi (Dragon Creek) County in Fujian Province who had asked to be sent home to do the job. The Ming government provided them with food and transportation to return to their native place; after going home and sacrificing to their ancestors, some of them then returned to Java.

That there were such men from Fujian's Longquan County who could rise to high office in Java was no doubt attributable to the large number of Chinese who had taken up permanent residence there. Again, in 1439, when the vice commissioner of Bengal, one Song Yin, asked to be allowed to build a ship and be relieved of his official duties, he received everything he asked for because he was Chinese. There most likely were many Chinese living in this small state on the Bay of Bengal for one of them to have been appointed vice commissioner.

During the first half of the Ming, overseas Chinese emigrants generally set up Chinese communities in the most important places, like Malacca, Palembang, and Samboja, along the ocean trade route. These people left home primarily to follow the "oceanic silk road." The Ming court forbade sea travel, so when Chinese merchants emigrated, it was very difficult for them to return. Thus, the sort of absconding mentioned above was common. After the establishment of the ocean trade routes, trading activity became very active and increasingly international. Various contemporary powers—Portugal, Holland, Britain, and also Japan—were in intense competition. These maritime powers were quite opportunistic, and there was really little difference between a national merchant and a pirate. The Chinese coastal population was swept up in this rising tide. Precisely because Ming officials tried to close the ocean borders, the profits to be made on the sea by Chinese merchants were that much greater. Thus, much manpower and materiel was thrown into this dangerous but lucrative ocean trade.

The activities of Chinese merchants and pirates on the high seas were closely related to those of the so-called Japanese pirates (*Wokou* or *Wakō*, in Japanese) of the history books. *Wokou* (*wo*, dwarf, being a derogatory Chinese term for the Japanese) was what the Chinese called the Japanese pirates who menaced China's coasts. Before the opening of the great ocean routes, Japan occupied a position remote from East-West trade. Even though Marco Polo called Japan "the Island of Gold and Silver," Japan's role in East-West trade was marginal, and China did not consider its trade with Japan to be very important. When Japanese trading ships came to China, in addition to their officially authorized goods, the merchant also had to carry private cargo in order to make a real profit. Since such smuggling of private goods was illegal, problems with the Chinese authorities was unavoidable. Thus, as early as 1369, when the Ming sent an official memorandum to Japan to establish diplomatic relations, the

Japanese reaction, under the Ashikaga *shogun* Yoshimitsu (r. 1368–1408), was both to send an ambassador bearing tribute goods and to return some seventy Chinese nationals who had been kidnapped from coastal areas such as Mingzhou and Taizhou. Despite this gesture, Japanese pirate raids continued. At the beginning of the Ming, the Ashikaga shogunate (*bakufu*) ruled Japan, and the military ethos was very strong. It was common for Japanese warriors to put to sea and steal whatever booty they could find. For this reason, to protect its coastal provinces, the Ming established military garrisons all along its long coast and continued to forbid its people to go to sea.

After the opening of the ocean routes, there was no distance the long sailing ships could not travel. The Portuguese established a base at Malacca, the Spanish did the same in Luzon (Manila, the Philippines), and the Dutch set up a colonial government at a place they named Batavia (Jakarta, Indonesia, was called Batavia from 1619 until 1942). From these bases they could reach China and Japan. Japan was no longer on the margin but now ranked as one of the states that made use of this international sea network. Japan was near China, and this gave the Japanese an advantage in the international smuggling practiced on China's coasts. They rapidly became the main element in the illicit activities of Chinese merchants and pirates.

From the Jiajing emperor's reign (1522–1567) on, the depredations of the *Wokou* grew increasingly rampant. Violent incursions flared up all along the coast for more than a decade, all because of the new trade situation and the profits to be made from exploiting it in this manner. According to contemporary records, only about one in three of these *Wokou* were really Japanese pirates; of the remaining 66 percent, most of them were Chinese pirates and the merchants who colluded with them—where there is profit to be gained, there are always people willing to take the risks involved.

At first, the merchants who entered this risky business were primarily residents of Fujian and Guangdong. According to early official records, in 1501 one Li Zhaotie, a native of Xinfeng County in Jiangxi, persuaded a Javanese smuggler to bring in foreign goods for sale in Guangdong; in 1509, the Malacca tribute official was one Xiao Minghua, a native of Wan'an County in Jiangxi; the Anhui merchant brothers Xu Hai (?–1556) and Xu Dong amassed a large store of goods, built a ship, put to sea from Guangdong to collude with the pirates—and they were actually related to the Ming merchant Wang Zhi (?–1559) from Anhui, who also became a notorious pirate. In 1522, Fang Gantong from Guangdong took to sea and joined together with the foreigners to pillage up and down the coast; this is perhaps the first recorded case of Chinese and foreign pirates working together. In 1534, pirates and smugglers from Zhili (modern Hebei), Fujian, and Zhejiang traded foreign goods all around, murdering civilians and resisting arrest—by this time, the activities of the merchant pirates was endemic.

By this point, the Portuguese had already captured Malacca, and in 1535 they bribed Chinese officials in Guangdong and took Macau (Aomen in Chinese) as a base for trade with China. From 1524 on, Shuangyu Island (near Ningpo in Zhejiang) was the principal harbor for Portuguese and Japanese merchants and pirates. The Chinese pirate Li Guangtou was one of the chief operators there. In April 1548, Zhu Wan, as grand coordinator (literally, "touring pacifier") of Fujian, "inflicted a great defeat on the Chinese and Portuguese pirates of Shuangyu Island," and in the next year he also defeated a pirate fleet operating off of Quanzhou and Zhangzhou. Zhu Wan's successful battles did not stop the international piracy. Soon after came the collusion of Wang Zhi and the Japanese mentioned above. In 1569, Nagasaki became the center of Japan's international trade. The Spanish in the Philippines built the city of Manila, and from then on many Chinese merchant ships frequented its harbor. The number of Chinese going abroad and of Chinese merchants working overseas continued to grow, reaching into the hundreds of thousands. In 1605, the Spanish massacred more than twenty thousand Chinese, and thus we can see that by that year the number of overseas Chinese must have been very large.

Several important events occurred during the seventeenth century: the Dutch joined entered into the Far Eastern ocean trade, Hideyoshi Toyotomi took power and brought order to Momoyama Japan, and not long after that the British also entered East Asia. All this created a changeable situation and many troublesome incidents in the Pacific Ocean regions.

The earliest Chinese national to go to sea and become a real power was the pirate leader Lin Feng (Limahong, or Lim Ah Hong in Cantonese) and his fleet. In 1574, the Ming navy chased him to his base at Wanggang (Spirit Harbor, today's Huweiliao in Budai, Jiayi County) in Taiwan; later his fleet entered Manila, from where the Spanish expelled him. In 1576, the Chinese fleet's commander, Wang Wanggao (fl. 1575), united with the Spanish to defeat Lin Feng on the high seas.

Lin Feng commanded only one of many Chinese merchant/pirate fleets. Other pirate commanders included Lin Daogan (fl. 1550–1560), Li Dan (?–1625), Yan Siqi (?–1625), Liu Xianglao, (?–1635), Zheng Zhilong (1604–1661)—also called Nicholas Gaspard, he was the father of Zheng Chenggong (Koxinga, 1624–1662)—and others who had large fleets that contended on the high seas with the various international powers.

Their bases were either on China's coastal islands or in the above-mentioned Nagasaki and Manila harbors, and their methods of operation blurred the lines between merchant activity and piracy. Take Li Dan for example. This Quanzhou adventurer (also known as Andrea Dittis) had legitimate business enterprises in both Manila and Nagasaki. In 1624, when the Dutch wanted to establish a base in the Penghu archipelago (the Pescadores) between Taiwan and the Chinese mainland but were met by a superior Chinese battle fleet, Li Dan led them toward Dayuan (Tayouan) on the southern tip of the island at Anping, now a district in Tainan City. Here the Dutch built Fort Zeelandia and established a colonial rule that lasted until 1662.

Zheng Zhilong was undoubtedly the man with the greatest accomplishments among these merchant and pirate leaders. Under Li Dan, Zheng worked with the Dutch in the Pescadores as an interpreter. It is said that he won Li Dan's complete trust and even became his godson. When Li Dan died, Zheng inherited his fortune, his fleet of ships, and his workers. After establishing himself and with Taiwan as his base, Zheng Zhilong frequently pillaged the cities of coastal Fujian and Guangdong. Later, he surrendered to the Ming, became a merchant again, and established a command center in his native Anping County in Quanzhou. Under the Ming banner (title) of admiral of the coastal seas, he rid the coastal waters of many of his old pirate friends, including Liu Xiang and the Yang brothers. After its defeat by the Manchu invaders, the Ming dynasty collapsed, but the prince of Tang declared himself emperor in Fujian, relying primarily on Zheng Zhilong's military forces. In 1646, his short-lived regime was destroyed by the Manchu army. Zheng Zhilong, desirous of riches and fame, surrendered to the Qing and was taken to the north. His son, Zheng Chenggong (1624–1662, later known as Koxinga, *Guoxingye*, Lord with the Imperial Surname), continued to fight for the Ming against the Qing, and consequently Zheng Zhilong was executed by the Qing court in 1661.

We are all very familiar with how Zheng Chenggong (Koxinga) took Taiwan from the Dutch; there is no need to belabor it here. There are two main reasons that he was able to land at Lu'ermen harbor in 1661, accept the Dutch surrender in February 1662, and end thirty-eight years of Dutch rule. First, there were already many Han Chinese living in Taiwan; many of them were farmers, some were merchants. Men such as Yan Siqi and Zheng Zhilong had long before used Taiwan as a base for their mercantile and pirate activities, and mainlanders continuously moved to Taiwan. Second, the Dutch interpreter, He Bin, who advised Zheng Chenggong to seize Taiwan, was a seafaring merchant who was used to acting as an intermediary between the Dutch and the mainland Chinese. With He Bin's guidance, Zheng Chenggong was able to navigate into Dayuan (Tayouan)'s Lu'ermen harbor.

In the late Ming, armed Chinese merchant/pirate groups made their way amid the fierce competition between the Western powers and Japan. At the same time, they had to contend with the Ming government's interdictions and official efforts to outlaw them. Nevertheless, they were able to amass truly remarkable power. At the height of Zheng Zhilong's influence, only ships flying the Zheng family flag were allowed to navigate in Chinese waters without incident. After Zheng Chenggong captured Taiwan, his anti-Qing, pro-Ming activities relied mainly on the thousands of ships he owned and directed.

All of these armed groups developed and prospered by making various temporary alliances amid the treacherous atmosphere of international sea trade. In terms of military prowess, their ships were equipped with the most advanced firepower of the time. They carried on an extremely lucrative and multisided trade. They sold Chinese products (raw silk, silk textiles, and porcelain) to European merchants while transporting Southeast Asian commodities (deer skins and camphor from Taiwan, medicines and spices from the Southeast Asia) to China and Japan. In all this trade, Mexican silver was the common currency of exchange. The preconditions for this roundabout trading were the Chinese and Japanese policies of isolation. The incremental development of a network of international trade gave these adventurers a golden opportunity to operate beyond the law, and, acting as part merchant and part pirate, they carved out an extremely profitable niche for themselves.

At the very time when the Western powers were competing mightily to establish colonies in Asia, the Ming court was carrying out a policy of outlawing and suppressing those Chinese who had already established overseas enterprises; at times, as when Zheng He took the Chinese leaders of Palembang back to Beijing, they even executed returned overseas Chinese. Under such conditions, the Chinese could only carry on illegal activities and rely on civilian wealth and commodities to compete with the Western powers and Japan. After the sixteenth century, China no longer had the opportunity to join in the competition on the high seas.

4. The First Wave of Westerners Arrive in China

The Roman Catholic Society of Jesus' (the Jesuits) transmission of Western culture should be considered the first shock wave of China's encounter with European culture. The influence of this first wave of Western contact extended to Catholic Christian doctrine, Western science and industrial arts, and a rudimentary understanding between China and Europe.

Francis Xavier (1506–1552) was the first missionary to attempt to transmit Christianity in China, but he became ill and died in Guangzhou without ever traveling to the Chinese interior. Michele Pompilio Ruggieri (1543–1607) and Matteo Ricci (1552–1610) reached Macau in 1579, were permitted to enter Zhaoqing on the Pearl River delta, and in 1583 established the first Roman Catholic church in China. Shortly after that, Ruggieri was ordered back to Rome, never to return. Ricci, however, was very successful in establishing cordial relations with Chinese literati such as Xu Guangqi (1562–1633), Li Zhizao (fl. 1620s), and others. He introduced Western culture to many contemporary Chinese intellectuals. Ricci's influence was far reaching, and he may be regarded as the father of modern Sino-Western cultural exchange.

After Ricci, some eighty or more Catholic missionaries came to China, most of them members of the Society of Jesus who came to carry on Ricci's work of transmitting Western scholarship and knowledge of Western culture to China's literati elite; they also worked at the Ming Imperial Directorate of Astronomy. There were also members of the Franciscan and Dominican orders preaching Christianity in Fujian, Guangdong, and Zhejiang, but they were involved primarily with merchants, sailors, and the general public and not with the intellectual elite.

The missionary methods of these two types of Catholic orders (the Jesuits and the other two) were extremely different, and, more importantly, they had divergent interpretations of Catholic doctrines. Their internal struggles led during the Kangxi era (1662–1722) to the celebrated Chinese

Rites Controversy (see chapter 7), which ended with a papal bull condemning Confucian rites and the Kangxi emperor's 1721 decree banning further Catholic missions in China. Thus ended Matteo Ricci's efforts at Sino-Western cultural exchange.

The activities of the Catholic missions in China are discussed here under three headings: proselytizing, introducing Western science and industrial arts, and acting as intermediaries for Sino-Western understanding.

Catholic Doctrine Introduced Into China

Ruggieri preached in the Church of the Holy Flower (*xianhuasi*) in Zhaoqing. He also had printed in Chinese the *Catholic Commandments as Transmitted by the Church Fathers* (*Zuchuan Tianzhu shijie*) and the *A Veritable Record of the Holy Catholic Religion* (*Tianzhu shengjiao shilu*)—the first two Chinese works intended to explain and spread Roman Catholicism. Ruggieri was fluent in Chinese, but he had not yet completely mastered the art of writing in Chinese, and these works were not altogether clear and coherent. Nevertheless, many important Christian concepts were given a Chinese vocabulary—the Christian God as Lord of Heaven (*Tianzhu* or *Tianshen*), holy water (*shengshui*), the Ten Commandments (*shijie*), and the Trinity (*sanwei yiti*)—and this was a great boon to the transmission of Christianity in China.

Matteo Ricci remained in China for twenty-seven years and made the acquaintance of many Chinese scholars. His *The True Doctrine of Catholic Christianity* (*Tianzhu shiyi*) appeared in 1595; its explications of Catholic Christianity makes use of several familiar terms from Chinese canonical texts. Ricci's method of teaching Christian doctrines was similar to the late Han and Wei-Jin introduction of Buddhism to China by "matching the meaning" (*geyi*) of Daoist terms. Ricci borrowed many terms from Confucianism, and his presentation of Christian doctrines was influenced by Confucian concepts. Ricci borrowed the words *Shangdi* (Highest Ancestor), *Tian* (Heaven), *Di* (Ancestor), and *Dao* (Way) from the ancient *Book of Documents* (*Shangshu*) and *Book of Odes* (*Shijing*) to explain the Christian doctrines of one and only God (monotheism) and unique Truth. Although these borrowed terms made it easier for the Chinese to understand this Western religion, some of the analogies also led to misunderstandings.

After Ricci's death, Niccolo Longobardi (1559–1654) took over his Jesuit work of preaching Catholic Christianity in China. Some contemporary priests doubted that terms such as *Shangdi* and *Tian* accurately represented the Christian ideas of Heavenly Lord or God (*Deus*) or whether the Chinese classics even contained the same concepts—the Lord God, angels, and immortal soul—as Christian doctrine. Sabbatino de Ursis (1575–1620) believed that Chinese culture did not. After discussions with Chinese scholars including Xu Guangqi and Yang Tingyun (1557–1627), Longobardi himself came to believe that the Christian God (*Deus*) should be translated with the Daoist term *Taichu* (Great Beginning), as in the phrase "In the Great Beginning there was the Way (Dao)." For him, Chinese *Tian* (Heaven) and *Shangdi* (High Ancestor) could not stand for God. Longobardi's book *Confucius and His Principles* (*Kongzi ji qi jiaoli*) was intended to explain the concepts of Confucianism and to demonstrate the conceptual differences between China and the West. Matteo Ricci believed that in Confucian rites (*liyi*), in which the Chinese sacrificed to Confucius and to their ancestors, it was not worship (*chongbai*) but only commemoration (*jinian*). These questions about Confucian rites and theories adumbrated the later Chinese Rites Controversy of the Kangxi era.

When Ricci and others were preaching Christianity in China, the Song Neo-Confucian School of Principle (*lixue*) had long since solidified its position as China's mainstream thought, but from the mid-Ming on, Wang Yangming's Neo-Confucian School of Mind (*xinxue*) was also attracting additional followers. The new realms of thought that Neo-Confucianism opened up greatly surpassed the contents of pre-Qin Confucianism. The long period of mutual interaction between Confucianism, Buddhism, and Daoism, with each accepting important elements of the others, gave each of them their own integral system. Chinese thinkers' main themes of debate and their dialectic methods for discussing them already formed a complex and theoretically integrated Chinese metaphysics.

When Buddhism entered China during the late Han and Wei-Jin era, that was the first time the China encountered Indian thought, and Chinese thought could not prevent absorbing Indian influences. By comparison, during the Ming, Chinese thought was deficient in the realms of politics, economics, and society but not in metaphysics. Catholic Christianity did not have any strong attraction for Chinese thinkers and their system of thought, nor did they need this foreign system of thought to make up for shortcomings in their own beliefs. Thus, the work of the Catholic missionaries was not very easy.

Those members of the Society of Jesus were themselves all very learned scholars, and they had some remarkable achievements even in that inauspicious environment. It is one of history's paradoxes that the nineteenth-century Protestant Christian missionaries who came to China on the heels of the superior economic and military strength of the Western powers did not need to have any profound learning or arguments in order to triumph wherever they went! It is enough to make the historian wring his hands and sigh.

Western Science and Industrial Arts

This wave of scientific knowledge brought into China by the Jesuits was centered on astronomy, but it also included mathematics, geography, agriculture, machinery, firearms, and medicine. The traditional Chinese cosmology was three dimensional (heaven, earth, and man; *tien*, *di*, and *ren*) and held that human and cosmic events mutually influenced each other. "To respectfully instruct the people in time" (*jingshou minshi*) was not only intimately related to agriculture, but changes in the axis of time could often reflect human events and the human body: whether or not human affairs were (or would become) harmonious could be determined by examining the changes and regularities of astronomical phenomena and the seasons. On this account, since ancient times the preparation of a calendar to describe very accurately astronomical phenomena and the seasons was a national priority. From the Han dynasty on, China had a general theory of the relations between astronomical phenomena and the calendar that relied on actual on-the-spot measurements to correct any imbalances in the official calendar. Both Indian and Moslem astronomy, introduced in the Tang and Yuan dynasties respectively, also influenced and improved Chinese astronomy.

The Jesuits in China were quite erudite and had an excellent knowledge of astronomy. This was especially so because contemporary Europe was just then in the throes of the debates surrounding the merits of the Copernican heliocentric and the Ptolemaic and Christian geocentric views of the cosmos. Xu Guangqi predicted a solar eclipse in 1629 based on Western methods and thus demonstrated the superiority of Western calendar making. Then Xu introduced and supervised Longobardi, Johann Adam Schall von Bell (1591–1666), and others in their reform of the official calendar. Their "Chongzhen Calendar" (*Chongzhenli*; the Chongzhen emperor Sizong reigned from 1628 to 1645) was never promulgated, because of the fall of the Ming, but Longobardi's "Timely Calendar" (*Shixianli*) based on it was promulgated in 1645. From then on, Jesuit scholars continued to work in the Qing Imperial Directorate of Astronomy, and Western calendar making had a profound influence on the imperial Chinese calendar.

The most noteworthy of the Jesuits' contributions was their use of the concepts of geometry to calculate the movements of the heavenly bodies. Traditional Chinese calendar making relied on algebraic formulas to calculate the orbital cycles of heavenly bodies. Geometric methods, however, produced more precise measurements, and their predictions were also more accurate. The Catholic missionaries could not, however, escape the restrictions that came from within their religion, because the Vatican continued to maintain Church dogma and refused to accept Galileo's (1564–1642) assertion that the Earth revolved around the sun. The best the Jesuits could do was to accept the compromise between the Copernican heliocentric universe and the Ptolemaic geocentric universe put forward by the Danish nobleman Tycho Brahe (1546–1601) and known as the Tychonian geoheliocentric system. Tycho's scheme kept the Earth at the center, with the moon and sun revolving around it, and the five other planets then known revolving around the sun. This may seem a regrettable compromise with reality, but it was perhaps the best that could be expected given contemporary knowledge and beliefs.

The Jesuits had to introduce the science of geometry for the sake of astronomical calculation. *The Principles of Geometry* (*Jihe yuanli*), jointly translated by Matteo Ricci and Xu Guangqi, initiated the study of Western geometry in China and is now a mathematical classic. Many Chinese mathematical terms derive from the book. They also translated some works concerned with mathematical survey and measurement techniques, such as *Principles of Right Triangles* (*Gouguyi*) and *Surveying Methods* (*Celiang fayi*), which introduced Western trigonometry to China. Ricci's *Atlas of the World* (*Kunyu wanguo quantu*) was the first Chinese atlas of the known world. In it, the map of China was also the first one ever drawn using the Mercator projection.

In the practical industrial arts, the book *Western Water Conservancy Methods* (*Taixi shuilifa*) by Sabatino de Ursis introduced Western reservoirs, water pumps, and siphoning methods of transporting water; it served as a model for the irrigation section of Xu Guangqi's 1639 *Comprehensive Treatise on Agricultural Administration* (*Nongzheng quanshu*). De Ursis also introduced distillation methods that had considerable influence on the production of Chinese medicines. The 1627 *Pictorial Explanations of Western Scientific Instruments* (*Yuanxi qiqi tushuo*), compiled by the celebrated scholar Johann Terrenz Schreck (1576–1630) and Wang Zhi (fl. 1620), was the first Chinese work to discuss Western physics, architecture, and mechanical engineering.

In the humanities, Nicolas Trigault's (1577–1628) 1626 *Aid to the Eyes and Ears of Western Literati* (*Xiru ermu zi*) was the first romanization (or Latinization) of Chinese. Ever since the North-South dynasties and under the influence of the translation of Indian Buddhist sutras, the Chinese had used the *fanqie* system (explained in chapter 4) to indicate the sound of Chinese characters. From Ming times on, Chinese phonetics could be indicated with romanization. The scholar Fang Yizhi's (1611–1671) *Rhyme Chart* (*Xuanyun tu*) and *Book of the Four Tones* (*Siyun dingben*) initiated the science of modern Chinese phonology. Fang was influenced by Western learning and was well versed in philosophy, science, music, and medicine, in every area of which he had his own individual interpretations. His *Comprehensive Refinement* (1666, *Tongya*) and *Notes on the Principles of Things* (1664, *Wuli xiaoshi*) are remarkable achievements in combining Chinese and foreign thought.

In the Catholic missionaries' preaching of their religion and transmission of Western knowledge were many areas that did not accord with traditional Chinese learning. Naturally, some Chinese scholars were not happy about these missionary activities. Vice Minister Shen Que (fl. 1620) of the Ministry of Rites in Nanjing soon attacked these missionaries, once in 1616 and again in 1621. He arrested some missionaries and Chinese Catholics, ordering that the missionaries be taken back to Macau to be expelled from China. Fortunately for them, Xu Guangqi and others appealed to the emperor on their behalf, and Catholics labeled Shen's actions "religious persecution." Attacks on Catholic missionaries by scholars such as Yang Guangxian (1597–1669) and others from 1664 on, during the Kangxi reign, including the bitter Chinese Rites Controversy, were related to this "religious persecution."

Sino-Western Understanding

During this period, China and the West began to have a rather comprehensive general mutual understanding. Prior to the opening of the oceanic trade routes, the European understanding of things Chinese largely depended on reports by Middle Eastern and Central Asian intermediaries and, of course, on Marco Polo's wildly popular thirteenth-century classic *The Travels of Marco Polo*. After the sea routes became active, Portuguese and Spanish merchants made direct contact with China, but their knowledge was restricted to matters of trade and only included the coastal areas; they knew nothing of China's vast interior. These merchants and sailors had little learning and, aside from trade conditions, had no clear understanding of Chinese government and culture. We can see the shortcomings of their knowledge from the maps of the Orient prepared by them.

The Catholic missionaries who came to China were learned men and thus able to gradually obtain a deeper understanding of Chinese culture; they also ventured into the interior away from the harbor cities and were able to observe the geography and the lives of the people. After a long period of observation, the missionaries came to have a thoroughgoing understanding of the Chinese geography, political system, and modes of thought. Matteo Ricci wrote *Records of China* (*Zhongguo zhaji*, available in English as *The Diary of Matthew Ricci*). With later additions by Nicolas Trigault, this work offered the West a comprehensive report on Chinese geography, local government, social customs, science and industry, religious beliefs, and philosophy—it was indeed the forerunner of modern Western Sinological research. Ricci was especially interested in Confucianism, and he translated many Confucian classics. From his introduction, the West finally began to have a general understanding of the civilization of this ancient nation. He edited the China section of his *Atlas of the World*, and the later maps used by Western merchant seamen were greatly revised on the basis of the greater accuracy of Ricci's map. In 1641, the Jesuit Alvaro de Semedo's (1585–1658) Portuguese book *The Chinese Empire* was published and immediately translated into Spanish, Italian, French, and English. It offered another comprehensive view of Chinese geography, government, society, daily life, arts and crafts, language, and ethnic groups. It also presented a thorough picture of the activities and difficulties of Catholic missionaries in China. This was the most complete contemporary record on China. Trigault, Semedo, and others all eventually returned to Europe and transmitted their knowledge. They traveled widely, reported on their Chinese experience to the Catholic missionary world, and gave their colleagues a relatively more accurate understanding of China and its culture.

The Catholic missionaries also introduced China to the natural and human geography of Europe. Ricci's *Atlas of the World* used romanization for Chinese place names, and this was the first time that the Chinese could see the contemporary Western situation and China's position relative to the West. The 1623 *Records of the West (Zhifang waiji)* by the Jesuit scholar Giulio Alenio (sometimes Aleni, 1582–1649) offered a narrative explanation of the items included in the *Atlas of the World*; it covered the important historical events and the customs of peoples of five continents. His *Questions and Answers on the West (Xifang wenda)* was an introduction to Western customs, cultural and governmental establishments, astronomy, and geography. It is so minutely detailed and comprehensive that it may well be considered an encyclopedia. Alenio's *Outline of Western Learning (Xixue fan)* introduced the scholarly subjects taught in European universities—rhetoric, liberal arts, philosophy, sciences, medicine, law, Christian classics, and theology—giving a fairly inclusive rundown of the content of the European scholarly curriculum.

Through the mediation of these Catholic missionaries, the educated elites of China and Europe were finally able to go beyond the fabrications of travelers' anecdotes and obtain concrete information about conditions on the other side of the great ocean. Only a mere eighty or so Roman Catholic missionaries came to China during the Ming dynasty, but fortunately they were all men of great learning and were able to carry on scholarly communication with learned Chinese such as Xu Guangqi, Li Zhizao, Yang Tingyun, Fang Yizhi, and others. Thus, a small group of elite scholars were able to make great achievements in mutual understanding between China and the West. The curiosity and thoughtfulness of these Chinese and foreign scholars who avoided prejudice and were willing to work hard to master each others' languages and carry on such wide-ranging cultural interactions is something quite rare in human history!

Unfortunately, during the Chinese Rites Controversy of the Qing emperor Kangxi's reign, the Vatican refused to allow Catholic missionaries in China to accommodate Chinese customs, and so the Qing court restricted the preaching of the missionaries. From that time on, China and the West never again experienced a cultural exchange based on a scholarly foundation. In the nineteenth century, Western imperialism invaded the East, and Catholic and Protestant missionaries entered China behind the superior European economic and military might. The relative strength of host and guest had been reversed, and the interaction between the two was now characterized by great prejudice and distortion. In light of this later situation, the special characteristics of the first wave of cultural influence from the West in China is all the more worthy of our continued reflection.

5. Ming Industrial Development

Important Ming books that discuss industrial and craft technology include the following: Song Yingxing's (1587–1666) *Exploitation of the Works of Nature* (1637, *Tiangong kaiwu*, available in English as *T'ien-kung k'ai-wu: Chinese Technology in the Seventeenth Century*), Xu Guangqi's *Comprehensive Treatise on Agricultural Administration* (1639, *Nongzheng quanshu*), and Mao Yuanyi's (1594–1640?) *Treatise on Armament Technology* (1621, *Wubei zhi*). That a large number of books on production techniques appeared during the late Ming is a noteworthy phenomenon in itself, especially since production activities, from handicrafts and agriculture to the armaments industry, were in no way mutually supportive. Industrial production was, however, already an important aspect of China's overall production activities.

Take the different categories and headings in Song Yingxing's *Exploitation of the Works of Nature*, for example. Contemporary industries included at least the following: salt manufacture, sugar making, oil pressing, textiles, dye making, mining, smelting, metallurgy (casting), tool making, coal mining, papermaking, painting, ink making, armament manufacture, pottery and porcelain making, boats and carts, pearls and jade, and so on. These were both categories of specialized techniques and of particular industries. According to a popular saying, in the early Ming, there were thirty-six categories of artisan; by the end of the dynasty, there were said to be three hundred and sixty categories. That is a measure of just how detailed and meticulous the division of specialized labor was in the Ming.

The Ming followed the Mongol Yuan system, so the government and the imperial house supervised many official workshops. These official workshops sought only the finest workmanship and did not stint on the costs of manufacture; their techniques were also constantly improving. From the artifacts found in a recently uncovered Ming official kiln at Jing-dezhen in Jiangxi, we can see that out of every hundred items produced, only four were deemed good enough to send to the capital for imperial use! All Ming artisans worked for the government in a system of conscription. When an artisan served his or her time working for the government, he or she would come in contact with officially controlled technology. As popular, nongovernmental production industries gradually developed, artisans who had worked in official workshops were able to transfer to non-governmental industries. The frequent improvement in Ming industrial technology probably came about because the developments in handicraft techniques were continually passed on to the nongovernmental arena; of course, a large market also stimulated production and helped raise the quality of industrial technology. The Ming market economy will be discussed in the next section.

The textile industry was undoubtedly the Ming dynasty's most highly developed. Official textile workshops were located throughout the country, with the greatest concentration and the most important in Jiangnan, south of the Yangzi. Nongovernmental textile workshops, whether for silk or cotton, were also centered in the Yangzi River delta, where the competition spurred on the most high-quality weavers.

Take Shengze Township in Suzhou, for example. The manmade looms of their small- or large-scale weavers were said to "use their skills" to "clothe the world." Shandong, Shanxi, Sichuan, Fujian, and Guangdong all had their own special textile products. For silk textiles alone, there was raw silk (*si*), thick loosely woven silk (*juan*), damask (*ling*), muslin (*luo*), light silk (*chou*), satin (*duan*), brocade (*jin*), velvet, and sheer silk gauze (*sha*); in muslins alone, there were five or six further specialty products, such as flowery, plain, autumn, stiff, and soft muslin. Besides all these silks, there were also many cottons, wools, and linens that developed as specialty items depending on various local environments.

The *Comprehensive Treatise on Agricultural Administration* and the *Exploitation of the Works of Nature* both describe the process of silk weaving. During the stage of reeling the silk from the cocoons, one person (almost always a woman) supervised the boiling of the cocoons, another person located the ends of the threads, and a third person reeled up the silk. The one who boiled the cocoons could perform two tasks, making a better division of labor and conserving everyone's effort. One person could then tread the spindle wheel with her feet and separate the ends of the threads with her hands; the rate of this style of work was faster than using a spindle wheel turned by hand. There were small-scale "waist looms" (*yaoji*), which one person used her lower back to operate and control several warps and woofs at the same time. Jacquard or "flower" looms (*huaji*) were very large, complex looms capable of producing several layered patterns of different colored threads (called jacquard weaves, a form of weaving that leaves a protruding pattern). Such looms required two people to operate: one squatted at the head of the loom to guide the differently colored threads, while the other sat in front of the loom pedaling the treadle with her feet and throwing the shuttle with her hands. The most complicated of these looms were constructed in four tiers and known as "transformation looms" (*gaiji*).

According to the *Comprehensive Treatise on Agricultural Administration*, the tools for handling cotton were also improving. The so-called mixing wheel or spinning wheel was a type of treadle-powered cotton gin (short for engine). The operator peddled the treadle with her feet, while her left hand turned a crank handle and her right hand spun the cotton bolls. The treadle-operated spinning wheel left the hands free to guide the many strands of thread and was a fast and efficient spinning method.

After the cotton cloth was ready, it had to be dyed; that was another specialized industry. There were a great many different colors—blue-green (*qing*), red (*hong*), jade green (*cui*), yellow (*huang*), and so on—all from plant materials, and they also were divided into different hues. There was a regional division of labor, with the weaving done in Songjiang (near modern Shanghai) and the dying done in Wuhu (in modern Anhui). After being dyed, the final step was the rolling process. Long bolts of cotton cloth were rolled flat using heavy stone rollers to make the cloth extremely close and fine with a high luster. After that, of course, the cloth would be made into clothing, shoes, and stockings by women needle workers based at home. For example, "dragon gate" linen from Songjiang was very light, thin, and white. Shopkeepers contracted the work out to women to make stockings and then sold them as summer garb.

Ming porcelain making was another very important consumer industry. Porcelain was made throughout the country in both the north and south. Hebei's Cizhou kiln carried on the Song porcelain-making tradition; Fujian's Dehua kiln and Guangdong's Raoping kiln also made porcelain for the overseas trade. Zhejiang's Longquan kiln made celebrated

Song porcelains, and it persisted into the Ming. Jiangxi's Jingdezhen, with its superior-quality, fine, soft white kaolin clay, became the center of the Ming porcelain industry and is still operating today.

Ming porcelains were thin and delicate—thanks first to the exquisite whiteness of the kaolin clay and second to the high temperatures at which they were fired. Tapped with a finger, they ring like crystal. The Ming glazes were pure and unmixed and had a bit more blue-green and gray than Song wares. Ming white glaze, like Blanc de Chine, is smooth as jade or silk, with a perfectly even color and luster. When colored glazes were added, they were quite elegant, no matter if they were blue and whites or had painted-on, colored designs. Ming blue-and-white porcelains are famous throughout the world for their fine hues.

The reigns of the Yongle and Xuande emperors each had their own special product depending on the nature of the metal alloys used. They achieved remarkably fresh color schemes using different amounts of iron, cobalt, and manganese. The color was applied under the glaze in these blue and whites. *Doucai* (dueling colors, also called bean colors) porcelains had the color put on under or over the glaze; both produced bright, flowing color patterns. Surviving Yongle white wares are as thin as eggshell; you can see the glaze but not the clay under it, and it was called "sweet and white" (*tianbai*). The Yongle and Xuande ruby reds and ruby blues were fired using the high-temperature flame-reduction technique, while Chenghua peacock greens and Hongzhi light yellows were single-color glazes fired at low temperatures. The five-color wares of the Jiajing era were painted with even more skill and were predominant for a time.

The key to firing porcelain is in controlling the kiln temperature. Kilns constructed in the Ming dynasty were mostly either "dragon kilns" or "serpent kilns"—long, brick, tunnel-like constructions built to raise the accumulated heat inside the kiln. They also used chimneys and vents to regulate the temperature inside the kiln. The temperature was highest in the middle of the kiln; it perhaps produced more broken pieces, and the success rate was actually lower. Only very experienced technicians were able to obtain just the right temperature. Since the key to firing porcelain was high kiln temperatures, kiln making required bricks that could withstand such heat, and laying bricks for a kiln required much experience. The celebrated Jingdezhen kilns have lasted for over a century precisely thanks to this kind of accumulated technological experience.

Pottery manufacture, like the unglazed purple sand (*zisha*) tea pots of Yixing (in Jiangsu near Taihu Lake), was wholly another technology. Although it did not require such high temperatures, choosing the best clays, making beautiful shapes, and maintaining just the right heat were all elements of a highly complex industrial art. The same was true of the "pure clay" inkstones (*chengniyan*) of Henan. They were made of clay dug up from the bottom of the Yellow River, but the art of washing and preparing the clay required exquisite esthetic skill. Even the bricks used to construct imperial palaces were made from this "pure clay" from the Yellow River bottom. The pottery and porcelain industries of the Ming had indeed reached a high level of both artistry and practical use.

The common element in all of these industrial arts was a detailed division of the labor sequence. In the manufacture of porcelain, for example, the following sequence was followed: choosing the kaolin clay, kneading the clay, firing and processing the unburned earthenware, etching in the patterns or pictures, painting the pictures, adding colors, adding glaze or painting colors over the glaze, boxing and arranging in the kiln, sealing the kiln, burning off the firewood, and opening the kiln. According to the *Exploitation of the Works of Nature*, "To complete one piece of porcelain required seventy-two separate operations," and every operation was performed by a different technical expert; if one mistake was made, all the previous operations would have been in vain!

Smelting and casting metals was another important Ming industry. The city of Daye in Hubei was the most important iron-mining area, accounting for one-third of all Ming production; Foshan in Guangdong was a center for casting iron products. Yunan produced more than two-thirds of all the Ming silver and tin, and zinc was produced in Hunan. All of these mining areas were in mountainous regions of the southwest.

Ming iron smelting was done primarily in upright furnaces equipped with wooden piston bellows that greatly increased the flow of air. Large piston bellows required four men to operate and could produce three hundred millimeters of mercury pressure—the highest output of any bellows in the world at the time. Pink stones (*yingshi*, lustrous stones) were fired along with the iron ore to lower its melting point. Chinese iron smelting had generally used charcoal for coking, but during the Ming dynasty great quantities of processed coal (coke) was used. The pig iron produced in this way was not as free of impurities as that produced using processed charcoal, but somewhat greater quantities could be produced this way, because it could be fired in upright furnaces at higher temperatures. According to Fang Yizhi's Notes on the Principles of Things, Ming pig iron produced wrought iron with a rather higher carbon content, because willow sticks were used to stir the molten mixture; the willow wood was carbonized in the process, and that increased the hardness of the resulting wrought iron. Ming iron and steel technology employed the method of "pouring steel" (guangang). Pig iron and wrought iron were smelted together, or strips of wrought iron mixed with pig iron were thrown into the fire together, or molten pig iron was blended into molten wrought iron. These methods were probably easier and more productive than the Song method of mixing molten wrought iron and pig iron together in trays. Refining coke from coal was a major part of steelmaking. Ming rectangular furnaces used to make coke from coal were similar in design to the long "dragon kilns" used in firing porcelain; they also used vents to control the temperature while slowly baking coal to produce coke.

Adding tin to pure copper produces bronze; adding zinc produces brass. Brass has more uses than bronze, because it can be more easily worked into tools and implements. Chinese copper coins have been made of brass ever since the Ming. Large structures can also be made of copper. The largest such copper structures are the "Golden Pavilions" (Jindian) in Kunming (Yunan) and Wudang (Hubei). Zinc was obtained in the Ming through a process of distillation. The Exploitation of the Works of Nature records that the Ming method of distilling zinc did not use an inverted distiller but rather collected the cooled and congealed zinc in a crucible. The zinc thus obtained was 97 to 98 percent pure, and this method was both fast and convenient.

Foshan township in Guangdong was the center of iron-goods production. There were metalworking shops toiling night and day everywhere in Foshan. The various specialty workers had a detailed division of labor. Workshops that cast pots did not forge knives, and even in the pot-casting shops, the casting of pots with or without handles was done by different specialist workers. The ironworking industry was just as compartmentalized as the porcelain industry. The work was divided into many specific operations, and each step in the overall process was supervised by an individual expert craftsman. The division of labor was, in the first instance, based on technical skill, but during the Ming dynasty the craft workers had a guild system that guaranteed their monopoly of certain types of work and safeguarded their employment. This situation was not limited to the above crafts but existed throughout all the various handicraft industries—for example, the lacquer ware and furniture industries.

After China's traditional handicraft technologies underwent this guild transformation, even though the workers wanted to constantly improve their skills, it was also easy for them to refuse to accept new and improved techniques. Furthermore, because the master and his disciples complemented one another, or because fathers passed on the skills and the trade to their sons, it was difficult for a particular craft's skills and techniques to spread beyond the guild—but it was easy for them to be lost.

In general, Chinese industrial technology in the Ming dynasty was far ahead of the contemporary world. The fact that China's handicraft industries were not able to undergo the industrialization that took place in Western Europe is a topic worthy of our serious consideration. At least in terms of energy sources, even though China did sometimes use water to turn grindstones and operate stone pestles, by far the most common sources of power were always human beings and domestic animals. Coal was already widely used as a fuel during the Ming dynasty, but they never attempted to convert the energy from heat into the power of motion. It is generally believed that China's population was so large that they did not worry about having insufficient manpower and thus never tried to develop labor-saving mechanical devices. As we have seen above, however, during the development of traditional handicraft industries, the desire to produce more products with less work certainly did exist and led to the development of ingenious precision apparatuses. Thus, a large population and an abundance of labor power are not necessarily the answer to this problem. Perhaps the minute division of labor in China's traditional industries led to excessive fragmentation. Every stage in the work process was self-governing, and there was no overall production plan. Every link in the chain of production was also a small unit (a family or small workshop) that did not possess the requisite financial resources to invest in new technologies.

The Jesuits who came to Ming China brought a great deal of European industrial knowledge with them. Much of it was introduced in Johann Schreck's 1627 *Pictorial Explanations of Western Scientific Instruments* and Xu Guangqi's 1639 *Comprehensive Treatise on Agricultural Administration* mentioned above. If we examine Ming China's production industries, we will find, however, that this new knowledge from abroad did not stimulate China's relevant industries in any noticeable way. For example, European machinery was mostly made of iron, but China's was generally made of wood; European machines were equipped with drive wheels and screws, but China's machines did not have any fittings for drives and screws. Thus, it was not easy for Chinese mechanical devices to make use of energy from high temperatures or from high-speed rotational designs. From this, we can see that Xu Guangqi, Wang Zheng, and others who introduced Western industrial technology were all Confucian literati who did not normally have any contact with artisans and craft workers. For this reason, the new knowledge entering China could not be transmitted to the industrial world that was actually engaged in manufacturing. In short, traditional Chinese intellectuals were separated from the manufacturing process, and there was no mechanism for the mutual stimulation of learning and the industrial arts. Perhaps this is why, after the Ming dynasty, China was always behind Western Europe in the very important area of industrialization.

6. The Ming Market Economy

Some time ago, Chinese historians hotly debated the concept of the so-called sprouts of capitalism, and it was generally believed that the pattern of the Ming economy exhibited the characteristics of capitalism. However, if the Ming already had the germs of capitalism, why did China not develop into a full-fledged capitalist system such as flourished in Europe? This is an extremely complex issue that involves many different elements, not least of which is the precise definition of "capitalism." In this section, we will not pursue this matter but will be confined to a discussion of the Ming dynasty and particularly the economic situation from the mid-Ming on.

Chinese oceanic trade gradually flourished from the Southern Song on. During the early Ming, Zheng He's great fleets visited most of the important ports on the oceanic trade route. The goods that China imported on this trade route included medicines and spices—ambergris, frankincense, and pepper—as well as things like tortoiseshell, pearls, and jewelry. At the same time, the commodities China exported included items such as silk, porcelain, iron implements, and lacquer ware. Silk and porcelain were sold as far away as the Middle East and Europe via the Persian Gulf and the Red Sea. Iron implements were sold in various places in Southeast Asia. This was the normal trade situation in the Song and Yuan times.

As the sixteenth century began, the Pacific Ocean opened up, and the long Chinese ships sailed around the Cape of Good Hope, entered into the Atlantic Ocean sea lanes, and carried Chinese mercantile commodities and the spices of the South Sea islands straight to the European markets. Several places in Southeast Asia, like Luzon (the Philippines), Sumatra, and Malacca, were important transshipment areas. Aside from the usual South Sea products, China's chief import at this time was American silver (Mexican silver dollars). Japan's trade with the West also plied these water routes along the China coast, and Sino-Japanese trade also grew more active than it had been during Song and Yuan times. Trouble with Japanese pirates (*Wokou*, many of them Chinese) began in the early Ming and was extremely rampant in the mid-Ming. If we consider this illicit trade as an index, we can see that the scope of Sino-Japanese trade in the Ming had developed far beyond anything that could reasonably be encompassed by the old term "tribute system."

Whether legal or illegal, a flourishing foreign trade necessarily stimulated commodity production. Since silk and porcelain were China's main foreign-trade commodities, the silk and porcelain industries grew and flourished along with the trade. Jiangnan was the base of operations for the Ming textile industry, while Jiangxi, Fujian, and Guangdong were the bases for the porcelain and metallurgy industries. Thus, the southeastern region and southern China both experienced rapid growth at this time.

The handicrafts of Jiangnan were of high quality and elegant workmanship and came in a multitude of colors. These southern commodities were highly prized in China and foreign lands; the more beautiful they became, the more expensive they were. The artisans constantly improved the quality of their work, and the prices rose concomitantly, producing a cycle that led to a rapid accumulation of capital and daily growth in the scope of these Jiangnan industries.

China's traditional division of labor was one of peasant cottage industries in which "men till the farm and women weave," but in the Ming Jiangnan textile manufacturing grew into a system of industrial workshops for which the owners invested capital to purchase looms, hired workers, enforced a specialized division of labor, and produced commodities for the open market. For example, most of the urban population of Wujiang (in Suzhou), Shengze (in Jiangsu), and other such areas became involved in the silk industry. Rich men were the employers, and the workshops employed highly skilled permanent mechanics as well as short-term day laborers or pieceworkers. There were also brokers who bought and sold silk goods; even young children helped out. A story in Feng Menglong's (1574–1646) collection of short fiction, *Lasting Words to Awaken the World* (*Xingshi hengyan*, 1627) describes the rise of a family that started by raising silkworms, then bought one silk loom, and eventually ended up running a workshop with many looms and employees. This fictional account quite accurately reflects the contemporary situation. According to essays of the time, such as Zhang Han's (1510–1593) "Dream Words from Pine Window" ("*Songchuang mengyu*," with a 1593 preface), the sale of high-quality textiles could earn a 20 percent profit!

China's cotton industry had begun in Jiangnan during the Yuan dynasty. Because cotton was produced for the common people, the demand was very great, and it became a major peasant handicraft industry. The cotton was cultivated in the north, and the cotton cloth was produced in the south. According to Xu Guangqi's 1639 *Comprehensive Treatise on Agricultural Administration*, this was because the northern climate was dry and unsuited to weaving cotton cloth, but the south was warm and humid, and the cotton thread produced there did not easily break, and thus the cloth had a fine, close weave that wore very well. This was another example of regional specialization that spurred on the growth of an internal market-exchange network.

Flourishing local industries were also seen in the porcelain production at Jingdezhen in Jiangxi. According to contemporary records, there were kilns everywhere; their fires lit up the night and their smoke blotted out the sun. The kiln operators amassed great amounts of capital, employed hundreds of workers, and their shipments of materials and fuel were constantly seen on the roads. Their customers arrived from all corners of the world in ships and carts to transport and sell the porcelain goods to internal and foreign markets. The same situation prevailed in the iron industry of Foshan in Guangdong—knives, scissors, agricultural implements, and tools piled up at Foshan and were shipped out for sale to internal markets and to the various Southeast Asian countries. Almost everyone in Foshan was involved in the iron industry. Because of the far-flung nature of the iron market, blacksmith guilds were located in every major port.

Just as cotton was grown in the north and processed in the south, the raw materials for the abovementioned industries did not necessarily come from their work area. The silkworms and cocoons for Shanxi's Luzhou silk industry came from Sichuan, and the pig iron for Foshan's iron industry was shipped in from Daye in Hubei. All this activity stimulated a thriving internal trade. A great deal of labor was needed in these industrial areas, and many local peasants turned to industrial work, so much so that these areas had to import their food from outside. Jiangnan was a fabled "land of fish and rice," but at this time its rice came in from the Huguang administrative region (now Hunan and Hubei), and its wheat came from the lower reaches of the Yellow River and the Huai River area. In the same way, cotton cloth for the north was shipped up from the south. There had been famous porcelain kilns in the north in ancient times, but during the Ming, nearly all of the nation's porcelain serving dishes came from Jiangxi, Zhejiang, Guangdong, and Fujian, with Jingdezhen alone as the major supplier for the entire country.

The large scale of these industries was not only attributable to their profits from China's internal market; sizeable profits also came in from their overseas sales operations. Legal and illegal, direct and indirect ocean trade made silk and porcelain the leading products of China's foreign trade. The chief commodities that the abovementioned European and Japanese merchants purchased in Ming China were raw silk and various silk fabrics. So-called trade porcelains were exclusively produced for sale abroad. They often had Islamic or European designs, such as rosaries patterns, auspicious Arabic sayings, pictures of the Virgin Mary, or European street scenes. The porcelain shards unearthed near the Red Sea coast were left behind when Chinese porcelain was transshipped overland from this area. Ships brought up recently from the floor of the South Sea are also full of such porcelain items.

From the above, we can see from the American silver entering Ming China that this foreign trade was much more profitable than the previous spice trade and that it directly benefited the common people. During the Ming, the south and the southeast and grew rich from the development of foreign trade industries; this trade also greatly stimulated China's internal exchange of commodities, such as the shipment of food grains to the south from the north and the middle reaches of the Yangzi River.

Ming merchants and their industrial management methods had a distinctively "modern" bent. Investors could go in together and set up a structure quite similar to today's joint-stock corporations; they could hire experts and operate their businesses like contemporary corporate managers. In some enterprises—general merchandise, for example—every commodity was managed by an expert unit. Qian Yong's (1759–1844) *Random Jottings from Lü Garden* (*Lüyuan conghua*) has a section on Sun Chunyang's (fl. 1600s) Southern Goods Shop. Qian records how this Suzhou shop bought and sold a large number of commodities, including "goods from North and South," "maritime goods," "pickled and preserved [meats]," "marinades and sauces," "foods preserved in sugar or honey," and candles. There were subdivisions for each category of goods, and such specialization was the norm both between enterprises and within the same enterprise. These shops kept excellent accounts, entering their income and expenditures every day at the close of business in a manner similar to modern double-entry bookkeeping systems.

In the Ming dynasty's vibrant commerce, besides their profits from foreign trade, merchants also had other sources of venture capital to inject into their enterprises. The salt industry was a government monopoly, but it still depended on private merchants. As an obvious example, the government used special salt monopoly licenses to persuade merchants to ship food grains to the north to provision the military—this policy was called "opening the middle" (*kaizhong*). The merchants, upon receiving the licenses, however, enlisted the resettled northern colonists to work the agricultural colony lands. The merchants then took their grain harvests to provision the northern armies. In this way, the merchants both saved the expense of transporting grain from the south and enjoyed the government-granted salt monopoly. In the process of this north-south exchange, the profits gained by the salt merchants were immediately turned into venture capital to be remitted back to their firms or loaned out to other enterprises. The Shanxi and Anhui merchants were particularly expert in these transactions. Both Shanxi and Anhui had insufficient agricultural land and thus had traditions of emigrating to look for methods of survival elsewhere. Thus the Shanxi and Huizhou money-exchange businesses and pawnshops came later on to assume the functions of banks. The *Taihang Collection* (*Taihang ji*) of Wang Daokun (1525–1593) from Anhui tells a great deal about these mercantile exchanges and gives us a good picture of the contemporary network of economic activity.

These liquid assets were not only a prime source of venture capital for the internal market, but there were also merchants who invested their capital in international trade. In general, the Shanxi merchants dominated the inland trade in the north and the west and traded Chinese goods for commodities such as furs and woolens. The Anhui merchants—like the Xu brothers with their shipbuilding discussed above—used their wealth to invest in South Seas maritime trade activities.

In Song society, Confucian scholars and merchants operated in quite different realms. The former demanded of themselves that they become "sages within and kings without" and set as their goal the management of the state and improvement of the nation; Neo-Confucianists of the School of Principle did not deign to talk of profit. The atmosphere after the mid-Ming was very different, and the Jiangnan literati gentry were quite willing to invest their surplus capital in mercantile activities. If there were several brothers in a gentry family, at least one would serve in office, one would engage in trade, and the others would manage the family's agricultural lands. In this way, not only did such a family have close connections in three professions in society, but Confucian values were also extended into merchant circles.

Professor Yu Ying-shih has noted that the standards of the "entrepreneurial tradition" (*chuangye chuitong*) that Ming merchants held themselves to in their business dealings was similar to the Confucian scholars' concept of practical statecraft for the good of the nation. What Yu calls the spirit of having a "merchant's talent with a scholar's soul" (*shihun shangcai*) probably ran through all Ming merchant activities. In his discussion of the origins of capitalism in Europe, Max Weber (1864–1920) asserted that the Protestant work ethic, especially that of the Calvinist followers of John Calvin (1509–1564), was one of the motivating forces behind capitalist business activities. This motivating force resided not only in the virtues of hard work and frugality but more in the sense of vocation that these men held themselves to be bound by. As the Ming merchants' activities unfolded on a grand scale, Yu Ying-shih pointed out, their consciousness of themselves was congruent with Weber's Protestant ethic.

When historians discuss the "sprouts of capitalism," they also generally examine the phenomenon of urbanization. The nature of Ming urban development and geographical distribution is seen to be essentially a continuation of the Song and Yuan situation. The most important Ming cities still served as collection and distribution centers located on the main roads across the country; added to these were a few additional cities serving as industrial centers. Beijing became the most important political city, Hangzhou lost this status, and Nanjing served as the capital for only short period of time. The most notable aspect of Ming urbanization was that small townships were concentrated in the Jiangnan areas of Hangzhou, Jiazhou, Huzhou, and Suzhou, Songzhou, and Taizhou. This led to the linkage of the areas with the highest population density, from Lake Taihu to the Yangzi River delta, into one long strip of land where industry, commerce, and agriculture were all very highly developed. During the Ming, the waterways of this vast area were woven into a close-knit transportation network. In this area, the differences in standards of living between the city and the countryside were much less than in the rest of China.

Paper currency began to be used during the Song and Yuan period, and the Ming carried on the Yuan currency system. The Ming government controlled the province of Yunnan, with its rich silver- and copper-mining industries, however, and large quantities of American silver entered China from across the ocean. During the Ming, Chinese paper currency was then converted to a mixed-metal currency (usually called "copper cash"—coins with a hole in the middle strung together on strings) consisting of part silver and part copper, thus avoiding the tendency toward depreciation that occurs if too much paper currency is put into distribution.

China continually produced commodities to be sold abroad, and silver continually entered China. Ming China experienced a long period of trade surplus and concomitant economic growth. When the leading regions of the south reached a high enough degree of economic development, the wave of growth spilled over into nearby areas that also opened up industries they never had before. For example, originally cotton was shipped in from the north to be woven into cloth in Songjiang and then shipped north again. Some time later, Hebei and Shandong began to weave their own cotton cloth for sale in nearby markets. This kind of development is similar to the theory that "a rising tide lifts all boats" in our contemporary "third wave" of industrialization.

In sum, Ming economic development continued the process begun in the Song and Yuan eras, especially that of the Southern Song. One new element that emerged at this time was the opening of the ocean trade routes and the extension of China's foreign trade market to Europe and the Americas; this gave China a favorable balance of trade and a large influx of silver. China had entered the burgeoning world economic network. Southern China, especially Jiangnan, directly absorbed the profits from this trade surplus and rapidly grew into China's leading economic region. Regional economic disparities grew, and the south's wave of prosperity washed over nearby regions and stimulated their economic development.

However great the effect of these changes was in China's vast and complex cultural, social, and economic system, they were still not enough to disturb the stability of the system as a whole. Capitalism may have sprouted, but it could not grow into maturity.

7. Economic Differences Between Northern and Southern Society

In such a vast nation as China, all the different areas could not possibly develop at the same pace, and there were, since ancient times, regional variations in prosperity and decline. Before the North-South dynasties era, the richest and most flourishing region was the Central Plain of the Yellow River valley. In the widest sense, the Central Plain included today's so-called five northern provinces (Shanxi, Shaanxi, Shandong, Hebei, Henan); in the narrow sense, it comprised the region of the central reaches of the Yellow River, with Luoyang as its center. From the mid-Tang on, the north was racked by war and chaos and grew gradually impoverished. Wars were less frequent in the south, and the climate was mild and well suited to agriculture. Thus the south gradually surpassed the north in both population and wealth.

The economic discrepancy between north and south was quite obvious during the Ming. Economic development and urbanization in the south was discussed above; this section will explore the situation in the north.

When the Mongols ruled China, they divided it into two areas: the north, which was seized directly from the Jurchen Jin, and the south, which was originally Southern Song territory—the Mongols called the Han Chinese by the insulting term *Manzi*, or southern barbarians. The *Diary of Marco Polo* demonstrates this division by referring to the north as Khitan and the south as Manzi. During the Yuan dynasty, the former Jin territories were occupied by generals of the Mongol "Han Army" and Mongol military units called *tümen*, or "ten thousand families," but the south still followed the Southern Song administrative system of prefectures and counties. The difference between these two areas was that the southern administrative system was more stable than the northern system, and thus the south had a chance to recuperate. In the north throughout the Yuan, the common people had to bear the burden of corvée labor services.

Near the end of the Yuan, there were frequent wars in the north, and, although there were many men-at-arms fighting the Yuan and contending for the throne in the south, there were very few battles in the central regions of the south. The battles of the civil war waged by the prince of Yan (Chengzu, the future Yongle emperor) from 1399 to 1402 (when he conquered Nanjing) took place primarily in the eastern provinces, and, again, the central regions of the south were not greatly influenced by this internal strife.

During the early Ming, the north was comparatively poor; because the Yellow River regularly burst its banks, the area between the Yellow and Huai rivers was one of frequent natural disasters. The north was also rapidly depopulated because of migration southward, leading Zhu Yuanzhang to enforce a large-scale resettlement of population to the north. At first, he resettled people from Jiangnan to fill up his old home of Fengyang in Anhui. The migrating population was very great, however, and there were many such resettlements; thus the people of the Shanxi plateau ended up emigrating to the provinces of Shandong, Hebei, and Henan. This area was not only a site plagued by fierce fighting in the north but was also greatly damaged by droughts and floods. Before Pan Jishun's (1521–1595) water projects "controlled" the Yellow River, the ecological conditions of this area were quite terrible, and immigrants continually had to be brought in to maintain the population. According to legend, the people of this area say that their ancestors all came from "beneath the great scholar trees" of Hongdong County in Shanxi, Great Scholar Trees being the name of the place from which their Ming migration began.

Zhu Yuanzhang set up many border garrisons and had the military families till the soil, so the garrisons could be self-sustaining. In the early Ming, there were some three million people stationed in these border garrisons. Major garrisons were set up along the line of the Great Wall in Liaodong, Xuanfu, Datong, Yansui, Ningxia, Gansu, Ji, Taiyuan, and Guyuan, as well as the southern coast from Shandong down to Guangdong. A great number of people were stationed from east to west along the northern border. These military garrison families were no doubt immigrants collectively resettled from the south. The natural environment of the north was very harsh, and by the mid-Ming, the garrison command system had broken down, the land tilled by the military families suffered either from salinization or desertification, and the people's lives had become extremely difficult.

The Ming government's "open the middle" policy used salt monopoly licenses as compensation to encourage merchants to ship grain to fill the

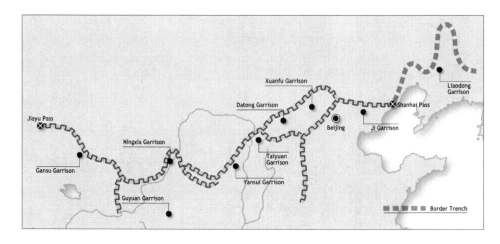

FIGURE 6.5 The Nine Garrisons of the Ming Dynasty

granaries in the important military areas of the north and around the capital. These merchants "opened the middle" by employing northern garrison families to grow and store grain for them. To shorten the transportation distance, these garrison agricultural lands were spread out all over the north, especially in Shanxi, Shaanxi, Hebei, and Liaodong. The garrison families in the various areas themselves recruited poor peasants to till the soil, and the surplus left over after the peasants handed in the grain was just enough to keep them adequately fed and clothed but not enough to amass any surplus.

From the mid-Ming on, the imperial princes were granted land, mostly in Hebei, Shandong, and Henan, sometimes as much as a thousand *qing* (16,700 acres). Near the end of the Ming, the land of one prince occupied one-tenth of all the arable land in Henan Province. The princely landholdings in Hebei and Shandong were not as great as in Henan, but the Ming "imperial manors" constituted a direct grant of agricultural land to the ruling family. Most of these imperial manors were near the capital, and thus there were many of them in the areas directly administered by Beijing, in modern Hebei Province.

Besides these imperial manors and princely lands, the Ming imperial relatives, meritorious officials, close friends of the emperors, and powerful eunuchs all had gifts of land bestowed upon them. They all lived in the capital, and their land grants were mostly close to the capital territory. Thus, these powerful families (eunuchs included) controlled most of the land in Hebei directly administered by Beijing. As a consequence, most northern peasants were long-term manorial tenants whose lives were very difficult, eking out a living with no surplus capital at their disposal. Aside from the rich consumers at the top of society, throughout the north, resources for the common people's economic development were extremely deficient.

The situation in southern China was quite different. According to the Ming "Ancestral Injunctions," land in the south directly administered by Beijing could not be bestowed as gifts to individuals. It was not the case that there were no big landlords in the south, but there were no military families, imperial manors, friends of the emperor, and so on. On that account, the percentage of land tilled by independent peasant owners (*zigengnong*) was higher than in the north.

The Ming household registry (census) system was not very accurate. Judging from the figures given in the *Veritable Records of the Ming* (*Mingdai shilu*), incorrect numbers were compiled almost everywhere. The recorded figures for the southern population were much lower than the actual population living there, and all of these unregistered people were people who escaped government taxation.

The most flourishing Ming handicraft industries—silk, porcelain, paper, and lacquer ware—were, because of environmental conditions, mostly located in the south, especially in the southeast, Fujian, and Guangdong. Cotton was grown in the north but woven into cloth in the south. The southern climate was mild, with a long period of sunshine and relatively abundant rainfall; southern agricultural production was thus higher than in the north, not to mention all of the handicraft commodities just discussed. It was therefore impossible to lessen the economic disparity between north and south. This was similar to the situation in Europe, where the economic level of agricultural and pastoral places such as Spain was much lower than that of both the Mediterranean commercial cities and the northern European industrial cities. This situation in China and Europe arose because certain handicraft industries, under the influence of a flourishing international trade, were transformed into preindustrial economic units. The areas where this occurred opened a great gap between the commercial and industrial regions and the regions of traditional agricultural and pastoral economic activity.

Throughout northern China, as noted above, the rich and well connected amassed large parcels of land, while the peasant farmers who worked these imperial manors barely made enough to eke out a living, thus creating a very uneven economic situation. The north could only supply raw materials to the south, such as raw cotton. This uneven trade of raw materials for finished products could only increase the economic discrepancy between north and south. It was only near the end of the Ming that northern merchants began to produce cotton at home, but northern cotton production could never catch up with the southern product.

The same sort of situation occurred in urbanization. In the south, especially in Jiangnan, both large and small towns were connected in a close-knit land and water transportation and communication network. The standard of living in the rural areas of Jiangnan, Fujian, Zhejiang, and Guangdong that were connected by ocean and river routes was not much lower than that in the urban areas, and news and information passed easily from the cities to the countryside. A most salient example of this was that local music and opera—*Kunqu* (*Songs of Kun*) from Mount Kun near Suzhou in Jiangsu, *Geyang* opera from Shanxi, *Nanguan* or "southern pipes" music, and Cantonese operas—were not only performed in the cities; there were also traveling troupes that performed them all over the countryside. Correspondingly, the quality and the dissemination of education in the south was much superior to the north. The south also had an obvious lead in the greater variety and vitality of popular thought.

The northern part of the area between the Yellow and the Huai rivers, where north and south came together, had very a poor natural environment because of the frequent flooding of these two rivers. Only in the cities and towns connected by the Grand Canal were there many merchants who made good profits. One stretch of land to the west on the middle reaches of the Han River near Nanyang and Xiangfan (a city in Hubei) was a transitional area between north and south. This region was not directly affected by Yellow and Huai river flooding, and it received adequate irrigation from the Han River. The western edge of this region—Mount Ba (eastern Sichuan) and the Qingling Mountains (in Shaanxi), a natural barrier between the Central Plain and the valley of the Han River—had high mountains and deep valleys. There, in the "Old Forest" between Sichuan and Hubei, now known as Shen Nong's Terrace forest district, the terrain is almost impenetrable and transportation quite inconvenient. The most impoverished northern inhabitants of the lower reaches of the Yellow River and the loess plateau of Shaanxi (the upper and middle reaches of China's Yellow River and China proper) often employed Nanyang, Xiangfan, and places further west of them as areas of sanctuary and escape from the law. They could usually survive there, but if things grew worse, they could retreat even deeper into the "Old Forest" on the Sichuan-Hubei border or the mountainous regions of western Hunan, where the long arm of the government could not reach them. Going even further down from Henan and Hubei, they could enter the mountainous regions of Hunan and Jiangxi. In short, when the destitute peasants of North China reached the end of their rope and risked breaking the law to survive, they could use the mountains of Huguang Province (now Hubei and Hunan) as a convenient hideout. Going west into northern Hubei or eastern Sichuan or south into the mountains of Hunan and Jiangxi, they could also take shelter in the rugged terrain and scrape out a living beyond the reach of the main transportation thoroughfares.

Their were many such émigré peoples scrabbling for a living in the above areas—including lineage groups and minority peoples of the Three Kingdoms era, popular generals who led migrant groups during the North-South dynasties period, and the Hakka and other such people after the Song dynasty.

There were many peasant uprisings from the very beginning of the Ming dynasty. The White Lotus Rebellion was an apocalyptic religious movement that stirred up the most impoverished peoples of the Shandong and Hebei region and Chuan-Chu, that is, the border areas of Sichuan, Shaanxi, Henan, and Hubei—precisely the remote outlaw hideout discussed above.

The large-scale armed rebellions of impoverished peasants led by the "Yellow Tiger" Zhang Xianzhong (1606–1647) and the "Roaming King" Li Zicheng (1606–1644) at the end of the Ming were labeled "roving bandit" (*liukou*) rebellions because of their extremely fast mobility, suddenly appearing in the east and just as suddenly in the west. Examining the area of their activities, we see that in expansion they roamed through all five northern provinces, and in straightened circumstances they retreated to the "Old Forest" and slipped into the mountainous regions of Chuan-Chu. These vast peasant rebellions were not really organized by any religious faction but were purely desperate revolts by poverty-stricken peasants. Having at first the abovementioned northern hideout as their base of sanctuary from the law, they developed mobile peasant guerilla warfare involving great armies. This prairie fire grew into a great conflagration that finally consumed the Ming imperial regime.

The economic discrepancy between north and south lasted from the Ming right through the Qing dynasty. Although the Qing capital was established in the north, at Beijing, and the government did its best to ship food grains via the Grand Canal to the capital area, the Qing could not narrow the economic gap between north and south. China's political power was often in the north, but its cultural and economic center remained in the south. It would be no exaggeration to say that the north and the south had very different overall styles of living.

Although there were many peasant uprisings at the end of the Ming, their activities were mainly confined to the north; if they invaded the southern border areas, they soon retreated north or simply dispersed and were never able to penetrate the southern heartland. When the Manchus came in through the northern Shanhai Pass, they encountered virtually no opposition, but in the south, the Han Chinese resistance was extensive and long lasting. The Ming loyalists fought fiercely in the mountains and on the high seas for an entire decade. From this we can also see the great difference in ethos between north and south.

8. The Transformation of Ming Thought

The Ming founder, Zhu Yuanzhang (Hongwu), and Chengzu (Yongle) used honors and ranks to attract the literati to join the government bureaucracy. Zhu Yuanzhang employed the literati to establish a civil bureaucratic system much larger than that of the Yuan dynasty—from the center to the periphery, every level of administration was under literati control. Both Hongwu and Yongle were ambitious and suspicious rulers who did not encourage the development of thought and knowledge. Ming officials were treated like servants by the emperors, who could appoint and dismiss them at will, and if they displeased an emperor they could be bastinadoed publicly at court. Even though there were officials who functioned as chief ministers, they were hardly treated with polite respect by the emperors; later on, when the eunuchs usurped power, the civil officials were even more badly harassed and humiliated by these imperial family slaves. Even though they were the ruling gentry in their local regions, the literati never had an opportunity to express and carry out their ambitions at court.

Not long after the establishment of the dynasty, the Ming rulers ceased to emphasize discussions of current affairs in the imperial examinations. Instead, they ordered the examinees to hold forth on Confucian thought using the so-called eight-legged essay (*bagu wen*) format. The essays written by imperial decree in Xiao Shizhong's *Great Compendium of the Four Books* (*Sishu daquan*), *Great Compendium of the Five Classics* (*Wujing daquan*), and the *Great Compendium of Neo-Confucianism* (*Xingli daquan*), commissioned by Yongle in 1414, all regarded the School of Principle of Zhu Xi and the Cheng brothers (Cheng Yi and Cheng Hao) as orthodox thought. On this account, the great scholar Gu Yanwu (Gu Tinglin, 1613–1682) lamented that "the eight-legged essay flourished and the ancient wisdom was discarded; the compendiums were published and the study of the classics perished." The imperial examination system began to stifle Chinese thought during the Ming dynasty, but its custom was so ingrained that it remained inescapable during the Qing: thus the eight-legged essay shackled Chinese culture for over a century.

In a bureaucratic system dominated by such a narrow orthodoxy, there were very few independent scholars. High officials of the early Ming, such as Xia Yuanji (1366–1430), Yang Pu, Yang Shiqi, and Yang Rong, were extremely cautious men of unexceptional speech and action. Although the early Ming Xie Jin (1369–1415) and the mid-Ming Yu Qian (1366–1430) were given the opportunity to employ their talents, they were still not allowed to die natural deaths. It is, then, no surprise that in the late Ming we see only clever and manipulative ministers and no great statesmen. Even someone such as Zhang Juzheng carried out his reforms as a political manipulator, but after his death his corpse was barely cold before he and his sons faced impeachment charges.

Wang Yangming's School of Mind was, of course, a challenge to the orthodox School of Principle. Confucian thought had been influenced by Buddhism and Daoism ever since the Tang and Song dynasties, and the Chan Buddhist concept of individual autonomy was certainly a stimulus to the School of Mind. Wang Yangming was quite successful as a general and as the governor of Jiangxi, but he developed his new ideas while in exile and no doubt in reaction to the prevailing orthodoxy. His School of Mind together with the already widespread Chan Buddhism was a great shock to contemporary intellectuals.

The Song philosopher Lu Xiangshan's ideas provided the origins of Wang's philosophy, but during his time Lu's philosophy was no match for that of Zhu Xi and the Cheng brothers. How, then, during the Ming dynasty, did Wang Yangming's School of Mind gradually come to rival and even surpass the School of Principle? One reason was that there were bound to be some reactions to such a repressive orthodoxy. During the Song dynasty, Zhu Xi's ideas flourished among the civilian population, but Ming officialdom employed them to establish the authority of the regime. Although the power and influence of this orthodox thought was accepted and defended by the majority of the literati (or gentry) class, it also provoked resistance in some quarters.

The historically interesting aspects of Ming thought, especially social thought, lie not in the orthodoxy but in the trend toward alternative thinking. By the sixteenth century, the search for individual subjectivity had enormous vitality in scholarly and cultural circles.

Wang Yangming's school of learning (or Yangming studies, Yangming xue; ōyōmei-gaku in Japanese) was itself a vast theoretical system that had a profound influence on Chinese thought over the past four centuries. It even traveled east across the sea to become one of the most important elements of Japanese culture. The Yangming school is one of the mainstream schools of Chinese thought, and many discussions of philosophy and thought make reference to it. Since this book is concerned with popular social thought, I want to briefly discuss the faction of Yangming thought known as the Taizhou School, founded by Wang Gen (Xinzhai, 1483–1541). Taizhou is near Yangzhou, north of the Yangzi River, in Jiangsu Province.

Many of the disciples of the Taizhou School, from Wang Gen on down, came from the ranks of the common people, and they also taught among the general public. The Taizhou School scholars did not aim at the imperial court but rather at influencing the common people and improving moral customs. These men were high-spirited, vigorous, and independent in thought and action. In his *Records of Ming Scholars* (*Ming ru xue an*), Huang Zongxi (1610–1695) has the following to say of them: "After the Taizhou School, their followers could fight dragons and snakes with their bare hands. Passed on to the School of Yan Shannong [1504–1596] and He Xinyin [1517–1579], Confucian orthodoxy [*mingjiao*] could not restrain them." Indeed, in the Ming intellectual world, which abounded with hypocrites and conformists, the sometimes impetuous and sometimes overcautious men of the Taizhou School were certainly capable of making the deaf hear and awakening the world! Their influence extended beyond the scholarly world and led to a change in the atmosphere of Ming cultural circles.

Wang Gen was born into the family of a salt drier who worked in the Ming salt fields. His family was quite poor, and he went into his father's trade while reading the Confucian *Analects* on his own and taking every opportunity to ask others about the meaning of the classics. When he later became a follower of Wang Yangming, Wang Gen had already formulated his own system of thought. He accepted the idea of innate knowledge (*liangzhi*) and believed that when the heart-mind inclined toward something, that was desire, and when something appeared to the mind, it was unreal. Having no inclinations and no false appearances, one reached the unbounded everlasting (*wuji*); at that point, if one reached the Great Ultimate (*Taiji*) and emptied one's mind of all phenomena, innate knowledge would naturally flood in upon one. This mode of thinking is virtually identical to that of Chan Buddhism.

Wang Gen also advocated moral self-cultivation (*xiushen*), that is, making one's self secure (*anshen*). If one could practice moral cultivation and make one's self secure (*an*), then one's mind and body would both be secure. One first preserves (*bao*) one's own self, and then the whole world (all under heaven) can be at peace (*an*). At the same time, Wang believed that one's self and the Way (Dao) were one substance (*ti*)—"everything is learning and everything is the Way" (*ji shi shi xue, ji shi shi Dao*). This Way is the Way of concrete things. If one's self (body) is not preserved and secure, how can one expand the great Way? If the Way and the self are both respected, then one can almost expand the Way.

Wang Gen believed that the Way was realized in the ordinary daily life of the common people. The happiness sought by Confucianism is the happiness that comes from practicing what one has learned. That includes understanding and experiencing, through the unity of body and mind, the exuberant life of the universe in which "the kites fly and the fish jump." Thus, Wang's self-cultivation and nurturing of the Way consisted in immersing one's subjective mind, unsullied by the filth of the world, into the human world while simultaneously uniting with the universe in order to attain a realm of great joy.

The later Taizhou School generally developed in the direction of the purely natural (*ziran*). Luo Rufang (1515–1588) believed that the child's innate (good) knowledge (*chizi liangxin*) was immediately available and that the physical heart and body could directly comprehend metaphysical nature (*xingti*). Geng Dingxiang (1524–1596) asserted that hidden within the obvious phenomena of the common people's daily activities was the

Way of Heaven (*tiandao*) that Zhang Zai spoke of when he said that "the people are my brothers, and I share the life of all creation [*minbao wuyu*]." Thus, Geng believed that the heart-mind, human nature, and heaven are one and that from introspection it is possible to understand the ultimate truth (*zhenji*) of the cosmos. These two men represented the mainstream of the Taizhou School. Wang Dong (1502–1581), however, advocated self-prudence or self-care of the mind (*shendu*) to make clear distinctions between good and bad volitional ideas (*yinian*), thus emphasizing self-restraint. His thought was close to that of Liu Zongzhou (1578–1645) of the Eastern Zhe (Zhejiang) School and to Zhu Xi's School of Principle.

The most radical members of the Taizhou School were He Xinyin and Li Zhi (1527–1602). He Xinyin advocated securing the body to establish one's basic nature (*anshen liben*); that is, beginning from man's original nature (*benxing*), he recognized that all human beings desire sounds, colors, smells, tastes, and ease and comfort. To deal with these desires, we should follow to the utmost our inborn nature, the nature (*xing*) be-stowed on us by heaven; we do not need to eliminate all human desires but rather to practice moderation. Believing that to "regulate all under heaven" (peace on earth, we might say) is a desire common to all man-kind, He Xinyin also advocated an idealistic social movement. He set up an assembly hall and donated money to establish an autonomous clan community. He hoped to bring all the traditional social classes—literati, peasants, artisans, and merchants—into one communal association (*hui*) with a system of rules for periodic meetings and a rotating leadership. The head of the association would be called teacher (*shi*) or ruler (*jun*), but the ruler and the common people would be equal; they would all belong to the same family or household (*jia*). Thus the ruler and the officials (the leader and the common people) would teach one another and be friends; then society would reach the utopian state of "all under heaven returning to benevolence [*tianxia gui ren*]." He Xinyin's egalitarian and autono-mous ideal society could naturally not be tolerated by the Ming imperial regime, and in the end he was smothered to death in prison, thus paying the ultimate price for his independent thought.

Li Zhi (styled Zhuowu, 1527–1602), originally surnamed Lin, was born into a Moslem family. His thinking was even more radical than that of He Xinyin. He developed the Taizhou idea of following one's original nature into his own theory of the "childlike heart" (*tongxin*). He taught that the childlike heart "rejects the false and preserves the true." The "truth" of

Li Zhi's childlike heart was meant to stand in stark contrast to the "false-ness hypocrisy" of his contemporary Confucian orthodoxy and the Neo-Confucian School of Principle. Confucianism (see *Analects* 9.4) already had four things one should be free of (*siwu*): arbitrary opinions (*wuyi*), dogmatism (*wubi*), obstinacy (*wugu*), and egotism (*wuwo*). Li Zhi believed that a person could only retrieve his natural and original childlike heart by getting rid of arbitrary opinions (*yi*) and dogmatic certainties (*bi*) while at the same time breaking away from the Taizhou School's excessive ob-stinacy (*gu*) and egotism (*wo*). From the "truth" of one's original childlike heart one could obtain a state of original truth (*benzhen*) free from the pollution of worldly reputation or emolument. Li Zhi's childlike heart was actually a vision of romantic longing. How to successfully combine the idea of moral self-cultivation with the concept of retrieving one's childlike heart remained one of the most difficult problems for the School of Mind.

Li Zhi extended the meaning of his concept of the childlike heart by asserting that customs regarding food and clothing were ethical common-places that anyone could know from birth. Therefore, the Way was not far from man, and man was not far from the Way—indeed, man was the center of everything. People cannot live without desires, and everything should follow its natural course; there should be no ceremonial rites, laws, punishments, or ethical norms to restrain the rights and privileges that are an individual's natural birthright. Today, we might think of Li Zhi's ideas as a sort of universal human rights theory that challenged traditional mo-rality, but at the time his views were regarded as a shocking and offensive affront to generally accepted ethical norms. He suffered the same social rejection as He Xinyin, cutting his own throat and dying in prison!

The intellectual origins of these men who broke through the tradition to open up new forms of thought were not at all Confucian. Wang Yang-ming's School of Mind was in the first place considerably influenced by Daoism and Chan Buddhism, and many members of the Taizhou School were similarly inclined. Geng Dingxiang blended Confucian and Bud-dhist thought to construct his own system. He used Buddhist learning as a metaphor for Confucian ideas, asserting that the cosmos is simply "my heart-mind" (*wu xin*) and that the *Great Learning*'s phrase "to dwell in the highest good" simply represents Confucius's idea of the everlasting Pure Land. He borrowed the *Heart Sutra*'s assertion that the five components of intelligent being (*wu yun*) are empty (*kong*) and the phrase "before the feelings of pleasure, anger, sorrow, and joy are aroused, it is called equilibrium" (*zhong*, centrality, mean) from the *Doctrine of the Mean* (*Zhongyong*; see Wing-tsit Chan's *Source Book*, 98) in order to expound the idea that when the heart-mind is selfless, then the benevolence (*ren*) of human nature will begin to flow without cease.

Geng Dingxiang merely used Buddhist terms as metaphors to interpret Confucian concepts, but Jiao Hong (1541–1620) went even further in the direction of combining the three schools of Confucianism, Buddhism, and Daoism. He believed that the concepts and topics each school discussed in their different ways represented similar concerns that were thus not in conflict but mutually quite compatible.

Li Zhi's family had believed in Islam for many generations, but after he encountered Wang Yangming's thinking, he came to greatly admire Wang Ji (Longxi, 1498–1583) and began gradually to examine Buddhist theories and accept their ideas—he mixed the Three Teachings without constraint. The attitude of Li Zhi, Luo Rufang, and others like them was extremely broadminded and did not insist on Confucianism as the orthodox system of thought. By the late Ming, when Fang Yizhi (1611–1671) brought the Three Teachings together, the intellectual nourishment of their transcendent views did not come from the *Analects* and *Mencius* but rather from the *Book of Changes, Zhuangzi*, and Tiantai and Hua Yan Buddhism. By that time, the Jesuits had brought Western scientific knowledge to China, and Fang Yizhi was quite well versed in astronomy and calendar making. Although he did not care much for Western religion or philosophy, he was very favorably impressed with the Jesuits' empirical (practical measurement) methods of research. We can fairly say that Fang Yizhi's scholarship had broken through the constraints of traditional Confucian learning.

After the mid-Ming, with this search for individual subjectivity combined with southern China's economic prosperity, the literati no longer focused exclusively on scholarship and academic activities. On this account, the literature, drama, and art of the second half of the dynasty saw the rise of a romantic ethos.

The literature of the first half of the Ming was dominated by the official or "cabinet" prose style (*taigeti*) and is not worth mentioning. Even though writers such as Li Mengyang (1472–1530) and Wang Shizhen (1528–1590) tried to break away from this moribund literary style, ironically under the banner of neoclassicism, they were not sufficiently creative. When the three Yuan brothers—Yuan Zongdao (Boxiu, 1560–1600), Yuan Hongdao (Zhonglang, 1568–1610), and Yuan Zhongdao (Xiaoxiu,

1570–1630)—established the Gongan Literary School (from Gongan in Hunan), Ming literature finally began to rid itself of the defect of excessive imitation. They wrote informal prose essays (*xiaopinwen*) full of clarity and genuine expression of feelings; they also collected popular songs and sayings and contributed to a literary renewal.

Of even greater interest are the Ming works of both long and short vernacular fiction. Shi Nai-an's (ca. 1296–1372) *Water Margin (Shuihu zhuan)* and Luo Guanzhong's (ca. 1330?–1400?) *Romance of the Three Kingdoms (Sanguo yanyi)* both appeared in the early Ming, and both developed out of the Yuan and Song vernacular *huaben* short stories. Wu Cheng-en's (1500–1582) *Journey to the West (Xiyouji)* and *Gold, Vase, and Plum (Jin Ping Mei,* multivolume translation by David Roy under the title of *The Plum in the Golden Vase)* together with *Water Margin* and *Romance of the Three Kingdoms* were linked together as the four great masterpieces of the Ming dynasty. *Journey to the West* and *Gold, Vase, and Plum* are both romantic novels of contemporary social criticism and are written in a style fundamentally different from earlier narratives. *Journey to the West* brilliantly satirizes the hypocritical thought and actions of contemporary secular and religious life in a playful and richly imaginative style. Its multifaceted thought relies on various levels of metaphor and allusion taken from the Confucian, Daoist, and Buddhist traditions. *Gold, Vase, and Plum* was already popular before the end of the Wanli era in 1620, but the work is still a matter of scholarly debate. Using highly colloquial, sometimes quite vulgar language, this book describes contemporary sexual relations and scathingly satirizes the corruption prevalent in both official and gentry life—as such, it is a most rebellious work of fiction.

Feng Menglong's (1574–1646) *Three Words (San yan)* collection—*Illustrious Words to Instruct the World (Yushi mingyan,* 1620), *Comprehensive Words to Admonish the World (Jingshi tongyan,* 1624), and *Lasting Words to Awaken the World (Xingshi hengyan)*—as well as Ling Mengchu's (1580–1644) *Two Striking the Table (Erpo)* collections—*Striking the Table in Amazement at the Wonders (Po'an jingqi,* 1628) and *Second Collection of Striking the Table in Amazement at the Wonders* (1632)—were both extremely popular collections of vernacular short stories. Feng was a friend of Li Zhi and also opposed to Cheng-Zhu Neo-Confucianism; Ling was, by contrast, a defender of the Way. Nevertheless, they both wrote in vernacular Chinese, opening up a long tradition of vernacular literature (*baihuawen*). Carrying on the *huaben* tradition, the material for their stories was taken directly from the daily lives of the common people and reflected the thoughts and actions of popular society.

In drama or opera, ever since the rise of Yuan drama (called *Yuanqu*, Yuan songs), China's stage art was quite mature. During the Ming, southern drama (*nanqu*, southern songs) gradually flourished. Most of the repertoire consisted of plays based on popular romances (*chuanqi*, romance, coming to be the general term for southern drama during the Ming), and every area had its local opera. In the mid-Ming, after Kunqu opera was reformed by Wei Liangfu (fl. sixteenth century) and other Jiangnan writers by the addition of song techniques from both north and south as well as popular Jiangnan folksongs, it rapidly assumed the status of China's mainstream opera.

Jiangnan was very prosperous, and with the enthusiastic encouragement of refined literati and scholars, Kunqu was not only performed on the public stage but also on the home stages of elite families. Many writers then tried their hand at writing operas. Of them, Tang Xianzu (1550–1617) was the most accomplished. Tang was by nature upright and outspoken, and, not surprisingly, had a checkered official career, having been several times dismissed from his post. Late in life he gave up the idea of serving in office and devoted himself to writing plays (that is, operas). His *Four Dream Plays of Linchuan (Linchuan si meng)* were extremely popular and have come down to us as dramatic classics. Tang was influenced by the Taizhou School, was antitraditional, and had a romantic spirit that especially emphasized *qing*, love or feelings. Tang's *Nanke [Southern Branch] Dream (Nanke ji)* and *Handan Dream (Handan ji)*, both derived from Tang *chuanqi* short stories, deal with the transience of life and evince a Buddho-Daoist indifference to fame and fortune. His *Purple Jade Hairpins (Zichai ji)* is based on the Tang *chuanqi* "Story of Huo Xiaoyu" (*Huo Xiaoyu zhuan*). Taking the woman's point of view, it expresses the inequality of love relationships between men and women. Finally, Tang's *Peony Pavilion (Mudanting)* is generally regarded as the greatest masterpiece of Kunqu opera. Not only does it praise romantic love and directly challenge Neo-Confucian norms, but, more importantly, Tang allows the heroine, the maid Du Liniang, to die for love and to be reborn, because the power of love is greater than that of death.

Kunqu opera was able to flourish in this its golden age both because of the cultural ethos of the times and because it could rely on the great wealth available in contemporary Jiangnan.

There were similar advances in painting after the mid-Ming. Early Ming painting was dominated by the academic style (from Hanlin Academy)—meticulously detailed and finely finished works that lacked originality. After the mid-Ming, the four masters of the Wu School (of Jiangsu)—Shen Zhou (1427–1509), Wen Zhengming (1470–1559), Tang Yin (Bohu, 1470–1523), and Qiu Ying (1494?–1552)—appeared and became dominant for some time with their "literati painting" (*wenrenhua*) style. Tang Yin's style was casual, free and easy, and independent; he strove to express his individual temperament and subjective artistic conception, which deeply resonated with Wang Yangming's teachings. A little later, Xu Wei (Wenchang, 1521–1599) employed gracefully floating brush techniques to pour out his inner feelings without seeking exact resemblances to nature. His work was even more in keeping with the antitraditionalism of the Taizhou School as he sought to find the perfect representation of his own autonomous spirit. Chen Hongshou (Laolian, 1598–1652) strove to paint a realm beyond appearances similar to the Daoist idea of obtaining the meaning and forgetting the words or the Chan Buddhist admonition not to be trapped in the net of words. His style evinces quite a bit of the spirit of modern abstract art.

The art of landscape gardening flourished in Ming-dynasty Jiangnan, and the gardens of Suzhou are still one of China's most important cultural inheritances. In a limited space, these private gardens, perhaps better called garden parks, create a complete world, one not of real mountains and rivers but of exquisitely designed natural scenery. Lake Taihu's artificial mountains of piled stones, neither beautiful nor ugly in their own right, allow free range for the viewer's own esthetic appreciation. This also demonstrates the landscape artists' respect for the subjectivity and individuality of those who view their work.

The cultural atmosphere of the late Ming was, of course, not confined to one pattern. Although everyone was not part of the antitraditional, individualistic, freedom-seeking trend discussed above, such ideas did permeate late Ming thought, literature, and art. They represented resistance to the various pressures of traditional authority and Confucian ethical norms as well as continued reflection during that process of resistance. When the wild and daring forged ahead, the timid and cautious were restricted in their activities. At its height, this atmosphere led to the emergence in 1604 of the Donglin Academy (*donglin* for eastern grove, a willow grove in Wuxi) founded by Gu Xiancheng (1550–1612), Gao Panlong (1562–1626), and others who espoused the Neo-Confucian morality of Zhu Xi. Putting their lives at risk through their words and deeds in a manner that contemporary hypocrites could not possibly match, they fought against official treachery with righteous indignation.

During the Ming-Qing transition, as the nation collapsed into chaos and war, besides grieving for this loss, Gu Yanwu (1613–1682) and Huang Zongxi (1610–1695) undertook a profound self-critical examination of Chinese culture, including especially the system of government and mode of thinking. In their spirit of rejecting the old and moribund and establishing the new, they both continued and criticized the cultural ethos from the Jiajing through the Wanli eras (from 1522 to 1620). Their style of thinking can certainly be characterized as an enlightened spirit of China's near ancient history. If it had not been for the harsh suppression of the Manchu Qing authorities, which brought this period of reflective cultural examination and attempts at innovation to an abrupt end, the development of later Chinese culture might not have involved another three centuries of rigidity.

9. The Ming Dynasty and Hapsburg Spain

In this section, we compare Ming China and Spain under the Hapsburg monarchy for two reasons—first, the two spanned a similar age in history, and second, the economy of both countries was influenced by a large influx of silver from the Americas. The development of the two nations' political systems was, however, completely different.

The Ming dynasty endured for almost three centuries, from 1368 to 1644, and Hapsburg rule in Spain lasted over two hundred years, from 1467 to 1700. During the sixteenth and seventeenth centuries especially, the two nations experienced very great economic transformations, and they were very active on the international stage.

Zhu Yuanzhang established the Ming imperial regime after the foreign conquest of the Mongol Yuan and thus returned the Chinese empire to ethnic Han Chinese rule. The emperor's authority and the Confucian-trained bureaucracy had long since become entrenched in Chinese culture. The Yuan regime was established by Mongols, however, and its basic character was really not the same as that of a traditional Chinese dynasty. Even though Khubilai Qaghan and his sons accepted many elements of traditional Chinese dynastic rule, the Mongol Yuan was still essentially a conquest dynasty. Zhu Yuanzhang's Ming dynasty restored China's unified imperial government; it controlled most of the territory governed by Chinese dynasties prior to the Yuan; in ethnic composition, the Han Chinese were again the leading element; and, finally, its culture was an integrated system combining Confucianism, Daoism, and Buddhism.

To put it simply, after a long period of change and integration, Chinese culture and society had reached a high degree of internal consistency. In this integrated structure, the imperial dictatorship (autocracy) controlled all political power, and Confucianism was the main form of Chinese thought. From the mid-Ming on, the economy of the south flourished greatly, and both the north-south population distribution and allocation of wealth became skewed in favor of the south. Both the rise of Wang Yangming's School of Mind and the trend toward individual subjectivity in the culture of the south challenged the abovementioned cultural consistency and even broke through China's overall holistic synthesis. Although these developments weakened the constitution of the Ming dynasty, they did not lead to the establishment of a pluralistic political and cultural structure. Poverty in the north gave rise to large-scale peasant uprisings, "roving bandits" marauding through more than ten provinces and finally toppling the Ming dynasty. The devastation of these rebel bands reached only to Jiangnan and Hunan and did not penetrate the rich heartland of the south. Thus, when the cavalry of the Manchu's eight banners poured through the Shanhai pass into North China, they encountered almost no resistance, but the southern resistance to Manchu rule lasted for a decade. The Chinese empire was, however, an integrated body, and when the northern regime collapsed, it was as though the linchpin of a chariot had broken in two—the southern resistance was doomed to failure!

Spanish history was completely different from China's Ming dynasty. The rise of Spain involved a tangled web of complicated marriage alliances and inheritances that united many areas into one territory under one monarch. Philip II (b. 1527, r. 1556–1598) came to the throne during a flourishing period of Spain's Golden Age (*el siglo de oro*). At that time, the Spanish crown controlled European Spain, Portugal, the central portion of the Italian peninsula, and the Lowlands in Europe (Holland and Belgium), along with colonies such as the Philippines (named after King Philip) and various possessions in the Americas. Austria and the Holy Roman Empire in Central Europe were also under the control of

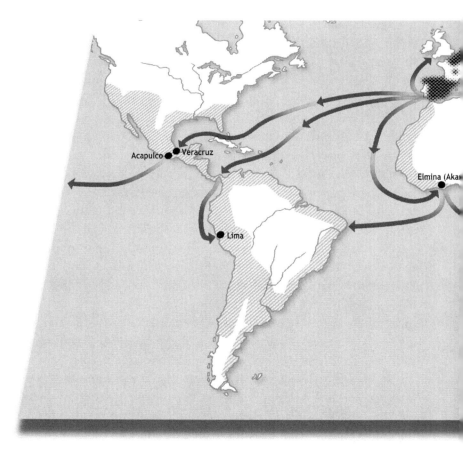

FIGURE 6.6 The Spanish Empire of Phillip II and the Ocean Trade Routes

the same Hapsburg family. The ruling family of England had made a marriage alliance with the Spanish crown: Mary Tudor, later Mary I—"Bloody Mary"—accepted the hand of Philip II and was styled Queen of Spain. France and Spain had a common border, and the two nations fought many fierce wars. The Habsburg dynasty came to an end with the War of the Spanish Succession, in which the Bourbon dynasty of Louis XIV's France took over Spanish rule.

The three great powers England, France, and Austria had changeable relations with Spain—sometimes they were relatives by marriage, sometimes they were sworn enemies. The large territory controlled by Spain had many different ethnic groups with different languages, religions, and economic conditions. The feudal aristocrats also maintained their power

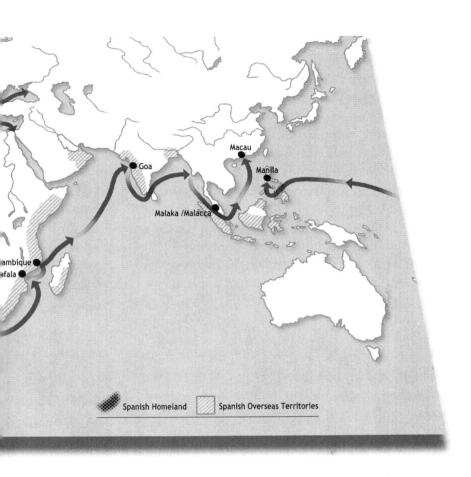

Spanish Homeland | Spanish Overseas Territories

bases in the various regions of Spain and elsewhere. The Spanish empire was indeed a pluralistic and hybrid system, and the crown never truly commanded authority over all of its parts, nor did it ever really come together as a unified whole.

Spain's wars were unceasing. At the beginning, the Spanish expended a great deal of effort to expel Islam from the Iberian peninsula (the Reconquest took some eight hundred years), but to the end of the Hapsburg monarchy the Moors (Moslems) who converted to Christianity remained a disgruntled minority that could not be assimilated into Spanish society. There were also many Protestants, like the Calvinists of Central Europe, among the northern subjects of the empire. Spain's Catholic monarchs dedicated themselves to the preservation of the orthodox faith, and so they established the Spanish Inquisition (an ecclesiastical tribunal) in 1487 and did everything possible to wipe out the new Protestant Christianity. Local aristocratic rulers exercised their own powers, however, and did not always obey the commands of the royal house.

To this internal squabbling was also added a powerful external threat—Spain still had to deal with competition from the forces of Islam. The Ottoman Empire under Suleyman I (1494–1566) commanded a great fleet of ships in the Mediterranean Ocean, and the European powers were no match for them. It was not until the great maritime Battle of Lepanto (1571), fought to the south of Greece, when the Spanish fleet and its allies smashed the Ottoman navy, that the Christian nations no longer had to worry about Ottoman might in the Mediterranean. The Spanish "Invincible Armada" was itself defeated in 1588 by the English at the Battle of Gravelines, after which much of it was lost, and it was never as strong again.

By the end of the seventeenth century, the two-hundred-year hegemony of Spain was coming to an end. The great wealth that Spain took out of the Americas supported its hegemony but did not bring economic prosperity to the nation.

The gold and silver of the Americas flowed out of that New World into Spain and China. China's vigorous international trade strengthened the coastal economy such that the silk and porcelain industries prospered, and the benefits of this prosperity extended to the lives of the common people. The Yuan and Ming dynasties both used paper currency, but after the large influx of American silver, silver replaced paper as the medium for large denominations. With a dual monetary system in which silver and copper cash circulated freely, the Ming and Qing economies had an abundant source of specie for development. China's foreign trade market and monetary system both expanded and stimulated southern China's economy, leading to three hundred years of economic prosperity.

The Ming dynasty's financial administration does not seem to have profited from this South China economic boom. Three things account for this anomalous situation: first, a great deal of money was expended on warfare; second, official corruption was customary and endemic; and third, the main sources of government tax revenues remained land and corvée taxes, and the government never established a rational system of commercial and industrial taxation. The third of these causes was related to the structure of the Ming financial administration and was probably the key problem.

The situation in Spain was again different from that in China. Spain and Portugal, with both Mediterranean and Atlantic coastlines, were pioneers in the opening of oceanic trade and the first to profit from it. Gold and silver from the New World, plus the profits from Far Eastern trade, supported Spanish hegemony, but this great wealth did not transform the structure of economic production in Spain. Pastoralism remained the chief source of income for regional aristocrats. They did not even promote agriculture, much less think of promoting industrial production. The large quantities of gold and silver that Spain took in were either expended to support the luxurious lifestyle of the royal house and the aristocracy or passed on into the coffers of the commercial cities of Central Europe and the Mediterranean. These cities only produced consumer goods, and the wealth they took in from the emperor and the nobles was immediately reinvested in production. As the industrial and commercial economy of Europe grew in accordance with the policies of mercantilism, the benefits did not go to Spain but to the commercial cities and harbors scattered about the Habsburg domains. As Spain's power waned, Holland, Portugal, and England each created an "East India Company" as a tool to promote the expansion of both their economic markets and their colonial projects. The prosperity of their commercial port cities was closely related to this colonial and economic activity.

The Spanish and the Portuguese opened up many new sea lanes, and their navigation stimulated the shipbuilding industry and its related enterprises; at the same time, practical mathematics and astronomy, both necessary for navigation, also made great progress. In scholarship, however, the Jesuits were most important. The Spanish monarchs were the greatest supporters of the Roman Catholic conservative factions. At that time, the struggle between the Jesuits and the Dominican Order was raging, and the Dominican missionaries in China took every opportunity to attack the Jesuits. In these disputes, the Spanish rulers consistently supported the conservative Dominicans against the more liberal Jesuits. In the history of Sino-Western cultural exchange, missionaries of the Society of Jesus performed a great service to both sides—introducing Western scholarship to China and Chinese learning and industrial techniques to Europe. In spite of this, Chinese cultural influences flourished in France rather than in Spain. The chief reason for this was the anti-intellectualism of Spain's conservative Catholics.

During the late Ming, China experienced a movement in favor of individualism in both thought and culture. This thought tide started in the southeast, but, given the restrictive conditions of Chinese history, it did not give rise to a European-style Enlightenment movement nor any sort of political liberalism. Contemporary Spain was also facing a burgeoning ethnic nationalism and civil consciousness (*shimin yishi*). The former developed into a motive force for the establishment of ethnic or national sovereignty of nations, and the latter gave rise to ideas of democracy and human rights. The Spanish ruling elite was completely oblivious to the growing strength of these two trends, but Protestant activities and contemporary industrial and commercial cities sent out their clarion call.

This phenomenon was somewhat similar to the Chinese situation. The Ming imperial regime employed eunuchs as tax supervisors, and the way they fleeced the people triggered popular revolts. These mass movements were actually something new. The contemporaneous large-scale community organizations of the Jiangnan intellectuals in the Donglin group (branded a party or faction, *dang*, by their opponents) and the Restoration Society (*Fushe*) were also new phenomena that deserve our attention. The orthodox and conservative elements among the Ming ruling stratum and intellectuals were unaware of the forces they might give rise to. When the Manchus entered China and established the Qing dynasty, the late Ming "new tide" was unable to develop any further, and Chinese history stalled. By contrast, the European "new tide" grew into a torrent that raged on as the Enlightenment and the Democratic Revolution. The Spanish empire fell behind these great changes and was pushed to the margins of European history by the Western and Central European powers.

Spain once commanded great riches of gold and silver, but today only the golden splendor of its imperial palaces remains to remind us of its time of awe-inspiring brilliance. The Spanish baroque style of art and architecture was rich and beautiful, though it was also mired in a mannerism of ornate minor details that was similar to the style aspired to during the Qianlong era (1736–1795) of the Qing dynasty—far inferior to the beautiful simplicity of Ming furniture or the pure elegance of Ming blue-and-white porcelain.

There were some outstanding accomplishments in fiction, prose, and drama during the late Ming, all of which participated in the movement in favor of individualism and offered critical reflections on tradition and authority. At about the same time in Spain, Miguel de Cervantes (1547–1616) published his masterpiece *Don Quixote de la Mancha* (in two volumes, 1605–1615). This long, humorous, picaresque novel (regarded as the first modern European novel) cast a panoramic glance at an age that had just passed or was quickly fading—it is both a lament and a satire for that age, very much in the *Shijing* style known as "elegant lament." The literary immortal Cervantes fought in the Battle of Lepanto, where he was shot three times and lost his left arm. Having such a great man to chronicle Spain's grandeur and decline makes the reader sigh at the changes in history.

10. Taiwan Enters Chinese History

In the records of Chinese history, the island of Taiwan is not mentioned for a very long time. It was once believed that Chinese power entered Taiwan during the Three Kingdoms and Sui eras. But during the ocean voyages of those times, did Chinese fleets actually land in Taiwan? Or did they land somewhere among the Ryūkyū Islands (including Okinawa)? There is still no way to confirm either view. Although Taiwan is close to Fujian and Zhejiang, there are no mainland historical records of it. This is probably attributable mainly to the fact that the Taiwan Strait is narrow and its deep waters flow southward very rapidly. Most premodern sailing vessels could not easily navigate against the prevailing currents but only go along with them or drift off course. Putting to sea from Fujian, they would be carried south and most likely land in the modern Philippines or hug the sides of the Malay archipelago through the South China Sea to reach various areas in Southeast Asia. Vessels setting out north from Zhejiang and Fujian could follow the East China Sea and sail diagonally across to Japan and the Korean peninsula. This sea route was interrupted by many islands with many different cross currents. Though their room for maneuver was winding and complex, the currents were not too strong, and the ships would not drift off course; in fact, a skilled navigator could take advantage of these variable currents to make easy progress. For all these reasons, whether they embarked from Fujian or Zhejiang going north or south, Chinese vessels had no reason to pass near Taiwan. Taiwan entered "World History," then, after the European countries started to ply the ocean trade routes and "discovered" the Americas. Once the Pacific

Ocean on Taiwan's northeastern side was opened up as a common passage for high-masted sailing vessels, Taiwan became the key to unlocking the North and South China seas.

Which ethnic groups constitute Taiwan's aboriginal or indigenous peoples is a question the anthropologists have not answered for certain. If we consider the distinctive features of Taiwan's Neolithic culture from three to four thousand years ago, then it would seem to be fairly well connected to the Fujian culture of the same period. The Penghu archipelago lies in the Taiwan Strait, and stones from its quarries are abundantly found in stone articles from Taiwan's Neolithic age. Jade articles from Taiwan's ancient east-coast culture are carved in a manner similar to those from the Liangzhu Neolithic culture of Zhejiang (c. 3400–2250 B.C.E.). According to the speculations of historical linguists, the original language of the Austronesian language group can be traced back to Taiwan. Two thousand years ago, during the First Emperor of Qin and the Martial Emperor of Han's time, the so-called Bai Yue (hundred Yue people, a generic term for southern ethnic groups) often ran away to escape the repression of the Qin and Han dynasties. Those Bai Yue who stayed put mixed with the ethnic Hans as they migrated south and developed into the southern Chinese, who spoke various different dialects. The Bai Yue, who were moved to the Han-occupied Huai and Han river basins, were absorbed into the other northern peoples. Those Bai Yue who live in today's Hunan, Jiangxi, and Anhui provinces were also finally absorbed into the Chinese population during the Three Kingdoms and Southern Dynasties period. Were the ancestors of Austronesian peoples in Taiwan actually the remnants of the Bai Yue? And did they follow this island chain and migrate throughout these southern islands? These are questions for archaeologists and historical linguists to investigate.

Taiwan and mainland China may have had some interactions in historical times prior to the Ming dynasty. Song copper coins and porcelain shards are often found in archaeological sites in Taiwan. Song China was the center of an East Asian economic sphere, and Song coins were a freely exchanged international currency found everywhere from the northern steppes east to Japan and south to Southeast Asia. The inhabitants of contemporary Taiwan may well have had trade relations with Penghu or Fujian, but we do not know what commodities were exchanged or what the scale of this trade might have been.

European sea power entered East Asia during the second half of the Ming. The profits from maritime trade were very great, and not only the Portuguese and the Spanish merchants prospered from it; the *daimyo* leaders of various Kyushu provinces (Han) also shared in the bounty. China's wealthy Anhui merchants, such as Wang Zhi and Xu Hai (?–1556), also engaged in this sea trade. Thus there were many maritime merchant organizations going up and down China's eastern coast exporting silks and porcelains and importing spices, medicines, gold, and silver — vast amounts of American silver especially poured in. The Ming court's foreign-trade policies were sometime lax and sometimes strict; sometimes they closed the sea coast, and sometimes they lifted these restrictions. When coastal trade was forbidden, these maritime merchant groups became pirate smugglers whose numbers included many Chinese adventurers. They organized those of the coastal inhabitants who were anxious to make a profit and, with large ships in the deep water and small boats in the coastal shallows, looted coastal villages and intercepted and plundered merchant cargo ships. Some of these armed groups that raided up and down the Chinese coast during the Jiajing reign (1522–1567), men such as Chen Lao, Lin Daogan, and Lin Feng, used Penghu and the bays and harbors of southern Taiwan (from Jiayi to Gaoxiong) as their bases of operation.

In the sixteenth century, Taiwan still belonged to its aboriginal peoples. Their settlements were scattered around the plains and hills on the western coast. Later on, the Han Chinese called them Pepo or Pingpu, "plains (lowland) tribes." They had no unified, "national" political structure. They engaged in intergroup warfare; we do not know much about them, but these wars are mentioned in their oral folklore. Taiwan produced enough food to maintain many aboriginal peoples, but they did not make any commodities to sell to outsiders, and thus the island remained outside of the international trade network. After the oceanic trade routes opened up, Chinese and Japanese maritime traders began to land in Taiwan to pick up and transport the island's rattan, deerskins, sulfur, and camphor to sell on the mainland and in Japan. Fujian fishing boats and armed maritime groups that often moored in Taiwan's harbors gradually started to establish more than seasonal lodgings. Some of them even imported tools and animals from the mainland, cleared farmland, and settled down permanently. Men like Lin Daogan and Lin Feng, mentioned above, probably took up their permanent residence in just this manner, not just temporarily resting their boats but establishing permanent bases where they could be safe and have an abundance of life resources. A story about Lin Daogan's sister burying gold and silver still persists to this day in Gaoxiong.

In the second half of the sixteenth century, Holland gained its independence from the Spanish empire and very rapidly entered the ranks of the great sea powers operating in the Far East. With the support of its government, the Dutch East India Company's commercial operations soon outstripped those of Spain and Portugal. At this time, Taiwan was dragged into the ongoing international competition. Spain already held the Philippines as its colony, with Manila as its base of operations; from there they transported goods across the sea and over land at the narrow isthmus of Central America. Portugal had Macau as its base for sea transport east of India. It was quite convenient for Spain and Portugal to obtain Chinese and Japanese goods from their bases at Manila and Macau. The Dutch had a colony at Batavia (now Jakarta) in Indonesia, but it was inconveniently far from East Asia. They wanted a base on the coast of China, and they attempted to take Penghu twice (1604 and 1622) but were rebuffed by its Chinese defenders. In 1623, the Chinese maritime merchant Li Dan, who was quite knowledgeable about Taiwan, guided the Dutch to Dayuan (Tayouan, modern Anping) where they built Fort Zeelandia and began their colonial rule in Taiwan. Their plan was to remain in Taiwan indefinitely. The sandy Tayouan Bay was unsuitable for mooring large ships or even a great number of smaller vessels, so Batavia remained the Dutch East India Company's headquarters.

In southern Taiwan, the Dutch first subdued the local people by force of arms and then organized and controlled them through missionary activity. The aboriginal villages were given autonomy but were required to obey the commands of the Dutch East India Company. The Dutch settlers gradually moved north, and the local people were coerced into accepting their rule. The Dutch did not have very many officers in Taiwan, and in everything they obeyed the commands of the governor-general of the Dutch East India Company at Batavia. They controlled southern Taiwan for forty years, until they were expelled by Koxinga in 1662.

The Dutch primarily used Taiwan as a base for contact with the Chinese coast, transshipping goods and attacking Spain and Portugal's forces. Aside from that, they do not seem to have had any plans for occupying the entire island. In 1628, the Spanish occupied the area around Tamsui (Danshui, the Freshwater River) in northern Taiwan and established a trading post. The Dutch sent a military force to attack them but were unable to expel them. In 1638, the Dutch again attacked the Spanish base at Jilong (Keelung), and this time the Spanish abandoned Taiwan; the Dutch still did not, however, succeed in establishing a colonial regime in the northern part of the island.

In seventeenth-century East Asia, Manila, Macau, Hirado, Nagasaki, and Tayouan were all centers of maritime activity. At that time, larger numbers of mainland Chinese from Fujian and Guangdong emigrated to Manila and Tayouan; there were more than ten thousand overseas Chinese in each city, and they were by no means all members of maritime trading groups. Most of them were artisans, merchants, fishermen, and peasants whose activities supported the maritime trade. The main activities of the Chinese engaged in international maritime trade were procuring, shipping, and selling silk and other commodities produced in China as well as shipping and selling goods brought by foreign fleets to supply the overseas Chinese. In short, they operated in a manner similar to what would be called compradors (agents for foreigners) in the nineteenth century. Since these maritime activities were carried out in a legal gray area, these Chinese compradors lived on the margin between legitimate and illicit business.

Zheng Zhilong and his son Zheng Chenggong (later to be known as Koxinga) were both involved in this late Ming seafaring activity. The abovementioned Li Dan, who guided the Dutch into Tayouan, was the most important person involved in this business. He had enterprises in Manila, Hirado, Amoy, and Tayouan, and Zheng Zhilong was his subordinate. When the Dutch occupied southern Taiwan, Zheng Zhilong became their interpreter and moved first from Hirado to Penghu and then to Tayouan. Soon after that, he resigned his post as interpreter went into the maritime trade business on his own. When Li Dan died in Hirado, Zheng Zhilong succeeded him as head of his many enterprises. In 1626, Zheng Zhilong's armed forces attacked Quimoy (Kinmen), Amoy, Dongshan, and other areas in Fujian. The Ming forces could not eliminate Zheng's power, not even in alliance with Dutch military forces. Thus, the Ming court offered Zheng Zhilong an amnesty and tacit recognition of his strength on the coast of Guangdong. With Anping in Fujian as their home base, the Zheng forces controlled the seas off of an area stretching from Quimoy to Amoy. Their fleets ranged up and down these coastal waters, and no merchants could operate there without flying the Zheng colors.

In Hirado, Zheng Zhilong was very familiar with the Japanese overlords. He married a Japanese woman surnamed Tagawa, and she gave birth to Zheng Chenggong in 1624. The Ming court having issued a prohibition on entering or leaving by sea, Zheng Zhilong ran a large-scale smuggling operation, primarily supplying the Dutch East India Company with raw silk. He also destroyed the fleet of his main competitor, Liu Xianglao (?–1635), monopolized the trade between Fujian and Taiwan, and entered the Taiwan-to-Japan trade by shipping deerskins and silk. Zheng Zhilong moved with his family to Tayouan, where they had close relations with the many overseas Chinese living there. The Zheng family's special relationship with and influence on Taiwan laid the foundation for Koxinga's establishment of his regime in Taiwan.

During this period, as the Ming dynasty was coming to an end, the Zheng family fleets, along with those of Spain, Holland, and Japan, operated freely up and down the Chinese coast, sometimes as friends and sometimes as enemies, and all the while the Zheng family's strength increased. In 1644, Li Zicheng conquered Beijing, the Chongzhen emperor hanged himself, and the Prince Fu was declared emperor in the secondary capital of Nanjing. The following year, Manchu forces moved south to attack the Southern Ming loyalists. The Minister of War, Shi Kefa (1601?–1645) died in the battle to defend Yangzhou. With the southern capital taken by the Manchus, Zhang Huangyan (1620–1664) and others in Jiangxi and Zhejiang gave Prince Lu the title Protector of the State (*jianguo*). Zheng Zhilong was in Fujian and supported Prince Tang's regime, thus changing from being an armed smuggler on the high seas to the main support for the remnants of the Ming court. When the Manchus attacked Fujian, however, Zheng Zhilong surrendered to them and was sent back to Beijing, where he was given many rewards but ultimately executed.

Prince Tang had a high regard for Zheng Chenggong and made him *Guoxingye* (Lord with the Imperial Surname, hence Koxinga). After Zheng Zhilong was taken to Beijing, Koxinga continued to fight for the Ming against the Manchus, using the Quimoy-Amoy area as his base of operations. After Prince Tang died, Prince Lu put himself under Koxinga's protection. From its small corner of China, Koxinga's regime perpetuated the Ming reign and attempted mightily to restore it to power. In 1658, he dispatched an army to attack the Manchus at Nanjing, but, because of strategic errors, the battle was a disaster, and his forces retreated back to Fujian. This series of events finally led to Koxinga's occupation of Taiwan and the establishment of the Ming-Zheng regime.

Around this same time, Holland won out over Spain in their long competition and became an important Pacific Ocean power. The center of Dutch activity in the Far East was still Batavia in Indonesia, but Tayouan had already become an important base for them on the East Asian trade routes. They had defense troops stationed and many ships moored there, and Chinese maritime coastal goods poured in to Taiwan. Although they employed missionary cultural work to appease the indigenous population, the Dutch regime also used ruthless military force to pacify any resistant native groups. In 1636, they made a punitive expedition against the southern Taiwan Xiaolong people and Lamey (Lamay) Island (Xiao Liuqiu) off the southern coast of Taiwan. In what is known as the Lamey Massacre, the Dutch slaughtered the island's population in exactly the same way that in 1621 they had massacred over ten thousand Bandanese people on the Banda Islands near Java. The Dutch tried to establish their own style of governance on Taiwan by selecting indigenous people who went along with them and organizing them into assemblies, but they did not respect the tribal tradition that prescribed that only the elders were to be looked up to as leaders.

There were already many mainland Chinese immigrants on Taiwan when the Dutch arrived. The Dutch discriminated against them as either representing the Ming court or the Zheng family; they did not trust them—but they did tax them heavily. The Dutch ships often plundered the villages of coastal Fujian. In 1622, they raided Zhangzhou Prefecture and took all of the oxen, pigs, chickens, and ducks of Amoy's Gulangyu Island back to Taiwan for their own use. In similar fashion, the Spanish twice massacred the overseas Chinese of Manila, killing over twenty thousand the first time and over ten thousand the second. Because of these incidents, the Chinese held a bad opinion of both the Dutch and the Spanish.

After Koxinga's defeat at Nanjing and retreat back to Quimoy and Amoy, He Bin, the former Dutch interpreter in Tayouan, took the Dutch leaders to negotiate with Koxinga for an end to his blockade of Taiwan. In 1660, He Bin again visited Amoy and presented his plan for Koxinga to navigate into Tayouan's Lu-ermen harbor. Koxinga laid siege to the Dutch

Fort Zeelandia for several months in 1661 to 1662 and forced the Dutch to surrender and leave Taiwan.

In 1662, Koxinga, as prince of Yanping, established a kingdom (given many different names by later historians) that putatively extended the Ming dynasty until 1683. In the Battle of Penghu that year, a fleet commanded by the Qing admiral Shi Lang (1621–1696) defeated the Zheng forces, and Koxinga's fourteen-year-old grandson, Zheng Keshuang (1669–1707), surrendered Taiwan to the Qing, thus bringing this twenty-two year kingdom to an end.

When the Zheng family came to Taiwan, they brought no fewer than a hundred thousand people with them. Adding in the people who came to Taiwan from the coastal regions of Fujian and Zhejiang during the course of more than two decades and the mainland Chinese already on the island, there were about two hundred thousand Han Chinese living in Taiwan by the late seventeenth century. Most of them were concentrated in southern Taiwan, from Jiayi south to the Gaoxiong and Pingdong regions. Northern Taiwan was still mainly occupied by the aboriginal tribes; the Han Chinese did not begin their gradual move north until after the Qing dynasty took control of the island.

Koxinga set up a Ming-style administration on Taiwan consisting of one prefecture and two counties. The people who followed Koxinga were originally military fighting groups, and when they arrived in Taiwan many of them set up garrisons on the basis of their original military organizations. The names of these groups still remain to this day as place names in the Gaoxiong and Tainan regions—Zuoying, Xinying, Qianzhen, Houzhen, Qianjing (or Qianjin), Yuanjiao (or Yuanchao), and so on were all garrisons where soldiers were stationed. Most of these early garrisons were in southern Taiwan, but some soldiers were garrisoned in central and northern Taiwan, where they opened up agricultural land and established village settlements, thus becoming pioneers in the Han Chinese opening up of northern Taiwan. The Zheng family's relationship with these settlements went from one of military organization to the establishment of a colonial *fengjian*-type system.

The core of the Zheng regime was ostensibly patterned on the Ming's six ministries system and civil bureaucracy, but it was not a truly civil bureaucratic system. In the first place, there were very few civil officials among Koxinga's subordinates. Even if those maritime adventurers were given the titles of a civilian bureaucracy, the Koxinga regime remained a military one led by a courageous leader and his many soldiers and sailors well versed in waging war. His one regular staff officer, General Chen Yonghua (1634–1680) from Fujian, and Prince Lu's followers from Zhejiang who threw in their lot with Koxinga were few in number and could not change the essentially military nature of the Zheng regime.

Koxinga, and later his eldest son, Zheng Jing (ca. 1643–ca. 1682), made great profits in the international trade along China's southeastern coast. After Koxinga moved to Taiwan and in order to provide for themselves, besides clearing farmland in southern Taiwan, setting up irrigation projects, and planting rice and hemp, the Zheng regime also planted tea and sugarcane and refined camphor and sugar. International trade remained the mainstay of their economy. Early on, the Zheng family had set up five commercial enterprises—dubbed metal, wood, water, fire, and earth (*jin, mu, shui, huo, tu*)—for the acquisition of silk goods. Meanwhile in Amoy, they set up five ocean fleets—dubbed benevolence, duty, rites, wisdom, and trust (*ren, yi, li, zhi, xin*)—to transport large quantities of these and other goods and sell them on the foreign market at very great profit. In 1663, when the Qing armies attacked Amoy, the Zheng family and a good part of their forces withdrew to Taiwan. The Qing prohibited going to sea and removed the coastal villages inland in an attempt to cut off the lifeblood of the Zheng regime. Under this strict embargo, however, the profits from smuggling were even greater. Not only did the Zheng regime not suffer from the maritime prohibition, but they were able to monopolize the trading opportunities; the European and Japanese maritime traders actually came to rely on them for products.

That the Zhengs could survive in the coastal regions of Quemoy, Penghu, and Amoy for several decades was primarily attributable to these rich sources of revenue from international trade. During their heyday, the Zhengs and the fleets commanded by their various "admirals" plied the seas at will between Japan, Indonesia, Luzon, Malacca, and so on. When the Zheng regime collapsed, some of their fleets surrendered to the Qing, but many of them were taken over by various Kyushu *daimyos*, greatly augmenting Japan's international trading power.

Koxinga was originally a Confucian scholar, but when he threw himself into the Ming loyalist resistance against the Manchus, he burned his Confucian robe and donned military garb; he ruled Taiwan in military fashion with little time for teaching. When Zheng Jing took the throne, he employed Chen Yonghua as his advisor, paid a great deal of attention to culture and education, and established many schools to educate the common people. Chinese religious beliefs, whether Buddhist or Daoist, also became widespread throughout Taiwan, and from then on Taiwan entered the Chinese cultural orbit. Another significant element of the Zheng regime's rule was that the Taiwanese aborigines began to intermix with the Han Chinese. Even if conflicts were unavoidable during this process, at least there were no class distinctions between the native people and the colonists. This was something unknown in the European colonial project.

Zheng Zhilong rose to prominence through an enterprise on the margins of the law, and his son Koxinga fought loyally for the Ming against the Qing and opened Taiwan up to the mainland Chinese. While the Zheng regime lasted, it brought Taiwan, a region that had never before belonged to China, into the Chinese cultural orbit. This last chapter of Ming history is, thus, worthy of discussion from the point of view both of Chinese history and world history, because it highlights the entrance of the former into the narrative of the latter. From this time on, the development of Chinese and world history could never again be detached from each other.

Suggestions for Further Reading

Brockey, Liam Matthew. *Journey to the East: The Jesuit Mission to China, 1579–1724.* Cambridge, Mass.: Belknap Press, 2007.

Brook, Timothy. *Praying for Power: Buddhism and the Formation of Gentry Society in Late Ming China.* Cambridge, Mass.: Harvard University Asia Center, 1994.

——. *Vermeer's Hat: The Seventeenth Century and the Dawn of the Global World.* Toronto: Viking Canada, 2008.

Chan, Wing-tsit. *A Source Book in Chinese Philosophy.* Princeton, N.J.: Princeton University Press, 1963.

Clunas, Craig. *Superfluous Things: Material Culture and Social Status in Early Modern China.* Urbana: University of Illinois Press, 1991.

Crossley, Pamela Kyle. *The Wobbling Pivot, China Since 1800: An Interpretive History.* New York: Wiley-Blackwell, 2010.

Crossley, Pamela Kyle, Helen F. Siu, and Donald S. Sutton, eds. *Empire at the Margins: Culture, Ethnicity, and Frontier in Early Modern China.* Berkeley: University of California Press, 2006.

De Bary, Wm. Theodore, ed. *Self and Society in Ming Thought.* New York: Columbia University Press, 1970.

Dreyer, Edward. *Early Ming China: A Political History, 1355–1435*. Stanford, Calif.: Stanford University Press, 1982.

——. *Zheng He: China and the Oceans in the Early Ming Dynasty, 1405–1433*. London: Pearson Longman, 2007.

Elliott, Mark C. *The Manchu Way: The Eight Banners and Ethnic Identity in Late Imperial China*. Stanford, Calif.: Stanford University Press, 2001.

Hsia, C. T. *The Classic Chinese Novel: A Critical Introduction*. New York: Columbia University Press, 1967.

Huang, Ray. *1597, A Year of No Significance*. New Haven, Conn.: Yale University Press, 1981.

Ko, Dorothy. *Teachers of the Inner Chambers: Women and Culture in Seventeenth-Century China*. Stanford, Calif.: Stanford University Press, 1994.

Mote, Frederick W., and Denis C. Twitchett, eds. *The Cambridge History of China*, vol. 7: *The Ming Dynasty*, part 1. Cambridge: Cambridge University Press, 1988.

Schneewind, Sarah. *A Tale of Two Melons: Emperor and Subject in Ming China*. Indianapolis, Ind.: Hackett, 2006.

Tsai, Shih-shan Henry. *Perpetual Happiness: The Emperor Yongle*. Seattle: University of Washington Press, 2001.

Twitchett, Denis C., and Frederick W. Mote, eds. *The Cambridge History of China*, vol. 8: *The Ming Dynasty*, part 2: 1368–1644. Cambridge: Cambridge University Press, 1998.

Von Glahn, Richard. *Fountains of Fortune: Money and Monetary Policy in China, 1000–1700*. Berkeley: University of California Press, 1996.

7

China Enters the World System, Part 2

THE SEVENTEENTH TO NINETEENTH CENTURIES

Compared to the rapid development of the West during this period, China's entry into the world system was slow and gradual, because its comprehensive cultural system, which had developed over the previous two millennia, had become fixed and rigid. As a result, the new ways of thinking that had entered China from the outside world were unable to flourish. These were the final centuries in which traditional Chinese culture and government could continue to function.

1. Characteristics of the Manchu Qing Dynasty

Over the course of China's history, many governments and dynasties have risen and then been toppled. Most of these dynastic changes have been the result of a strong local power entering China and establishing its rule, some lasting and some brief. Among these invading powers were several from the northern steppes. Long before the period covered in this chapter, leaders from the Huns (Xiongnu) and the Jie ethnic group established two of the sixteen kingdoms that controlled various areas of China during the Six Dynasties period (317–589 C.E.). Subsequently, the Mongols divided their conquered lands into khanates under members of the ruling family, as they swept over the Eurasian continent. The Yuan dynasty (1279–1368) was one of these states. Mongol rule, however, was brief, since it did not establish an effective system of governance. In contrast, the peoples who later swept down from the forests, grasslands, and rivers of the northeast did succeed in setting up a lasting dynasty in China, the Qing (1644–1911).

Much earlier, the Northern Wei dynasty of the northern Xianbei (Särbi) people, as well as the Northern Zhou and the Northern Qi, which evolved from the Wei, ruled northern China for several hundred years. Subsequently, the Liao dynasty of the Khitan ethnic group dominated northern China, coexisting over a long period with the Song dynasty in the North China Plain. Subsequently, the Jurchen-controlled Jin dynasty continued the Liao line of control, until fully half of China was under northern domination. This succession of northern conquerors, from Xianbei to Khitan to Jurchen, was in effect the vanguard of the Manchu Qing dynasty. But the special skill of the Qing dynasty's rulers was their ability to establish effective structures for organization and management, which enabled them to set up the longest-lasting dynasty in Chinese history.

The peoples of these northeastern cultures, who were united by their Tungusic languages, combined agriculture, nomadic herding, and hunting and fishing in their way of life. This was in contrast to the earlier invaders from the northern steppes, who relied primarily on nomadic herding. Thus the northeastern peoples were already much closer in their culture and economy to the Han peoples of the North China Plain. Before the Manchus set up the Qing government, they had already established a settled way of life in villages, built up a fairly high level of trade with the Han Chinese to the south, and, most importantly, acquired a healthy respect for Han Chinese culture. As a result, they were much better able than the Mongols to adapt to Chinese ways of life.

But the Qing method for controlling China was hardly a new development in Chinese history. As early as the period of conflict following the Eastern Han, when northern ethnic groups took over most of China, they too generally employed a dual system of administration. When the five non-Chinese peoples (*wuhu*) established states in China, each of these states was ruled jointly by a Han Chinese emperor and a *shanyu*, a Xiongnu title for a ruler from the northern ethnic group. These governments were generally able to control the northern armed forces through their military organization and control the Han Chinese through the local levels of government. The Han Chinese governments of that period were able to maintain their civil structure through coalitions with the areas controlled by the powerful local clans and to protect themselves militarily with their frontier forts.

To strengthen the civil structure of the Northern Wei, Emperor Xiaowen (Tuoba Hong, 467–499) moved the capital from Pingcheng to the safer location of Luoyang and replaced the system of local administration with a more centralized rule over his territory. The Tuoba (Tabgatch) military chieftain Erzhu Rong (493–530) then used guards from the six military districts on the northern frontier to seize control of Emperor Xiaowen's new government. These northern guardsmen, however, resented being sidelined under a centralized government structure and rebelled. The subsequent Northern Zhou set up a garrison militia system (*fubing*) whose members were rewarded with tracts of land to farm during peacetime. This created a dual governmental structure, with frontier garrisons that were independent of the local administration, which gradually fostered a division between civil and military functions rather than between Han Chinese and the northern non-Chinese.

The two following dynasties of Liao and Jin both established their structures of power according to a division between southerners and northerners, so that there were two governmental units, one to administer the north and one to administer the south. Individual areas also had military administrations for garrisons, such as the Jurchen Jin military structure of companies (*mouke*) made up of one hundred households and battalions (*meng-an*) made up of one thousand households. These were outside the jurisdiction of the Han Chinese local administration.

The dual administrative structure, or diarchy, set up by the Manchu Qing dynasty lasted until the fall of that dynasty in 1911. The bannermen of the eight Qing Banners (*qi*) and the Han Chinese Banners, whether in bureaucratic office or posted to a frontier garrison, continued as members of their banner groups and were permanently attached to their original jurisdiction. They were bound to service for their whole lives and unable to change their local administrator or their relationship with him. The Manchu bannermen dominated most of the administrative units in charge of Han Chinese affairs, assuming the bureaucratic responsibilities of these offices; the bannermen's admission and retirement, advancement and demotion were all determined according to standards different from those of the Han Chinese officeholders.

The Qing empire's system of government also had dual tracks for entering office. When the administrators of the six ministries (*liubu*) and the nine chief ministers (*jiuqing*) took office, the Manchu and the Han would handle administrative duties together. Each province was under a local high-ranking official, and from the beginning to the middle years of the Qing, this officer was typically a Manchu. The Han officials could take office as commanders of border provinces, though there were fewer of these officers. Compared to the Han administrators, the generals assigned to garrison duty and guarding the borders had a broader range of potential responsibilities. They were not only responsible for commanding maneuvers to secure the outpost camps, but at times they would concurrently be in charge of levying duties at places of entry into China and along the major routes of communication. This level of responsibility was beyond that permitted to the Han Chinese, since bannermen in the Han military units were unable to rise to ranks as high as general.

Traditional customs of the Qing-dynasty Manchu local areas could be seen even in the power structure for the emperor himself. During the early years of the reign of Nurhaci (Nurhachi, 1558–1626), who initiated the overthrow of the Ming dynasty, the leaders of all eight banner divisions would deliberate governmental policy together in council. This collective form of leadership is expressed in the group of buildings known as the Pavilions of the Ten Princes, constructed for the leaders of the eight bannermen and the two assistant kings, which is preserved in the Manchu imperial palace of Shenyang (Mukden), in northern Liaoning Province. Huang Taiji (1592–1643, r. 1626–1643), the son and successor to Nurhaci, began the gradual consolidation of power, even to the point of concentrating it in himself as emperor, but despite this long-term tendency toward centralization, there was always an administrative staff at the center of power. These included cabinet members from the early Council of Ministers (a military emergency office) after the Yongzheng emperor (r. 1722–1735), and there were princes who served in supporting positions, even to the point of acting as regent before the accession of a young emperor. In addition, there was the princes' level of hierarchy in the administration, which was above that of the highest officers. This kind of local nobility participated in both the civil and the military aspects of governance from the inception of the Qing to its fall. However, during the latter part of the Taiping Rebellion in the mid-nineteenth century, with the political situation changed greatly, Han Chinese ministers, such as Zeng Guofan, Li Hongzhang, and Zhang Zhidong, began to be appointed as grand councilor in the interior and provincial governor on the frontiers. In response to this situation, as the Qing empire began to decline, noble families from Manchuria grouped together in clan associations to regain power as best they could.

In addition to governmental organizations, the basic territorial structure of the empire itself expressed this duality of Manchu and Han roles. The Qing divided the traditional area of China proper into a system of provinces, prefectures, and counties (*sheng, fu, zhou,* and *xian*), while the areas to the north of this, which were the homeland of the Manchu and referred to as "The Homeland of the Rising Dragon," were administered by chiefs of the Eight Banners. The areas outside the traditional boundaries of China fell under members of the imperial family, while peripheral areas became the manors of bannermen, who appointed people to manage these estates. Beginning with people sent there because they were dissatisfied with Qing rule, the Han Chinese in these areas were composed of exiled criminals instead of the normal population that might have migrated there. Not until the end of the Qing dynasty did this population change, when large numbers of Han Chinese from Shandong Province secretly crossed the borders and emigrated there without official permission. The generals and city administrators, both in the areas outside of China proper and the manor areas, were directly responsible to the Manchu nobles, following the old system that emphasized cities and towns. These outer areas were in effect sealed-off Chinese states.

Looking at another aspect of this situation, from the time the Qing dynasty's Manchu imperial house established its reign, it maintained direct communications with the Mongolian and Tibetan areas. At the beginning of the Qing, both the Han Chinese who had been accepted as residents of the outer areas and the Han Chinese who had been reduced to the status of bondservants of Manchu bannermen were organized into Han military forces. During the second phase of Qing expansion, southern Mongolia was gradually brought under their control. During the reign of the Manchu leader Huang Taiji, just before the Qing gained control of China, the areas of Ar Horqin, Harqin, Aohan, Naiman, and Khalkha formed a union and twice defeated the Mongol forces of Ligdan Qaghan (Chinese Lindan, 1588–1634), a descendent of Chinggis Qaghan from Chahar. After being badly defeated, Ligdan Qaghan then fled west to Qinghai

(Kokonor), and the southern area of Mongolia fell into the hands of the Manchu Qing. From this point on, the Manchus controlled the eastern part of what is now called Inner Mongolia, and they used the Mongols' military strength and their superior horses to harass the northern frontier of the late Ming dynasty, encircling the northern and eastern regions. The pressure of Huang Taiji's military victory over the Ming dynasty led to a reorganization of the Mongol lands to the south of the Gobi Desert, and apart from the forces under the generals Gelaqin and Tumote, able-bodied men from all of the Mongol areas were incorporated into the troops of the Eight Banners. The Mongols acknowledged Huang Taiji as their qaghan, thus combining the Mongols and the Manchus into what was effectively a single people. After the Qing dynasty was established, the Manchu imperial family and the noble families of Inner Mongolia continually intermarried. Many of the Manchu Qing empresses and the consorts of princes were from Mongol noble families, and the Qing princesses and female members of the imperial family were married off to scions of Mongol aristocratic families. This form of marital diplomacy was originally the mainstay of alliances on the steppes, and the marriage ties that developed over a hundred years greatly strengthened the hold of the Manchu Qing emperors over the Mongol areas.

The Qing influence over the land of the Mongols gradually extended north of the Gobi Desert to the Khalkha Mongols, who comprise most of the peoples in the current state of Mongolia. From the fall of the Manchu Yuan dynasty to the Ming, this area had seen unification under leaders such as Esen Qaghan, Alta Qaghan, and Dayan Qaghan, though it eventually split into three constantly warring regions: Inner Mongolia, to the south of the Gobi Desert; the area to the north of the Gobi Desert, occupied by the Khalkhas and previously referred to as Outer Mongolia; and the western regions, occupied by the Eleut Mongols. Following the establishment of the Manchu Qing dynasty, the Khalkha Mongols served that dynasty faithfully and paid tribute regularly. But the situation remained unstable, however, and during the reign of Emperor Kangxi (r. 1661–1722), the Eleut Mongol tribe of Zunghars from the west continually raided the Khalkhas, pushing their tribes into the areas south of the Gobi Desert. After the Qing court was established, it began to develop alliances with the Mongol tribes and changed their original tribal structure by dividing them according to the Eight Banners into a military hierarchy modeled on that of the Manchus.

The nomadic herders of the western Mongol Eleut tribes were not only the last to submit to Qing rule, but they also rebelled many times afterward, forcing the Qing Manchus to expend a great deal of energy in subduing them. The Heshuot tribe of Eleut Mongols, who originally lived in the area of modern Xingjian, moved south into Qinghai and Tibet during the reign of Huang Taiji's son, the Shunzhi emperor (r. 1644–1661). Their leader, Gushri Qaghan, paid tribute to the Qing and in turn received a subsidiary title, and thus the Qinghai region effectively returned to Manchu Qing control. In contrast, the Zungar tribe of Eleut Mongols, who originally pastured their flocks in the western reaches of Xinjiang and western Siberia, were unwilling to submit to Qing rule and mobilized a menacing force along China's western border. Though Emperor Kangxi and his son, Yongzheng, mounted three military campaigns to bring these regions into line, it was not until the following emperor, Qianlong (r. 1735–1796), that the Zungar's own internal conflicts forced them finally to surrender to the Qing and incorporate their local areas into the system of the Eight Banners. The Durbot tribes of the Eleut Mongols, unable to fend off the attacks of the Gar tribe, also submitted to Qing rule during Qianlong's reign, and some of the regions assisted the Qing, swearing allegiance to the banners. The Terhut Eleut tribes, who pastured their livestock along the Ejile River, could not withstand the pressure from Russian forces and in 1770 moved to territory under Qing control, changing their tribal system to the system of Manchu banners.

Thus, in the hundred years from the establishment of the Qing dynasty to the middle of the Kangxi reign, the Mongol tribes to the south, north, and west of the Gobi Desert, forces that had maintained their autonomy and threatened both the East and the West for five centuries, became completely subsumed under the Qing authority and social structure.

This merging of the Mongols and the Manchus is a highly significant event in China's history. In the times when the Xiongnu, the Proto-Turks, the Qitans, and then the Mongols had flourished, China's northern grasslands and the northeastern forest regions had been united. Under Qing rule, they drew together within the borders of China and formed a rear guard for China's natural resources. Supported by the southern tribes, the northern areas were reclaimed, and the Zungar tribes were forced to submit. This created an entirely new state of affairs, in which the grasslands surrounding the Gobi Desert in all directions were firmly under the leadership of the Manchu Qing court.

Tibet went through a different process in its path to integration under the Qing. This sparsely populated high plateau with its arid climate had, from ancient times, handled its own affairs. During the Tang dynasty, after the rise of the Tubu (Tibetans, from Bod), this area grew into a great state in this hinterland region, such that even the mighty Tang empire had been hard pressed to beat back the Tubu forces approaching the gates of their capital, Chang-an. Although the Tubu peoples were reduced militarily after the medieval period, their religion, the Vajrayana branch of Buddhism from the Tibetan region, which was introduced into China during the Mongol Yuan dynasty, spread rapidly. This branch of Buddhism had developed in India later than the Mahayana Buddhism that was the main branch in China and had been the state religion of Tibet and the Mongol regions. With the Mongol conquest of China, it became the religion of the rulers. When the Yuan dynasty fell, although the Mongol tribes also lost their political unity, the Gelugpa, or Yellow Hat, sect of Vajrayana Buddhism became a common faith uniting the Mongol peoples, and by the missionary activities of lamas, the Manchus were later converted to Buddhism.

In the early Qing, under the reign of the Shunzhi emperor, the Zangba qaghan from the Heshuot Mongol tribe seized political power in Tibet, with the Dalai Lama under him as the central religious leader. When the Gushri qaghan assumed leadership following the Zangba qaghan, the Zungar Mongols responded to this opportunity by invading Tibet. Up to this point, the Qing policy toward Tibet had been to remain uninvolved and respect the position of the high lamas. In the tenth year of Shunzhi's reign (1652), in a gesture of magnanimity the Qing court invited the Dalai Lama to Beijing. Following this, when Kangxi subdued the Zungar Mongols, the Qing helped to establish the theocratic government of Tibet with the Dalai Lama as its head, and, shortly after this, they set up the Panchen Lama to share power with the Dalai Lama. These actions established the image of the Qing emperor as the protector for the Gelugpa sect.

During Qianlong's reign, the Qing further extended their influence in Tibet's religious affairs by setting up a system to draw lots from a golden vase when there were disagreements on the succession of reincarnated lamas, so that the Qing Manchu court could in effect override religious power. This dual control succeeded in solidifying the influence of the Manchu Qing emperors, and thus, working through the religious control of the Gelugpa sect, the Mongol and Manchu Vajrayana Buddhists were

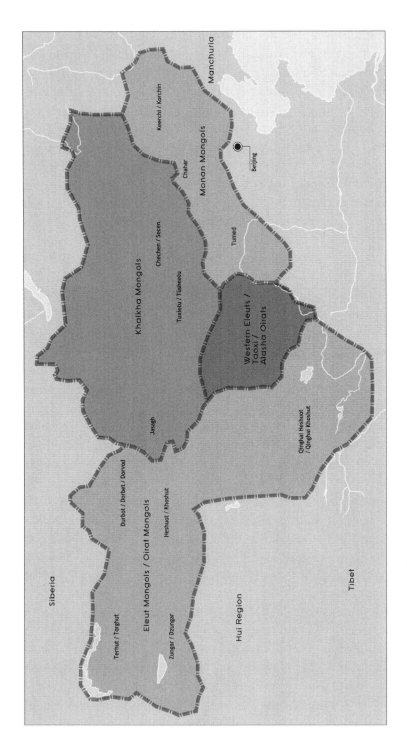

FIGURE 7.1 Various Mongol Tribes in the Early Qing

eventually convinced that the Qing emperor was indeed the protector of Buddhism. This further consolidated the Manchu Qing position as the common ruler of the Manchus, Mongols, and Tubu (Tibetans).

By this point, Manchu Qing control had spread over a vast territory extending from Manchuria in the far east to Tibet in the west. The might of the Qing exceeded even that of the Tang, whose Emperor Taizong had been given the title Heavenly Qaghan in recognition of the Mongols' submission to him. This was the first time that the Tibetan high plateau had been united with the Mongolian steppes, and it was established on a foundation much more solid than that of the administration of Chinggis Qaghan, which had relied entirely on military might to establish and hold together its great empire.

To sum up, when the Manchu Qing swept down into China and took the imperial throne from the Ming, they followed their original method for controlling areas outside their homeland, here using Han Chinese administrative structures to rule over the Han Chinese. Though the Manchus were indeed a conquering force from outside China, they formed a true Chinese dynasty that was based on the system wherein the emperor, in this case the great Qing emperor, would oversee the world. The other significant aspect of Manchu Qing rule was the unification of the Manchu, Mongol, and Tibetan regions. This was accomplished by linking the great Manchu qaghans with the lamas' spiritual influence, by the family ties established through marital diplomacy, by the use of rituals preserved from the Mongol state audiences, and by the reciprocal tribute from and gifts to frontier regions. All of these combined to enable the Qing to control about two-thirds of the steppes of the Great Khanate at that time.

Manchu-Mongol-Tibetan affairs were administered by the Court of Colonial Affairs (*lifan yuan*), the Imperial Household Department (*neiwu fu*), and the system of the Eight Banners, all of which were under the direct supervision of the Manchu Qing emperor, a situation that differed fundamentally from the Han Chinese system of central government. This Great Khanate had not only Beijing as its capital but also a summer capital at Chengde, along with the ancient royal palaces of the Mongols and a capital in Lhasa in Tibet. Manchu nobles held state audiences in all of these locations, repeatedly confirming the imperial mandate of the Qing dynasty's Manchu emperors. These two systems, one for the Han Chinese areas and one for the Manchu-Mongol-Tibetan areas, were the core of the dyarchic legal system of the Qing dynasty. It was the hallmark of the development of the Qing dynasty and a form of governance not frequently seen in other periods of world history.

2. The Development of Taiwan

From the first year of Kangxi's reign (1662), when Zheng Chenggong (Koxinga, 1624–1662) attacked and occupied Taiwan, until Kangxi was twenty-two (1683), Koxinga headed a hereditary government that managed to extend a vestige of the Ming dynasty's control over this maritime region for twenty-two years. In 1684, two years after the Qing finally gained control over the island, they set up a rudimentary administrative system of a single prefecture and three counties, with Taiwan as an adjunct to Fujian Province. They also fostered the trade route between Taiwan and Amoy (Xiamen) in Fujian, just across the Taiwan Strait, and maintained control of the island with a single officer commanding a troop of soldiers in rotating duty.

During the two centuries of Qing rule, Taiwan's population grew rapidly, so local administrative units were added gradually according to the hierarchy of prefecture, subprefecture, county, and department (*fu, zhou, xian, ting*). Finally, in 1885 the whole island was upgraded to a separate province (*sheng*) in itself. Before Koxinga arrived, the population of Taiwan did not exceed fifty thousand, and when he arrived he brought with him a hundred thousand troops. By the early years of the nineteenth century, only a hundred years later, Taiwan's estimated population had exploded to more than two million. By the end of the nineteenth century, the registered population alone had risen to more than 3,200,000. This surge of population, apart from the indigenous population of a hundred thousand and the positive birthrate, can be attributed to the many immigrants from Fujian and Guangdong.

The seventeenth and eighteenth centuries saw general population growth throughout the world, and perhaps the most dramatic area of change was in the New World, where immigrants from Europe and their descendents rapidly replaced the indigenous peoples of North and South America. In East Asia, despite the Ming interdiction of maritime commerce, there were still many immigrants who went to all areas of Southeast Asia. When the Qing took power, Manchus and Mongols moved south into the original area of China. In the interregnum between the

Ming and the Qing, there were constant, drastic internal upheavals, with masses of peasant soldiers under the rebel leaders Zhang Xianzhong (1606–1647) and Li Zicheng (1606–1645) terrorizing vast areas of Sichuan, Hubei, and Shaanxi. After episodes of horrible violence, people fled in every direction, leaving vast, depopulated wastelands in these provinces.

During the early years of the Qing dynasty, specifically the reigns of Kangxi, Yongzheng, and Qianlong, as law and order were finally restored and the common people could return to a normal life, the population increased substantially. The entire registered population of China during the Ming dynasty had ranged between seventy and eighty million people; thus China's population of three hundred million by 1795 at the end of Qianlong's reign (1796) represents a dramatic increase. Such a fundamental change may be attributable in part simply to the way statistics were compiled, but the increased food supply was also a factor. These issues were related to two campaigns during the Kangxi and Yongzheng reigns, which promulgated the slogans "The population of a flourishing world will never need to pay higher taxes" and "Disperse able-bodied men over all the land." The first of these campaigns was intended to prevent the tax-evading population from continuing to remain unregistered; the second sought to promote new areas of land that had become available for agricultural cultivation. With the opening of the great ocean routes, a number of new crops were introduced to China—crops such as corn, yams, and potatoes, which could be grown on hillier, colder, and drier areas than were suitable for rice; this increased food supply could now support a larger population.

At the beginning of the Qing, the population of Hubei and Hunan together was more than ten million, and a great number of these people moved into the area along the Han River and the Sichuan basin, following another government emigration campaign under the slogan "With Hubei, Hunan, and Guangdong, we shall fill up Sichuan." In addition, Han Chinese who had lived in the valley of the Yangzi River gradually moved up into previously unsettled mountain areas, now that corn and other new crops could be grown at these higher elevations. These settlers encroached on China's southwestern mountain region and put pressure on the indigenous tribes either to assimilate with the Han Chinese or move deeper into the mountains. During the Qing dynasty, troops were used to force the conversion of native areas into regular administrative units in this southwestern mountain region, which expanded the

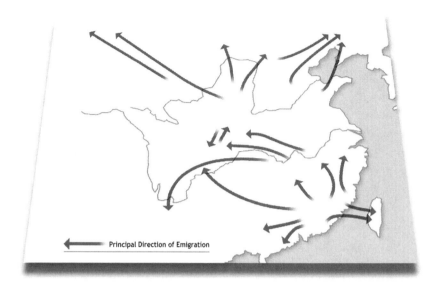

FIGURE 7.2 Early Qing Emigration Patterns

territory directly under government control and enabled further increases in population.

The immigrants to Taiwan from Fujian and Guangdong were also a part of this great wave of human migration. During the rule of Koxinga, when the Qing court's prohibition of maritime activity was much more strictly enforced, residents of the coastal towns were forced to leave their homes. Had these former coastal residents who then moved into mountainous regions been unable to avail themselves of the newly introduced crops, they would have been hard pressed to avoid starvation. After the Qing had taken control of Taiwan, despite the government's interdiction of maritime traffic, the population pressure in Fujian and Guangdong encouraged large numbers to emigrate to Taiwan. At the beginning of the Qing administration of Taiwan, there were only twelve thousand registered households, including sixteen thousand adults, though this figure can hardly be an accurate reflection of the actual population, as the troops who had accompanied Koxinga to Taiwan themselves numbered over a hundred thousand. To this Han Chinese population must be added the residents of the over 130 settlements of lowland indigenous tribes, each of whose settlements was inhabited by between a hundred and a thousand inhabitants, totaling more than a hundred thousand people. When the populations of the Han Chinese and the indigenous people are added together, it appears that the population of Taiwan during the early Qing was approximately three to four hundred thousand. In 1811, the local authorities in Taiwan tallied the total population of the island, finding two million residents. Thus in the four generations between the Qing takeover in 1683 and the census of 1811, the population increased four- or fivefold. Such a tremendous increase cannot be attributed to childbirth alone; most of it must have been caused by emigration from China. The magnitude of this immigration to Taiwan from Fujian and Guangdong, in terms of its effects on the population density of a limited geographic area such as this island, is an especially noteworthy element in Taiwan's history.

The Qing court did not initially encourage immigration to Taiwan. When the Koxinga government fell, the Qing court had not yet developed an active strategy to maintain control over the island. But Shi Lang (1621–1696), the naval leader who had defected from Koxinga to lead the Qing takeover of the island, persuaded Emperor Kangxi that establishing a civil government over Taiwan would be in the best interests of Chinese security. If the Dutch were to reoccupy this fertile island several hundred miles long, such a base of operations could have drastic repercussions for the security of China's coastal regions. The Qing court therefore dispatched ministers to Taiwan to incorporate it as a part of Fujian Province, though they were still concerned about the barrier of the Taiwan Strait, which could leave Taiwan vulnerable to attack in the future by individuals such as Koxinga and make it difficult to administer. Despite these security issues, the troops that were initially dispatched to the island were insufficient even to maintain local order, and it was not until after the insurrections of Zhu Yigui in 1721 and Lin Shuangwen in 1786 that the Qing court finally sent a large number of troops to the island. Despite inconsistencies in the immigration policies of the Kangxi, Yongzheng, and Qianlong reigns, they generally forbade ordinary people from crossing over to Taiwan. But these legal provisions were insufficient to stem the flow of people driven out of their native areas and across the Taiwan Strait in search of a new life on the island.

Looking at other areas of the world, we could note that the European countries with strong naval forces at that time—Spain, Portugal, Holland, and England—all had governments that actively intervened to encourage the movement of immigrants to new lands they controlled. Even the government of the newly independent United States used its influence to increase immigration to its western territories. In contrast, not until large-scale immigration to Taiwan had already occurred on its own did the Qing court finally set up local administrative units in their new territory. Comparatively speaking, Qing China had essentially no clear direction in its policies for emigration to open up new lands.

After occupying the island and setting up a minimal administration, the Qing court did occasionally step in to patch up differences that arose between Han settlers and the aboriginal tribes, but it generally adopted a laissez-faire attitude to affairs on the island. The tribes who lived on the lower plains were called Pepo or Pingpu (plains or lowland tribes) or Shoufan (acculturated natives). They were already using agriculture and had a society organized around villages when the Chinese arrived. The mountain tribes differed from those in the plains not only ethnically but in their ways of life, since they depended more heavily on fishing and hunting and had a tribal form of society; they were referred to as Shengfan (uncultured natives). Each social unit of these tribes had between several hundred to over a thousand individuals, and there was little social organization at levels higher than the village.

The Puyuma tribe (in Chinese, *Beinanzu*), which was centered around the location of modern Taidong, on the eastern coast of the island, was a much more populous tribe that occupied a relatively large territory and whose leader was referred to as the Puyuma king (*Beinan wang*). In dealing with these indigenous groups, the Qing court followed the model they had used in relating to the indigenous chieftains in southwestern China, recognizing their autonomous authority and granting them seals of authority as local officials (*tuguan*) or local leaders (*tumu*). Qing officials called subprefects for the regulation of natives or inspectors of natives were used to maintain order and mediate disputes between the Han Chinese and the indigenous peoples. Around the areas inhabited by indigenous peoples, these officials would erect markers to indicate the boundaries of their territory, and where the lowlands met the highlands were also "red lines" or earthen ramparts to prevent the Han Chinese from intruding into the mountains.

These policies of the Qing court were ineffective in preventing the Han Chinese from gradually encroaching into the indigenous areas and taking land away from the native peoples. Given their better-organized military forces, the Han Chinese were able to maintain their control over

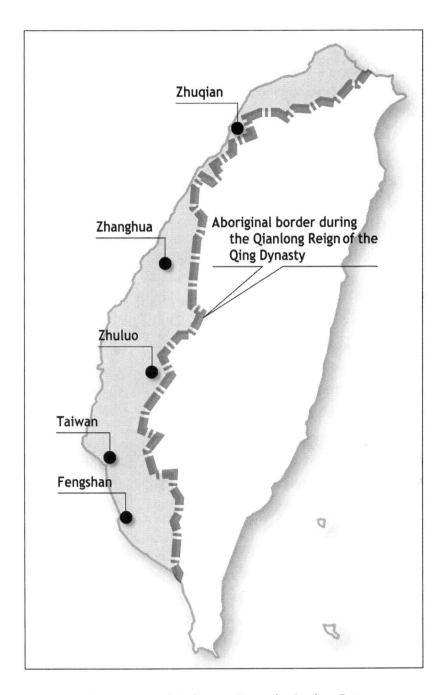

FIGURE 7.3 Taiwan Aboriginal Settlements During the Qianlong Reign

the indigenous peoples, and the entire island gradually evolved into a territory dominated by Han Chinese. The Pepo (Pingpu) tribes in the lowland became almost completely Sinicized, and their descendents differed little from the Han Chinese. In contrast, the mountain peoples were restricted to highland valleys and the narrow strip of lowlands on the eastern coast, which were separated from the rest of the island by a high mountain range, and they eventually became a disadvantaged minority in Taiwan.

The Han Chinese gradually extended their control northward from their base in the south. When the Qing initially took the island, the northern boundary of their domain was a town called Zhuluo, today the city of Chiayi, but they then moved into the central plains, around the modern city of Changhua, as they edged forward. At the beginning of the eighteenth century, the Han Chinese had broken through to the northern tip of the island to control the territory around the port cities of Tamsui (Danshui) and Keelung (Jilong). Finally, in a large-scale move at the end of the eighteenth century, the Han Chinese opened up the Kavalan tribal area in the Lanyang plain on the eastern coast around the current city of Yilan (from Kavalan). Generally speaking, the latter half of the eighteenth century, from the middle years of Kangxi's reign to the middle of Qianlong's, saw the main thrust of Han Chinese moving to open up Taiwan for settlement. The undeveloped plains from south to north had all fallen under Chinese domination, and after Qianlong it remained only to open up the mountain areas and the rest of the eastern coast.

The Han Chinese who immigrated during the Kangxi, Yongzheng, and Qianlong periods were mostly driven by privation on the Chinese mainland. The ocean current—the Black Current—that flows southward in the Taiwan Strait speeds up dramatically as it is funneled through the strait. Thus small craft carrying unauthorized immigrants were often unable to work their way across the strait, and it was difficult to avoid being driven by the current, which might push them out to the open ocean, founder them on shoals, or trap them in the rolling breakers before they reached land. The Han immigrants who managed to escape the driving winds and waves then had to face backbreaking toil and the threat of malaria, which together undoubtedly led to a high rate of attrition among the immigrants. There may not have been a large proportion who were actually able to establish their livelihood on Taiwan. There is an old saying in Taiwan: "Three remained, two died, and five went back," indicating that only about thirty percent of those who crossed the strait managed to continue living there.

These illegal immigrants initially were mostly unmarried men, though after the prohibition of private immigration to Taiwan was lifted, women also began to arrive. These single men worked to break the virgin soil of the plains or clear the dense growth of the mountains, though there were also a few who began trading with the indigenous peoples or who scraped by as agricultural laborers for aboriginal landlords. Many of these young men married into the Pepo (Pingpu) tribes, perhaps living with their wife's family and eventually inheriting their land. Thus after a forty- or fifty-year process of development, the Han Chinese eventually became widely distributed across western Taiwan.

Late in Kangxi's reign, wealthy and powerful people of Fujian and Taiwan invested collectively to enlist able-bodied men to open up island land for agriculture in the area around Banxian (the modern city of Zhanghua) and in the Taipei basin. The extended family groups directing the development of farmland were responsible for enlisting thousands of agricultural workers from Fujian and Guangdong to develop irrigation systems; the Babao irrigation ditch in Changhua remains an example of their labors.

The overseers of these projects directed large numbers of workers to open up vast tracts of farmland, and after the land was put into use, the workers would have a small area apportioned to each of them, as well as having sharecropping lands allotted to them. As a result, a three-level system of tenancy relationships developed in the northern and central areas of Taiwan. At the top, the large landowners who had organized the reclamation projects controlled vast tracts and employed hundreds or even thousands of laborers. Since these large landowners took shares of the harvest, they were in effect feudal lords, and the locations of their manor houses (*gongguan*) are still reflected in some place names. Next in the hierarchy, the agricultural laborers who had opened the land also became landowners, and they then could rent out their land to even smaller tenant farmers, who were lowest on this scale. These Taiwanese landowning despots drove their workers, victimized the original indigenous inhabitants, and, given their unchecked power, scorned even the authority of government officials. The local officials in Taiwan were low in the Qing bureaucratic ranks, and they were generally rotated frequently, so that postings to Taiwan were almost like foreign travel. Unable to develop a power base, they could not help but depend on the wealthy and overbearing great landlords. This situation continued up to the Japanese occupation of Taiwan at the end of the nineteenth century, when the highest level of landlords began to lose their grip on power and the middle rank of landowners could begin to function as the actual owners of their property.

Great local autonomy was a common characteristic of Taiwan's newly opened society. Since the government exercised little authority, local despots used their power to pull together collective organizations in their areas to help them make better use of their land. These social ties were reinforced by ethnic ties, as the earliest wave of immigrants to Taiwan in the seventeenth and eighteenth centuries came mostly from areas in Fujian, first from Quanzhou and then from Zhangzhou. Eventually, they were succeeded by Hakka Chinese from Guangdong. Although the first arrivals to Taiwan were young unmarried men, with the increased power of wealthy families to recruit immigrants, eventually groups of people from the same clan or village would come to Taiwan en masse. The arrivals from these three areas of China each tended to settle in certain areas of Taiwan, according to the order of their arrival and the order in which areas of Taiwan were settled. Thus the arrivals from Quanzhou were mostly in southern Taiwan, those from Zhangzhou in the central and northern regions, and Hakkas in the upland areas.

In actual practice, the towns in which these peoples lived were closely spaced and tightly interlinked, and given this closeness there was great competition for arable land and irrigation water. Each of these groups from the three different areas was bound together by complex networks of family, origin, and geographic proximity, and thus they could quickly muster bands of armed men numbering in the hundreds or even thousands when disputes arose, disputes that could become almost small-scale wars. Since the people from Fujian were much more numerous than the Hakka, when popular uprisings occurred that had to be quelled by the local officials, the officials could always find allies in the Hakka. And since the Hakka spoke a dialect of Chinese different from the Fujian immigrants, governmental conflicts thereby promoted an increased separation between linguistic groups. This reflected the essential fact that the public authorities were unable to rely solely on the force of law to preserve order, and thus local groups would resort to violence in the struggle for agricultural resources, which devolved into ceaseless conflict as each side fought for what it considered its fair share. Many of the social organizations that developed in the process of settling the land had similar characteristics, and it is not such a long stretch from the situation of that period to more recent times. The imprint of these conflicts between ethnic groups left in the collective memory has had an extraordinary effect on Taiwanese society.

By the nineteenth century, most of Taiwan had been opened up for agricultural use, with only the eastern coast and the high mountain regions remaining undeveloped. The world economy of the nineteenth century already showed signs of an emerging globalization, and many of Taiwan's products had entered the network of international business transactions. The warm climate of Taiwan, with its long growing season and abundant rainfall, yielded agricultural products of great variety and quantity. The rice harvest quickly increased to the point where it could be exported to Fujian and Guangdong, further to Jiangsu and Zhejiang, or even as far north as Beijing and Tianjin. Taiwan's sugar production also increased rapidly, soon penetrating the markets of China, Japan, and Southeast Asia. Taiwan initially imported tea plants from Fujian, and at first its production could not rival that of Fujian or Zhejiang. Foreign trading companies from England and America developed the practice of ordering tea in advance, the so-called monopoly (*baozhong*), and Taiwan's Black Dragon (*wulong*) tea gained a significant place in the international tea market. The camphor trees abundant in Taiwan's forests provided both an aromatic oil used extensively in pharmaceutical preparations and lumber popular for shipbuilding and furniture. These products were Taiwan's major exports in the nineteenth century. These phenomena show that there are similarities with the contemporary situation in many aspects of the settlement of Taiwan. The model of development that arose from these characteristics also has many parallels with the development of the Caribbean islands in relation to the Central American economy at the same point in time, and it has certain marked differences from developments in China's southwestern and northeastern frontier regions.

To sum up this section, when Koxinga lost control of Taiwan, it became Qing territory, and this caused a large influx of immigrants, which rapidly brought the island into the orbit of Chinese society. To administer the territory, the Qing court initially set up a hierarchy of prefectures, subprefectures, counties, and departments, similar to the mainland's system, for governing the Han Chinese on the island. Cultural pressure from Han immigrants on the indigenous Pepo (Pingpu) lowland tribes gradually led them to assimilate into Chinese society. As a result, when Taiwan became settled, it was transformed into a thoroughly Chinese territory. Moreover, in the areas populated by immigrants, the local social strata were empowered by the arms-length administration of Qing officials. This, on the one hand, brought about bitter quarrels over natural resources, and on the other it led to a vivid and colorful sense of local consciousness. The early Portuguese and Spanish who preceded Koxinga on the island were primarily missionaries and expeditionary forces, numbering only a few thousand, and they had essentially no influence on the ethnicity or culture of the Taiwanese. Then the lowland Pepo (Pingpu) indigenous population was absorbed by this new wave of mainly southern Chinese immigrants — the Han from Fujian's Quanzhou and Zhangzhou and the Hakka from Guangzhou. Chinese culture has a great ability to include and absorb different cultures, and the local cultures from Fujian and Guangdong that the immigrants brought with them became the main components of the Taiwanese culture that developed, one that established a firm identification with the mainstream of Chinese culture.

3. Ethnic and Cultural Conflicts in the Early Qing

The territory of China proper has been invaded many times by northern ethnic groups, who then established governments over the areas they had conquered. During the Northern Dynasties, as well as the Liao and Jin dynasties, the territory they controlled was limited to the northern part of China, but after the Song dynasty fell to the Jurchen Jin, which in turn was replaced by the Mongol Yuan dynasty, all of China was ruled by ethnic groups that were not Han Chinese. During the Yuan, the Han Chinese people felt deeply the pain of the repeated dissolution of their nation and worked strenuously so that it could rise again, until finally Zhu Yuanzhang (1328–1398) led the uprising that founded the Chinese Ming dynasty. During this period of foreign conquest, the distinction between Chinese and foreign cultures naturally was an issue much more pressing to the officials and scholars than to the ordinary people, and for these literati issues of ethnicity and culture were generally discussed together under the same rubric. In contrast, although the ordinary people also felt the humiliation of foreign exploitation, that change actually made little difference to the rhythms of their daily lives.

When the Manchus burst out from the northeast after a decade of planning, they took advantage of the straitened circumstances of the Ming court, which was beset by peasant uprisings led by Zhang Xianzhong and Li Zicheng. The betrayal by the Ming general Wu Sangui (1612–1678), who opened the Shanhai Pass gate in the Great Wall in 1644, offering the Manchu forces easy entry into China, allowed them to take power quickly from the already enfeebled Ming. The early part of the Manchu takeover of the north saw almost no resistance from officials or the common people: they were exhausted, and their loyalty was compromised by the corruption of the late Ming government. In 1645, the Qing court promulgated an order that all adult males should adopt the Manchu practice of shaving their foreheads and braiding the rest of their hair in a queue, as well as wearing clothing in the Manchu style; this was met with great objection in all areas. The resistance was fiercest in Jiangnan, and though Qing troops were sent to quell the uprising, turmoil dragged on for over ten years there. This degree of resistance had not occurred when the Mongols established the Yuan dynasty, and the nature of this resistance indicates the development of a Han ethnic consciousness, brought into relief by the enforced wearing of queues and changes of dress for the men.

Patterns of daily life may be the most direct gauge of a culture. The Yuan Mongols had taken a very laissez-faire attitude toward the Han Chinese, allowing them to lead their daily lives largely unhindered, leaving the scholars to continue studying the Chinese tradition as before, and certainly not meddling with their clothing or hairstyles. During this period there were individuals such as Xu Heng (1209–1281), who worked under the first Yuan emperor, Kublai Qaghan, to reestablish the Chinese National Academy (*Guozixue*). These people persistently sought to continue Confucian studies and preserve the Chinese cultural tradition, hoping to draw the foreign government into this culture. The Manchu Qing order to change men's hairstyles and clothing initiated the "choice," enforced by the death penalty, referred to as "Keep your head or your hair." For most Han Chinese, the emotional distress of losing their culture was a far greater torment than the loss of the imperial dynasty. The Three Massacres at Jiading by Qing troops as a punishment for resisting the Qing government, or the eighty-three days of siege of Jiangyin (in Jiangsu), where tens of thousands of Han Chinese defending the city of Jiangyin were killed, indicate the force of the Han resistance to the Qing takeover of their culture. The Han scholars who took refuge in the mountain wildernesses or desolate coastal areas were driven there as the only means of protesting this assault on their native culture. The essay "When the State Falls, So Falls All Under Heaven," by the great scholar from the late Ming Gu Yanwu (1613–1682), who refused to cooperate with the Qing government, considers Chinese culture to be "all under heaven" (*tianxia*). In addition, he states that the preservation of the state is the responsibility of the ruling classes, both the monarch and his officials, though "even the lowest commoner has a responsibility to participate" in the preservation of all under heaven.

The distinction between *Zhongguo* China and the *Yi* "barbarians" is made clear as early as the great moral principles presented in the Pre-Qin Confucian classic *The Spring and Autumn Annals*. Here, being from within China (*nei Huaxia*) or from outside of it (*wai Yidi*) divides mankind into the two basic cultural spheres. The matrix for this view may be the Zhou feudal relationships, which were formed around the Zhou kings as the central pivot for the joint entity of the feudal order, which was composed of the ruling classes related to the Zhou royal court. The peoples and states outside the community of this joint entity were outsiders, and the feudal nobles within this community were encompassed by the system of rituals held in common by the Zhou people. During the Spring and Autumn period, regional cultures in the south had grown apart from the center. The powerful state of Chu had established its own culture, drawing in smaller states such as Chen and Cai that had originally been part of the central orbit. At this time, Mencius castigated his contemporary Xu Xing (fl. late fourth century B.C.E.), a philosopher and early agricultural theorist in Chu, and others for having become one with the barbarians. The concept of being an outsider or barbarian was determined by one's cultural allegiance as well as by birth.

In times when China was controlled by foreign ethnic groups, these dual cultural standards for Chinese and outsiders led some historical figures to take the position that it was best to adapt oneself to a foreign occupation as a temporary tactic. Many of the outstanding individuals discussed above, such as Xu Heng, who served as an official during the Mongol Yuan dynasty, chose to preserve the Confucian tradition by cooperating with foreign rulers. In addition, the noted Confucian scholar Hao Jing (1223–1275) took office under the Yuan court and even acted as Kublai Qaghan's ambassador to the Southern Song dynasty, an action that must have required a great deal of deliberation on his part. He elected to do so because he considered Kublai a worthy monarch capable of bringing social stability to the people. He chose his course of action based on the Confucian exhortation to bring peace to all under heaven and adopted a new culturally defined identity. His choice could also be seen as consistent with the viewpoint expressed in *Mencius*, which states that though the mythical sage kings Shun and his successor Yu had both come from lands outside of China, they each became exemplars of virtuous Chinese emperors.

During the early Qing, most of the Han Chinese took positions somewhere between the two extremes of withdrawing completely from official life and wholeheartedly serving the new government, and each individual had to find a direction and an identity suitable to his own moral stance. There were notable extremes. Wang Fuzhi (1619–1692), the great philosopher of the late Ming and early Qing, tenaciously resisted the Manchu government and sought to preserve the Ming reign by meeting with troops under Li Zicheng, whose peasant rebels had facilitated the Manchu conquest by sacking Beijing. Wang urged them to cooperate and share power with the Southern Ming emperor Longwu (r. 1645–1646). Viewing the situation from the standpoint of preserving ethnic self-rule, Wang could put aside Li Zicheng's role in bringing down the Ming. Then, when the Southern Ming fell to the Qing shortly thereafter, Wang Fuzhi disappeared deep into the mountains of Hunan to live as a recluse and work privately on his philosophical works. His statement that "the Six Classics call me to begin a new life" indicates the new attitude that his secluded scholarship brought to his preparation of commentaries on the classics. Outwardly, his thinking in this work generally followed the lines of the Han Confucians, although in essence it was inspired by the ideals of the Song Neo-Confucian masters. Dissatisfied with the doctrines of Wang Yangming (1472–1529) on innate moral knowledge (*zhiliangzhi*), Wang Fuzhi promoted the thought of Zhang Zai (1020–1077) in an effort to establish the core values of Chinese culture. His books *Essays on Reading the Comprehensive Mirror for Aid in Government* (*Du tongjian lun*) and especially *Essays on the Song Dynasty* (*Song lun*) describe the rise and fall of ancient and recent dynasties and were in effect a critical evaluation of the process that led to the demise of the Ming dynasty. Even more relevant were his judgments on ancient figures according to the principle of distinguishing between Chinese and foreigners, or natives and outsiders (*Hua Yi neiwai*). According to Wang Fuzhi's critical evaluation, the principle of distinguishing between Chinese and foreign peoples was higher than even the Confucian principle of the relation between ruler and minister. For example, he praised the usurper emperor Liu Yu (363–422) of the Liu-Song dynasty during the period of the Northern and Southern Dynasties because he had moved north to invade the Chinese heartland of the North China Plain when that area was held by invaders from the north and west. Wang also praised Han Tuozhou's (1152–1207) attempt to retake the North China Plain from the Jurchen Jin during the Southern Song dynasty, even though the campaign was a disaster for the Southern Song. And he sharply denounced Qin Kuai (1090–1155), whose execution of the patriotic general Yue Fei (1103–1142) in an effort to appease the Jurchen Jin dynasty gave him the reputation as one of the most notorious traitors in Chinese history. Similarly, he referred to Xu Heng as a "despicable Confucian" for his complicity with the Mongol Yuan dynasty, acting as a "Chinese who had turned barbarian." Worst of all, he considered that Sang Weihan should be damned for ten thousand generations for supporting the Later Jin (936–947) ruler Shi Jintang's (892–942) policy of conceding the Sixteen Prefectures (from modern Beijing to Datong) to the Khitan Liao and becoming a vassal of the Khitan. Wang Fuzhi's lifelong refusal to recognize the legitimacy of the Manchu Qing regime was thus the extension of his principle of preserving the integrity of the Han people (*minzu*).

At the fall of the Ming, another scholar, Gu Yanwu (1613–1682), participated in resistance movements against the Qing in Jiangnan, and after this last gasp of the Ming had been stamped out Gu wandered from place to place, meeting those who preserved the final sparks of defiance against the Qing. His main literary work combined a historical phonology of the Chinese language with the study of the classics, historiography, and geography, applying this encyclopedic knowledge to his goal of bringing order to the world. Countering the prevailing intellectual currents, Gu Yanwu strongly criticized the empty talk of the reigning Song-Ming Neo-Confucianism, maintaining that the disorder brought to China by invading tribes had originated with the "pure talk" (*qingtan*) mysticism of the Wei-Jin period, which had turned the direction of study away from its proper focus on statecraft. Gu Yanwu considered the overly academic Ming scholarship to be a trivialization of the original tradition of Confucius and Mencius, just as thinkers of the Wei-Jin period had trivialized the original tradition of Laozi and Zhuangzi. His work on the classics and especially on phonology sought a return to the original meaning of the classical texts. It was for this reason that the reformist scholar Liang Qichao (1876–1929) considered Gu Yanwu to have opened a new direction in Qing Confucian studies that sought the original meaning of texts (*puxue*). Liang wrote that "the Qing Confucians defined themselves by their commitment to a scholarship of textual criticism to indicate their differences with the (Song) literati, and it was Gu Yanwu who opened this way." It was this renewed understanding of Confucianism that Gu Yanwu, as he pondered the fall of his nation, came to see as the vital line of Chinese culture; it was his hope that from this renewed conviction, the original sense and root meanings of the classics could be recovered.

Gu Yanwu based his consideration of applied statecraft on his studies of history and historical geography. In his signature work, *Record of Knowledge Acquired Day by Day (Rizhilu)*, he meticulously analyzed and ordered his ideas on history and on human affairs, including systems of government offices, as well as the course of historical affairs from beginnings to conclusions, concentrating in particular on practical matters. Systems of taxation, the iron and salt monopolies, transportation of grain by waterways, military affairs: these and more were matters that Gu viewed from the painful perspective of the demise of his dynasty, considering the advantages and disadvantages of the Chinese systems of government as part of his own self-reflection and criticism. Like Wang Fuzhi, he viewed China's defense against outsiders as being a matter of even more gravity than the relations between a ruler and his ministers. In the section on the Pre-Qin political theoretician Guan Zhong (725–645 B.C.E.) in *Records of Knowledge Acquired Day by Day*, Gu Yanwu stated that "The distinction between ruler and minister concerns essentially one person, whereas the defense of China against barbarians concerns all under heaven." Gu Yanwu thus took as the core of his philosophy the concept of all under heaven, a term that covers all affairs, from the life of common people to the vital force of China's culture itself. Consequently, he considered that the Chinese imperial system needed to change back to a more locally based system of government.

Gu Yanwu's work on geography recorded what he had seen and heard in the many regions he visited in his peripatetic life, and since he included information on strategic passes and important routes for communication, it is possible this may have been part of a plan eventually to overthrow the Qing. But more broadly, this work presents a discussion of the society and economy of all these regions. These pragmatic tasks of investigation were not ones that could have been accomplished by a scholar working only from textual sources, and they show Gu Yanwu's reflection on and criticism of current affairs.

Refusing to have any association with the Qing court and living only with others faithful to the vanquished Ming dynasty, Gu Yanwu never forgot his goal of restoring the Ming. He befriended worthy community leaders and traveled extensively, crossing mountains and fording rivers, always striving to further his cause. In contrast to Wang Fuzhi, Gu's deep reflections on Chinese culture and centralized political power all had a sense of personal self-examination and criticism. In the scope within which he worked, the works of Gu thus might even be considered of more importance than those of Wang.

One of Gu's close friends and associates in his quest was Huang Zongxi (1610–1695). At the end of the Ming, Huang went to great lengths to gather a local militia to support the prince of Lu's doomed resistance against Qing rule. After repeated frustration at the failure of all of the Southern Ming's rebellions, Huang turned his energies toward teaching and writing. Like Gu Yanwu, he gave deep consideration to the rise and fall of Chinese culture and governments. Huang also bitterly resented the empty scholasticism to which the Neo-Confucian schools had been reduced and instead urged clear historical studies promoting practical applications of statecraft (*jingshi*). "Study must be based on considerations of governance so it will not end up in empty talk; it must be supported by historical documents so it will be suited to the needs of actual affairs." In his Confucian studies, Huang compiled and arranged his *Records of Ming Confucian Scholars* (*Mingru xue-an*) and began compiling the *Records of Song and Yuan Scholars* (*Songru xue-an*). These magisterial works, which organized the different schools and branches of scholarship during the Song, Yuan, and Ming, were seminal contributions to the historical study of Chinese thought.

Huang Zongxi's reflections on gain and loss in human affairs are contained in his book *Waiting for the Dawn: A Plan for the Prince* (*Mingyi daifang lu*). In this great work, after pointing out the flaws of Chinese culture and government, he puts forth his own reformist ideals. The scope of this book is vast, including government, administration, military affairs, the economy, society, and many other topics, all as part of his proposal for fundamental changes to these systems. Put in modern terminology,

Huang hoped that China could develop a democratic government and society with a cultural elite, using the schools as the locus of political discussion and eventually transforming the autocratic imperial system into one with a rather high degree of local autonomy. The first two words of the Chinese title refer to the *Yijing* hexagram *Ming Yi*, or "Darkening of the Bright." This hexagram symbolizes the need to wait for the proper time to act, stating,

> The trigram for darkness, Kun, is in the upper position and below it the trigram for fire, Li. This is the image for Darkening of the Bright. One should maintain constancy in the face of adversity. The commentary states: This symbolizes the need to wait for the proper time to act. The Bright goes into the earth; this is the darkening of the Bright. One should be cultivated and bright within; but yielding and compliant on the outside. When beset by adversity, King Wen was thus. By practicing constancy in the face of obstructions, one can maintain one's brightness in the dark.

Huang saw his own time as a period when the light had been hidden and thus felt it was necessary to await a more appropriate time for action.

By the time this book was completed, all of the regimes led by Ming loyalists had fallen, and Koxinga had died. Huang must have resented bitterly that the times would not be ripe for him and that he could only leave his unfulfilled ideal for those who would come after him. In quoting the title of this hexagram, the title of Huang's book thus alludes to the longing for a new ruler, but could this new ruler come from the Manchu-controlled Qing dynasty, or was it to be someone from a civilization yet to come? Huang did not make this clear. But given Huang's central goal of supporting the cause of the Ming, he was not one to mourn over the fallen dynasty while expecting to be invited to serve the new Manchu government. Another phrase from the hexagram *Ming Yi* states, "In the midst of difficulties, yet maintaining the propriety of his character, thus was Jizi." This refers to a prince of the fallen Shang court, Jizi, who accepted a request to provide King Wen of the Zhou with consultation on the principles of proper governance. Similarly, in his later years Huang expressed his approval of the governance of the Kangxi emperor and received liberal support from the Qing court. It has been conjectured that in his view, the happiness and welfare of the common people were more important that the principle of remaining true to his own ethnic culture. From the viewpoint of history, the rise and fall of dynasties was inevitable, and these changes did not need to be his central concern.

The degree to which these three men identified with and cared for their people and culture demonstrates their essential difference from the attitude of most others at this time, who generally had quite a different relationship to the new dynasty. Most scholars maintained only superficial support for Confucian ideals, quickly abandoning their seclusion after the fall of the Ming to seek the honor and wealth that success in the government examinations could bring. By enrolling in the public-service examinations under the Manchus, they could become the dignitaries of the new dynasty. Moreover, the Manchu Qing also employed conciliatory means to appease the Han Chinese. In addition to holding examinations for government positions, they also won over a number of well-known scholars with their support for the compilation of an official history of the Ming and several other major research projects.

After recuperating during the reign of Kangxi, the life of the common people returned to normal as they became accustomed to Manchu rule, and the pain of losing their dynasty was forgotten by a new generation. The Qing generally followed Ming governmental policies, and the official interpretation of the classics accepted for the examinations was still based on Zhu Xi's interpretations of the Confucian classics, the *Four Books*, whose central point was the maintenance of social order through the traditional hierarchy of human relationships. In this view, when the proper relationship between the ruler and his subjects has been established, the divisions between ethnic groups would not be sufficient to disrupt the basic scheme of human relationships.

But sentiment for overthrowing the Qing to restore the Ming had not entirely vanished, and rebellions arose that called for support by hailing "the Third Crown Prince Zhu," a purported son of the last Ming emperor. For example, there was the abortive 1728 attempt of the schoolteacher Zeng Jing, a follower of the scholar Lü Liuliang (1629–1683) from the Ming-Qing transition, to persuade one of the Yongzheng emperor's trusted generals, Yue Zhongqi (1686–1754), to rise and lead his troops in revolt. Moreover, there was a bewildering variety of rumors that circulated among the common people: that the after the death of the first Qing emperor in China, Huang Taiji (also, Hung Taiji, 1592–1643; r. 1626–1643), Grand Empress Dowager Xiao Zhuang Wen (1613–1688) had married the prince regent, her brother-in-law Dorgon (1643–1650); that the love affair between the Shunzhi emperor (1638–1661, r. 1644–1661) and his concubine Dong Xiaowan had led to his taking vows as a monk; that there was great strife between the sons of Kangxi; that Yongzheng had obtained the throne illicitly; that Lü Liuliang's daughter Lü Siniang had attempted to assassinate Yongzheng; that Qianlong was actually a Han Chinese surnamed Chen; and others. This swirling mass of strange and unfounded gossip that circulated was merely a reflection of the Han Chinese ridicule of the Manchu Qing control. Another aspect of this undercurrent of opposition was the ceaseless stream of admonishments that reflected the suspicions and jealousy of the Qing court as they continually exerted themselves to repress the Han ethnic self-consciousness. One of the most notable of these tracts, *Record of Great Rightness Dispelling Superstition* (*Dayi juemi lu*), written by the Yongzheng emperor in response to Zeng Jing's attempted rebellion, mentioned above, stressed the Confucian notion that "there is a fixed and proper relationship between the sovereign and his subjects" (*jun chen zhi yi yi ding*) in order to coerce the Han Chinese into following the Manchu Qing system of ethical conduct. Following Qianlong's reign, movements to overthrow the Qing were limited to peasant rebellions, pulled together by underground loyalist organizations such as the Heaven and Earth Society (*Tiandihui*); the scholars from the upper social classes had already resigned themselves to the current state of affairs.

4. Qing Scholarship

The rapid ascendancy of Wang Yangming's School of the Heart-Mind (*xinxue*) effectively replaced the Neo-Confucianism of the Cheng brothers and Zhu Xi as the dominant mode of philosophical thinking during the Ming. Although Wang's philosophy made a major contribution by encouraging greater freedom of expression, its success was at the same time limited by a lack of scholarly rigor. Furthermore, under the influence of the Ming fashion for hypothetical discussions, a tendency no less marked than that of the Wei-Jin period, scholars were more apt to overlook real-world issues. Then, after the fall of the Ming, scholars such as Gu Yanwu and Huang Zongxi reflected on the flaws of the Ming administration and Chinese culture in general, pointing out that the root of China's defeat had lain in the tendency of literati to debate empty intellectual issues while neglecting pragmatic affairs.

During the early Qing, the Yan-Li school, named after Yan Yuan (1635–1704) and Li Gong (1659–1733), reacted to the tendencies of previous Ming scholarship by demonstrating that the theory and practice of a school of thought could be based on the needs of more practical scholarship. The pre-Qin Confucian doctrines had tended to focus on moral conduct and scholarship, and in this sense they conveyed the sense that perception and action were reciprocal conditions, one concerned with the inner world and the other with the outer. Early Confucian scholarship had been a form of critical introspection distinctly different from the tradition of knowledge and cognition that had developed in the West since the age of Greek philosophers. In the scholarship that developed based on intellectual analysis, the Cheng brothers, Zhu Xi, Lu Jiuyuan, and Wang Yangming all made significant contributions, but if scholars exerted themselves only analytically and neglected the importance of application, then the early Confucian emphasis on working on both inner and outer aspects could not be realized. Even during the Ming, while the school of Wang Yangming was still flourishing, scholars such as Liu Zongzhou (1578–1645) were already unwilling to limit themselves to scholarship based only on texts and verbal debates, and they changed their focus to emphasize individual self-cultivation based on sincerity and rectification of the mind. These scholars, who opposed the more traditional academic view, not only emphasized the importance of meticulous introspection on one's individual accomplishments and failings but also urged scholars to encourage one another in tempering their actual moral conduct. Then after the fall of the Ming, Liu Zongzhou's student Huang Zongxi saw that even this emphasis on the practice of integrity had been unable to save Chinese culture from disgrace. In his late years, Huang produced his work of deep self-reflection, *Waiting for the Dawn: A Plan for the Prince*, discussed above.

Two other scholars who shared his sympathies, Yan Yuan and Li Gong, appeared on the scene unexpectedly from rural Hebei with no connections to the late Ming schools of the Jiangnan region. They came from an area in which the relatively new northern Quanzhen sect of Daoism had flourished ever since the Jin and Yuan dynasties and where the local customs were plain and honest. When the Manchu Qing government took over China, given the unfairness with which it redistributed land

and the harshness by which it sought out those who attempted to evade its administration, even the common people directly experienced the bitterness of losing their native dynasty. Thus Yan and Li were unsparing in their criticism of the former Ming literati's lofty discussions of the heart-mind and human nature. Yan Yuan's sarcastic statement on the late Ming intellectuals that they "idly discussed human nature, their hands in their sleeves; and then when faced with danger, fulfilled their responsibility to the emperor by dying" illustrates the attitude of these two scholars. Yan Yuan's self-discipline was especially strict, and he made his living by farming and teaching, customarily wearing coarse clothing and eating plain food, pushing himself in hard physical labor. His manner of conduct allowed him, without casually slighting or being disrespectful of others, to engage in mutual admonitions with his associates when they met. This followed the Confucian exhortation to maintain high standards in one's individual behavior and associations with others, and through this emphasis on ethical conduct Yan aimed to rectify the failings of other scholars' empty rhetoric.

Yan Yuan also criticized the current government. Broadly speaking, he stressed that scholarship had the responsibility of attending to both statecraft and the affairs of common people. Two of his essays, "Preserving Scholarship" ("*Cun xue*") and "Preserving One's Nature" ("*Cun xing*"), stress the inseparability of study and practice. His educational curriculum included not only the traditional six Confucian arts (*liuyi*) of ritual, music, archery, charioteering, calligraphy, and mathematics (*li, yue, she, yu, shu, shu*) but also practical subjects such as military affairs, economics, industrial technologies, and agricultural production. What he cared for most deeply was the principles of having correct morality, making proper use of one's resources, and developing one's material well-being. Beyond his care for personal morality and livelihood, he stressed that it was even more important to expand outward from the individual to a broader social context, from the family to the state. With this expansion, one could begin to correct the morality of the state through education, organize the usefulness of the state through administration, and support the livelihood of the state through production and its material benefits. This was in fact the traditional Confucian aspiration of working from inner sagehood toward outer rulership.

Yan Yuan's student, Li Gong, followed his teacher in developing practical studies, though he gave greater emphasis to the need for combining study and practice without emphasizing one over the other. In his thinking, study (*xue*) consists of the examination of material things (*gewu*) and the attainment of knowledge (*zhizhi*); knowledge (*zhi*) is relevant to one's practice of moral conduct and consists of sincerity (*chengyi*), rectification of one's heart-mind (*zhengxin*), and self-cultivation (*xiushen*); action (*xing*) that will benefit the whole world consists of regulating one's family (*qijia*), governing the state (*zhiguo*), and bringing peace to all under heaven (*ping tianxia*). It was in order to fulfill this aspiration that Li Gong stressed the six arts of the pre-Qin Confucians together with the Song Confucian recitation of poetry and quiet meditation, contrasting the liveliness of the former with the stiffness of the latter.

Had the Yan-Li School developed further, the Qing educational system might have undergone a revolutionary change in response, and the face of Qing scholarship and culture would have been vastly different. It is indeed unfortunate that this school, which so emphasized the practical aspects of study was, in the end, unable to develop further or open up a new direction for the mass of "vulgar Confucians." The type of scholars who received degrees through the examination system of the Qing court did so, as before, by mastering the formulaic composition of poetry and the traditional eight-legged essay, with Zhu Xi's explanations of the classics serving as the orthodox text. Since achieving wealth and status, often through the road opened by scholarship, was the goal pursued by the masses, the line of thinking put forth by Yan and Li could hardly succeed as a mainstream school of thought. Correspondingly, among the literati who were recognized by a degree from the official examination system, even the best of them were little better than a scholar such as Tang Bin (1627–1687), a noted Neo-Confucian scholar upright in his official government duties. The worst were like Li Guangdi (1642–1718), who merely composed essays following the Neo-Confucian formulae but knew how to wangle a lucrative official position. They were also not ashamed of selling out their friends to gain undeserved merit. Such scholars were limited to pure scholarly investigation with little practical application. In the three hundred years of Qing examinations, pedantic scholars like Tang Bin and Liu Guangdi were in the majority. It was not until the Daoguang reign period (1820–1850) that further calls for practical statesmanship would be heard. Yu Zhengxie (1775–1840) and Gong Zizhen (1729–1841), two scholars of the School of Evidential Learning (*kaozheng xue*), were also concerned with the decline of China at that time and attempted to correct the enfeebled tradition of scholarship.

In contrast with this earlier pedantry, the broad success of evidential learning scholarship can be said to be the high point of Qing scholarship. This school, which focused on determining the correct versions of classical texts and the original meanings of words in them, originated in the Zhejiang city of Qianjia. It spread rapidly to supplant the formerly dominant Neo-Confucian scholarship, which was more concerned with moral principles. The rise of this new school is generally explained as a result of the strict regulations on scholars, forbidding the free discussions that had characterized the late Ming, and leading Qing scholars to seek shelter in the less restricted field of evidential learning. But, while this explanation is not unreasonable, the rise of evidential learning also follows a previous line in the development of scholarship, and it cannot entirely be explained by pressure from the Qing government.

Looking back fifteen hundred years from this period, the trajectory of scholarship in the Western and Eastern Han dynasties can be helpful in understanding the way that scholarship changed direction in the Qing. During the Western Han, Dong Zhongshu (179–104 B.C.E.) had established the study of metaphysics in early China as part of state-recognized scholarship, and this type of scholarship then developed in two directions. On the one hand, the New Text (*jinwen*) school of interpretation of the classics evolved, concerning itself with deep meanings that these scholars perceived in subtle patterns of phrases within the classics, leading often to far-fetched interpretations. On the other hand, the apocryphal commentaries on the classics (*chenwei*) tended to extrapolate from the classics in an even more arbitrary fashion. To counter this direction, Eastern Han scholars strove to clear up corruptions in the classical texts by using philological analysis, thereby restoring these texts to their original state. This direction of Eastern Han scholarship was again reversed during the following Wei-Jin period, with its predilection for speculative discussion on metaphysical subjects.

The Qing dynasty inherited the late Ming fashion for casual conversations on moral principles and for putting systems of thought into more orderly arrangements. Although Gu Yanwu was mainly intent on countering this pedantic tendency through applications of his scholarship to statecraft in the late Ming and early Qing, he also cautioned scholars against quoting the classics out of context to suit their own intentions. In addition, he made a systematic investigation of the ancient Chinese rhyme patterns and attempted to find patterns in the evolution of China's state administration. Thus Gu's scholarship can be considered one of the starting points for the Qing evidential scholarship.

The fields of research contributing to evidential scholarship included historical phonology, etymology, and textual criticism. More broadly speaking, the verification obtained through evidential scholarship was also related to understanding historical events, bureaucratic administration, and social customs, as well as geographical changes over time. This methodology, since it was an approach to scholarship concerned with proof, worked from textual materials in order to deduce credible conclusions from the evidence. Thus, although evidential scholarship was sometimes referred to as "simple scholarship" (*puxue*), the modern scholar Hu Shi (1891–1962) considered it to be a "scientific method of study." Within the traditional three divisions of Chinese learning—moral reasoning, rhetoric, and textual criticism—rhetoric was related to the study of creative literature, whereas textual research was the basic skill needed for moral reasoning. The importance of textual research in this scheme lies in that without reliable versions of the classical texts, that is, versions that could be established only by the use of evidential scholarship, discussions of the moral reasoning that lay behind these texts would find it difficult to avoid poorly founded speculation, and thus the explanations would be inevitably subjective. Since this moral reasoning was the basis for proposing social and political systems, evidential scholarship was much more significant than simple pedantry.

One of the proponents of Qing evidential scholarship, Yan Ruoju (1636–1704), devoted himself to researching a single of the earliest classics, the *Book of Documents* (*Shangshu*), and his *Critical Investigations of the Old Text Book of Documents* (*Shangshu guwen shuzheng*, 1743) was the first scholarly work to generate conclusions via logical deductions from a large body of evidence. The brothers Wan Sida (1633–1683) and Wan Sitong (1638–1702) were both students of Huang Zongxi. The elder brother was a scholar of the classics who sought correct explanations of the classics through his comprehensive knowledge of these texts; the younger was a historian who sought to understand the actual nature of more recent historical events by consulting large amounts of historical materials. During the reign of the Qianlong emperor, the great figure in evidential scholarship, Dai Zhen (1723–1777), unequivocally stated that if moral reasoning was not to be groundless speculation, it could never be separate from the classics. Moreover, all scholarship must begin with careful textual analysis and close distinctions of meaning, so that in the end the scholar could directly "hear the Dao," as the *Analects* referred to the ultimate goal of the scholar. This level of ability was something that the great figures of Qing evidential scholarship strove for and that many attained. But after evidential scholarship had become an established, orthodox school of thought, these scholars, whose work was so closely tied to the detailed proof of actual facts, tended to become trapped in narrow specialization, putting all their efforts into the consideration of minutiae. To lose oneself in exhaustive studies of details of the classics as a means to find the roots of their meaning then changed to what was merely evidential scholarship for its own sake, and the meticulous study of details led to few further developments in scholarship.

Another aspect of official scholarship during the Qing dynasty was the editorial activities that brought together earlier texts into great collections, referred to as *congshu*, a great many of which were compiled during this period. During the Kangxi and Yongzheng reigns, in addition to the "strategic planning" (*fanglue*) collection, which propagated knowledge of military skills, there were regular dictionaries, specialized rhyming dictionaries, literary encyclopedias, and collections of annotations to the classics. Of these massive works, the most notable from the Kangxi reign were the *Kangxi Dictionary* (*Kangxi zidian*), the *Peiwen Rhyme Book* (*Peiwen yunfu*), the *Imperial Encyclopedia* (literally, "the imperially approved synthesis of books and illustrations past and present," *Gujin tushu jicheng*), and the *Complete Tang Poetry* (*Quan Tangshi*). During the Qianlong reign, official bibliographic efforts to collect previous texts on more specialized subjects were even more comprehensive, including *The Complete Martial Arts* (*Shiquan wugong*) and texts on all aspects of ritual. In addition, the massive collection of works on government administration and policies, the *Ten Encyclopedic Histories of Institutions* (*Shitong*), begun in the Tang, was extended, expanding the original contents by several times. The largest and most comprehensive of these collections was *The Emperor's Four Treasuries*, the *Siku quanshu*. This required thirteen years of concentrated effort by a large team of scholars to collect texts from all over the empire, compare and select variant versions, and then recopy them by hand into seven copies. The resulting collection of 3,457 works in 79,070 chapters (*juan*) was divided into the four basic categories of classics, history, philosophy, and literature (*jing, shi, zi, ji*), and the modern reprints of the original text run to 1,500 volumes. The efforts of scholars for this undertaking were primarily focused on the verification and reassembling of these texts, together with annotating and arranging them. The rise of evidential scholarship was clearly related to this great project, which had a profound effect on the direction of scholarly research in the Qing.

Because they were brought together during the editing of texts, Qing scholars formed their own scholarly community. Dai Zhen, as an example, continued the research tradition set out by Gu Yanwu, Yan Ruoju, and Wan Sitong: his contemporaries included the philologist Qian Daxi (1728–1804), the *Yijing* scholar Hui Dong (1697–1758), the chief editor of the *Siku quanshu* Ji Yun (1724–1805), and many others; and his disciples included the philologist Wang Niansun (1744–1832) and Duan Yucai (1735–1815), the annotator of the second-century C.E. dictionary *Shuowen jiezi*. An example of the strength of this scholarly community was the mid-nineteenth-century *Qing Imperial Annotations to the Classics* (*Huangqing jingjie*), together with its continuation volumes. Though these texts came two centuries after Gu, they were based on a scholarly lineage between student and teacher as well as on communication between contemporaries in this scholarly community, which had continued to develop from the early Qing. In Chinese culture, the last time there had been an academic social entity with long-term continuity in any way resembling this one would have been the Neo-Confucian scholars of the Northern and Southern Song.

A scholarly community of such a large scale and extended time span would naturally tend to shape the direction and characteristics of the scholarship of its age. To have some perspective on the Chinese situation, we could look at a similar scholarly association in seventeenth-century England. This was the Royal Society of London for the Improvement of Natural Knowledge, originally formed in 1660 by twelve English scientists and dedicated to what it referred to as "Physico-Mathematical Experimental Learning." These scholars drew from one another's different fields of knowledge and promoted a new form of science based on experimental evidence. The astronomer Christopher Wren (1632–1723) was the first president of the society; founding members included Isaac Newton (1643–1727), Thomas Henry Huxley (1825–1895), Robert Boyle (1629–1699), and other significant figures in the history of science. Despite its importance, it remained essentially a private institution until 1850, when the British government made a grant of one thousand pounds to support its scientific work. Prospective members of the society were required to have their nomination supported by three members and be passed by a vote of all the members. The society began to receive regular governmental support in the mid-nineteenth century, when Charles Darwin (1809–1882) was one of its members.

Comparing the work and aspirations of these two scholarly communities, one Chinese and one English, we can see some of the great differences between the Eastern and Western traditions of scholarship. The English scholars of the Royal Society were searching for principles that lay behind interactions of the material universe, using knowledge based on the actual results of experiments. In contrast, the community of Chinese scholars of evidential learning based their research on texts transmitted over thousands of years and devoted themselves to making annotations and correct commentaries to these texts. They were little concerned with ideals or theoretical concerns and even less with opening new fields of knowledge. Though Qing scholarship was certainly extremely careful and precise, the idea that evidential scholarship was in some way related to or a forerunner of the scientific method was a later notion, originating with Hu Shih and other scholars in the first half of the twentieth century.

The Qing scholars instead considered themselves to be part of the academic tradition of "Han Learning" (*Han xue*), a term used to differentiate this tradition from the Neo-Confucian philosophical speculations of "Song Learning" (*Song xue*)—and both were still entirely different from experimental science. Qing evidential scholarship emphasized the small details of research, with less concern for the Way (*dao*) or Principle (*li*). They also neglected the goal of using the well-edited classic text as material for reflection on their own conduct. Within the tradition of Qing scholarship, a spirit of ultimate concern for humankind had been lost. The Qing scholarly tradition could be said to be intent on rectifying the errors of the Neo-Confucian tradition stretching from the Cheng brothers of the Northern Song, through Zhu Xi and Lu Jiuyuan of the Southern Song, down to Wang Yangming in the Ming. But the tendency of evidential learning to fall into pedantic trifles severely diminished these scholars' ability to criticize effectively actual problems in their government and society.

5. The Popular Culture of Local Organizations, Religious Sects, and Secret Societies

In addition to the work of the evidential scholars and editors discussed above, the mid-Qing reigns of the Qianlong and Jiaqing emperors were the high point of a broadly based movement to compile local histories (*difangzhi*). Also called local gazetteers, these texts focused on individual counties or municipalities, combining chronicles of events in their history with descriptions of their geography, local products, family genealogies, and distinguished individuals. Their compilation during this period was so extensive that almost all subsequent local histories are merely revisions of these Qing works. The most outstanding of the many scholars who compiled these works, Zhang Xuecheng (1738–1801), considered that local histories should be "the *complete* history of a place." In contrast, the official dynastic histories were histories of the entire Chinese world, in which the information on local areas was combined into national histories. This increased interest in local histories during the Qing was a reflection of the increased interest in studying all things local. Since these local histories were less a part of the Confucian rubric of an idealistic and nationalistic world view, local people were here better able to find in them an expression of the actual conditions of their lives.

When people left their native areas to work elsewhere, they formed fraternal organizations in these distant places with others from home. During the Qing, all cities had village assembly halls (*xiang huiguan*) erected by these local fraternities, and in Beijing were halls that served as centers both for government officials who had come to the capital from the provinces and for examination candidates from the same common area. In addition to the camaraderie provided by these associations, since areas generally tended to have certain specialty trades, the local fraternal organizations also supported the activities of these trades. Just west of Shanghai, my birthplace of Wuxi was known for its blacksmiths, who were distributed along the Yangzi River. When these smiths moved to other areas of this river system, such as Chongqing or Hankou, the Wuxi assembly (*tongxianghui*) they set up there functioned essentially as a trade guild (*gonghui*), and their halls became gathering places for people of this trade. Since the patron deity of blacksmiths was the Daoist fire god Huo De, the Wuxi fraternal halls also were places of his worship.

The best known of these local fraternal organizations during the Qing was for people from Shanxi. The businessmen of Shanxi were famous all over China for their financial acumen, and they became highly influential through the series of private lending institutions they set up in many areas. The people of Shanxi had as their patron deity Guan Di, the deified General Guan Gong (d. 219 C.E.) of Three Kingdoms fame, who came from Xie County in Shanxi and was also the main deity of the Shaanxi assembly. Beginning in the Qing, Guan Di evolved from his original status as a god of war to a god of wealth, though the connection to Shanxi people's beliefs is still a subject of debate. Traditionally, the specialized professions in China tended to have a collective nature that was highly regional, and thus the mutual assistance provided by these local fraternal organizations enabled professions to extend the scope of their influence. These organizations, however, may also have increased the independence and closed nature of their trades.

Another type of grassroots social organization, one very different from these local, trade-based fraternal organizations, was the popular religious movement, of which there were a great many during the Qing. One of the larger and more open movements was the cult of Mazu, which was especially strong in southern China, since it originally developed in Quanzhou Prefecture, in Fujian. During the Song dynasty, there was a female deity, said to have been a woman named Lin Moniang living on the island of Meizhou just off the coast of Fujian. Although she was initially a protector deity for sailors and fishermen, the way in which she was regarded changed gradually, and she became a maternal goddess. The Mazu temples of Fujian and Taiwan developed into a broad network, establishing subsidiary temples through a system known as "division of incense" (fenxiang), which linked these temples together in branches resembling a genealogical tree. As a result, the Mazu temples became important centers of community social life. In the areas where the worship of Mazu was strong, there would be regularly scheduled religious activities called "making the rounds" (xunjing), which combined elements of pilgrimage, procession, and social gathering, thereby strengthening the sense of local identity through a community of believers. Using these and other religious activities, local leaders could build up both their own influence and the cooperative spirit of the worshipers. Thus these religious communities formed social entities through which the local residents cooperated on a range of activities from water rights to charitable works, which bound the communities into more unified economic bodies. The traditional system of local markets in China had its basis in just such local social structures.

The "division of incense" system for establishing new Mazu temples created a network that extended from Tianjin and Yantai in northern China as far south as the ports of Southeast Asia that were home to communities of overseas Chinese. These areas, though widely separated, were all places frequented by people from Fujian and Taiwan who made their living from the sea and thus made offerings at Mazu temples. As a consequence, the ability to mobilize manpower or finances that derived from connections within this vast network exercised a great social influence.

Similar religious systems, large and small and centered on other deities, were spread broadly over China. Some of the larger sects in the north were those devoted to the Dragon Kings (*longwang*), who ruled the seas of the four cardinal directions, or the goddess of Mount Tai, called the Primordial Goddess of the Morning Clouds (*Bixia Yuanjun*). In the south were devotees of Xu Zhenjun (Xu Sun, 239–374), a Daoist immortal whose cult had been popular as early as the Tang. Overall, these believers were connected to a vast network of other believers through their pilgrimage activities. With the smaller sects, in a local region there could be groups of believers in a certain deity who would participate in the temple associations or attend the regular festivals, thereby cultivating distinctly local activities. For example, in Wuxi, in addition to the blacksmiths' offerings to Huo De, the birthday of another deity, Zhang Dadi, was celebrated jointly by members of all the other sects, thereby strengthening the communal sense of local identity.

The effects of geography, commerce, and religious activities combined in this way to foster a strong sense of localism, which provided a social identity that became an alternative to the nationalism of imperial power. As a result, the strength of this local social cohesion could impede the efforts of the central government to control a region, even to the extent of nullifying the exercise of government power.

Another form of social power that became much more apparent during the Qing was the interaction between religious believers and the development of religious sects that had great political effects beyond their influence on local culture. Though Confucianism certainly embodied a strong sense of religious belief, its teachings and rituals made clear the extent to which it was an orthodox doctrine of the central government.

Government power was firmly held by the alliance of imperial power with the influence of Confucian scholars who had risen through the ranks of official examinations and the bureaucracy. The other two religions of China, Buddhism and Daoism, were fundamentally otherworldly; after a period of accommodation and change, the orthodox sects of Buddhism and Daoism had become thoroughly accustomed to coexistence and working within the framework of the central government.

Among the common people, a great variety of religious beliefs had arisen and blended with one another since the Song dynasty. One of the earlier of these syncretic movements was the Xiajiao sect, founded by Lin Zhaoen in the late Ming, which sought to combine Confucianism, Daoism, and Buddhism. The strength of this melding of China's three main teachings can be seen in essentially all of the subsequent popular religions. The combination of Confucian ethical principles, Buddhist teachings on the karma of reincarnation, and the Daoist cosmology and emphasis on physical cultivation produced a broad religious outlook that permeated the worldview of almost all the Chinese peoples. The popular sects more familiar today, even those outside of China such as the Tenrikyo of Japan or the I-Kuan Dao in Taiwan, could all be said to be descendents of this great syncretic movement of Chinese religions. During the Qing, one of the most popular types of printed material was the morality tract, and the most widespread of these was the *Treatise on Actions and Their Retributions (Taishang ganyingpian)*, another example of the syncretism of Chinese popular religions.

Beyond this combination of the three main Chinese religious traditions, popular religions in the Qing included even more complex sets of beliefs influenced by Zoroastrianism and Manichaeism. These messianic religions had entered China from Central Asia very early on and thus they also had a long period in which to accommodate themselves to the central government. Their notions of fate and redemption permeated Buddhism at a very early date, influencing the formation of Maitreyan sects, which emphasized the coming of a future Buddha. Their influence also extended to figures that bridged the gap between humans and deities, such as the Daoist "immortal" Li Babai. This messianic tendency also underlay the Northern Song popular uprising of Fang La in southern China. At the end of the Yuan dynasty, the uprising led by Han Lin-er (d. 1366) that was to lead to the establishment of the Ming dynasty was based on Zoroastrianism (*Mingjiao*). During the Qing there was a similar series of very active secret religious societies collectively referred to as the White Lotus Society, all of which were severely repressed by the government as they arose. The large-scale White Lotus Rebellion of more than ten million people, which began during the Qianlong reign in 1796, was initially spread over Sichuan, Hubei, and Shaanxi. The Qing court dispatched large armies in an effort to control the situation, but religious believers continued to arise, and the military campaign to put down this revolt lasted over ten years before finally achieving peace. Although the rebels relinquished control of their territory, the sect moved underground and continued to emerge from time to time. Then, in 1813, during the Jiaqing reign, the Heavenly Principle sect (*Tianlijiao*) revolt led by Li Wencheng in Hebei, Shandong, and Henan provinces gathered enough support to endanger Beijing. The late nineteenth-century Boxer Rebellion was also a descendent of the White Lotus Society.

The White Lotus Society's teachings included the apocalyptic belief that the Maitreya Buddha would return to the world, at which point the forces of light would conquer the forces of darkness. Though superficially similar, this dualistic view was in fact entirely different from the traditional Chinese view of the complementarity between Yin and Yang (dark and light forces), because the traditional view held that these two opposites were mutually cooperative and productive. The White Lotus Society, similar to Zoroastrian or Manichean sects, had a belief in what it called the "Three Ultimates," which were the three worlds of the green, red, and white Yang principles, also representing the three times of past, present, and future. The green Yang was personified by the Buddha of the past, Randeng (Sanskrit, Dipankara); the red Yang by the Buddha of the Present, Sakyamuni; and the white Yang by the Buddha of the Future, Maitreya. Each of these three epochs had a certain ability to relieve mortal sufferings, bringing to the Way those who did good and sending evildoers to their just punishments. This doctrine of the three epochs resembles the Buddhist notion of past, present, and future times, each represented by a manifestation of the Buddha. However, the traditional Buddhist understanding is that there were seven Buddhas of the past, none of whom had the name Randeng. Since the two characters in the name of this White Lotus deity both indicate brightness, it appears that his name is similar to the reverence for fire or light in Zoroastrianism. Moreover, the White Lotus concepts and symbolism were not simply received from Zoroastrianism whole; rather, they were a form of revealed teach-

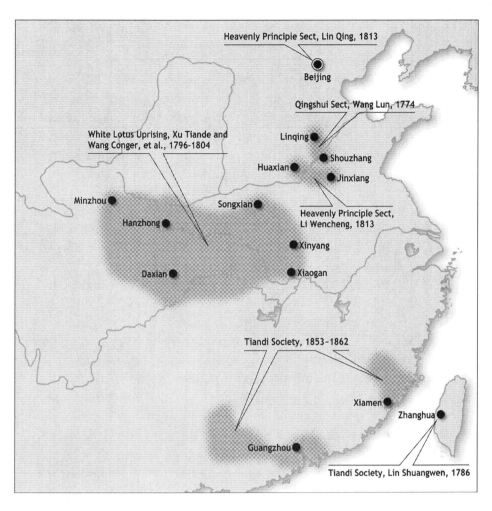

FIGURE 7.4 Map of Qing Dynasty Popular Religious Rebellions

ing that combined several aspects of traditional religions. For example, the White Lotus Society propagated the two-part notion of "the Eternal Progenitor and the realm of True Emptiness," the first part of which is derived from the *Laozi* and the second part from the Buddhist view that "all transmigration comes to an end, and all things are empty." Moreover, the White Lotus moral code is essentially that of Confucian ethical principles. Overall, we can see how this popular religious sect blended many strains from diverse religions. It was not a logically consistent philosophy that appealed to the educated upper classes, but its doctrines had a magnetism that could, and indeed did, draw in great masses of the common people.

Though the early nineteenth-century White Lotus Rebellion that arose during the Jiaqing reign was successfully suppressed, its adherents scattered to hide themselves throughout China, and they continued to develop under the cover of local religious sects. The I-Kuan Tao (Yiguan Dao, the Pervasive Truth) sect, now popular in Taiwan, is one example of this. According to this group's own explanation of their tradition, it was originally called the Xiantiandao (Way of Former Heaven), and its teachings include the notion of the "Eternal Progenitor and the realm of True Emptiness," along with other doctrines apparently derived from the White Lotus Society. In addition, the combination of Confucianism, Daoism, and Buddhism is also central to their doctrine. The connection between this sect and the White Lotus Society groups is further demonstrated by the fact that in 1802, while the White Lotus Rebellion was raging in Sichuan, Hubei, and Hunan, twelve of the founders of the Xiantiandao sect were banished to Guizhou, indicating that it had begun activities under this name by that time. It was at this point that the Yiguan Dao sect began to proselytize actively in Sichuan, Hubei, Hunan, and Fujian. In 1831, the Xiantiandao was also suppressed, and its leader, Chen Bin (fl. 1830s) was exiled to the frontier to serve in the army. In the years from 1843 to 1845, the Xiantiandao suffered severe persecution, and many of its leaders were put to death. This brief sketch of but one of the Qing popular religious sects indicates their remarkable ability to change names to avoid government persecution, permitting them to spread and evolve.

The Yiguan Dao has continued to develop in Taiwan and other areas of the world and currently has no fewer than a million adherents. If we consider the way in which it developed as a means to understand the organization and form of activities of the White Lotus sects at that time, it would appear that the many branches of the White Lotus Society could have developed independently into their own sects without the restrictions of a central organization. All of the sectarian branches could then shape themselves according to requirements of the areas where they were located. Their thinking could be profound or shallow, their doctrines complex or simple; their only common point was an adherence to a vegetarian diet. This type of gradual development that put down deep roots wherever it went was one of the hallmarks of Chinese popular religions.

When we consider the development of the White Lotus Society from its origins in the Song dynasty down through the Qianlong and Jiaqing reigns of the Qing and then through its later transformations, we can see that it was a social force whose importance would be difficult to overestimate.

Another direction in which popular religion developed during the Qing was the Heaven and Earth Society (Tiandihui), which sought to overturn the Qing and restore the Ming dynasty. The first large-scale activity of the Tiandihui in Taiwan was the rebellion led by Lin Shuangwen in 1786, which continued for over a year and managed to take over almost the entire island before the Qing court dispatched a large army to suppress it. From this point on, the activities of the Tiandihui or its branches continued uninterrupted. During the reign of the Xianfeng emperor (r. 1851–1862), the Taiping Rebellion was closely connected with the Tiandihui, although it was a movement on a massive scale that—at least nominally—worshipped the Christian God. Moreover, the early revolutionary movement of Sun Yat-sen (1866–1925), itself a militarized secret society, was in fact composed of the local chapters of the Tiandihui, which was sometimes referred to as the Hongmen.

The doctrines and slogans of the Tiandihui clearly reflect its desire to overthrow the Qing and return the Ming dynasty to power. Its activities were mostly in the southern provinces such as Hubei, Hunan, Fujian, and Guangdong, though they also extended to Southeast Asia and the overseas Chinese communities in North America. According to this association's own account of its rise, after the Shaolin temple had been destroyed by Qing troops as they were suppressing the Xilufan Rebellion, the Shaolin monks did not return their arms and instead attempted to seek retribution on the Qing. Although this account is difficult to verify, what is certain is that after Qing power had been thoroughly established, groups of Ming loyalists were driven underground. Thus, the Tiandihui was highly secretive and protected itself by employing a highly complex series of passwords and rituals. Its membership was primarily composed of a broad range of working-class people such as farmers, tradesmen, soldiers, and others, though there were also a few Confucian gentry. Although the Tiandihui associations were scattered and went under other names, such as the Hongmen, when members traveled they could be assured that the brotherhood would provide them with shelter and protection. Determining the actual numbers involved in the Hongmen is extremely difficult, since divulging that kind of information during the Qing would have meant breaking a solemn vow, and even for the Republican period, figures are difficult to obtain. But the gradual growth of power in this deeply rooted and extensive popular organization was clear for all to see.

Another of the Qing popular organizations, one that differed in several aspects from the Hongmen-Tiandihui network, went under several names, primarily the Water-Transport League (Caobang, Anqingbang, or just Qingbang, the Green Gang). During the Qing, the northern city of Beijing continued to be supplied with rice from the southern agricultural regions by barges plying the Grand Canal. The bargemen along this route, numbering in the tens of thousands, had a guild-based sect of Daoism that honored a Ming-dynasty founder, Luozu. As the Caobang writings describe its own origins, there were three clans of bargemen, surnamed Qian, Fan, and Weng, that controlled shipping on the Grand Canal. According to tradition, the Qing government was afraid that if control of this shipping fell into the hands of the Hongmen, it could be enough to bring the dynasty to its knees, so it relied on the Caobang to protect this vital transportation link. Subsequently, the membership of this organization expanded greatly to include various forms of land and water transport, as well as inns, teahouses, taverns, and other businesses along these routes. Its codes and passwords used for communications and to identify members were closely guarded secrets, no less than those of the Hongmen. The subordinate routes within each region maintained their autonomy, without an overall national organization. The Caobang and the Hongmen organizations appear to have maintained a long-term agreement for their mutual coexistence, and there is a saying, "Like the red flowers, green leaves, and white lotus roots, the three families both spring from the same source." In this sentence, red stands for Hongmen and green for Qingbang; the lotus roots indicate their historical connection to the earlier White Lotus Society. The actual relationships between these groups are now almost impossible to penetrate, but we can see that these popular secret societies in fact relied on one another for their mutual protection from the Qing government authorities.

In sum, local societies during the Qing included three broad types: groups from a common place of origin, religious sects, and secret societies. At the same time, these three types are difficult to discuss individually, since in actual practice most societies combined at least two of these aspects. For example, the organizations for people with a common place of origin were also connected with temples for religious ceremonies. The

offerings to the protector deities of certain professions were both cooperative and competitive; both were interlaced with the activities of hometown
organizations and were part of the underground cults and secret societies.
All of these organizations existed in a world apart from that recorded in
the official histories, in an environment that was forbidden and seldom
spoken of openly. In contrast to the traditional arrangement of government power in China, which is a pyramidal system, these popular societies were based on an organic network of roots and branches. The social
space of these two worlds was very different, and while each could develop
to some degree independently in its own directions, they were not necessarily mutually exclusive. Though organizations of the common people
have been a facet of the social life of China from early times, their activities were much more apparent during the Qing dynasty.

6. China's Diplomatic Relations with European Nations

China's interchange with the West during the mid-Qing dynasty occurred
through overland and maritime movements of people and goods. Unlike
other European nations at this time, Russia's relationship with China was
based almost exclusively on contact by land, and during the reigns of the
Kangxi, Yongzheng, and Qianlong emperors, Russia was in fact the nation
with the most significant foreign relations with China.

Russia's drive to the east, which had begun in the late sixteenth century,
extended toward China from the Ural Mountains, until Russia had gradually assumed control over Siberia. Four centuries earlier, after the Mongols had swept westward to the edges of Europe, the lands that Chinggis
Qaghan left to his eldest son, Jochi (ca. 1185–1227), covered most of the
territory within the current borders of Russia. Jochi's son Batu Qaghan
(c. 1205–1255) established the Kipchak khanate, sometimes referred to as
the Golden Horde, to rule over this area. The Mongols never developed
an effective form of government for their khanates, and as a result this
large territory disintegrated step by step into smaller autonomous areas.
As that occurred, the Slavic nobles on the western front of the Kipchak
khanate gradually reassumed power. From the fifteenth through the sixteenth centuries, under the control of Ivan III (Ivan the Great, r. 1462–
1505) and his grandson Ivan IV (Ivan the Terrible, r. 1533–1584), Russia
took shape as a nation with a centralized government. Then in 1613, at the

beginning of the Romanov dynasty, Russia began to expand its boundaries, with the goal of becoming the leading nation of Eastern Europe. The main events of this process took place during the reigns of Peter the Great (r. 1689–1725) and Catherine the Great (r. 1762–1796).

Although Russia focused most of its expansionist energies toward the West and its European culture and toward the south, to obtain ports in the Baltic and Crimean seas, in those directions it met determined opposition from Sweden and the Ottoman Empire, respectively. To the east, however, it encountered little opposition, and by seizing the vast reaches of Siberia, it extended its control to the Pacific Ocean. There were several factors responsible for the ease with which Russia expanded eastward. The first was that Siberia is composed primarily of northern forests quite different from the Mongol steppes, which made it of less interest to the Mongols and China to the south. The Mongol Yuan dynasty had referred to the local tribes, such as the Buryats or the Yakuts, as "peoples of the forests," and even though these tribes lived on the frontiers of the Mongol herders, the Yuan administration never considered them to be of any importance. Moreover, following the Wanli (1572–1620) era of the Ming, the Mongol political power had disintegrated to the point that over the entire range of the steppes there was not a single leader capable of commanding a substantial following. With the Siberian peoples fragmented into individual territories, there was no power capable of stemming the Russian incursion.

This Russian expansion to the east was initially motivated by commercial concerns. The northern forests of Siberia were home to many fur-bearing animals, such as sable, fox, bear, and deer, whose pelts were valuable commodities in the European markets. Wealthy Russian merchants allied themselves with the landowning nobility, called boyars, and supported by Cossack cavalry they moved to claim the eastern lands. The Cossacks had originally lived in the central Russian river basins of the Don and the Volga, one of the steppe regions of Eastern Europe. Their lifestyle could accommodate itself to conditions in the eastern regions, and by this time the increasing strength of the Russian central government had reduced the Cossack tribesmen to the status of mercenary cavalrymen, making them ideal candidates for the military vanguard of Russia's westward expansion.

In 1579, the Cossack leader Ermak Timofeeyvich was subsidized by the wealthy Stroganov merchant family to lead an expeditionary force of mounted Cossacks armed with Western firearms westward into Siberia. As a result of this and subsequent campaigns, by the mid-seventeenth century Russia had established its control over Siberia. Subsequently, in 1618 a diplomatic mission led by Ivan Petlin left the Russian-controlled area of southwestern Siberia on its way to China. Passing through the Chinese trading post of Jiangjiakou on the northwestern border of Hebei, they entered Beijing, the first diplomatic envoy from Russia to enter China. In 1649, Yerofey Khabarov (1603–ca. 1671) led an expedition down the Amur River, even establishing the fortified town of Albazin, where this river meets the Pacific Ocean. At this time, the Manchus had just recently moved south to take control over China as the Qing dynasty and thus were not concerned with the Russian expansion to their north. Though diplomatic relations had not yet been established, trade was beginning to flourish, with the Chinese exporting tea and spices in addition to large amounts of silk and cotton, while the Russians sent back furs, silver, and gold.

After establishing Albazin in 1652, over the next ten years the Russians also built a fort and a town at the river port of Nerchinsk. With Russia continually pressing to extend its influence and control, the potential for border conflicts with China began to increase.

After suppressing the three main uprisings of Ming loyalists, the Qing court at last turned its attention to the danger of Russia's encroachment on Manchuria and in 1685 sent troops to drive the Russians from Albazin. This was the first military engagement between China and a European nation. Four years later, the Russians sent a diplomatic mission to China to negotiate peace and determine their national boundaries in the Amur region. These negotiations resulted in Treaty of Nerchinsk, signed in 1689, requiring the Russians to dismantle their settlement at Albazin. This was the first time that China had signed a treaty with a Western nation, and the treaty was written in both Manchu and Russian—although Latin was used for the formal version, as the Manchu envoys had used Jesuits as their translators with the Russians.

After concluding the Treaty of Nerchinsk, Russia sent several missions to China to discuss details for opening up further trade and to resolve finally matters relating to the boundary between the two countries. Following the subsequent Treaty of Kyatkha in 1727, the Chinese allowed cross-border trade, but only at the single city of Kyatkha, and to settle the border, the Qing court had to concede a large area of steppes, now known as Tuva in Russia, that lies to the northwest of Mongolia. The Qing court also permitted Russia to establish an embassy in Beijing. This embassy compound included a Russian Orthodox church, and it allowed Russian students to become more skilled in the Chinese language. The diplomatic parties from Russia could reach Beijing by two routes, a northern one through Siberia and a southern one through Mongolia that reached Beijing via the city of Zhangjiakou in northern Hebei. Although the Qing court now allowed trade at the border, when the diplomatic missions entered China, this did not open the Beijing market to Russian merchants. The Sino-Russian trade that did develop was, however, highly profitable for the Russian side. In the trading done at the border city of Kyatkha, on the northern, Siberian route, the Chinese offered mainly silk, cotton, and herbs; Russian exports included woolens, furs, livestock, and iron items. By the end of the eighteenth century, the trade with China had expanded to the point where it was responsible for fully 25 percent of Russia's customs duties.

Apart from the official foreign affairs described above, Russia still maintained designs to expand the sphere of its influence. The Dzungars, one of the Oirat tribes of Mongolia, were militarily the strongest and had their homelands in the far western reaches of China, now western Mongolia. The Qing dynasty had several times successfully attacked Khalkha tribes of the northern Gobi and Dorbod tribes of the southern Gobi. But despite numerous military campaigns throughout the Kangxi, Yongzheng, and Qianlong reigns, the Dzungars could not be similarly suppressed. In fact, the reinforcements that permitted the Dzungars to maintain their resistance were being furnished by Russia, as were most of their firearms. The Turghuts, another of the Oirat Mongol tribes, who pastured their flocks along the lower reaches of the Volga to the west of modern-day Kazakhstan, were under great stress because of the eastward movement of Russian forces, who pressed the Turghuts into slavery. Thus in 1770, during the Qianlong reign, the Qing court allowed almost two hundred thousand of these tribespeople to move eastward into Chinese territory and settle west of the Gobi. These complex conflicts and relocations of people are one of the indications of the frictions that were growing between China and Russia, even though they had established diplomatic relations.

Apart from these simmering conflicts, relations between China and Russia during the Kangxi reign generally were relatively stable, as both parties were clear as to the other's situation. Toward the end of the Kangxi reign, in 1712, the Qing court sent a party under the Manchu official Ayan Gioro Tulišen (1667–1741) into Russia to investigate conditions there. Three years after his return to China, Tulišen published his famous travel observations on Russia's geography, culture, and products. Following this, Tulišen participated in Sino-Russian exchanges and became one of the foreign-policy experts of that period. Similarly, Russia sent numerous groups to China to obtain detailed information and report back to Russia. Discussions between the two nations were thus based on a sufficient common ground of understanding so that they were able to negotiate effectively with each other and maintain peaceful relations despite their inherent conflicts.

In contrast, along the southern seaboard, China's relationships with Western nations had many more strains both because interchange was only by long-distance naval communication and because there were several European powers in competition for the Chinese trade. European relations toward the south initially centered around Macao, which had fallen under Portuguese control during the Ming and become the southern entry point for Europeans to China. The Jesuit scholars and missionaries who entered China during the Ming generally did so through Macao, and for many years European trading was transacted primarily there and in neighboring Guangzhou (Canton). Though trade was still limited at this point, the European understanding of China that was transmitted by these missionaries and businessmen had developed greatly by the mid-Qing, and Chinese scholars of that time had come to understand many aspects of European culture. By the beginning of the Qing, the balance of Western naval power had undergone a major transition, because the former supremacy of Spain and Portugal was being eclipsed by Holland, which had already taken over southern Taiwan as a base for their trading operations. When the Qing government retook Taiwan, the Dutch repeatedly urged that they be permitted to cooperate in a joint military presence on the island, but they were rebuffed and had difficulty finding another base close to China for their operations. It was at this point that England began to emerge as a naval power in the Far East, expanding its maritime trade vigorously. The British East India Company had much earlier established major trading centers in India, including one in Bombay, in the late seventeenth century, and by the early nineteenth century England would replace Holland and Portugal at points such as Cape Town and Singapore

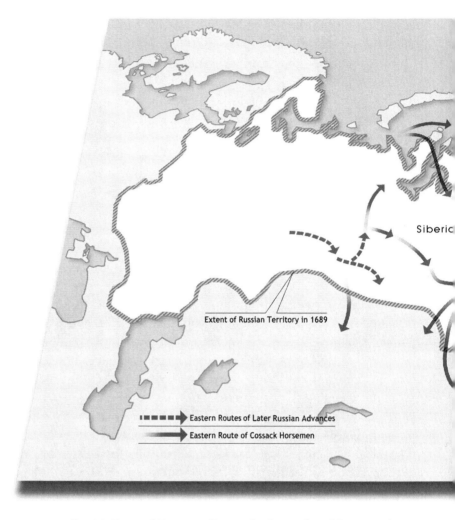

Siberia

Extent of Russian Territory in 1689

■ ■ ■ ■ ➡ Eastern Routes of Later Russian Advances
➡ Eastern Route of Cossack Horsemen

FIGURE 7.5 Russia's Eastward Expansion During the Sixteenth and Seventeenth Centuries

along the route to China. From England's standpoint, the China trade had great potential, even more than the trade with colonial India, but to access China, they needed to open a door to this trade.

In the early eighteenth century, the Qing government began to relax its ban on foreign trade, planning to designate several ports for that purpose, including Guangzhou (Canton), Xiamen (Amoy), and Ningbo. In 1755, during the early Qianlong reign, a British East India Company fleet

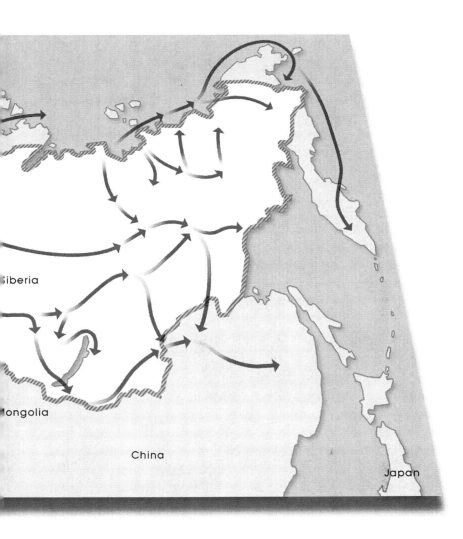

Siberia

Mongolia

China

Japan

reached the southern coast of China and took advantage of this new openness by refitting their vessels at Ningbo and completing their trading there. The next year, English ships returned, this time with a request that they be permitted to establish a permanent base at Ningbo. The Qing government would not accede to this and permitted trading only at Guangzhou. Shortly afterward, the English merchant James Flint sailed to Tianjing in an attempt to appeal directly to the Qing court for a relaxation of trade restrictions in the southern ports. For this violation of protocol by appealing directly to the emperor, in 1759 the Qianlong emperor severely punished his officials in Guangdong, condemned Flint to a three-year jail term in Macao, and then expelled him from China after his sentence had been served.

Following this, the Qing court promulgated a set of regulations for foreign traders to prevent them from creating further disturbances: by imperial edict, foreign trade was to be restricted to Guangzhou (Canton). Though other European countries such as France, Germany, Holland, Sweden, and Demark were also involved in the China trade, Britain's share was far greater, and it continued to press strongly for permission to establish permanent bases for its envoys. There was a broad range of Chinese export goods that the European traders were competing for at this time, including silk, porcelain, and other handicrafts, not to mention tea; Chinese imports were primarily limited to spices and silver.

By the latter part of the eighteenth century, England's Industrial Revolution was largely complete, and international exports were vital if England was to maintain its economic expansion, which made the potential Chinese market especially important. In 1792, King George III of Great Britain accepted the suggestion of the British East India Company and dispatched Sir George Macartney (1737–1806), an experienced diplomat and colonial administrator, as the head of a diplomatic party to China aboard a British man-of-war. When they arrived in Beijing in 1793, Qianlong was seventy-two years old, and his favorite minister, Heshen (1750–1799), had already insinuated himself into many of the functions of government. It also happened that this year was the celebration for the sixtieth year of Qianlong's reign, and so the arrival of the English diplomatic party could be interpreted as homage from a foreign power to the Heavenly Emperor. Thus the Qing court treated the British mission as tribute bearers and required Macartney to submit to an extended formal ceremony of kowtowing (touching his head to the ground) before the emperor, which Macartney refused to do. Finally, to resolve this impasse, a simplified ceremony was agreed upon to permit an imperial audience for Macartney. To support mutual trade, Britain had a number of requirements: their embassy should be established in Beijing; British trading should be permitted in Ningbo, Tianjing, and Danshan, an island port in Zhejiang Province; land would be granted for residential settlements in Danshan and Guangzhou (Canton); a commercial bank would be established in Beijing; and

England would be granted preferential customs rates. These English demands were rejected out of hand by the Qing court, which declared, "There is nothing that we do not produce within the imperial kingdom; we should not permit these mere foreigners to trade with their trifles."

Relations with England were stalemated for another twenty years, until 1816, when the British government made another attempt to open diplomatic relations by sending Earl William Pitt Amherst (1773–1857) with gifts of tribute on a British warship. Again, the mission failed, at least in part because of the inability of the two sides to come to agreement on protocol for the minister's reception by the emperor, similar to the disagreements that had disrupted the Macartney mission, and Amherst had to return having penetrated no further into China than his reception at the seaport.

The inability of these two missions to begin negotiations with China was attributable on the one hand to the Manchu chauvinism of the Qing court and the imperial view that it was the holder of a heavenly mandate and, on the other hand, to the overconfidence of the British in presenting one-sided demands in the expectation that they would be readily accepted by China. Both sides were poorly informed and overconfident. The ministers of the Qianlong court had become accustomed to a very comfortable lifestyle and had little motivation to understand the situation of the world outside China—an attitude far different from the curiosity for foreign knowledge that had been displayed during the Kangxi reign. The British crown, for its part, was well aware of its colonial abilities and was accustomed to taking an arrogant attitude toward Eastern nations. It understood the situation only on the basis of the potential economic benefits, with none of the interest that the broader European intellectual community displayed for a knowledge of Chinese culture. Blind to all but their own short-term interests, Britain and China had come to an impasse in their relations.

The Macartney and Amherst missions had included a number of specialists, and during the Macartney mission's travels to and from Beijing they gathered a substantial amount of information about many aspects of Chinese society, including government policies, military equipment, troop disposition, and economic production. This gave Britain a more detailed and realistic understanding of China and made it aware that the great Qing empire, though it had passed through more than a century of prosperity and stability, had now begun to decline from its former strength and vigor. It could no longer succeed in warding off the greater economic and military might of the European nations. Thus, England's next step would be to break down the door of Chinese exclusionism with military coercion, using gunboat diplomacy to force China into accepting its one-sided demands so it could profit from the Chinese markets.

When we compare the process of the Anglo-Chinese negotiations with that between Russia and China, the great difference is clear: so much depended on how well both sides understood the other. The mutual misunderstandings between the Chinese and the English were numerous, and most of them stemmed from each party's overestimation of its own position. An earlier China, at the time of Kangxi, when the basis of diplomacy with Russia was established, had been better able to understand itself and the other party and to handle foreign relations according to pragmatic concerns. In contrast, burdened by his own exaggerated sense of self-importance, the Qianlong emperor had difficulty effectively relating to foreign powers. Though the Qianlong era is generally considered one of China's periods of great strength, the progressive decay that was to plague the nation for the next century had already begun. In China's earlier contacts with Russia, it had been dealing with a nation not unlike itself: if not an equal, at least on the same plane. But when it faced Britain, it was confronted with a nation that had a far different concept of imperial foreign relations.

7. Qing Domestic Trade

During the late Qing dynasty, European navies linked Asia and the West, permitting the flow of silver into China from mines in the Americas in return for the products of East Asia. This marks the beginning of a truly global world economic system. Within China, the primary beneficiary of this development was the southeast, which saw a dramatic increase in prosperity. The economic activities of the Qing dynasty were built upon the foundations of the Ming, which is generally considered the most economically advanced period of Chinese history, comparable to the high point of mercantilism in the West.

Economic activities during the Qing can be considered from the standpoint of the domestic and the international markets, and we will first discuss the expansion of China's internal markets and their complexity. By the late Ming, China had already introduced New World food crops such as corn, sweet potatoes, potatoes, and peanuts, which enabled agriculture in mountainous or lowland areas unsuitable for the cultivation of rice or wheat. This permitted a movement of peoples to upland and river areas to the west, and thus the Qing population grew rapidly, as influenced also by other factors discussed in section 2 of this chapter.

With this expansion of the population, production for the consumer market increased accordingly, as did the overall economic system. The Qing dynasty's receipts from the salt tax were a significant item in the national revenue for two reasons: first, because apart from the land tax, the government had very few other sources of tax revenue, and, second, because it was such a broadly used commodity. As the population increased, salt consumption went up proportionally, and the receipts from salt levies are thus data by which we can measure population growth. These increased salt levies clearly reflect the expanding Qing economic system.

When the Qing brought the Tibetan and Mongolian peoples under their control, this put an end to the long-term border threats on the north and east, and the border tribes of these two regions began a process of centralization. With these new peaceful relations, the economies of these areas began to connect with China's domestic market. In the mountainous regions of the southwest, Han Chinese moved in to settle along the roadways that led to the outside world, clearing the bamboo forests and opening the land for agriculture. As these Han Chinese became established in this new territory, the native peoples were influenced by Chinese culture, and with the gradual changes to their lifestyles, they increasingly relied on the Han Chinese for implements of daily life. The island of Taiwan, though not large, helped relieve the population pressure from China's overcrowded southern coastal areas. These regions of the northwestern border, the mountainous southwest, and Taiwan thus were annexed to become parts of the greater Chinese economic system.

The broad and sparsely populated spaces of the northeast, however, were the homeland of the ruling Manchus, and in principle the Qing government forbade entrance to Han Chinese. Nevertheless, the Manchu princes and nobility still needed to recruit non-Manchu laborers to work on the grazing lands of their country estates that enabled them to preserve their aristocratic way of life. Although the northeast never formed a major part of the economy in Qing China, agricultural workers from north-central China, particularly the Shandong peninsula, gradually moved into the northeast as its importance grew.

The Ming disturbances along the coastal areas gradually simmered down after the Qing had retaken Taiwan and the Qing navy began to suppress the last bands of pirates and other armed bands. The raids of Cai Qian (1761–1809) on Taiwan during the first decade of the nineteenth century were the last maritime insurrection. From the beginning of the Qianlong reign, peace was established in the southeastern coastal regions, and these settled conditions helped to ensure further the safety of the shipping lanes. The situation with overland transport was similar; communications between Mongol regions and the center of China were safe, though the routes north and south to and from the Mongolian steppes were rugged. Communication to the east and west was easier, and major trade routes were established leading west from the Mongolian border. These routes were economically important, especially since they connected to the Gansu corridor that had formed the northern route of the Silk Road as early as the Tang dynasty. Since the Qing government continued the policy of gradually replacing the original social structures of the mountainous southwest with local Han administrations, this area continued to develop urban centers. As the network of smaller roads branching off the trade routes expanded, safer commerce was greatly facilitated. Naturally, the opening and improvement of these land and sea routes benefited China's internal communications as well as its commercial exchange.

The example of cotton fabric can illustrate the complex interactions that determined the movement of goods in China's domestic markets. During the Qing dynasty, cotton fabric and goods woven from it were an important commodity on the domestic market. Since the everyday clothing of the common people was made from cotton fabric, there was a great deal of it sold. Though most of the raw cotton fiber produced in China was from the northern plain, the southern climate was much better for the spinning and weaving process, since higher humidity made the cotton fibers relax and become more elastic. The movement of raw cotton from the north to the south and finished cotton fabric from the south to consumer markets over all of China was one of the major items of trade at this time. (Cotton fabric was also produced in the Shandong region, but its quality was far below that of the south.)

Another of the main items in the domestic trade was grain. Although Jiangnan was principally a rice-producing area, the cotton-weaving industry siphoned off a large amount of the available labor force, and given the region's increased population, its own rice production was not sufficient for the local market. It was thus necessary to bring rice from Hubei and Hunan to feed the people, and shipping rice downstream from the middle reaches of the Yangzi also became another significant economic activity of the domestic market.

One of the main factors in foreign trade at this time was the large amounts of silver entering China as payment for its exports, since in China silver was traditionally the standard precious metal. Given the large scale of this trade, almost 60 percent of the silver mined in North and South America made its way into China. Thanks to its long-term favorable balance of trade, China accumulated a substantial surplus of silver that could be used for currency. Silver was generally used for higher denominations of currency, but it was not convenient for coins in daily use, which were generally of copper. Japan produced copper during the Tokugawa period (1603–1867), and although the Tokugawa shogunate had officially imposed a policy of cutting Japan off from foreign trade, Chinese commercial ships could obtain special authorizations for limited trading. The more than seven hundred thousand kilograms of copper annually brought into China from Japan to use for minting currency is an indication of the great scale of the Chinese market.

There are three main reasons for the great size of the Qing economic system: the greater population and expanded area of cultivated land; the great increase in urbanization, especially since a higher density of urban centers was required to make the market system function effectively for the distribution of goods; and the separate road networks that were connected together and extended, substantially increasing the speed and density of the routes for distribution of raw materials. These factors enabled the Qing economy to continue growing for over a hundred years.

International trade was also much more active during the Qing than during the Ming. As discussed above, the overland trade routes from North China helped to pacify the Mongol borderlands and unify the central region. China's export goods, such as brick tea and woven fabrics, could pass through Mongol regions and then be transported along the roadways that crossed the steppes. After crossing the Russian border, they could be transported to the markets of Eastern and Central Europe. The formal treaties between the Qing government and Russia negotiated during the Kangxi reign all had clauses to regulate trade and establish designated points of entry, such as Kyatkha. As an indication of the volume of trade over this east-west route, there were thousands of camel caravans in peak years.

Furthermore, tea's movement into Europe via land from North China is reflected by the way European languages use two different sounds to refer to tea—*cha* (*chai* in Russian) from the northern Chinese dialect and the English "tea" from southern dialects.

For maritime international trade, the Qing government dictated that Guangzhou (Canton) should be the primary port of entry. Although other cities such as Ningbo also had harbor facilities, the Qing government was unwilling for them to be used for international trade. This restriction of foreign relations was similar to the intransigence that characterized China's reaction to the Macartney mission and other diplomatic negotiations with European countries at that time. Though this insistence by the Qing government was outwardly based on the need to control the "foreign barbarians," the close relations between the court and the Chinese trading houses in Guangdong were actually more important: these companies were unwilling to relinquish any of their profitable special privileges. With the establishment of sea routes to China from Europe, merchants from several European nations arrived in succession; the Spanish, Portuguese, and Dutch, and then the English gradually assumed positions of dominance. Apart from traditional goods such as silk and porcelain, the English merchants also brought back tea, which was shipped to both Europe and the colonies in North America.

Since the sea route was not as long and arduous for transporting heavy porcelain goods, and as with proper packing there was less danger of breakage than when shipped overland, despite the danger of shipwreck a substantial volume of porcelain was transported by ship, and porcelain made up a large portion of the total amount of goods shipped by sea. In addition to porcelains from the famous kilns of Jiangxi or Zhejiang, goods produced in Guangzhou also included glazed ware from Guangdong and Fujian. Guangzhou production was primarily devoted to goods for the European market, decorated according to European tastes and in China considered to be lower-grade commercial wares. Many of the artisans who decorated these pieces were in fact from Europe, and so Western artistic traditions entered China through Guangdong, marking the beginning of what was to become the artistic style of Guangdong.

For internal trade, in addition to the general characteristics of the markets for individual products, as these markets expanded and the regional goods became more specialized, local manufacturers invested further in developing these regional specialties. Thus the division of labor needed to produce these goods further increased the trade of these regions. As one example, Shanxi produced both copper and vinegar, and when copper is exposed to vinegar, a green product called verdigris (copper carbonate or copper chloride) forms on surface. After it is scraped off, it can be used as a dye for fabric. The businessmen of Shanxi then purchased ferromanganese alloy from Sichuan to make a red dye and thereby began to develop an independent business in dyestuffs that were marketed throughout China under well-known brand names. One of the most famous of these enterprises was the Xiyuecheng Dye Company of Pingyao, better known as the first Qing banking institution (*piaohao*).

The rise of commerce during the Qing dynasty was one of the reasons for the development of the ten major commercial leagues (*shangbang*) at this time, of which those of Shanxi and Huizhou were the strongest. The ways in which two of these leagues developed indicate the main characteristics of Qing commerce.

Shanxi's broad central plain is generally dry, poorly irrigated, and surrounded by mountain ranges. Because it is not part of the major road network, communication is difficult and internal commerce limited. The surprising success of the Shanxi trading league (*Jinbang*), which eventually surpassed the other trading leagues of the time can be attributed to the commercial activities of these merchants in areas of China outside their home base. The origins of this league can be traced back to Ming efforts to supply their nine divisions of frontier troops, for which they set up a system of "salt certificates" that had to be purchased before selling salt and also enlisted trading families to transport supplies to frontier garrisons. Since the northern garrisons of Datong and Xunfu and the western garrisons of Shanxi and Yulin were closer to Shanxi, these merchants could lease land just within the Great Wall to grow supplies for the military, thereby saving on the cost of transportation to the garrisons while also making substantial profits on the "salt certificates" obtained through the government. Using this as capital, the Shanxi merchants made further profits on the shipping of salt and brick tea, buying hides, leather, and draught animals in the Mongol border regions to send back to the internal regions. Thus, the influence of these Shanxi traders was felt over all the northern border regions.

During the rapid rise of the Manchus, Nurhaci (r. 1616–1626), who was to become the first Qing emperor, required large volumes of provisions for his troops, and the assistance of Shanxi merchants in transporting supplies from the interior regions was essential. As a result, when the Manchus had taken control of China, there were eight clans of Shanxi merchants that received the status of imperial businesses to use in their activities on the Mongol trading routes. Since there were no longer armed conflicts between the Mongols and China, garrison cities mostly devoted to trading in tea and horses sprang up along these routes, also providing waystations for travelers and further assisting the Shanxi traders. Necessities for the Mongol aristocracy as well as the common people were all transported by these trading families.

The Shanxi commercial travelers came mainly from the cities of Pingyao, Taigu, and Qixian, but they moved rapidly over many other areas, making contacts with people who could assist them. The wealth of these Shanxi families was accumulated primarily in the form of silver, which was distributed over many areas of Qing China, especially after the Qing had suppressed the early revolts and could turn their attention to the redevelopment of commerce in their newly acquired domain. From the Jiaqing (r. 1796–1820) to the Daoguang (r. 1820–1850) emperors, the Shanxi merchants developed a network of private exchange shops, referred to as *piaohao*, which functioned first to provide commercial remittances from one area to another, making profits on the exchange rates between the silver and copper currency in various areas. These *piaohao* then expanded into providing small loans, which yielded very favorable profits. With the unsettled national conditions following the reign of the Xianfeng emperor (r. 1850–1861), these *piaohao* rendered a variety of services to assist local authorities, receiving special privileges from both the provincial and national treasuries. By the last years of the Qing, the *piaohao* were handling most types of financial affairs.

The Huibang, another of these trading leagues, was based in Wannan, a mountainous area of Anhui in the south with little arable land, surrounded by unbroken mountain ranges and traditionally described as "eight parts mountains, one part tea plantations, and one part fields." The local people, like the Shanxi traders, had to leave their home region to do business. During the Ming, there was little business that the Huibang traders did not deal in, and, in fact, they even went so far as to underwrite a rebellion during the Ming. Though Anhui is a very mountainous region, it is connected to both the Yangzi River and the Zhejiang region, which was the most economically developed area of China. During the Qing, the most profitable trade was that of salt, and the major salt shipments of the Yangzhou region were controlled by Anhui merchants. The Huibang

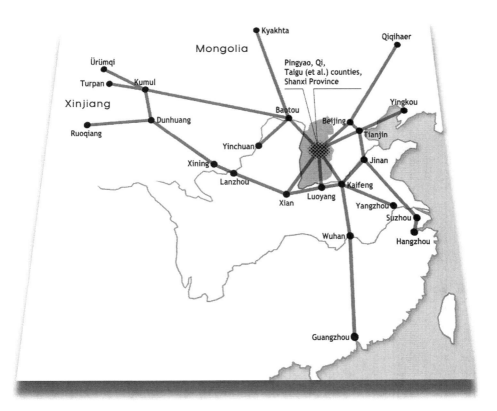

FIGURE 7.6. Major Routes of the Shanxi Traders

merchants supported one another through their network of people from the same native areas. They engaged in a great range of trades up and down the Yangzi from Sichuan to Jiangnan, as portrayed along with other Ming-dynasty business activities in the *Records of Taihan* (*Taihan ji*) by the Ming author and Huibang merchant Wang Daokun (Taihan, 1525–1593). The Anhui merchants branched out into many financial activities, the most famous being pawn brokerages (*dangpu*) that made small loans as a means of putting their excess capital into play so it could earn interest.

Interregional trade to exchange surplus goods for those in short supply and to move capital requires a system of credit and financial networks. The successful southern traders from the Wannan region were similar to their northern counterparts from Shanxi, and each of these groups had its own commercial territory. Originally constrained by limited economic opportunities in their home areas, both commercial leagues were forced

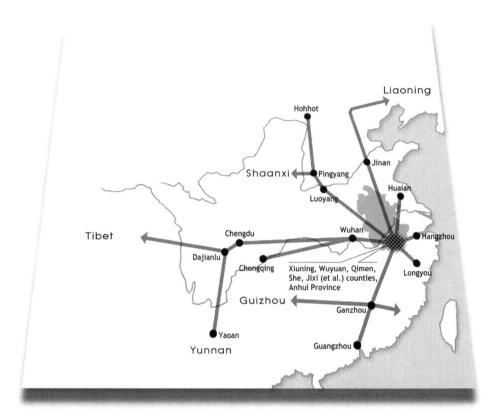

FIGURE 7.7 Major Routes of the Huizhou Traders

to seek outside opportunities. Both were characterized by flexible adaptation to a broad range of businesses, and they relied on a network of connections with people from their home territories. Both obtained substantial profits from the salt trade, and they used their personal connections with other traders to develop networks of financial exchange. The history of these two trading leagues reflects the vitality of the mid-Qing economy, and their decline during the late Qing represents the end of the traditional Chinese financial system.

8. China's Cultural Interaction with the West

The Jesuits who came to Ming China, including Matteo Ricci (1552–1610) in 1583, brought with them much contemporary Western scientific knowledge, and this was a vanguard of the greater changes to come. When the Manchu forces had taken central China and established the Qing dynasty, they continued many of the Ming policies, including support for the astronomical work of Johann Adam Schall von Bell (1592–1666). The year after the Shunzhi emperor (r. 1644–1661) was enthroned, Bell was appointed head astronomer of the Imperial Board of Astronomy. From this point on, Bell and other Jesuits, including Ferdinand Verbiest (1623–1688), were to hold this post in succession, so that it came to be seen as an accepted practice. From their training in Europe, the Jesuits were well qualified in this and other types of scientific work, including astronomy, calendrical calculations, and mapping surveys.

Communication between the Jesuits and Qing Chinese scholars, however, was not as close as it had been with the Ming scholars such as Xu Guangqi or Li Zhizao, both of whom worked closely with Matteo Ricci and even converted to Christianity. Following the death of the Shunzhi emperor, one of the regents he had appointed for Kangxi, Oboi, began to assume power. At this time, also, the anti-Christian official Yang Guang-xian (1597–1669) was vigorously opposing the work of Bell and the Jesuits who were revising the Chinese calendrical system, going so far as to bring the Jesuits to trial. In 1664, the Qing court imprisoned these scholars under the sentence of execution and ordered all of the Jesuit missionaries from other provinces to be sent to Guangdong under guard in preparation for their banishment to Macao, which would have terminated the Jesuit presence in China. But after the personal intercession of the emperor's grandmother, the Jesuits were pardoned, although some of the Chinese officials who were their converts had already been executed. The year following this pardon, the judgments that had been made against the European missionaries were reversed, and Yang Guangxian, whose rhetoric had inspired them, was executed. In 1669, at the death of von Schall, his assistant Ferdinand Verbiest (1623–1688) was appointed to replace him as director of the imperial observatory, and the other missionaries were allowed to return to their missions in the provinces. This, for a time, turned the tide of resistance to Western influence, with the debate being settled by the accuracy of the observatory's calendrical predictions; the more modern information of the Jesuits held the day against the older Chinese system.

The Kangxi emperor was himself quite fond of scholarship, took an interest in the Western-style calendar, and even personally tested the effectiveness of Western medicine. His interest in these subjects was very deep, and during this period the influence of the missionaries on the Chinese emperors was at its highest level. The conflict between Christian beliefs and traditional Chinese rituals now referred to as the Rites Controversy came to a head during the latter part of the Kangxi reign. The Jesuit's defeat in this debate within the Catholic Church was a great blow to them and to the influence of Western scholarship in China. It was a setback that would take two centuries to overcome.

Much more than simply a theological divergence, the Rites Controversy was a very clear case of cultural conflict and as such is worthy of further explanation. When Matteo Ricci and the other early Jesuit missionaries began their work in China, it was necessary to translate all of the Christian terminology into a language that lacked certain similar concepts. Initially, two words in common Chinese use, *tian* (heaven) and *zhu* (lord), were combined to indicate the Christian monotheistic God; later, the Chinese classical terms for the highest god, *tian* or *Shangdi*, were also used to refer to the Christian God. In addition, the early Jesuit missionaries did not forbid their converts from making offerings to Confucius or their ancestors, considering that both of these were ceremonies of commemoration rather than religious observances. By the late Ming, missionaries from the Dominican order, which had long been in competition with the Jesuits, also entered China to proselytize. The Dominicans were deeply opposed to both the Jesuit translations and their permissiveness toward Chinese traditional rituals, and at the Vatican they accused the Jesuits of perverting religious doctrine. This conflict between orders was fanned by internal conflicts within the Vatican and expanded to affect the disputes, both open and covert, between the Vatican and nobility in various European countries. In 1704, the Vatican forbade the use of the Jesuit's terms *tianzhu*, *tian*, and *Shangdi* and also forbade Christians to make offerings to Confucius. When the Vatican emissary arrived in China to propagate the papal bull of 1715 to this effect, Kangxi responded by giving the Christian missionaries the choice between remaining in China or obeying the orders set out in the new bull. The Vatican did not back down and even reemphasized this ban. By 1755, the Jesuit order in China had been directed to dissolve, and in 1773 the Jesuit order itself was almost completely suppressed in Europe. As a result of this internal turmoil, in the latter years of his reign, Kangxi forbade all Western missionaries in China, and it was not until the end of the Opium Wars in the mid-nineteenth century that China was again opened to Western missionaries.

The Rites Controversy incited heated arguments both in secular scholarship and between the different religious orders in Europe. At stake were issues of how to explain religious doctrines as well as the understanding of Chinese culture, making it a significant issue in European cultural history. It also led many scholars to criticize the exercise of power by the Vatican and, more broadly, by the Catholic Church itself.

On the Chinese side, because the Vatican was dispatching emissaries with orders to China, it appeared as if the Vatican was assuming it had the prerogative to make regulations regarding Chinese practices. Kangxi and his ministers were extremely offended by this. Of course, if the Vatican was to alter significantly the Chinese viewpoint, they had little choice but to forbid converts from making offerings to Confucius. But this ban's effects on Chinese scholarly debate were minimal, certainly much smaller than the waves it caused in European scholarship.

Most of the priests active in China at this time interacted primarily with the upper classes and attached themselves closely to the centers of government power. During Matteo Ricci's time, the Jesuits developed close communications with Chinese scholars. In addition, they also worked with technical experts who were part of the Imperial Board of Astronomy or were retainers at court, instructing them in Western mathematical techniques. But after the Manchus had established the Qing dynasty, the imperial examinations, on which scholars increasingly relied for social and economic status, were rigidly bound by Zhu Xi's Neo-Confucian interpretations of the Chinese classics. This "literary prison" of the Qing dynasty kept scholars from breaking free from the confines of officially sanctioned scholarship. Furthermore, the Chinese scholarly community, having seen how dearly those involved in the calendrical disputes of the early Kangxi years had paid, were further loathe to extend themselves beyond the safety of pedantic debates on academic and ceremonial questions. Although the Kangxi emperor had personally taken a broad interest in Western knowledge, there were very few in society who even had the opportunity to encounter this stimulus.

Of the novelties introduced to China by European clergy, almost all were matters relating to practical knowledge that could facilitate their entry to the court; even the astronomical studies were valued for their ability to make practical calculations. In terms of theoretical sciences, Western influences were very minor. Moreover, most applications of these practical innovations, such as the landscape design of the Summer Palace or the hydraulics of its fountains, were seen only in the imperial enclaves and extended very little into general society.

Of the long-lasting influences of Western sciences on China, the first was the calendrical system. From the point at which the Western methods were adopted by the Imperial Board of Astronomy, although China's official calendar retained its traditional combination of a lunar-solar system, the methods of calculating the astronomical phenomena on which the calendar dates were based were entirely Western, and the traditional ways of measurement together with the Arab astronomical knowledge that had entered during the Yuan dynasty were no longer used. From ancient times, the Chinese people had observed the official adjustments to the calendar, and from the point that the Western methods of calculation began to be used, the Chinese reckoning for the seasonal beginnings became very precise. After these changes were made, everyone simply took them for granted.

A second important area of Western influence on China was in cartography, though this was a field that even fewer Chinese were aware of. In 1689, the Jesuit missionary Jean-François Gerbillion (1654–1707) assisted the imperial diplomatic mission from Beijing in settling the boundary dispute with Russia, which is an indication of Kangxi's early awareness of the importance of determining more precisely geographical boundaries. In addition to regular applications of cartography in areas such as the planning or purchasing of land, training workers, or establishing geographic meridians, it was also necessary to have a national mapping project. In 1708, Kangxi ordered the Jesuit missionary Joachim Bouvet (1656–1730) to work with a Chinese team to begin the mammoth task of surveying the entire country. Ten years later, work was complete, and the *Comprehensive Atlas of the Imperial Territory of the Kangxi Reign* (*Huangyu quan lantu*) maps were published for most of the Qing territory, including Manchuria and all the provinces of Inner Mongolia. This was the first map of China based on accurate surveys, and work to expand its coverage to include the far western Qing territories was continued into the Yongzheng and Qianlong reigns. The progress under Qianlong was even more comprehensive; the *Qianlong Imperial Household Atlas of the World* (*Qianlong neifu yutu*), published under his orders, extended far beyond the boundaries of land under Qing control: westward to the Baltic Sea and the Mediterranean, north to the northern sea of Russia, and south to the Indian Ocean. This immense atlas, covering almost all of the Asian continent, was divided into many tracts and maps at smaller scales. This project provided training for later generations of Chinese mapmakers and established a foundation for the preparation of later maps.

For thousands of years, China had developed under the idea that it was an empire in the center of "all under heaven" and that regions on its periphery were, to greater or lesser extents, barbarian. Now, in the eighteenth century, China was developing a clearer sense of its own boundaries. The way these two great atlases had determined the territory of China by drawing precise boundaries was in fact an unprecedented change, establishing China's identity as one nation among others in the world and similarly indicating its ethnicity.

The cultural interchange between China and European countries during the seventeenth and eighteenth centuries took on special historical significance. The Jesuits were required to send frequent reports back to Rome on the activities of their members in China, India, and other areas; in addition to missionary activities, these reports also contained detailed information on what the Jesuits had observed in the areas where they were working. Beginning in 1702, these letters were published in France in twenty-six collected volumes, printed in series until 1743 under the title of *Lettres édifiantes et curieuses*. In 1753, the Jesuit historian Jean Baptiste Du Halde (1674–1743), working in France, used selections from these reports to compile an encyclopedic presentation of China's geography, history, government, and material culture in four volumes, entitled *Description de la Chine*. Following this, over the four decades between 1776 and 1814, another French compendium of knowledge about China, the series *Une grande collection: Mémoires concernant les Chinois*, was published. These three great works together comprised the first body of detailed knowledge on the culture and national conditions of China available in the West.

Most of the scholarly community in Europe was in contact with members of the religious orders, and the universities in most areas also had significant relationships with them. The intelligentsia of Europe had already formed a scholarly and intellectual community, and the Jesuits, who were known for their erudition, were a vocal faction in this community, much more so than the other religious orders. The three French compendia of knowledge on China could thus stimulate a vigorous and objective

European interest in China. Moreover, the customs and political structure of Europe of the eighteenth century were permeated by the influence of religious orders, and the Jesuit introduction to Chinese culture formed the basis on which Voltaire (1694–1778) and Montesquieu (1689–1755) launched much of their contemporary social criticism. The Jesuit reports contained much praise of Chinese customs. As a result, the Confucian ideals, philosophy, and spirit of humanism; the scholarly diligence of the emperor Kangxi; and the government administered by Confucian officials selected through a national examination together formed an ideal model for an enlightened monarch to govern society according to humanistic goals. Moreover, some aspects of Chinese philosophy also stimulated European thinkers; for example, the arrangement of trigrams in the *Book of Changes* was influential in the development of binary mathematics by Leibniz (1646–1716). China's industrial production and artistic styles, completely different from those of Europe, also provided a basis of comparison for the Enlightenment thinkers to present their criticisms of these facets of European culture. Artistically, development of the Rococo style in European architecture and interior design was influenced by elements of the Chinese aesthetic.

Though the affection for things Chinese was popular in Europe for a certain period, scholars there were also conscious of the negative aspects of Chinese culture. While praising many of the ideal elements of Chinese society, Montesquieu and Voltaire were also quick to point out the autocratic and dictatorial qualities of the Chinese imperial system. Rousseau (1712–1778) noted even more pointedly the great divergence between the idealized views of China and its reality. Moreover, from the midpoint of the Qianlong reign, the Jesuits had begun to observe clearly the signs that imperial China was in a state of decay and that Chinese culture had essentially ceased to develop. Accordingly, by the beginning of the nineteenth century, Europe's evaluation of China had already shifted from admiration to disparagement.

In sum, the Jesuits first brought to China a new awareness of Western culture, which stimulated China, even though its effects were limited mainly to practical matters and did not yet lead Chinese scholars to make serious comparisons between their world and that of the West or to make a penetrating consideration of the current state of Chinese culture. In contrast, the thinkers of the European Enlightenment took Chinese culture as material from which to make unsparing criticisms of their own cultural situation, criticisms that led to revolutionary cultural changes there.

At this strategic juncture, Europe was developing the mainstream of contemporary civilization, whereas China was not yet aware of the momentous changes at work in the world, trapped as it was in the Chinese empire's obsolete sense of self-importance. In 1792, when the British sent Sir George Macartney to lead their mission to China, it was with the hope that commercial relations could be established. Because the Qianlong emperor viewed them as merely a tributary group from a small and distant island, the trading requests of the British mission were denied. The disappointed British, though unsuccessful in their diplomatic objectives, saw only too clearly the crippling ignorance and self-importance of the Chinese imperial system. Accompanying this delegation was a young man who was received with great affection from Qianlong, a man who was ten years later to become a member of Parliament. On the eve of the First Opium War, this man stated the situation clearly: China was like a feeble old man who would fall at the first blow.

9. Qing Popular Culture

The dynasties of China all had their own popular cultures, and these traditions were expressed in a great variety of ways: the folk songs and narratives passed down through generations and the folk religions that could be seen in the dramatic performances popular among the common people, to name just a few. Following the urbanization and commercialization of society that occurred during the Song, many of the oral performance traditions evolved into professional dramatic arts. In the Ming, with its more advanced commercial economy, especially in the southern cities, popular performances developed to an especially high level. This was part of a general trend for culture overall to be oriented increasingly toward popular culture and to the culture of entertainment. This trend continued into the Qing, where it developed its full force and influence, permeating both fiction and painting and emerging as a fully developed and integrated tradition of popular culture. The vigor of this "lesser tradition" both coexisted with and competed with the established position of the "greater tradition" in upper levels of society.

By the Ming there were already many works of popular literature, such as the *Romance of the Three Kingdoms* (*Sanguo yanyi*) or the *Water Margin* (*Shuihu zhuan*, also translated as *Outlaws of the Marsh* or *All Men Are Brothers*), but the language in these works was partly literary and partly popular, still at some distance from everyday speech. Even in the great short-story collections of the Ming—Ling Mengchu's (1580–1644) two *Striking the Table in Amazement at the Wonders* collections (*Erpo*) and Feng Menglong's (1574–1646) *Three Words* collection (*Sanyan* or *Gujin xiaoshuo*)—although there are some elements from the Song's popular storytelling tradition, the writing differs quite substantially from spoken language. The large corpus of Ming opera libretti includes a great many for *kunqu*, a style of opera that developed based on local theatrical performances into one of the great flowerings of Chinese opera. But all of the more noted authors of *kunqu* were members of the scholarly elite, and their elegant libretti—*Peach Blossom Fan* (*Taohua shan*), *Palace of Eternal Youth* (*Changsheng dian*), and so on—could not but be considered overly refined by most of the common people, so it would hardly be appropriate to consider them as part of popular culture.

In the Qing, however, the vernacular language was used in many literary works, especially long works today loosely considered novels. One of the greatest of all Chinese novels, the *Dream of the Red Chamber* (*Honglou meng*), together with well-known classic novels such as the satire on Confucian elite *The Scholars* (*Rulin waishi*), the allegorical fantasy *Flowers in the Mirror* (*Jinghua yuan*), or the tale of adventure *Hero Boys and Girls* (*Ernü yingxiong zhuan*), all are written in the spoken style of language. Literature written in the vernacular was not something that suddenly emerged from the 1919 May Fourth Vernacular Movement; it already had a very rich and well-established tradition.

The popular form of drama combining spoken and sung passages, sometimes referred to as chantefable (*shuochang*), of course used a dialect that could be understood by most audiences. Wealthy people during the Qing, in both urban centers and small towns, commissioned performances in this genre. Thus whether in urban quarters or within temple festivals, as part of the small seasonal celebrations by ordinary people or the great feasts of wealthy families, all of these would have troupes come from near and far to perform for the gatherings. These performances were marked by regional differences, especially between north and south, but all used common themes such as the advancement of young men through the examination system, retribution for good and evil, and Buddhist and Daoist influences.

Not only are these performance activities a part of the historical record for many areas of China, but they play an important role in Qing novels. In *Dream of the Red Chamber*, we read that, in addition to maintaining troupes of performers, the great families would give private dramatic performances on their own. In the text of *The Peach Blossom Fan*, one of the masterpieces of *kunqu* opera, all of the famous female performers were professional actors, the teachers were professionals, and the character Liu Jingting was in fact a famous performer of Yangzhou *pingtan*, a form of traditional Chinese opera during the Ming-Qing transition. In *Palace of Eternal Youth*, one "plucking rhyme" (*tanci*) section recalls the great *kaiyuan* era (713–741) of the Tang emperor Xuanzong (r. 712–756). Rather than say it represents a Tang performance, it would be better to say that the piece reflects the great contemporary popularity of Hong Sheng's (1645–1704) works.

At least as influential as the elite *kunqu* performances was the literature created for chantefable performances. The most noted master of this genre during the Ming-Qing transition was Gu Fuxi (fl. mid-seventeenth century), who retired from a small government post to his native area and then wove curious events from the bureaucracy into drum ballads (*guci*), traveling from place to place performing these chantefables. The *Peach Blossom Fan* author Kong Shangren's (1648–1718) *Story of the Tree Bark Hobo (Mupi sanke zhuan)* recalls Gu Fuxi's work *The Tree Bark Hobo's Drum Ballads*, which was in effect a history that narrated events from ancient times to the present as a drum ballad, giving them his own critical commentary. But Gu's work had long been on the list of banned texts, and it was not until the late Qing that printed editions began to appear. There were also similar works in this genre of popular presentations of historical material, such as Yang Shen's (1488–1559) *The Twenty-one Histories in Ballad Form (Nianyi shi tanci)*.

Historical romances were also frequently material for chantefable lyrics. For example, the extensive material reworked by Liu Jingting included histories of the Western Han dynasty, the Three Kingdoms, and the Sui-Tang period; the stories of General Yue Fei (1103–1142); and the *Water Margin* as material. During this period, the Ming loyalist General Zuo Liangyu requested Liu to perform for his troops and treated him as an honored guest, because his performances could inspire his soldiers.

Another type of historical romance concerned "pure officials" (*qingguan*) and wandering warriors (*xiake*). The most famous of these was the series of stories concerning deeds of the incorruptible Judge Bao (Bao Gong; real name, Bao Zheng; 999–1062) and a group of wandering warriors who assisted him. Narrated by the storyteller Shi Yukun (fl. 1870), these stories were copied out at the time and published widely as *The Aural Record of the Lord of the Dragon Pattern* (*Longtu erlu*). Later on, because more of the stories concerned wandering warriors than Judge Bao, the series was revised and published as the *Three Heroes and Five Gallants* (*Sanxia wuyi*). From this type of story about honest officials and wandering warriors derived popular works such as *The Crime Cases of Lord Shi Shilun* (*Shigong an*) and *The Crime Cases of Lord Peng* (*Penggong an*), two of the most important pieces in the body of chantefable historical romances.

In the north, the majority of these storytelling lyrics are historical romances, while in the south the majority of them are romantic love stories. It would be difficult to make a clear separation between these two types of narrative, however, and the south is certainly not without its stories from history, nor the north without love stories. The most famous of these love stories, especially in the south, is the *Legend of the White Snake* (*Baishe zhuan*); its lead role of Madame Bai, transformed from a white snake demoness, originally from another Song legend, appeared in many chantefables. Many of these love stories derive from earlier texts, especially the two *Striking the Table in Amazement at the Wonders* collections and the *Three Words* collection. The most overwhelmingly popular of themes within them is that of the poor struggling scholar and the beautiful young woman who befriends and helps him pay for his studies, a trope that is woven into the *Dream of the Red Chamber* as well. Transformed by masters of the storytelling form, some of these narratives departed from the original texts and grew into new string-music versions such as the *Three Smiles* (*San xiao*) and others.

In addition, many young women of good families with no other outlet for their talents also employed the "plucking rhyme" (*tanci*) genre to compose long rhyming stories. These include Chen Duansheng's (1751–ca. 1796) *Twice-Destined Marriage* (*Zaisheng yuan*), Qiu Xinru's (ca. 1805–ca. 1873) *Flowers from My Pen* (*Bi sheng hua*), and Tao Zhenhuai's (fl. 1644) *Heaven Rains Flowers* (*Tian yu hua*). Meng Lijun, the heroine of *Twice-Destined Marriage*, dresses as a man to place first in the official examinations and becomes a general in the military, thus expressing the author's discontent at the unequal status of women. These works, written by women in the inner quarters, though not produced by professional performers, frequently furnished the professional performers with their texts.

In 1790, on Qianlong's fifty-fifth birthday, the Four Great Anhui Troupes came to Beijing to perform in his honor. Following the celebrations, these troupes remained in the capital, forming the basis of what became a national art, now referred to as Peking opera. These performing groups came from the southern part of Anhui, which was also home territory to the Qing leagues of Anhui merchants, who had penetrated to all quarters of China for the salt trade. There were also other noted regional troupes at that time, including ones supported by the salt merchants of Yangzhou, and these performed before Qianlong during his official tour of the south. But the Anhui troupes were well positioned for broader contacts, being located near the Yangzi River and the southern terminus of the Grand Canal, and they had already been influenced by the operatic styles of other areas. Thus, when they came to the capital to celebrate the emperor's birthday, they had absorbed stylistic influences from the earlier operatic forms of Shaanxi's *hanxi* and *qinqiang* and Suzhou's *kunqu*, together with vocal and instrumental influences from many regions. Having blended elite and popular singing styles as well as combining string and wind accompaniments, they were well suited for the role of a national theater. Peking opera made use of the finest aspects from different areas, making it more refined than simply a regional style, and its lyrics also were easier to understand than those of the *kunqu* style, so that it became the most popular form with audiences ranging from the palace elite and wealthy businessmen to servants and peddlers.

The themes contained in the lyrics of Peking opera are quite extensive, including northern and southern tunes and using many types of historical narratives from the story-telling texts (*huaben*), bringing the descriptive techniques of the chantefable into a staged performance. The popularization of these tales by their appearance as *tanci* material also made them more familiar to audiences of Peking opera. This style of opera spread over both North and South China, to theaters both large and small, assimilating the various regional performance styles and narrative materials to become a rich form of popular art.

This tradition was widely disseminated together with other forms of popular culture such as paper cutouts, woodblock prints, or figurines made out of clay, dough, or sugar. To take woodblock prints as an example, prints from the Taohuawu area of Suzhou or the Yangliuqing area of Tian-jin used the characters and storylines of the Peking opera to create many themes popular with the common people. In addition, the masks used in performances reflect popular conceptions of personality types.

Influenced by the almost-universal influence of Peking opera, after the mid-Qing, Chinese people were much more familiar with a great cast of folk heroes, including Guan Gong, Zhu Geliang, Bao Gong, Yue Fei, Li Kuei, Liang Shanbo, Zhu Yingtai, Yang Guifei, and many others, in part historical and in part fictional. The Chinese intellectual system had already divided subtly into two streams: the historical and moral under-standings of the intelligentsia and those of the common people.

The historical systems of the "great tradition" held by the upper strata of society can clearly be seen through judgments contained in Sima Guang's (1019–1086) *Comprehensive Mirror for Aid in Government (Zizhi tongjian)*. Here the rise and fall of dynasties are shown as a result of governmental corruption and lack of care for the common people; self-indulgent emper-ors and treacherous officials are contrasted with wise emperors and virtu-ous officials to clarify this cause and effect. These historical situations are presented in order to use the rise and fall of dynasties as an instructional model.

The historical views of the ordinary people, on the other hand, can be seen throughout many narratives, such as the Ming text *The Investiture of the Gods (Feng shen bang)*; the Qing *States of the Eastern Zhou Dynasty (Dong Zhou lieguo zhi)*; the Ming *Romance of the Three Kingdoms (San-guo yanyi)*; the Qing Yongzheng–era novel of Sui-Tang history, *Complete Story of the Tang (Shuo tang yanyi quan zhuan)*; the historical romance of loyal Song generals, *Generals of the Yang Clan (Yan jia jiang)*; the Re-publican-period *Legend of the Flying Dragon (Fei long zhuan)*; the Ming *Crime Cases of Judge Bao (Baogong an)*; and the Qing *Story of General Yue Fei (Shuo yue)*, *Heroes of the Great Ming (Da ming yinglie zhuan)*, and *The Iron Crown (Tie guan tu)*. In these stories, in contrast to the scholarly histories, the changes of history are resolved by personal feelings of gratitude and blame or by the process of karmic retribution. To give an example, in the *Romance of the Three Kingdoms*, the ways that three great statesmen—Han Xin (d. 196 B.C.E.), Peng Yue (d. 196 B.C.E.), and Ying Bu (202–196 B.C.E.)—died during the wars at the founding of the Han dynasty were brought forward in time to the end of the Han, when it was split into three kingdoms, showing how each of these three had obtained revenge after his death. Similarly, the Empress Fu is presented as the reincarnation of Empress Lü of the early Han. There is also the example of Emperor Yang of the Sui, who was strangled at the fall of his dynasty and then reincarnated as Yang Guifei, the Tang imperial concubine who caused a national uprising but then could not escape the same fate of being strangled.

In official histories, a Song general Yang Ye (?–986) is recorded as having been killed in battle. But in the popular historical narratives, the stories of the Yang family generals are extended to the point where they make up an extremely important part of the popular version of Song history. In this version, the generals of the Yang family are the sole remnants of military power protecting the Song, and the men of this family all sacrifice themselves on the battlefield. The widows of this family then take up the responsibility of defending their country, even though treacherous officials at court continually work against the family. Fortunately, deities including the Eight Wise Kings protect the family at all turns. This story of the Yang family generals then gives rise to other similar narratives for different dynasties, such as the Xue family generals and the Yue family soldiers, reprising the tribulations of the Yang family.

These tales of chivalry (*xiayi*) represent ideas of justice imbued in the minds of the common people. Court cases contained in the Ming collection *Crime Cases of the Lord of the Dragon Diagram (Longtu gong-an)* gave rise to the stories of the great Judge Bao, who defies those in power to preserve justice, and these stories then are combined with tales of wandering warriors offering their services to protect Judge Bao, evolving into tales of chivalrous warriors who themselves resolve court cases. The myriad of upright officials and chivalrous warriors make it clear that the common people did not rely on the legal system for justice but rather hoped to find it by imperial decrees, treasured swords, or brilliant and just officials who could resolve all difficulties and redress injustice on the spot.

In addition to class differences, there was great inequality between the sexes in Chinese traditional society. Women were generally unable to work outside the home or develop a profession. When they were married, the marriage contracts made clear that their fate had been in the hands of their parents, to be handled as their parents ordered without input from the women. In popular narratives, however, the situation is very different: young women are able to provide financial assistance to struggling scholars and to steer the direction of their own fate. There are also stories such as that of the brave woman Wang Baochuan, who raises the ideals of love and marriage to a level higher than the relations of ordinary women in actual life. In Chen Duansheng's *Twice-Destined Marriage*, the heroine's martial and literary prowess make even the men bow their heads to her in respect. The women Fan Lihua and Mu Guiying even overpower brave generals with their military skills, leading these men to ask for their hands in marriage. These are some of the ways in which literary genres from popular culture expressed a protest against the orthodox social mores of the time.

But positive moral values were also an important component of the common people's tradition. The story of the sworn brothers of the peach orchard in the *Romance of the Three Kingdoms* shows the sense of honor and justice (*yiqi*) that was stressed in this popular literature. Here the value placed on personal loyalties was higher even than the traditional Confucian bonds between ruler and minister or husband and wife. In the narrative performances and staged dramas, many of the heroes place their sense of justice as the highest moral value in their lives, being willing even to die for the bond of friendship. In contrast, treacherous villains are always denounced by upstanding commoners.

The Buddhist sense of fate and karmic retribution runs deep in popular culture as well. The desire for revenge against wrongdoing, as described above, is seen in this sense as an explanation for the succession of dynasties as well as being a component of human relations. Thus the relationship between the fictional character Luo Cheng and the Tang emperor Taizong (Li Shimin, 599–649, r. 626–649) was depicted as being too long and too deep to have been exhausted in just one lifetime, which is why Luo Cheng was reincarnated as Taizong's great general, Xue Rengui (614–683) and then twice afterward as other great generals. Similarly, Judge Bao was said to have come to earth from the Great Bear constellation, and the great general of the Southern Song, Yue Fei, was the reincarnation of a marvelous golden roc, all supernatural explanations for their extraordinary abilities.

Most of these folk traditions stray from the orthodox views of social order, coming closer to natural human emotions and giving direction to the behavior of ordinary Chinese people. Heroes of this folk culture, who are lauded for their upright relations with others, ascend to become deities revered by ordinary men and women. Guan Gong, for example, is a deity revered through history for his uprightness; he and many others under a great variety of honorary titles became local deities for various areas. The most extreme example of this connection between religion, fiction, and politics is that the deities worshipped by the fighters during the Boxer Rebellion were almost all characters from the recited narrative and dramas, not part of any standard religious sect or figures recognized by the standard histories. As we can see from these examples, the popular culture that came to fruition during the Qing is extremely diverse in its sources and interactions, far beyond simple characterizations.

10. The Contemporary West

From the seventeenth century to the mid-nineteenth, while China was enjoying the benefits of the prosperity it had developed during the Kangxi period, Europe was going through momentous changes. By the mid-nineteenth century, the West had passed through two centuries of dramatic change; it had already entered the modern world and taken on an entirely different aspect from that of a century or two before.

The religious and political changes from the Reformation, together with the formation of major states, carried Europe into a new period as the influence of the Vatican and the Holy Roman Empire both declined. England, France, the German territories, and Russia were now on course to becoming world powers based on their nationalism, mercantilism, and overseas expansion. The results of these struggles for authority established the loci of power that were to become the nation-states of the modern world. At the same time, revolutions in America and France led to unprecedented developments in democratic systems of government.

Of all of these changes, the earliest was the Enlightenment of the seventeenth and eighteenth centuries. The brilliance of this period of human history is marked by great names in the sciences and philosophy: Rene Descartes (1596–1650), Benedict de Spinoza (1632–1677), John Locke (1632–1704), Thomas Hobbes (1588–1679), and Sir Isaac Newton (1642–1727), as well as Voltaire and Rousseau. Through the brilliance of their ideas, they and others proposed social ideals, many of which still guide the modern world. The spirit of scientific investigation replaced the earlier fragmentary and dogmatic systems of theology. The common people began to gain the right to determine the government of their country by voting. Though these ideals have as yet to be fully realized, people were by this time seeking to group themselves together and rule themselves by means other than mere force or religious belief.

As Europeans more fully exploited the ocean shipping routes to develop their foreign trade, a commercial economy began replacing the formerly dominant agricultural economy. Fostered by this mercantile spirit, the Industrial Revolution in Europe advanced the means of production to a much higher level. With an expanded view of imperial possibilities, the great mercantile and industrial powers of Europe established colonies to control the markets for their products and loot the natural resources of Asia, Africa, and the Americas. This potent mixture of nationalism, mercantilism, and violence ushered in a scene in human history on which the final curtain has yet to fall.

In the northwestern corner of continental Europe, Holland was a small and vigorous nation whose strength was based on its maritime commerce, and at the time of the Ming-Qing transition, several of its trading companies had combined to form the Dutch East Indies Company. Though ostensibly a trading company, it used naval force to take control of the shipping routes from the formerly dominant countries of Spain and Portugal. As a joint stock corporation, the company had received a monopoly for international activities from the Dutch government and on this basis could sell shares to private investors. This model of corporate organization enabled the participation of any person who had the financial means to invest, and the strength that was thus mobilized was far greater than what the royal houses of Spain or Portugal could field.

But Holland, with its small territory and population, was unable to contend with Britain, whose merchants formed their own East India Company, originally called the Governor and Company of Merchants of London Trading Into the East Indies. In 1600, Elizabeth I (r. 1558–1603) granted this company a monopoly on international trade, a right that was continued until 1833 and enabled the British royal government to penetrate much further and more deeply than it would have been able to with armed forces alone. The economic principles behind this action were put forth in Adam Smith's (1723–1790) *The Wealth of Nations* (or, more fully, *An Inquiry Into the Nature and Causes of the Wealth of Nations*, 1776), which proposed that the people of a nation could create national prosperity by putting their efforts into an open economic market. By the time of Queen Victoria (r. 1837–1901), through this combination of capitalism and government support, Britain had established an empire on which "the sun never sets." It was in the middle of this period of great national confidence that the Macartney-led mission arrived in China to discuss the possibilities of opening trade and the Chinese court coolly rejected their overtures to begin relations.

In Asia at this time were three great empires, the Qing dynasty of China, the Mughal Empire on the Indian subcontinent, and the Ottoman Empire in the Middle East. Robert Clive (1724–1774) of the British East India Company used a strategy of dividing the many smaller rulers of the Mughal Empire to conquer the whole of that empire, and in 1773 the administration of the Indian territories by the British East India Company under British government supervision was formally established. In the next century, because of the administrative and financial difficulties of the company, control of the subcontinent was rescinded to the British crown, with Victoria as queen of India. To the west, the Ottoman Empire was affected not only by Britain but also by Russian and German incursions, and the Middle East fell apart into a number of kingdoms and protectorates. As the Ottoman Empire declined, these smaller kingdoms looked to Britain as an overlord to maintain stability in the Middle East. Of these developments to their west, China was foolishly unaware, and it was not until the latter part of the nineteenth century that calls from a few revolutionary figures began to rouse the populace to the fact that the Qing was about to fall under colonial control, as had the Mughal and Ottoman empires.

During this period, England saw a great rise in the influence of the middle class. Oliver Cromwell (1599–1658), for example, came from a background of minor country gentry and increased his economic status through the sale of property. After being elected to a seat in the House of Commons, he came into his own as a leader and led Parliament in a revolution that sent King Charles I (1600–1649) to the executioner's block. Cromwell thereby became the Lord Protector of the Commonwealth of England for the five years from 1653 to 1658, and this Calvinist Puritan ruled England as if he were king. Though Charles II (r. 1660–1685) was restored to the throne soon after Cromwell's death, the British monarchy was never to regain its former power, much of which was relinquished to the partially elected Parliament.

But the first true democratic revolution did not occur until the American War of Independence. When the thirteen British colonies arose in the rebellion of 1776, which began with the Battle of Concord in Massachusetts, it was the first revolution that led to a stable democracy. At the Continental Congress of 1787, the thirteen states agreed upon what was the first complete written constitution for a nation, realizing the ideal of a "social contract" with the establishment of the United States of America. This new confederated republic was governed by a democratically elected president together with state representatives in the Senate and House of Representatives. The shock of this revolution in North America was felt across the Atlantic, and it proved a stimulus to the following French Revolution.

The internal turmoil of the French Revolution, which lasted ten years, from 1789 to 1799, began with the storming of the Bastille and sent Louis XVI (r. 774–1791) to the guillotine. Though it initially may have appeared to be taking a course similar to Cromwell's revolution of the previous century, the Reign of Terror in Paris made clear that the populist direction in which the revolution had turned could also lead to self-destructive social turmoil. The direction of the French Revolution then changed dramatically when Napoleon Bonaparte (1769–1821) became emperor. Spread by the expansion of his empire, the revolutionary thinking of France permeated all of Europe. Although Napoleon's empire fell to pieces within a decade, the ideal of a democratic government and the Napoleonic code of laws was the beginning of the end of the union of royal privilege and the religious right of the Catholic Church, which had dominated Europe since the fall of the Roman Empire. With the ensuing wave of revolutions that swept over Europe, the old political landscape was completely remade into a system of nations that, to varying degrees, incorporated the principles of democratic representation. This process eventually led to the European Union of today.

In the seventeenth and eighteenth centuries, the country that was to become Germany was limited to the duchy of Prussia, which was the main Teutonic state and whose leader was the most influential elector of the Holy Roman Empire. Declaring itself the Prussian kingdom in 1701 and then the German Empire in 1871, the German state went through an extensive program of militarization and industrialization to become the most powerful nation of Europe, glorifying a Germanic tradition of bearing arms. At the beginning of this process of unification, Prussia's Frederic II (r. 1740–1786) was the foremost of the "enlightened monarchs." Although Prussia had joined forces with Britain to defeat the armies of Napoleon, these two countries were in competition for colonial territories in the Middle East and Africa. Chancellor Otto von Bismarck (1815–1898) guided Germany through the latter half of the nineteenth century with a government that, though not democratic, was perhaps the most effective in Europe. Germany began to stress its ethnic unity and presented itself both as a model for democratic nations and as having inherited the mantle of the Holy Roman Empire, referring to its king as a Kaiser, in reference to the ancient Roman title of Caesar. This national rise, which occurred while Chinese scholars of the Qianlong and Jiaqing eras (1736–1830) were developing the school of evidential scholarship, was little understood in China, and it was not until the publication of Wei Yuan's (1794–1856) 1844 *Illustrated Treatise on the Maritime Kingdoms* (*Haiguo tuzhi*) that China was even clearly aware of Germany's existence.

In terms of the development of democracy, America and the German empire might be placed toward opposite ends of a spectrum. Russia would be even beyond Germany toward the absolutist end of the spectrum. Germany had a class of local nobility, similar to China's class of scholar-officials, and their leadership formed a counterbalance to that of the national central government; in Russia, the large landholders were much more closely under national control. The Russian empire was vast, largely overlapping the area that had been under the control of the Mongol Golden Horde, and it would have been difficult for the democratic process to take root there. The Russian Orthodox priests, who owed their authority to the Russian crown, could not compete with this royal power. Thus Peter the Great (r. 1689–1725), although he pushed forward a great revolution in the Westernization of Russia, had little reason to change the fundamental characteristics of its government. It could be that the Qing government's understanding of European politics was based largely on its knowledge of Russia, such as that obtained when the Qing court sent its Manchu representative Ayan Gioro Tulišen to the Russian legation in Beijing in the early eighteenth century to learn of the Russian situation. Although Russia in the next century may have changed little from China's early understanding of it, China did not recognize the great changes that had taken place in other areas of Europe.

The last of the Western nations that we should consider in relation to China is the United States. This new democratic republic, established largely by European immigrants, was essentially an extension of European culture. Although the newborn union of thirteen states initially had little influence beyond the Atlantic seaboard, by the early nineteenth century, this nation began to come into its own. The Louisiana Purchase of 1803

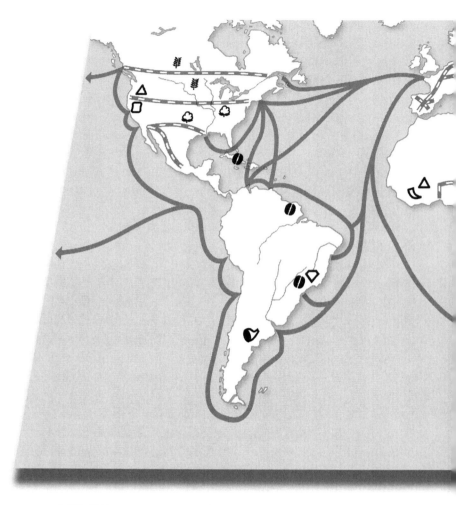

FIGURE 7.8 World Economic System in the Second Half of the Nineteenth Century

acquired it the area of its current central and southern states, and as it expanded westward, it converted the forests and prairies of that central area into great stretches of farmland. At the same time, the growing industry in the east converted the cotton grown in the south to textiles for export to Europe. The conflict between the industrial interests of the North and the agricultural interests of the South strained relations between the states of these two areas and led to the Civil War, after which America developed with new vigor. The discovery of gold in California stimulated a great

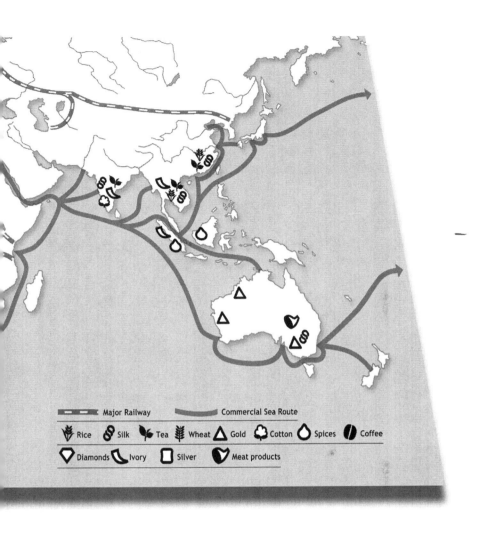

Major Railway **Commercial Sea Route**

Rice Silk Tea Wheat Gold Cotton Spices Coffee

Diamonds Ivory Silver Meat products

migration that effectively tied together the nation from the Atlantic to the Pacific. To the Chinese during the first half of the nineteenth century, it would have been incomprehensible that the rapid expansion of this new nation would lead it to be a major world power within the century. It would also have been impossible to foresee that this new nation would provide a model that the later revolutionaries of China would seek to emulate or that its example would help foster the establishment of a democratic republic in China.

The world of the first half of the nineteenth century already had an extensive global economic system. International trade, based on ever-increasing maritime shipments of cargo, brought silver from the Americas to China and Chinese products to Europe. Although the Suez and Panama canals had yet to be opened, as early as the Napoleonic occupation of Egypt, Europeans had begun planning ways to cut a canal that would connect the Mediterranean and the Red Sea, greatly shortening the passage from Europe to the East. Closer to China, England had already established Singapore as a means to control trade that passed through the Straits of Malacca between the Pacific and Indian oceans. All these developments were extensively discussed by the politicians and businessmen of Europe, but the Chinese of that time had little understanding that the outside world was rushing headlong into a period when global empires were being fueled increasingly by private capitalism. Even less could they realize that soon China itself would almost be swamped by this great wave.

The reigns of the Kangxi, Yongzheng, Qianlong, and Jiaqing emperors were a magnificent time for China. The economy was flourishing at unprecedented levels, the population was rising in all quarters, and the people lived and worked in peace. But the Chinese had become too reliant on the comfort of their easy way of life, disdaining to understand the affairs of the greater world around them. They little knew that on the other side of the world great changes were in progress that before long would impinge on China from the outside. Knowledge of the outside world in China during the Qing was largely built on what was known in the Ming, which was in some respects more advanced. There are two factors that may be responsible for this. The first is the broad erudition of the Jesuits who came to China during the Ming and the extensive knowledge of European affairs that they brought with them. Moreover, there were Chinese scholars of that time who were greatly interested in this new knowledge. But following the rupture of relations between the Qing court and the Vatican following the Rites Controversy, since there were few means of support outside of the court, Chinese intellectuals rarely came in contact with Western missionaries. In addition, after the suppression of the Jesuits, among the missionaries who came to China were fewer men of scholarly ability. Furthermore, and perhaps more important, was the great variety and rapidity of changes in the West. These were not limited to the establishment of democratic governments but also included a number of different schools of thought that were incompatible with Catholic doctrine. Thus the missionaries could hardly have been expected to give a full presentation of the changes sweeping over Europe at that time.

The second factor contributing to the Qing dynasty's greater ignorance of the situation in the West was the fact that, during the Ming, officials dealing with foreign affairs had gathered a great deal of their information from overseas traders from Spain, Portugal, Holland, and Japan. During the Qing, because foreign trade was largely restricted to the thirteen chartered trading houses granted this right by the government, these "imperial merchants" had contact only with Cantonese customs inspectors and the Imperial Household Department that supervised foreign traders, rather than with scholar-officials at the court. Satisfied with the great profits they reaped from this limited trade, the imperial traders had little incentive to expand or open up new commercial opportunities. For example, a considerable amount of foreign trade developed in the city of Nanjing, located to the north of the center of foreign trade in the far south and then referred to as Nankeen, whereas the monopolized interests in Guangzhou (Canton) were not interested in marketing commodities other than silk. As another example, the Western maritime trade was supported by a well-developed system of insurance for cargoes and vessels, and Western banks were accustomed to financing this trade through loans. Chinese companies, on the other hand, considered commercial trading to be an isolated discipline, and though they were not ignorant of these Western commercial practices, they showed little interest in gaining experience. The Chinese traders lacked interest in novel business practices, thanks to their smug satisfaction with their current wealth, and they had even less curiosity about other areas of Western knowledge.

Thus, while Europe and America were making great advances on many fronts, an overly confident Qing China remained in a deep sleep. When compared to its previous strength, there is little wonder that the West considered it to be a "sleeping dragon."

Suggestions for Further Reading

Cohen, Paul. *History in Three Keys: The Boxers as Event, Experience, and Myth.* New York: Columbia University Press, 1997.
Crossley, Pamela Kyle. *The Manchus.* Oxford: Blackwell, 1997.

Elliott, Mark C. *Emperor Qianlong: Son of Heaven, Man of the World*. New York: Longman, 2009.

——. *The Manchu Way: The Eight Banners and Ethnic Identity in Late Imperial China*. Stanford, Calif.: Stanford University Press, 2001.

Elliott, Mark C., James Millward, Ruth Dunnell, and Philippe Forêt, eds., *New Qing Imperial History: The Making of Inner Asian Empire at Qing Chengde*. London: Routledge Curzon, 2004.

Elman, Benjamin A. *On Their Own Terms: Science in China, 1550–1900*. Cambridge, Mass.: Harvard University Press, 2005.

Elvin, Mark, and William Skinner, eds. *The Chinese City Between Two Worlds*. Stanford, Calif.: Stanford University Press, 1974.

Fairbank, John K. *Trade and Diplomacy on the China Coast: The Opening of the Treaty Ports, 1842–1854*. Cambridge: Harvard University Press, 1953, 1964.

——, ed. *The Cambridge History of China*, vol. 10: *Late Ch'ing, 1800–1911*, part 1. Cambridge: Cambridge University Press, 1978.

Fairbank, John K., and Kwang-Ching Liu, eds. *The Cambridge History of China*, vol. 11: *Late Ch'ing, 1800–1911*, part 2. Cambridge: Cambridge University Press, 1980.

Hevia, James. *Cherishing Men from Afar: The Qing Guest Ritual and the Macartney Expedition of 1793*. Chapel Hill, N.C.: Duke University Press, 1995.

Kuhn, Philip. *Soulstealers: The Chinese Sorcery Scare of 1768*. Cambridge, Mass.: Harvard University Press, 1998.

Mann, Susan. *Precious Records: Women in China's Long Eighteenth Century*. Stanford, Calif.: Stanford University Press, 1997.

Perdue, Peter. *China Marches West: The Qing Conquest of Central Asia*. Cambridge, Mass.: Belknap Press, 2005.

Pomeranz, Kenneth. *The Great Divergence: Europe, China, and the Making of the Modern World Economy*, rev. ed. Princeton, N.J.: Princeton University Press, 2001 [2000].

Rawski, Evelyn. *The Last Emperors: A Social History of Qing Imperial Institutions*. Berkeley: University of California Press, 2001.

Skinner, G. William. *Marketing and Social Structure in Rural China*. Ann Arbor, Mich.: Association for Asian Studies, 1964, 2001 [1965].

Spence, Jonathan. *The Death of Woman Wang*. New York: Viking, 1978.

——. *God's Chinese Son: The Taiping Heavenly Kingdom in Hong Xiuquan*. New York: Norton, 1996.

8

A Century of Uncertainty

1850 TO 1950

The West's Industrial Revolution and subsequent capitalist imperialism determined the fate of the entire world for a hundred years. China was beaten down by these twin pressures. In the hundred years after the mid-nineteenth century, as China strove to adapt to this new world situation—through internal self-examination and reflection and through study abroad and emulation—the entire fabric of Chinese civilization was torn to pieces. China's self-reorganization and progress toward joining this new world first had to endure the terrible hardships of the first half of the twentieth century. Only then did signs of hope and renewal gradually appear.

1. Troubles Internal and External

The year 1795 (the sixtieth and last year of the Qianlong emperor's long reign) has generally been regarded as a time of great prosperity for the Qing dynasty (1644–1911). In actual fact, China's cultural vitality was exhausted, and her real economic power was on the decline. During the reigns of the Jiaqing and the Daoguang emperors (1796–1820 and 1821–1850), China's national strength progressively weakened; a most obvious example of this was the greed and incompetence of officialdom and their extremely poor administrative performance. Although the White Lotus Rebellion in Hubei, Sichuan, and Shaanxi from 1796 to 1804 did not have too many adherents, it exhausted the Qing armies, which wasted time and resources before finally defeating a basically untrained force of peasant rebels. The rebellion demonstrated that the Qing armies were no longer invincible. The main force fighting the rebels was the Green Standard Army, a standing infantry during the Qing dynasty originally made up of Han Chinese not related to the Manchu banner units. This situation was a key to the rise of the Han Chinese and decline of the Manchus in the late Qing.

Aside from the military, the huge civil bureaucracy, except for the Manchu royal family, came primarily from Han Chinese civil service examination graduates. The examination system was designed to be procedurally fair and had long been used to recruit men into the higher ranks of society. However, the examination system recruited officials on the basis of their recitation of Zhu Xi's version of Neo-Confucian doctrine as the only repository of orthodox ideas, and this produced an ossified mode of thinking among the intellectual stratum of society. As a result, the culture of the upper strata of Qing society was characterized by a rigid ideology resistant to change. A minority of independently minded individuals tried to break out of this intellectual cage, but they were hardly able to tear down such a solid structure.

China suffered very sound defeats in the Opium Wars of the 1840s and 1850s. China had already entered the global economic system during the Ming, but after the Opium Wars, China was dragged into the imperial competition of the great powers, a greatly humiliating experience that had a profound effect on the psychology of the Chinese people and led to a century of confusion and uncertainty.

From the middle of the nineteenth century to the middle of the twentieth century, China was forced to undergo six wars of aggression—the Anglo-Chinese War (Opium War, 1839–1842), the Anglo-French expedition to China (1856–1860, called the Second Anglo-Chinese War or the Arrow War), the Sino-French War (1884–1885), the First Sino-Japanese War (1894–1895, after which Taiwan was ceded to the Japanese), the invasion of the Eight-Nation Alliance (1900–1901, following the Boxer Rebellion), and the War of Resistance Against Japan (1937–1945). Each of these foreign wars of aggression was bigger than the one previous, and the devastation visited on Chinese society was also more serious.

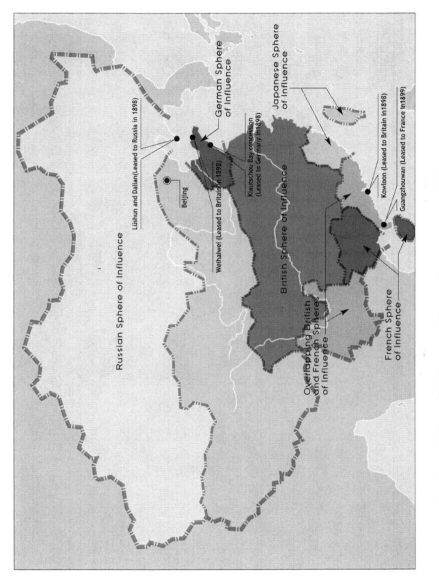

FIGURE 8.1 Great Power Spheres of Influence in China in the Late Nineteenth Century

During this century of foreign invasions, China also suffered from a series of internal wars and calamities—the Taiping Rebellion (1850–1864, in which there were forty times more casualties than in the American Civil War); the Nien Rebellion of northern China (1851–1868); the Boxer Rebellion (1898–1901); the Republican Revolution (1911, the *xinhai* year, that led to the collapse of the Qing dynasty); the Warlord Era of chaotic fighting from 1916 to 1928; the Nationalist Party's (KMT, Kuomintang or Guomindang) Northern Expedition of 1926 to 1928; and the Nationalist-Communist Civil War (April 1927 to May 1950), which ended with the Chinese Communist Party victory, the declaration of the People's Republic of China, and the Republic of China's escape to Taiwan. If we examine the chronology of these successive internal and external calamities, they can be seen to be intimately related—an internal civil war occurs immediately after and as the apparent result of each foreign invasion.

The Opium War was Qing China's first defeat. Twenty years earlier, the Qing court had discussed the harm that opium did to the country and issued an order forbidding its sale and use. Lin Zexu (1785–1850) carried out the order to proscribe opium; he was very thorough in both his foreign negotiations and his military defenses, but the Qing court still did not have a nationwide plan of action. Soon after that, when negotiations broke down in Guangzhou, a small British armed force moved north by ship along the Chinese coast as easily as it would have along an uninhabited island. The Chinese weapons were no match for those of the British, but the keys to China's defeat in the Opium War were that the government did not have any mechanism for unified mobilization, and the officials and the public, the cities and the countryside, also lacked communication and integration. China at that time was not really an integrated nation, because it had neither a mobilization mechanism nor intelligence about its own and its enemy's actual situation. It was already a society in disintegration and could not ward off an external attack.

The breakup of a society demonstrates that it does not possess a common and collective unifying consciousness. There were many discussions about Chinese culture during the last stage of the Ming dynasty, and many scholars reflected deeply on Chinese culture before and after the demise of the Ming. After the reign of the Kangxi and Yongzheng emperors (1662–1735), Chinese thought followed only one line, the study of trivial minutiae occupied all intellectual resources, the economy prospered, and society was happy with its leisure activities—there were very few individuals who cared to think deeply about fundamental problems in such an environment. As a consequence, China was left with only an autonomic nervous system keeping its body lumbering along involuntarily but lacked any mode of voluntary thought able of leading it in a different direction.

The Taiping (Heavenly Peace) Rebellion was a reaction to this defeat. Its leader, Hong Xiuquan (1814–1864), and his followers came from the Guangzhou area. They were familiar with the Western powers and aware of the importance of religion in Western culture. Thus, the doctrines they proclaimed actually aimed to attract their followers through "worshiping God." The Taiping organization, nevertheless, remained confined to the usual characteristics of traditional Chinese popular religious rebellions. Because the upper and lower strata of Qing society were isolated from each other, the Taiping movement was unable to expand into the upper levels of society. Its spiritual resources could not blend into Chinese culture, it could not attract the intellectual elite to join its cause, and its population base could not extend beyond the two provinces of Guangdong and Guangxi. The Taiping Rebellion moved the Han Chinese Zeng Guofan (1811–1872) and Zuo Zongtang (1812–1885) to organize the Hunan Army (*Xiangjun*), with village militia commanded by rural gentry at its core. They attracted followers under the banner of defending Confucian culture and eventually defeated the Heavenly Kingdom of the Taipings.

The Boxer Rebellion followed another model. "Boxers" comes from the Chinese Yihetuan, the "Society of Righteous Harmonious Fists." Western Protestant missionaries followed the Western gunboats into China and won over the people's faith not with the strength of their doctrines but with the support of superior European military and economic might. The work of the Western missionaries gave rise to many "religious incidents" (that is, protests by Chinese) that eventually culminated in the rise of the Yihetuan. This "nativist movement" blindly and totally rejected all things foreign. Since the followers of the Yihetuan came from the countryside and the lower classes, their demands were not only unable to attract the intellectual elite but actually gave rise to their opposition. At the same time, given the rigid political organization and social disintegration throughout the country, each local area, north and south, solely took care of itself, with the local gentry everywhere looking out for their own private interests. When the Boxer Rebellion led to an invasion by the Eight-Nation Alliance, the Qing court was unable to mobilize sufficient resources to resist them.

China was defeated by Western powers from across the sea and suffered from the terrible destructive force of modern weapons. After that, the court and the public felt that the development of a powerful national defense based on fighting ships and heavy artillery was the most important national imperative. During their battles against the Taipings, Zeng Guofan, Zuo Zongtang, Li Hongzhang (1823–1901), and other leaders had gained valuable experience in the practical use of weapons in war. Their postrebellion Self-Strengthening Movement (*ziqiang yundong*) thus adopted the celebrated slogan of "employ the best technology of the barbarians to defeat the barbarians" (*shi yi zhi changji yi zhi yi*). However, their efforts at building a national defense system based on a modern army and navy were unable to pass the test of either the Sino-French War (1884–1985) or the First Sino-Japanese War (1894–1895)—the Chinese northern and southern fleets were almost totally annihilated.

Reflecting on this painful experience and considering the successes of the Meiji Restoration (1862–1869) in Japan, intellectual circles began to realize that the strength of a nation does not reside only in a powerful military establishment. It was even more important to have a unifying sense of national spirit and a comprehensive state system to accompany this spirit. For this reason, the ill-fated Hundred Days' Reform (*wuxu bianfa*, the *wuxu* year being 1898) took political reform to be the road to self-strengthening. The main element of Liang Qichao's (1873–1929) subsequent "theory of a new people" (*xinminshuo*) was his advocacy of new citizens (*xin guomin*) for a new nation.

The 1911 Republican Revolution was an explosion of pent-up longings for change. Had Sun Yatsen's (1866–1925) revolutionary ideals been limited to the expulsion of the Manchus, he would probably not have surpassed the Taipings. His principle of "people's rights" (*minquan*) resonated with the reflections of Huang Zongxi (1610–1695) and others, and his principle of "people's livelihood" (*minsheng*) harmonized with China's traditional egalitarianism. Sun's principle of nationalism (*minzu zhuyi*, literally, "people-race/nation-ism") aroused Han Chinese indignation against their Manchu rulers and was the main reason that the national revolution was able to overthrow the Qing dynasty. Nationalism, or the concept of a nation-state composed of one people (*minzu*), began in Europe as the reaction of various nations (peoples, *zu*) to the papal system of the Roman Catholic Church. The Chinese imperial system was regarded as a universal order (universal kingship), but the Chinese Nationalist Revolution appropriated the Western concept of nationalism (*minzu zhuyi*) to make China into a nation-state that could oppose the colonial imperialism of the Western powers. From then on, Chinese efforts to construct a national people (*guozu*) could never be separated from the concept of nationalism.

After the 1911 revolution, the Republic of China was hurriedly established as a nation-state, and China's several-thousand-years-old imperial system came to an end. The republican system was really not fully implemented, though, and the ever-menacing great powers continued to bully and humiliate China. That this wounded and battered nation was not actually destroyed was attributable primarily to the force of its new nationalism. Even while great and small warlords made war on one another, none of them dared to fly in the face of overwhelming national public opinion and invite foreign armies to invade China.

Sun Yatsen set up his regime in Guangzhou (Canton) and struggled against the Beiyang Army, controlled by the Beiyang Clique in the north. That Sun was able to attract the attention and support of the entire nation from his corner of a rugged and poorly defended coastal region was because his principles of nationalism and his ideal of nation building were directly connected to his contemporaries' hopes for saving the nation from extinction. That the Nationalist Party under Chiang Kai-shek (Jiang Jieshi, 1887–1975) was able to accomplish successfully the Northern Expedition (from 1926 to 1928) and defeat many regional warlords was also attributable to the people's desire to save the nation. It was this set of circumstances that finally brought the powerful warlords Feng Yuxiang (1882–1948) of north-central China, Li Zongren (1890–1969) of Guangxi, and Yan Xishan (1883–1960) of Shanxi to cease fighting Chiang Kai-shek and one another and join with Chiang against the Beiyang Clique. This also made it possible for the "Young Marshall" Zhang Xueliang (1901–2001) to bring the Northeast (Manchuria) under submission to Chiang's government.

From the Mukden Incident in 1931 (known in China as the September 18 Incident) that led to the establishment of the Japanese puppet regime of Manchukuo (Manzhouguo) to the Marco Polo Bridge Incident of July 7, 1937, imperialist Japan pushed forward step by step in an attempt to swallow up China piecemeal. The more powerful the Japanese forces became, however, the more determined was the Chinese resolve to save the nation. During the eight-year War of Resistance Against Japan, China experienced the most extreme hardships. Chinese forces were not ready for war yet, but they were forced to rush into battle by a public that

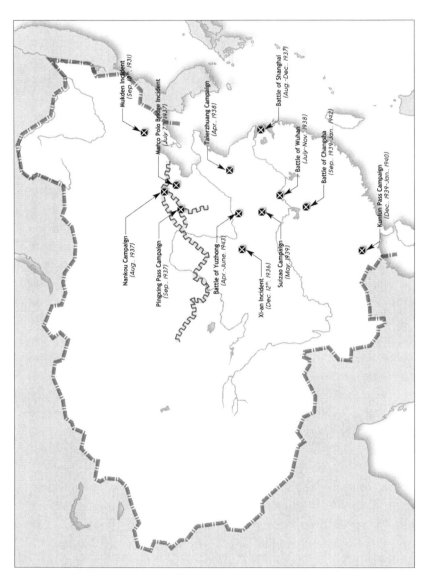

FIGURE 8.2 Major Battles in the War of Resistance Against Japan

could no longer bear the Japanese insults and provocations. In the fiercely fought three-month Battle of Shanghai (August to November 1937), which pitted Chinese small-caliber weapons against Japan's air, naval, and armored guns, large numbers of China's elite troops were killed, and her fledgling air force was almost completely destroyed. After that, the Chinese people were united in their resistance, and many regional warlords began to support the War of Resistance without even receiving orders from the central government. From the second year of the war on, as Japanese advances slowed after the capture of Nanjing, Chiang's National Revolutionary Army (*Guomin gemingjun*, NRA) adopted the strategies of "trading space for time" and "winning by outlasting," making the war into a test of endurance. China's military strength was insufficient, but it relied on its great size and population to hang on for eight long years. The Nationalist armed forces suffered over three million casualties, including over one hundred generals, and civilian casualties from Japanese bombardments or refugee starvation reached at least thirty million.

The Chinese forged a powerful national consciousness over the course of this long war. European national states were based on only one people (nation, *minzu*), but throughout its history China had considered itself a universal nation of "all under heaven" (*tianxia*). Many different peoples or ethnic groups (*zuqun*) were included under the universal order known as China (literally, "central states," hence the name Middle Kingdom). Of course, China was also a cultural concept, but it could encompass many regional variations. The twentieth-century Chinese national people (*guozu*) actually grew into the most populous community in the world.

The Chinese Communist Revolution began with the establishment of the Chinese Communist Party in 1921. Before the War of Resistance, the Chinese Communist Revolution had been one element of the international Communist movement. After more than a decade, the Communist Party's internationalist revolution was unable to obtain the support of the common people. On the eve of the War of Resistance, the Communists completed their historic Long March and established their base in Yan-an, in Shaanxi Province.

On December 12, 1936, in the celebrated Xi-an Incident, Zhang Xue-liang and Yang Hucheng (1893–1949) arrested Generalissimo Chiang Kai-shek and forced him, on the basis of nationalist sentiment, to agree to join forces with the Communist armies and fight against Japan. Under the banner of nationalism, the Communist guerrilla bases steadily expanded.

At the same time, from their experience in using the villages as their base, the Communists learned how to mobilize the power of the peasants and nationalized (indigenized) their international communism. Nationalism was, thus, probably the most important reason that the Communists were able to defeat the Nationalists in the Chinese Civil War (1946–1950). In September 1949, when Mao Zedong announced to a meeting of the Chinese People's Political Consultative Conference that "from now on, the Chinese people have stood up" rather than "socialism has stood up," it was because he had captured "all under heaven" by appealing to Chinese nationalism. This was an appeal that had been forged by a century of experience, and its power was undefeatable.

The Chinese Confucian concept of "all under heaven" was a universal order that had no need to appeal to a national people. From the Qin and Han empires on, the concept of "China" had to accommodate the cultures of many different ethnic groups living on this piece of land in East Asia. The Han series of Five Emperors (*Di*) arranged various ethnic groups into one interconnected genealogy, with the Yellow Emperor designated the supreme ancestor. This genealogical construction was employed by Zhang Taiyan (Zhang Binglin, 1868–1936) and others to replace the reign names of the Qing imperial house with a reign that began with the Yellow Emperor. To this day, many ethnic Han Chinese consider themselves the descendants of the Yellow Emperor, and many non-Han ethnic groups have constructed their own theoretical genealogies to link their origins with those putative Han Chinese origins.

In recent history, China attempted to construct a national ethnic group by combining many nationalities into one. This direction was just the opposite of the European nations' attempts to escape the Roman Catholic world order by constructing separate ethnic (hence national) origins. Thus, the Chinese revolution started by opposing the Manchus and supporting the Han Chinese and developed into a movement in opposition to Western imperialism based on two demands put forth by Sun Yatsen: that "all internal ethnic groups should be equal" and that China should "align with all the nations of the world that treat our nation with equality." China's transformation into a huge pluralistic community was something rarely seen in the world up to that time.

The trajectory of this series of transformations was that each foreign humiliation led to an internal reaction such that, step by step, the country went from seeking substantial military might toward the emulation of

Western political systems. After that, Sun Yatsen's pluralistic order evolved on the basis of the concept of the nation-state (*minzu guojia*). From then on, China no longer had to rely on the entire panoply of narrow Western ethnic nationalism, such as the Germanic ideal in Germany. Nor did it have to rely on religious belief to sustain its nationalism, as with Jewish nationalism (Zionism). China's path was one that could easily link up with contemporary "globalization" and can still be further developed in the future.

2. China's Modern Economic Transformation

The Opium War started because Great Britain dared to offend world opinion and go to war over the buying and selling of opium. As pointed out in the previous chapter, because of an influx of silver from the New World, China experienced a favorable balance of trade over an extended period of time, and that led to economic prosperity in its eastern coastal regions. During the reigns of the Jiaqing and Daoguang emperors (1796–1850), world silver was in short supply. Great Britain, with no colonial possessions in South America, suffered a particular shortage of silver. The opium trade thus grew into a mechanism for the British East India Company to pay off Britain's Chinese debts.

In China's case, the shortage of silver had already created a currency shortfall and economic retrenchment, but opium could not be made into currency. Thus, for China, the Opium War brought nothing but calamity, not only because of the intrinsic poisonous effects of opium addiction but also because the economic effects of the war caused China to fall into a negative balance of trade. According to the Qing statesman Wei Yuan's (1794–1856) observations, foreign imports into China in 1847 (not including opium) could be valued at more than twenty million *yuan*, and China still had a large trade surplus. According to Chinese customs figures, this trade surplus no longer existed after 1878; from that time until the First Sino-Japanese War broke out in 1894, trade deficits increased at an annual rate in the tens of millions of *yuan*.

A much more significant and long-lasting influence of the Opium War was the transformation of China's economic structure. From earliest times, China's market economy relied on agricultural products and commodities produced by rural handicraft industries. All of these products traveled through a chain of rural markets until they reached consumers all over the country. This market network was the channel for the distribution of the natural resources and wealth of the nation. China was a vast geographical area with an enormously large economic system, and this great system was able to operate quite well solely on the basis of interregional trade. To cite the example of silk cocoons from Jiangnan: they were first bought up in the villages by brokers concentrated throughout southern China; larger urban brokerage firms then sold them to silk merchants who traveled to markets in Jiangnan; these merchants then shipped them off to various localities. Peasant handicraft industries in the villages could also weave reeled silk threads into ordinary-quality silk cloth that they supplied to urban workshops for further refinement before it was sent off for sale all around the country. The operation that worked in the opposite direction along with the above process was that of foodstuffs and processed agricultural products from Huguang Province (modern Hubei and Hunan): they were extracted from the villages, worked on in the small towns, sold in urban markets, and then peddled to supply the agricultural villages of Jiangnan.

This vast marketing and distribution mechanism operating at different levels of Chinese society made it possible for the products of the various geographical areas of China to go freely wherever needed, thus creating one enormous market network. This network was already in existence from as early as the Han dynasty. As the Ming and Qing market economy prospered, this vast network operated quite smoothly. The money-exchange shops of Shanxi and Ningpo and the merchants of Anhui all operated within this network of exchange, transferring various forms of venture capital and making great profits in the process. Even the owners of grain storehouses and the large cocoon merchants of Jiangnan not only engaged in the storage and purchasing business but also transferred much venture capital through borrowing and loaning out funds. In this way they encouraged the easy movement of commodities across the market network as well as the transfer and redistribution of wealth throughout the country.

In the nineteenth century and especially after the Opium War, the Chinese economy was subject to serious external interference. After 1840, opium occupied the highest value in Sino-British trade for some twenty years. After that, large quantities of machine-made goods, products of the Industrial Revolution in Europe, began to be marketed in China. They often supplanted traditional Chinese commodities because of their superior quality and lower prices. Chinese rural industries produced many types of traditional commodities, including textiles, processed goods (pickled foods), bamboo and wooden implements, and many other items for household use. Textiles, clothing, and footwear were the most important of these native commodities. The division of labor in the villages was summed up by the saying "men plant, and women weave." The income earned from the marketing of such side products played a large part in the structure of this small-peasant-producer economy. The first wave of products from the European Industrial Revolution were just such commodities—foreign linen, foreign woolens, foreign umbrellas, leather shoes, candles, buttons, and so on—all of them supplanting indigenous products. The situation depicted in the folk song—"Elder sister weaves cloth, elder brother sells linen . . . local linen is expensive, foreign linen is cheap; nobody wants the local product, and brother and sister go hungry"—sums up exactly the rural immiseration depicted in the often-reprinted 1939 report on rural conditions, *Peasant Life in China: A Field Study of Country Life in the Yangtze Valley*, by China's first anthropologist, Fei Xiaotong.

From 1914 to 1919, because of World War I in Europe, many Western products were not marketed in China. By this time, China's own light industries—factories for textile weaving, milling grain into flour, making matches and soap, as well as small-scale machine-making factories—had developed, but they were all located near the coastal treaty port cities rather than in the interior. Thus the rural villages in the interior still did not share in the wealth created by these new industries. No matter whether the wealth flowed abroad or remained in the coastal urban areas, with no income from side products and relying only on the harvests from tilling their small parcels of land, most peasants were unable to maintain even a modest standard of living.

In a modern transportation system, large quantities of goods can be shipped directly to the cities along the railway and highway routes. Thus, the large traditional village market system, originally a network connecting points and areas throughout the nation, was separated and cut off by a linear system of rail, road, and boat transportation. Of course, before the modern transportation lines had completely penetrated the interior, the traditional market network could still exist. Nevertheless, the nationwide market network having been ruptured, not only was much of the national wealth being funneled abroad, creating an unfavorable balance of trade, but the internal flow of wealth was also disrupted. It was no

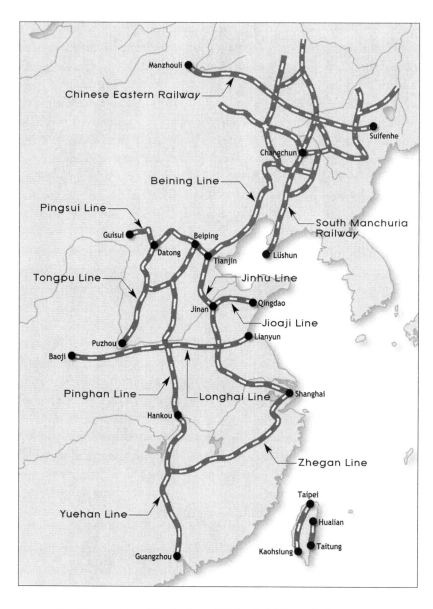

FIGURE 8.3 Geographical Distribution of Major Rail Lines, 1876–1937

longer possible to rely on interregional trade to redistribute continuously the national wealth. Every country is bound to experience some regional wealth disparities, but in China the disruption of its traditional market network led to a situation (existing to this day) in which the coastal areas are wealthy and the interior and isolated regions of the country languish in long-term poverty. At the same time, the wealth disparity between the urban and rural areas became painfully obvious. In short, there was no way for nineteenth-century China to remedy the situation of an unfavorable balance of trade and the flow of wealth outside the country.

During the late Qing and early republic, many of China's railway companies took on foreign loans, and the steamships plying the inner waterways were all owned by foreign merchants, like the Taigu, Yihe, and Riqing (Swire, Jardine, and Japan Shipping) companies. As China's main transportation arteries fell into foreign hands, shipping profits became one more drain on Chinese wealth. At the same time, the carters, boat people, horse and foot travelers—and the innkeepers serving them—were all rendered unemployed as China's interior transportation industries were depressed. China's traditional market network was intimately connected to such traditional transport, and as the transport industry declined, the traditional communication network was disrupted and retained only the ability to carry on small-scale local transportation and communication.

Although the vast market network had broken up, some remnants of it could still be seen in the interior. Professor C. K. Yang (1911–1999) investigated the market structure of Zoupin County, in Shandong Province, in the 1930s and found that regular markets were still being held. The inhabitants of peasant villages gathered at these markets to sell their products and to buy items of daily use and raw materials for their handicraft industries. These regional networks involved areas the size of a county or larger. According to the American scholar G. W. Skinner's report on markets in Sichuan Province in the 1940s, the market network there comprised at least four levels—villages, small townships, large cities, and regional centers.

During the War of Resistance, the Japanese occupied China's coastal cities and most important land and water transportation routes. The Chinese interior could not communicate with the outside world and returned in effect to its earlier state of trade autarky, with these various levels of regional markets for collection and distribution of goods resuming their earlier functions. The holding of market fairs in various provinces in the southwest also resumed. In the guerrilla regions behind enemy lines, the Japanese army patrolled the roads and railways, creating many sealed-off areas in which the circulation of goods also relied on a multilayered market mechanism. In these cases, of course, they were no longer able to link up to form a nationwide market network.

China's traditional market network was not limited to the economic realm, however; it also served to facilitate the flow of information and the movement of people with various skills. Such movement was constantly carried on by the small local communities that comprised the most basic units in Chinese society. After the middle of the nineteenth century, China's nationwide network was gradually transformed, but these small regional communities continued to exist, albeit in different shapes. From ten to a hundred "natural villages" would group themselves together into multifunctional regional organizations. There were water conservation and distribution collectives in Shanxi and Shaanxi and similar groups in southern Taiwan organized to share irrigation channels, combines in southern Fujian for the preservation of common markets for the distribution and sale of porcelains and other local products, associations for sacrifices to Guan Di (the god of war) or the Dragon King in North China, village alliances for martial-arts training and self-defense in the Hakka areas, China's communes of recent times, and ward heelers who manipulate the votes in local elections in Taiwan—all of these various local groups had overlapping functions, and all of them represented basic units of grassroots Chinese social structure. The tradition of holding village fairs (markets) every ten days has actually been preserved to this day in China's southwest.

China's traditional economic structure was gradually transformed as China's internal economy, with its foundation in village agriculture and peasant handicraft industries, disintegrated. After the Opium War, the Chinese economy entered the far larger world economic network. From then on, the Western production revolution and the capitalist market economy permeated China, their influence beginning in the coastal treaty ports and then spreading to the large cities of the interior. After 1990, this new system proliferated in midsized cities throughout the nation.

Under the Japanese colonial regime, Taiwan's agricultural labor was appropriated to supply raw materials for the Japanese capitalist agricultural processing industries, such as sugarcane for sugar production. The long arm of private Japanese corporations (*kabushiki-gaisha*) reached down to the household level. On the other hand, under the Japanese colonial policy of "industry for Japan, agriculture for Taiwan," rice production remained the leading element in Taiwan's economy. Other measures, such as water conservancy, fertilizer distribution, seed development, and pest eradication, also brought colonial government intervention down to the agricultural villages. Various multifunctional popular communities, however, such as temple associations, water conservancy collectives, and self-defense units (like the six Pingdong Hakka regional militia, *liudui*, of southern Taiwan), still continued to operate at the grassroots level.

The contemporary Chinese economy, which is based on its urban areas, began with the importation of foreign commodities into the Chinese market. Two other factors that helped to transform the pattern of the Chinese economy were the construction of a modern transportation system and modern industrial production. Both began with an influx of foreign capital investment and were gradually expanded and developed by the Chinese themselves.

During the nineteenth century, after China opened the treaty ports, the industrial world was riding the crest of a great wave of railroad building. At the end of the nineteenth and the beginning of the twentieth centuries, either with foreign capital loans or with national capital, China constructed a number of east-west and north-south railway lines in the eastern half of the country. These included today's Tianjin-Shanghai, Beijing-Hankou, Guangdong-Hankou, Jiangsu-Gansu (Longhai), and Zhejiang-Jiangxi lines. These rail lines, combined with the Yangzi, Pearl, and other inland waterways and coastal shipping lanes, served to connect the many geographical regions of the eastern half of China.

The enormous carrying capacity of these long lines of transportation formed a new economic network. The internal exchange of regional goods and materials combined with international trade transformed the Chinese economic market into one in which large urban megacities serve as centers of collection and distribution. The range and variety of commodities available in this huge economic supply and sales system differ greatly from earlier times. Compared with China's traditional economy, its modern economic system is more complex, pluralistic, and flourishing.

The second major element of change was the transformation to modern industrial modes of production. Modern Chinese industrialization began with the late Qing national defense industry. Shipbuilding and weapons factories in Jiangnan, Fujian, and Hubei led the first phase of Chinese

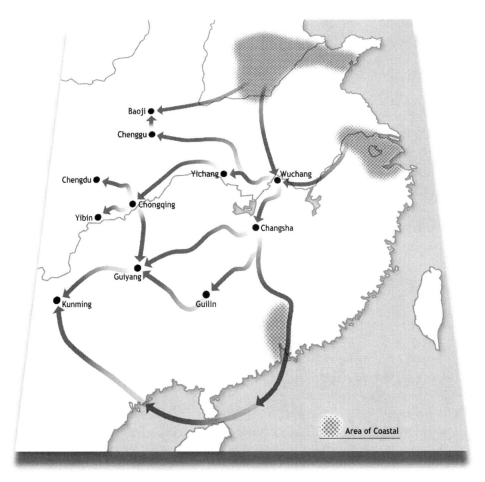

FIGURE 8.4 The Movement of Chinese Industries to the Interior During the War of Resistance Against Japan

industrial production. Although these early industries were quite large, they were difficult to maintain and did not continue to develop. Light industry for the manufacture of consumer commodities for everyday use soon constituted the main element in Chinese industrialization. Factories for the production of noodles, textiles, matches, electricity, machinery, chemicals, and processed agricultural commodities, operated first with foreign capital and later with Chinese government and private investment, sprang up all over the Yangzi delta, from Beijing to Tianjin and in the Wuhan regions. During the war in Europe, from 1914 to 1919, foreign investment stopped, and light industry with Chinese investment was given an opportunity to develop. In terms of the world market, these industries were not very large, but they still transformed the pattern and content of the Chinese economic system. Five or six large urban areas became the foundation of Chinese industry and replaced the former base of cottage industries in rural villages.

Although the scope and quality of this Chinese industrialization were rather modest in terms of the contemporary world, nevertheless the shock that these changes gave to Chinese society was both profound and irreversible. They brought about a rupture in the Chinese economy. Three strata—the interior and the coastal regions, the villages and the cities, and agriculture and industry—split into two separate production and marketing systems. The economy of the coastal industrial cities gradually extended into the interior, but its rate of expansion was quite slow. The traditional economic pattern continued to exist only in the regions between the interior heartland and the large urban areas.

Two events that greatly influenced the Chinese economy occurred during the War of Resistance from 1937 to 1945. First, the traditional market network began to function again in the interior and the guerrilla areas, greatly bolstering Chinese endurance to resist Japanese aggression. Second, thousands of coastal factories were moved to Sichuan, reassembled there in the southwest, and put into production. These dilapidated factories established a foundation for industry in China's interior. On this account, one result of eight years of war was to stimulate China's coastal industries to develop into the interior, and this development served as a catalyst for China's industrialization after 1950.

3. Changes in China's Educational System

Late Qing China was faced with conditions unprecedented in Chinese history and was failing everywhere on the military front. Even though the Qing court was obstinate and ineffective, it was forced to institute various reforms and do its utmost to confront the challenges it faced. Thus in 1862, the Qing court set up the School of Combined Learning (*Tongwen Guan*) in Beijing; the next year it established the School of Broad Learning (*Guangfangyan Guan*) in Shanghai and another School of Combined Learning in Fuzhou the year after that. All of these schools were set up to train experts in Western languages. In 1867, the Qing court established the Academy of Naval Administration (*Chuanzheng xuetang*) in Mawei harbor in Fuzhou, and in 1869 the Jiangnan Manufacturing Bureau (*Jiangnan zhizaoju*) was established in Shanghai to train modern engineers. After that, military academies and specialized training schools were set up in many places around the country, all for the purpose of "employing the best technology of the barbarians to defeat the barbarians."

The Tongwen Guan was primarily concerned with languages and hoped to produce diplomats for negotiations and the translation of Western-language materials. The general and statesman Li Hongzhang had a broader vision, however. He advocated teaching not only languages but also Western natural sciences, including mathematics, astronomy, and physics, as well as industrial engineering and other subjects. He hoped to train a cadre of experts who would be able to oversee the manufacture of modern Western-style steamships and weapons. Li wanted to establish an Academy of Science inside the Tongwen Guan, but his plan was defeated after opposition from the Grand Secretary Woren (1804–1871) and others. Nevertheless, the Tongwen Guan did eventually add mathematics, international law, medicine, physiology, astronomy, and physics to its curriculum. As a result of these measures, some Chinese schools began to teach Western academic subjects in 1870, and after that many military academies, especially naval academies, began to offer modern mathematics, mechanical engineering, physics, geography, and so on, thus offering another powerful channel for instruction in the "new learning."

In 1874, Tang Tingshu (Tong King-sing, 1832–1892), Xu Shou (1818–1884), and others established the Shanghai Polytechnic Institution; their curriculum went beyond simply studying Western industrial arts, and they taught students in subjects such as astronomy, mathematics, medicine, manufacturing, chemistry, weaponry, and geology. At this same time, Western churches also began to establish parochial schools in China, such as St. John's University in Shanghai. St. John's first set up faculties of Western learning, national learning, and theology, but later it expanded into the four faculties of literature, science, medicine, and theology, with curriculums including Western languages, mathematics (algebra and calculus), Western science, astronomy, chemistry, mechanics, geology, and navigation. Tianjin's Beiyang Academy of Western Learning (now Tianjin University) began by teaching industrial engineering, Western learning, mining, mechanical engineering, and law. The curriculum of these private and parochial institutions of higher learning already approximated our contemporary university faculties of humanities, law, science, engineering, and medicine, and the subjects they taught went far beyond the national defense industry and foreign affairs.

In 1898, the Qing court established the Imperial Capital University (*Jingshi da xuetang*, until 1912 the name of today's Peking University). Replacing the ancient National University (*Guozijian*), it offered seven branches of study: Chinese classics, literature, law and government, commerce, agriculture, Western science, and industrial engineering. Some other provinces also established such universities (*Da xuetang*); for example, the Hunan-Hubei University (*Lianghu xuetang*) in Hubei (1902) offered courses in Chinese classics, history, mathematics, physics and chemistry, law, financial administration, and military affairs. Compared with the private and parochial universities, these government-sponsored universities added only Chinese classical studies to their curriculums. In 1912, when Cai Yuanpei (1868–1940) created the new educational system, universities were organized into the six faculties of humanities (literature or arts), law, sciences, engineering, medicine, and agriculture. In 1917, when he became chancellor of the Imperial Capital University and its name was changed to Peking University (*Beijing daxue* or *Beida*), he established only the two faculties of humanities (literature, arts) and science; the university actually did not have the four practical faculties of engineering, commerce, medicine, and agriculture.

From the above, we can see that in less than a generation higher education in China developed away from serving the narrow interests of national defense and foreign affairs and into a new educational system quite similar to that of Western universities. Universities, colleges, and various specialized schools for training in industry, commerce, law, government administration, and medicine sprang up all over the country; by 1909, China already had some 123 institutions of higher learning, with an enrollment of more than twenty-two thousand students. This number of students already surpassed the number of successful candidates in the imperial provincial examinations. By 1907, there were thirty thousand middle, elementary, and normal schools nationwide, with an enrollment of a million students. Many foreign missionary–sponsored universities — St. John's, Yanjing (now Peking University), Jinling (now Nanjing University), and Furen Catholic University — were also established in the last years of the nineteenth century. There were already more than a thousand parochial elementary and middle schools and colleges, with a combined enrollment of twenty to thirty thousand students.

During the early years of the republic, these late Qing school and enrollment numbers continued to rise. After the National Revolutionary Army's 1928 victory in the Northern Expedition, modern education advanced by leaps and bounds. The number of government, private, and parochial schools at all levels increased tenfold, and student enrollment increased even more. On the eve of the War of Resistance, there were more than one hundred thousand resident university students. After the abolition of the traditional examination system in 1905, modern school education soon became the mainstream form of Chinese education.

The curriculum of China's new educational system was adopted from Western schools and, after Chinese classical studies was removed, the new system of higher education bore no relation to China's traditional studies. Elementary and middle-school curriculums were all designed for students to graduate to postsecondary education. Since higher education was completely Westernized, elementary and middle schools naturally followed suit. Elementary-school primers like the *Three Character Classic* (*Sanzi jing*), the *Hundred Surnames* (*Baijia xing*), the *Thousand Character Classic* (*Qianzi wen*), and the *Thousand Poets* (*Qianjia shi*) were first replaced by picture books with vocabulary items like "man," "hand," and "ruler" and then later by texts like "the dog barks and the cat jumps." Textbooks for the middle-school curriculum of national studies, English, mathematics, sciences, chemistry, history, geography, and so on were prepared on the basis of contemporary knowledge. This new education system was based on Western models and used Western texts as blueprints. Teaching materials for parochial schools were generally imported directly from abroad, and the instruction was done in a foreign language. For example, in a middle school in southern China, the English textbooks were British and published in India; the chemistry and mathematics (algebra and analytic geometry) and the introductory biology texts were all published in the United States. One-third of the subjects the students studied was from English textbooks.

The educational level of students taught in this fashion was comparable to the upper third of students in Western countries, but graduates of upper middle schools who returned to the rural villages of the Chinese interior not only would have no place to practice their skills but would also experience a great sense of alienation from their surroundings. Such students could only live in the big coastal cities and could not return to their rural homes. Scholars studying nineteenth- and twentieth-century Chinese education have all noticed a major problem: the rupture between the coastal areas and the interior, the cities and the countryside. They had become two separate worlds. China's villages had already lost the children who went off to receive a modern education and training. The distribution of schools in the first half of the twentieth century was as follows: small towns and villages had elementary schools; county seats had lower middle schools; provincial capitals had upper middle schools, specialized training schools, normal schools, and possibly universities; and big cities had universities. Beijing (then Peiping), Tianjin, Shanghai, and Nanjing had the finest universities. According to the level of their education, elementary school graduates no longer returned to the villages, middle school graduates no longer returned to the small towns, graduates of special training schools and above no longer returned to the county seats, university graduates no longer returned to the provinces of their origins, and, finally, returned overseas students were confined to four or five major cities.

This situation was quite different from how it had been in the past. If we examine the traditional imperial examination system, we see that most of the *xiucai* (flowering talents), the graduates of county-level examinations, remained in their rural homelands. Most *juren* (presented scholars), graduates of provincial-level examinations, also stayed in their county seats. They held offices in different parts of the country, but upon retirement, they not only returned to their county of origin but even to their old (natal) homes. Thus, the traditional educated elite continued to be primarily affiliated with their native homes. They were the local leaders and maintained large, close-knit networks of communication and association. An obvious example of the working of such networks was when Zeng Guofan and other Hunan gentry appealed for help against the Taipings in their homeland. Hundreds of men answered their call, joined them in common cause, and they were able to organize the Hunan Army in their little corner of China. Before and after the 1911 revolution, the gentry elite of many provinces advocated a written constitution and later joined the revolution, amply demonstrating the power of regional elites at the time.

The phenomenon of a modern education system leading to alienation between the intellectual class and their rural homelands was not confined to China alone. In the process of learning from Western Europe, both Poland and Russia experienced the same phenomenon—the term

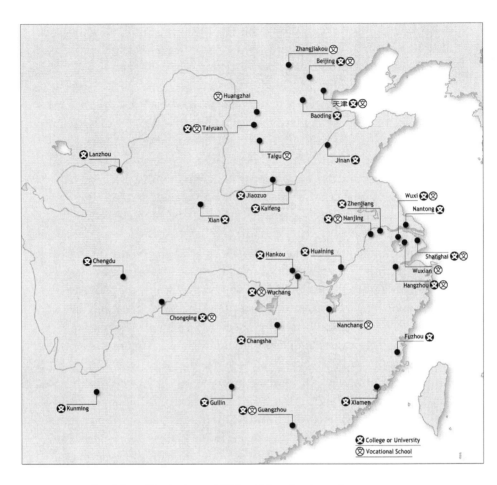

FIGURE 8.5 Map of Institutions of Higher Education in 1936

"intelligentsia," first applied to this Eastern European intellectual class, came into English from Polish and Russian. In the process of "Angliciza-tion," there were also many displaced intellectuals in India. China is too large, however, and the wholesale transformation of the country could not be accomplished in a short period of time. Thus, the rupture that began in the late nineteenth century between the coastal cities and the interior, or the cities and the villages, still prevails today. The trouble with this situa-tion is not that the educated population works mostly in the coastal cities; the real problem is that for many years the rural countryside has experi-enced a steady loss of talented people. This has produced a desertification of rural talent (a brain drain) comparable to the erosion of fertile land that leaves behind nothing but barren soil.

China paid a high price for its movement toward modernization. First, it could not halt the process of modernization in favor of its traditional culture. Second, the problem of rural decline and poverty caused by uneven modernization cried out for a solution. Before the War of Resistance, a few areas in the interior, such as Guangxi, Shanxi, and West Hunan, attempted some rural development, but the results were not particularly striking. In several guerrilla areas behind enemy lines during the war, outside leaders attempted to rebuild the local social order and economy under blockade conditions. As soon as the war was over and these once self-sufficient areas came into contact with the outside world, however, they were again marginalized by the wealthy coastal cities. Perhaps the continuing transformation of China's coastal cities and the spread of its effects to the extent that the relative distance between rural and urban gradually lessens offers the best hope for the solution of this difficult problem.

Considering the successes of China's modern education, we can say that from the late nineteenth into the twentieth century, China produced two or three generations of excellent human capital. In the academic world, China already has several high-quality universities and graduate institutions for the education of the next generation of human talent. When the graduates of China's premier universities go abroad to Europe and America for advanced studies or scholarly research, they hold their own with the best local scholars. Modern academic research is already well established in China, and, although they are relatively few in number, Chinese research institutions are of very high quality. In some fields of study, such as archaeology, geology, and mathematics, Chinese scholars have made outstanding achievements on the international stage.

On the road to industrialization, China's modern education system also trained an able cadre of experts in specialized areas of technology. From the 1890s through the 1920s, Chinese railroad and harbor construction relied on foreign engineers, but from the 1950s on, Chinese industrial construction no longer relied on foreign assistance. In similar fashion, in iron smelting, machine building, industrial chemistry, weaving, and other manufacturing industries, the technological experts trained in Chinese schools were already able to operate quite smoothly. The well-known chemist Hou Debang (1890–1974) earned worldwide respect in 1933 for his discovery of a method for improving the ammonia-soda process for producing sodium carbonate (soda ash or washing soda).

After its victory in the Northern Expedition, the Nationalist government in Nanjing attracted a large number of returned overseas students as high-level personnel, established many universities, and trained many midlevel government functionaries. This group of modern-educated individuals organized a brand-new administrative mechanism that was qualitatively on a par with governments throughout the contemporary world. During its ten years of national reconstruction (the Nanjing decade), the currency was unified, the Central Bank of China was established, and the national tax system was continually improved. Natural-resource committees employed a cadre of superb personnel to prospect for mineral resources, improve waterways, set up a national industrial system, and integrate advanced and less-advanced enterprises. This effort made it possible in one short (but still insufficient) decade for China to be at least somewhat prepared for the coming explosion of the War of Resistance against Japanese aggression. When full-scale warfare began, hundreds of coastal-area factories were dismantled and transported in their entirety into the interior. All of these accomplishments were possible because China had spent over half a century building up a high-quality modern educational system; even though it was still not large enough, it was able to function very well in support of the national welfare.

The historian Huang Renyu (Ray Huang, 1918–2000) maintained that the regime led by Chiang Kai-shek set up the "superstructure" for the modern Chinese nation-state. China's new education system was undoubtedly the most important force supporting this superstructure. Professor Huang also maintained that the Chinese Communist regime led by Mao Zedong (1893–1976) established the "base" of this new nation-state with the peasants as the foundation. The integration of these two strata of the Chinese social structure will depend on further development. Only when these two strata are welded together can the rupture between China's coastal cities and its interior regions, the urban and the rural, finally be healed.

4. The Militarization of Modern China

In Chinese history, the end of the Han dynasty through the Three Kingdoms era and the end of the Tang dynasty through the Five Dynasties era represent periods of military control. Not only did warlords occupy the land, but the power of the various states was held in military hands for more than a century. Modern Chinese history has also been a militaristic era, and it has also lasted for more than a century—from the Taiping Rebellion and the rise of the Hunan Army to the middle of the twentieth century and beyond.

What is meant by "militarization" here refers to the phenomenon of military men (including civilians who became military leaders) using armed force to achieve a large measure of autonomy and gradually plundering the nation's economic resources and dominating part or even all national power. This process of militarization began with the rise of Zeng Guofan's Hunan Army.

When the Qing armies entered China and conquered the Ming by force of arms, their military strength was organized under the Manchu banner system. Their eight Manchu, Chinese, and Mongolian banners numbered only a little more than two hundred thousand men, but all the ethnic Manchu men were soldiers, and they were all members of the ruling strata that governed China. This may be regarded as the militarization of an ethnic group. During the conquest of northern Xinjiang (Galdan's Dzungar khanate) under the Kangxi emperor (r. 1662–1722), the Manchu bannermen were still the backbone of the Qing armies, and the Han Chinese troops were only auxiliaries. In the Qianlong emperor's time (r. 1736–1795), the quality of the Manchu banner troops declined because of their overindulgence in the pleasures of life, and the empire had to depend on the Chinese troops of the Green Standard Army as its main fighting force. In all of the campaigns of this era, the ethnic-Chinese Green Standard Army was commanded by decorated Manchu noblemen. After the Jiaqing and Daoguang emperors (combined reigns 1796–1850), Han Chinese generals commanded the empire's chief fighting forces.

The Taiping rebels wreaked havoc all the way from Guangxi north toward Beijing, and the Manchu Qing armies could only chase and harass them, not stop them. Zeng Guofan, Zuo Zongtang, and other local Hunan literati with no other backing were actually able to organize a powerful Hunan Army and contend with the Taipings across hundreds of miles of territory. In the end, these "Hunan braves" defeated and subdued the vast Taiping Heavenly Kingdom. This military movement had several important new characteristics. First, the rise of the Hunan Army was organized completely by private individuals; the official Qing armed forces were only auxiliary to them. The Hunan Army's systems of operation, training, and supply were all planned and executed solely by Zeng Guofan, Zuo Zongtang, and their associates. The officers of all ranks were chosen to serve from among the relatives, close friends, and followers of Hunan Army commanders; none of them were transferred in from the regular reserve army. The army's commanding officers were all united by personal relationships rather than the government's military command system. Second, except for early on when they accepted the assistance of local officials such as Guan Wen (1798–1871) and Hu Linyi (1812–1861), the Hunan Army provided for its own salaries and food rations. The army itself also procured all of its weapons, ammunition, and other logistical materiel. Third, during the fighting, the Qing court granted the Hunan Army commanders the title of provincial governor or viceroy (*dufu*; for example, Zeng Guofan was viceroy of Zhili, now Hebei Province) and gave them the power to commandeer local resources.

After the defeat of the Taipings, the commanders of the Hunan (Xiang) and Anhui (Huai) armies (the latter created by Li Hongzhang) spread out around the country as governor generals of the southeast and operated almost like modern *fengjian*-style princes. During the Boxer Rebellion, when the Eight-Nation Alliance captured Beijing, these southeastern governor generals were actually able to unite their provinces for self-protection and disobey the Qing court's orders. The Hunan and Huai army commanders were among the most active governor generals to participate in the late Qing Self-Strengthening Movement. These generals were able to achieve a high level of autonomy, amass considerable military power in Hunan and Anhui provinces, and use that power to commandeer the resources of other provinces without the Qing court's authorization.

When the Hunan Army was created, it was divided into battalions (*ying*), with each battalion having a normal complement of five hundred men who were recruited from his local population by the battalion commander himself. Zeng Guofan led about ten of his followers, and they organized some ten battalions, with the entire army comprising only a few thousand troops. As the Hunan Army engaged the Taiping armies from South Hunan, they followed the Yangzi eastward, the battle lines became very drawn out, and the army greatly expanded in numbers. Toward the end of the campaign, the Hunan Army was distributed throughout the middle and lower reaches of the Yangzi, and its troop strength had reached more than three hundred thousand. Adding to this number Zuo

Zongtang and Li Hongzhang's troops from Zhejiang and Jiangsu respectively, and this formidable military force led by the Hunan Army actually commanded some five hundred thousand troops.

After the defeat of the Taipings, Zeng Guofan demobilized most of the Hunan Army, but Li Hongzhang's Anhui Army continued to grow, becoming the main Qing army. Zuo Zongtang reorganized a portion of the old Hunan Army to participate in the Qing campaigns in Xinjiang. This was still a force of some two to three hundred thousand men, and it was spread out over an even greater stretch of territory than before—north to Zhili (Hebei); west to Shaanxi, Gansu, and Xinjiang; and to the various provinces in the south and southeast. Even General Liu Mingchuan (1836–1896) led troops from Taiwan to join the Hunan and Anhui armies. "Taiwan braves" under the leadership of the father-and-son team of Lin Wencha (1828–1864) and Lin Chaodong (1851–1904) were attached to these two armies and fought the Taipings on the mainland.

The Hunan Army employed two methods to raise money. First, they set up customs stations on the main communication arteries and exacted new *likin* transportation taxes from traveling merchants. Second, they took advantage of the Qing court's authorization of the sale of blank certificates of office and gave out different official ranks in order to obtain contributions—this amounted to the sale of offices by the governor generals. Besides these methods, the army could also impose taxes and requisition supplies from the local populations near where they were stationed. They did this openly, even without government authorization. The governor generals of the Hunan and Anhui army network used the funds obtained in this manner under the umbrella of normal government taxation to finance the Self-Strengthening Movement's reconstruction efforts. Thus, the Jiangnan Manufacturing Bureau in Shanghai, the Mawei Shipbuilding Factory in Fuzhou, and lamp factories, telegraph offices, steamship companies, railroads, and so on of various other regions carried on the first wave of China's modern industrialization. At the same time, this network of "famous officials" led by Zeng Guofan, Zuo Zongtang, and Li Hongzhang also expanded their own base of operations and their considerable personal power. All of these enterprises and activities grew out of the Hunan Army's military mobilization of a thousand "Hunan braves."

After Zeng Guofan, Zuo Zongtang, Li Hongzhang, and others, men such as Zhang Zhidong (1837–1909) and Yuan Shikai (1859–1916) began their rapid rise to power. Zhang Zhidong was based in Hubei, where he organized and trained his New Hubei Army with a strength of not less than seventy to eighty thousand troops. Combined with the Hanyang Steel Factory, the Hanyang Arsenal (in contemporary Wuhan, the capital of Hubei), and many new schools, the middle Yangzi also became a base for new political policies. In 1911, the New Hubei Army would launch the Republican Revolution and bring an end to two thousand years of Chinese imperial history.

Yuan Shikai's power was entirely based on military strength. In 1895, he was appointed to command the first New Army. Later, as viceroy of Zhili (Heibei), he expanded his warlord army, making the Beiyang Army, stationed near the capital area, China's most modern fighting force, with a strength of some one hundred thousand troops. Yuan relied on various enterprises and local agriculture in the Tianjin area to become the most powerful general in North China. When the Qing court suspected him of betraying them, Yuan advanced by retreating—he returned to his native Henan on the pretext of treating a foot illness. When the revolution erupted in Wuchang, the Qing court was unable to mobilize the Beiyang Army and had to recall Yuan to lead it. Taking advantage of the situation, Yuan Shikai engineered the abdication of the last emperor of China, six-year-old Puyi, and used his military strength to have himself made the first president of the new republic (in place of Sun Yat-sen). He later declared himself emperor but never took the throne. All of Yuan's various machinations were made possible by the strength of his warlord Beiyang Army.

Yuan's attempt to be crowned emperor failed, and he died angry and humiliated, but the Beiyang military clique was not disbanded. Beiyang warlords such as Feng Guozhang (1859–1919), Duan Qirui (1865–1936), and Cao Kun (1862–1938) held the rank of army commander in the provinces while contending for the chief executive's power in the capital. During the warlord era at the beginning of the republic, warlord cliques fought for power and territory from about 1916 to 1928. The Beiyang Clique had subdivisions in many provinces and continued to expand its armies until their military strength reached five to six hundred thousand troops, arguably the largest military organization in the early republic. The Beiyang warlords soon split into the Anhui, Zhili, and other cliques, which fought one another for supremacy. The second generation of warlords, including Wu Peifu (1874–1939) and Sun Chuanfang (1885–1935), staked out their separate territories in northern, central, and southeastern China, where they usurped political power through military force, controlling the heartland of China for over a decade.

Besides the Beiyang warlords, Zhang Zuolin (1875–1928) commanded the Fengtian Army of more than a hundred thousand troops in Manchuria. From there, he contended for power with the Beiyang and Zhili cliques. Zhang invaded North China twice (1920 and 1922), defeating Duan Qirui the first time but later losing to Wu Peifu and retreating to Manchuria. Zhang Zuolin's Fengtian Army was not limited to ground troops; he also commanded a small-scale navy and a few fighter planes. The Shenyang Arsenal, which served Zhang's armies, was the nation's largest at that time, and his other industrial enterprises were quite formidable. Zhang relied on this military and industrial strength to make his way resourcefully in the three-way struggles between the Beiyang and Anhui cliques and Sun Yat-sen's Canton regime. When he was killed in a Japanese-organized railroad explosion at Huanggutun Station near Shenyang on June 4, 1928, his son, the "Young Marshal" Zhang Xueliang (1901–2001), capitulated to Chiang Kai-shek. Consequently, Chiang was able to overcome the other warlord enemies facing him at the time and unite China.

Yan Xishan (1883–1960) took advantage of Shanxi's natural terrain, which is easy to defend but hard to attack, to seal himself off for ten years. Yan commanded over a hundred thousand troops. He joined the final stage of the National Revolutionary Army's Northern Expedition and attacked Beijing from the north. Later, however, he joined with Li Zongren's (1890–1969) New Guangxi Clique and Feng Yuxiang's Northwest Army (or Guominjun, Nationalist Army) to attack Chiang Kai-shek in the Central Plains War (May to November 1930). After being defeated by Chiang's forces, Yan Xishan retreated again to Shanxi. During the War of Resistance, Yan maintained his independence facing the Nationalists under Chiang, the Communists under Mao, and the Japanese puppet government of Wang Jingwei (1883–1944).

Li Zongren, Bai Chongxi (1893–1966), and others relied on their strength as battalion commanders to control Guangxi. They inherited the Guangxi Army forces and used them to move up the upper reaches of the Yangzi in Guangdong and occupy the southwest. They fought well with Chiang Kai-shek in the Northern Expedition but later combined with Feng Yuxiang and Yan Xishan to oppose Chiang in the Central Plains War. During the War of Resistance, the Guangxi troops were the main

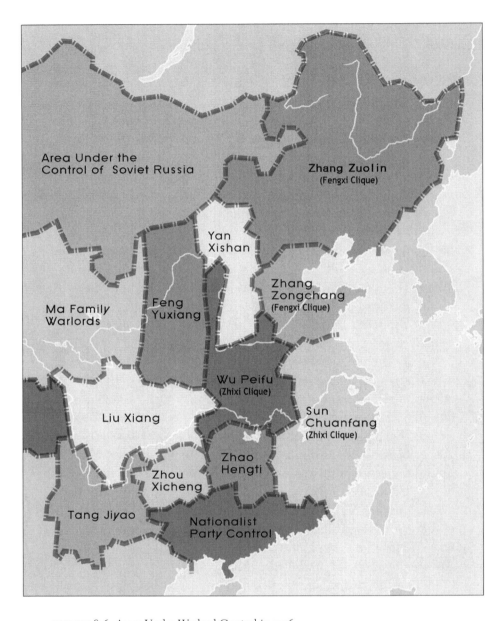

FIGURE 8.6 Areas Under Warlord Control in 1926

force in theater number 5. Their one hundred thousand troops guarded the Yangzi River gateway to Sichuan but maintained their base area in Guangxi.

Feng Yuxiang grew up in the military rank and file. He served as a midlevel officer in the Beiyang Army, and then later on he and Hu Jingyi (1892–1925) betrayed the Zhili Clique and established their own Northwest Army. Feng frequently changed his position and his friends and enemies, fighting in many different areas without a fixed base, finally ending up in the northwest. At the most he commanded around two hundred thousand troops, but their military strength was uneven. Feng was allied with Chiang Kai-shek during the Northern Expedition but later joined forces against him; then, still later, Feng went back over to Chiang's side. In any case, Feng represented a military force that could not be ignored at the time.

After Yuan Shikai declared himself emperor, Sun Yat-sen organized a government in Guangzhou (Canton), but he had no armed forces and had to rely on the Guangxi, Guangdong, and Yunnan militarists for support. Sun received help from the Comintern (Communist International) under the direction of the Soviet Union, established the Whampoa Military Academy, appointed Chiang Kai-shek its commandant and, starting with five thousand rifles, created a military force that belonged to his Nationalist Party. Chiang Kai-shek built on this base to develop the National Revolutionary Army (NRA). After defeating Chen Jiongming (1878–1933), a former Sun ally who opposed Sun's warlord connections, Chiang launched the Northern Expedition and completed the unification Sun had sought.

Graduates of Whampoa Military Academy all pledged their loyalty to Chiang Kai-shek. After establishing Nanjing as the capital of the Republic of China, Chiang was the supreme commander, the generalissimo, of the NRA and, with a hundred thousand troops under his command, the ruler of the nation's heartland. The Beiyang Clique collapsed, and Chiang maintained his hold on military power as chairman of the Military Affairs Committee in the Nationalist government. The National Revolutionary Army was a Nationalist Party army and, as such, pledged its loyalty to Chiang as his personal army. This was the basis for Chiang's dictatorship, and the older leaders of the Nationalist Party could do nothing but acquiesce to this state of affairs.

Sun Yat-sen set up his government in the south, unarmed and defenseless, by relying on the popular desire for revolution and his own personal prestige. Although he appealed to people from all over China, he was always dependent on other forces and unable to carry out his plans. Chiang Kai-shek originally had no great prestige within the Nationalist Party, but with the support of the Whampoa Military Academy, he was unstoppable.

Chiang's rise to power and position is a perfect example of the effects of militarization in China. After the Northern Expedition, the military leaders from various regions held a conference to discuss the reorganization of the nation's military forces. Chiang Kai-shek advocated a reduction of troop levels to eight hundred thousand men, but his proposal was rejected. Chiang wanted to maintain his own military strength while reducing the numbers in the armies of other commanders. This led to widespread anti-Chiang feelings and the outbreak of the Central Plains War, which pit Chiang's troops against the combined armies of Feng Yuxiang, Yan Xishan, and Li Zongren. No fewer than a million troops were engaged in this bloody and costly civil war. This number does not include the forces serving in smaller regional warlord armies, such as those stationed in the so-called defense areas. Thus, the overall military strength of China at that time totaled probably more than one and a half million men.

After the Northern Expedition, the Chinese Communists concentrated their scattered military forces in the Jiangxi Soviet and continuously fought with the Nanjing government. The Communist First Front Red Army (later the People's Liberation Army) had at least two hundred thousand troops at the beginning of the Long March from Jiangxi to Yan'an (Shaanxi) in October 1934. With losses on the Long March but adding in the troops commanded by Zhang Guotao (1897–1979), the entire Communist army numbered some one hundred and fifty thousand.

During the War of Resistance, the Communists and the Nationalists carried on an uneasy united front against the Japanese. The Red Army expanded its numbers in various guerrilla areas and was reputed to have ninety thousand troops. During the occupation, the Japanese established several puppet governments, all of which had some military strength — these included Manchukuo in Manchuria, the Provisional Government of the Republic of China in Peiping, and Wang Jingwei's collaborationist Government of National Salvation in Nanjing. Manchukuo had the most military might, with some four hundred thousand troops at the end of the war. Thus, the combined armed strength of the Communist and the puppet regimes was quite large.

During the major engagements they fought against the Japanese in eight years of war, the Central Government's National Revolutionary Army lost most of its elite troops. Many of these losses were suffered in the first stage of the war, when they pit their blood and guts against greatly superior Japanese forces at the battles of Peiping, Shanghai, Xuzhou (in Jiangsu), and Taierzhuang (near Xuzhou). After losing the four-and-a-half-month-long battle to defend Wuhan, the key city on the Yangzi, in which the NRA under Chiang's personal command committed more than a million troops, Chinese officers and men were extremely exhausted; they had used up all their reserves, but much of the ground army escaped, and they continued to fight on. In their eight years of resistance to the Japanese, the NRA suffered more than three million casualties—90 percent of all Chinese army casualties—but they still managed to field three to four million troops. In light of all this, we can estimate that during the War of Resistance there was a total of seven to eight million troops in the various armies operating in China. This is more military strength than ever before in Chinese history.

Soon after the end of the anti-Japanese war, full-scale civil war (1946–1950) broke out between the Communist and the Nationalist parties for control of postwar China. Both sides easily fielded armies of one to two hundred thousand troops in their various battles. In one of the three largest Communist assaults, the Liaoning-Shenyang (Liaoshen) Campaign (or Battle of Jinzhou), the Nationalist Fifth Army was totally destroyed. In the Huaihai Campaign (Battle of Xupeng or Xu-Bang), the Communist armies under the command of Marshal Liu Bocheng (1892–1986) and Political Commissar Deng Xiaoping (1904–1997) surrounded and annihilated several major Nationalist armies under the command of General Huang Wei (1904–1989). More than a million troops fought on both sides.

After taking power and establishing the People's Republic of China, the Communist government set up a number of military regions, each of which had several hundred thousand troops. There were then probably three million active-duty soldiers in the entire country. The Republic of China's Nationalist government moved to Taiwan, and the over nine hundred thousand remaining troops crossed the Taiwan Strait with the government. Altogether, there were a remarkable number of active-duty, battle-hardened Chinese soldiers.

In sum, the militarization of China took place after the civilian government regimes had lost their legal legitimacy. As Mao Zedong famously
said, power came from the barrel of a gun. Those with real military power
also controlled the national resources. From the Taiping Rebellion on,
China marched step by step toward militarization—not only did the number of armed soldiers gradually increase, but whoever controlled these
military forces was also able to obtain economic resources and political
power. Even the development of industrial enterprises and education had
to find developmental opportunities in an environment of militarization.

For over a century, China had experienced a long period of warfare
during which the land was divided, national resources were parceled out,
and the nation was greatly weakened. Nevertheless, under these inauspicious conditions and with limited capital, men such as Liu Mingchuan
in Taiwan, Zhang Jian (1853–1926) in Nantong (Jiangsu), and Lu Zuofu
(1893–1952) in Beipei (part of Chongqing, in Sichuan) still managed to
carry out some constructive regional development. The national construction and development accomplished during the Nanjing decade was
carried out under the military dictatorship of Chiang Kai-shek. Other development in Guangxi and Shanxi was carried out under the military
regimes of the Guangxi Clique and Yan Xishan respectively. Even during
the War of Resistance and with the enemy at the gates, some agricultural
areas (like West Henan) and some guerrilla areas behind enemy lines
were still able to carry out various reforms and maintain relative stability
under extremely trying conditions. All of these constructive efforts demonstrated the resilience of the Chinese people under the wartime conditions
of national division.

China's vast military forces were, in the final analysis, a tremendous
waste of national manpower. China's inability to properly develop during
the hundred plus years from 1840 to 1950 was in large part attributable
to the dissipation of huge quantities of the national treasure in order to
maintain the armed strength of large military establishments. Militarization involved the use of military force to coerce people into accepting rule
by warlord regimes, and such coercion did not lead to normal systems of
administration. Recent Chinese history is actually the history of the use
of military coercion. That the nation could survive for a hundred years
without being swallowed up by foreign powers is remarkable. This is a
historical irony that was neither planned nor predictable, and it should

not be used as a rationale for regarding militarization as a permanently normal condition.

5. The Vigorous Expansion of Urban Culture

China's most celebrated modern cities gradually came into prominence during the nineteenth and twentieth centuries. In the first rank was the metropolis of Shanghai, in a class by itself. In the second rank were cities such as Beijing, Tianjin, Nanjing, Shenyang, Guangzhou, Wuhan, Xiamen (Amoy), and Qingdao. Finally, in the third rank, were cities such as Chongqing, Xi'an, Harbin, Kunming, Fuzhou, Ningpo, Taiyuan, and so on. Only members of the first and second ranks could rightly be called metropolitan cities at that time; members of the third rank were all regional centers beyond the major cities.

There have, of course, been many major cities throughout Chinese history: Chang-an, Luoyang, and Yangzhou during the Tang dynasty; Bianliang (Kaifeng), Hangzhou, Guangzhou, and Quanzhou (Zaytun) during the Song and Yuan dynasties; Nanjing and Beijing during the Ming and Qing dynasties—all of these can be considered world-class cities for their time. They had large populations and flourishing trade and industries that compared very well with major contemporary cities of Europe and the Middle East. Most of these major cities in Chinese history were either centers of government or involved in world trade. Most cities that served as regional centers were primarily concerned with military government while also carrying out some commercial functions.

With the exception of the two capitals of Nanjing and Beijing, most of the major cities of the nineteenth to twentieth centuries rose and grew prosperous through international trade. Shanghai and Tianjin were originally small towns; their rise as important and prosperous big cities depended completely on their status as world trade ports. Shanghai is a special example: this coastal county seat vaulted forward to become China's premier trade port city thanks to the chance circumstances of its location.

The nature of world trade in the nineteenth and twentieth centuries was different from China's traditional foreign trade relations. In earlier Chinese foreign trade, the foreigners who came to China were all merchants. In the late Qing, China was forced by the superior military might

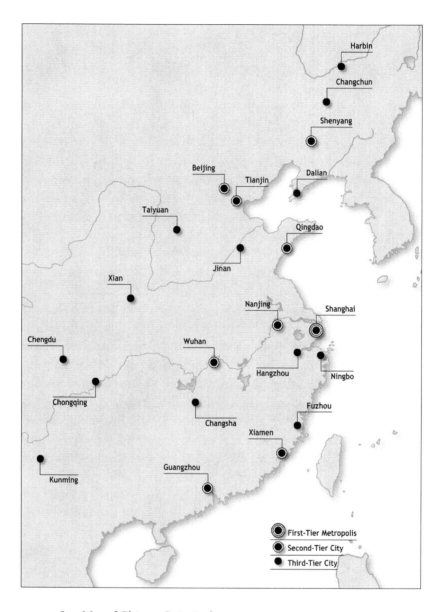

FIGURE 8.7 Map of Chinese Cities in the 1930s

of Western powers to open up treaty ports for foreign trade. The Western powers relied on the superiority of their Industrial Revolution production methods and the power of their capitalist economic system to put China at a very severe disadvantage. These treaty ports served as the entry point for the spread of Western power and influence throughout China. Thus, treaty ports were subject to extreme pressure as they transmitted these Western influences—commodities, industries, political systems, and ideas—into the Chinese interior. In the process of modernization, China went through a century of transformation, and these great treaty ports were the chief conduits of the new and the modern.

Shanghai, Tianjin, Guangzhou (Canton), Wuhan, and Xiamen (Amoy) all had Foreign Concessions, or quasi Foreign Concessions such as Gulangyu Island in Amoy harbor, where foreigners lived in great concentrations and where Chinese law could not reach. The largest Foreign Concession was in Shanghai—its territory was vast, and it housed British, French, and Japanese Concessions and its own municipal council or city government, just as if it was a foreign territory inside China. Foreign merchants flocked to these concessions, and foreign companies had branch offices—"foreign firms" (yanghang)—in them. Many foreign banks—City Bank of New York, Hong Kong and Shanghai Banking Corporation (HSBC), Yokohama Specie Bank, General Bank of the Netherlands, and the Bank of France—all set up shop in these concessions where they remitted funds, made loans and investments, and carried on all the usual world trade practices. Thus, these financial institutions were an integral part of China's modern international market economy. Protected by extraterritoriality (making them exempt from Chinese law), these foreign concessions were both international and Chinese at the same time. This dual character gave them the right to plunder the wealth of China and also provided a safe haven for Chinese nationals who wished to escape from the war chaos and bad government of China.

In these cities, Chinese and foreign capital was used to set up both light and heavy industries. The large numbers of workers and clerks that concentrated in these cities made up China's first urban proletariat. The protest activities of these workers—labor shop closings—were also seldom seen in Chinese history. The great population mobility associated with these large cities also provided excellent breeding grounds for secret societies and criminal gangs. The traditional Green Gang (Qingbang) and the Hong Gang (Hongmen) groups, including the Heaven and Earth

Society (Tiandihui), were based in Shanghai. They also spread to other treaty ports and became a powerful underground force in Chinese society. These cities, then, had a dual power system that included the official government and secret underground societies. With several layers of authority—Chinese, foreign, official, and popular—none of which was overly efficient, these treaty ports all provided a great deal of space for uncontrolled, often criminal, activities.

The population of these treaty port cities increased rapidly. In the 1930s, after a century of absorbing people from the interior, the cities of Shanghai, Tianjin, Wuhan, Canton, Amoy, Nanjing, and Beijing counted their populations in the tens of millions. Their surrounding regions of the Yangzi delta, the Bohai plain, and the Pearl River delta contained two to three times the population of the treaty ports. The regional centers in the interior also had populations of ten or more million. The combined population of the great cities, their surrounding hinterlands, and the other regional centers made up about 10 percent of China's total population. The population increase in these areas was primarily attributable to an influx of people from China's far-flung interior. Since the eighteenth century, China's population increased very rapidly, and the excess population migrated into the southwestern provinces, the mountainous regions of the interior, Manchuria, and Inner Mongolia; the nineteenth-century treaty port cities became one more magnet for internal migration. This tenth of the population living in the big cities was, however, the leading force in the modern transformation of China.

Most of these large cities were linked by railroads, highways, and ocean or river communication routes. Beijing and Tianjin both had north-south railways to Nanjing and Wuhan, then from Wuhan to Canton and from Nanjing to Shanghai and Hangzhou. Along east-west routes, Beijing had railways to Taiyuan, Zhang Jiakou, Baotong, and Shenyang, then from Shenyang north to Harbin and south to Lüshun and Dalian. The eastern stretch of the Jiangsu-Gansu (Longhai) line went from Lianyungang to Zhengzhou, Luoyang, and Xi'an, and the Zhegan (Zhejiang-Jiangxi) line went from Hangzhou to Jiangxi and then on to Liuzhou (Guangxi). North-south ocean routes linked Dalian, Tianjin, Qingdao, Shanghai, Amoy, Canton, and Hong Kong. Yangzi River shipping lines went north from Shanghai upstream to Nantong, Nanjing, Jiujiang, Hankou, Yichang, and Chongqing, and the Xijiang (West River) line went west from Canton to

Guangxi. This vast communication and transportation network covered half of eastern China, a region inhabited by at least three quarters of the Chinese population.

Nearly all of modern China's industries are located in or on the periphery of these major cities. Jiangnan had flour milling, textiles, matches, porcelain, electricity, machine manufacture, and shipbuilding industries, and Shanghai was the center of industry for Jiangnan. Canton was the center of tobacco (cigarette), textiles, and agricultural products–processing industries. Foreign capital built the first factories in these areas, but Chinese government and private capital soon developed their own industries. Foreign commodities were shipped into these treaty ports and, added together with the industrial products produced in these areas themselves, transported into China's vast interior via the network described above. Thus were supplied new industrially produced commodities of everyday use that came to determine the new modern lifestyle of the Chinese people. That the tastes and fashions of China's modern consumer culture were modeled on those of Beijing, Shanghai, Canton, and Hong Kong stemmed from the fact that these commodities of everyday life came primarily from these great cities. They were the models, and Shanghai was the model of the models.

Almost all of modern China's universities are in these large urban areas. Beijing has Peking University (still the official name), Qinghua, Yanjing, Furen, and Beijing Normal; Nanjing has Jinling or Nanjing University and Central; Tianjin has Nankai; Shanghai has Jiaotong, St. John's, Soochow (Dongwu) University, Tongde, Tongji, Fudan, and Guanghua; Wuhan has Wuhan University and Wenhua; Canton has Zhongshan University and Lingnan; Chongqing has Chongqing University; Qingdao has Shandong University; Xiamen has Amoy University—this list includes all of China's premier institutions of higher learning as of the 1930s. The May Fourth Movement began at Peking University and spread out to influence the entire country. Beijing advocated Western learning, and Nanjing favored the national cultural heritage; polemics between northern and southern academic factions was a major element of the Chinese intellectual world of that time. Shanghai's universities particularly stressed Western languages and literature, and its medical school was also a major teaching center. The engineers trained at Jiaotong University were the main force behind China's modern construction developments. The research achievements and the talented scholars trained in modern China's academic world radiated out from these urban centers to the entire country, and these universities attracted the most promising young people and continually increased the cadre of university-educated individuals.

The most important function of these large cities was the accumulation and distribution of new ideas and information, and this function was carried out by the publishing industry, especially the new periodical press. China was the birthplace of paper and printing, and the dissemination of ideas and information took place throughout Chinese history. When Western ideas flooded into China in modern times, simply relying on the resources of institutions of higher education would have been insufficient for their influence to reach the entire country. Such influence and many new ideas reached the various strata of Chinese society indirectly through the widespread dissemination of printed materials. The tremendous influence of the printing industry, especially the periodical press, in spurring on the modern transformation of China should not be forgotten by modern historians.

The forerunner of the modern Chinese periodical press was the publication by the English missionary Robert Morrison (1782–1834), in Malacca in 1815 (and until 1826), of the first Chinese-language periodical ever issued. Entitled *A General Monthly Record, Containing an Investigation of the Opinions and Practices of Society* (*Cha shisu meiyue tongji chuan*), this periodical was intended for the overseas Chinese of Southeast Asia, and it was also sent to Canton, where it circulated among the intellectual circles of Guangdong. In 1833, the missionary Karl Gützlaff (1803–1851) brought out the *Eastern Western Monthly Magazine* (*Dong Xi yang kao meiyue tongji chuan*)—the first periodical published on Chinese soil. The *New Shanghai News* (*Shanghai xinbao*) came out in 1861. It was not only the first periodical published by Chinese themselves, but it was published in Shanghai, and from then on the center of the Chinese periodical publishing industry moved to Shanghai. The first edition of the *Shanghai Journal* or *Shun Bao* (*Shenbao*), founded by Ernest Major (ca. 1830–1908) and others, came out in 1872. This paper was extremely well received and remained the leading paper in the Shanghai newspaper world for over eighty years, from 1872 until its demise at the hands of the victorious Chinese Communist Party in 1949.

Shanghai newspapers had already come to rely on advertisements as their main source of revenue, and with this professionalization the newspaper business was no longer dependent on government or missionary funding. The media industry now stood on its own and, in the capitalist market economy, achieved freedom of speech. From then on, Shanghai became the nation's public opinion leader. By the 1930s, Shanghai's *Shanghai Journal* (*Shenbao*) and *News* (*Xinwen bao*, 1893–1949) and Tianjin's *L'Impartial* (*Dagong bao*, 1902–1966) and *Current* (*Shishi xinbao*, 1907–1949) all had a nationwide circulation no longer limited to the big cities.

In the first decade of the twentieth century, a great number and variety of periodicals were published in Shanghai. Among the most noteworthy of them are *Current Affairs* (also called *China's Progress*, *Shiwu bao*, founded in 1896 by Kang Youwei and edited by Liang Qichao) and *Youth Magazine* (*Qingnian*, founded in 1915 by Chen Duxiu), which was soon to move to Beijing and be retitled *La Jeunesse* or *New Youth Magazine* (*Xin qingnian zazhi*). The former was the mouthpiece of the Hundred Days' Reform, and the latter advocated the New Culture Movement. Both of them represented milestones in the history of modern Chinese culture. New Youth's sister periodical, *Science Monthly* (*Kexue yuekan*) was published by a group of scientists who formed the Science Association (*Kexue hui*, 1915–1960). It was published for some thirty-five years and was one of the most important sources for the dissemination of modern scientific knowledge in China. Members of the Science Association were familiar with many branches of science, and it became the most influential scientific association in modern China. There was even a *Scientific Monthly* in Taiwan in the 1960s. The ideas of free thought and scientism (*kexue zhuyi*) propagated by *New Youth* and *Science Monthly* had a profound influence on modern Chinese ways of thinking. All of these various ideas radiated out to the entire country from their starting point in Shanghai.

The publishing companies (often with their own chains of bookstores) that issued and sold their publications were the backbone of the publishing industry, and Shanghai was China's publishing Mecca. Hong Kong and Macao were originally the center for modern Chinese publishing, but Shanghai superseded them during the late Qing. Besides books on technology translated and printed by the Jiangnan Manufacturing Bureau in Shanghai, the public also had works produced by lithographic printing by the Combined Learning Publishing House (Tongwen shuju). In 1882, the *Shenbao* began to issue editions done in great quantities by machine printing, and this made it possible for readers to purchase inexpensive works on both national and Western learning. Works printed in Shanghai could then be shipped north to satisfy the Beijing and Tianjin markets.

After the first Sino-Japanese War of 1894–1895, the population clamored for the new learning, and the Shanghai Commercial Press was founded in 1897 to answer their needs, first by issuing English-language textbooks and Chinese-English dictionaries and then many more books and periodicals. Another category of important books published by Commercial Press was translations of world classics, such as Yan Fu's (1854–1921) translation of John Stuart Mill's *On Liberty* (1859) and Lin Shu's (1852–1924) many translations of Western literature, which were very popular throughout the country and had considerable influence for a time. The third major type of works Commercial Press published was school textbooks, which were used in schools throughout the nation. Among the periodicals published by Commercial Press, *Eastern Miscellany* (*Dongfang zazhi*, 1904–1948), *Education Magazine* (*Jiaoyu zazhi*), *Short Story Monthly* (*Xiaoshuo yuebao*, edited by Mao Dun), and *Youth Magazine* (*Shaonian zazhi*) were the most popular, though in different spheres with different readers. *Eastern Miscellany* was especially influential.

Chess Street in Shanghai was the center of the Chinese publishing business; by the 1930s, the Commercial Press, Kaiming, World, Zhengzhong, Guangwen, Guangya and Shenbao publishing companies were all located there. They published works ranging from the four divisions in China's traditional classification (*sibu*)—classics, history, philosophy and belle lettres—to children's reading materials, comprising the great majority of works published in China at the time. Works published outside of Shanghai did not amount to more than a small percentage of those from Shanghai. Shanghai works were, however, transmitted to the entire country by means of the urban network described above, and thus Shanghai basically determined the academic standards and the reading trends of the whole nation.

This urban network was also the locus for the growth and dissemination of drama, cinema, and other modern Chinese performing arts. Beijing opera came to Beijing near the end of the Qianlong emperor's reign, around 1790, when several troupes from Anhui entered the capital; there it developed into an exquisitely refined art. After the 1920s, the center of Beijing opera performance shifted to Shanghai. Even if highly gifted actors came to maturity in Beijing, they still had to perform in Shanghai to achieve fame. Great performers such as Mei Lanfang (1894–1961), Ma Lianlang (1901–1966), Zhou Xinfang (1895–1975), and Cheng Yanqiu (ca. 1904–1958) all gained great fame on the Shanghai stage. After China's victory in the War of Resistance, the Shaoxing opera (from Zhejiang) actress Yuan Xuefen (1922–) performed in Shanghai. She combined elements of Beijing opera and kunqu to raise Shaoxing opera to a new and higher artistic level. Kunqu was already mature at the end of the Ming dynasty and was in decline by the beginning of the Republican era when it was revived in Suzhou, but it was still necessary for Yu Zhenfei (1902–1993) and others to perform on the Shanghai stage before kunqu's artistic status could be successfully reestablished.

The first moving picture presented in China was a short foreign film put on screen at Tianjin's celebrated Quanxian Theater in 1906 as part of a variety show. The first Chinese feature film, a story of greed and murder entitled *Yan Ruisheng*, was shown in Shanghai in 1921. From then on, from silent films to talkies and from black-and-white to color films, Shanghai remained the main center of Chinese cinema. Few films were made in the interior during the War of Resistance, and Shanghai's Foreign Concessions remained the center of Chinese filmmaking. In the 1950s, Hong Kong emerged and quickly rose to prominence as a cinematic hub. The thematic elements of Shanghai films from the 1920s to 1950s continually changed in response to the times—they included everything from nationalism and social problems to romance, resistance, and revolution. Films shot in Shanghai showed on screens everywhere and elicited the tears, laughter, sadness, and joy of audiences all around the nation.

China's urban network of about a dozen major cities led and directed cultural change in the nineteenth and twentieth centuries. This vast network, with Shanghai as its leading element, spurred the transformation of the Chinese urban population. In their thoughts, tastes, and daily activities, they were transformed from living in their traditional ways to the modern lifestyles we are so familiar with today. The coastal cities and the interior heartland suffered a rupture at this time, but later on the interior areas were gradually drawn into the process of cultural change. The development that took place in China during the last two centuries is called "Westernization" by some and "modernization" by others, and it is difficult to come to any final conclusion on the benefits and drawbacks of either.

6. Modern Thought and Cultural Change

Suffering multiple encroachments by the Western great powers and Japan's repeated invasions, China felt severely the transformation of the age. On this account, Li Hongzhang lamented that China faced a situation unprecedented in two thousand years.

The defeats, disappointments, and subsequent dejection that the Chinese population suffered for over a century largely determined public and private behavior during this time. Gong Zizhen (1792–1841) and Wei Yuan (1794–1856) represented two different attitudes to China's predicament. Gong Zizhen found China's problems to come from within, especially from the imperial system of government and the immersion of the scholar class in the official examination culture. He employed ideas from the *Gongyang Commentaries* (*Gongyang zhuan*) and the *Spring and Autumn Annals* (*Chunqiu*), especially their concepts of change and statecraft, to describe China's crisis of internal collapse. Wei Yuan, in contrast, concentrated on "knowing one's enemy" and sought the reasons for Western strength and Chinese weakness in his studies of Western culture and political systems. He wrote an *Illustrated Treatise on the Maritime Kingdoms* (*Haiguo tuzhi*, 1844) to help his compatriots understand their opponents.

Zeng Guofan, Zuo Zongtang, Li Hongzhang, and others learned the lesson of the power of Western weapons from their actual wartime experiences. Then they set out to put Wei Yuan's slogan of "employ the best technology of the barbarians to defeat the barbarians" into practice. With his well-known slogan of *Zhong xue wei ti, Xi xue wei yong*—"Chinese learning as substance (fundamental principles) and Western learning as function (practical applications)"—the leading self-strengthener Zhang Zhidong (1837–1909) called for a compromise between Chinese and Western culture. He called for maintaining traditional Chinese morality through "rectifying people's hearts and minds" while "creating a new atmosphere" for the study of Western industrial systems. Zhang's *ti-yong* attitude was representative of the mode of thinking of more than one generation of Chinese intellectuals.

The reform leader Kang Youwei (1858–1927) explicated the "Three Ages of the *Gongyang Commentary*" as a path of progress from an Age of Chaos (*luanshi*) through an Age of Peace and Order (*xiaokang*) to a final utopian Age of Great Unity (*datong*, a universal commonwealth).

His theories were an amalgam of Confucian and Buddhist metaphysics combined with selected Western scientific knowledge and, with them, he established the theoretical foundations of the Hundred Days' Reform. Ultimately, Kang considered Western culture and society to be more progressive than their Chinese counterparts.

Kang's contemporary Yan Fu made his greatest contribution by translating Western scientific classics into Chinese. His most influential translation was *Evolution and Ethics* (1893) by Thomas Henry Huxley (1825–1895). In his *Tianyan lun*, Yan selected and translated Huxley's celebrated essays on the Darwinian theory of evolution and its ethical implications and interspersed his translations with his own opinions. Through translating Huxley, Yan Fu also introduced the theories of Charles Darwin (1809–1882) on biological evolution, especially the concepts of "struggle for existence," "natural selection," and "survival of the fittest." Yan employed the doctrine of "social evolution" to describe the competition between the great powers of the world and to remind his compatriots that they had to strive for victory in order to strengthen and preserve the Chinese nation.

Yan Fu's translation of *Evolution and Ethics* came out a little later than Kang Youwei's modern discussion of the Three Ages theory. The theory of evolution introduced by Yan Fu, however, provided another theoretical foundation for Kang Youwei's reformist ideas, and, thus, Kang incorporated social evolution as expounded by Yan into his *Confucius as Institutional Reformer* (*Kongzi gaizhi kao*) of 1898.

Liang Qichao (1873–1929) relied even more on Yan Fu's version of evolutionary change in his calls for political reform and cultural progress. Many intellectuals at that time accepted and praised to the skies the concept of social evolution. As a result, the struggle between Chinese and Western culture, originally concerned with their parallel development, changed, after the publication of *Evolution and Ethics*, into a consideration of two unequal developments, in which Chinese culture was regarded as backward (insufficiently evolved) and Western culture as progressive (leading the social-evolutionary parade).

Liang Qichao was modern China's most prolific scholar, with more than ten million published words. He himself admitted that, being mired in China's environment of "academic famine," he was extremely interested in the new Western knowledge introduced by Yan Fu. As a consequence, every cause he advocated throughout his whole life was always preceded by the word "new" (*xin*). Aside from reform (*weixin*) itself, with his theory of the "new citizen" (*xinmin*) Liang strove to define a new Chinese citizen and establish a Chinese national consciousness. His goal was to transform China from a polity self-described on the basis of culture as "all under heaven" (*tianxia*) into a modern nation-state based on political sovereignty and equal to the contemporary (Western) world powers. Liang Qichao's "new citizen" regarded the model of Western nation-states as the most progressive (evolutionarily advanced) stage in history so far and the traditional Chinese state model as one to be eliminated by natural selection. However, in 1918, Liang visited Europe and witnessed firsthand the problems inherent in Western capitalist societies, such as the great income disparities between rich and poor and rampant materialism. After that, his views changed, and he came to believe it necessary to rely on Eastern civilization to rectify the shortcomings of Western civilization. Thus, he returned to the view that China and the West had parallel rather than unequal development paths. There are still people who are either for or against these two opposing views held by Liang Qichao at different times in his life.

The May Fourth New Culture Movement of the 1920s and 1930s was one of the most important events in the history of modern Chinese culture. It had three main components: First, the rejection of traditional Chinese culture, with some extremists calling for total Westernization and throwing traditional Chinese string-bound books into manure pits. Second, advocacy of vernacular (*baihua*, plain talk) writing. Third, Hu Shi's (1891–1962) proposal to import "Mr. De" (democracy) and "Mr. Sai" (science) in order to save China. The first two elements rejected the past; the third welcomed the modern. The overall theme was to make China progress along the universal social evolutionary path described by social Darwinism. For the Chinese nation to survive in the modern world, China had to follow the Western model of "modernization." This mode of thought regarded the West and the modern, or "modernization," (*xiandaihua*) as one and the same. By the middle of the twentieth century, this form of "modernization theory" was fashionable throughout the world.

Many people were opposed to the May Fourth advocacy of vernacular literature. Zhang Junmai (Carsun Chang, 1887–1969), Liang Shuming (1893–1988), and the Nanjing professors of the Critical Review circle (their journal, *Xueheng zazhi*, had the English title *The Critical Review*) all questioned the validity of this change, and thus began the polemics on Chinese and Western culture. Chinese intellectuals of the 1930s also had a polemical debate on the pattern of Chinese social development. This debate was centered around the historical materialism of Karl Marx (1818–1883) and the attempt to fit Chinese social development into the so-called universal pattern of history. Carsun Chang and others initiated another China-versus-the-West polemic between "science and metaphysics." Science here meant "scientism" and reflected the European nineteenth-century optimism that science could solve all human problems, making virtually a religion out of science!

These beliefs in social evolution and scientism dominated Chinese intellectual circles for more than a century and have not yet completely disappeared. In terms of modern Chinese social thought, these two beliefs to a great extent distorted the development of culture and scholarship.

The chief accomplishment of the May Fourth New Literature Movement was the substitution of vernacular Chinese (close to the spoken language) for literary (or classical) Chinese (*wenyan*, written language only) as the vehicle for writing modern Chinese literature. This momentous change divided the past and present of Chinese literature. If we compare Hu Shi's *Fifty Years of Chinese Literature* (*Wushi nian lai Zhongguo zhi wenxue*) and Qian Jibo's (1897–1957) *History of Modern Chinese Literature* (*Xiandai Zhongguo wenxue shi*), Hu covers the period 1873 to 1923 and Qian covers 1911 to 1930, and they are both concerned with changes in literary styles during those fifty years. Their points of view are, however, dramatically different. Hu Shi follows the direction of progress or evolution and maintains that the transition to vernacular literature is the necessary path to the new and the modern. Qian holds, on the other hand, that change does not have to be a rupture with literary origins and that classical literature (*guwen*) also went through a process of change. His emphasis is on inheritance and continuity, not on rupture and rejection.

In retrospect, the vernacular language has indeed become the vehicle for modern Chinese literature, and the May Fourth New Literature Movement has triumphed. From another point of view, however, poetry (*shi*) was traditionally the most refined and polished genre and set the norm for classical literature. But there are very few outstanding and immortal vernacular poems. This fact might lead us to wonder if, after cutting itself off from the arterial stream of its literary heritage, the vernacular language still has enough nourishment.

That said, there is indeed a wealth of vernacular fiction (*xiaoshuo*) and some remarkable achievements. Because vernacular fiction originated with the art of the traditional storyteller (*shuoshu*), there was fiction in the spoken language of its time long before the May Fourth Movement. The great mid-Qing works of fiction, like the *Dream of the Red Chamber* (*Honglou meng*) and the *Marriage That Awakens the World* (*Xingshi yinyuan zhuan*), although not related to the storyteller's performances, were nevertheless written in the vernacular language. From the late Qing to the Republic, the publishing industry flourished, the urban population increased, and there was a great market for fiction, both long (novels) and short (story collections). There were also many literati who lived in the cities and made a living at writing, producing an abundance of works of fiction. There were, of course, some serious works with high literary value among them, but the most common genres were those that satisfied the popular taste for entertainment: fiction of manners, martial arts or knight-errant fiction, and romance fiction of the "mandarin ducks and butterflies" variety; all of them were written in the vernacular language. From the late Qing to the 1940s and 1950s, fiction writing followed a process of development from simple literary Chinese through a period of mixed vernacular and literary language to the final stage of pure vernacular. This process clearly illustrates the influence of the May Fourth New Literature Movement.

In the development of drama, the stage plays or "spoken drama" (*huaju*) of the New Literature Movement were enriched by importation via Japan of the European-style stage plays of the Norwegian dramatist Henrik Ibsen (1828–1906) and others. This new Chinese stage drama could neither link up with the traditional Chinese drama performances of the Yuan and Ming dynasties nor absorb the Western dramatic traditions of ancient Greece or Shakespeare. Thus, modern Chinese drama has never really established itself as a major art form.

Aside from the activities of the May Fourth Movement, modern Peking opera and kunqu also went through considerable transformation. Stimulated by economic market forces, these two dramatic genres continually appropriated new resources and developed their traditions into extremely elegant and refined art forms. Most of the literati and actors who participated in these two performing arts were extremely well versed in Chinese traditional learning while at the same time not opposed to reform. Thus, they were easily able to take advantage of the finest elements of tradition and the most promising new directions. These two performing arts were not really influenced by the literary revolution and can be said to have adapted to their new circumstances and made the best of it for their own development.

The cinema was a new genre of performing arts, and its technology was solely derived from the West. The themes of early Chinese cinema were, however, thoroughly traditional. Early Chinese films included sensationalist stories like the murder drama *Yan Ruisheng* (1921) and social morality tales such as *Love and Responsibility* (*Lian-ai yu zeren*), which were very close to traditional Ming and Qing stories. Later on, in keeping with the trends of the time, were films such as the *Song of the Fisherman* (*Yuguangqu*, 1934) that criticized social injustice and patriotic films full of nationalist sentiment. The latter were especially abundant during the war against Japan. After China's bitter victory in the war, films depicting the hardships of wartime refugees and the general postwar social malaise appeared. Showing at the same time were popular films that movingly depicted the common people's resistance against bad government. Especially powerful was *The Spring River Flows East* (*Yijiang chunshui xiang dong liu*, 1947) in two parts—*Eight War-Torn Years* (*Banian liluan*) and *The Dawn* (*Tianliang qianhou*). All of these works adopted Western cinematic techniques to the themes of traditional Chinese literature, producing an art that skillfully blended China and the West, the old and the new.

In the development of painting, the "Four Wangs" (Wang Shimin, 1592–1680; Wang Jian, 1598–1677; Wang Hui, 1632–1717; and Wang Yuanqi, 1642–1715) of the Qing dynasty imitated both the ancients and one another without breaking any new ground. The works of Zheng Banqiao (Zheng Xie, 1693–1765), Jin Dongxin (fl. 1736), and some others had, however, already broken through the restraints of tradition and struck out on new artistic paths. After the opening up of the sea routes, Western painting came to China, and Chinese artists mastered the techniques of oil painting. The most accomplished modern painters were those, like Xu Beihong (1895–1953), Huang Binhong (1865–1955), and the Lingnan School, who blended the ideas of Western painting into their ink-and-color paintings on cotton paper in the Chinese style. Qi Baishi (1864–1957) started with seal carving, and Zhang Daqian (1899–1983) learned from the wall painting of Dunhuang—both of them drew inspiration from traditional Chinese artistic techniques to find their own unique style and establish themselves as major figures in modern Chinese art. All of these artists successfully combined the old and the modern in their works.

To sum up, the tides of modern Chinese thought received the greatest shock ever in Chinese history. To strengthen themselves and save their beleaguered nation, Chinese intellectuals could not but follow Western examples and try to master Western models of thought. Their sense of national crisis caused many of them to abandon their own tradition and embrace Western culture. Thus, regarding the conservative as backward and emulating the West as modern became the common practice of the day, and the theory of social evolution served as justification. The result of this was a "revolution" that cut the present off from China's past. The May Fourth Movement was both the central headquarters and the most effective advocate of this trend. Vernacular Chinese replaced the classical language as the vehicle for both literature and everyday communication. In other areas of cultural activity, however, such as drama, cinema, and painting, a successful blending of old and new, Chinese and Western led to some very fine accomplishments. From this we can see that both ardent revolution and gradual adaptation were capable of moving toward a new culture in tune with the times.

The May Fourth Movement raised high the banners of science and democracy, but neither of them developed very smoothly. Scientism was a kind of faith resembling religious belief that could not provide a good foundation for the birth and healthy flourishing of modern academic science, and democracy was reduced to vague electioneering activities. Perhaps this was because those who advocated democracy at the time did not seriously study its long historical development, which involved many changes and took place under many diverse conditions in Western political history. They thought democracy could simply be transplanted to China in a short time and all at once!

7. The Chinese and Russian Revolutions Compared

The word *geming*, which is now used for the Western idea of political revolution, originally meant the removal of the Mandate of Heaven, the ancient Chinese concept of dynastic legitimacy. In modern times, political revolution generally includes the following elements: a group of people are dissatisfied with their current political system and social order, they mobilize the masses (the lower classes) under the banner of a particular ideal (or ideology), and they then rely on the strength of the masses to overthrow the ruling group and set up a new political regime. When the new regime takes power, it usually carries out a social revolution to transform social values and thoroughly implement the ideals of the revolution. In recent world history, since the eighteenth century, their have been several such revolutions, but the four that have had the most far-reaching influence are the American Revolution, the French Revolution, the Russian October Revolution, and the Chinese Communist Revolution. In this section, I will attempt a sketch of the Russian Revolution and then discuss the causes and results of the Chinese Revolution for comparison.

Russia was a latecomer to power in Europe. Emperor Peter the Great (1672–1725) emulated Western Europe and rapidly transformed his country into one of the great powers. The Russian empire expanded eastward as far as Kamchatka and the Kuril Islands between Kamchatka and Hokkaido, becoming a powerful nation on China's northern border. During the nineteenth century, Russia took part in the "Great Game" of European powers warring with one another for hegemony. In this way, Russia squandered a great deal of its military might and was forced to invest large amounts of capital in industrial development that its national treasury could scarcely afford. Russia was defeated in two devastating foreign wars—the Crimean War (1853–1865) and the Russo-Japanese War (1904–1905)—causing a great decline in national power. In World War I (1914–1918), Russia was pushed steadily back and had insufficient reinforcements in the rear areas.

While Russia's national strength was suffering a great decline because of the war, inflation was rampant at home. In March 1917 (February by the Russian calendar, hence the name February Revolution), the workers and the hungry masses of Petrograd (St. Petersburg) rose up in rebellion; they were joined by soldiers and members of the capital guard, and their rebellion brought about the collapse of the Romanov dynasty. A provisional government was formed with the participation of many political parties who still wanted to carry on the war. In November (October by the Russian calendar, hence the October Revolution), however, the provisional government collapsed, and the so-called majority Bolshevik (later Communist) Party, led by Vladimir Ilich Lenin (1870–1924) and Leon Trotsky (1879–1940) and claiming to represent the Russian proletariat, took power by force of arms.

In 1918, after the Communist Party took power in Russia, they set up the system of Soviet dictatorship and abolished private property. Under the Communist system, however, Russia's economic production capacity did not increase. Thus, from 1921 to 1928, the Soviet government reverted to Lenin's New Economic Policy (NEP) and permitted privately owned small businesses to continue to operate, with the state controlling the large industries. In 1928, Joseph Stalin (1879–1953) came to power, instituted a planned or command economy, and carried out rapid rural collectivization and industrialization focused on heavy industry. From then on, until its collapse in 1989, the Soviet Union was ruled by a totalitarian dictatorship.

That the Russian empire took this inexorable road to revolution was closely related to the fact that most Russian peasants depended on their landlord's manors for their existence. Although serfdom had been abolished in 1861 and the peasants were technically free, their conditions were not good, and the majority of them did not yet know how to participate in social activities. The prerevolutionary Russian intellectual class received a French and Western European education, was alienated from native Russian culture, and had little to do with the peasantry. The traditional Russian bureaucracy was even more dependent on the imperial government and had no independence. Thus, when the masses rose up in revolt in 1917, Russian society had neither an autonomous administrative system that could act on its own nor a powerful middle class to maintain social stability.

The modern Chinese revolution had its own pattern of development, with some similarities with and some differences from revolution in Russia. There were three stages of revolution in China from 1911 to 1949: the establishment of the Republic of China (ROC) in 1911, the Nationalist Party's Northern Expedition of 1928, and the Communist Party's establishment of the new regime of the People's Republic of China (PRC) in 1949. If we include the unsuccessful "revolution" of the Heavenly Kingdom of the Taipings in the mid-nineteenth century, the modern Chinese revolution could be said to have lasted for an entire century. From 1950 to the death of Mao Zedong in 1976, the Maoist Chinese Communist Party led China through a relentless series of chaotic and disruptive campaigns, the most extreme being the Great Proletarian Cultural Revolution from 1966 to 1976. After that, Deng Xiaoping restored a semblance of order, stability, and economic advance. In this light, we can say that the overall process of modern revolution in China actually lasted even more than a century.

The traditional Chinese peasantry were not really attached to the landlords' manors as in Russia. The tenant-farming peasant families sought to maximize the profits from the labor-intensive farming of their small plots of land as part of a village market economic system in the same way the self-cultivating peasants did. The peasant households had to sell their crops and their cottage-industry goods together at village markets. Village society had its market exchange associations and its networks of social relationships. From these networks, the peasants received market advantages as well as information relevant to their daily lives. The traditional Chinese gentry literati class operated as the leading element within this society characterized by local market networks—they organized local social forces and managed local affairs. The gentry literati was made up of literati who had passed the civil examinations and incumbent as well as retired officials and their family members. They established various networks of relationships—ranging in scope from small local villages to the entire nation—based on their status as fellow bureaucrats, relatives, close friends, and trusted advisors. The social power of the gentry literati was such that it could balance or even resist the power of the central government. Such a force was completely missing in traditional Russian society.

After the abolition of the traditional examination system, the prerevolutionary modern Chinese intellectual class studied mainly Western subjects in school and lived primarily in large or small urban areas. They became easily alienated from rural society—this was one thing they had in common with the prerevolutionary Russian intellectual class. These alienated Chinese intellectuals, however, were often the sons or grandsons of the abovementioned gentry literati. They could take advantage of the networks of gentry literati relationships for mutual assistance and indirect linkage with their rural societies—this was an element that differed greatly from the situation of prerevolutionary Russian intellectuals.

In the section on "militarization," above, we saw how the Hunan Army that defeated the Taipings came into existence when gentry networks organized the peasants into China's first "militarized" community. The Hunan Army and its offshoot the Anhui (Huai) Army were not made up of professional soldiers; their strength came from manpower and resources that were mobilized by the gentry networks in order to establish an armed force outside of the official national army system. The post of governor general in the late Qing, especially in Zhili (Beijing, Tianjin, Hebei, Henan, and part of Shandong) and the various southeastern provinces were all occupied by men from this gentry literati bloc. In this way, beyond the power of the Qing royal house, China had another separate power structure.

Normally these governor generals followed the Qing court's orders, but sometimes they acted independently, in their own interests. In 1906, when the dynasty was in deep decline, the Qing court was forced to carry out a series of reform measures. When the court promised to establish a constitution, provincial assemblies were set up in various provinces. The first of these were in Jiangsu, Zhejiang, Hubei, Hunan, and Sichuan, just where these governor generals and the gentry literati were most powerful. The establishment of these provincial assemblies confirmed the power of provincial "militarization" and the provincial gentry literati behind it.

When the Eight-Nation Alliance suppressed the Boxer Rebellion at the turn of the twentieth century and the governor generals of the southwestern provinces declared their neutrality, this was already a declaration of local power beyond the reach of the central government. The New Army (of Hubei) that started the 1911 revolution represented the second generation of these "militarized" governor generals. When Wuchang rose in rebellion, various provinces followed suit and declared their independence, and in that way the local military and civilian social power described above came together to overthrow the imperial regime in Beijing. This entire revolutionary process, which resulted in the establishment of the Republic of China, was quite smooth, and China did not actually experience any great degree of chaos at that time.

The new republic was unable to reestablish a national government, however, because the local "militarized" forces were too powerful. After the founding of the republic, the two decades in which warlords controlled many parts of the country represented the expansion and intensification of the process of "militarization." The 1911 revolution, "militarization," and the expansion of the power of society were all inescapably linked.

The Nationalist Party's Northern Expedition was the second stage in the modern Chinese revolution. Urban forces participated in it from its inception, and urban elements enthusiastically promoted and responded to it. Chiang Kai-shek established his capital at Nanjing and took control of the resources of Jiangnan and Guangdong to support his government. The rank-and-file members of his new government were nearly all returned overseas students and urban intellectuals. These people who were originally alienated from China's rural hinterland actually had the opportunity to design a new national government's administrative system! This was a golden opportunity that the so-called minority Mensheviks in Russia, intellectuals who advocated Westernization, never had.

The most influential element of reconstruction during the Republic of China's Nanjing decade was the establishment of a comparatively modern political and economic government mechanism. This included especially the Central Bank of China, which unified the currency; many new universities; and a team of professional experts whose duty it was to carry out national reconstruction. Many newly established universities set up specialist research institutes where a large number of "technical bureaucrats" (in the Committee on National Resources and various economic, industrial, and commercial boards) promoted the search for new natural resources and the work of industrial construction. The real strength of the new national government was based on the major cities along the east coast, which were on the navigable rivers and the main railroad lines. Alienation was not a problem during this period; the problem was rather how the cities could absorb the countryside. This was an enormously difficult problem given China's vast rural population, and the Nanjing decade was too short a time to accomplish this ambitious goal.

While China suffered extreme hardships during the Anti-Japanese War, there were also some unforeseen benefits. Large numbers of coastal residents moved into the interior, bringing with them their talents, technological know-how, and modern concepts. For example, the factories that had been moved to the interior remained there after the war and laid the foundation for the industrialization of the interior. To support higher education, the government established a national bursary so that over ten thousand college students could complete their education. This system provided a large pool of postwar talent that benefited both the mainland and Taiwan. The transformation of China's alienated intellectuals into a group that was fully integrated into society was the chief characteristic of the second stage of the modern Chinese revolution.

The Chinese Communist Revolution began with a number of unsuccessful armed uprisings in cities and rural areas until the establishment of the Jiangxi Soviet (1931–1934) with the support of the Communist International, but their real power to achieve the revolution was created during the Anti-Japanese War, when they organized peasant support in their guerrilla areas behind enemy lines. Because the invading Japanese armies controlled the coastal regions and the major cities along the railroad lines and monopolized the chief lines of communication, the Nationalist government in Chongqing lost its lines of communication and saw its territory cut into a number of sealed-off areas. For this reason, the rural areas were freed from the economic pressure of supplying the cities and reverted to their former communal economy of rural market networks. The Communists learned how to organize and mobilize the peasants in their guerrilla areas, and the rural society's handicraft-exchange mechanism, formerly subservient to the cities, was actually revived.

On the periphery of this vast rural base, the Nationalist army was unable to find entry and was forced to move reinforcements and supplies a long way around these areas to maintain its fighting strength. In contrast, the Communist armies within their rural base areas had only to maneuver around the villages and could thus force the Nationalist armies into an unfavorable position. The groundwork for the coming Communist victory in the Civil War was thus already in place.

The Chinese Communist leadership, especially Mao Zedong, came from the countryside. After they came to power, they continued to use their rural experiences as a guide for their national reconstruction. The Maoist Communist Party's two decades of repeated campaigns were nothing more than attempts to transform China on the basis of these rural experiences! This Maoist Communist developmental path was quite different from Stalin's emphasis on Russia's industrial base.

The continuities of these three stages of the modern Chinese revolution are much greater than the radical ruptures. Ray Huang's contention that Chiang Kai-shek established the urban "superstructure" and Mao Zedong established the rural "base" for the modern Chinese nation-state is confirmed by the process described above. Deng Xiaoping's reforms have seemingly swung the pendulum back to the Nanjing era. Some portions of today's rural villages have been transformed into semiurbanized areas (as in Zhejiang), and other portions of China's rural areas have simply been pushed to the side (as in Henan). Only when the pendulum swings into the center will China have completed its terribly difficult hundred-year-long journey.

8. China's Hundred Days' Reform (1898) and Japan's Meiji Restoration (1868–1873)

The Meiji Restoration (Japanese *Meiji Ishin*, "renewal by enlightened rule"; Chinese *Mingzhi weixin*) from 1868 to 1873 opened up a new era in Japanese history. The term *weixin*, translated as "restoration," derives from the *Book of Songs* (*Shijing*, Mao edition no. 241): "The Zhou is an ancient state, but its Mandate is new [*ming wei xin*]." The Meiji Restoration is indeed named for a seizure of power from the bottom up that brought the Tokugawa shogunate (*bakufu*) to an end, restoring imperial power to Emperor Mutsuhito, or the Meiji emperor (r. 1867–1912).

On July 8, 1853, the American commodore Matthew C. Perry (1794–1858) sailed a squadron of ships into Edo (modern Tokyo) bay and demanded that the Japanese open trade relations with the United States. Perry's threats to bombard Japanese cities from his "black ships" gave the Japanese an overwhelming sense of national crisis; it was no less a shock to them than the Opium War was to the Chinese. The Tokugawa regime was powerless to deal with this grave situation. A pair of feudal lords (*daimyo*) from the domains (*han*) of Chōshū (on Kyūshū island) and Satsuma began a revolt under the slogan of "defend the emperor and resist the foreigners." They forced the Tokugawa shogunate to return real power to the long-time puppet Emperor Kōmei (Emperor Meiji's father, who died shortly afterward). The new Meiji political regime carried out a policy of total Westernization, changed the political system, built a new army and navy, revived national industries, and transformed a regime that had for centuries followed Chinese models into the first Westernized nation in the Far East.

Twenty some years later, Japan challenged China for hegemony in the region. In 1895, Japan defeated China's new Beiyang Navy, occupied Korea and Taiwan as colonial possessions, and received an indemnity of several million pounds of silver from China. Japan thus became an instant colonial empire that would lord over East Asia for fifty years to come. Japan advanced as follows: defeating Russia in 1905, invading Manchuria in 1931, launching an all-out war on China in 1937, bombing Pearl Harbor in 1941, fighting total war on land and sea in an attempt to establish a pan-Asian empire. This dream was ultimately reduced to ashes under the mushroom clouds of the atomic bombing of Hiroshima and Nagasaki in August 1945.

Japan's rapid rise and fall was a holocaust for East Asia. Nevertheless, the success of the Meiji Restoration helped inspire China's Hundred Days' Reform of June 11 to September 21, 1898. During that brief time, the Guangxu emperor (1875–1908), with Empress Dowager Cixi's permission, called on the support of Kang Youwei, Liang Qichao, and other reformers and issued a series of decrees ordering a wide-scale reform of the imperial system. After the rise of much conservative opposition and after General Yuan Shikai attached himself to the Manchu General Ronglu (1836–1903), Cixi was able to make use of the New Beiyang Army to seize power and put an end to the reform effort. Emperor Guangxu was put under house arrest until his death in 1908, and the reformer Tan Sitong (1865–1898) and five others were publicly executed on September 28, 1898. Thus, this short-lived *weixin* ended in tragedy!

That the Japanese and Chinese nineteenth-century reforms had such completely different outcomes has long been a topic of discussion among historians. First let's consider their similarities. The supporters of the Meiji Restoration leaders were young men from peripheral domains who were greatly alarmed by the foreign military threat and the Tokugawa regime's incompetence. They gathered around the intellectual Yoshida Shōin (1830–1859) to discuss strategies for preserving their country. Likewise, in China a group of young men in the south worried about the increasingly dangerous foreign incursions and the Qing court's incompetence. They gathered around Kang Youwei in Guangzhou (Canton) and tried to devise ways to prevent China's further decline.

The Japanese domains on Kyūshū were far away from the center of Tokugawa power in the Kantō region, but the people there had learned a great deal about Western affairs through profitable trade with foreigners. Nagasaki harbor had long been visited by ships from Holland and other Western countries, and there were even Europeans living there. *Rangaku* or "Dutch studies"—as early Japanese studies of Europe were known— began in Nagasaki. Thus, the men of Kyūshū were well acquainted with international affairs. After the Portuguese occupied Macao during the Ming, the Jesuit missionaries entered Ming and Qing China from that quarter. After the Opium War, China ceded Hong Kong to the British, and it became a base for foreign merchants seeking trade with China. Although Guangzhou is far to the south, its close proximity to both Hong Kong and Macao meant that Cantonese Chinese both had the easiest access to knowledge of Western affairs and felt most deeply a sense of national crisis. Although Guangdong was one of China's wealthiest provinces, it was very far from the Qing regime's center of power in Beijing; in this sense, it had much in common with the Kyūshū domains.

With the support of the reform advocates, Emperor Meiji was transformed from a puppet emperor into the symbol of the new regime. The Guangxu emperor, Zaitian, the son of Prince Chun, was chosen by Dowager Empress Cixi to ascend the imperial throne at the age of four. He grew up under Cixi's regency, but, as soon as he actually began to rule, he was determined to bring about reforms that he hoped would quickly rejuvenate the country. He acted decisively and trusted completely his new civil officials. The Japanese reformers raised the slogan "defend the Emperor and resist the foreigners" to restore the emperor and establish the legitimacy of the Meiji Restoration. Guangxu's position as emperor also had its legitimacy. When Cixi wanted to force his abdication, the governor generals of the southeast forestalled her plans by maintaining the position that "the distinction between ruler and minister is firmly fixed, and it would be hard to defend against foreign criticism."

All of the above similarities in the late nineteenth-century Chinese and Japanese reform situation only makes us more puzzled as to why one succeeded so well and the other failed so badly. Moreover, in their subsequent development, China and Japan followed completely different paths! Let's try to delineate their different processes of development.

First, the situations of the Meiji and Guangxu emperors were quite different. Under the slogan of "defend the emperor and resist the foreigners," the Tokugawa shogun was nothing more than a powerful official who had usurped imperial power. Once a genuine emperor came forth, the shogunate was unable to maintain its legitimacy. Guangxu was Cixi's adopted son, however, and parent-child relationships received the highest preference in the Chinese moral order—even though he was the emperor, he still had to obey his mother.

Second, at the beginning of the Tokugawa shogunate, the feudal lords of the various domains in the Kantō region, hereditary vassals of the shogun Tokugawa Ieyasu, were good fighters who defended the shogunate. As time went on, they collected their tax money, indulged in luxurious living, and lost their fighting abilities. At the end of the Tokugawa era, even the generals chosen to lead the army were only court favorites and not genuine soldiers. Thus, when the Kyūshū lords banded together and demanded that the military return the government to the emperor, the shogun did not have the military might to resist them. In contrast, after the defeat of the Taiping Rebellion, many Chinese provinces were thoroughly "militarized." In Zhili (Hebei) especially, the governor general (viceroy) there guarded the gates of Beijing, and he had a large army at his disposal and thus could do more or less whatever he wanted to. During the Hundred Days' Reform, Cixi made her trusted ally General Ronglu the governor general of Zhili. Even if Tan Sitong had been able to enlist Yuan Shikai in support of Guangxu, Yuan's troops would have had little chance of defeating Ronglu's army. At the time, only the governor general of Hunan, Chen Baozhen (1831–1900), supported the reforms; the rest of the southeastern governor generals sat back and did nothing. Guangxu lacked military support; Cixi had the power of the Zhili governor general's army behind her. Guangxu's plight was therefore the exact opposite of Emperor Meiji's favorable position.

A third important element was that the Japanese *daimyo* (feudatories) and their followers were part of a feudal system. They were all soldiers of their lord and master; they normally lived at his castle and had no other base in society. The Tokugawa shoguns originally commanded great armies, but after ruling for a long time, these warriors were replaced by bureaucratic officials who lived off of the *bakufu* but could not mobilize any military support for the regime. Since the Tokugawa shogunate did not have either powerful support from *daimyo* of their own clan nor warriors who could mobilize society in their favor, it is easy to see that they could not sustain their power. The medieval German landed nobility (Junkers) of Prussia were "an army in the countryside" quite similar to the garrison militia in China since the Tang dynasty. They were an important force in the assertion of Germanic sovereignty in Germany. The main difference between the Japanese *daimyo* samurai class and the Junkers was that the samurai lived at the shogun's court and did not command real power in the countryside.

The Ming and Qing gentry were not at all military men; they were rather a local social elite. They had definite leadership abilities and formed networks of relationships based on clan, occupational, and friendship connections. The support or opposition of these gentry literati was decisive in times of political transition and dynastic change. In the last decades of the Qing dynasty, the government's administrative abilities were quite insufficient, but the powerful moral restraints on Confucian officials was still in force. This can be illustrated by the way that Zeng Guofan scrupulously abided by his duty as the emperor's servant and disbanded his Hunan Army when they had defeated the Taipings, after he was in control of the entire southeast. Under these conditions, if revolution did not come from the bottom of society, the imperial bureaucracy of the gentry literati, unlike the Japanese *daimyo*, were not very likely to start a revolution from the top.

The ideals represented by the Hundred Days' Reform still revolved around the options of either the conservatives or the foreign-learning factions. The conservative faction, men such as Woren (1804–1871) and Wang Xianqian (1842–1917), all resolutely believed that China's traditional orthodoxy was immutable; for them, any emulation of the West was an unconscionable heterodoxy that should not be allowed. The foreign-learning faction, men such as Zhang Zhidong and the majority of the governor generals, bought machines and built factories hoping to build modern ships and armaments, revitalize commerce and industry, and prevent China's economic profits from flowing out of the country. Their ideal, we recall, was "Chinese learning as substance (fundamental principles) and Western learning as function (practical applications)," and they really did not endorse the idea of transforming China's governmental system to follow Western models. These were the two major trends of gentry literati thought, and those who favored reform were decidedly not in the majority. Thus, Guangxu, Kang Youwei, and Liang Qichao were unable to enlist the great power of the gentry in support of their reform measures. When Cixi attacked the reform movement, the great majority of the governor generals did not support Guangxu because at that time they were only in favor of learning the foreigners' technology but were not in favor of reforming the Chinese government system on foreign principles.

After the failure of the Hundred Days' Reform, the conservatives took advantage of the Boxer "nativist movement" to support the Qing and destroy the foreigners, raising the ire of the Eight-Nation Alliance. After the disastrous Western military invasion, many people began to favor reform, and the Qing court started to discuss the establishment of a constitution. This may be said to have been an extension of the reform movement. With the Republican Revolution of a few years later, the Qing's so-called constitutional plans were rendered empty talk.

From the Hundred Days' Reform to the establishment of a constitution, this brief period of incomplete reform at the end of the Qing dynasty was only a ripple in the tide of Chinese history. Shen Jiaben's (1840–1913) revision of the *Great Qing Legal Code with Substatutes* (*Da Qing Lüli*, translated as *The Great Qing Code* by William C. Jones in 1994) introduced Continental European legal canons and thus constituted the first modern Chinese set of legal statutes. The civil, criminal, and procedural laws of the Republic of China basically followed Shen Jiaben's legal categories. Not long after the establishment of the republic, China fell into the chaos and disintegration of the Warlord Era. Nevertheless, aside from the lawless actions of some warlords, legal cases in most regions of the country generally adhered to the new legal statutes. The judicial precedents of the Court of Judicial Review in Beijing were still quoted in courts of law even in places where the orders of the Beiyang regime could not reach.

Another accomplishment of late Qing reform was the establishment of the basic outline of modern Chinese higher education. The curriculum of the Imperial Capital University (Peking University) became the model for other universities throughout the nation. Cai Yuanpei's establishment of China's new university educational system was based on this foundation, with the addition of some minor changes.

In general, the efforts of the late Qing reform movement were abortive. If there had been no 1911 revolution and China had followed a developmental path that included the establishment of a constitution, its direction would have been decided by the social elite (the old gentry and, later, the modern intellectuals), and it would have developed quite differently. Since the history of this period has now gone by, however, there is no need to speculate about what might have been.

The Meiji Restoration established a modernized Japan. Twentieth-century Japan moved, however, steadily toward military dictatorship from 1925 until the so-called February 26 Incident, a coup d'état attempt by the ultranationalist Kōdō-ha faction of the Imperial Japanese Army. Right-wing Japanese military factions murdered three out of five sitting prime ministers and two out of three ministers of finance, and the brother of another prime minister narrowly escaped being assassinated thanks to mistaken identity. These political figures who advocated peace and political liberalism were eliminated one by one as the Japanese military took control of the emperor and created a warlord dictatorship, thus ending Japan's incipient progress toward a constitutional monarchy. Japan's wild and unchecked military expansion then led step by step to total war and then step by step to total defeat. The Meiji Restoration was initiated by a group of young samurai, and the nature of their Bushido (Way of the Warrior) philosophy bequeathed its militaristic genes to later generations and helped lead to this historical turn toward war. The historical causes and effects of the nineteenth-century Japanese and Chinese reform movements, over the short and the long term, continue to be understood and explained in different ways.

9. A Century of Change in Taiwan

From the 1850s to the 1950s, Taiwan experienced change on a magnitude rarely seen anywhere else. As an island province of Qing China, Taiwan was twice invaded by foreigners (the French and the Japanese), then it was ceded to Japan by the Qing court, became a Japanese colony, and was forced to assimilate to the Japanese empire. After participating in World War II and being returned to the Republic of China under Nationalist Party rule, Taiwan experienced the tragedy of the February 28 Incident (1947) and its aftermath. China's Nationalist-Communist civil war dragged Taiwan into an extended period of opposition to mainland China. From 1945 on, Taiwan also experienced another process of assimilation, this time to Chinese culture as represented by the ruling Nationalist Party. In 1950, Taiwan had only gone through the first half of these many ups and downs. What Taiwan's future direction would be was not yet clear.

Immigrants across the Taiwan Strait from Fujian and Guangdong in the nineteenth century raised Taiwan's population to three million. Taiwan's lowland aboriginal people were already steeped in Han Chinese culture, even to the extent of identifying with the Han people. Waves of immigrants from Fujian and Guangdong brought their local customs and way of life with them. Entering a Minan settlement was just like visiting a village near Amoy or Quanzhou, and walking into a "guest settlement" was just like visiting a Hakka village in Mei County in Guangdong. They worshipped their ancestors and recalled the counties their illustrious ancestors came from; they sang mountain songs, listened to the "southern pipes" (*nanguan*) music of Fujian, and practiced Eight Warriors (*bajiajiang*) boxing techniques. They sacrificed to Mazu, to the Lord Who Preserves Life, to the Master of Clear Water, and other gods of their native places. They were born and died there, raised their children and cared for their elderly, toiled mightily and thoroughly laid down roots in this new home, singing, weeping, and establishing their race there.

The Chinese immigrants' earthen defense lines steadily expanded deeper into the mountains. Increasing numbers of unmarried young men recruited from Fujian and Guangdong cleared more land and turned the wilderness into good arable fields. They were called "Arhat feet" (*luohan jiao*) because, being homeless, they slept in Buddhist temples at the feet of the Arhats. The old *Zuozhuan* poem describing the Shaanxi plateau of three thousand years earlier—"With wattle carts and tattered clothes, they clear the forests"—is perfectly appropriate to describe the lives of these pioneers.

Even though Taiwan had all the usual Qing administrative units—prefectures, districts, departments, and subprefectures—the real power of the Qing court authorities was limited. In the nineteenth century, Taiwan society was under the control of powerful, semifeudal local families such as the Lins of Wufeng Township (in contemporary Taizhong County), the Lins of Banqiao, the Wus of Yilan (from the aboriginal tribal name Kavalan), among others. These great landowners possessed tens of thousands of acres of land (measured in *jia* or *morgen*, a Dutch measure of varying size) and employed thousands of farming families. The offices (*gongguan*) where they collected rents from their tenants are still preserved in many place names. Back in their native locales on the mainland, especially in the important seaports, these great families all had commercial shops, and the ships traveling across the Taiwan Strait brought rice, tea, sugar, camphor, sulfur, and so on from Taiwan to places such as Amoy, Shantou, Shanghai, and Tianjin. When the government built city walls, roads, and bridges, these great families were required to make large financial donations. Nevertheless, it was these great families that ruled Taiwan and not the Qing authorities.

In the newly formed immigrant society of Taiwan, people from the same native villages banded together to form communities, working the fields, locating water sources, building village defense works, and collectively protecting the areas they opened up with such backbreaking work. The different ethnic groups frequently battled one another for possession of land and water. Since weapons were plentiful, many people were killed in these battles; those who died were worshipped in temple sacrifices as "heroic martyrs" (*yimin*, literally "just" or "righteous people") or "Lords of the People" (*dazhongye*). At one point in 1835, however, in Xinzhu County, the leaders of the rival Fujian and Hakka factions finally made peace, organized the Jin Guang Fu *gongguan* (the characters for gold, Guangdong, and Fujian can also mean "great golden good fortune"), and developed the surrounding mountain lands together.

The people of this developing island prized especially physical strength, ambition, and leadership ability. The immigrants to Taiwan relied upon their courage and strength and honored their promises, but they were not good with words nor were they interested in being so. Thus, although nineteenth-century Taiwan was the Qing dynasty's newest province, its customs were crude. Very few provincial examination graduates (*juren*), presented scholars (*jinshi*), Hanlin scholars, or high officials lived there. There were rich and extravagant great families on the island, but no gentry literati class like that of the intellectual families on the mainland.

Many incidents occurred along China's ocean borders in the nineteenth century, including a French invasion of Taiwan in 1884. The Qing court then decided to make Taiwan an official province and sent Commander Liu Mingchuan (1836–1896) to be the first governor general. Liu developed Taiwan and brought modernization to the province. During his tenure in office, Taiwan built many Chinese firsts: the first passenger railroad line from Keelung to Xinzhu; the first city, Taipei, that was built as a result of urban planning; the first aboveground telegraph line, transmitting from Taipei to Gaoxiong and later from Tamsui to Fuzhou and Tainan to Penghu by means of undersea lines. Coal from the mines of northern Taiwan made Keelung a major collier port. All of these new facilities provided excellent conditions for foreign merchants, and many of them set up enterprises in Taiwan. International tea merchants took over the export business in Taiwan tea, and Taiwan's Black Dragon (*wulong*) tea became world famous, as did Taiwan camphor.

After the Beiyang Army was defeated in the first Sino-Japanese War of 1894–1895, the Qing court offered to pay a variety of indemnities, but Japan insisted on taking Taiwan. Japan wanted to colonize Taiwan in order to secure a base for its continued southern expansion. China bore the pain of ceding Taiwan to Japan, and the entire Chinese people felt the sadness of it for fifty years. After learning that this cession had been finalized, the governing elite on Taiwan established the Taiwan Democratic Republic (Taiwan Minzhu Guo) and declared Taiwan an independent republic—the first republic in Asia! Even though they knew they had no chance of success, Taiwan's armed forces and people resisted the superior Japanese armed might for over three months, inflicting over thirty thousand casualties on the Japanese and suffering over ten times that many deaths themselves.

The Japanese did not declare the end of martial law on Taiwan until after ten years of occupation. At the beginning of the Japanese occupation, Taiwanese popular resistance did not stop for some time—men including Jian Dashi (1870–1900), Ke Tiehu (1876–1900), and Lin Shaomao (1865–

1902) continued to lead volunteer guerrilla forces in uprisings against the Japanese. The Japanese army's suppression of resistance was ruthless. They systematically burned to the ground village after village, especially the Hakka settlements where resistance was greatest. The saddest thing that happened during this period was the resurgence of interethnic strife. Some elements among the common people either betrayed their fellow Taiwanese by serving as informants for the Japanese or took advantage of the Japanese war of suppression to occupy the lands of other ethnic groups. Some even murdered women and children, expressing the worst side of human nature!

Even after the end of the period of suppression, the 1911 Chinese Revolution and the establishment of the Republic of China gave rise to another wave of anti-Japanese resistance on Taiwan. All of these uprisings failed, but they put the Japanese authorities on the alert that the people of Taiwan had not yet completely capitulated.

Japanese colonial policy on Taiwan also had its civilized side. Count Gotō Shinpei (1857–1929), chief of civilian affairs in Taiwan, began his social policies with the goal of completely assimilating Taiwan, to make it an extension of metropolitan Japan. There were many admirable elements of Japan's colonial rule on Taiwan, such as universal public education, great improvements in public health, and a harsh but fair legal system, all of which were welcomed by the populace. On the other hand, the people of Taiwan were only second-class subjects of the Japanese empire; they did not have the right to vote and could not hold higher than mid-level official positions. Taiwan's middle and elementary school system had two parts, schools for Japanese students with good facilities and excellent teachers and schools for Taiwanese students. These latter schools were inferior in every way. During the "Pacific War," the Japanese on Taiwan received food rations in greater quantity and higher quality than those distributed to the Taiwanese. All of this was part of the sorrow of being a colonized people!

To establish a stable rule, the Japanese authorities first set about to cultivate a new Taiwanese social elite. The place of the great landowners and tenant cultivators was taken by midlevel landowners. Qing-dynasty degree holders either returned to the mainland or lost their social status; they were replaced by men who received "gentlemen's awards" (shinshō) from the Japanese authorities. It was impossible for this new Taiwanese elite to enter the colonial ruling class, so their sons became doctors and lawyers or developed new business enterprises. Most members of this new elite went to Japan and received excellent educations. Their behavior was generally upright, honest, and decent, and they had refined cultural tastes. They constituted a stable force in an ordered society, and they did not expect themselves to "take the whole world as their responsibility." The cultivation of this stable and peaceful local elite to maintain the status quo was one of the main reasons for the success of Japanese colonial rule in Taiwan.

The Japanese also vigorously promoted a "national language movement" (*kokugo undō*) to make the Taiwanese population learn Japanese; prizes were awarded to every "national language family" (*kokugo katei*) that mastered Japanese. Any Taiwanese family willing to forsake its Chinese surname for a Japanese surname was also awarded the status of *kōmin*, "people of the emperor," sometimes translated as "imperial citizens." *Kōmin* enjoyed many special privileges almost on a par with imperial Japanese subjects, and for this reason some families tried very hard to assimilate. They made offerings before the holy talisman at Shinto shrines, thus abandoning the gods and ancestors that they previously worshiped. At the beginning of the *Kōminka* (assimilation) Movement, not very many Taiwanese received the *kōmin* status; when Japan invaded China, only about 4 percent of the Taiwan population were *kōmin*. When the Pacific War began, however, the movement accelerated greatly, and by the end of the war about 10 percent of the population were *kōmin*. Nevertheless, the Japanese *Kōminka* Movement on Taiwan was still a success: of all the countries in the world that emerged from colonialism, only on Taiwan do the former *kōmin* cherish the memory of their Japanese colonial masters and forget that they were only second-class subjects of the Japanese empire!

Before the Japanese occupation, Taiwan was a Chinese cultural area, and the chief language, writing system, and daily customs were all similar to those in southern China. Although the Japanese vigorously promoted assimilation policies, many Taiwanese people still did not want to give up their Chinese culture. While the Japanese carried out their "national language" (Japanese) education program, the Taiwanese still taught their children to read Chinese books in their private family schools. While the books, periodicals, and newspapers were all in Japanese, some men who had received excellent Chinese educations formed Chinese poetry associations and wrote and chanted their Chinese poems together. Although they could not have them printed, they could still produce poetry collections and play poetry-writing games for their own amusement. Chinese-style traditional popular religious ceremonies also never ceased, and Chinese operas never lost their audiences.

Taiwan intellectuals paid close attention to cultural activities on the mainland, and important discussions and works from the mainland all gave rise to reactions on Taiwan. When notables such as Sun Yatsen, Liang Qichao, and Gu Hongming (1857–1928) visited Taiwan, the local elite organized large assemblies to listen to them. Taiwan's intellectuals were even more interested in the May Fourth Movement. The vernacular literature of Zhang Wojun (1902–1955) and others was written in response to the new mainland literary trends. After the Nationalist victory in the Northern Expedition, many of Taiwan's youth returned to the mainland to study and remained there to work. Zhang Wojun, Lian Zhendong (1904–1986), and Liu Na-ou (1905–1940) were among those too numerous to mention who took this path.

The Taiwanese elite also worked hard to obtain human rights for the people of Taiwan. Lin Xiantang (1881–1956) and others organized a Taiwanese Cultural Association in 1921 to work for the right of the Taiwanese to vote, a Taiwan Representative Assembly, and to secure equal status for the people of Taiwan in the Japanese empire. The left-wing branch of the Taiwan labor movement strove to secure the right of Taiwanese to work in Japanese factories and to receive proper work benefits. Whether it was the professional elite or the manual workers, the people of Taiwan did not want to give up their individual dignity or their human rights—they did not want simply to be tame and docile subjects (*kōmin*) of the Japanese emperor.

When Japan invaded China, many Taiwanese merchants and doctors were working in China, especially in Manchuria, a puppet regime created by Japan in northeastern China. They were both Japanese citizens and ethnic Chinese, and their status was rather ambiguous. The Japanese also called up Taiwanese men to fight in China, and there were Taiwanese who considered it an honor to serve as imperial soldiers in the Pacific War.

The Wushe Incident occurred in 1930. That year in Wushe, a mountainous region in central Taiwan, the Atayal aboriginal people rose up in violent resistance against the Japanese after being insulted by a Japanese army officer. The Japanese suppressed their resistance with great brutality, employing heavy weapons and poison gas and completely destroying the village. Considering together the resistance of the people of Wushe and the willingness of some other Taiwanese to join the imperial army makes one sigh at the differences in human nature. In this same line of thought, what a historical paradox it was that some Taiwanese sang Japanese military songs during the tragic events of February 28, 1947!

In 1895, the Qing dynasty ceded Taiwan to the Japanese, and in 1945 Taiwan was returned to China; Taiwan changed countries twice in fifty years, and on neither occasion was it the people of Taiwan's choice. This prompted Wu Zhuoliu (1900–1976) to call Taiwan "The Orphan of Asia," a phrase also given to the title of his popular 1945 autobiographical novel. The pain and sorrow the Taiwanese people felt in their hearts has been the cause of many bitter tears. The February 28 Incident of 1947 was the great tragedy of postwar Taiwan. When the people of Taiwan were first returned to China, it was like a lost son suddenly returning to his old home to meet relatives he had never met before. Their enthusiastic expectations are easy to imagine. The Chinese soldiers who followed Chief Executive and Garrison Commander General Chen Yi (1883–1950) to Taiwan, however, were mostly local troops from Fujian who were not well trained and lacked discipline. They could in no way be compared to the image of the Japanese imperial soldiers that the people of Taiwan had in their minds, and they left them terribly disappointed. Before the Japanese invaded China, they had already carried out a propaganda campaign about the backward nature of the Chinese "slaves of the Qing dynasty" and their impoverished, stupid, and incompetent nature. This Japanese view was still the impression many Taiwanese people had of mainlanders at the time of the February 28 Incident.

Because of the mistaken intelligence they received, the Nationalist Army handled the February 28 Incident very badly. During the colonial era, the Japanese had nurtured a pool of assimilated (*kōminka*) local Taiwanese elites, who made up about 7 percent of the total population at the time of the Pacific War. Many of the Taiwanese local leaders at the time of the February 28 Incident were from this stratum of society, and their views of China and Japan were not without bias. When the Nationalist government took over Taiwan, they relied primarily on the assistance of a different group of local people. For this latter group to establish their own social status, they had to get rid of the former elite and take their place. When a great number of the original Taiwanese elite were killed during the February 28 Incident, who was it that had compiled the list of names of local leaders to be eliminated? Who benefited after the incident was over? It is obvious that they were the same people. The February 28 Incident has ever since remained a rupture in the cross-strait relationship between Taiwan and China—it is such a deep wound that time does not seem to be able to heal it.

In the final analysis, Taiwan changing countries twice without the consent of the local population became the main reason for strained cross-strait relations with China and for internal ethnic conflicts in Taiwan. The deeper background to cross-strait problems is that people on the two sides of the Taiwan Strait both have fifty years of different collective memories and different expectations and wishes for the future. It will not be an easy task to eliminate their mutual misunderstandings and heal the wounds of separation! Will their history move toward conciliation or conflict and destruction? This will ultimately depend on the collective wisdom of people at every level of both societies.

Suggestions for Further Reading

Brown, Jeremy, and Paul G. Pickowicz. *Dilemmas of Victory: The Early Years of the People's Republic of China*. Cambridge: Cambridge University Press, 2007.

Bray, Francesca. *Technology and Gender: Fabrics of Power in Late Imperial China*. Berkeley: University of California Press, 1997.

Cohen, Paul. *History in Three Keys: The Boxers as Event, Experience, and Myth*. New York: Columbia University Press, 1997.

Dikötter, Frank. *The Age of Openness: China Before Mao*. Hong Kong: Hong Kong University Pres, 2008.

Fairbank, John K., ed. *The Cambridge History of China*, vol. 10: *Late Ch'ing, 1800–1911, part 1*. Cambridge: Cambridge University Press, 1978.

Fairbank, John K., and Albert Feuerwerker, eds. *The Cambridge History of China*, vol. 13: *Republican China, 1912–1949, part 2*. Cambridge: Cambridge University Press, 1986.

Fairbank, John K., and Kwang-Ching Liu, eds. *The Cambridge History of China*, vol. 11: *Late Ch'ing, 1800–1911, part 2*. Cambridge: Cambridge University Press, 1980.

Hsia, C. T. *A History of Modern Chinese Fiction*. 3rd rev. ed. Bloomington: Indiana University Press, 1999.

Lary, Diana. *China's Republic*. Cambridge: Cambridge University Press, 2007.

MacFarquhar, Roderick, and John K. Fairbank, eds. *The Cambridge History of China*, vol. 14: *The People's Republic, part 1: The Emergence of Revolutionary China, 1949–1965*. Cambridge: Cambridge University Press, 1987.

———. *The Cambridge History of China*, vol. 15: *The People's Republic*, part 2: *Revolutions Within the Chinese Revolution, 1966–1982*. Cambridge: Cambridge University Press, 1991.

Mann, Susan. *Precious Records: Women in China's Long Eighteenth Century*. Stanford, Calif.: Stanford University Press, 1997.

Naquin, Susan, and Evelyn Sakakida Rawski. *Chinese Society in the Eighteenth Century*. New Haven, Conn.: Yale University Press, 1987.

Peterson, Willard J., ed. *The Cambridge History of China*, vol. 9: *The Ch'ing Empire to 1800*, part 1. Cambridge: Cambridge University Press, 2002.

Rubinstein, Murray A., ed. *Taiwan: A New History*. Armonk, N.Y.: M. E. Sharpe, 1999.

Spence, Jonathan. *God's Chinese Son: The Taiping Heavenly Kingdom in Hong Xiuquan*. New York: HarperCollins, 1996.

———. *Mao Zedong*. New York: Viking, 1999.

Strauss, Julia, ed. *The History of the People's Republic of China, 1949–1976*. Cambridge: Cambridge University Press, 2007.

Taylor, Jay. *The Generalissimo: Chiang Kai-shek and the Struggle for Modern China*. Cambridge, Mass.: Belknap Press, 2009.

Twitchett, Denis, ed. *The Cambridge History of China*, vol. 12: *Republican China, 1912–1949*, part 1. Cambridge: Cambridge University Press, 1983.

Xiaotong, Fei. *Peasant Life in China: A Field Study of Country Life in the Yangtze Valley*. With a preface by Bronislaw Malinowski. London: Routledge, 1939.

Afterword

Across several thousand years of history, Chinese culture experienced innumerable ups and downs, and the Chinese people who lived within this cultural sphere also experienced innumerable vicissitudes of life. Looking back on the developmental path of Chinese culture, the most striking feature is its broadminded inclusiveness. When the Chinese encountered different cultures, they were generally able to absorb their best features and incorporate them into their own cultural system. Furthermore, when a Chinese system of thought became overly dominant and moribund, they were also able to reform it and thus give Chinese culture a new opportunity to flourish.

In the last one hundred and fifty years, however, shaken by the onslaught of Western influence, some Chinese came to doubt the value of their own cultural tradition; some even repudiated that tradition. Chinese culture was almost in danger of disappearing off the face of the earth. Before the nineteenth century, to be sure, the Chinese were proud that they were the center of "all under heaven" and that their history was the history of a great civilization. After the nineteenth century, however, China faced the new world and had to accept a different reality. Thus, Chinese schools and textbooks began to offer "World History" and "Chinese History" as parallel curricula. From then on, Inside and Outside, the Chinese Self and the Other, were completely separate or even oppositional entities. If China had any contact with the outside world, it was generally one of opposition or confrontation. The frustration and humiliation China suffered in its foreign relations from the nineteenth century on produced a complex emotional mixture that combined feelings of inferiority with empty arrogance, and this further strengthened and deepened the attitude of isolation and conflict mentioned above.

The twenty-first century is an era of increasingly rapid globalization, and few regions of the world can remain isolated. China was once a world unto itself, the center of East Asia, and Chinese culture followed its own developmental process. Nevertheless, China could never really stand alone, independent from the rest of the world; Chinese history from beginning to end was always a constituent part of the common collective experience of humankind. If the Chinese today still think that the process of their historical experience went on in isolation, they will be unable to understand correctly either themselves or other peoples. The Chinese must adjust this attitude and come to understand themselves and other regions of the world in light of the intimate relationships between China and the outside world. Humanity had a common origin, and, after spreading out to occupy every region of the earth, we are now in the process of coming together to form a common society. Human beings in the various regions of the world have traveled different roads, but now we are finally moving in a common direction. We used to have our own histories, but essentially these independent histories were only different chapters in the common history of humanity.

Western culture has been hegemonic for a very long time. In today's globalized world, however, it must accept the different ideas and actions of its "others" in order to remedy the defects it has accumulated over several hundred years. At this same time, China is in the process of breaking away from one of the harshest dictatorships in human history. This struggle is not yet over, but the process of change is still moving forward. Chinese people everywhere in the world, as well as China's East Asian neighbors who live within the Chinese cultural sphere, are also engaged in a process of readjustment. As responsible "others," they are experimenting with different forms of coming together, self-reflections, and expressions of concern. Behind this phenomenon are long-pent-up tensions that can, given some chance of expression, offer a great deal of positive potential. Following this direction of development, today's globalization may perhaps turn out to be the most inspiring event in human history. At a time when various cultures of the world are mutually stimulating and moving one another, human society is finally on the road to becoming a single human family in which the essence of each cultural system will become a common resource for all humankind. At this historical turning point, cultural systems that have been in a subordinate position for a long time are no longer simply to be preserved in museums. They have acquired new vigor and are able to carry on a meaningful dialogue with the "mainstream" cultures of recent centuries. Through this dialogue, they can correct their mutual shortcomings.

We hope that the contemporary capitalist market economy, with its technological civilization and industrial production, together with a democratic political system of national scope can incorporate China's humanistic spirit of "taking responsibility for all humanity" (*yi ren wei ji ren*) and "not doing unto others what you would not want done to yourself" (*ji suo buyu wu shi yu ren*) so as to remedy the ills brought on by its loss of God. We hope it can also incorporate the Indian cultural concept that all sentient beings are equal in order to tame its mounting arrogance. We hope it can also incorporate Islamic culture's respect for nature to correct its waste of natural resources and environmental degradation. This important vocation will require the awareness and cooperation of all mankind. The evils of humanity's past mutual slaughter are already too great. To save ourselves from collective extinction, however, we must now learn to assist one another to prosper through mutual forgiveness and mutual trust and thus complete the next great breakthrough in human civilization. In the first such great breakthrough, over two thousand years ago, several important pioneering sages of civilization defined the values necessary for human survival. Facing our great contemporary crisis of destruction leading to global collapse, this new breakthrough can not only save us from apocalyptic extinction; it can also put into actual practice the values defined by those ancient sages. This will make it possible for the world that human beings have ruled for millennia to create the new Heaven and Earth and the new Garden of Eden that humanity has always longed for—in Chinese terms it will make possible an age of Grand Unity in which "the world is shared by all alike" (*tianxia wei gong*). Emerging from its recent calamity, China must redouble its efforts in this regard.

The snow now melting in the Bayan Har Mountains (the source of the Yellow River, in Qinghai Province) will soon flow into the great ocean. In the mutually connecting oceans of the world, the waters of the Yangzi and Yellow rivers will mix with the waters of other regions. At that time, the waters of China's rivers and the waters of other regions, such as the Indus, the Ganges, the Nile, the Persian Gulf, the Red Sea, the Mediterranean, the Mississippi, the Amazon, the Congo . . . will be indistinguishable! Likewise, the rivers of the ancient past (*wangu jianghe*, the Chinese title of this book) do not belong to China only—they belong, through our contemporary global convergence, to all of humanity.

Index

Chahai culture, 37
Champa, 266, 280, 348, 350 (map)
Chan (Zen) Buddhism, 200, 301, 303, 324, 385, 387
Chang-an, 131, 139–40, 172, 221 (fig.), 250, 285, 537
Changsha, 289
chantefable (shuochang), 485–86
Chao Yuanfang, 214–15
chariots, 68, 71–72, 223
Chen Bao (mythical creatures), 142
Chen Baozhen, 562
Chen Duansheng, 486–87, 490
Chen family, 297
Cheng, King, 81
Chengbeixi culture, 28 (fig.), 42
Cheng Hao, 385, 442
Cheng Yanqiu, 545
Cheng Yi, 385, 442
Chengzu. See Yongle emperor
Chen Hongshou, 393
Chen Lao, 403
chenwei texts, 138, 160, 162
Chen Yi, 571
Chen Zhi, 318
Chen Zuyi, 349
Chiang Kai-shek, 507, 509, 526, 536, 556, 558; and Central Plains War, 531, 534; and National Revolutionary Army, 533; and Northern Expedition, 533; rise to power, 534; and Whampoa Military Academy, 533–34
chickens, 32, 110, 130
childlike heart (Li Zhi's concept), 387–89
children. See education
"Chinese," definition of, 8–9
Chinese Civil War. See Nationalist–Communist Civil War
Chinese Communist Party, 504, 509–10, 535
Chinese cultural exchanges with the outside world, 5–6; Bronze Age, 71–72; Catholic missionaries (Ming dynasty), 356–64, 370–71, 476–77; and ceramic technology, 230–31, 233; cultural interactions with the West (Qing dynasty), 476–83; and glassmaking, 219, 233; influence of non-Chinese people of the north, 144–51, 236, 263, 274–75 (see also steppe peoples; Yuan dynasty; specific peoples); late Qing dynasty transformation to Western-style education system, 519–26; and military technology, 71–72; and northwestern trade routes, 16, 150 (see also Silk Road); and papermaking, 232–33;

and printing, 298; and religious traditions, 16 (see also Buddhism); and silk making, 233; and southeastern coastal region, 15; and sugar production, 230, 233; Western science and industrial arts introduced to China, 359–61, 370–71, 390, 476–77, 480–81. See also Buddhism; Europe; India; trade, international
Chinese culture, prehistoric, vii, 9–66, 35 (map); agriculture, 12–13, 15, 26–33, 60–64; artwork, 13–14, 55, 57; Bronze Age, 34; early China compared to ancient Mesopotamia, 60–66; fixed settlements, 26–33; lifeways, 11, 17, 27, 37; modern human species distribution, 20–21 (map); and myths and legends, 45–51, 48 (map), 65; natural geography of Chinese culture, 10–18; Neolithic agriculture and fixed settlements, 26–33; origins of differing worldviews of northern vs. southern peoples, 13–14; Paleolithic period, 18–26; relationships between regional and local Neolithic cultures, 34–45; rise of complex societies, 51–59; six major systems of regional cultures, 35 (map), 36–45; tools, 19, 21–22, 32–33
Chinese culture (16th through 3rd centuries B.C.E.), vii–viii, 68–119, 74 (map), 76 (map); artwork and decorative items, 69–70, 88; Bronze Age beginnings, 68–72; Chinese cultural system and Western Zhou political structure, 78–84; clothing, 111; compared to emerging civilizations in the Middle East, 113–19; corvée labor system, 105; daily life of common people, 108–12; division of China into prefectures and counties, 102–4; economics, 105; feudal system, 80–82, 84–86; feudal system, breakdown of, 87–88, 100–105; food and agriculture, 108–10; household registry system, 101, 104–5, 107–8; housing, 111; human sacrifice, 77, 88; and Mandate of Heaven (Tianming) concept, 79–80, 82–83; oracle bones, 73–76, 110; organization of government and daily life, 101–8; pottery, 70, 111; property ownership, 105; religion, 77; rise of southern cultures and merge with central plains, 96–101; role of regional cultures in forming unified Chinese cultural order, 84–90; seasonal festivals, 112; Shang dynasty as core of ancient Chinese culture, 72–78; social classes, 104–5; systems of thought, 90–96,

Chinese Rites Controversy, 357, 358, 361, 363–64, 478–79, 498

Chinggis Qaghan, 147, 270–73, 322; descendents and their khanates, 270, 273–74, 325, 416–17, 459; Qiu Chuji's advice to, 305; technical talent highly valued, 312

Chiyou, 46, 47–48, 48 (map), 49

Chongli, 50

Chongzhen emperor, 406

Christianity, 117, 177, 258, 259, 305, 359. *See also* Catholic missionaries; Chinese Rites Controversy

chronology, vii–xi

Chu culture, 43, 45, 46, 50, 97–101

Chu kingdom (Five Dynasties period), 265, 278

Chu state (Spring and Autumn period), 50, 97–102, 209, 434

cifu poetry, 101

cinnabar (mercuric sulfide), 201–2

Cishan culture, 28 (fig.), 47, 62

cities: cities in the 1930s, 536 (map); late medieval period, 289, 321, 325–26; medieval period, 221–22; modern expansion of urban culture, 537–45; and performing arts, 544–45; population of, 540; secret societies/criminal gangs, 539–40; and transformation of economic system in the late 19th and early 20th century, 517–19; and transportation networks, 540–41; treaty ports and Foreign Concessions, 539–40. *See also* port cities and harbors; *specific dynasties and cities*

civil bureaucracy: Han dynasty, 126, 183–84; Ming dynasty, 336–38, 384–85; Qing dynasty, 440, 502; Song dynasty, 290–300, 321; and stagnation of thinking, 337–38, 385, 502; Tang dynasty, 255; Yuan dynasty, 322. *See also* examination system and civil bureaucracy; government and territorial administration

Cixi, Empress Dowager, 559–61, 563

clan system and great families, 88; bargemen clans, 458; and Chu kingdom, 98; conflicts between early vs. late settlers in the south, 241; decline in power, 254, 275, 293, 306–7; and end of the Han dynasty, 185, 323; families' relations with imperial power, 81, 100, 127, 183–84, 321; and family education, 296–97; and gentry literati class, 184, 207, 208, 300, 321, 562; great power from Eastern Han to North-South dynasties, 195–96; Han clan organization

distinguished from Qin feudal system, 183; and Han distribution of labor, 129; and He Xinyin's utopian community, 388; and Manchuria, 416; and personal names, 107; regional warlords under northern conquest dynasties, 274; self-contained communities, 189, 195–96, 224, 241; Shanxi merchant clans, 474; Song dynasty changes, 321, 323–24; southward migration of great families, 194–96, 241; and Taiwan, 430, 566–67; and Zhou dynasty, 81–83, 85–86, 100

Classic of Mountains and Seas (Shanhaijing), 49, 142, 144

climate, 32, 33, 99, 193, 431

clothing: and disruption of domestic economy by influx of European commodities, 513; late medieval period, 315–16; Manchu braided queue and clothing required for all adult men (Qing dynasty), 433; medieval period, 216–19; Neolithic period, 40; Qin-Han period, 166–67; Warring States period, 111, 166

coal, 368–70

coastal regions, geography and prehistoric culture, 11, 12 (map), 14–15, 36, 43. *See also* port cities and harbors; southeastern cultural region; southern cultural region

Collected Commentaries on the Materia Medica (Zhang Zhongjing), 215

Collected Prescriptions (Zhouhuo fang; Ge Hong), 213

communication: and contrast between China and ancient Middle East, 113–15; and contrast between China and Roman Empire, 178–79; disruption of traditional communication networks, 515–16; extensive networks in the south (Ming dynasty), 382; Han dynasty communication with the West (overland routes), 146–47(maps), 148–49; and Han dynasty southward expansion, 151; and late medieval trade networks, 273–76; Qing dynasty, 470; and relationships between Neolithic cultures, 34–45. *See also* maps of trade routes and lines of communication; roadways; trade, domestic; transportation; waterways

Communist Party, 554. *See also* People's Republic of China

Communist Revolution, 557–58

community organizations: commercial leagues (*shangbang*), 473–74; late medieval period, 323–24; late 19th century, 516;

local, trade-based organizations, 450–51; Mazu temples, 451–52; and popular religious sects of the Qing dynasty, 451–57; village assembly halls, 450

Comprehensive Mirror for Aid in Government (Zizhi tongjian; Sima Guang), 488

Comprehensive Treatise on Agricultural Administration (Nongzheng quanshu; Xu Guangqi), 361, 364–66, 370, 373

Confucianism, viii, ix, x, 203, 338, 385–89; academies, 295–97; and Buddhism, 198, 301, 303, 389–90; *chenwei* texts, 138, 160, 162; and Chinese Rites Controversy, 357; contrast to philosophy and religion in the West, 178; and cooperation with foreign rulers, 434–35; core concepts, 92–93, 183, 303, 338; and Daoism, 305; and examination system (*see* examination system and civil bureaucracy); and filial piety, 183, 198; and Han dynasty, 134–38, 162, 176, 183, 203; in Japan, 248; in Korea and Japan, 248; late medieval development, 292–303, 321–22, 326; loss of position as official ideology during North-South dynasties, 196; loss of vitality during Eastern Han, 203; and Mandate of Heaven (*Tianming*) concept, 90–91; and Ming dynasty, 336–38, 358, 376, 385–89, 395; Neo-Confucian schools of thought, 326, 336–38, 358, 376, 385–89; New Text School, 138; and north/south contrast in Chinese worldviews, 13, 100; origins of, 90–95, 118; and Qing dynasty, 436–49; relationship with the court, 178, 183, 452–53; "sage on the inside/king on the outside" concept, 321, 338, 376; six Confucian arts, 443; and Song dynasty, 295–300, 321, 326, 338; and status of women, 306; and syncretic movements, 203, 453; virtues of humanity and rightness (*ren* and *yi*) in pre-Han times, 183; Zhang Zai's "Western Inscription," 302. *See also* Cheng Hao; Cheng Yi; Lu Jiuyuan; Lu Xiangshan; Wang Yangming; Zhu Xi

Confucius, 87, 94–95

Confucius as Institutional Reformer (Kongzi gaizhi kao; Kang Youwei), 547

conscription, 106, 152, 258, 365

Continuation of Ancient Mathematics (Jigu suanshu; Wang Xiaotong), 212

cooking, 109, 150, 167–68, 216–18, 317–18

copper, 68–69; copper coins/cash, 280, 283–84, 343–44, 369, 377, 382–83, 471;

"Golden Pavilions" made from, 369; imported from Japan and Korea, 280, 284, 471; and medieval trade, 280, 284, 288

corn, 32, 340–41, 342, 423, 469

corruption, 312, 398, 488, 501

corvée labor system, 104, 105, 225, 378

cosmology, 136, 141, 142, 211, 214

Cossacks, 460–61

cotton: cotton clothing, 220; Ming dynasty, 342, 366, 373; Qing dynasty, 462; and regional division of labor, 373, 377, 470; Tang dynasty, 229; technology for separating cotton from its seeds, 342; treadle-powered cotton gin, 366; and weaving, 229, 313

creation stories, 11, 45–46

The Crime Cases of Lord Peng (Penggong an), 486

The Crime Cases of Lord Shi Shilun (Shigong an), 486

Crime Cases of the Lord of the Dragon Diagram (Longtu gong-an), 489

Cromwell, Oliver, 493

Cultivation of Golden Yams (Jinshu Chuanxilu; Chen Shiyuan), 340

currency. *See* money

cycles, theory of, 123, 126, 134–35, 136–37, 163

Dadiwan culture, 28 (fig.), 52–54, 53 (fig.), 59

Dai, Lady (tomb), 144, 167

Daily Jottings (Liuqing rizha; Tian Yiheng), 341

daitian system (agricultural technique), 129

Dai Zhen, 447

Dali kingdom, 252, 264 (map), 266, 267, 288

dance, 210

Dangxiang people, 191, 247 (map)

Dao-an, 197, 199

Daoguang emperor, 501, 511

Daoism, viii; alchemy, 163, 201–3; and apocalyptic beliefs, 163, 202; and Buddhism, 159–65, 186, 201, 301; and Chu state, 100; complexity of, 201; and Confucianism, 305; core concepts, 94, 201, 202; Dark Learning (Neo-Daoism), 160–61, 203; and Five Agents, 95; and Han dynasty, 134–36, 159–64, 176, 202; and *Huainanzi,* 135; and Jin and Yuan dynasties, 304–5; late medieval period, 300–305, 321–22; and literature/performing arts, 485; and nature, 95, 201; and North-South dynasties, 203; persecution of Daoists, 300; popularization of, 304; Quanzhen (Complete Truth)

Daoism (*continued*)
sect, 304–5; and quest for longevity, 201, 202, 304; religious (*daojiao*) distinguished from philosophical (*daoxue*), 186; and shamanistic arts, 162–65, 201, 301; and southern culture, 101; and syncretic movements, 203, 453; Taiyi (Great Unity) sect, 304–5; Talisman (*fulu*) School, 201, 203; and Tang dynasty, 202; temples and community cohesion, 221, 324; Way of the Celestial Masters (*Tianshidao*), 162, 201, 202, 300; Way of Great Peace (*Taiping dao*, Yellow Turbans), 162–64, 300; and Yin-Yang, 95; Zhenda (Truly Great) sect, 305

Daosheng, 199
Dark Learning (Neo-Daoism), 160–61, 203
Darwin, Charles, 547
Dashi (Arab states), 246 (map), 250–51, 276
Dawenkou culture, 28 (fig.), 38, 48 (map), 49, 52, 59, 74–75
Daxi culture, 28 (fig.), 33, 42
Dayan Qaghan, 270
death, beliefs about, 143–44
Decline and Fall of the Roman Empire (Gibbon), 182
deities: ancient beliefs, myths, and legends, 11, 45–50, 95, 158–59; Buddhist-Daoist hierarchy, 203; Guan Di (patron deity of Shanxi), 451; Lin Moniang (Song dynasty), 451; and literature/performing arts, 490–91; north/south contrast, 101; and popular religious sects of the Qing dynasty, 451–52; Qin-Han period, 141; and religious Daoism, 162–63; Shang dynasty, 77; temples and the rise of complex societies, 54–55; Warring States period, 161; Zhou dynasty, 79
democracy, 439, 495, 548, 552
demographics: cities, 540; and economics in the medieval era, 225; Han dynasty, 128, 151, 339; Ming dynasty, 339–45, 423; Qing dynasty, 469, 471, 498; Song dynasty, 339; Taiwan, 422, 425
Deng Xiaoping, 535, 554, 558
de Semedo, Alvaro, 362–63
The Destruction of the Soul (*Shen mie lun*; Fan Zhen), 199
de Ursis, Sabatino, 361
dictionaries and encyclopedias, 447–48
Dingling people, 149
Di people, 188, 217, 234
Disciplinary School of Buddhism, 200

disease epidemics, 150–51, 153, 189, 193, 218–19, 234
divination, 77, 79, 126, 137, 141. *See also Book of Changes*; oracle bones
Doctrine of the Mean (*Zhongyong*), 297, 301
dogs, 29, 61, 110, 130
Dominicans. *See* Catholic missionaries; Chinese Rites Controversy
Dong family, 274
Donghu people, 149
Donglin Academy, 393
Dong people, 240
Dong Zhongshu, 135–37, 141, 142, 211
donkeys, rental of, 223
Dragon Kings (*longwang*), 452, 516
drama. *See* performing arts
Dream of the Red Chamber (*Honglou meng*), 484, 485, 486, 550
Dream of Splendors Past in the Eastern Capital (*Dongjing Meng Hua lu*), 289
Dream Pool Essays (*Mengxi bitan*; Shen Kuo), 311
droughts, 379
dualism, 95, 115, 117–19
Duan family, 265–66
Du Fu, 206
Dutch East Indies Company, 492
dyeing techniques for textiles, 229, 365, 473
Dzungars, 462, 527

Early Qin kingdom, 188
eastern cultural region, 38, 38 (map)
Eastern Han dynasty (25–220 C.E.), viii; and Buddhism, 186; and Confucianism, 139, 160, 203; disease epidemics, 150–51, 189, 193, 218–19; elites, 195–96; food, 216; government and territorial administration, 184, 185; medicine, 213; and Neo-Daoism, 203; and non-Chinese northern "barbarians," 186, 233; population decrease, 189; rebellions, 162, 185; scholarship, 445; and southward migration, 152, 189, 192–94, 240; split into three kingdoms, 182; study of omens forbidden, 126
Eastern Jin dynasty (317–420), ix, 241; and Buddhism, 197–98; divisions of non-Chinese southern peoples, 240; government and territorial administration, 194; investiture system, 249; and southward migration of Han people, 194; warfare, 193; and Way of the Celestial Masters Daoism, 201
Eastern Western Monthly Magazine, 542

Eastern Wu kingdom, 153, 243

Eastern Zhou dynasty (770–256 B.C.E.): daily life of common people, 108–12; "the rites were ruined and the music shattered," 86; and role of regional cultures, 84–90; and shared culture of the elite, 85; and Three Dynasties concept, 83. *See also* Spring and Autumn period; Warring States period; Zhou dynasty

economics: Europe, 345–46, 350–55, 381, 462–64, 468, 492; Japan, 277, 280, 284, 352–54; Korean peninsula, 277, 280, 284; late medieval period, 275–92, 312–13; medieval period, 224–33; Middle East, 279–80; Roman Empire, 187; transformation in the late 19th and early 20th century, 511–19; unfavorable balance of trade, 513; wealth disparities between urban and rural areas, 515. *See also* industry; maps of trade routes and lines of communication; money; salt trade; trade; trade, domestic; trade, international; *and following headings*

economics (Han dynasty), 127–33, 178–79, 186–87, 224, 226

economics (Ming dynasty): closure of ports, 334–35, 348–52; and Confucianism, 376; industrial development, 364–77; maritime trade, piracy, and smuggling, 349–56, 371–72, 403, 406; market economy, 371–78; north-south trade, 373–75

economics (Qing dynasty): domestic trade, 468–76, 475 (map); international trade, 462–67, 471–72; local, trade-based organizations, 450–51; relaxation of ban on foreign trade, 464–66, 472

economics (Song dynasty), 285–90, 346–48, 371

economics (Sui dynasty), 225–28

economics (Tang dynasty), 225–31, 276

economics (Warring States period), 105

economics (Yuan dynasty), 346–48, 371

economics (Zhou dynasty), 88

education: and alienation from rural society, 522–25, 555; Confucian academies, 295–97; family education (medieval era), 296–97; and industry, 525–26; late Qing dynasty transformation to Western-style system, 519–26; and monasteries, 295–97; schools for specialized subjects, 297, 308, 520; and shared culture of the elite during Zhou period, 86; Song period, 294–98; Sui-Tang era, 308; and Taiwan, 568–69; Tang period, 211, 215–16, 294–95; textbooks, 544; universities, 294, 295, 520–21, 524 (map),

540–41, 564; Yan Yuan's emphasis on practical studies (Qing dynasty), 443–44

Egypt, 17, 114, 117, 277

The Elders of Xiangyang (Xiangyang qijiu zhuan), 185

Elephant Mountain Academy, 296

Eleut Mongols, 417–18, 420 (map)

The Emperor's Four Treasures (Siku quanshu), 447–48

energy resources, 370. *See also* coal

England. *See* Britain

Enlightenment, European, 400, 482, 491–92

Eridu, 62 (map), 64

Erligang culture, 42

Erlitou culture, 28 (fig.), 42, 72, 73

Essays on Chinese History (Liang Qichao), 3

ethnic groups: blood ties vs. geography for identifying ethnicity, 325; ethnic and cultural conflicts in the early Qing, 432–41; ethnic mixtures of Zhou period elite, 85; and Han dynasty southward expansion, 151–55; and Manchu banner system, 527; and nationalism in the 20th century, 509–10; and northern conquest dynasties, 269–75, 322–27; and Taiwan, 402, 430–31; and theoretical interconnected genealogy, 510. *See also specific regions and ethnic groups*

eunuchs, 258, 337, 338, 380, 400

Europe: barbarian invasions, 149–50, 158, 177, 188; beginning of Sino-Western understanding, 362–64, 480–81; Catholic missionaries to China (Ming dynasty), 356–64, 370–71; and Christianity, 177; comparison of Ming dynasty and Hapsburg Spain, 394–401; comparison of Qing dynasty with contemporary West, 491–99; concept of nationalism, 506–7; Enlightenment, 400, 482, 491–92; Foreign Concessions in port cities, 539; immigration policies, 425; Industrial Revolution, 492, 512–13, 539; legal codes, 563; maritime trade, 345–46, 350–55, 463–66, 492; and modern thought and cultural change in China, 546–52; papermaking transmitted to, 232; Protestant Reformation, 491; Qing dynasty relations with European nations, 459–68; regional variation in economics, 381; scholarship in, 448–49; *semu* merchants, 277; superior weapons of, 314; and transmission of Western industrial arts, 359–60, 370–71; World War I, 513, 518–19. *See also specific countries*

Guangxi Army, 531–32, 536

Guangxi Province, 154, 525, 531–33; climate, 32; Neolithic agriculture, 32; Paleolithic sites, 24; and Qin-Han southward expansion, 151; and Taiping Rebellion, 505, 527

Guangxu emperor, 559–63

Guangzhou (Canton), 15, 537; emigration to Taiwan from, 432; Foreign Concessions, 539; foreign merchants living in "foreign quarters" (*fanfang*), 281; and lack of Chinese traders' interest in commodities other than silk, 499; and late medieval era, 275, 289; as medieval port city, 223, 278; and Qing dynasty relaxation of ban on foreign trade, 464–66, 472; as second-rank city of the modern era, 537; and Taiping Rebellion, 505; universities, 541

Guanmiaoshan archaeological site, 43

Gu Fuxi, 485

Gu Hongzhong, 223, 315

guild system, 369–70, 373, 450–51

Guizhou Province, 22, 24, 195, 243, 266, 456

Gu Kaizhi, 209

Gun (water god), 50

gunpowder, 314

Guodian texts, 91–92

Guo Shoujing, 310, 311, 312

Gu Xiancheng, 393

Gu Yanwu, 343, 394, 434, 436–38, 441, 445–46

Hainan Island, 32, 157, 342, 348

hair styles, 167, 433

Hakka people, 195, 218, 383, 516; and Taiwan, 430, 432, 565, 566, 568

Halaf culture, 69

Hallan Cemi archaeological site, 61, 62 (map)

Han dynasty (206 B.C.E..–220 C.E.), viii, 126, 148–49, 152, 173 (map); agriculture, 127–33; animal husbandry, 130; artwork, 209; and Buddhism, 158–66, 186; burial customs, 143; calendrical system, 137–38; center–periphery issues in governance, 127; ceramics, 230–31; cities, 131; clan system, 129, 183; clothing, 219–20; collapse of Qin-Han imperial order, 181–88; communication with the West (overland routes), 146–47(maps), 148–49; and Confucianism, 139, 160, 162, 176, 203; contrast to Roman Empire, 171–79; daily life, 166–71, 216; and Daoism, 134–36, 159–64, 176; disease epidemics, 150–51, 153, 189, 193, 234; and dynastic change, 126; economics, 127–33, 178–79, 186–87, 224, 226; establishment of, 182; examination system and civil bureaucracy, 126, 183–84; foreign relations, 267; founder of, 123; government and territorial administration, 123–27, 151–55, 174–75, 183–85, 226, 245; handcrafts, 130; investiture system, 249, 267; and localism, 182–85; male–female division of labor, 129–30; and Mandate of Heaven (*Tianming*), 126, 136–37, 143; medicine, 141, 150, 215; military, 125, 152; myths and legends, 46, 47, 142; northern nomad cultural interaction with Chinese culture (Qin-Han period), 144–51; "peace and kinship" marriage alliances, 234; philosophy, 133–39, 176–77; political unification of China, 97; popular beliefs, 142; population changes, 128, 189, 192, 339; rebellions, 124, 133, 162, 163, 192, 193; religion, 139–44, 158–66; roadways, 132 (map), 151–54, 187; and *Romance of the Three Kingdoms*, 488; rule of "all under heaven" concept, 123; ruling class, 123–24; southward expansion and migrations, 6, 125, 151–58, 189, 192–94, 233; village administration, 323. *See also* Eastern Han dynasty; Han people; Western Han dynasty

Han family, 274

Han Gaozu, 204

Hangzhou, 15, 286, 299, 341, 376, 537, 540

Han people, 191; acculturation to non-Han cultures, 236; clothing, 219–20; conflicts between early vs. late settlers in the south, 241; continuation of culture following Han dynasty's loss of power, 126; culture mixed with Yi cultures, 89; and decline of the Manchus, 502, 506; great families self-protection behind fortifications in the north, 196; and Green Standard Army, 527; hybridization of culture with Hu cultures following Han dynasty's loss of power, 188–91; immigration to Japan and other East Asian nations, 248; Mongol derogatory term for (*Manzi*), 378; and Qing dynasty movement, 469; and Qing dynasty takeover of Han culture, 433–41; and Qing dynasty territorial administration, 413–16; reestablishment of dynasty ruled by Han Chinese after fall of the Yuan dynasty, 330; southward migration of great families, 194–96, 241; in Taiwan, 355, 407–8, 410, 422, 424–29, 565–72; term explained, 234; and theoretical interconnected genealogy, 510; Yuan dynasty's laissez-faire attitude toward, 433

Han River, 31–32, 43, 97, 98, 131, 382, 402, 432
Han Wudi, 184, 186, 201
Han Yu, 208, 301–2
Hao Jing, 434–35
Heaven and Earth Society (Tiandihui), 457–58
Heavenly Principle sect, 454, 455 (map)
Heavenly Qaghan (*Tian kehan*), 244, 250, 262
Hebei Province, 28–29; and An Lushan Rebellion, 236; as disaster-prone region, 379; and Early Shang culture, 73; hybridization of Han and Hu cultures, 191; land grants to imperial princes and other favored people (Ming dynasty), 380–81; mathematicians from, 309–10; and myths and legends, 47; Neolithic sites, 28; as non-Chinese territory during the Sui-Tang period, 236, 238; northern cultural interaction with Chinese culture (medieval era), 263; Paleolithic sites, 24; piracy and smuggling, 353; porcelain production, 366; prominent families under conquest dynasties, 274; Qiang and Särbi immigration into, 188–89; and regional warlords, 238, 274; and rise of complex societies, 54; Tang period loose-reign prefectures (*jimizhoufu*), 263. *See also* Warring States period
He Bin, 355, 407
He Chou, 219
hemp clothing, 110, 220
Hemudu culture, 28 (fig.)
Henan Province: Bronze Age archaeological sites, 70; as disaster-prone region, 379; and Early Shang culture, 73; geography and prehistoric culture, 36; land grants to imperial princes and other favored people (Ming dynasty), 380–81; late medieval period, 290; Neolithic sites, 29, 74; and Song capital city, 285; and Xia culture, 72
Hexi Corridor. *See* Gansu Corridor
He Xinyin, 388
History of the Former Han (Han shu), 154, 159, 294
History of the Later Han (Hou Hanshu), 234
History of Modern Chinese Literature (Xiandi Zhongguo wenxue shi; Qian Jibo), 549
Hlai (Li) people, 313, 342
Hmong people. *See* Miao (Hmong) people
Holland: and Batavia, 352, 404, 407; Dutch East Indies Company, 492; immigration policies, 425; Lamey Massacre, 407; loss of Taiwan, 354–55, 404–5, 463; maritime trade, 350, 351, 353, 492
"Holy Mother" worship, 323–24
Honghuatao archaeological site, 42
Hong Kong, 15, 543, 545, 560
Hongmen, 457–58, 539–40
Hongshan culture, 28 (fig.), 37, 45, 48 (map), 49, 54–56, 64
Hongwu emperor (Ming Taizu; Zhu Yuanzhang): and civil bureaucracy, 336, 384; isolation policy, 334, 348–49; as regional warlord, 274–75; resettlement policies, 379; style of governance, 336–38; victory over the Mongols and establishment of Ming dynasty, 330, 394–95, 432
Hongxi emperor, 336
Hong Xiuquan, 505
Hongzhou (modern Nanchang), 226, 231, 279, 281, 286, 297
horses: and clothing, 220; as late medieval transportation, 316; and northern nomad culture, 145; polo, 223; prehistoric cultures, 17; salt traded for, 288; and Silk Road, 148; silk traded for, 276; southerners' fear of, 223; Tang period, 223; tea traded for, 276, 279, 288; Warring States period, 110; and wheeled vehicles, 170
Hou Debang, 525–26
Houji, 50, 79
household registry system, 101–8, 225, 381
housing, 28–29, 33, 53–54, 96, 111, 169–70, 221–23
Houtu (god of earth), 51
Huainanzi (Liu An), 134–35, 141, 168
Huai River, 97, 263, 344, 374, 402; natural disasters, 379, 382
Huang Binhong, 551
Huang Chao Rebellion (874–884), 278
Huang Daopo, 313, 342
Huang Di. *See* Yellow Emperor
huangdi title for emperor, 122
Huang Renyu (Ray Huang), 526, 558
Huang Taiji, Emperor, 415–17
Huang Zongxi, 386, 394, 438–42, 506
Huating culture, 42, 57, 59
Hua-Xia culture, 45, 48, 68, 89
Hubei Province: climate, 32; and Early Shang culture, 73; food imports from, 471; iron mining/metallurgy, 368, 374; late medieval period, 290; Neolithic agriculture, 31–32; Paleolithic sites, 22; and rise of the Chu state, 50; siege of Xiangyang (1267–1273), 314

eval era, 266; Chinese immigrants to, 248, 348; cities modeled on Tang cities, 221; and Confucianism, 248; copper exports, 280, 284, 471; February 26 Incident, 564; First Sino-Japanese War, 502, 506, 567; invasions of Korea (1500s), 335; and investiture system, 249; and late medieval economics, 277, 280, 284; and late medieval multistate system, 266; and Legalism, 248; maritime trade, 351–54; Meiji Restoration, 506, 558–65; metallurgy, 248; military, 562, 564; and Pacific War, 569, 570; papermaking transmitted to, 232; philosophy, 386; pirates, 334, 351–52, 372; puppet governments in China, 531, 534; relations with Sui dynasty, 247–48; relations with Tang dynasty, 247–48; shoes, 220; sphere of influence, 503 (map); and Taiwan, 502, 516–17, 565–72; Tenrikyo sect, 453; War of Resistance Against Japan, 502, 507–9, 508 (map), 515–16, 518 (map), 519, 526, 534, 557; writing system, 248, 266

Jarmo archaeological site, 61, 62 (map)

Java, 348, 350, 350 (map)

Jericho archaeological site, 61, 62 (map)

Jesuits, 357–64, 370–71, 390, 476–77, 480–81

jewelry, 25, 279, 371

Jiahu archaeological site, 74, 96

Jiang clan, 81, 85, 88

Jianghan culture, 41, 45, 49

Jiangnan, 345; agriculture, 345; food imports, 374, 470–71; landscape gardening, 393; as leading economic region during Ming dynasty, 377; opera, 392; resistance to Qing rule, 433, 436; textiles, 365, 372, 373; transportation networks, 382

Jiangsu Province, 24, 57, 59, 241, 288

Jiangxi Province, 31, 32, 73, 151, 290, 367, 372, 374

Jiangzhuo archaeological site, 74

Jiang Ziwen (deity), 141

Jiankang. See Nanjing

Jiao Hong, 390

Jiaozhou prefecture, 154, 241, 266, 287–88

Jiaqing emperor, 501, 511

Ji clan, 81, 83, 85

Jie people, 188, 234, 235, 412

Jin Dongxin, 551

Jin dynasty (1115–1234), ix, 187, 263, 264 (map), 267, 269–75, 413–14; artwork, 209; and Daoism, 304–5; government and territorial administration, 271, 414; invasion of China, 286, 294; medicine, 213, 319;

military, 292; money, 284; scholarship, 215; stories of the supernatural, 206–7; and trade networks, 276

Jin dynasty (220–420). See Eastern Jin dynasty; Western Jin dynasty

Jing, King, 143

Jingdezhen, 286; as center of porcelain production, 367, 373, 374

Jingnan kingdom (Five Dynasties period), 265

Jin state (Zhou period), 89, 99, 103, 106

Jochi, 459

Jones, William C., 563

Judaism, 176–77, 258, 277

Judge Bao, 486, 489, 490

Jurchen Jin dynasty. See Jin dynasty

Jurchen people, 317, 322

Kaifeng. See Bianliang

kaiyuan era (713–741), 237, 244, 295

Kampuchea (Cambodia), 348, 350 (map)

Kang, King, 81

Kangxi emperor, 417–19; and cartography, 480; Catholic missionaries banned, 357; and Chinese Rites Controversy, 361, 363–64, 478–79; curiosity about foreign knowledge, 467, 477–78; and military, 527; and Russia, 462–63, 471; and Taiwan, 422, 425

Kang Youwei, 543, 546–47, 559–60, 563

kapok tree, 342

Kara Khitai. See Western Liao dynasty

karma, 453, 490

Kazakh people, 147

Kazuo Dongshanzui archaeological site, 55

Kejia (guest households) people, 241

Khalkha Mongols, 417, 420 (map)

Khitan (Qidan) people, 238, 244, 247 (map), 263, 269, 317, 322. See also Liao dynasty; Western Liao dynasty

Khmer, 266, 280, 350 (map)

Khubilai Khan. See Kublai Qaghan

Khwarezmian empire (840–1211), 268, 269

kilns, 230–31, 367. See also porcelain

kinship relations. See clan system and great families

Kong Shangren, 485

Korean peninsula, ix, 243; and Buddhism, 200–201, 248; Chinese immigrants to, 248, 348; and Confucianism, 248; friendly relations with medieval China (after unsuccessful Sui-Tang invasions), 246–47, 266; and investiture system, 249; Japanese invasion (1500s), 335; and late medieval

Liu Jinting, 485
Liu Mingchuan, 567
Liu Song dynasty (420–479), 247
Liu Xiang, 532 (map)
Liu Xianglao, 354, 406
Liu Yuan, 234–35
Liu Zhang, 140–41
Liu Zhongzhou, 442
Li Ye, 308–10
Li Zhi, 388–89
Li Zhizao, 356, 363, 477
Li Zicheng, 383, 406, 423, 435
Li Zongren, 531, 534
Long March, 534
Longobardi, Niccolo, 358, 360
Longqing emperor (Muzong), 349
Longshan culture, 28 (fig.), 38, 70, 71
looms, 365
Love and Responsibility (*Lian-ai yu zeren*;
  film), 551
Lü, Empress Dowager, 124
Lu, Prince, 406
Lü Buwei, 135
Lü Guang, 239
Lu Jiuyuan, 296, 297, 303. *See also* School
  of Mind
Luo Guanzhong, 391
Luo Rufang, 387–88, 390
Luoyang, 131, 537; Buddhist temples, 200; lay-
  out of, 221; as Northern Wei capital, 414;
  sack of (311), 193–94, 241; Six Garrisons'
  invasion, 237; Tang dynasty quarters, 222
  (fig.)
Lu state, 85, 87, 102, 112
Lu Xiangshan, 303, 385
Luxinan culture, 38
*Luxuriant Dew of the Spring and Autumn An-
  nals* (*Chunqiu fanlu*; Dong Zhongshu),
  135–36

Macao, 15, 463, 543, 560
Macartney, Sir George, 466–68, 483, 493
Ma family, 274
Mahayana Buddhism, 419
Maitreya Buddha, 453–54
Majiabang culture, 28 (fig.), 41, 41 (map)
Majiayao culture, 28 (fig.), 69
Malacca, 281, 350, 350 (map), 352, 353
Ma Lianlang, 545
Manchukuo, 534
Manchu people: rise in the mid-Ming,
  332–33, 417, 433; and Russia, 461; victory

over the Ming, 314, 354, 384, 395, 433;
  writing system, 273. *See also* Qing dynasty
Manchuria, 273, 421, 461, 507, 531, 534, 559,
  570
Mandate of Heaven (*Tianming*): and concepts of fate and human nature, 91–92;
  and Confucianism, 90–91; defined/
  described, 80; and *geming*, 552; and
  Guodian texts, 91–92; and Han dynasty
  concerns with dynastic change, 126,
  136–37, 143; and mutual misunderstandings of Qing court and British diplomats,
  467; and state religion, 161; and Tang
  period, 255; and theory of cyclical change,
  123; and Zhou defeat of the Shang, 79–80,
  82–83, 90–91
Manichaeism, 259, 301, 306, 453–54
Manila, Philippines, 352, 353
Man people, 152, 240
Maoran people, 191
Mao Yuanyi, 364
Mao Zedong, 510, 526, 531, 536, 554, 558
maps: Great Wall, 331; institutions of higher
  learning, 524; Mercator projection, 360;
  modern human species distribution,
  20–21; Qing dynasty popular religious
  rebellions, 455; regions of rice and millet
  cultivation, 31; Ricci's *Atlas of the World*,
  360, 362–63; spread of Buddhism into
  China, 164–65; and Western influence in
  cartography, 480–81. *See also following
  headings*
maps of states, settlements, cultures, territory, and spheres of influence: ancient
  Middle East, 116; Austronesian language
  group, 156–57; cities in the 1930s, 536;
  Great Powers' spheres of influence in
  China (late 19th century), 503; Han and
  Roman empires, 172–73; Islamic Empire,
  256–57; Liangzhu cultural sequence, 56;
  major systems of regional cultures, 12, 35;
  Mesopotamian archaeological sites, 62;
  Ming dynasty border garrisons, 380; Ming
  dynasty South Seas, 350; Mongol tribes
  of the early Qing dynasty, 420; Neolithic
  archaeological sites, 30, 37–39, 41–42, 44;
  Neolithic cultures and legendary characters, 48; Paleolithic archaeological sites,
  23; Qin dynasty, 124; regions under warlord control (1926), 532; Russia's eastward
  expansion, 464–65; Shang culture, 74, 76;
  sixteen northern prefects of Yanyun, 239;

development, 364–77; interdiction on sea travel lifted (1567), 349; isolation policy, 281, 330–39, 348–49, 352; land grants to imperial princes and other favored people, 380–81; literature and the arts, 337, 390–93, 484, 489; and Manchus, 314, 332–33; metallurgy, 368; money, 377, 398; Mongol threat, 335; music and opera, 382, 392, 484; north–south economic disparities, 378–83; "opening up the middle" policy for repopulating the north, 344, 375, 379–80; outlaws/bandits in border areas, 382–83; overseas settlements, 350–51; overseas settlements, outlawed, 355–56; peasant uprisings, 383, 395, 400, 433, 435; piracy and smuggling, 349–56, 372, 403, 406; population growth, 339–45, 423; porcelain production, 366–67; power of emperors and style of governance, 336–38, 384; printing industry, 299; resistance to repressive imperial governance, 337–39 (*see also* peasant uprisings *and* transformation of thought *under this heading*); rigidity, conservatism, and inward-looking nature, 329–39; South Seas, 350 (map); and superior weapons of the Europeans, 314; and Taiwan, 405–10; taxes, 398; territory of, 340; textiles, 342, 365–66, 372, 373; transformation of thought, 384–94, 400; transportation network, 377, 382; voyages of Zheng He, 281, 332–33 (map), 334, 348, 371

Ming Taizu. *See* Hongwu emperor

Ming Yi hexagram, 439

Mingzhou (modern Ningbo), 15, 223, 278, 281, 286, 289, 464–65, 472, 512, 537

mining, 368

Min kingdom (Five Dynasties period), 265, 278, 286

missionaries, 359, 521. *See also* Catholic missionaries

Mohe people, 248

Mohist school of thought, 93, 100, 161

Mojiaoshan archaeological site, 57, 58

money: copper coins/cash, 280, 283–84, 343–44, 369, 377, 382–83, 471; Han dynasty, 224; Mexican silver as currency, 355, 374, 377, 398, 403, 468, 471; Ming dynasty, 377, 398; paper currency, 377, 398; Qing dynasty, 471; silk as currency, 224, 228; Yuan dynasty, 284, 377, 398

Mongols, 11–12, 12 (map), 322, 416–22; conquest dynasties, 269–75, 322–27, 378;

and Lamaist Buddhism, 335; and Qing dynasty, 273, 416–22, 420 (map); threats to Ming dynasty, 335. *See also* northern cultural region; steppe peoples; Yuan dynasty

monotheism, 119

Monthly Instructions for the Four Classes of People (Simin yueling), 167, 171

morality: conflict between Confucian filial piety and Buddhist monasticism, 198; and cultural conflicts in the early Qing, 435–41; Han vs. Qin virtues, 183; and Ming dynasty transformation of thought, 386–90; and modern thought and cultural change, 546; and popular literature, 490; and social relationships (Zhou period), 86; and state religion, 161; and White Lotus Society, 455. *See also* Confucianism; Mandate of Heaven; philosophy and political philosophy; religion

Mozi, 93, 161

mulberry trees, 344

mules, 148, 228

Mulian Rescues His Mother, 198

Murong people, 235

music, 25, 206, 208, 210. *See also* opera

Muzong, Emperor (Longqing emperor), 349

myths and legends, 11, 45–51, 48 (map), 65, 141–42

Nagasaki, Japan, 353

names, personal, 107, 199, 248, 278

Nanchang. *See* Hongzhou

Nangong Shuo, 214

Nanjing (Jiankang), 286, 289, 376, 499, 533, 537, 541, 556–57

Nanzhao kingdom, 73, 84, 210, 240, 247 (map), 249–51, 265–66; successor state (*see* Dali kingdom)

nationalism, 506–10

Nationalist–Communist Civil War, xi, 504, 535, 557–58

Nationalist Party, 507, 526, 554, 556. *See also* Northern Expedition

National Revolutionary Army, 509, 531, 533, 535, 571

natural disasters, 379, 382

nature worship, 95, 158, 161

Neo-Confucianism, 302–3, 321, 326, 336–38, 358, 376, 385–89, 502

Neo-Daoism, 160–61, 203

Neolithic period, vii, 27, 28 (fig.); agriculture and fixed settlements, 26–33, 30–31 (maps), 40–42, 127, 145; clothing, 40; and

Neolithic period (*continued*)
north/south contrast, 13–14, 32–33; pottery, 40; relationships between regional and local cultures, 34–45; six major systems of regional cultures, 35 (map), 36–45; and writing system, 74–75; Yangzi River basin cultures, 97
New Book on Nourishing Our Elders (*Shouqin yangsheng xinshu*; Zou Xuan), 318
New Hubei Army, 530, 556
New Shanghai News, 542
newspapers and periodicals, 542–43
New Text School of interpretation, 445
New Youth Magazine, 543
Nien Rebellion, 504
Night Revels of Han Xinzai (Gu Hongzhong; scroll painting), 315
Nile River, 114, 117
Ningbo. *See* Mingzhou
Ningzhen culture, 42
Niuheliang archaeological site, 55
nomadism. *See* steppe peoples
noodles, 216–17
North China Plain, 39 (map), 39–40, 43, 45
northeast region, 12 (map); Balhae (Bohai) kingdom, 248; extent of high Tang culture influence in Asia, 247 (map); geography and prehistoric culture, 14–15, 36–37; as Manchu homeland, 469; Ming aboriginal-office system, 245. *See also* Khitan (Qidan) people; Manchu people; Manchuria; Qing dynasty
northern cultural region, 36–38, 378, 379; and An Lushan Rebellion (*see* An Lushan–Shi Siming Rebellion); artwork and decorative items, 101; buildings, 96; and Confucianism, 100; conquest dynasties, 188–91, 190 (map), 238, 263, 269–75, 322–27, 378 (*see also* Jin dynasty; Liao dynasty; Yuan dynasty); and cotton cultivation, 373; and early agriculture, 62, 64; extent of high Tang culture influence in Asia, 246–47 (map); and medieval foreign relations, 242–47; and medieval trade, 279; movement of northern non-Chinese people into China (medieval era), 233–40, 324–25; north–south economic disparities (Ming dynasty), 378–83; northern nomad cultural interaction with Chinese culture (Qin-Han period), 144–51; "opening up the middle" policy for repopulating the north (Ming dynasty), 344, 375,

379–80; and outward-looking nature of non-Chinese peoples, 326–27; poetry, 101; and rise of complex societies, 54–55; small population compared to the south, 344–45, 379; spread of culture from, 113; and Tang period loose-reign prefectures (*jimizhoufu*), 262–63; and warfare, 344, 378–79; and writing system, 99. *See also* Huihe people; Jin dynasty; Liao empire; millet; Mongols; steppe peoples; Tujue people; Yuan dynasty
Northern Expedition, 504, 507, 526, 531, 554, 556, 570
Northern Qi dynasty (550–557), ix, 189, 191, 236, 413
Northern Song dynasty (960–1127), ix, 263, 265, 285, 288, 308
Northern Wei dynasty (386–534), ix, 189, 191, 217, 236, 413, 414
Northern Yinyangying culture, 41
Northern Zhou dynasty (556–581), ix, 189, 191, 196, 236, 300, 413
North-South dynasties (420–589), 182, 187; buildings, 221; clothing, 219, 220; and Daoism, 203; decline of Confucianism as official ideology, 196; elites, 195; food, 218; scholarship, 215; ships, 223; silk as commodity and currency, 228; stories of the supernatural, 206–7; vehicles, 223; warfare, 193–94
northwest region, 11, 12 (map), 16, 36–37, 238–39. *See also* Tubu (Tibetan) people; Tujue people
Nurhaci, 273, 415, 473
Nüwa (goddess of creation), 11, 45–46, 49

offerings, 50, 140–41, 161
"Old Forest" between Sichuan and Hubei, as bandit hideout, 382–83
On Cold Pathogenic Damage (*Shanghan lun*; Zhang Zhongjing), 151
On Diseases of Heat and Cold (*Shanghan zabing lun*; Zhang Zhongjing), 213
One Hundred Prescriptions (*Zhouhou yibai fang*; Tao Hongjing), 213
"opening up the middle" policy for repopulating the north, 344, 375
opera, 544–45; *kunqu* opera, 382, 392, 484, 486, 545, 550–51; Peking opera, 486–87, 550–51
Opium Wars, x, 502, 504, 511–12, 560
oracle bones, 72, 74–76, 98
oral tradition, 209

The Origins and Symptoms of Diseases (Zhu-bing yuanhoulun; Chao Yuanfang), 215
Ottoman Empire, 345, 398, 460
Outline of Western Learning (Xixue fan; Alenio), 363
oxen, 170, 316

Pacific islands, 157–58
Pacific War, 569, 570
Paekche kingdom. See Baekje (Paekche) kingdom
pagodas, 221
painting, 209, 210, 393, 551
Palace of Eternal Youth (opera), 485
Palembang, 349–50, 356
Paleolithic period, 18–27
Pan Geng, King, 74
Pangu, 45
paper, 231–33, 279
pastoralism, 11, 16, 27. See also steppe peoples
The Peach Blossom Fan (opera; Kong Shan-gren), 485
peanuts, 341–42, 469
pearls, 279, 281, 371
peasants: cottage industries, 228, 230, 233, 372, 373, 555; difference between Russian and Chinese peasants, 554–55; and disruption of domestic economy by influx of European commodities, 513; Ming dynasty, 343–44, 381–82; uprisings, 383, 395, 400, 435, 502, 557–58
Peiligang culture, 47, 62, 96
Peking Man, 20–22
Peking opera, 486–87, 550–51
Peking University, 521, 541, 564
Pengtoushan culture, 28 (fig.), 42
People's Liberation Army, 534
People's Republic of China, xi, 504, 535, 554
Pepo (Pingpu) tribes of Taiwan, 426, 428, 431–32
pepper, 282, 371
performing arts: chantefable, 485–86; early 20th century, 550–51; medieval period, 210; Qing dynasty, 483–88, 544–45. See also opera
Persia, 113, 115, 250
Peter the Great, 460, 495, 553
Philip II of Spain, 395–96
Philippines, 352, 353, 404, 407
philosophy and political philosophy, 136–37; ancient Middle East, 115, 117; and Chu state, 100; and comparison

of the Tang and Islamic empires, 259; Confucianism and debates of the Hundred Schools, 90–96; and dualism, 117–19; Han dynasty contrast to Roman Empire, 176–77; Han dynasty intellectual integration, 133–39; "Han Learning" vs. "Song Learning," 449; "Heaven and Mankind are one" doctrine, 96; impact on European thinkers, 482; and individualism, 94, 203–4; late medieval pluralism and integration, 300–307, 321–22; Legalism, 107, 134; Ming dynasty transformation, 384–94; modern thought and cultural change, 456–552; Qing dynasty scholarship and political thinking, 436–49; Song dynasty Neo-Confucian schools of thought, 297–98; theory of cyclical change, 126, 134–35, 136–37, 163; traditional divisions of Chinese learning, 446; Warring States period schools of thought, 93–96, 107, 122, 134; Yin-Yang school of thought, 95. See also Buddhism; Confucianism; Daoism; Five Agents doctrine; Legalism
pi, value of, 212, 214
Pictorial Explanations of Western Scientific Instruments (Yuanxi qiqi tushuo; Schreck), 361, 370
pigs, 29, 32, 61, 110, 130, 169
Ping, King, 84
piracy and smuggling, 334, 349–56, 372, 403, 406, 409, 470
poetry, 85, 101, 204–8, 486–87, 549, 569–70. See also Book of Songs; Songs of Chu
political philosophy. See philosophy and political philosophy
polo, 223
population statistics. See demographics
porcelain: colors, 367; division of specialized labor, 368; importance in medieval commerce, 277–78; Islamic or European designs, 374, 472; late medieval period, 313–14; and maritime trade, 231, 371–72, 374, 472; medieval period, 230–31; Ming dynasty production, 366–67, 373, 374; protoporcelain, 110; types of kilns, 367
port cities and harbors: ancient coastal cities and harbors, 15; Foreign Concessions, 539; foreign merchants living in "foreign quarters" (fanfang), 281; medieval coastal cities and harbors, 277–80; Ming dynasty closure of ports, 334–35, 348–52; modern era cities, 537, 539–41

Portugal: immigration policies, 425; and Macao, 463; and Malacca, 352, 353; maritime trade, 350, 351, 399, 404; overseas colonies, 352

potatoes, 341, 423, 469

pottery: and development of bronze casting, 70–71; inscriptions on, 49, 74–75; Ming production, 368; protoporcelain, 110; and relationships between Neolithic cultures, 34, 40, 43; and rise of complex societies, 52. *See also* porcelain

poverty, 525

predestination, 163, 306

prehistoric cultures. *See* Chinese culture, prehistoric

Primordial Goddess of the Morning Clouds (*Bixia Yuanjun*), 452

The Principles of Correct Diet (*Yinshan zhengyao*; Hu Sihui), 318–19

printing, 298–99, 304

property ownership, 105

Protestant missionaries, 359

Protestant work ethic, 376

Prussia, 494–95

publishing industry, 542–44, 550

Pugu people, 237

Pure Land Buddhism, 200, 301, 303

Puyuma tribe of Taiwan, 426

Qarahoja, 239, 275

qi (vital force), 96, 141–42, 144, 163, 303, 306

Qiang people (proto-Tibetans), 186, 188, 217, 234, 242. *See also* Nanzhao kingdom

Qian Jibo, 549

Qian Long, 375

Qianlong emperor, 418; and British diplomats, 466–67, 483; and cartography, 480–81; and military, 527; and Peking opera, 486; prosperity under, 501; and Taiwan, 425; and White Lotus Rebellion, 454

Qi Baishi, 551

Qidan people, 191

Qijia culture, 28 (fig.), 70

Qin dynasty (221–207 B.C.E.), 124 (map); burial customs, 143; clan system, 183; and control of natural resources, 127; daily life, 166, 170; end of, 182; expansion of Chinese culture, 6; and Legalism, 134; melding of cultural groups, 45; military, 123; northern nomad cultural interaction with Chinese culture, 144–51; political unification of China, 97, 102, 173; popular beliefs, 142; religion, 139;

reorganization of territory, 104, 121–22; rule of "all under heaven" concept, 123; terracotta army of First Emperor, 123, 143; theory of cyclical change, 123; unification of Chinese cultural system, 121–23; unification of writing system, 122; village administration, 323

Qingbang. *See* Green Gang

Qing dynasty (1644–1911), viii, x; capital cities, 421; Chinese Rites Controversy, 357, 358, 361, 363–64, 498; comparison of Chinese and Russian Revolutions, 555–57; comparison of Hundred Days' Reform and Meiji Restoration, 558–65; comparison of Qing dynasty with contemporary West, 491–99; and Confucianism, 436–49, 452–53; dictionaries and encyclopedias, 447–48; domestic trade, 468–76, 475 (map); and economic transformation, 511–19; education, 443–44, 519–26; Eight Banners, 414–15, 421, 527; emigration patterns, 423–26, 424 (map); ethnic and cultural conflicts, 432–41; examination system and civil bureaucracy, 440, 444, 479; government and territorial administration, 413–17, 421, 556; Great Powers' spheres of influence in China (late 19th century), 503 (map); Hundred Days' Reform, 506, 543, 547, 558–65; ignorance of outside world, 495, 498–99; intermarriage between Manchu imperial family and noble Mongol families, 417; international trade, 462–67, 471–72; last emperor's abdication, 530; literature and the arts, 484–91; local, trade-based organizations, 450–51; Manchu braided queue and clothing required for all adult men, 433; military, 502, 504, 506, 527–30; and modern thought and cultural change, 546–52; money, 471; and Mongols, 273, 416–22, 420 (map); mutual misunderstandings with England, 465–68, 483, 493; and north–south economic disparity, 384; overconfidence of, 499; painting, 551; performing arts, 483–88, 544–45; piracy and smuggling, 409, 470; population increase, 469, 471, 498; prohibition of maritime activity, 424; proliferation of rumors and gossip, 440–41; prosperity of, 498, 501; provincial assemblies, 556; rebellions, 454–57, 455 (map), 502–4, 527–30, 554 (*see also* Boxer Rebellion; Taiping Rebellion); relaxation of ban on foreign trade,

464–66; religious sects, 451–57; resistance to Qing rule, 433–41 (*see also* rebellions *under this heading*); and Russia, 459–63, 468, 471, 495; scholarly community, 448–49; scholarship and political thinking, 436–49, 479; secret societies, 457–59; Self-Strengthening Movement, 506, 528–29, 546; and stagnation of thinking, 502; and Taiwan, 408–9, 469; taxes, 469; and Tibet, 252; transportation, 540–41; unification of Manchu-Mongol-Tibetan areas, 416–22, 469; victory over the Ming, 354; wars, 502–4 (*see also* Opium Wars); weakening of, 468, 482–83, 501–2, 504–5. *See also* Manchu people

Qingliangang culture, 45

Qinglongquan culture, 43

Qin Jiushao, 308

Qin Shihuangdi, First Emperor of Qin, 122, 123, 126, 142, 201; terracotta army of, 123, 143

Qin state, 85, 104, 106; defeat of other states and unification of Chinese cultural system, 121–23 (*see also* Qin dynasty)

Qi state, 88, 99, 106

Qiu Chuji, 305

Qiu Xinru, 486

Qiu Ying, 393

Quanzhen (Complete Truth) sect of religious Daoism, 304–5

Quanzhou (Zaytun), 15, 537; emigration to Taiwan from, 430, 432; foreign merchants living in "foreign quarters" (*fanfang*), 281; and late medieval era, 289; Mazu cult, 451; as medieval port city, 278, 281, 286; ships at, 347–48

Questions and Answers on the West (*Xifang wenda*; Alenio), 363

Qu family, 239

Qujialing culture, 28 (fig.), 43, 45

Qu Yuan, 49, 50, 204

quzhong system (agricultural technique), 129

railways, 514 (map), 515, 517, 540–41

Random Jottings from Lü Garden (*Lüyuan conghua*; Qian Yong), 375

rebellions, ix–x; An Lushan rebellion (*see* An Lushan–Shi Siming Rebellion); Boxer Rebellion, 454, 491, 504–6, 528; Han dynasty, 133, 162, 163; Ming dynasty, 383, 395, 400, 433, 435; Nien Rebellion, 504; Qing dynasty, 454–57, 455 (map), 502, 504; Rebellion of the Seven States, 124;

Rebellion of the Six Garrisons (524), 191, 236–37; Republican Revolution (*see* Republican Revolution); and roadways, 133; Taiping Rebellion, 457, 504, 505, 527–29, 554; Taiwan, 425; and Talisman School of religious Daoism, 203; Way of the Celestial Masters (Way of the Five Pecks of Rice) rebellion, 133, 201; White Lotus Rebellion, 454–56, 502; Xilufan Rebellion, 457; Yellow Turban uprising, 185

Record of Knowledge Acquired Day by Day (*Rizhilu*; Gu Yanwu), 437

Records of Daily Learning (*Rizhilu*; Gu Yanwu), 343

Records of the Grand Historian (*Shiji*), 46, 130, 138, 139, 159

Records of the West (*Zhifang waiji*; Alenio), 363

Red Army, 534

Red Turbans, 306

reincarnation, 163, 198–99, 453, 489, 490

religion: ancestor worship, 95, 158–59, 161; in ancient Middle East, 64; apocalyptic religions, 163, 202, 301, 306, 383, 454; Catholic doctrine introduced to China, 357–59; Chinese Rites Controversy (*see* Chinese Rites Controversy); and community cohesion, 323–24; and comparison of the Tang and Islamic empires, 259; Han dynasty, 139–44, 158–66; heavenly bureaucracy, 162–63; introduction of Buddhism, 158–66, 196–203; introduction of Islam and Nestorian Christianity, 305; late medieval pluralism and integration, 300–307; and literature/performing arts, 490–91; messianic sects, 453–54; nature worship, 95, 158, 161; North-South dynasties, 203; popular religious sects (Qing dynasty), 451–57; Qin dynasty, 139–44; and rebellions, 163, 203, 453–57, 505; and rise of complex societies, 52; sacred places, 139–41; Shang dynasty, 77; state religious ceremonies, 161; syncretic movements, 203, 453; in Taiwan, 410; Warring States period, 112; Zhou dynasty, 79. *See also* Buddhism; Daoism; deities; divination; folk beliefs; human sacrifice; Manichaeism; Mohist school of thought; myths and legends; philosophy and political philosophy; White Lotus Society; Zoroastrianism; *specific sects*

ren (humanity), 92, 94, 118, 183

Renzong, Emperor (Hongxi emperor), 336

Republican Revolution, x, 504, 506–7, 530–34; compared to Russian Revolution, 552–58

Republic of China, xi, 504, 554, 556

rhinoceros horn, 281

Ricci, Matteo, 356–58, 360, 362–63, 476

rice, 31 (map); as mainland staple, 14; need for food imports to industrial areas, 374, 470–71; and Neolithic cultures, 29–32, 41, 62–63; origins of cultivation, 62–63; as staple, 96, 109, 168; and Taiwan, 431, 517; types of, 31–32, 63, 316

Rites of Zhou (*Zhouli*), 169

rituals: Chu state, 100–101; conflicts with Christianity (*see* Chinese Rites Controversy); and Daoism, 163; *di*, 140; jade ritual objects (*cong, bi, huang, guan, yue*), 57–58; Qin-Han period, 140–41, 161; ritual centers and the rise of complex societies, 52, 54–55; and Song dynasty neoclassicism, 300; state religious ceremonies, 161; Warring States period, 94, 110, 112; Zhou dynasty, 85, 95, 105–6. *See also* ancestor worship

roadways: Han dynasty, 130–33, 132 (map), 146–47(maps), 148–49, 151–54, 172, 187; medieval period, 226, 228; Qing dynasty/ modern era, 470, 540–41; and rebellions, 133; Warring States period, 131. *See also* Silk Road

Romance of the Three Kingdoms (*Sanguo yanyi*), 488

Roman Empire, 171–79, 182, 185–87

Ronglu, General, 561–62

Rouran people, 237, 242

Rousseau, Jean-Jacques, 482

Ruggieri, Michele Pompilio, 356–57

Rules of Conduct for Palace Women (Zhan Hua), 209

Russia: China's knowledge of Europe based on knowledge of Russia, 495; comparison of Chinese and Russian Revolutions, 552–58; and displaced intelligentsia, 523–24; eastward expansion, 460–61, 464–65 (map); relations with China (Qing dynasty), 459–63, 468, 471; sphere of influence, 503 (map); trade, 462

Russian Orthodox church, 462, 495

Ryukyu Islands, 348

sacred places, 112

Saisiyat people, 155–56

salt trade, 250, 277, 279, 288, 476 (map), 486; and Anhui merchants, 474–75; Qing dynasty, 469, 473–76; salt monopoly licenses and "opening up the middle" policy, 375, 379–80; salt tax, 469; and Shanxi merchants, 473

Samboja, 348, 350 (map)

Sangha, 312

Sang Weihan, 436

Sanxing culture, 148–49

Särbi (Xianbei) people, ix, 189, 235, 242, 265, 272, 413

Sassanid empire, 250

scholarship. *See* Confucianism; examination system and civil bureaucracy; philosophy and political philosophy; *specific schools of thought*

School of Evidential Learning (*kaozheng xue*), 444–49

School of Mind (*xinxue*), 297–98, 303, 358, 385–86, 389, 395, 441

School of Principle (*lixue*), 297–98, 358, 376, 385, 388, 389

Schreck, Johann Terrenz, 361, 370

science: late medieval period, 307–15; and late Qing dynasty transformation to Western-style education system, 520–26; and May Fourth New Culture Movement, 548; medieval period, 210–16; scientism, 549, 552; Western science and industrial arts introduced to China by Jesuit missionaries, 359–60, 370–71; Western scientific works translated into Chinese, 547. *See also* astronomy; cosmology; medicine; technology

Science Monthly, 543

secret societies, 457–59, 539–40

sedan chairs, 316

Selections of Refined Literature (*Wenxuan*), 298

Self-Strengthening Movement, 506, 528–29, 546

semu merchants, 276–77, 322

serfdom, 128

Seven Martial States, 102, 122

Shaanxi Province: and Early Shang culture, 73; economic resources, 288; immigrant prefectures, 245; movement of northern non-Chinese people into, 240; Neolithic agriculture, 31–32; Neolithic sites, 29, 74; and origins of Zhou kingdom, 78; Paleolithic sites, 22; and southward migration of Han people, 192; Tang period loose-reign prefectures (*jimizhoufu*), 263; Tibetan control of, 250–51

shamanism, 57, 136, 140–41, 162–65, 301

Shandong Province: Bronze Age archaeological sites, 70; as disaster-prone region, 379; and Early Shang culture, 73; geography and prehistoric culture, 36, 38; land grants to imperial princes and other favored people (Ming dynasty), 380–81; Paleolithic sites, 24; Qi state, 88; regional warlords under northern conquest dynasties, 274; rise of complex societies, 52

Shangdi (High God), 161, 357

Shangdingdong Man, 24, 25

Shangdong culture, 28 (fig.)

Shanghai: film industry, 545; as first-rank city of the modern era, 537, 543, 545; Foreign Concessions, 539; Fuyuanshan archaeological sites, 59; and modern expansion of urban culture, 537–45; newspapers and periodicals, 542–43; performing arts, 544–45; publishing industry, 542–44; secret societies/criminal gangs, 539–40; universities, 541

Shanghai Commercial Press, 544

Shanghai Journal, 542–43

Shang kingdom (ca. 17th to 11th century B.C.E.), vii, 45, 72–79; agriculture, 128; archaeological sites, 72–73; bronze casting, 71; dynasty as core of ancient Chinese culture, 72–78; and Fu Sinian's cultural opposition theory, 83; government, 76–77; human sacrifice, 77, 88; legendary founder, 50; location of culture, 73, 74 (map), 76 (map); pottery, 110; religion, 77; social structure, 77; and Three Dynasties concept, 72; time divisions of, 73–74; war chariots, 71; Western Zhou defeat of the Shang, 78–80, 82–83, 90–91; writing system, 74–75

Shang people, 85

Shanxi Province: and Early Shang culture, 73; geography and prehistoric culture, 36; immigrant prefectures, 245; merchants, financial institutions, and commercial leagues, 375–76, 451, 473–74, 475 (map), 512; Paleolithic sites, 22, 25; patron deity of, 451; Qiang immigration into, 188; silk industry, 373; Tang period loose-reign prefectures (*jimizhoufu*), 263

Shanyue people, 152

Shaohao, Emperor, 48–49

Shao Yong, 302

she (community organizations), 323–24

sheep, 32, 61, 110, 130, 145

Shen Jiaben, 563

Shen Kuo, 308, 309, 311

Shen Nong, 46–47, 49, 50

Shen Nong's Materia Medica (*Shen Nong bencaojing*; Zhang Zhongjing), 215

Shen Que, 361

Shenxiu, 200

Shen Yue, 206

Shen Zhou, 393

Shi family, 274

Shijiahe culture, 28 (fig.), 32, 43

Shi Nai-an, 391

ships. *See* boats and ships

Shi Siming, 238

Shi Yukun, 486

shoes, 220

Shuangyu Island, 353

Shu clan, 98

Shu-Han dynasty, 239–40

Shu kingdom, 182, 185. *See also* Three Kingdoms era

Shun, Emperor, 46, 48

Shu people, 240

Shu Zhe, 216–17

Siam, 348, 350 (map)

Siba culture, 70

Siberia, 460–61

Sichuan basin, 36, 42–43, 114, 154, 239, 288, 423

Sichuan Province: Ba-Shu culture, 43, 154, 195; coastal factories moved to during War of Resistance Against Japan, 519; geography and prehistoric culture, 36; late medieval period, 288; movement of northern non-Chinese people into, 239–40; Paleolithic sites, 24; silkworms, 373

Sidun archaeological site, 58–59

silk, 110, 371; central government's production of (Tang period), 224–25; importance in medieval commerce, 228, 276–77, 279; and maritime trade, 371–72, 374; as medium of exchange, 224, 228; Ming period industry, 365–66, 372–73; products (satin, damask, gauze, etc.), 220, 229, 365; Qing dynasty trade with Russia, 462; and regional division of labor, 373, 512; silk clothing, 167, 220; silk painting, 209; silk production described, 365–66; traded for horses (Tang period), 276

Silk Road, 16, 146–47(maps), 148, 150; and Buddhism, 159–60; economic beneficiaries of, 250, 252; foods introduced via, 219; "oceanic silk road," 347–48; Qarahoja, 239; and Qing dynasty networks, 470; and Roman Empire, 172; silk transported over, 224; "Third Silk Road" (Nanzhao kingdom), 251

Silla (Xinluo) kingdom, 247 (map), 248

silver: export of, 281, 283–84; Mexican silver and maritime trade, 355, 374, 377, 398, 403, 466, 468, 471; opium trade and the shortage of silver, 511; silver mining, 368

Sima Guang, 294, 488

Singapore, 498

Sino-French War, 506

Six Garrisons, 236; Rebellion of the Six Garrisons (524), 191, 236–37

Sixteen Kingdoms era, 189

Sixteen Prefectures, 285

Skinner, G. William, 131, 515

slavery, 240, 323

The Slave's Contract (*Tongyue*; Wang Bao), 169, 171, 229

Smith, Adam, 492

smuggling. *See* piracy and smuggling

social classes: and Buddhist monks, 197–98; difference between Russian and Chinese peasants, 554–55; differing historical and moral understandings of intelligentsia and common people, 488; education and alienation from rural society, 522–25, 555; four traditional classes (scholars, farmers, workers, merchants), 171; gentry literati in the modern era, 555; and Han dynasty diets, 167; and household registry system, 104; late medieval period, 307, 312–13; late medieval period intellectual class (during and after the Song), 292–300, 321; medieval era power structure of great families and the state, 196; Ming dynasty mixing of gentry and mercantile activities, 376; Ming dynasty peasant farmers, 343–44, 381–82; and Ming dynasty transformation of thought, 388; Qin state, 106; Shang social structure, 77; Song dynasty powerful families replaced by urban residents and local gentry, 307; Song dynasty separation of scholars and merchants, 376; and southward migration of Han elite, 194–96; and Taiping Rebellion, 505; and Taiwan, 429–30, 565–66, 571; Tang period, 254, 300; Warring States period, 104–5; Zhou

period, 104–6. *See also* clan system and great families; merchants; peasants

social evolution, ideas on, 546–52

Society for the Worship of Mazu, 324

Sogdian people, 238, 242–43, 275, 277

solar eclipse of 1629, 359

Song Collection of Essential Documents (*Song huiyao*), 277, 281

Song dynasty (960–1279), ix; artillery and firearms, 314; astronomy, 310–11; boats and ships, 316; borders of, 251; capital city (Bianliang), 285; cities, 289, 321; civil bureaucracy and intellectual class, 290–300, 321; clothing, 315–16; conflicts with northern non-Chinese peoples, 265; and Confucianism, 292, 295–300, 302–3, 321–22; daily life, 315–20; and declining power of great families, 275, 293, 307, 321, 323; deity Lin Moniang, 451; economics and trade networks (internal), 285–90; economics and trade networks (international), 275–84, 346–48, 371; education, 294–98; establishment of, 263; ethnic relations, 268; food and drink, 282–83, 316–18; government and territorial administration, 290; high living standards, 320; and late medieval multistate system, 262–69; literacy rate, 298, 299; medicine, 319; metallurgy, 313; military, 290–91, 292; money, 284, 377; Mongol conquest of, 265, 271, 288; neoclassical tendencies and inward-looking nature, 326, 338; Neo-Confucian schools of thought, 297–98, 302–3, 322; oral tradition, 209; overseas settlements, 348–49; population statistics, 339; porcelain, 313–14; Song-Liao Treaty of Shanyuan (1005), 265; taxes, 284, 288–90; transportation, 316; tribute paid to neighboring states, 265, 267, 276, 279; village-compact organizations, 300; weaving industry, 313; women in, 315–16. *See also* Northern Song dynasty; Southern Song dynasty

Song Huizong, Emperor, 304

Song of the Fisherman (*Yuguangqu*; film), 551

Songs of Chu (*Chuci*), 101, 204–5, 207

Song Taizu, 292, 293

Songtsän Gampo, 250

Song Yingxing, 364

Songze culture, 28 (fig.)

sorcery, 201

southeastern cultural region, 41 (map), 41–43; and early agriculture, 64; and Ming

transportation (*continued*)
vehicles, 122; wheeled vehicles, 71, 122, 148, 170, 223, 316. *See also* boats and ships; horses; roadways; waterways
Treaty of Kyatkha (1727), 461
Treaty of Nerchinsk (1689), 461
trebuchets, 314
tribute: and *fenjian zhidu* system of Western Zhou, 81, 105; and Ming dynasty overseas settlements, 349, 350; Song dynasty tribute paid to neighboring states, 265, 267, 276, 279; tributary states, 249, 266, 267, 335
Trigault, Nicolas, 361, 362–63
The True Doctrine of Catholic Christianity (*Tianzhu shiyi*; Ricci), 357
Tubu (Tibetan) kingdom, 249–52, 264 (map)
Tubu (Tibetan) people, 191–92, 237, 239, 240, 246 (map), 265, 276. *See also* Nanzhao kingdom
Tujue people (Türks), 246–47 (map); and Arab Islamic empire, 268–69; China's relations with, 237, 250; and rise and fall of pastoral confederacies, 237, 238, 242, 272; steppe empire of, 191–92, 243–44; and trade networks, 276
Tulišen, Ayan Gioro, 463, 495
Tuoba (Tabgatch) people, 191, 236–37, 242, 414
Turghuts, 462
Tuva, 462
Tuyuhun people, 191, 235, 237, 247 (map), 265
Twice Destined Marriage (*Zaisheng yuan*; Chen Duansheng), 486, 490

Ubaid culture, 62 (map), 63–64, 69
Umayyad caliphate, 250, 253–55, 256–57 (map)
United States, 493–97, 559
universities, 520–21, 540–41, 564
Upper Cave Man, 23–25
Ur, 62 (map), 64
Uruk, 62 (map), 64, 69
Uyghur people, 147, 273. *See also* Huihe people

Vajrayana Buddhism, 419
vegetables, 109, 218, 318
vegetarianism, 317
Verbiest, Ferdinand, 477
Vietnam, 154, 241, 266, 287–88, 335. *See also* Annam peninsula

Voltaire, 482
von Bell, Johann Adam Schall, 360, 477

Waiting for the Dawn: A Plan for the Prince (*Mingyi daifang lu*; Huang Zongxi), 438–39, 442
Wang Anshi, 290, 293, 294, 295
Wang Bao, 169, 171, 218, 229
Wang clan, 194
Wang Dong, 388
Wang family, 274
Wang Fuzhi, 435–36
Wang Gen, 386–87
Wang Hui, 551
Wang Jian, 551
Wang Jingwei, 531, 534
Wang Mang, 137–38, 182
Wang Shimin, 551
Wang Xiaotong, 212
Wang Yangming, 298, 303, 338, 358, 385–86, 389, 393, 395, 441
Wang Yuanqi, 551
Wang Zhi, 352, 353, 361
Wan Sida, 446
Wan Sitong, 446
war chariots, 68, 71–72, 223
warfare: Bronze Age, 68, 71; and cultural exchanges, 71; Five Dynasties era, 263, 526; gunpowder, 314; and household registry system, 102; and militarization of modern China, 526–37, 556; North-South dynasties, 193–94; Three Kingdoms era, 193, 526; warlord armies of the early 20th century, 528–35; Warring States period, 106; wars of the late 19th and early 20th century, 502–11, 526–37; Western and Eastern Jin dynasties, 193; Yuan dynasty, 344, 378–79; Zhou dynasty, 106. *See also* Opium Wars; rebellions; War of Resistance Against Japan
warlords, 526–27; and militarization of modern China, 526–37; military leaders of Hebei Province, 238, 274; regional warlords under northern conquest dynasties, 274, 292, 305; and Song military units, 291; warlord era (1916–1928), xi, 504, 507, 530–37, 532 (map), 556, 564; and War of Resistance Against Japan, 509, 534–35. *See also* Warring States period
War of Resistance Against Japan, 502, 507–9, 508 (map), 515–16, 518–19, 526, 531, 534, 557

Wu state (Warring States period), 99, 101
Wuyue culture, 41, 45
Wuyue kingdom (Five Dynasties period), 265, 278–79, 286
Wuzong, Emperor, 300

Xavier, Francis, 356
Xia dynasty (ca. 2070–ca. 1600 B.C.E.), vii, 45, 47, 72–73, 74 (map), 83
Xiajiadian culture, 28 (fig.), 37–38, 70
Xiajiao sect, 453
Xiamen (Amoy), 405, 409, 422, 464, 537, 539–41
Xianbei (Särbi) people, ix, 189, 235, 242, 265, 272, 413
Xiangyang, siege of (1267–1273), 314
Xianrendong culture, 28 (fig.)
Xianrong people, 89
Xiantiandao set, 456
Xiaoheyan culture, 28 (fig.)
Xia people, 85
Xie clan, 194
Xieli (Illig) Qaghan, 244
Xilufan Rebellion, 457
Xin dynasty (New dynasty; 9–23 C.E.), 182
Xingyang, 131
Xing Yitian, 167
Xinjiang, 16, 144–51, 245, 527
Xinlongwa culture, 28 (fig.), 37
Xintai man, 24
Xiongnu people, viii, 146, 149, 186, 188, 191, 234, 242, 272, 412
Xi people, 240
Xi Xia state, 264 (map), 265, 276, 279, 284, 285
Xizong, Emperor, 240
Xuande emperor (Xuanzong), 240, 251, 258, 336
Xuanyuan, 47
Xuanzang, 197, 200
Xuanzong. See Xuande emperor
Xu Beihong, 551
Xu clan, 98
Xu Dong, 352
Xue clan, 240
Xu Guangqi: books translated by, 360; *Comprehensive Treatise on Agricultural Administration*, 361, 364–66, 370, 373; and Jesuits, 356, 358, 361, 363, 477; solar eclipse prediction, 359; and sweet potatoes, 340
Xu Hai, 352

Xunzi, 93, 100, 134
Xu Wei, 393
Xu Zhenjun, 452

yams, 340–41, 423
Yan, Emperor, 46–49, 48 (map)
Yandi, 65
Yan family, 274
Yan Fu, 547
Yang, C. K., 131, 515
Yang Guangxian, 361, 477
Yang Hucheng, 509
Yang Hui, 309–10
Yangming school, 386–90. *See also* Wang Yangming
Yang Pu, 336
Yang Rong, 336
Yangshao culture, 28, 28 (fig.), 39, 40, 43, 45, 47–49, 48 (map), 59
Yang Shen, 485
Yang Shiqi, 336
Yang Tingyun, 358, 363
Yang Ye, 489
Yangzhou, 15, 223, 279, 281, 286, 537
Yang Zhu, 94
Yangzi River basin, 1–3, 12 (map); agriculture, 12–13, 30, 32, 193; cultural development during the Warring States period, 96–101; geography of, 11–13, 114; indigenous peoples, 193; and origins of differing worldviews of northern vs. southern peoples, 13; and origins of mainstream Chinese culture, 45, 96–101; prehistoric cultures, 11–13, 28 (fig.), 30, 32, 33
Yan-Li school, 442–44
Yan people, 85
Yan Ruisheng (film), 545, 551
Yan Siqi, 354, 355
Yan state, 89
Yan Xishan, 531, 532 (map), 534, 536
Yan Yuan, 442–44
Yao, Emperor, 46, 48
Yao people, 240
Yaoshan archaeological site, 58, 59
Yellow Emperor (Huang Di), 46–49, 48 (map), 65, 510
Yellow River basin, 1–2, 12 (map); agriculture, 12–13; flooding, 379, 382; geography of, 11–13, 113–14; and origins of differing worldviews of northern vs. southern peoples, 13; and origins of mainstream Chinese culture, 45; prehistoric cultures,

Zhou, Duke of, 81, 84

Zhou Dunyi, 302

Zhou dynasty (1045–256 B.C.E.), viii, 78–84; buildings, 111; calendrical system, 111; clans, 80–81, 83, 85, 88; cultural development of the south, 96–101; defeat of the Shang, 79–80, 82–83, 90–91; early rulers, 81, 83; economics, 88; fall of the Western Zhou, 84–86; feudal system, breakdown of, 84–88, 101–2; feudal system (*fengjian zhidu*), 80–82, 104–6, 434; government, 80–81, 86–87, 95, 100–108; household registry system, 101–8; literature and the arts, 85–86, 88, 101; and Mandate of Heaven (*Tianming*) concept, 90–91; and North China Plain culture, 45; origins of Zhou people, 40, 49, 78–79; position of major Western Zhou states, 81 (map); re-emergence of human sacrifice, 88; rise of Confucianism, 87, 90–95; rituals, 95, 101, 105–6; role of regional cultures, 84–90; schools of thought, 117–18; shared culture of the elite, 85–86; social classes, 104–6; and Three Dynasties concept, 72, 83–84; warfare, 106. *See also* Eastern Zhou dynasty; Spring and Autumn period; Warring States period; Western Zhou dynasty

Zhoukoudian (cave system), 21, 25

Zhou people, 40, 49, 78–79, 85

Zhou Xinfang, 545

Zhuangzi, 13, 94, 134, 162

Zhuanxu, Emperor, 48–50

Zhu Danxi, 319

Zhukaigou culture, 70

Zhurong (god of fire), 49–50, 98

Zhurong league, 65

Zhu Shijie, 308–10

Zhu Wan, 353

Zhu Xi: and academies, 296; contrast to Lu Jiuyuan, 303; and examination system, 336–37, 385, 440, 444, 479, 502; main thesis of, 303; and "sage on the inside/king on the outside" concept, 338; School of Principle commentaries as orthodox state teachings, 297–98, 336–38, 385

Zhu Yuanzhang. *See* Hongwu emperor

zinc, 369

Zoroastrianism, 117, 119, 258–59, 306, 453–54

Zou Xuan, 318

Zu Chongzhi, 212, 214

Zungar Mongols, 418–19

Zuo Commentary, 48, 85–86

Zuo Zongtang, 456, 505, 506, 527–29